An Exposition of the Gospel of John

William Kelly

w.K.

Edited, with additions,
by E. E. Whitfield

Scripture Truth Publications

AN EXPOSITION OF THE GOSPEL OF JOHN

First published 1898 by T. Weston, 53 Paternoster Row, London

Special cheap edition published 1923 by F. E. Race, London House Yard, Paternoster Row, London E.C.

Reprinted 1966, C. A. Hammond Trust Bible Depot, 11 Little Britain, London E.C.1

Second edition (edited, with additions, by E. E. Whitfield) published 1908 by Elliot Stock, 62 Paternoster Row, London, E.C.

Special cheap edition published c.1916 by Alfred Holness, 13 and 14 Paternoster Row, London E.C., and R. L. Allan & Son, 141 and 143 Sauchiehall Street, Glasgow

Re-typeset and transferred to digital printing 2013

Third edition published April 2013

ISBN: 978-0-901860-52-1

© Copyright 2013 Scripture Truth

A publication of Scripture Truth

All rights reserved. No part of this publication may be reproduced, stored in a retrieval system, or transmitted, in any form or by any means, electronic, mechanical, photocopying, recording or otherwise without prior permission of Scripture Truth Publications.

References to The Authorised Version (A.V.) are to The Authorised (King James) Version. Rights in the Authorised Version are vested in the Crown. Reproduced by permission of the Crown's patentee, Cambridge University Press.

References to the Revised Version (R.V.) are to "The New Testament of our Lord and Saviour Jesus Christ, Translated out of the Greek: Being the Version Set Forth A.D. 1611, Compared with the Most Ancient Authorities and Revised, A.D. 1881". Oxford: Oxford University Press, 1881 or "The Holy Bible containing the Old and New Testaments translated out of the original tongues : being the version set forth A.D. 1611 compared with the most ancient authorities and revised". Oxford: University Press, 1885.

Old Testament quotations, when not from the Authorised Version, are taken from "The Holy Scriptures, a New Translation from the Original Languages" by J. N. Darby (G Morrish, 1890)

Cover photograph of 2nd Century Papyrus Fragment of John's Gospel 18:31-33 recto (left) and 18:37-38 verso (right) reproduced by courtesy of the University Librarian and Director, The John Rylands University Library, The University of Manchester

Published by Scripture Truth Publications
31-33 Glover Street,
Crewe, Cheshire CW1 3LD

Scripture Truth is an imprint of Central Bible Hammond Trust, a charitable trust

Typesetting by John Rice
Printed by Lightning Source

FOREWORD TO THE THIRD EDITION

Our purpose was to re-publish the second edition of William Kelly's *Exposition of the Gospel of John*, edited by Edward Elihu Whitfield, a friend of the author's over the last thirty-five years of his life, and incorporating almost four hundred editorial additional notes. Despite the first edition's relative freedom from typographical errors, the same is not so of the second, particularly in the capitalization of the initial letter of some words and the italicization of emphasised words which it introduced. It was therefore necessary to carefully compare the texts of the two editions. Discrepancies have been resolved, in most cases, in favour of the first, often after extensive searches and comparisons of various Greek texts of the Gospel and textual commentaries to which references are made. In the process it became clear that several references to quoted texts of Scripture required amendment – a task greatly assisted by the ready availability of computer-based texts of the Scriptures.

William Kelly's footnotes, referenced by letter (e.g. [a]) in this edition, have been placed at the end of each chapter, thus enabling those who just wish to read the main body of text to do so, whilst still providing easy access to his (mainly textual) additional comments.

E. E. Whitfield's additions to the text are enclosed in square brackets []. Scripture references he added as footnotes are now included in the main body of the text.

In this edition further Scripture references and explanations of obsolete English words have been added, enclosed in curly brackets {}. Capitalisation, introduced extensively in the second edition, has been applied consistently. Arabic numerals in Scripture references replace Roman to facilitate ease of reference.

The combined Indexes of Exposition and Notes have been separated so that the first part of this edition is essentially the text of the first edition plus indexes, and the additional Notes of the second edition, together with its indexes, form the second part.

As not all readers will have access to Whitfield's editions of William Kelly's *Exposition of the Gospel of Mark* and *Exposition of the Gospel of Luke*, an additional section has been included containing Whitfield's Notes from those editions to which reference is made in the Appendix of Additional Notes.

We are grateful to the late Edwin Cross for his suggestion that it would render a great service to all lovers of the Word if the next reprint of the *Exposition* was of the second edition containing E. E. Whitfield's additional notes. His initial support was invaluable in this project. It is our prayer that this new edition will encourage all our readers to grow in their appreciation of the eternal Son of God.

John Rice

March 2013

INTRODUCTION TO THE 1966 REPRINT OF THE FIRST EDITION

It is a source of humble thankfulness to the publishers that another re-issue of William Kelly's Exposition of the Gospel of John is called for from both sides of the Atlantic.

In this studiously prepared work the author set out in his mature and scholarly style what he had gleaned over many years of the perfections of the eternal Son of God as He walked through this evil world in holy Manhood.

The promise of the Father had been fulfilled ere the New Testament scriptures were written, and in the fourth Gospel the aged Apostle recalls under His inspiration the things he had seen and heard, that we might share with him the Father's delight in His Son, and believing we might have life through His name. However much believers down the ages have loved to trace the steps of Him Who manifested the light as well as the love of heaven, a further meditation with this Exposition in our hands cannot fail to increase the richness of that true knowledge of Him which will bow our hearts in adoring worship.

As the author desired in his original Preface, may the Father's Name be glorified as "honour is truly paid to the Son" by those who have received Him, and who treasure this profound record of His matchless ways among men.

H. Harle

FOREWORD TO THE 1923 EDITION

The Fourth Gospel has a sweetness and a beauty all its own. It is loved by the simple and prized by the mature. The infant in grace lisps its easy words and the man of God still longs to know its heights and depths. It is a Gospel, strange as it may seem to some, penned specially for believers that they might be taught to believe: "These are written that ye might believe that Jesus is the Christ, and that believing ye might have life through His name" (John 20:31; see also 19:35). Yet while "believe" is one of the characteristic words of the Gospel, "faith", though so frequent in all other parts of the New Testament, does not occur once.

It has been called the "Gospel of the Rejection", because the Lord Jesus is shown in its history to have that character from the beginning, while the Synoptists show its gradual development. The Gospel has many peculiarities which mark it out as an exceptional book, such as the word "disciples" for "apostles", "signs" for "miracles", "similitudes" for "parables", etc. The first verses of the first chapter open a window into the eternity of the past, and in the seventeenth chapter we are permitted to hear the voice of communion in the Godhead. Seven signs only are selected by John from the multitude the Lord performed during the days of His ministry, and one which was wrought after His resurrection.

John was inspired to present the Saviour in this Gospel as the eternal Son of God, yet as One on Whose bosom he could recline, though when he afterwards beheld Him in His official dignity, he fell at His feet as dead (Revelation 1:17).

Mr. Kelly in his Exposition shows in detail how this Gospel was framed that men might honour the Son even as they honour the Father.

W. J. Hocking

July, 1923

"These have been written that ye may believe that Jesus is the Christ, the Son of God; and that believing ye may have life in His Name."— 20:31

AUTHOR'S PREFACE

The work now before the Christian did not consist of discourses taken down in shorthand and corrected, as many books of mine have been. It was written with care from first to last, with the deep conviction how little my plummet, perhaps anyone's, can sound its revealed depths. Still, its communications are freely given by the God and Father of our Lord Jesus, that we might know them through the Spirit in our measure. May the truth, and nothing but the truth, commend itself to the conscience and heart of all God's children. It is a day when many, listening to the tempter, have found a hard saying in the matchless words of life eternal, and even gone back, so as to walk no more with the Lord. May they so learn, as it were from His own lips, that the words He has spoken are spirit and are life. Of these sayings none is more eminent a witness among the inspired than the apostle, and of his inspired writings none so rich in these sayings as his Gospel. May grace use whatever help may be in this exposition to better appreciate the name of our Lord Jesus Christ. No reader is likely to feel its shortcomings so much as the writer, but he also feels that the Father delights in honour truly paid to the Son. This throughout he has sought humbly and heartily, counting on the Spirit's presence and power, Who is here to glorify Him.

LONDON, *April*, 1898.

PREFACE TO THE SECOND EDITION

The Exposition of the Fourth Gospel issued, within the last ten years, by Mr. William Kelly happily contained his own translation of the Greek text preferred by him, with critical apparatus. Each of these is reproduced in the new edition, whilst the footnotes now record also the voice of the Syriac codex of Sinai among the ancient versions, besides the respective readings adopted for their texts by Professor B. Weiss (1901) and Professor Blass (1902). Such additions are enclosed in crotchets {square brackets[]}, which are used also for the few alternative renderings here added in harmony with the Exposition. Quotations from the Old Testament have been treated as in the recently published volume of the same writer's *Exposition of Mark*. {"Any deviations from the Authorised Version of Old Testament passages quoted are drawn from the ... {J.N. Darby} translation (London: G. Morrish, 1890)."} The few marginal references to parallel passages of the Synoptics, the Appendix and Indexes are likewise new features.

The expositor had before him the English works in chief repute relating to this Gospel that had appeared down to the time of the publication of his book. The outlook has been extended to the latest—in particular German and American—literature noticed in the Appendix. Although, as a learned dignitary has just been saying from his pulpit, "the Gospel of St. John is the one book in the Bible which stands in least need of the apologist", there has been a keen attack upon it in recent years, so that the Notes at the end are largely devoted to an examination of the criticism in fashion, by many regarded with deep concern.

Mr. Kelly had the happiness of being outside the ranks of those who have "to do the best they can for the side on which they are retained." Neither adhesion to ecclesiastical tradition nor academical influences hampered his independence, which was therefore no more governed by antecedent theories of the conventional "apologetic" than by those of the rigidly "critical" type. His robust religious belief was as far from being synonymous with "dogma" on the one hand as with "mysticism" on the other. In conflict with current unbelief, he did not understand any process of buttering bread on both sides: he seriously and consistently did battle for the Faith of the Gospel, as he understood that, "once for all delivered to the saints." A melancholy feature at the present day is the readiness of some without pain to write in derogation of the faith in which they were reared; with such Mr. Kelly had nothing in common.

The editor associates himself closely with the standpoint of the Exposition; his notes, as a Scottish review of the volume on *Mark* has stated of the Appendix there, are "in logical development of Mr. Kelly's views." He has endeavoured to speak plainly, yet with becoming respect towards scholars whose statements are combated. One may value the better aspects of a method, whilst questioning the application of it in the light of actual results obtained.

PREFACE TO THE SECOND EDITION

How a singularly precious book of Holy Scripture served William Kelly's ministry may be learned from this Exposition, which is reissued in the hope that it will continue to afford help to those at least who care for neither sentimental tradition nor traditional sentiment, but do love the Christ of God.

E. E. Whitfield
January, 1908

CONTENTS

	Page
Foreword to the Third Edition	3
Introduction to the 1966 Reprint of the First Edition	5
Foreword to the 1923 Edition	7
Author's Preface	10
Preface to the Second Edition	11

EXPOSITION BY WILLIAM KELLY

Introduction	17

Translation and EXPOSITION

The First Chapter	26
The Second Chapter	61
The Third Chapter	72
The Fourth Chapter	117
The Fifth Chapter	150
The Sixth Chapter	182
The Seventh Chapter	218
The Eighth Chapter	241
The Ninth Chapter	273
The Tenth Chapter	293
The Eleventh Chapter	318
The Twelfth Chapter	338
The Thirteenth Chapter	358
The Fourteenth Chapter	395

CONTENTS

The Fifteenth Chapter 424

The Sixteenth Chapter 453

The Seventeenth Chapter 481

The Eighteenth Chapter 515

The Nineteenth Chapter 535

The Twentieth Chapter 562

The Twenty-First Chapter 600

Indexes to the Exposition

Index of Scripture Quotations 627

Index of Greek and Hebrew Words 632

Index of Subjects 633

APPENDIX OF ADDITIONAL NOTES BY EDWARD ELIHU WHITFIELD

Editions of Authors Used 651

NOTES 661

Indexes to the Notes

Index of Scripture Quotations in the Notes 819

Index of Greek and Hebrew Words in the Notes 824

Index of Subjects in the Notes 826

Referenced Notes on the Gospels of Mark and Luke

Notes on the Gospel of Mark 843

Note on the Gospel of Luke 907

AN EXPOSITION OF THE GOSPEL OF JOHN

INTRODUCTION

That the fourth Gospel is characterised by setting forth the Lord Jesus as the Word, the Only-begotten Son, God Himself, on earth can be questioned by no intelligent Christian. It is not as Messiah, Son of David and of Abraham, yet withal the Jehovah of Israel, Emmanuel; nor yet as the Son devoted to the service of God, above all in the gospel; neither is it as the Holy Thing born of the Virgin by the miraculous agency of the Holy Ghost, and in this sense too Son of God, that He is presented, as in each of the other inspired accounts respectively by Matthew, Mark, and Luke. In the Gospel of John[1: This and all other reference figures relate to the Editor's notes respectively so numbered in the Appendix.] His divine nature shines from under the veil of flesh, as He moves here and there, evermore displaying the Father in His Person and words and ways; and then, on His going above, giving and sending the Holy Ghost to be with and in His own for ever.

Hence it is that He is here declared the giver of eternal life to the believer, who is accordingly entitled in virtue of this new life to become a child of God. For it is no question here of dispensational dealings, nor of testimony to the creature, nor yet of the moral perfections of the man Christ Jesus. All these have their fitting places elsewhere; but here the Spirit of God has in hand a deeper task—the manifestation of the Father in the Son, and this as the Word become flesh and tabernacling here below, with its immense consequences for every soul, and even for God Himself glorified both in the exigencies of His moral being and in the intimate depths of His relationship as Father.

Further, we may take note of the divine wisdom which wrote and gave such a Gospel at a comparatively late date,[2] when the enemy was seeking to corrupt and destroy, not by Pharisaic or Sadducean adversaries, nor by idolatrous Gentiles, but by apostates and antichristian teachers. These, under the highest pretensions to knowledge and power, were undermining the truth of Christ's Person, on the side both of His proper Deity and of His real humanity,[3] to the ruin of man and to the most thankless and daring dishonour of God. No testimony came in more appropriately than that of John, who, like the writer of the earliest Gospel, was an eyewitness,[4] and even above all others familiar, if one may reverently so say, with the Lord Jesus as man on earth. Yet none the less, but above all, is he the instrument of attesting His divine glory. The bearing of both on the closing efforts of Satan, even then and thenceforward prevalent (1 John 2:18), is also most evident and of supreme importance. The Lord, on the other hand, as ever in His grace, met the efforts of Satan by a fuller assertion of "That which was from the beginning," for divine glory in the clearing, comfort, and consolation of the family of God—yea, of the babes. For what greater security than to find themselves the objects of the Father's love, loved as the Son was loved, Himself in

INTRODUCTION

them, and they in Him, Who on departing assures them of the abiding presence of that other Paraclete, the Holy Spirit?—a blessedness so great that He declares His own deeply missed absence "expedient" for them in order to secure it.

Consequently, along with the reality and manifestation of eternal life in man, in Christ the Son, there is the careful, complete, and distinct abolishing of Jewish or any other relationships for man in the flesh with God; while it is shown clearly both in the introduction and at the end of the Gospel that the dispensations of God are not overlooked, nor Christ's relation to them, His Person, Divine yet a man, being the pivot on which all turns.

Indeed, it was a great oversight of the ancient ecclesiastical writers to regard John as the evangelist who views the Lord or His own in their heavenly connections, ill as the eagle could symbolize any such thing; though even Augustine accepted the fancy, as Victorinus seems first to have suggested it. But theologians do not at all agree; for Irenæus will have Mark to be the eagle, and Andreas follows in his wake. Williams of late—and he is not alone—revived the interpretation of Augustine, who strangely applied the man to Mark and the ox to Luke, where the converse would have been at least more plausible. Many more applications equally wild prevailed; but they are hardly worth recording.

For the "living creatures" in Revelation 4 and elsewhere have no real or intended relation to the four Gospels. These present to us the grace of God which appeared in Christ among men, and the redemption which He accomplished in the rejected Messiah. The cherubim, on the contrary, are revealed when the throne on high assumes a judicial character in chastisements, preparatory to the Lord's taking the kingdom of the world and appearing from heaven for that reign. They symbolize the divine attributes in figures taken from the heads of creation. Ingenious but superficial analogies cannot avail against the entire moral bearing of their associations as contrasted as grace is with judgment.

But the characteristic truth which it is hard to overlook in John, with a slight exception here and there, is God manifesting Himself in His Son, yet man on earth; not man in Him the exalted Christ on high, which is the line assigned to the apostle Paul, and among the inspired accounts of the Lord to the end of Luke and even, in a measure, of Mark. Therefore we may notice that there is no Ascension scene (though abundantly supposed) in John any more than in Matthew, though for wholly different reasons. For the first Gospel shows us the Lord in His final presentation, risen indeed but still maintaining His links of relationship with the disciples or Jewish remnant in Galilee, where He gives them their great commission, and assures them of His presence with them till the consummation of the age. The last shows us Him uniting in His person the glory not only of the risen man and Son of God, the last Adam, but also of the Lord God, Who as the quickening spirit breathes the breath of a better life in resurrection power into His disciples, and thereon gives also a mystical view of the age to come, with the special places of both Peter and John.

It is God on earth, therefore, that appears in the account of our Lord here, not (save for exceptional purposes) man glorified in heaven, as in the writings of St. Paul.[5] Hence in the first chapter, so remarkable for the fulness with which the titles of Christ are brought before us there, we do not read of Him either as priest or as Head of the Church—relations which are exclusively bound up with His exaltation above and service at the right hand of God. John presents all that is divine in Christ's person and work on earth; and as he gives us the setting aside of the first man in his best shape, so also the absolute need of the divine nature if man is to see or enter the kingdom of God. What is essential and abiding naturally flows from the presence of a divine Person revealing Himself here below in grace and truth.

Again, the character of the truth before the Holy Spirit evidently excludes any genealogy such as is found in the Gospels of Matthew and Luke, who respectively traced our blessed Lord down from Abraham and David, or up to Adam, "which was (the son) of God." Here John gives no such birth-roll; for how trace the line of Him Who in the beginning, before a creature existed, was with God and was God? If Mark is devoted to the details of His service, especially His service in the gospel, accompanied by suited powers and signs (for He would arouse man and appeal to unbelievers in the patient goodness of God), he in the wisdom of the same Spirit was led to omit all record of His earthly parentage and early life, and at once enters on His work, only preceded by a brief notice of His herald, John the Baptist, in his work.[6] Hence, as the Lord was the perfect Servant, so the perfect account of it says nothing here of a genealogy; for who would ask the pedigree of a servant? Thus, if His service seems to keep it out from Mark, His Deity, being the prominent truth, renders it unsuitable for the Spirit's purpose by John. It is only from all the four that we receive the truth in its various fulness:[7] only so could even God adequately reveal to us our Lord Jesus Christ. In the Gospels He is given us in view not merely of our need, but of the divine love and glory.

The contents of this Gospel may be more clearly apprehended by the summary that follows.[a] Chapters 1-4 precede the Galilean ministry of our Lord given by the three Synoptists. John the herald was still baptizing, and free (chapter 3:23-24); while our Lord was on His way to Galilee (chapter 4) through Samaria. Chapters 1 to 2:22 are preliminary; 1:1-18 being the wondrous and suited preface of His personal glory, seen in the chapter throughout. Then from verses 19-42 is John's testimony historically—not to others only about Jesus, but to Himself {or, following *Lectures Introductory to the Study of the Gospels*: to others, for himself he was not the Christ, but for Jesus he says no more; to his disciples, Jesus is the Lamb of God, even the Son of God}—and its fruit. From verse 43 Christ calls individually and gathers, wherein He passes from the truth of His position as the Christ in Psalm 2 to the wider and higher glory of the Son of Man in Psalm 8. Then we have in chapter 2:1-22 the marriage in Cana of Galilee which manifests His glory, and His execution of judgment in purifying the temple, as risen from the dead.

From chapter 2:23 is shown the impossibility of God's trusting man as he is, and in chapter 3 the necessity of his being born anew to see or enter the kingdom of God, even on its earthly side. The cross of the Son of Man is no less requisite; but God's Only-begotten Son is given in His love to save the world. Only faith in His name is indispensable. It is not a charge of law violated, but of light come and hated, men's works being evil. But John, the Bridegroom's friend, rejoices to be eclipsed by His glory Who comes from heaven and is above all, not only the Sent One with God's words, but the Son of His love to Whom the Father has given all things. To believe on Him, therefore, is to have life eternal; to disobey Him in

INTRODUCTION

unbelief is to have the wrath of God abiding on him. Such is the introduction.

Chapter 4 is the Son of God humbling Himself in grace to draw a reprobate Samaritan to God, in order to worship Him and as Father too in spirit and truth, Jerusalem being now gone, as her rival was nothing. For He is the Saviour of the world. Yet the courtier in Capernaum proves that his faith in the Saviour for his sick son, though in Jewish form, was not in vain. He does not despise feeble faith.

Chapter 5 shows us Jesus the Son of God, not a healer only, but quickening the dead souls that hear Him now, and raising to a life resurrection at His coming; while those who hearken not and live wickedly He, the Son of Man, will raise to a resurrection of judgment. The grounds of faith are therefore added in the rest of the chapter.

In chapter 6 the sign of the bread He gave the great crowd introduces the teaching of Himself, incarnate, the True Bread from heaven, and in death His flesh truly food and His blood truly drink, followed by His ascension. He is the object of faith thus, as the Quickener in the preceding chapter.

Thence chapter 7 lets us into His sending down the Holy Spirit from Himself in glory before the Feast of Tabernacles is literally fulfilled. Such is the power for witness, as in chapter 4 for worship. In these four chapters the Lord is set as Himself the truth of which Israel had possessed forms.

In chapters 8 and 9 His word and His work are rejected respectively and to the uttermost. Nevertheless the sheep, which receive both to their blessing, He not only keeps but leads outside the fold to better still, one flock, one Shepherd. Nothing can harm. They are in the Father's hand and in the Son's (chapter 10).

Chapters 11 and 12 give us the testimony to Christ, as Son of God in resurrection power, as Son of David according to prophecy, and as Son of Man bringing in through His death a new, unlimited, and everlasting glory, which His joint-heirs should share with Him.

From chapters 13 to 17 is unfolded the Lord's position in heaven, and what He is for us then and there—an entirely new thing for the disciples who looked for the kingdom here and now. He is our Advocate (1 John 2:1), and washes by the word our feet defiled by the way; and when Judas is gone out, opens His death as morally glorifying Himself, glorifying God in every way, and His glorification in Him as the immediate consequence. But He is coming (chapter 14) to receive them to Himself in the Father's house, the proper Christian hope. Meanwhile Christ promises another Advocate, or Paraclete, to dwell with them and be in them for ever, Who is the present power of Christianity, and works in the obedience of the Christian. In chapter 15 we have the Christian position on earth contrasted with Judaism. It is not union but communion with Christ to bear fruit, and render testimony to His glory: moral government is in question rather than sovereign grace. Chapter 16 treats of the presence of the Spirit, what it proves to the world, and how He deals with the believers who now ask the Father in Christ's name. Chapter 17, in Christ's outpouring to the Father, gives our place with Him, and apart from the world, in past, present, and future unity, both privilege in heaven with Him by and by, and our wondrous blessedness even now.

Chapters 18 and 19 characteristically sketch the closing scenes of His varied mock trials after His willing surrender, and the humiliating experience of His disciples; then the death of the cross, and its fruit, as well as the beloved disciple's witness, to whom He confided His mother. Chapter 20 presents Him risen, His message through Mary of Magdala, and His manifestation to the gathered disciples on the Resurrection, and in eight days to Thomas, the type of Israel seeing and believing. Chapter 21 adds the mystical picture of the millennial age, when the Gentiles become Christ's, and the net is not broken as heretofore. As an appendix, we have Peter restored and reinstated, with the assurance that in the weakness of age grace would strengthen him to die for his Master, Whom he failed thus to glorify in the day of his more youthful self-confidence. John is left in no less mysterious guise, though it was not said that he should not die, but in suspense. "If I will that he tarry till I come, what is that to thee? follow thou Me." So we know that the same pen, which God employed to set out the Son of God in His personal glory and ineffable grace, was to give us, after the translation of the heavenly on high, the divine government which will at length invest Christ and them with the world's kingdom, in the day when He will be the manifest centre of all glory—heavenly and earthly. For this and more we find in the Revelation.[8]

NOTES ON THE INTRODUCTION

a [*Cf.* subsequent *God's Inspiration of the Scriptures* (Divine Design, § 31. JOHN), pp. 347-357 {pp. 286-293, 2007 edition, Scripture Truth Publications }]

THE FIRST CHAPTER [a]
VERSES 1-5.

"In the beginning was the Word, and the Word was with God, and the Word was God" (verse 1).

The Word, the expression of the Godhead, has eternal being, distinct personality and proper Deity, not merely θειότης [Romans 1:20], but θεότης [Colossians 2:9]. We see One Who was before time began. It is not even the beginning of creation, but before then, when the Word was with God before all things were made by Him. Look back as we may before creation, the Word was—not ἐγένετο, *existed*, as One that had commenced to be, but ἦν, *was*, the Word increate—yea, the Creator. Further, He "was with God," not exactly here with the Father as such; for Scripture never speaks with such correlation. "The Word was with God." Father, Son, and Holy Ghost were there; but the Word was with God, "and the Word was God." He was no creature, but essentially Divine, though not He alone Divine. Other Persons there were in the Godhead.[9]

"The same was in the beginning with God" (verse 2);

not at a subsequent date, but "in the beginning," when no creature had commenced its existence. For this truth we are entirely indebted to God. Who could speak of such things but God? It is He Who uses John to write, and all He says is worthy of implicit faith. The Word "was in the beginning with God." His personality was eternal, no less than His nature or being. He was no mere emanation, as the Indo-Aryans dreamed in the earliest form of their thoughts known to us. For God thus was not really supreme and free, but subject to restraint necessarily incompatible with sovereignty, and ever tending to that pantheism which, making the universe to be God, denies the only true God. Thus, He was merely Tad (That), an abstract energy, yet not in self-sufficiency, but in longing for others to emanate—Brahma, Vishnu, and Siva, the Creator, the Preserver, and the Destroyer. In the Hindoo system developed later, as the Divinity was thus imaginatively resolved into emanations, so is the universe itself pantheistically to be an emanation rather than a creation formed by divine will, power, and design. All is flux and illusion. What a contrast is its Triad with the Trinity, the Father, and the Son, and the Holy Spirit, one God! And its Avataras, even that of Krishna, late as the legend rose, how remote from the Incarnation! Thereby God and man stand for ever united in one Person, by His death the Reconciler of all creation, heavenly and earthly, and of those who by grace are to reign with Him over all things to the glory of God the Father.[b]

Then as an added and after communication we are told that

> "all things were made by Him, and without Him not one thing was made which hath been made" (verse 3).

The Word was not made, but Himself made all.[c] The Word is the Creator of all that has had a derived being. He created all. No creature received being apart from Him. The Word was the agent. Had He not been God, this must have been a work impossible to Him. Had He not been "in the beginning with God," it could not have been in any special way attributed to Him, the eternal Word. But creation is here affirmed as His work, not in a positive way only, but without exception for every creature. So in Colossians 1:16-17 we are told that "by (ἐν, in virtue of) Him were created all things, the things in the heavens and the things on the earth, the visible and the invisible, whether thrones, or lordships, or principalities, or authorities; all things have been created through Him, and for Him; and He is before all things, and by (ἐν) Him all things consist (or, are held together)." What repeated and irrefutable proofs of Deity![d]

Each of these scriptures gives us precise instruction of the highest kind. Even Genesis 1, though it points in verses 1 and 2 to states of creation indefinitely anterior to Adam, only begins with John 1:3. But of the details that followed in time no scripture gives us such complete information. What was before creation is wholly omitted by Moses. John 1:1-2 shows us eternity before creation, as well as creation itself (verse 3), in the most precise terms.[9a]

But there is much more than the power of an eternal Being. For we come now to a thing higher and more intimate: not to what was brought into being[9b] through Him, but to what was in Him. "This is the true God and eternal life" (1 John 5:20).

"In Him was life."[e]

THE FIRST CHAPTER

The only life here noticed is that which, being eternal, is capable of knowing, enjoying, serving, and worshipping God, suited to His presence, and to be there for ever. Believers have life; but it is in the Son, not in them but in Him. Here, however, it is not pursued beyond its source in Him; its communication will soon follow in due course. The Spirit is occupied with the character of His person. Only He adds at this point the deeply interesting announcement,

> "and the life was the light of men" (verse 4).[11]

Not angels but men were the object. He does not say life but light of men. The life was only for those that believe in His name: the light goes far beyond. That which makes manifest is light. So in Proverbs 8, the beautiful introduction of Wisdom, Whom Jehovah possessed in the beginning of His way before His works of old, not more His delight than Wisdom's delights were with the sons of men.

But men, in fact, were in a fallen condition, and at a distance from God; and so it is intimated here that a worse darkness reigned than the gloom which covered the deep before the six days' work began.

> "And the light shineth in darkness, and the darkness comprehended (that is, apprehended) it not" (verse 5).

Darkness is neither the mother of all, as the heathen said, nor a malignant Demiurge, the never-ceasing opponent of the good Lord of light.[f] It is really the moral condition of man, fallen as he is, a negation of the light, differing wholly from the physical reality, inasmuch as it is of itself unaffected by light. Grace only, as we shall see by and by, can deal effectually with the difficulty.

Here it may be noticed that John does not discourse of life absolutely, but of life in the Word, which life is affirmed to be the Light of men. It is exclusive of other objects—at least, the proposition goes not beyond men. So in Colossians 1 Christ is said to be the image of the invisible God, Who is here only revealed to perfection in man and to men. He is the light of men, and there is no other: for if man has what Scripture calls light, he has it only in the Word, Who is the life. Beyond controversy God is light, and in Him is no darkness at all {1 John 1:5}; but He dwells in unapproachable light, Whom no man has seen, nor can see {1 Timothy 6:16}. Not so with the Word of Whom we are reading. "The light shineth in the darkness, and the darkness comprehended it not." Observe the striking precision of the phrases. It appears in darkness—such is its nature; "it shines," not "it shone"; whereas the abstract form is changed for the historical, when we are told that the darkness apprehended it not.

Thus we have had the Spirit's statement of the Word, as related first to God, next to creation, lastly to men, with a solemn sentence on their moral state in relation to the light. and not merely to life.

Verses 6-8.

We are next presented with John sent from God to testify of the Light.

> "There was a man sent from God—his name John. The same came for witness that he might witness about the Light, that all might believe through him. He was not the Light, but that he might witness about the Light" (verses 6-8).

God, Who is love, was active in His goodness to draw attention to the Light; for deep was man's need. Hence there was a man sent from Him—his name John.[12] He, as we are told elsewhere {John 5:35}, was the burning and shining lamp (ὁ λύχνος); but the Word was the Light (τὸ φῶς) concerning Whom he came to bear witness. For his mission is here viewed in relation, not to the law or any legal purpose, but to the Light (and hence its scope is far beyond Israel), that he might witness concerning the Light, that all[12a] might believe through him. It is a question of personal faith in the Saviour, not merely of moral exhortation to the multitude, tax-gatherers, soldiers, or any others, as in the Gospel of Luke. Every scripture is perfect, and perfectly adapted to the divine purpose of glorifying Jesus.

VERSES 9-13.

The Light is here the object of God's gracious purpose. John is but an instrument and witness; *he* was not the Light, but that he might witness concerning the Light.

> "The true Light was that (or, He was the true Light) which, coming into the world, lighteth every man" (verse 9),

in exclusion of Philonism and Platonism, as we have seen before of eternal matter and Manicheism. The law dealt with those under it—that is, with Israel; the Light, on coming into the world—a cardinal point in the teaching of our Apostle (1 John 1:1-4; 2:8, 14, etc.)—casts its light on every man. Coming, or a comer, into the world is used by the Rabbis for birth as man; but for this very reason it would be the merest tautology if viewed in apposition with π. ἄνθρ. "every man."[g] It qualifies the relative, and affirms that as incarnate the true Light lights every man—that is, sheds light on him.

The result, however, in itself is, and can only be, condemnation by reason of opposition of nature; for, as we are told,

> "He was in the world, and the world was made (or, brought into being) through Him, and the world knew Him not. He came unto His own, and His own received Him not; but as many as received Him, to them He gave authority to become children of God, to those that believe on His name; who were born not of blood, nor of flesh's will, nor of man's (ἀνδρὸς) will, but of God" (verses 10-13).

What infinite and loving condescension that He, the eternal Word, the true Light, should be in the world[14]—the world which receiveth its being from Him! How dense its ignorance that the world knew Him not, its Creator! But He had one place on earth which He was pleased to regard as His own peculiar (τὰ ἴδια)[15]: there He came; and (οἱ ἴδιοι) His own people (it is not said knew Him not, but) received Him not! It was rejection, not ignorance.

This prepared the way for the manifestation of a new thing, men from out of the ruined world separated to a new and incomparably nearer relationship with God, to whom, as many as received Christ (for it is no question of "every man" here), He gave right or title to enter the place of God's children, to those that believe on His name. Nor is this a mere external position of honour, into which sovereignty might choose, so as to maintain by adoption family name and grandeur. It is a real communication of life and nature, a living birth-tie.[16] They were τέκνα Θεοῦ, God's children. It is not that they had been better than others. They had been once alienated, and enemies in mind by wicked works. They believed on Christ's name; they were born of God. It was a work of divine grace through faith. Receiving the Word, they were begotten of God. Natural generation from either side, effort of one's own, influence of another however exalted, had no place here.

John nowhere describes believers as *υἱοί* but as *τέκνα*, for his point is life in Christ, rather than the counsels of God by redemption. Paul, on the other hand (as in Romans 8), calls us both *υἱούς* and *τέκνα Θεοῦ*, because he is setting forth alike the high place given us now in contrast with bondage under the law, and also the intimacy of our relationship as children of God. On the other hand, it is notable that Jesus is never called *τέκνον* (though as Messiah He is styled *παῖς*, or Servant), but *υἱός*. He is the Son, the Only-begotten Son in the bosom of the Father, but not *τέκνον* as if He were born of God as we are. Thus it is the name of nearest but derived relationship. This is quite confirmed by the immediately following statement of John, "who were born ... of God." So indeed it will be seen invariably elsewhere, despite the Authorised Version, which wrongly represents *τέκνα* by "sons" in his First Epistle, chapter 3. They believe on His name, after the manifestation of what the Word is.[17] Every creature source is shut out, as well as all previous relationship closed and done with; a new race is brought in. They were men of course, and cease not to be men as a fact; but they are born afresh spiritually, born of God most truly, partake of the divine nature (2 Peter 1) in this sense, as deriving their new life from God.

Life, as we may observe ever throughout the writings of John and Paul, is wholly distinct from simple existence. It is the possession of that divine character of being, which in the Son never had a beginning, for He was the eternal life which was with the Father and was manifested to us {1 John 1:2}. He is our life {Colossians 3:4}; because He lives, we also live {John 14:19}. It is true in Him and in us: in Him essentially, in us derivatively through grace; yet this is not so as to be for a moment independent of Him, but in Him. Still we have the life now; nowhere is it taught that we shall be born of God, only that as believers we are. "Begotten" now, as distinct from "born," is false, absurd, and without a shadow of scripture to support it.

Verses 14-18.

From the revelation of the Word in His own intrinsic nature, we now turn to His actual manifestation as man here below. The Incarnation is brought before us, the full revelation of God to man and in man.

> "And the Word became flesh and tabernacled among us (and we beheld His glory, glory as of an only-begotten from beside a father), full of grace and truth" (verse 14).

Here it is not what the Word was, but what He became. He was God; He became flesh[18] and dwelt[18a] among us, full of grace and truth.

It was no transient vision, however momentous, as on the holy mount. It was a contemplation[19] of His glory vouchsafed to His witnesses, not of an earthly conqueror, nor Messianic even, but glory[20] as of an only-begotten from beside [παρά] a father.[21] No sword girds His thigh, no riding to victory, no terrible things in righteousness: the incarnate Word dwelt among us, full of grace and truth. Such is He that was in and from the beginning, and thus known. He was the King undoubtedly, but not so portrayed here. He is infinitely more than King, even God, yet God on earth, man dwelling among men, full of grace and truth. So only could God be displayed, unless in judgment which had left no hope but only destroyed to the bitter end at once and unreservedly. For infinitely different purposes had He come, as this passage itself declares in due season, perfectly knowing and feeling the universal evil of man. He tabernacled among us full of grace and truth. It was not a visit or a theophany, as in Old Testament experiences. So He here manifested God, Who is love. But grace is more; it is love in the midst of evil, rising above it, going down under it, overcoming it with good.

And such was Jesus, sojourning on earth, full of truth withal; for otherwise grace was no more grace, but a base imitation, and most ruinous both for God and to man. Not such was Jesus, but full of grace and truth, and in this order too. For grace brings in the truth and enables souls to receive truth and to bear it, themselves as sinners judged by it. He, and He only, was full of grace and truth. To make it known, to make God Himself thus known, He came. For as grace is the activity of divine love in the midst of evil,[22] so truth is the revelation of all things as they really are, from God Himself and His ways and counsels down to man and every thought and feeling as well as word and work of man—yea, of every invisible agency for good or evil throughout all time, and throughout all eternity.[h] So He dwelt among us, full of grace and truth.

Nor did God fail to render testimony to Him thus.

> "John witnesseth about Him, and hath cried, saying, This was He of whom I said, He that cometh after me is become before me, for He was before me" (verse 15).

Most strikingly is John introduced with his testimony in each of the great divisions of the chapter. Before it was to the abstract revelation of the Light. Here it is to His actual presentation to the world, and as it is historical, so we have what John cries, not merely a description as before. He says, "This was He of whom I said," etc. The coming of Jesus after John was no derogation from His glory, but the very contrary. No greater prophet than John the Baptist had arisen among those born of women. But Jesus is God. If He was pleased therefore to come after John in time, He had become incomparably before him in place and title; nay, He was really before him, but this only because He is Divine.

The last verse (15) appears to be a parenthesis, however full of instruction. But the direct line of truth runs, "full of grace and truth …

> and of His fulness all we received, and grace for grace" (verse 16).

An astonishing truth! He is the gift and the giver—full of grace and truth; and of His fulness did we all receive.[i] Such is the portion of the least believer. The strongest is only the stronger, because he better appreciates Him. For there is no blessing outside Him, and consequently no lack for the soul that possesses Jesus. If the Colossian saints, if any others, seek to add any other thing to the Lord, it is a real loss, not gain. It is but to add what detracts from Him. For Christ is all ($τὰ\ π.$), and in all.

The expression "and grace for grace" has perplexed many, but without much reason; for an analogous phrase occurs, even in profane authors not infrequently, which ought to satisfy any inquirer that it simply means grace upon grace,[24] one succeeding to another without stint or failure—super-abundance of grace, and not a mere literal notion of grace in us answering to grace in Him. It will be noticed, further, that Scripture speaks of grace upon grace, not truth upon truth, which last would be wholly unsuitable; for the truth is one, and cannot be so spoken of. The same apostle wrote even to the babes, not because they did not know the truth, but because they do know it, and that no lie is of the truth. The unction, which they, in fact, received from Him, teaches them as to all things, and is true, and is not a lie {1 John 2:21, 27}. But as grace brings the truth, so the truth exercises in grace. How blessed that of His fulness all we received, and grace for grace!

Wholly different was seen at Sinai,

> "for the law was given through Moses, grace and truth came through Jesus Christ" (verse 17).

Not that the law is sin. Far be the thought. It is holy, and the commandment holy and just and good. But it is altogether impotent to deliver man or to reveal God. It has neither life to give nor object to make known. It requires from man what he ought to render both to God and to his fellows; but in vain is it required from man, already a sinner before the law was given. For sin entered the world through Adam no less surely than the law was given through Moses. Man fell and was lost; none could bring eternal life but Jesus Christ the Lord.[25] Even this was wholly unavailable to man without His death in expiation of sin. Here, however, we have not yet reached the work of Christ, nor the message of grace that goes out to the world grounded on it in the gospel, but His Person in the world; and to this the testimony is "grace and truth came (ἐγένετο) through Jesus Christ." There, and there only, was the divine love superior to man's evil; there, and there only, was everything revealed, and in its due relation to God, for such is the truth. Truly Jesus is a divine Saviour.

But there is yet more than this. God Himself must be known, not merely fulness of blessing come in Christ, or souls be brought into the blessing by redemption. Yet man as such is incapable of knowing God. How is this difficulty to be solved?

> "No one hath seen God at any time: the[j] Only-begotten Son[k] Who is in the bosom of the Father—*He* declared (Him)" (verse 18).

Thus only can God be known as He is, for Christ is the truth, the revealer and revelation of God, as of everything in God's sight. Nowhere does Scripture say with rationalists and, one regrets to add, with theologians, that God is the truth.[26a] Not so: God is the "I AM," the self-subsisting One; He is light, He is love. But Christ is the truth objectively, as the Spirit is in power, working in man. And Christ has declared God, as One Who as the Son *is* in the bosom of the Father, not Who *was,* as if He had left it; as He left the glory and is now gone back into glory as man. He never left the Father's bosom. It is His constant place, and His peculiar mode of relationship with the Father. Hence we by the Holy Ghost are in grace privileged to know God, even as the Son declared Him, Who perfectly, infinitely, enjoyed love in that relationship from everlasting and to everlasting. Into what a circle of divine association does He not introduce us! It is not the Light of men, not yet the Word acting, or becoming flesh, but the Only-begotten Son Who is in the Father's bosom, declaring Him according to His own competency of nature and the fulness of His own intimacy with the Father. Even John Baptist, as having his origin in the earth, was of the earth and spoke as of it.²⁶ᵇ Jesus alone of men could be said to come out of heaven and be above all, testifying what He had seen and heard, as the Holy Spirit also does. It was for Him to declare God, and this in His own proper relationship.

If the verses which precede comprise the divine preface, the sections which follow may be viewed as an introduction. The Baptist, in answer to the inquiring deputation, gives an explicit, though in the first place negative, testimony to the Lord Jesus. A singularly fitted vessel of witness to the Messiah, as he was himself filled by the Spirit from his mother's womb, he was sustained as scarce another had ever been in nothing but the function of making straight the way of Jehovah.²⁷

Verses 19-28.

"And this is the witness of John when the Jews²⁸ sent from Jerusalem priests and Levites that they might ask him, Who art thou? And he confessed, and denied not, and confessed, I am not the Christ. And they asked him, What then? Art thou Elijah? And he saith, I am not. Art thou the prophet? And he answered, No. They said therefore to him, Who art thou, that we may give an answer to those that sent us? What sayest thou of thyself? He said, I (am the) voice of one crying in the wilderness, Make straight the way of Jehovah, as said Isaiah the prophet. And they were sent from among the Pharisees; and they asked him and said to him, Why then baptizest thou, if thou art not the Christ, nor Elijah, nor the prophet? John answered them, saying, I baptize with (ἐν) water: in the midst of you standeth, Whom ye know not, He who cometh after me, of Whom I am not worthy to unloose the thong of His sandal.

These things took place in Bethany,[1] across the Jordan where John was baptizing" (verses 19-28).

Thus did God take care to rouse a general expectancy of the Messiah in the minds of His people, and to send them the fullest witness. And never was there a more strictly independent witness than John, born and brought up and kept till the fit moment to testify of the Messiah. For while the minute questions of those sent by the Jews from Jerusalem show how men's minds were then exercised, how they wished to ascertain the real character and aim of the mysterious Israelite, himself of priestly lineage, and thereby, as they ought to have known, excluded from the Messianic title, there was no vagueness in the reply. John was not the Anointed. This was the main aim of their search; and our Gospel very simply and fully attests his reply.

There is somewhat of difficulty in the next answer. For when asked, "Art thou Elijah?" he says, "I am not." How is this denial from the lip of John himself to be reconciled with the Lord's own testimony to His servant in Matthew 17:11-12? "Elijah truly shall first come and restore all things. But I say to you, that Elijah is come already, and they knew him not, but have done unto him whatsoever they listed. Likewise shall also the Son of Man suffer of them. Then the disciples understood that He spoke to them of John the Baptist." And they were right. The key appears to lie in Matthew 11:14: "And if ye will receive it" (says the Lord in vindicating John at a time when, if ever, he seemed to waver in his testimony; for who but One is the Faithful Witness?) "this is Elijah which was (*literally*, is) to come." Such a word, however, needed ears to hear. Like the Lord (Son of Man no less than Messiah), his testimony and his lot were to be in unison with an advent in shame and sorrow as well as in power and glory. The Jews naturally cared only for the latter; but, to avail not only for God, but for the true wants of man, first must Jesus suffer before He is glorified, and comes again in power. So Elijah came to faith ("if ye will receive it") in the Baptist, who testified in humiliation and with results in man's eyes scanty and evanescent. But Elijah will come in a manner consonant with the return of the Lord to deliver Israel and bless the world under His reign. To the Jew, who only looked at the external, he was not come. To point to the Baptist would have seemed mockery; for if they had no apprehension of God's secrets or His ways, if they saw no beauty in the humbled Master, what would it avail to speak of the servant? The disciples, feeble though they might be, enter into the truths hidden from men, and are given to see beneath the surface the true style of the servant and of the Master to faith.

Nevertheless John does take his stand of witness to Jesus, to His personal and divine glory; and to this end, when challenged who he was, applies to himself in every Gospel the prophetic oracle attached to him: "I (am the) voice of one crying in the wilderness, Make straight the way of Jehovah."[30] Jesus was Jehovah, John no more than a voice in the desolation of the earth—yea, of Israel—to prepare the way before Him.

They further inquire why he baptized if neither the Messiah, nor Elijah (that is, the immediate precursor of the kingdom in power and glory over the earth—Malachi 4), nor the prophet (that is, according to Deuteronomy 18, which, however, the apostle Peter in Acts 3 as clearly applies to the Lord Jesus, as the Jews seem to have then alienated it from the Messiah).[31] This gives John the occasion to render another testimony to Christ's glory; for his answer is, that he himself baptized with water; but there stands[32] among them, yet unknown to them, One coming after, Whose sandal-thong he was not worthy to unloose.

It is evident that John's baptism had a serious import in men's minds, since, without a single sign or other miracle, it awakened the question whether the Baptist were the Christ. It intimated the close of the old state of things and a new position, instead of being the familiar practice which traditionalists would make it. On the other hand, Scripture is equally plain that it is quite distinct from Christian baptism: so much so that disciples previously baptized with John's baptism had to be baptized to Christ when they received the full truth of the gospel (Acts 19). The Reformers and others are singularly unintelligent in denying this difference, which is not only important but plain and certain. Think of Calvin's calling it a foolish mistake, into which some had been led, of supposing that John's baptism was different from ours! The confession of a coming Messiah widely differs from that of His death and resurrection; and this is the root of differences which involve weighty consequences.

From verses 19 to 28 John the Baptist does not rise beyond what was Jewish and dispensational. The next paragraph brings before us the testimony which he rendered when he saw Jesus approaching. And here we have Christ's work viewed in all the extent of gracious power which might be expected in the Gospel devoted to showing out the glory of His Person.

Verses 29-34.

"On the morrow he seeth Jesus coming unto him, and saith, Behold, the Lamb of God that taketh away the sin of the world" (verse 29).

THE FIRST CHAPTER

There was no image more familiar to a Jew's mind than that of the lamb. It was the daily sacrifice of Israel, morning and evening. Besides, the paschal lamb was the pledge for the fundamental peace of the year; even as its first institution was coeval with the departure of the sons of Israel from the house of bondage. We can understand, therefore, what thoughts and feelings must have crowded on the heart of those who looked for a Saviour now, when Jesus was thus attested by His forerunner, "Behold the Lamb (ἀμνὸς) of God." In the Book of Revelation He is frequently viewed as the Lamb, but there with a pointedly different word (ἀρνίον), the holy earth-rejected Sufferer, in contrast with the ravening wild beasts, civil or religious instruments of Satan's power in the world (chapter 13). Here the idea seems to centre not so much in the slain One exalted on high as in the sacrifice: "Behold the Lamb of God that taketh away the sin of the world."

John does not say "that will take," still less "that has taken"; nor does the notion seem at all tenable that He was then taking sin away.[33] It is, as frequently in John and elsewhere, the abstract form of speech; and the meaning should be understood in its fullest extent, irrespective of the time of its accomplishment. There was the Person, and this His work. Thus the testimony looks onward to the effects of the death of Christ as a whole; but these were not to appear all at once. The first result was to be the gospel, the message of remission of sins to every believer. Instead of the sin of the world only being before God, the blood of the Lamb is set; and God could therefore meet the world in grace, not in judgment. Not only was love come in Christ's Person as during His life, but now the blood also shed whereby God could cleanse the foulest; and the gospel is to every creature God's proclamation of His readiness to receive all, and of His perfectly cleansing all who do receive Christ. In fact, only those that are His now, the Church, receive Him; but the testimony is sent forth to all the creation.

When Christ comes again in His kingdom, there will be a further result; for all creation will then be delivered from the bondage of corruption, and Israel will at length look upon the Messiah Whom they pierced in their blind unbelief. The blessing resulting from the sacrifice of Christ will then be far and wide extended, but not complete. Only the new heavens and new earth (and this exceeds the limited scope of the Jewish prophets, but is the full meaning which the Christian apostles give the words) will behold the ultimate fulfilment; and then indeed it will be seen how truly Jesus was "the Lamb of God that taketh away the sin of the world." For then, and not till then, will sin have disappeared absolutely and all its active consequences. The wicked having been judged and cast for ever into the lake of fire, as well as Satan and his angels, righteousness will then be the footing of God's relationship with the world, not sinlessness as at first, nor dealings in Christ in view of sin as since and now, but all things made new.

Observe, however, that the Baptist does not say the "sins" of the world. What a fatality of error haunts men when they venture to handle the truth of God after a human sort! It is not only in sermons or books that one finds this common and grave blunder. The solemn liturgies of Romanism and Protestantism are alike wrong here. They alter and unconsciously falsify the word of God when directly referring to this scripture. In speaking of believers both the apostles Paul and Peter show that the Lord Himself bore their sins upon the cross. Without this, indeed, there could be neither peace secured for the conscience nor a righteous basis for worshipping God, according to the efficacy of the work of Christ. The Christian is exhorted to come boldly into the holies by the blood of Jesus, which has, at the same time, purged his sins and brought himself nigh; but this is only true of the believer. In total contrast is the state and condition of the unbeliever, of every man in nature. He is far off, in guilt, in darkness, in death. The language of the liturgies confounds all this, according indeed to the practice of their worship; for the world is treated as the Church, and the Church as the world. Were Christ the Lamb that takes away the sins of the world, all men would stand absolved before God, and might well therefore boldly approach and worship; but it is not so. The blood is now shed for the sin of the world, so that the evangelist can go forth and preach the gospel and assure all who believe of pardon from God; but all who refuse must die in their sins, and only the more terribly be judged because they refused the message of grace.

But God never forgets the personal dignity of the Lord Jesus here. Hence John the Baptist adds,

> "This is He of Whom I said, After me cometh a Man who is become before (or, hath taken precedence of) me, for He was before me.ᵐ And I knew Him not, but that He might be manifested to Israel, therefore came I baptizing with (ἐν) water" (verses 30-31).

There is no reference here to His Messianic judgment, as in other Gospels, which, on the other hand, are silent as regards a testimony like this to His glory. Undoubtedly also John did call souls in Israel to repent in view of the kingdom as at hand; but here the one object is the manifestation of Jesus to Israel. It is an absorbing topic of this Gospel indeed. The previous unacquaintance of the Baptist[34] with Jesus made his testimony so much the more solemn and emphatically of God; and whatever the inward conviction he had as the Lord came for baptism, it did not hinder the external sign nor the witness he bears to His Person and His work as he had borne before it.

Hence we read,

> "And John bore witness, saying, I have beheld the Spirit descending as a dove out of heaven, and it abode upon Him. And I knew Him not; but He that sent me to baptize with ($ἐν$) water, *He* said unto me, Upon whomsoever thou shalt see the Spirit descending and abiding on Him, this is He that baptizeth with ($ἐν$, the) Holy Spirit. And I have seen and borne witness that this is the Son of God" (verses 32-34).[35]

Such was the suited sign for the Saviour. Ravens might have been employed in God's wisdom to feed the famished prophet at another dark day; but not such was the appearance of the Spirit descending from heaven to abide on Jesus. The dove only could be the proper form, emblematic of the spotless purity of Him on Whom He came. Yet did He come upon Him as man, but Jesus was man without sin; as truly man as any other, but how different from all before or after! He was the Second Man in bright contrast with the first. And He is the last Adam: in vain does unbelief look for a higher development, overlooking Him in Whom dwelt all the fulness of the Godhead bodily.

Observe, again, the Spirit came before the death of the Lord Jesus. If Christ died, He died for others. If He suffered and became a sacrifice, it was not for Himself.

Jesus needed no blood in order that He might subsequently be anointed with the holy oil. He was Himself the Holy One of God in that very nature which in every other case had dishonoured God.

But if the Spirit abode on Him as man, this is He that baptizes with the Holy Spirit. None could so baptize but God. It were blasphemy to say otherwise. It is the fullest prerogative of a divine Person so to act; and hence John the Baptist utterly disclaimed it, and in every Gospel points to Jesus only as the Baptizer by (ἐν) the Holy Ghost, as himself had come baptizing with water. It is the mighty work of Jesus from heaven, as He was the Lamb of God on the cross.

Thus, though the immediate aim of John's mission with baptism attached to it was for the manifestation of Jesus to Israel, he testifies to Him as the Lamb of God in relation to the world, the Eternal at whatever time He came (and surely it was the right moment, "the fulness of the time," as the great apostle assures us—Galatians 4:4), not merely as the object of the Holy Ghost's descent to abide on Him, but as baptizing with the Holy Ghost. "And I have seen and borne witness that this is the Son[n] of God." Such was His everlasting relationship: not the Son of Man Who must be lifted up if we are to have life eternal, but the Lamb of God and the Son of God. On the other hand, it is not here the Father declared by, or revealing Himself in, His Only-begotten Son, but *God* in view of the broad fact of the world's sin, and Jesus His Lamb to take its sin away. So the baptism of the Holy Ghost is not quickening, but that power of the Spirit which acts on the life already possessed by the believer, separates from all that is of flesh and world, and sets in communion with God's nature and glory as revealed in Christ. He was as man on earth, not only Son of God, but always conscious of it; we becoming so by faith in Him are rendered conscious of our relationship through the Holy Ghost given to us. Nevertheless even Him, as the Gospels show, the descent of the Spirit Who anointed Him placed in a new position here below. All here is public announcement and reaches the world in result.

VERSES 35-39.

We have had before us John's testimony reaching out far beyond the Messiah in Israel; we see now the effect of his ministry.

> "Again, on the morrow, stood John and two of his disciples; and, looking at Jesus as He walked, he saith, Behold, the Lamb of God! and the two disciples heard him speak, and followed Jesus. But Jesus, having turned and beheld them following, saith to them, What seek ye? And they said to Him, Rabbi (which is to say, being interpreted, Teacher), where abidest Thou? He saith to them, Come and see. They went therefore° and saw where He abode, and abode with Him that day. It was about the tenth hour" (verses 35-39).

It is not the fullest or clearest statement of the truth which most acts on others. Nothing tells so powerfully as the expression of the heart's joy and delight in an object that is worthy. So it was now. "Looking at Jesus as He walked, he saith, Behold, the Lamb of God!" The greatest of woman-born acknowledges the Saviour with unaffected homage, and his own disciples that heard him speak follow Jesus. "He must increase, but I must decrease." And so it ought to be. Not John, but Jesus, is the centre: a man, but God, for none other could be a centre without derogation from the divine glory. Jesus maintains that place, but this as man too. Wonderful truth, and for man how precious and cheering! John was the servant of God's purpose, and his mission was thus best executed when his disciples followed Jesus. The Spirit of God supplants human and earthly motives. How, indeed, could it be otherwise, if one really believed that He in His Person was God on earth? He must be the one exclusive and attractive centre for all that know Him; and John's work was to prepare the way before Him. So here his ministry gathers to Jesus, sending from himself to the Lord.

But if in the Gospel of Matthew the Lord has a city if not a home, which we can name, here in that of John it is unnoticed where He abode. The disciples heard His voice, came and saw where He abode, and abode with Him that day; but for others it is unnamed and unknown. We can understand that so it should be with One Who was not only God in man on earth, but this wholly rejected of the world. And so divine life effects in those that are His: "therefore the world knoweth us not, because it knew Him not" (1 John 3:1).

Verses 40-42.

Nor does the work stop there or then.

> "Andrew, the brother of Simon Peter,[36] was one of the two that heard (it) from John and followed Him. He first findeth his own brother Simon, and saith to him, We have found the Messiah (which interpreted is Christ),[37] and he led him to Jesus. Jesus, looking at him, said, Thou art Simon,[38] the son of Jonah (or, John);[p] thou shalt be called Kephas, which is interpreted Peter (or, Stone)[39]" (verses 40-42).

Deeply interesting are the glimpses at the first introduction to Jesus of those souls who receiving Him found life eternal in Him, and were called afterwards to be foundations of that new building which would supersede the old, God's habitation in the Spirit. But all here concentrates in the Person of Jesus, to Whom Simon is brought by his brother, one of the first two whose souls were drawn to Him, however little yet they appreciated His glory. Yet was it a divine work, and Simon's coming was answered with a knowledge of past and present and future that told out Who and What He was, Who now spoke to man on earth in grace.

Here the same principle reappears. Jesus, the image of the invisible God, the only perfect manifestation of God, is the acknowledged centre beyond all rivalry. He was to die, as this Gospel relates (chapter 11), to gather in one the scattered children of God; as He will by and by gather all things in heaven and all things on earth under His headship (Ephesians 1:10). But then His Person could not but be the one centre of attraction to every one who saw by faith what He is entitled to be for every creature. Only He was come not only to declare God and show us the Father in Himself the Son, but to take all on the ground of His death and resurrection, having perfectly glorified God in respect of the sin which had ruined all; and thereon to take His place in heaven, the glorified Head over all things to the Church His body on earth, as we know now. On this, however, as involving the revelation of God's counsels and of the mystery hidden from ages and from generations, we do not enter, as it would carry us rather to the Epistles of the apostle Paul, the vessel chosen for disclosing these heavenly wonders.

Our business now is with John, who lets us see the Lord on earth, a man but very God, and so drawing to Himself the hearts of all taught of God. Had He not been God, it would have been robbery not only from God but sometimes also from man. But not so: all the fulness dwelt in Him—dwelt in Him bodily. He was therefore from the beginning the divine centre for saints on earth, as afterwards when the exalted Man the centre on high, to Whom as Head the Spirit united them as members of His body. This last could not be till redemption made it possible according to grace, but on the basis of righteousness. What we see in John attaches to the glory of His divine Person: otherwise to bring to Jesus would have been to separate from God, not to Him, as it is. But, in truth, He was and is the sole revealed centre, as He was and is the only full revealer of God, and this because He is the true God and life eternal, though He Who was manifested in flesh and so meeting and winning man to God by His death.

Verses 43-51.

> "On the morrow He[q] would go forth into Galilee, and Jesus findeth Philip and saith to him, Follow me. Now Philip was from Bethsaida,[40] of the city of Andrew and Peter" (verses 43-44).

It is an immense thing to be delivered by Jesus from the waste of one's own will or from the attachment of the heart to the will of a man stronger than ourselves; an immense thing to know that we have found in Him, not the Messiah merely, but the centre of all God's revelations, plans, and counsels, so that we are gathering with Him because we are gathering to Him. All else, whatever the plea or pretension, is but scattering, and therefore labour in vain, or worse.

But we need more, and find more in Jesus, Who deigns to be not only our centre, but our "way," on earth indeed, but not of the world, as He is not. For such He is, no less than the truth and the life. What a blessing in such a world! It is now a wilderness where is no way. He is the way. Do we fear where to walk, what step to take? Here are snares to seduce, there dangers to affright. Above them says the voice of Jesus, "Follow Me." None other is safe. The best of His servants may err, as all have. But even were it not so, *He* says "Follow Me." Christian, hesitate no more. Follow Jesus. You will find a deeper and better fellowship with those that are His; but this by following Him Whom they follow. Only look well to it that it be according to the word, not your own thoughts and feelings; for are they better than those of others? Search your motives according to the light where you walk. "If thine eye be single, thy whole body shall be full of light" [Matthew 6:22]. But singleness is secured by looking to Jesus, not to ourselves or others. We have seen enough of ourselves when we have judged ourselves before God. Let us follow Jesus: to Him only and absolutely, a divine Person on earth, it is due. It is the true dignity of a saint; it is the only security for him who has still to watch against the sin that is in him; it is the path of genuine humility, and of real love, and of faith. In this shall we be sure of the guidance of the Spirit Who is here to glorify Him, taking of His and showing them to us.

He that has found and follows Christ soon seeks and finds others. But they are not always prepared to follow at once. So Philip proves here with the son of Talmai, here called not Bartholomew but Nathanael.[41] And hence, too, we learn that a man otherwise excellent may be hindered by not a little prejudice. It is a wholesome lesson neither to be hasty in our expectations nor to be cast down if a good man be slow to listen, as we may often prove.

> "Philip findeth Nathanael, and saith to him, We have found Him, of whom Moses in the law and the prophets did write, Jesus from Nazareth, the son of Joseph" (verse 45).

Nathanael was not at all prepared for this. Most surely did his heart look for Him of Whom Moses and the prophets wrote; but that the Christ was Jesus from Nazareth, the son of Joseph, he had yet to learn. He believed in the glory of Messiah's Person, as far as the Old Testament had revealed it beforehand: it had never occurred to him how Messiah could be "from Nazareth," not to speak of "the son of Joseph." For that village was despicable in the eyes even of a despised Galilean, who doubtless felt the more its miserably low moral repute because of his own practical godliness. Had Philip said "from Bethlehem, the Son of David," no such shock could have been given to the expecting Jew. But in truth, the Lord is here viewed as wholly above all earthly associations, and therefore He could come down to the lowest. For He was the Son of God Who came to Nazareth, and only so could be said to be "from Nazareth" any more than "the son of Joseph."

However this may be, Nathanael does not withhold his expression of hesitation.

> "And Nathanael said to him, Can there be any good thing out of Nazareth? Philip saith to him, Come and see" (verse 46).

But there was another also to see. For Jesus, Who saw Nathanael coming to Him, gave him to hear words of grace about himself which might well surprise him in His greeting,

> "Behold, an Israelite indeed, in whom is no guile" (verse 47b).

If the Spirit of prophecy wrought according to Psalm 32, soon was he to know the Spirit of adoption and the liberty wherewith the Son makes free.

> "Nathanael saith to Him, Whence knowest Thou me? Jesus answered and said to him, Before that Philip called thee, when thou wast under the fig-tree, I saw thee" (verse 48).

He is God always and everywhere in this Gospel. Unseen, Jesus had seen Nathanael. He had seen him where evidently he thought himself seen by none; but He who heard the musings of his heart in that spot "under the fig-tree" saw him: the irresistible evidence of His own glory, of omniscience, and omnipresence. Yet was He Who saw him evidently a man in flesh and blood. He could be none other than the promised Messiah—Emmanuel, Jehovah's fellow, "Ruler in Israel, whose goings forth have been from of old, from everlasting" [Micah 5:2]. His prejudice instantly vanished away as mist before the sun in its strength. He might not be able to explain the connection with Nazareth, or with Joseph;[42] but a good man would not, none but a bad one could, resist the positive light of One Who thus knew all things, and told it out in grace to win the heart of Nathanael and of every one who hears His word and fears God since that day to this.

But there is more conveyed here. Surely the fig-tree is not a fact only, or an isolated circumstance, but clothed with the significance usually found in it, at least, in

Scripture. In the great prophecy of our Lord, the fig-tree is employed as the symbol of the nation, and so one cannot doubt it is here. If Nathanael were there musing in his heart before God on the expected Messiah and the hopes of the elect people, as many, indeed all men, were at that time through the impulse of John the Baptist, nay, even whether *he* were the Christ or not (Luke 3:15), we may conceive the better with what amazing force the words of Jesus must have appealed to the heart and conscience of the guileless Israelite. This appears to be powerfully confirmed by the character of his own confession.

> "Nathanael answered (and saith to)[r] him, Rabbi, Thou art the Son of God, Thou art the King of Israel" (verse 49).

It was a confession precisely of the Messiah according to Psalm 2. He might be Jesus of Nazareth, the son of Joseph; but He could be, He was, none other than "My (Jehovah's) King," "the Son" (verses 6, 12), though not yet anointed on Zion, the hill of Jehovah's holiness.[43] Nathanael was prompt and distinct now, as slow and cautious before.

Nor did the Lord check the flow of grace and truth, and Nathanael must borrow vessels not a few, till there was not one more to receive the blessing that would still overflow.

> "Jesus answered and said to him, Because I said to thee, I saw thee under the fig-tree, believest thou? thou shalt see greater things than these. And He saith to him, Verily, verily,[44] I say to you, (Henceforth)[s] ye shall see heaven opened, and the angels of God ascending and descending upon the Son of Man" (verses 50-51).

Was Messianic glory the horizon of that which Nathanael's soul saw and confessed in Jesus? Not "hereafter," but if any word here, "from the present," "from that out," should the disciples see, if earthly power were still delayed, the opened heaven, and the homage of its glorious denizens to the rejected Messiah, the Son of Man.[45] Him all peoples, nations, and languages should serve, when He should enter on His everlasting dominion which should not pass away, and His kingdom which should not be destroyed. Truly these are "greater things"; the pledge of which Nathanael saw thenceforth in the attendance of God's angels on Him Whom man despised and the nation abhorred to their own shame and ruin, but to the working out of heavenly counsels and an incomparably larger sphere of blessing and glory than in Israel or the land. These the reader may see in Psalm 8, especially if he consult the use made of it in 1 Corinthians 15, Ephesians 1, and Hebrews 2.

NOTES ON THE FIRST CHAPTER

a [*Cf. Lectures Introductory to the Study of the Gospels,* {Second Edition, 1873}, pp. 408-429.]

b ["I cannot but regard John 1:2 as a striking and complete setting aside of the Alexandrian and Patristic distinction of λόγος ἐνδιάθετος and λόγος προφορικός. Some of the earlier Greek fathers, who were infected with Platonism, held that the λόγος was *conceived* in God's mind from eternity, and only *uttered*, as it were, in time. This has given a handle to Arians, who, like other unbelievers, greedily seek the traditions of men. The Apostle here asserts, in the Holy Ghost, the *eternal personality* of the Word *with* God" (*Lectures Introductory to the Study of the Gospels,* p. 409, note).]

c I think the remark not only unhappy but worthy of reprobation, wherein it is said that evil itself implicitly (and not all matter only) was made by the Word. This is false philosophy, the Hegelianism even of many who oppose Hegel. Evil has nothing to do with creation, save as it is an inconsistency with it. The question now is not of evil in the sense of physical punishment; for this is pre-eminently sent of God. But moral evil in any being is a contradiction of the relationship in which God set that being. It is therefore neither in God nor of God, being failure relative to what previously existed as the fruit of God's pleasure, Who nevertheless permits it in view of government and redemption. Thus the angels left their first estate. Satan stood (or stands) not in the truth, and Adam fell from his original innocence. This is in no way a limitation of divine power; but, contrariwise, the error I am combating does limit His goodness or His truth. Impossible that there can be in or from God the contrary of what He is, and He is good, He only; in the creature it can easily be, and it is, where creation is not sustained by God, or delivered by His grace.

d [*Cf. Notes on Colossians*, pp. 19-21.]

e The arrangement of verses 3-4, which Lachmann, Tregelles, and Westcott and Hort [*Notes on Select Readings*, p. 73 *f.*] prefer (partly because of the absence of interpunction in some very ancient MSS., partly because some copies, versions, and fathers, expressly so take it), is ὃ γέγονεν ἐν αὐτῷ ζωὴ ἦν. [So AC^{pm}DG^{pm}L, Vulg. Syr^{cu} Sahid.] But with Tischendorf and others [as Weiss and Blass][10] I unqualifiedly decide for a colon or full-stop after γέγονεν, and begin a new sentence with ἐν αὐτῷ ζωὴ ἦν. [So Weiss after C^{corr}EGHKM Syr$^{pesch\ hcl}$.] There is an intended contradistinction between what was made or brought into being *through* the Word with life *in* Him, which is lost when the new sentence begins with ὃ γέγ. Is it not false doctrine so to reduce life in the Word? Further, it is not Johannean, if grammatical, to take γέγονεν ἐν αὐτῷ as "made by Him." Again, this life, which would mean the living universe (in itself a strange, unscriptural, and senseless phrase), must then be the light of men, contrary to the express teaching, just after, that the Word exclusively was the light. On the other hand, the phrase, as it usually stands, is in the fullest harmony with the style of the Evangelist elsewhere, as Dean Alford has pointed out.

f [See note {i below} on verse 16.]

g There seems to be no force in taking ἦν with ἐρχόμενον as equivalent to an imperfect "came," even if an independent clause such as ὃ φ. π. ἄνθρ. might legitimately come between the verb and the participle; which, as far as I know, has not yet been produced, Mark 2:18 (which Lücke advances and Alford approves) being in no way parallel. But were it so, where is the propriety of telling us in this wondrous prologue, where each brief clause—yea, word—is brimful of the profoundest truth, that the true Light which lights every man was in process of coming (*not* of manifesting Himself, which is quite another thought) into the world? On the other hand, the construction given in the Authorised Version, though vouched by ancient translations, Western and Eastern, and even by Greek fathers, seems not really admissible. It would require the article with ἐρχόμενον. The anarthrous participle does not mean "that cometh," but "as" or "on coming," which could have no proper meaning in connection with ἄνθρωπον. For how strange the doctrine resulting, that every man on coming into the world of darkness has or receives the light of Christ! With ὃ it teaches a momentous truth, and this extinguishing, not suggesting, the Quaker idea. For it is the Word in His own nature, not an inward light, Who pours it on every man. He alone coming here is the true Light for man, and sheds it on all, high or low, Jew or Greek. It is like the sun's light for all mankind, but in a spiritual way.[13]

h [See further, exposition below of 14:6.]

i Before our Apostle died Gnosticism was sowing its baneful seeds, it would seem even before St. Paul's death. Early in the second century we know that Basilides had developed the system so far as to separate Jesus from Christ, the latter an emanation ["Æon"] from God united to Jesus at His baptism, and returning to the Fulness on high before His death on the cross.[23] Thus the Incarnation was annulled no less than the Atonement. But even Christ in this impious reverie was not the true God, but only an emanation, sent to make known the good God, and expose the Demiurge [Jehovah], who made the world, with all its evils, inseparable from matter. One readily sees how the doctrine of the apostles cuts off by anticipation this irreverent and destructive falsehood by stating the simple truth of Christ's Person and work, though only the germs may have then appeared.

j [ὁ omitted by ℵ^{pm}BC^{pm}L.]

k ℵBC^{pm}L, 33, Syrr. $^{not\ cu.}$ Æth. ^{Rom} have the strange reading θεός, God, which Tregelles, Westcott and Hort adopt, the latter having written a learned monograph in its defence. [So Weiss and Zahn.] As the variant seems to be out of all correlation to "Father," the weight of evidence is against it. [Blass reads "the Only-begotten, Who," etc., with ℵ^{corr}A, etc. See further Note 26 in Appendix.]

l The best reading according to ancient authorities is *Βηθανίᾳ* (ℵ^pm ABC^pm EFGHLMSVXΓΔΠ^pm more than a hundred and thirty cursives, and many ancient versions), not *Βηθαβαρᾷ* or *Βηθαραβᾷ*. It was not the well-known village near Jerusalem, but another district of the same name beyond the Jordan.[29]

m It is interesting and instructive to note that to the Pharisees John is silent (verse 27) as to Christ's pre-existent eternity as the ground of His taking precedence of himself, though born after him. Compare verses 15, 30.

n [ℵ^pm Syr^sin have "chosen," followed by Blass.]

o ℵABCLT^b XΛ, 33, Memph. read *οὖν*, which inferior witnesses omit.

p [So Edd. as ℵB^pm L., 33, several Latt. Memph. Æth. "Jonah" is read in AB^corr XΓΔΛΠ. Syr^pesch pcl and Armen. Æth., and Epiph. Chrys. Cyr. Alex.

q The best copies do not read "Jesus" here, but in the next clause.

r There is not a little variation here in the copies, even the more ancient.

s The oldest copies [ℵBL] and versions [some Latt. Memph., etc.] omit *ἀπ' ἄρτι*, which, if read, must be rendered "from now" or "henceforth," not "hereafter." [The words are rejected by Weiss and Blass.]

THE SECOND CHAPTER [a]
VERSES 1-11.

The second chapter opens with a striking miracle—the water turned into wine. It is only given here. Jesus is God, the God of creation. He had shown His omniscience to Nathanael, now His omnipotence to others. It was "the third day," possibly the third since He had first seen Nathanael.[46] But the passage is so significant that one does not feel disposed to question the thought that the Spirit may here have meant figuratively the type of a day yet future when glory will appear, as distinguished from the day of John the Baptist's testimony, and that of the Lord and His disciples. For as the light shone in despised Galilee when He came in humiliation, so will it shine on the poor in spirit when He appears in glory; and judgment fall on the proud and lofty, on Jerusalem in its religious pretensions, so big and so hollow, till grace makes even her lowly before Him.

> "And the third day there was a marriage in Cana of Galilee,[47] and the mother of Jesus was there. And Jesus also was invited and His disciples unto the marriage" (verses 1-2).

It is the figure of things on earth: there is no picture of the heavens opened here. Hence we find the mother of Jesus[48] brought forward prominently as one at home in the scene.

> "And when the wine fell short, the mother of Jesus saith unto Him, They have no wine" (verse 3).

The first Adam always fails, and fails most where most is wanted. But Jesus will meet all wants, though His time is not yet come. Faith, however, never looks to Him in vain, and

> "Jesus saith to her, What have I to do with thee[49], woman? Mine hour is not yet come" (verse 4).

It is a remarkable answer, which Romanist theologians find very difficult to square with their doctrine and practice. He does not say, Mother. It is no longer a question of the first Adam: not that there was disrespect, but that Mariolatry is unfounded and sinful. Jesus was here to do the will of God. Blessing, He would show, comes down from the Father through the Son. Flesh and its relationships have nothing to do in the matter. All must be of grace.

> "His mother saith to the servants, Whatever He shall say to you, do. Now there were six waterpots of stone set there according to the purification of the Jews, holding each two or three measures" (verses 5-6).

The Jewish system was a witness of defilement; and its ordinances could do no more than sanctify to the purifying of the flesh.[50] This was human. Jesus was here for divine purposes, then in testimony, by and by in power.

> "Jesus saith to them, Fill the waterpots with water. And they filled them up to the brim. And He saith

to them, Draw now and carry to the master of the feast. And they carried. But when the master of the feast tasted the water that had become wine (and he knew not whence it was, but the servants that had drawn the water knew), the master of the feast called the bridegroom and saith to him, Every man at first setteth on the good wine, and when they have drunk freely, then the worse; thou hast kept the good wine until now"[51] (verses 7-10).

So will Jesus do on the richest scale in the day that is coming. He will reverse the sorrowful history of man. The wine will not fail when He reigns. There will be joy for God and man in happy communion together. Jesus will furnish all to the glory of God the Father. In that day, too, He will be the Bridegroom and the Master of the feast; and the joy of that day will find its root not only in the glory of His Person, but in the depth of that work of humiliation already wrought on the cross. There will be no secrets then. It will not be the servants only who will then know, but all, from the least to the greatest.

> "This beginning of signs[52] did Jesus at Cana of Galilee, and He manifested His glory, and His disciples believed on Him" (verse 11).

Faith grows where real (2 Thessalonians 1:3).

It will be noticed that our Gospel gives us most important particulars, unnoticed by all the others, which took place before His Galilean ministry commenced when John was cast into prison.[53] Thus we have John's testimony suited to the Lord's personal glory, about His earthly work for the universe even to eternity, and His heavenly work in baptizing with the Holy Spirit. We have had Christ's testimony "on the next day" after John's; and here "the third day."

The hour of Jesus is not yet come. The marriage at Cana was but a shadow, not the very image. For the true bridals here below, as well as on high, we must yet wait. The mother of Jesus, of the true male Son, will be there when the feast arrives. What has been is but a testimony, a beginning of signs, to manifest His glory. Jehovah's day for Israel will come.

Verse 12.

> "After this He went down to Capernaum, He and His mother and His brethren and His disciples; and there they abode not many days" (verse 12).

It may be noted that Joseph does not appear anywhere since the end of Luke 2 when the Lord was twelve years old. Doubtless he had fallen asleep meanwhile. Mary is again seen with Him. His absolute separation to the will and work of His Father in no way interferes with the earthly relations He had graciously taken. And so will it be with that which He represents.

But the marriage is only part of the display of His glory in the kingdom by and by; and of the judgment to be executed, He gives a token in the scene that follows, and this at the first Passover noted since that of His childhood. Our Evangelist is careful to mention this feast throughout our Lord's course (6:4; 11:55). Alas! how little the Jews entered into its meaning.

Verses 13-22.

> "And the Passover of the Jews[54] was near, and Jesus went up to Jerusalem. And He found in the temple the sellers of oxen and sheep and doves, and the money-changers sitting; and having made a

scourge of cords (or, ropes), He drove them all out of the temple, both the sheep and the oxen; and poured out the change of the money-changers, and overthrew their tables;[55] and to the sellers of the doves He said, Take these things hence; make not My Father's[56] house a house of merchandise. (And)[b] His disciples remembered that it is written, The zeal of Thine house will eat Me up"[c] (verses 13-17).

Not only is this clearing of the temple distinct from that which the Synoptic Gospels relate on His last visit to Jerusalem, but it is instructive to remark that, as they only give the last, John gives only the first. It is a striking witness by a significant fact, as we have already seen doctrinally in his introduction, that he begins where they end, not in a barely literal way, but in all the depth of what Jesus is, says, and does. The state of the temple, the selfishness which reigned there, the indifference to the true fear and honour and holiness of God while there was the utmost punctiliousness in a ritual show of their own invention, were characteristic of the ruined state of a people called to the highest earthly privilege by God's favour.

Solomon had acted at the beginning with a vigour which drove out the unworthy high priest in his day; when the kingdom was divided, Hezekiah and Josiah, sons of David, had each sought to vindicate the glory of Jehovah. Nehemiah, alas! under the protection of the Gentiles, had not been lacking, when the returned remnant so quickly manifested that the captivity on the one hand and God's mercy on the other had failed to lead them to repentance. Now the Son gives a sign as solemn for proud religious Jerusalem, as the miracle of the water changed into wine was full of bright hope for despised Galilee.

He does act as the Lord with divine rights, yet as the lowly Sent One and servant. Nevertheless He does not withhold the testimony to the glory of His Person in the very command not to make His Father's house a house of merchandise. He was the Son of God, announced as such, even as Nathanael had already owned Him, judicially dealing not merely on moral grounds, such as might be open to any godly Israelite, but openly as the One Who identified Himself with His Father's interests; and this was His house. So too, the Spirit of prophecy spoke of the rejected Messiah, as the disciples remembered at a later day.

> "The Jews therefore answered and said to Him, What sign showest Thou to us that Thou doest these things? Jesus answered and said to them, Destroy this temple (ναὸν), and in three days I will raise it up. The Jews therefore said, In forty and six years was this temple built,[57] and wilt Thou raise it up in three days? But *He* spoke of the temple of His body. When, therefore, He was raised from among (the) dead, His disciples remembered that He said this; and they believed the scripture, and the word which Jesus said" (verses 18-22).

The sign that He would give was His own resurrection-power, raising not others merely but His own body, the true Temple in which alone God was (for the Word was God).[58] That of which they boasted had but a name without God, soon to be formally pronounced "their" house (Matthew 23), and given up to destruction (Matthew 24). It is resurrection that defines Him Son of

God in power; and when He was raised, the disciples remembered His saying, as they yet more found the strongest confirmation of their faith in both Scripture[58a] and His word. His resurrection is the fundamental truth both of the gospel and of our distinctive place as Christians. No wonder that the Jews were jealous of it, and that Gentiles mock or evade it. May we ever remember it, and Him Who thus gives Scripture all its grace and power.

Verses 23-25.

We arrive now at a new division of the Gospel introduced by the prefatory verses as to man and his state, which conclude chapter 2. The coming and the inquiry of Nicodemus give rise to our Lord's testimony to the necessity of birth anew for the kingdom of God, to the cross, eternal life, the love of God, and the world's condemnation, closing with the Baptist's testimony to the glory of His Person.

> "Now when He was in Jerusalem at the Passover, at the feast,[d] many believed on His name, beholding His signs which He did. But Jesus Himself did not trust Himself to them,[59] inasmuch as He knew all (men), and because He needed not that any should testify of man, for Himself knew what was in man"[60] (verses 23-25).

It was at the city of solemnities; it was a feast of Jehovah, nay, the most fundamental of the sacred feasts; and the Messiah was there, the object of faith, working in power, and manifesting His glory in appropriate signs. And many believed on His name accordingly. It was man doing and feeling his best under circumstances the most favourable.[60a] Yet did not Jesus Himself trust Himself to them. Certainly it was from no lack of love or pity in Him; for whoever did or could love as He? And the reason, calmly given, is truly overwhelming: "inasmuch as He knew all men, and because He needed not that any should testify of man, for Himself knew what was in man." What a sentence; from Whom; and on what grounds! We do well to weigh it gravely: who is not concerned in it? It is the ordained Judge of quick and dead Who thus pronounces. Is it not all over with man?

One great fact, one truth, accounts for it; the total evil, the irremediable ruin, of man as such. The ways of the Lord are in the strictest accord with the words of the Spirit by the apostle Paul: "the mind of the flesh"—and this is all that is in man—"is enmity against God, for it is not subject to the law of God, for neither, indeed, can it be." Hence, "they that are in the flesh cannot please God" [Romans 8:7-8]. Its doings and its sufferings are selfish and worthless Godward. Its faith as here is no better; for it is not the soul subject to God's testimony, but mind judging on evidence satisfactory to itself. It is a conclusion that Jesus must be Messiah; not submission to, nor reception of, divine testimony. For in this case the mind sits on the throne of judgment, and pronounces for or against, according to its estimate of reasons favouring or adverse, instead of the soul setting to its seal (in the face of all appearances it may be, yea, of the most real difficulties) that God is true. For what ground to expect the love of the Holy One to the vile and rebellious? Christ received according to God's testimony, Christ in grace to the lost dying for the ungodly and the powerless, He it is accounts for, as He displays, all; miracles or signs not in the least. They arrest the eye; they exercise the mind; they may touch and win the affections. But nothing short of God's word judges the man, or reveals what He is in Christ to man thus judged; and this only, as we shall see, is of the Spirit, for He only, not man, has before Him the true object, the Son of God's love given in grace to a ruined and guilty world.

The truth is that our judgments flow from our affections. What we love we easily believe; what makes nothing of us we naturally resist and reject. As long as Jesus was deemed an ameliorator of humanity, there seemed to be the readiest, warmest welcome. Man would accredit Jesus if he thought Jesus accredited man. But how could he receive what makes nothing of himself, what condemns him morally, what keeps before him the solemn warning of eternal judgment and the lake of fire? No, he hates the testimony and the Person Who is the central object of it, and truth connected with it and Him. When broken down before God and made willing to own one's utter and inexcusable sins and sinfulness, it is a wholly different matter; and He Who was dreaded and repugnant is turned to as the only hope from God, even Jesus the Deliverer from the wrath to come. This is indeed conversion, and grace by quickening power alone effects it.

So it is when Christian doctrine is made to suit the world by being emasculated and changed to build up what in truth it judges. Then indeed it is no longer a seed that takes root and grows and bears fruit, but a mere leaven that spreads and may assimilate largely to itself. Such is Christendom, when human will was engaged on its side, and the religion became traditional.

But here it is the holy and awful witness of Jesus to man at his best estate, when no enmity had appeared, but all looked full of human promise. Here, again, we see John beginning where the other Gospels close. It is not Messiah rejected, but Jesus the Son of God, Who knows the end from the beginning, treating man as altogether vanity and sin; and this, because God is in none of his thoughts, but self without real sorrow or shame about his opposition to God, without any due sense of sin or consequently a serious care about it. He gathered from the evidence of the signs before him that none but Messiah could have wrought them; but such an inference did not affect his moral state either with God or with man. He was just as he had been with any other object for his busy mind to work on, but his nature unjudged, God no better known, and the enemy with just the same power over him as ever. As yet, it was man and not God; for there is no work of God till the word is received as it is in truth His, revealing His grace to man consciously needing it. Here was nothing of the sort, but a simple process of man's own mind and feelings, without a question of his sins or state before God, without the smallest felt need of a Saviour. Jesus knew what it was worth and trusted not Himself to man, even when he thus believed on Him. It was human faith, of which we have instances not infrequently in this Gospel as elsewhere, whilst as clearly we have the divinely given faith which has eternal life: this having to do with God, as that, being of man, rises not above its source. "Beware of men," said He to His apostles at a later day, Himself about to prove in the cross how truly from the first He Himself knew what was in man.

NOTES ON THE SECOND CHAPTER

a [*Cf. Lectures Introductory to the Study of the Gospels*, pp. 429-431.]

b ℵBLTX Memph. [Syr^{sin}] omit δὲ, which AEPΔ with some cursives and versions insert.

c [καταφάγεται: so W. and H. {Westcott and Hort}, and Weiss and Blass, after Syr$^{pesch\ hier}$, etc. Syr^{sin} has "hath eaten," as Psalm 69:9 in Heb. LXX, κατέφαγεν.]

d [Syr^{sin} has "in the days of the feast of unleavened bread."]

THE THIRD CHAPTER ᵃ ⁽⁶¹⁾
VERSES 1-21.

The worthlessness of believing on Christ because of evidence, we have seen. But in the crowd of such there might be souls who had the sense of wants awakened which led them to Jesus personally. And in Him was life: not merely all things brought into being through Him, and signs wrought and things done by Jesus, which, if written one by one in books, would be beyond the world's power to contain, but, beyond all, life in the Son for the believer. And such is the fact which is here recorded in detail.

> "But there was a man of the Pharisees, his name Nicodemus,⁽⁶²⁾ a ruler of the Jews. He came to Him by night,⁶³ and said to Him, Rabbi, we know that Thou art come a teacher from God, for none can do these signs which Thou doest, unless God be with him. Jesus answered and said to him, Verily, verily, I say to thee, Except one be born anew,⁶⁴ he cannot see the kingdom of God"⁶⁵ (verses 1-3).

It was a chief man from among the most orthodox in the chosen people; sufficiently in earnest to seek Jesus for truth, and still valuing the world enough to fear its condemnation and scorn. So he came by night to Jesus; yet did he take the ground of a persuasion he shared in common with his fellows because of the signs wrought by the Lord. He knew not that a deeper work was going on within, which drew him, not them, to Jesus. He, the teacher of Israel, recognised in Jesus One come a teacher from God, and God with Him: for any others born of woman a signal honour; for Jesus the proof that His true glory was unknown. As yet then Nicodemus was astray as to himself, as to the Jews, and as to Jesus. In short, the true God was unknown.

The Lord accordingly stops him at once with the declaration that man, any one, needs to be born from the outset and origin. Not teaching is wanted but a new nature, a new source of being spiritually, in order to see the kingdom of God. No inference, however logical, is faith. It is not even a conviction of conscience. It may be a conclusion fairly drawn from sound premises, from sensible facts of the weightiest kind before the mind; but neither God is known nor itself yet judged. The new character of life which suits the kingdom of God does not yet exist for the soul. In such a state teaching would but aggravate the danger or expose to fresh evil. The Word of God has never penetrated the heart of Nicodemus. He knew not himself utterly defiled, spiritually dead in sins. What he wanted was to be quickened, not to have fresh aliment {food} for the exercise of his mind. And Jesus, instead of commenting on his words, answered his true need, which he too would have sought himself, had he but known it.

If Nicodemus then took for granted his own capacity, as he then stood, to profit by the truth and serve God and inherit His kingdom, the Lord, with incomparable solemnity, assures him that the new birth is indispensable to seeing the kingdom. For God is not teaching or improving human nature. He had already tried it patiently; and the trial would ere long be absolutely complete.

The kingdom of God is in question, and not anything in fallen man. It was not yet established or displayed in power over the earth, as it will be at the appearance of Jesus. It was not yet preached to the Gentiles as it was after the cross. But it was come for faith in the Person of Christ, the pledge that it will be set up by and by in all its extent, its "earthly" and its "heavenly things." The kingdom of God was among them in Christ, Who demonstrated its power, the enemies themselves seen or unseen being judges. Why, then, did not Nicodemus see it? From no defect in the object of faith or in His testimony, by general conviction and confession, from no lack of signs attesting the presence and power of God. Alas! the defect is in man, and to man it is incurable; for who can change his nature? In fact, if it were possible, it could avail nothing. "Except one be born anew, he cannot see the kingdom of God." God only can give a new nature, and a nature suited to His kingdom. Without this none can as much as see it.

> "Nicodemus saith unto Him, How can a man be born when he is old? Can he enter a second time into the womb of his mother and be born?" (verse 4).

We learn hence that the intimation was the birth, not from above, but again; else the difficulty expressed in reply could have had no place. The truth is, however, that even if the fabled conversion of an old man into youth again could be true—yea, if the strange case suggested by the astonished Pharisee could have been turned by miracle into fact (as Jonah came forth alive from the great fish that swallowed him)—it would fail to meet the requirements of the kingdom of God, as we shall see expressly in the further explanation of our Lord. For it would be human nature still, let it be renewed in its youth or repeated in its birth ever so far or so often. A clean thing cannot come out of an unclean; and such is man's nature since the fall. Nor is aught God's way of renewal, but by giving a nature wholly fresh from its source; for the believer is born of God, not of corruptible seed, but of incorruptible by the living and abiding word of God.

> "Jesus answered, Verily, verily, I say to thee, Except one be born of water and Spirit, he cannot enter into the kingdom of God.[b] That which is born of the flesh is flesh; and that which is born of the Spirit is spirit" (verses 5-6).

Words of incalculable moment to man, of deep blessing where grace gives him ear to hear, and heart to receive and keep. Yet I scarce know a scripture more widely perverted than this has been to baptism, nor one where tradition is more dangerously false, though *quod semper, quod ubique, quod ab omnibus {what (has been held) always, everywhere, by all}* be as true of this as of any interpretation of Scripture that could be named. A double result would follow, that not a soul could enter the kingdom of God save such as are baptized; and, secondly, as the context would prove, that, the new nature being identified with eternal life, none of the baptized could perish—a statement which all but the most grossly ignorant or prejudiced must confess to be in both its parts opposed to other and clear scriptures, and to notorious fact.

Christian baptism (and this is what it is traditionally conceived to mean, not that of John or of the disciples) was not instituted, nor did the facts exist which it symbolizes, till the Lord died and rose. How, then, could Nicodemus by any possibility anticipate them or understand what the Lord gives as the clearing up of his difficulty as to being born anew? Yet the Lord reproaches him as "the teacher of Israel" with his slowness of intelligence. That is, he should (even as teaching Jews) have known these things, which he could not possibly know if the Lord alluded to a Christian institution as yet undivulged.[66]

The reasoning of Hooker[c] (*Works*, ii. 262, etc., Keble's ed. 5), as of others before and since, is beside the mark, and simply proves inattention to Scripture, and superficial acquaintance with the truth. It is not true that "born of water and Spirit," if literally construed, means baptism. Never is that rite set out as figuring life, but death, as in Romans 6, Colossians 2, and 1 Peter 3. "Know ye not that so many of us as were baptized unto Jesus Christ were baptized unto His death?" {Romans 6:3.} It is never the sign of quickening, but rather of identifying those quickened with the death of Christ; that they in virtue of Him might take the place of men dead to sin, but alive to God, and so reckon themselves by grace, for under this we are, not under law. Such is the apostolic doctrine. The words of our Lord do not, and cannot, teach otherwise, as they must if John 3:5 be applied to baptism. Take water here as figurative of the word which the Spirit uses to quicken, and all is clear, consistent, and true. Were it said in the Scripture that we are born of the Spirit by means of water, we should have some approach to what the Fathers drew from it, and what is necessary to bear the construction put on it in the Anglican and other formularies that apply it to baptism. Their dealing with it seems to be really "licentious," "deluding," and "dangerous," at issue with what our Lord says even in verse 5, still more with His omission of "water" in verse 6, most of all if it be possible with the place of baptism everywhere else given in Scripture. Baptism may be the formal expression of washing away sins, never of communicating life, which is unequivocally false teaching.

So it is in John 13 and 15, not to speak of chapters 4 and 7. Compare for the figure Ephesians 5:26, for the truth couched under it 1 Corinthians 4:15, James 1:18, 1 Peter 1:23. It is not a rite giving honour to an official class, but the word of God applied by His Spirit, bringing death on nature that we might live to God in Christ.

For Christ came by water and blood; He purifies and expiates (1 John 5). He is the truth, which the word of God applies in the power of the Spirit, judging the old nature and introducing the new. "I live, no longer I, but Christ liveth in me" (Galatians 2:20). One is the same person, but a life is communicated which he had not before, not of Adam, but of Christ, the Second Man {1 Corinthians 15:47}. He is begotten of God, made a partaker of the divine nature through the greatest and precious promises, having escaped the corruption that is in the world through lust {2 Peter 1:4}. Such is it to be born of water and of Spirit—an incomparably deeper thing than any form of truth, however it be prized in its place and for the object the Lord Who instituted it had in view. Baptism was the formal admission; it was the confession of Christ on the ground of His death and resurrection, not of quickening, which was true of all saints before Christ, when there was no Christian baptism. If baptism were really the sign and means of quickening, consistency would deny life to the Old Testament saints, or they ought to have been so baptized, which they were not. But this is clearly false ground. There is no reason to infer that the twelve were baptized with Christian baptism; they baptized others, but, it would seem, were not themselves. Were they not, then, born again? Nor did circumcision mean life; and so we know that souls were born anew even before it was imposed on Abraham already justified by faith.

Hence, too, it is important to observe that he who is thus born again is said to be born of the Spirit, omitting water, in verse 6. "That which is born of the flesh is flesh; and that which is born of the Spirit is spirit." The word (or water, emblematically) can do nothing toward quickening without the Spirit, Who is the efficient agent in communicating the life of Christ. Water cleanses, but of itself it is not capable of quickening; it is death to the flesh. There had been only flesh before; now, as believing in Christ, the man is born of God (1 John 5); and each nature retains its own characteristic. As flesh never becomes spirit, so spirit never degenerates into flesh. The natures abide distinct; and the practical business of the believer is to hold himself for dead to the one that he may live in the other by the faith of the Son of God, Who loved him and gave Himself for him.

Nor was Nicodemus to wonder that he and other Jews (not pagans merely, to which they would have assented at once) needed to be born afresh.

> "Wonder not that I said to thee, Ye must be born anew" (verse 7).

But if sovereign grace met that need, could it, would it, stop there? Certainly not. It would breathe the blessing as widely as the ravages of sin, according to the choice of God.

"The wind bloweth where it will, and thou hearest its voice, but knowest not whence it cometh, and where it goeth: so is every one that is born[d] of the Spirit" (verse 8).

Thus "every one" leaves room for any fallen man, a Gentile no less than a Jew. Whatever might be their distinction after the flesh, the Spirit thus freely flowing can bless those who are most distant, while the nearest is nothing without Him.

It has been already remarked, moreover, that in all this was no such special privilege as should have been beyond the ken of an intelligent Jew. Hence when

"Nicodemus answered and said to Him, How can these things be? Jesus answered and said to him, Art thou the teacher of Israel, and knowest not these things?" (verses 9-10).

Had he never read the promise to Israel in one prophet?—"I will pour water upon him that is thirsty, and floods upon the dry ground; I will pour My Spirit upon thy seed, and My blessing upon thine offspring" [Isaiah 44:3]. Had he forgotten the words of another prophet?—"Then I will sprinkle clean water upon you, and ye shall be clean: from all your uncleanness and from all your idols will I cleanse you. And I will give you a new heart, and will put a new spirit within you; and I will take away the stony heart out of your flesh, and I will give you a heart of flesh. And I will put My Spirit within you, and cause you to walk in My statutes and keep Mine ordinances, and ye shall do them. And ye shall dwell in the land that I gave to your fathers; and ye shall be My people, and I will be your God" [Ezekiel 36:25-28].

There can be no mistake that Israel will require the new birth in order to receive and enjoy aright even the earthly blessings of God's kingdom by and by, and that God will of His grace impart it to them for this end. Nicodemus, then, need not be surprised at the universal need of the new birth, even for the Jew, proclaimed by the Lord; but as the blessing is not of flesh, but of Spirit, grace will not restrain it from any on grounds that give weight to man. The Gentile will not be left out of such rich mercy, indispensable to the kingdom of God, which is of grace, not of law or flesh, as the Jew was apt to assume. "Ho, every one that thirsteth, come ye to the waters, and he that hath no money, come ye, buy, and eat; yea, come, buy wine and milk without money and without price" [Isaiah 55:1]. Is not this grace, and so expressed as to open the door to any of the nations? to sense of need, resourceless need, wherever found? Yet who did, who could, draw it out from the prophets and give the principle its absolute shape, as here to Nicodemus, but the One Who spoke? Others inspired of the Spirit were soon to follow; and of them all none more distinctly than the apostle Paul.

Thus far, then, Nicodemus as a Jew, as the teacher of Israel, should have known the nature as well as the necessity of the new birth. The ancient prophets were not silent about its application to Israel, even for the days when blessings shall be shed abundantly on them from God according to His promise. Not the heathen only, but His people (whatever might be their present self-complacency and the pride which wraps itself up in ignorance), are described as unclean, till He sprinkle clean water upon them, and put His Spirit within them. Undoubtedly, the Lord, as was due to His personal glory, presents the truth with incomparably greater clearness and depth, as well as with an all-embracing comprehensiveness; but what was presented ought not to have been strange to Nicodemus on his own ground. The new thing follows the cross, whether in statement or in fact, as we see it implied in chapter 4.

But even here the Lord intimates a knowledge to be communicated, as, in fact, it was, first by Himself in Person, then by the Holy Ghost through chosen witnesses, transcending that of the prophets and of a character, not measure only, quite different.

> "Verily, verily, I say to thee, We speak that We do know, and testify that We have seen; and ye receive not Our testimony" (verse 11).

It is no vision of things out of the ordinary sphere of him who was inspired to be a prophet, nor a message founded on the authority of Him Who sent His servant with a "Thus saith Jehovah." Jesus only, true man among men, could none the less say, because He was none the less God, We speak that which We know, and bear witness of that which We have seen.[67] He knew what was in man, needing no testimony about man (chapter 2); He knew what was in God, and alone of men could testify of Him without testimony about Him (chapter 3). I have known Thee, says Himself to the Father later on in this Gospel (chapter 17:25). But the world knew not the Father; least of all were the Father and the Son known by those who, in persecuting the disciples, thought to do God's service. But, blessed be His name, if none knew the Father but the Son, there were not lacking those to whom the Son reveals Him; and so the Holy Ghost, Who searches all things—yea, the depths of God—reveals what was previously hidden even from prophets, and gives to Christians the mind, or intelligence, of Christ.

For a divine Person knows in Himself all things in themselves; not as the prophets—from One without and above, Who gives the commission, vision, and message. These, therefore, might often speak that which they knew not, and learn on searching that "not unto themselves but unto us they did minister the things which are now reported by those that have preached the gospel by (ἐν) the Holy Ghost sent down from heaven" [1 Peter 1:12]. But Jesus spoke what He knew. Coming from God, and being Himself God, He knew the divine nature perfectly, and was here a man to reveal it to men. If none had seen God at any time, the Only-begotten Son Who is in the bosom of the Father has declared Him; He alone of woman-born had this competency, both as Son and as the image of the invisible God, in a sense not only pre-eminent, but exclusive, as the Epistles to the Colossians [Colossians 1:18] and the Hebrews [Hebrews 1:3] formally teach. And this He spoke in ineffable grace, expressing the grace and truth of Him Who is God and Father through a man's heart to the hearts of men. Of the glory, too, familiar to Him with the Father before the world was, He testified. For what was divine love keeping back from those about to share with Him the glory in which both will be displayed to the world, and to behold His glory as none else will see it? In heaven—yea, in its brightest glory—He was at home; and as He was about to prepare a place in the Father's house for His own, so He bears witness of what He alone had seen to those whom sovereign grace would call and fit to be with Him there.

And what a testimony is this twofold knowledge, to the Person of Jesus, absolute yet in relation! He is, indeed, the true God, but withal eternal life. It was not empirical, but intrinsic. As a divine Person alone could, He knew both man and God; and, after He has urged the indispensable need of being born anew, He speaks of God known above in nature and glory, as before it we had His knowledge of what was in man. How blessed to have such a knowledge communicated to us as now in Christ and Christianity! Would not man, needy, ignorant, blind, welcome such a boon? Alas! no: not even when grace brings it down and tells all out in the tones of human speech. "And ye receive not Our testimony." It declares God, and reveals the Father. It leaves no room for receiving glory one of another. It condemns man as he is, self-willed and proud, not only without heart for God, but unwilling to believe what is in His heart for man expressed in every word and way of Jesus. As the Apostle tells us, "The things of God knoweth no one but the Spirit of God. The natural man is far from receiving them, for they are foolishness unto him; neither can he know them, because they are spiritually discerned" [1 Corinthians 2:11, 14].

There is a natural repugnance in man's mind to divine testimony. The judgment depends on the affections, and the affections of man are estranged from God. Privileges do not alter this, nor the responsibility which flows from the relation in which one may stand to God. He must be born again. A divine nature cleaves to God; the life which comes from Him as its source goes up to Him in desire, if not always (till redemption is known) in confidence of heart.

Yet the Lord had not in this solemn declaration gone beyond the universal necessity of man for the kingdom of God; and therefore it was inexcusable in the Jewish teacher so to have overlooked its truth as to feel amazement at the Lord's assertion of it. He ought to have known from the ancient Scriptures, from the Psalms and Prophets especially, that Israel must be renewed in order to enter and enjoy their promised portion on the earth. "Truly God is good to Israel," as the Messiah's kingdom will manifest; but the assurance is restricted. It is "to such as are of a clean heart" (Psalm 73). So far will the mass of the Jews be from fitness for the kingdom, that the Spirit of Christ in the pious remnant does not hesitate to ask God's judgment and pleading of their cause against an ungodly or unmerciful nation (Psalm 43). They were no better, but guiltier, than the Gentiles. There were enemies within as well as without. "And I said, Oh that I had wings like a dove! I would fly away, and be at rest. Behold, I would flee afar off; I would lodge in the wilderness. Selah. I would hasten my escape from the stormy wind, from the tempest. Swallow (them) up, Lord; divide their tongue: for I have seen violence and strife in the city. Day and night they go about it upon the walls thereof, and iniquity and mischief are in the midst of it. Perversities are in the midst thereof, and oppression and deceit depart not from its streets. For it is not an enemy that reproached me; then I could have borne it: neither is it he that hateth me that hath magnified (himself) against me; then I would have hidden myself from him. But it was thou, a man, mine equal, mine intimate, my familiar friend. We who held sweet intercourse together. To the house of God we walked amid the throng" (Psalm 55:6-14). Thus to the saint's mind the city (the holy city in title—in fact, most unholy) is worse than the wilderness, dreary as it may be. Not Gentiles only, but Jews, need to be born afresh: otherwise the name of God is blasphemed among the Gentiles through them, as it is written (Romans 2:24).

THE THIRD CHAPTER

But it is striking to notice that the chapter of Ezekiel (chapter 36), already cited in part, which is naturally brought to illustrate these words of the apostle Paul, declares in the plainest and most unconditional terms that God will sanctify His great name which was blasphemed among the heathen, "Which ye have profaned in the midst of them; and the nations shall know that I (am) Jehovah, saith the Lord Jehovah, when I shall be hallowed in you before their eyes. And I will take you from among the nations, and gather you out of all the countries, and will bring you into your own land. And I will sprinkle clean water upon you, and ye shall be clean: from all your uncleannesses and from all your idols will I cleanse you. And I will give you a new heart, and I will put a new spirit within you; and I will take away the stony heart out of your flesh, and I will give you a heart of flesh. And I will put My Spirit within you, and cause you to walk in My statutes and keep Mine ordinances, and ye shall do them. And ye shall dwell in the land that I gave to your fathers; and ye shall be My people, and I will be your God. And I will save you from all your uncleannesses; and I will call for the corn and will multiply it, and lay no famine upon you. And I will multiply the fruit of the tree and the increase of the field, so that ye may receive no more the reproach of famine among the nations. And ye shall remember your evil ways, and your doings which were not good, and shall loathe yourselves for your iniquities and for your abominations. Not for your sakes do I this, saith the Lord Jehovah, be it known unto you: be ashamed and confounded for your ways, O house of Israel. Thus saith the Lord Jehovah: In the day that I shall cleanse you from all your iniquities I will also cause the cities to be inhabited, and the waste places shall be builded. And the desolate land shall be tilled, whereas it was a desolation in the sight of all that passed by. And they shall say, This land that was desolate is become like the garden of Eden; and the waste and desolate and ruined cities (are) fortified (and) inhabited. And the nations that shall be left round about you shall know that I Jehovah build the ruined places (and) plant that which was desolate: I Jehovah have spoken, and I will do (it)" [Ezekiel 36:23-36].

Further, these words of the prophet illustrate "the earthly things" in our Lord's conversation with Nicodemus.

> "If I told you the earthly things and ye believe not, how shall ye believe if I tell you the heavenly things?" (verse 12).

In speaking as He had of the necessity to be born afresh—born of water and of Spirit—the Lord had not gone beyond "the earthly things." The kingdom of God could not be entered or seen without that new birth. Of course, it is indispensable for heaven; but the Lord goes farther, and insists on it as essential even for the lower province of God's kingdom. Even the Jew must be born again, and for millennial blessings, too, as well as for eternity. So true is it that they are not all Israel which are of Israel, neither, because they are the seed of Abraham, are they all children.

We shall see, too, when our Lord proceeds in His discourse to touch on His cross and the love of God in giving His Son, that to be born anew does not adequately describe what is given to the believer, but life eternal. Substantially, no doubt, it is the same new nature which every saint has, and must have; but, now that the glory and work of Christ are revealed, its full character shines out. There is yet more, as we know, and the next chapter shows—the Spirit given, and the relationship of children of God enjoyed, and the results of the death and resurrection and ascension of Christ our portion even now. But I enlarge no more on this as yet. Only we here learn that the kingdom of God has its "heavenly things," no less than "the earthly things" of which the prophets spoke. Jesus the Son could have opened the heavenly things, but the condition of such as Nicodemus did not admit of it for the present. The Spirit revealed all these and other depths of God amply after the shed blood vindicated God and purged their consciences. Then were the disciples free to learn all in the power of Christ's resurrection and in the light of heaven. Such is Christian knowledge.

But even while Christ was here He intimated distinctly the Father's kingdom as a heavenly sphere where the risen saints are to shine as the sun, contradistinguished from the Son of Man's kingdom, which is clearly the world, out of which at His coming the angels shall be sent to clear away all offences and those that practise lawlessness (Matthew 13:41-43). Nay, in the prayer given to the disciples we may recognise a similar distinction, though not so sharply drawn out, for He bade them pray for their Father's kingdom to come, where they and all the risen saints would be glorified; and then, that His will be done as in heaven so on earth, which will only be secured at the completion of the age, when the Son of Man comes in His kingdom (Matthew 6:10). These together constitute the kingdom of God, which comprises, therefore, as the Lord here assumes, "the heavenly things" and "the earthly things." The reader will find abundant confirmation in Ephesians 1:10, Colossians 1:20, and Hebrews 12:22-24.

We are next given to learn Who it is that could speak with competent knowledge and authority of heavenly things. It is the Son of Man, the same Person, doubtless, Who deigned to be born of the virgin, the Son of David, the Messiah. But as Messiah He is to judge Jehovah's people in righteousness, and to reign with a power which cannot be disputed, save to the ruin of every rebel. For "the Spirit of Jehovah shall rest upon Him, the spirit of wisdom and understanding, the spirit of counsel and might, the spirit of knowledge and of the fear of Jehovah. And His delight will be in the fear of Jehovah; and He shall not judge after the sight of His eyes, neither reprove after the hearing of His ears; but with righteousness shall He judge the poor, and reprove with equity the meek of the earth" [Isaiah 11:2-4]. As such He presented Himself to Israel, but was rejected; and, as we know, they reject Him to this day. For man, being lost, proves himself wholly blind, and of men none more than Israel against their truest glory and best treasure—Christ the Lord. And thus we have seen it from the first in the Gospel of John, who was given to treat things as they are, and as they are in presence of grace and truth in His Person Who reveals the Father.

Here, accordingly, it is not a prophet revealing the future of the kingdom of Jehovah over the earth, or of the judgments which will introduce it, or of the evils which must be judged before the establishment of blessing in that day. It is more than a prophet who gives out what he receives responsibly to communicate from God to man. Jesus knows not merely what is in man on earth as none ever knew, as the Word made flesh alone did know, but what is in God above as only a divine Person could, yet now as man also. No prophet ever did, ever could, so speak as He; none but He so knew and so testified. He, therefore, could speak of things heavenly, as well as of the earthly, not as one inspired to tell of what was before unknown, but of that which He knew and saw in the communion of the Godhead. His becoming man in no way detracted from His divine capacity or rights; it was unspeakable grace to those for whose sakes He was come from God and went to God, not only the truth and witness of it, as He alone could be, but about to die atoningly, as we shall see shortly in this very context, that the believer might live eternally and righteously.

What could man, angel, or any other creature avail? It was His glory, His work. The man, Adam, whom Jehovah Elohim formed, He put in Eden, chief of all creatures around him which God had pronounced very good. But the heaven is Jehovah's throne, though neither it nor the heaven of heavens can contain Him.

> "And no one hath gone up to heaven but He that came down from heaven, the Son of Man that is[e] in heaven" (verse 13).

Men have been, and will be, caught up to heaven; angels have been sent down from heaven. To Jesus only it belonged to go up,[68] as He only came down. For He was a divine Person, and He came in love; and love is ever free as well as holy. "Lo! I am come to do Thy will, O God." In the volume of the Book it was written of Him alone. And He Who was thus pleased to be found in fashion as a man, taking the body God prepared Him, rejoiced ever to speak of Himself as the Sent One, the man Christ Jesus, Who came down from heaven to do, not His own will, but the will of Him that sent Him. He became servant, but did not, could not, cease to be God. But He is man withal, as truly as Adam; yea, He is what Adam was not—Son of Man, come of woman.

And so it is that in the form of the expression used He is stamped as having ascended to heaven, He only that descended from heaven: ἀναβέβηκεν[f] ... ὁ ἐκ τοῦ οὐρανοῦ καταβάς. For, as the Apostle asks, "That He ascended, what is it but that He also descended into the lower parts of the earth? He that descended is the same also that ascended up above all the heavens, that He might fill all things" {Ephesians 4:9-10}. Only, as the apostle Paul tells us, it is in connection with His work and the counsels of God, so John presents it in our Lord's words as connected with the truth of His Person—"the Son of Man that is in heaven." And an astonishing truth it is. To have said the Son *of God* that *was* in heaven would have been true; but what an infinite truth is that which is said, "the Son of Man that *is* in heaven"! Impossible to be said if He had not been God, the Son of the Father, yet, what was of the deepest moment, said of Him as man, the rejected Messiah, "the Son of Man that is in heaven." The Incarnation was no mere emanation of divinity; neither was it a Person once Divine Who ceased to be so by becoming man (in itself an impossible absurdity), but One Who, to glorify the Father, and in accomplishment of the purposes of grace to the glory of God, took humanity into union with Godhead in His Person. Therefore it is that He could say, and of Him alone could it be said, "the Son of Man that is in heaven," even as He is the Only-begotten Son that is (not merely that was[g]) in the bosom of the Father. He it is Who met, and more than met, the challenge of Agur (Proverbs 30), speaking prophetically to Ithiel and Ucal, "Who hath ascended up into the heavens and descended? Who hath gathered the wind in His fists? Who hath bound the waters in a mantle? Who hath established all the ends of the earth? What is His name, and what is His Son's name, if thou knowest?" It is God, not man, Who can take up the challenge; but it is God become man—yea, the Son of Man. How suited as well as competent is He to unfold all things, heavenly, earthly, human, and divine! He is, indeed, the Truth.

We saw that the ascension of the Lord is grounded on His descent from heaven, and that both flow from and belong to His Person as the Son of Man that is in heaven. But the Lord follows this up by setting out the mighty work He came to do for sinners, that they might have life eternal—by grace, indeed, but on the footing of divine righteousness.

> "And even as Moses lifted up the serpent in the wilderness, so must the Son of Man be lifted up; that every one that believeth on[h] Him should (not perish, but)[i] have life eternal.[69] For God so loved the world that He gave His[j] Only-begotten Son, that every one that believeth on Him should not perish but have life eternal" (verses 14-16).

The new birth had been already insisted on for man to see or enter the kingdom of God. But so is the cross also a necessity, if guilty man was to receive pardon from God whilst living to Him. They are alike indispensable. Compare 1 John 4:9-10. And Christ as He alone could be, so was He sent a propitiation for our sins. The Lord here illustrates the latter truth by the well-known scene in the wilderness, where God directed Moses, in his distress for the guilty Israelites bitten by the fiery serpents and dying in all quarters, to set a serpent of brass on a pole, that whoever looked might live. It was the figure of Himself, Who knew no sin, for us made sin, identified in divine dealing with the consequences of our evil in judgment on the cross. Impossible that sin could otherwise be expiated adequately. It must be by God's judging it in One capable of bearing what it deserved at His hands; and it must be in man, in the Son of Man, to be available for man. Yet, had it been any other than Jesus, it had been offensive to God, and not efficacious for man; for He only was the Holy One, and in no offering was there more jealous care that it should be without blemish. "It is most holy," says the law of the sin-offering. Adam fell, and all other men were shapen in iniquity, and in sin conceived.

In Him only of woman-born was no sin, not only no sins committed, but no sin in Him. Therefore was a body prepared for Him as for no one else when the Holy Ghost came on the virgin Mary, and the power of the Highest overshadowed her. Therefore also that Holy Thing which was born was called the Son of God; not only the Son of God before He was sent of the Father, but, when in grace the Word thus became flesh, perfect man, yet not the less truly God. For there was none other way, if the desperate case of man was to be remedied before God. It could only be righteously through atonement, and the Son of Man was the only fitting victim. For blood of bulls and goats is incapable of taking away sins, however such sacrifices might be beforehand instructive of man's need and of God's way. "Wherefore, when He cometh into the world, He saith, Sacrifice and offering Thou wouldest not, but a body didst Thou prepare Me. In burnt-offerings and sacrifices for sin Thou hadst no pleasure. Then said I, Lo I am come (in the volume of the Book it is written of Me) to do Thy will, O God" [Hebrews 10:5-7, quoting Psalm 40:6 *f.*].

Thus did the man Christ Jesus, Son of God withal, yea, God over all blessed for ever, deign to suffer once for sins, Just for unjust, that He might bring us to God. Only so could it be, for God could not make light of sin, however surely He can and does pardon sinners; but even He could not pardon consistently with Himself or

His Word, or the creature's real blessing, but through the blood of the cross. And therefore did the Lord say here to Nicodemus, who knew the Law, if he had little known the Prophets, "As Moses lifted up the serpent in the wilderness, even so *must* the Son of Man be lifted up." Thus did He redeem out of the curse of the law, having become a curse for us. It is not a living Messiah reigning over His people on earth, but He rejected by them, sinners and lost as they were now proved to be; it is Jesus Christ and He crucified, in that character or title which connects Him with the one object for a sinful man: or, as He says Himself here, "that every one that believeth on Him may not perish, but have life eternal." By Him only thus presented one comes to God, all his sins being judged and borne in His cross. Hence it is by *believing* on Him that one has life eternal. The believer looks out of himself to the Lord Jesus.

But this alone might leave the soul, though looking to Christ by faith, without liberty or peace, however truly blessed thus far. Hence the Lord reveals another truth. "For God so loved the world, that He gave His Only-begotten Son, that every one that believeth on Him should not perish but have life eternal."[70] It is no longer the abject and absolute need of guilty man, be he Jew or any other. There is now revealed the sovereign love of God, which confines not itself to any limits such as the law, or man under it, had contemplated, but goes out freely and fully to the world, where He was unknown and hated; and this, not in creation or providential mercies, but in such sort as to give His Son, His Only-begotten, "that every one that believeth on Him may not perish but have eternal life." It is grace to the uttermost. It is no question here of a needs-be. There was no moral necessity that God should *give* His Son; it was His love, not obligation on His part, nor claim on man's. Whatever need there was in man's state was amply met in the cross of the Son of Man, and therein was accomplished the atonement or propitiation for the sins of those who believe. But there is incomparably more in the Only-begotten Son given by the God of love, not to the elect nation, but to the world. Thus divine love is manifested as perfectly as His just and holy requirement in judging sin; and this in Christ, the Only-begotten Son of God, the suffering but now glorified Son of Man, both too displayed in and enjoyed by that life eternal which the believer has in Him.

The great truth has been cleared: not only that man, sinful man, needed an adequate atonement as well as new birth, but that God loved the world, the guilty, lost world of Gentiles no less than Jews, and loved it so that He gave His Only-begotten Son, that every one who believeth in Him should not perish but have eternal life. It is in the Son of God that both lines of the truth meet, for He is incarnate and crucified. Accordingly the true light shines, life eternal is given, God's love is known, redemption is accomplished, salvation is come. There is more in and by Him now than if the kingdom were set up in power, for which those waited whose expectations were formed and bounded by the Old Testament. "Loving-kindness and truth are met together; righteousness and peace have kissed each other"; and, though one could not say perhaps till "that day" that "truth shall spring out of the earth, and righteousness shall look down from the heavens" [Psalm 85:10 *f.*], yet one knows assuredly that "grace and truth came by Jesus Christ," and that righteousness is established and displayed in Him exalted on the throne and glorified in God Himself above. In the bright days of heaven upon the earth He is to judge His people and the world righteously, and will early cut off the wicked; for the quick must be judged by Him at His coming, as well as the dead at last, ere He gives up the kingdom to God.

But deeper purposes were in hand now that the Messiah is viewed as rejected by the Jews: eternal life in, and salvation by, the Son of God, Who dies atoningly on the cross.

> "For God sent not His^k Son into the world that He should judge the world, but that the world might be saved through Him" (verse 17).

And as a work beyond comparison deeper and with everlasting consequences was before God, so the objects of His grace are no longer within the circumscribed limits of the land of Israel. If He is to manifest Himself now as a Saviour God in His Son, it suits His love to send out the good news to the world as a whole. God was in Christ reconciling the world to Himself, not imputing their trespasses to them. Granted that Christ thus present was rejected; but the errand of love was in no way abandoned; rather did it enter on a new ground whence it could go forth in the power of the Spirit. For Him Who knew no sin God made sin for us (that is, in the cross), that we might become God's righteousness in Him.

Thus Christ as Saviour, not as Judge, expresses the characteristic testimony of God now made known to man and here declared by our Lord, in contradistinction from His predicted glory as Messiah and Son of Man, ruling as He will over the earth by and by in the age to come. This is followed up by the result for him who receives Christ now.

> "He that believeth on Him is not judged; but¹ he that believeth not hath been already judged, because he hath not believed on the name of the Only-begotten Son of God" (verse 18).

Not only is the believer not condemned, but he is not an object of judgment. He will give account, but is never put on his trial. This is explicitly taught in John 5, where the twofold issue is connected with the mystery of Christ's Person. As He is Son of God and Son of Man, so He gives life and will exercise judgment, the one for the blessing of believers as owning His glory, the other for His vindication on such as have dishonoured Him.

Thus, as His stooping to become man exposed Him to unbelief, it is as Son of Man that He will judge His despisers, which clearly does not apply to the believer, whose joy is even now and ever to honour Him as the Father. And as in this later chapter of John the believer is declared to have life eternal, and not to come into judgment, but to have passed out of death into life, so here "he that believeth not hath been already judged, because he hath not believed on the name of the Only-begotten Son of God." For John presents the Lord as declaring all decided by the test of His own Person received in faith or unbelievingly rejected. Good or evil in all other respects turns on this, as He shows soon after. There is no such touchstone, not even the law of God, weighty and incisive as it is. Hence we see the fallacy of the older divines, who drag in the law here as everywhere, and thus make it only a question of moral condemnation; whereas the very point of instruction is that it is Christ Himself believed or disbelieved, though no doubt conduct follows accordingly.

But here it is not death for not doing God's commandments, but the unbeliever already judged by Him Who sees the end from the beginning, and pronounces on all persons and things as they are before God. Only One can avail him who is dead in trespasses and sins; in nowise the law, which can simply condemn him whose walk is opposed to itself, but the Son, Who is life and gives life to the believer. But the unbeliever refuses the Son of God: carelessly or deliberately, in haughty pride or in cowardly clinging to other trusts, pleasures, or interests, it is only a difference of form or degree. For he has not believed on the name of the Only-begotten Son of God, Whose name is not hidden but preached. There is the fullest declaration of what He is, and is to sinners: so that all excuse is vain and can only add sin to sin. His very name implies, yea asserts, that He is the Saviour, a divine Saviour, yet a Man, and so for men. Nor can it be truthfully urged that there is any doubt as to God's feeling and mind; for it had just been said that God sent Him into the world to this end, whatever must be the character of His coming another day, when He will reckon with those who would have none of Him. But what is it to God that wretched, guilty, ruined sinners should despise and reject Him Who is at once the only Saviour of man, and the Only-begotten Son of God! When those who most need mercy least feel it, when they in their utter degradation refuse the Highest, Who comes down to them in the fullest love to bless, what remains but judgment for those who thus render God's grace null as to themselves, heightened as it is by the glory of Him Who in love came for their sakes, and deepened by the humiliation in which He designed to come?

I am aware that the Puritan divines drag in the law even here, and will have it that Christ, in illustrating the certainty of salvation for those that believe in Him, shows on the contrary the condemnation of unbelievers to be twofold, one by the law and the other by the gospel. Their idea is that the unbelievers are here declared to be condemned already by the sentence of the law, which they still lie under, and have it confirmed by the gospel, since they do not by faith lay hold on the offered and only remedy in Christ.

But there is no trace of such a scheme either here or anywhere else in Scripture, which teaches expressly that "as many as sinned without law shall also perish without law, and as many as sinned in the law shall be judged by the law ... in the day when God shall judge the secrets of men by Jesus Christ" (Romans 2:12-16). St. Paul's doctrine therefore excludes the assumption that every unbeliever is already under the law, which would intelligibly involve his being condemned by it, law affecting only those under it, whilst those who have it not are dealt with on their own ground. With this entirely agrees the language of our Gospel, which does not say a word about the law, even where a teacher of it was before the Lord inquiring into life eternal and salvation. It is solely a question of Christ.

> "And this is the judgment, that the light hath come into the world, and men loved the darkness rather than the light; for their works were evil. For every one that doeth evil hateth the light, and cometh not unto the light lest his works should be convicted; but he that practiseth the truth cometh unto the light, that his works may be manifested that they have been wrought in God" (verses 19-21).

THE THIRD CHAPTER

Inasmuch as the true light now shines—no longer the law in Israel, but the light come into the world, a criterion is in force which decides for every man. There is a far deeper question than a man's own state or conduct. Indeed, this, too, is already decided: man is no longer under probation, as the Jew was under law. He is lost: be he Jew or Gentile, he is alike lost. It is, therefore, a question of believing on Jesus, Son of God and Son of Man, Who (as we saw before) has been sent of God, not as He will be shortly to judge the quick and the dead, but that the world (not the elect nation now, but the world, spite of its ruin, in His grace) may be saved through Him. This tests to the core. All thus depends on believing on Him. If one believes not, one has been already judged. It is not merely to fail in duty, but to fight against the grace and truth come by Jesus Christ. It is to reject life eternal, and the perfect love of God, in the Only-begotten Son of God, Whose name one disbelieves or makes light of.

It is wholly vain to complain of lack of light. The very reverse is true. "This is the judgment, that the light hath come into the world, and men loved the darkness rather than the light, for their works were evil." Terrible revelation of their state! Alas! it was our state, our affections so utterly corrupt as to prefer the darkness to the light, and this from the guiltiest reason, and a bad conscience. For our deeds were evil. Assuredly the trumpet gives no uncertain sound. Have we heard its clear warning above, beneath, the din of this world? Have we submitted to the sentence of Him Who knows what is in man, no less than what is in God? Or are we unbroken still in self-righteousness and self-conceit? Do we dare to dispute the words of the Lord, solemn and plain—too plain to be mistaken? Would we put off the decision till the great white throne? And what will He then judge of the unbelief which thus virtually gives Him the lie? For no man that believed these words of His now would put off till then, but surely cast his soul on Him Who, if the Judge then, is Saviour, and nothing but a Saviour, to the lost one that now believes on His name.

But when eternal judgment does come, it is not true that then it is a question simply of man's unbelief. From the divine account given to us, we learn that the dead are judged according to their works. There is no such thing at any time as salvation according to our works; for all who reject Christ there will be judgment according to their works. They had refused the Saviour, they had despised the grace of God through religiousness or irreligiousness, through opposition or indifference. They are not found written in the book of life, they are judged out of the things written in the book according to their works. They are cast into the lake of fire. This is the second death, the lake of fire, the end of all who loved[71] the darkness rather than the light. For their works were evil: is not their judgment just? What is the Lord's moral analysis? "For every one that doeth evil hateth the light, and cometh not unto the light, lest his works should be convicted." How could such a one suit the portion of the saints in light? He hates the light which has come here: would he suit it or love it better on high? He is inwardly false and dishonest, deliberately and decidedly preferring to go on in his sins, instead of submitting to their complete detection by the light, that they might be blotted out and forgiven by the faith of Christ's blood. Is this truth in the inner man? Does it not rather prove that such as refuse Christ are of the devil as their father, and desire to do their lusts, instead of hearing the word of God and being subject to His Son?

On the other hand, "he that practiseth the truth cometh unto the light, that his works may be manifested that they have been wrought in God." For the faith that is of God's elect is never powerless but living, not only productive of results seen among men, but such as savour of their divine source and sphere. None makes more of the truth or of knowing God than John; none has a deeper horror of Gnosticism. It is life, life eternal, that one should know the Father, the only true God, and Jesus Christ Whom He sent; but His commandment is life everlasting, as our Lord could say of Him Who gave to Himself what He should say and what He should speak.

If we know these things, we are blessed if we do them. Unblessed is the forgetful hearer, who does not practise the truth nor come unto the light, but is rather gone away after considering himself, and straightway loses all remembrance of what he was like. Is it not too plain that his works are at best impulsive and natural? But he that practises the truth comes unto the light; walking therein he seeks to walk according to the light, trying by it his inward thoughts and feelings, motives and objects, words and ways. The realised presence of God imparts its colour to his works. They were manifestly wrought in God. They bear His image and superscription. Hence when all that are in the tombs hear the Lord's voice and go forth, it is for those that have practised good to a life-resurrection, for those that have done evil to a judgment-resurrection.[72] There was life in the one case, not in the other. He that heard the Saviour's word and believed the God Who sent Him has life eternal, and hence practises good. He who rejects the Son of God has no ground but man, and can have no power but Satan's; he has refused Him Who is God's wisdom and God's power. He might not like to be lost and judged; but he despises the only way of salvation open to any, the crucified Son of Man, the life-giving Son of God. He will not be able to refuse or despise His judgment by and by.

VERSES 22-34.

The next paragraph has for its object the homage rendered by the Baptist to the Lord. This the Spirit of God introduces by telling us the occasion of it.[73] The conversation with Nicodemus was in Jerusalem, and in this was unfolded the absolute need of both the new birth and the cross. Only that when the Lord speaks of these things, He could not but let us know that it is life eternal which the believer receives, and that He Himself was not more surely the Son of Man Who must be lifted up for man's desperate case than He is the Only-begotten Son of God given to the world in divine love. Salvation was in His mind, not judgment, though the unbeliever in Him must be, yea is, judged already; and this on the deepest of all grounds, the preference of darkness, that they might do their wicked works at ease, to the Light come into the world in Christ. The case, then, of every rejector of Him is thus solemnly decided.

It is evident that the Person of Christ is the key to all, and shines out more and more in the secret scene with Nicodemus. Still it seemed good to the Holy Ghost, Who gave a yet fuller witness to His glory by John at a critical moment, to reproduce this permanently for us with the circumstances which led to it. The thought might enter some minds that the Lord only used His predecessor to continue the work and outdo it. It was fitting, therefore, that John the Baptist should give a final testimony to Him where human nature is apt to be most grudging.

> "After these things came Jesus and His disciples into the land of Judæa, and there he was tarrying with them and baptizing.[74] And John also was baptizing at Ænon near Salim, because much water was there; and they were coming there and being baptized: for John was not yet cast into prison" (verses 22-24).

We have thus a view of what was going on previous to the public Galilean ministry of our Lord in the three Synoptic Gospels. They do not touch on any work of His before John's imprisonment, whilst the early chapters of the fourth Gospel are devoted to this, after the revelation of His Person and glories at the beginning.[75]

> "There arose then a dispute on the part of the disciples of John with a Jew[m] about purification. And they came unto John and said to him, Rabbi, He who was with thee across the Jordan, to Whom thou hast borne witness, behold, He is baptizing and all come unto Him" (verses 25-26).

A Jew's reasoning did not ruffle them, for their souls could not but feel the moral superiority of John's call and baptism to repentance in the faith of the coming Messiah; but the nearness of Jesus and the fact of His attractive power, veiled as it then might be, was a fact that disconcerted them, though the appeal to their master took the shape of zeal for one who had been prompt to own the dignity of Jesus when He came to John for baptism. But now He was baptizing, and all were flocking to Him: so complained John's disciples.[76]

Let us well weigh the reply.

> "John answered and said, A man can receive nothing unless it have been given him from heaven. Ye yourselves bear me witness that I said, I am not the Christ, but that I am sent before Him" (verses 27-28).

It was lowly yet wise withal; it put, as truth always does, both God and ourselves in the right place, thus securing a like recognition of His sovereign disposal of all and the contentedness of each with his own lot, and, it may be added, quiet firmness in the discharge of the duty which flows from it. For there is no greater error than the thought that our own will is really strong. Be it ever so, obedience is stronger still. "He that doeth the will of God abideth for ever" [1 John 2:17]. Out of this spirit of dependence and happy submission to God did John answer his disciples. If he were eclipsed as the morning star by the dawn of day, it was to fulfil, not to fail in, his mission. He, the servant and forerunner, had never set up to be the Master, as they could all attest, if they would.

Then John applies to himself a figure taken from the circumstance of a bridal feast to illustrate his relation to the Lord, in beautiful harmony with the Lord's own use of it elsewhere. Here, of course, all is connected with Israel, though, when the Church took the place of that nation, the Holy Spirit applies it freely to the new relationship constantly before us in the Epistles and the Revelation.

> "He that hath the bride is (the) Bridegroom; but the friend of the Bridegroom that standeth and heareth Him rejoiceth with joy because of the voice of the Bridegroom: this my joy then is ful-

filled. He must increase, but I decrease" (verses 29-30).

John was indeed the most favoured servant—yea, "the friend" of the Bridegroom. It was his joy, therefore, that the bride should be Christ's, not his, whose highest distinction was to be His immediate herald, seeing those days which kings and prophets had so ardently desired to see, seeing Him Who gave those days their brightness. It was his chiefest joy to hear His voice of love and satisfaction in those He deigned to love as His bride. His own mission was closed. If Simeon could depart in peace, John could say that his joy was fulfilled. It was right, it was necessary, that He should increase and himself decrease, though no greater was born of woman. Instead of feeling a pang, his heart bowed and delighted in it. By and by when Christ comes in power and glory, and sits on the throne of David as well as of the yet larger dominion of the Son of Man, "there will be no end of the increase of His government," as the prophet declares [Isaiah 9:7]. But John could say it now in the days of His humiliation, as his soul rests on the glory of His Person, and the Spirit leads him on in the sense of what was due to Him.

The glory of the Person of Christ shines with rich lustre here. It is not merely His nearness of relation to His people as distinguished from John, nor His increase while the greatest of woman-born decreases. He is superior to all comparison.

"He that cometh from above is above all" (verse 31a).

Neither Adam nor Abraham, Enoch nor Elijah, could take such a ground. They, like John, did not come from above, nor could any one of them be said to be above all.

Nor could our blessed Lord Himself be so described, as born of Mary, and heir of David, had He not been God—the great theme of our Gospel. But this it has been the grand aim to show He is: a truth of the deepest moment, we can say boldly, not only to us the children, but to God the Father. For thus and now are to be solved all the questions that had ever risen between God and man, insoluble till He appeared, and appeared a true man, Who is no less truly God, and thus both "from above" and "above all."

And it was fitting that John the Baptist's own lips[77] should give utterance to the incontestable supremacy of the Lord Jesus in presence of his own disciples, jealous of their leader's honour. Hence follows the explanation:

> "he that is of the earth is of the earth, and speaketh (as) of the earth; He that cometh of the heaven is above all" (verse 31b).°

The Lord may vindicate John; but John asserts the glory of Jesus, Who had lost none of His intrinsic and supreme dignity by deigning in divine love to become man. Like all other men, John could not claim to have any other origin naturally than the earth. Jesus alone is out of heaven; for such is the virtue of His Person that He raises up humanity into union with His divine nature, instead of being dragged down by humanity into its degradation by sin as some have vainly and evilly dreamt.

Nor is it of His person only that we are here taught. His testimony is invested with kindred value.

> "And what He hath seen and heard, this He testifieth; and no one receiveth His testimony" (verse 32).

THE THIRD CHAPTER

His is the perfection of testimony; for what was there of God, of the Father, and this in heaven, that the Son had not seen and heard? There could be no conceivable defect here in the glory whence He came, and in the grace with which He made all known to man. How withering, therefore, the sad result! For surely beforehand it must have been universally anticipated that all but the most besotted would eagerly welcome such a witness of things divine, heavenly, and eternal. But such is man's estate through sin, not only the savage and the brutal, not only the idolater or the sceptic, but those who pique {pride} themselves on their religion, whether it be theory or practice, ordinances or tradition, effort, ecstasy, or experience—"no one receiveth His testimony." How solemn the sentence! and the more so as being the unimpassioned utterance of holiness. Doubtless they knew not what they did in their dislike of, or indifference to, His testimony; but what a state man must be in, to have the heavenly and divine Saviour thus bearing witness of things most deeply needed by himself in relation to God and heaven and for ever, without ever finding out the worth of the Testifier or of the testimony! It is not that grace did not open some hearts, here and there, now and then; but the point here noted is the rejection of His testimony by man, not the reserve of sovereign mercy when all was lost in sin and ruin.

Faith is in no way a growth natural to the heart of sinful man. Without faith it is impossible to please God; and without His grace faith is impossible, such faith at least as pleases Him. For they that are in flesh cannot please God; but who are not in flesh till brought to God? Man conscious of sin and shrinking from divine judgment dislikes the God Whose punishment he dreads. His grace he sees no reason, as far as he is concerned, for believing; and no wonder he sees none, for it would not be God's grace if there were a ground for it in himself. Grace excludes the desert of him to whom it is shown, and this is as offensive to his own self-sufficiency as it supposes love in Him Whose displeasure he knows he deserves. Thus there is no disposition in his heart to believe in God's grace, ample to make him doubt; and the more, as he reasons on what God must be, and on what he himself has been toward God. Christ is not seen to change all, as the manifestation of love, and His death the ground of the righteousness of God which justifies the believer, spite of past sins and ungodliness.

His testimony therefore puts the heart thoroughly to the test; for it tells the truth of the sinner as decidedly as it announces the grace of God; and the heart resists the one and distrusts the other. The last thing submitted to is to think ill of oneself, and well of God. But this is just the effect of receiving the testimony of Christ. We then begin to take God's side against ourselves; for if there be genuine faith, there is genuine repentance, without which, indeed, the faith is human and worthless, as in John 2, where men believed beholding the signs wrought, and Jesus did not trust Himself to them. Such faith is not of God's Spirit, but merely of the mind drawing a conclusion from the probabilities of the case.[78] In it man judges, which pleases him, instead of his being morally judged, which is humbling and offensive. He sees no sufficient reason to reject the evidence, and, his will going along with it, he believes accordingly. As this was the case with many in Jerusalem at the Passover, so it is with multitudes throughout Christendom now and ever since. The vague creed which prevails generally awakens enough neither of interest nor of opposition to put men to the test. But when any great truth, even of that creed, is pressed on the conscience or comes distinctly before the heart, it will then be seen how little men believe what they in words accredit, only because they never seriously apply it to their souls before God.

Take the simple truth, for instance, of our Gospel, the Word, Who was God become flesh and dwelling among us; or, again, remission of sins in His name, the message to every soul, the possession of every believer: who doubts either as long as they are preached abstractedly in the pulpit? But the moment a man receives them for his own soul, and, though feeling and owning his sins more than ever, blesses God for forgiveness and rejoices in Christ—while he worships God and the Lamb, others shrink back and cry presumption! As if such truths were never intended for the heart and life and lips of every day, but only as a religious service, or, rather, a form for the multitude keeping holiday.

The fact is, however, that the grace and truth which came by Jesus Christ (being perfect in themselves and in Him Whose glory is adequate to display and make them good, as well as perfectly adapted to man, sinful and lost as he is) test him absolutely, "and no one receiveth His testimony." Where the quickening power of the Spirit acts, it is far otherwise. So proper is it to win the heart, that he who is not won shows that his will is against God and His grace and truth in Christ, hatred naturally and soon following. He who bows, being begotten by the word of truth, judges himself. He has received not man's word, but, as it truly is, God's word, which effectually works in the believer; or, as it is put here,

> "he that hath received His testimony hath set to his seal that God is true" (verse 33).

This is the essential character of real, living faith. His testimony is received because He gives it: nothing more simple, but we are not simple; nothing more right and due to Him, but we have been all wrong, and most wrong to Him. It is received because He says it, not because it seems reasonable, or wise, or good, or for evidence of any kind; though one need not say there are the fullest evidences, and the testimony is that which alone could suit God or man, if one be a sinner, the other a Saviour where His testimony is received. A divine faith is due to a divine testimony; but the faith which is grounded on human motives is not divine: only that which is founded on God's word truly searches heart and conscience. When a man is broken down to feel his own state of sin, as well as what he has done against such a God, the heart desires that the good news of the gospel should be the truth, instead of yielding to the indifference or active repugnance natural to it; and this is to believe with the heart (Romans 10:9-10).

Further, the ground of confidence is laid plainly and expressed fully. We are not left to inference.

> "For He Whom God sent speaketh the words of God; for God^p giveth not the Spirit by measure" (verse 34).

To receive the words of Jesus, then, is to receive those of God. What possible ground is there for hesitation? To faith alone belongs absolute certainty. And of this the Spirit is the power, as in Him perfectly, so in and by us as far as flesh is judged. He was the holy vessel of the Spirit, so that the testimony was poured out as pure as it was poured in, or, rather, as it is in Him Who is Himself the truth. As for what inspired men have written, it is just the same. "If any man think himself to be a prophet, or spiritual, let him acknowledge that the things that I write unto you are the commandment of the Lord" (1 Corinthians 14:37). In all others, whatever the power, there is no such guarantee against infirmity or mistake, though one may be perfectly kept and guided, where only and simply dependent: so real is the connection between the truth and the Spirit.

Verses 35-36.

We have had the supremacy of Jesus, and His testimony, so thoroughly marking Him off from all others. But there is more. He is "the Son," and the especial object of divine affection and honour. This follows; and here, accordingly, we rise far above His position either as the Messiah, the Bridegroom on the one hand, or the heavenly prophet on the other, Whose testimony absolutely detected every child of Adam, while it brought him that received it to the knowledge of God and His mind with divine certainty. Hence we hear of the Father and the Son.

> "The Father[q] loveth the Son, and hath put (*literally*, given) all things in His hand" (verse 35).

Jesus is the Heir of all, as the Son of the Father in a sense peculiar to Himself, the true Isaac Who abides ever, the beloved Son Who has all that He Himself has, and has all given to be in His (the Son's) hand.

Consequently it is no question here of blessing for any measured time or for glory on earth under His reign as King. All things come to the point at once and for ever before Him, Who is the object of testimony, and not the testifier merely.

> "He that believeth on the Son hath life eternal" (verse 36a).

One need not thus wait for the blessing in the days of the kingdom. Then, no doubt, Jehovah will command blessing, even life for evermore. But he that believes in the Son has eternal life now. For the same reason it is of all things the most fatal to refuse subjection to His Person now. Therefore is it added,

> "and he that believeth not on the Son shall not see life, but the wrath of God abideth on him" (verse 36b).

If disobedience is intended, it is to Himself as well as to His words, as, indeed, by the obedience of faith the apostle Paul meant not practical obedience, however important in its place and season, but subjection[79] to Himself—to the truth revealed in Him. He that refuses Him in unbelief abides in unremoved death and under the wrath of God, Who cannot but resent such insult of heart to His Son.

NOTES ON THE THIRD CHAPTER

a [*Cf. Lectures Introductory to the Study of the Gospels*, pp. 431-440.]

b [So most Edd., with majority of copies. Blass: "heaven," as in ℵ^{pm}. The Syrr. support "God," for which internal evidence is decisive. As to the "kingdom" here, *cf. Lectures on the Gospel of Matthew*: "He appears to speak of a kingdom which we do enter now" (chapter xvii., p. 366, {New Edition, 1896; p. 261, 1868})]

c Cartwright had said that irregular baptism had grown out of a false interpretation of John 3:5, "where certain do interpret the word water for (of) the material and elemental water, when as (whereas) our Saviour Christ taketh water there by a borrowed speech for the Spirit." This the reader will see to be imperfect; for water here is the figure of the word bringing the sentence of death on the flesh; and so is sinful man cleansed by Him out of Whose side flowed blood and water, as John testifies. On the general point says Hooker, "I hold it for a most infallible truth in exposition of sacred scripture, that where a literal construction will stand, the furthest from the letter is commonly the worst. There is nothing more dangerous than this licentious and deluding art, which changeth the meaning of words, as alchymy doth or would do the substance of metals, making of anything what it listeth, and bringeth in the end all truth to nothing. … To hide the general consent of antiquity agreeing in the literal interpretation, they cunningly affirm that 'certain' have taken those words as meant of material water, when they know that of all the ancients there is not one to be named that ever did otherwise either expound or allege the place than as implying external baptism" (*Of the Laws of Ecclesiastical Polity*, V. lix. 2, 3). Antiquity was perhaps as unanimous in applying John 6 to the Lord's Supper with as little solid reason. In neither case is it a literal construction, but a mere catching at a superficial resemblance; and in both cases the consequence is heterodoxy most perilous to souls, which has enormously helped on the ruin of Christendom as well as of deluded individuals. To deny that the Lord often elsewhere employed water figuratively is impossible; to maintain that He meant it literally here is to lower the sense immensely and to involve the worst consequences, as of an ordinance saving *ex opere operato* {by the very fact of the action's being performed}. It is remarkable, I would add, that the Gospel of John omits even the institution of baptism and of the Lord's Supper, dwelling beyond all others on life and the Spirit.

d [א, Syr^(ch sin) have, as some Old Lat., "of water and of the Spirit."]

e The Alexandrian (pr. m.) and a cursive of the Gospels (4949 in the British Museum) omit ὤν. Still more serious is the omission ὁ ὢν ἐν τῷ οὐρανῷ in the Sinai, Vatican, two other uncials [L,T.], a valuable Paris cursive [33], etc. There need be no hesitation, however, in accepting the mass of authorities [including Latt. and Syrr.] against these testimonies; which illustrate the danger of being carried away by a few favourites, be they ever so venerable and in general trustworthy. I am glad to see that Dr. Tregelles [as Tischendorf] inserts the clause; but it is hard to understand with what consistency it is done in his system of recension. [See W. and H., *Select Readings*, p. 75. Weiss and Blass omit the words; but Syr^(sin) has "the Son of Man who is from heaven."]

f We are not to suppose ἀναβήσεται here. The futurity of the Ascension is perfectly right in John 6. But here it is a proleptic character attached to the Person of the Lord; and hence to express this no tense was so proper as the perfect, the present continuance of a past act. The seeming anomalies of Scripture are most instructive when understood.

g It is surprising that Bengel should follow Raphelius in preferring "*qui erat*" to "*qui est*," as almost all the ancients, Greeks and Latins rightly insist.

h The Sinai MS. and the great mass of the uncials and cursives have εἰς here, as in verse 16; but the Vatican (B) and the St. Petersburg uncial of the sixth century (T) read ἐν αὐτῷ, supported by many Latin copies [besides Syr^(sin), and followed by Edd.]; as the Paris L has here in verse 16 ἐπ' αὐτῷ, the Alexandrian ἐπ' αὐτὸν here only, though T^b reads it in verse 16. A Bodleian cursive (47) omits the phrase in both cases.

i The clause μὴ ἀπόληται ἀλλ' here is wanting in four uncials of the highest character, seven cursives, and many versions, etc. [not Syr^{sin}]; but almost all read it in verse 16.

j The Sinai and the Vatican (B) omit αὐτοῦ, "His."

k The word αὐτοῦ ("His") is omitted by אBLT^b, five cursives and some fathers, but read by all other authorities [rejected by Edd.].

l אB, etc., omit δέ ("but"), which all else read [rejected by Edd.].

m There is equally good evidence from the most ancient and excellent witnesses for the plural form (א^{pm}G Λ^2 Π^2 1. 13. 69. 124. etc. It. Vulg. Syr$^{cu.}$ Cop. Arm^{usc} Æth. Goth. Orig.) in the common text as for the singular (א^{corr} ABEFHKLMSUVΓΔΛ^{pm}Π^{pm}, many cursives, Syr$^{sin\ pesch\ et\ phil.}$ and Arm$^{zoh.}$ Chrys. Nonn.) preferred by most critics, partly as being the less common of the two, and so more likely to be changed.

n The witnesses for omitting μοι include אEFHMVΓ, many cursives, etc., and are scarcely inferior, therefore, to those [including Syr^{sin}] in favour of the ordinary text.

o [Lachm., Treg., W. and H., Weiss: "is above all," from א$^{corr.}$ ABLΓΔΛΠ, etc., Vulg. Syr$^{sin\ pesch\ hcl\ hier}$ Memph. Æth. Goth. Chrys. Cyr. Alex.—Tischendorf, followed by Blass, omits the words according to א^{pm}D and a few cursives, some old Latt. Syr^{cu} Arm., Tertullian.]

p ["God": so Lachm., Treg., after AC$^{corr.}$DΓΔΛΠ, etc., Vulg. Syr$^{pesch\ hcl}$ Memph. Æth., Orig. Chrys. Tisch., W. and H., and Weiss omit, as אB$^{corr.}$C^{pm}LT, 1, 33, Cyr.

Alex.—Blass: "the Father," omitting "the Spirit," as B^{pm} Syr^{sin}.]

q [Syr^{sin} has "But He," followed by Blass.]

THE FOURTH CHAPTER [a]

We find ourselves still in that part of our Gospel which precedes the Galilean ministry of our Lord presented in the three Synoptic Gospels, though this journey through Samaria is conducting the Lord to their starting-point. In chapter 3:24 it will have been noticed that John was *not yet* cast into prison. When he was put in prison (Mark 1:14), and Jesus heard it (Matthew 4:12), He came into Galilee, preaching. Our chapter speaks of a previous moment, and, as usual, lets us into a deeper view of all that was at work.

Verses 1-3.

> "When therefore the Lord knew that the Pharisees heard that Jesus[80a] maketh and baptizeth more disciples than John (though Jesus Himself did not baptize, but His disciples), He left Judæa and went away (again)[b] into Galilee" (verses 1-3).

Little did the disciples know the depth of the glory that was in Him or the consequent blessing for man, though they zealously baptized and thus exposed their Master to the spleen of those who could ill brook His increase and honour. It will be noticed that not He but His disciples did baptize. He knew the end from the beginning; and this finds its appropriate statement here. They might baptize to Him as Messiah; but He, the Son of God, knew from the first that He must suffer and die as the Son of Man: so, indeed, He had already declared to Nicodemus with its blessed results for the believer. The baptism He instituted was, therefore, after and to His death and resurrection. The Son of God knew what was in man, even when he was disposed to pay Him homage because of the signs which He wrought. So did He know the effect of His disciples' activity on the religious men of that day.[81]

It was the jealousy of the Pharisees, then, which in reality drove the Lord from Judæa. What was that land longer? What without Him, above all when it rejected Him and He abandoned it? They might boast of the law, but they had not kept it; they might claim the promises, but He—the promised One and Accomplisher of all the promises—had been there, and they knew Him not, loved Him not, but were more and more proving their heart-estrangement from Him, their Messiah. What could the first covenant avail now? It must ensure their condemnation; it could work no deliverance. The Jew was to reap only ruin and death under its terms. We shall presently see more; yet here at the beginning of the chapter is the Son of God, through the ill-feeling of those who ought most to have appreciated His presence, forced out, we may say, from the people of God and the scene of His institutions, but in the power of life eternal, whatever the humiliation which the haughty religionists put on Him, who saw in Him a man only, little suspecting that He was the Word become flesh.

THE FOURTH CHAPTER

VERSES 4-6.

> "And He must pass through Samaria. He cometh therefore to a city of Samaria called Sychar[82] near the land which Jacob gave to Joseph his son. Now a fountain of Jacob was there. Jesus therefore being wearied with the journeying sat thus[83] at the fountain. It was about the sixth hour"[84] (verses 4-6).

He is as truly man as God, but the Holy One always and only. Weary and rejected, He sits there in unwearied love. The false pretensions before Him can no more hinder now than the proud iniquity He had just left behind. Jerusalem and Samaria alike vanish. What could either do for a wretched heart, a guilty sinner? And such a one approaches.

VERSES 7-10.

> "There cometh a woman out of Samaria to draw water. Jesus saith to her, Give Me to drink (for His disciples had gone away into the city to buy provisions).[85] The Samaritan woman therefore saith to Him, How dost Thou being a Jew ask to drink of me being a Samaritan woman? for Jews[86] have no intercourse with Samaritans.[c] Jesus answered and said to her, If thou knewest the gift of God, and Who it is that saith to thee, Give Me to drink, thou wouldest have asked of Him, and He would have given thee living water" (verses 7-10).

He that made the heart perfectly knows the avenue to its affections. And what grace can He not show Who came to give a new and divine nature, as well as to reveal God in love, where there was nothing but sin, self, and unrest? God in the lowliness of man asks a favour, a drink of water, of the Samaritan woman; but it was to open her heart to her wants, and give her life eternal in the power of the Holy Ghost, communion with the Father and His Son Jesus Christ.

"Beautiful upon the mountains are the feet of him that bringeth good tidings, that publisheth peace; that bringeth good tidings of good, that publisheth salvation, that saith unto Zion, Thy God cometh." So said the Spirit of prophecy by Isaiah of old [52:7]; and so it will be fulfilled in its fulness by and by, as even now it is in principle. But what a sight to God, and, indeed, to faith, the Son of God, when driven out by the jealous hatred and contempt of man, of His own people who received Him not, thus occupying Himself with an unhappy Samaritan who had exhausted her life in quest of happiness never thus found! Surprised, she inquires how a Jew could ask aught of one like her: what had she felt, had she then conceived Who He was, and that He knew to the full what she was? And how reassuring to her afterwards when she looked back on the path by which God had in gracious wisdom led her that day that she might know Himself for evermore!

Alone He spoke to her alone, beginning in her soul His work for heaven, for eternity, for God. No miracle of an external sort is wrought before the eyes, no sign is needed without. The Son of God speaks in divine love, though (as we shall see) intelligence is not till the conscience is reached and exercised. The law is good if one use it lawfully, knowing that its application is not to a righteous person, but to lawless and insubordinate, to impious and sinful, and, in short, to all that is opposed to sound teaching. But Christ is the best of all as the revelation of God in grace, giving all that is wanted, producing (not seeking) what should be, not to dispense with the absolutely needed lesson of what we are, but enabling us to bear it, now that we know how truly God Himself cares for us in perfect love, spite of all that we are.

This is grace, the true grace of God. No error is more complete or perilous than the notion that grace makes light of sin. Was it a slight dealing with our sins when Christ bore them in His own body on the tree? Did law ever strike such a blow at any sinner, as God when He, sending His own Son in likeness of flesh of sin and for sin, condemned sin in the flesh, and thus brought "no condemnation to those in Christ Jesus" [Romans 8:1-3]? Nay, it was expressly what the law could not do. The law could condemn the sinner with his sins; but God has thus in Christ condemned not only the sins, but the root of evil—sin in the flesh—and this in a sacrifice for sin, so that those who otherwise had nothing but condemnation inwardly and outwardly, past and present, in nature as well as ways, have now by grace "no condemnation". All that could be condemned has been condemned; and they are in Christ, and they walk not according to flesh, but according to the Spirit. This is now the law of liberty.

Here, doubtless, there was no such standing yet existing, or, consequently, possible to any. But the Son was here acting and speaking in the fulness of grace which was soon to accomplish all for the believer and give all to him. Yet He lets the Samaritan know that she knew nothing. For, whatever His goodness (and it has no limits), grace does not spare man's assumption; and the revelation it brings from God and of God never really enters till self is judged. Samaria and Jerusalem are alike ignorant of grace; and only Christ by the Spirit can open the heart to bow and receive it. "If thou knewest the gift of God": such is the reality and the aspect of God in the gospel. He is not an exacter but a giver. He is not commanding man to love Him, but proclaiming His love to man—yea, to the most wretched of sinners. He is not requiring the creature's righteousness, but revealing His own. But man is slow to believe, and religious man the slowest to understand, what makes nothing of himself and all of God. But such is the word of truth, the gospel of our salvation; such the free giving of God, which the Lord was then manifesting as well as declaring to the woman of Samaria.

But there was, and is, more. The knowledge of the gift of God, in contradistinction from the law on the one hand, or from blank ignorance of His active love on the other, is inseparable from faith in the personal dignity of the Son of God. Therefore does the Saviour, all-lowly as He was, add: "And Who it is that saith to thee, Give Me to drink." For without this nothing is known aright. Jesus is the Truth, and abides ever the test for the soul, which owns with so much the more decision and adoring thankfulness the glory of Him Who, true God, became man in infinite love that we might have life eternal in Him. For otherwise, we may boldly say, it could not be. The truth is exclusive and immutable; it is not only the revelation of what is, but of what alone can and must be, consistently with the real nature of God and the state of man. Yet is God acting in His own liberty, for His love is always free and always holy; and the truth can only be what it is; for it is He Who has brought down that love in man to men in all their sin and death and darkness.

It is the revelation of God to man in Him Who, though the Son of God, stooped so low to bless the most needy and defiled and distant from God as to ask a drink of water, that He might in this find the occasion to give even to such a one living water. For this, too, He does not fail to say, as a consequence, "If thou knewest the gift of God, and Who it is that saith to thee, Give Me to drink, thou wouldest have asked of Him, and He would have given thee living water." For grace, truly known in Christ, produces confidence in grace, and draws out the heart to ask the greatest boon of Him Who will never be below, but above, the highest position that can be conferred on Him. Never can it be that the faith of man equals, still less surpasses, the riches of the grace of God. If men, spite of their evil, know how to give good gifts to their children, how much more should the Father Who is of heaven give the Holy Spirit to those that ask Him? [Luke 11:13]. If a guilty Samaritan woman is assured by the Son of God that she, knowing the gift of God and Who He is that asked of her to drink when weary by the fountain, had but to ask of Him in order to receive living water, still none that so asked and received had anything like an adequate sense of that infinite blessing—the Holy Ghost given to be in the believer.

Such is the living water that Christ here speaks of—not power in gift, nor yet simply eternal life, but the Spirit given[88] of the Son to be in the believer as the spring of communion with Himself and the Father.

It is not, then, quite correct, as some have said, that Christ is here alluded to as meant by "the gift of God," the next clause being viewed as explanatory. Undoubtedly, He was the means of displaying it; but the first of the clauses in this rich word of our Lord sets forth the thought, so strange to man, of the free-giving of God. Nature, as such, never understands it; law alone makes it still less intelligible. Faith only solves the difficulty in the Person, mission, and work of Christ, Who is the witness, proof, and substance of it; but it is the gratuitous grace of God that is meant. Hence, the second clause, instead of being merely exegetic of the first, directs attention to Him Who was there in the utmost humiliation (weary with His journeying, and asking a drink of water from one whom He knew to be the most worthless of Samaritans), yet the Son of the Father in unshorn fulness of divine glory and of grace to the most wretched. And this was so true that she who was as yet blind to all this had but to ask Him and have the best and greatest gift the believer can receive—living water, not life only, but the Holy Ghost. Thus, while Christ is the way of it, the Trinity was really involved in making good these words of our Lord to the Samaritan woman, all the Godhead engaged in the proffered blessing.

VERSES 11-12.

> "The woman saith to Him, Sir, Thou hast no bucket, and the well is deep: whence then hast Thou the living water? Art Thou greater than our father Jacob, who gave us the well, and drank of it himself and his sons and his cattle?" (verses 11-12).

She comprehends none of the gracious words she had heard; they were not mixed with faith in her heart. She therefore reasons against them. If the water was to be drawn from Jacob's well, where was the bucket to let down, for the well was deep? Did He pretend to be greater than Jacob, or was His a better well than that which of old supplied him and his house—a well which was now theirs? Thus the mind argues against the Lord, according to the senses or tradition: so fatal is ignorance of His Person and of the truth. Circumstances are the trial of faith and the swamp of unbelief, which gladly avails itself (with or without any just title) of a great name and its gifts, alas! to slight a greater—yea, the greatest.

Verses 13-14.

Mark now the Saviour's grace. He develops with the utmost fulness to this dark soul the unspeakable gift of God, in contrast with her own thoughts, and with those of man generally.

> "Jesus answered and said to her, Every one that drinketh of this water shall thirst again; but whosoever drinketh of the water which I shall give him shall in no way thirst for ever,[d] but the water which I shall give him shall become in him a fountain of water springing up into life eternal" (verses 13-14).

Water of whatever spring nature boasts may refresh, but thirst will come again; and God has ordered for the creature that so it should and must be. But it is not so when one is given to drink into the Spirit. Christ gives the Holy Ghost to the believer to be in him a fresh fountain of divine enjoyment, not only life eternal from the Father in the Person of the Son, but the communion of the Holy Ghost; and hence the power of worship, as we shall see later in this very conversation. Thus it is not only deliverance from hankering after pleasure, vanity, sin, but a living spring of exhaustless and divine joy, joying in God through our Lord Jesus, and this in the power of the Spirit. It supposes the possession of life eternal in the Son, but also the love of God shed abroad in our hearts by the Holy Spirit Who was given to us.

Verses 15-19.

Even then the Samaritan remains as insensible as ever.

"The woman saith to Him, Sir, give me this water that I may not thirst nor come here[e] to draw. He saith to her, Go, call thy husband, and come here. The woman answered and said, I have not a husband. Jesus saith to her, Thou saidst well, I have not a husband; for thou hast had five husbands, and he whom thou now hast is not thy husband: this thou hast spoken truly. The woman saith to Him, Sir, I see that Thou art a prophet" (verses 15-19).

She would gladly learn how she might be relieved of her wants and of her labour for this world. As yet not a ray of heavenly light had entered her. Not to thirst nor to come here to draw formed the boundary of her desires from the Saviour not yet known to be a Saviour, still less the Only-begotten Son.

This closes the first part of our Lord's dealings with her. It was useless to say more as before. Jesus had already set before her the principle on which God is acting, and His own gracious competence to give her, on her asking, living water; He had also shown the incomparable superiority of His gift as being divine over any or every boon left by Jacob. But her heart did not rise above the sphere of her daily wants and earthly wishes. She was deaf to His words, albeit spirit and life, which disclosed what is eternal.

Had it been in vain, then, to have so spoken to her as He did in the fulness of God's love? Far from it. It was all-important, when a door was once opened within, to reflect and find that such riches of grace had been brought to her absolutely unsought. But it was useless to add more till then. Hence the Lord's abrupt and seemingly unconnected appeal, "Go, call thy husband, and come here." But was the digression apart from the question of her salvation? Not so. It was the second and necessary way with a soul, if it is to be blessed divinely. It is through an awakened conscience that grace and truth enter; and it was because her conscience hitherto was unreached that the grace and truth were not at all understood.

On the one hand, it was of all consequence that she and we and all should have the clearest proof that the testimony of the Saviour's grace goes out before there is any fitness to receive it; for this, as it magnifies God and His free-giving, so it abases and exposes the wholly evil and frightfully dangerous state of man.

On the other hand, it was equally momentous that she should be brought to feel her need of that free and wondrous grace of which the Saviour had assured her, in all its depths and amplitude and everlasting continuance, before she had judged herself as a sinner before God. To this point He now conducts her: for if it is impossible to please God without faith, without repentance faith is intellectual and worthless. It is man discerning evidence and accepting what he in his wisdom judges best; not a sinner who, met by sovereign grace, is judged, owning himself in his sins, but too glad to find the Saviour, the only Saviour, in Jesus Christ the Lord.

Yet the Lord still holds to grace. He does not say, "*Go*, call thy husband," without adding, "and come here." He does not repent of His goodness because she was dull; on the contrary, He was using the fresh and necessary means to have the need of such goodness felt. How painstaking is grace, working in the soul that it may enter and abide, now that it had been testified of in all its fulness, and without any preparation for it any more than desert in man!

The woman answering, "I have not a husband," is astounded to hear the withering reply, "Thou saidst well, I have not a husband; for thou hast had five husbands, and he whom thou now hast is not thy husband: this thou hast spoken truly." She was convicted. It was in demonstration of the Spirit and power. Yet were the words few and simple, not one of them harsh or strong. It was the truth of her state and of her life brought home most unexpectedly, as God knows how to do, and does in one form or another in every converted soul. It was the truth which spared her not and laid her sins bare before God and her own conscience. She did not doubt for a moment what it was that made everything manifest. She recognised it to be the light of God. She owns His words to be not man's wisdom, but God's power. She falls under the conviction, and at once confesses, "Sir, I see that Thou art a prophet." It was not the fact only, but the truth from God.

It is plain hence that "prophet" does not mean one only who predicted the future, for this was not in question, but one who told out the mind of God—one who spoke by the evident guidance of the Spirit what could not be known naturally, yet what therefore so much the more put the soul before God and His light. So Abraham is a prophet (Genesis 20:7), and the fathers generally (Psalm 105:15), and the Old Testament prophets in all their ministry and writing, not merely in what was prediction. The same thing is emphatically true of New Testament prophesying, as we may see in 1 Corinthians 14:24-25. That is communicated from God which judges the life, yea, the secrets of the heart before Him.

Recognising the divine power of His words, the Samaritan seizes the opportunity to have light from God on that which had not been without perplexity and interest even to her—the religious difference between her race and the chosen nation, and this not merely in homage to God but in formal or express public worship. She wants to have the question, old as it was, settled for her now. The Samaritan, like many another in grievous error, could talk of great antiquity. Happy the soul that has recourse for it to Jesus! He alone is the Truth. Others may deceive, themselves deceived.

To this end was Jesus born, and for this cause came He into the world that He should bear witness to the truth. What is more: "Every one that is of the truth heareth His voice." Alas! how different has it been with Christendom, corrupted first, then rent hopelessly, most haughty when it has most reason to be ashamed. Be it ours in such a state of ruin to keep His word and not deny His name.

A time of declension beyond all things tests the soul; for it seems proud to differ from the excellent of the earth, especially if they are many, and those who cleave to God's Word are few and have nothing to boast. For this very reason it is precious in God's eyes, and no small testimony to the absent Master. Still, it becomes all who differ from the mass to be sure of their ground, as this woman sought when she appealed to Jesus; and the Christian need seek no other—yea, is guilty and infatuated if, where men's uncertainty is so great and grave, he heed aught other—than Jesus speaking by His Word and Spirit.

Verses 20-26.

"Our fathers worshipped in this mountain; and ye say that in Jerusalem is the place where one must worship[89]. Jesus saith to her, Woman, believe me, an hour is coming when neither in this mountain nor in Jerusalem shall ye worship the Father. Ye worship what ye know not: we worship what we know, for salvation[90] is of the Jews. But an hour is coming and now is when the true worshippers shall worship the Father in spirit and truth; for also the Father seeketh such as His worshippers. God is a Spirit; and His worshippers must worship[90a] (Him) in spirit and truth. The woman saith to Him, I know that Messiah is coming, that is called Christ:[91] when *He* shall come, He will tell us all things. Jesus saith to her, I that speak to thee am (He)" (verses 20-26).

The Lord more than meets every desire of the Samaritan's heart. For here we have, not merely the vindication of Israelitish worship as compared with its Samaritan rival but the first unfolding of Christian worship ever given by God to man; and this as superseding not Samaritanism only but Judaism also— a change withal then at hand. Yet is all conveyed in language that was plain enough even to the soul thus addressed; while there is depth of truth which no saint has ever fathomed, however deeply he may have drawn on it and enjoyed it.

"The Father" was to be worshipped henceforth: of itself, what a revelation! It is no longer a question of the Jehovah God of Israel, nor even of the Almighty as was the name by which He was made known to the fathers. There is a richer display of God, and far more intimate.

THE FOURTH CHAPTER

It is not as the Eternal Who put Himself in covenant and government, Who will surely yet make good His ways with Israel, as He has chastised them for theirs. Nor is it the God Who shielded His poor pilgrims that hung on His promises in their wanderings among hostile strangers before their children formed a nation and received His law. It was God as the Son knew Him and was making Him known in the fulness of love and fellowship, Who would accordingly bring His own that were in the world into the conscious relationship of children as born of Him. (Compare John 1:12-13, 18; 14:4-10, 20; 16:23-27; 20:17-23.)

No wonder that, in presence of such nearness and the worship that befits it, the mountain of Gerizim melts and the sanctuary of Jerusalem fades away. For the one was but the effort of self-will, the other but the test and proof of the first man's inability to meet God and live. Christian worship is found on the possession of life eternal in the Son, and on the gift of the Spirit as the power of worship.

In verse 22 the Lord leaves it impossible for the Samaritan to draw the inference that, if Christian worship was about to be alone acceptable to God, independently of place or race, Samaritan had been just as good as Jewish. Not so. The Samaritans worshipped what they did not know, the Jews knew what they worshipped; "for salvation," as He added, "is of the Jews." They had "the adoption, and the glory, and the covenants, the law-giving, and the service, and the promises, whose were the fathers, and of whom as pertaining to flesh was the Christ Who is over all God blessed for ever. Amen" [Romans 9:4-5]. The Samaritans were mere imitators, Gentiles jealous of

Israel and hostile to them, without fear of God; else had they submitted to His ways and Word.

Thus God's privileges to Israel are vindicated; but none the less was the Lord at that time driven out by Pharisaic jealousy, and none the less had He set aside all pretension to traditional and successional blessing. He was there to communicate from God, not to accredit man; and, He being rejected, Jerusalem and Samaria alike vanish away. Old things are judged; all things must become new. God was in Christ reconciling the world to Himself, now that those who had the institutions of God are rejecting His counsel against themselves. And if that unbelief went to the uttermost in hatred of the Father and the Son, it would only bring out the fulness of divine grace and righteousness, leaving His love absolutely free to act supremely above all evil for His own glory, as we know is the fact in a crucified but risen Christ.

It is remarkable accordingly that the Lord does not say "Who," but "what." For in Judaism God dwelt in thick darkness, and the testimony rendered by the whole Levitical system (with its sacrifices and priests, door, veil, incense, everything in short) was that the way into the holiest had not yet been made manifest. When Christ died, it was: the veil was rent from top to bottom, and eternal redemption found; the worshippers once purged have no more conscience of sins, and are invited to draw near. Such is Christianity, God having revealed Himself as the Father in the Son through the Spirit. To know Him, the only true God, and Him Whom He had sent to reveal Him, even Jesus, is life eternal. And the mighty work which was done on the cross has dealt with all our evil, so that we are free to enjoy Himself. *We know therefore* Whom *we worship, and not merely* "what." When God was hidden in the thick darkness, and only the unity of His nature proclaimed, the Godhead remained vague. When the Father is revealed as now in the Son by the Spirit, what a difference!

Hence this exceeding blessedness is opened in its positive character in verses 23-24. For it is an hour when form is repudiated, as it could not be in Judaism. Reality alone is endorsed. National worship therefore is now an evident delusion, being but an effort to resuscitate what has vanished away as far as regards any recognition on God's part. It was owned in Israel under law for its own purpose; it will be so on the largest scale in the millennium; but it is not, if we believe the Saviour, during the hour which, then coming, now is. It is an hour now when the true worshippers worship the Father. Who and what are they? The doctrinal utterances of the Apostles answer with one voice that they are God's children, born of Him through the faith of Christ, and sealed by the Spirit consequently as resting on His redemption. So the Apostle says (Philippians 3:3) that we (in contrast with mere Jews or Judaizers) are the true circumcision, who worship by the Spirit of God, and boast in Christ Jesus, and have no confidence in flesh. But we must cite the New Testament as a whole to give the full proof, if one asks more evidence than the Lord affords in this context, though I feel assured that he who bows not to such a witness would not be won by ten thousand. A single word from God is more to the believer than every other evidence: how many would convince the unbeliever?

Further, what is said of the worship excludes all but true believers. For they are to worship in spirit and truth. How can any who have not the Spirit and know not the truth? Granted that the article is wanting. But this in such a case as the one before us adds to the strength of the statement, for it predicates a spiritual and truthful character of the worship. That is to say, the Lord's words express more than the necessity of having the Holy Ghost or of acquaintance with the truth, though this would suppose the Christian with his distinguishing privileges. But He says that they worship in that character, not merely that they have the Spirit and the truth in order to worship. Now, plainly, a real Christian might act unspiritually and not according to the truth. Even Peter and Barnabas failed at a grave crisis to walk according to the truth of the gospel. However true the worshipper then, if he were grieving the Spirit or dishonouring the Lord, this would not be to worship in spirit and truth. But it remains still more manifest that none but "the true worshippers" could so worship, though on a given occasion or in a given state they might not, in fact, as they ought.

Moreover, "also the Father seeketh such as His worshippers." Let us weigh it. Time was when every Jew went up to Jerusalem to seek Jehovah; time will be when all nations shall flow to the same centre when the Son of Man comes in power and reigns in glory. But the characteristic working of grace is that the Father seeks the true worshippers. Undoubtedly when sought they gather unto the name of the Lord, and enjoy His presence by the Spirit. It is not enough that they are washed, and not by water only but by water and blood, and thus are every whit clean; it is not only that they have the Spirit as the witness of the one efficacious sacrifice, and the spring of praise and power of continual thanksgiving; "also the Father seeketh such as His worshippers." What confidence for them! What grace in Him! Yet is His seeking such true of every

Christian. May they answer His grace by eschewing all that is unworthy of it in this evil day!

But there are other words of profound import. "God is a Spirit, and His worshippers must worship in spirit and truth." It is the nature of God which is here in question, not the relationship of grace which He now reveals in and by Christ. And this is not without the greatest importance for us. For He must be worshipped correspondingly; and He most fully provided for this, seeing that the new life we enjoy is by the Spirit and is spirit, not flesh (John 3:6); as, indeed, He begot us of His own will by the word of truth (James 1{:18}), and we are thus born again, not of corruptible seed, but of incorruptible, by God's living and abiding word (1 Peter 1:23). Assuredly we should walk and worship in the Spirit, if we live in the Spirit. He is given to us that we should judge and reject the first Adam, glorifying only the Second Man, our Lord Jesus. Nay, more, as God is a Spirit, spiritual worship is all He accepts. His worshippers "*must* worship in spirit and truth." It is a moral necessity flowing from His nature—a nature fully revealed in Him Who is the image of the invisible God; and we should not be ignorant of it and its character who are born of Him as believers in Christ.

The woman, struck by words plain, indeed, but no doubt far beyond her (for they reach up to God as surely as they come down to man), at once thinks of the Messiah, owns her confidence in His coming, and is sure that when He is come, He will tell us all things (verse 25). Would that all who believe on Him believed this of Him! Would that, when He has spoken peace to them, they turned not again to folly! And what folly greater than to turn from His words on this very theme, and in this very chapter, for instance, to follow the traditions of men and the ways of the world in the worship of God?

And now break on her ear and heart the last words needed to clinch all the rest and ensure her blessing evermore: "Jesus saith to her, I that speak to thee am (He)" (verse 26). It might be the lowest form of presenting the only One Who can avail the sinner; yet it remains ever true from first to last that every one who believes that Jesus is the Christ is begotten of God. And this the Samaritan did. Her heart was touched, her conscience searched, and now the grace and truth which came by Jesus Christ was all to her. All the blessing was hers in His person Who was then present and received by her in faith.

What a moment, a present Messiah,[92] and He speaking to a Samaritan woman, yea, on Christian worship!

Verse 27.

> "And upon this came His disciples, and wondered[f] that He was speaking with a woman: none however said, What seekest Thou? or why speakest Thou with her?" (verse 27).

Their wonder was that He spoke[g] with a woman:[92a] what was hers who knew that every secret of her heart was naked and open before Him with Whom she had to do? His grace, however, had fully prepared the way. He Who searched all the recesses of her soul had already encouraged her by revealing the richest grace of God the Father, Himself the only true Revealer of it, about to give the Holy Spirit that even she might receive and enjoy it truly. It was no question of seeking on her part at any rate: the Father was seeking such; nor was it of talking with her, but of revealing to her. The disciples had much to learn. Had they known the subject-matter of converse they might well have wondered incomparably more.

Verses 28-30.

> "The woman then left her waterpot, and went away into the city, and saith to the men, Come, see a man who told me all things that[h] ever I did: is not this the Christ?[93] They went out of the city and were coming unto Him" (verses 28-30).

The moral change was immense. A new world opened to her which eclipsed the present with new affections, new duties, the power of which asserted itself in lifting her entirely above the things that are seen, whatever might be the effect ordinarily, in strengthening to a better fulfilment of present earthly toil. But the revelation of Christ to her soul was both all-absorbing and the most powerful stimulus to make Him known to others. Where the eye is single, the body is full of light. She felt who needed Him most, and she acted on it forthwith. She left her waterpot, went off to the town, and told the men of Jesus. How well she understood Him! He had not formally sent her, yet she went boldly with the invitation. Nor was it merely that she bade them go: "Come, see a man." She would go along with them. Her heart was in the current of His grace, and counted upon the same welcome for others, unwarranted though it might appear, as for herself. Such is the power of divine love even from the very first.

Yet there was no enfeebling of the truth because of His grace. They, too, must prepare for what had searched her. "Come, see a man that told me all things that ever I did. Is not He the Christ?" Well they knew what she had been; and if He had so dealt with her, might not they also see and hear Him? Such a personal experience has great power, and it is safe, too, where it is not merely an appeal to the affections, but conscience is searched along with it.

VERSES 31-34.

> ⁱ"Meanwhile the disciples were asking Him, saying, Rabbi, eat. But He said to them, I have food to eat which ye do not know. Then the disciples said to one another, Hath any one brought Him to eat? Jesus saith to them, It is My food that I should doʲ the will of Him that sent Me, and finish His work" (verses 31-34).

How humbling to find His disciples at such a time occupied with the body and its wants. And this the Lord makes them feel by His answer. They knew not as yet such food, disciples though they were.[94] It is not as men often quote it, "His meat and His drink," for there was an inner spring of loving and delighting in His Father beyond doing His will and completing His work. But this was His food. He came to do His will. In this He was never wearied, nor should we be even now, whatever might be the fatigue of the body. For "He giveth power to the faint, and to them that have no might He increaseth strength." Without Him even the "youths shall faint and be weary, and the young men shall utterly fail. But they that wait upon Jehovah shall renew their strength; they shall mount up with wings as eagles, they shall run and not be weary, and they shall walk and not faint" {Isaiah 40:29-31}. Jesus knew this Himself in perfection, and here is a sample of it.

THE FOURTH CHAPTER

VERSES 35-38.

> "Do not ye say that there are yet four months and the harvest cometh? Lo, I say to you, Lift up your eyes, and behold the fields, for they are white unto harvest already.[k] He[l] that reapeth receiveth wages, and gathereth fruit unto life eternal, that both[m] he that soweth and he that reapeth may rejoice together. For in this is the saying true,[n] It is one that soweth and another that reapeth. I sent you to reap that on which ye have not toiled: others have toiled, and ye have entered into their toil" (verses 35-38).

Whatever might be the times and seasons of the natural harvest, the fields spiritually were ripe for the reaper. Man, the world, undoubtedly deserved judgment; but the very same state of sin which calls for judgment God uses for His call of grace. The gospel comes expressly on the ground of man's total ruin, and therefore levels all distinctions. Jew, Samaritan, Gentile—what are any now but sinners? The Jew had been under probation, but he was now rejecting the Messiah, the Son of God. All was lost; but the rejected Christ is the Saviour, and now there is salvation for any, and grace carries it among such as these Samaritans.

Not that grace had failed to work during the past times of probation. Man had broken down utterly; but God was preparing the way when it should be no longer experimental dealings and man's righteousness sought, but God's righteousness revealed in virtue of the work of Christ. His witnesses had not wrought in vain, however little seen the effects meanwhile.[95] But the true light was now shining, and things appeared as they are to the eye of grace. What a sight to Christ the Samaritans coming to Him—coming to hear One Who tells us whatever we did! The fields were white indeed.

It is remarkable that the Lord speaks about reaping now rather than sowing, though sowing, of course, goes on, and has its place elsewhere, as in Matthew 13. Of old it was rather sowing than reaping; now in this day of grace there is a characteristic reaping—fruit not only of God's past dealings, but of His coming and mighty work Who thus speaks to the disciples: "The reaper receiveth wages and gathereth fruit unto life eternal, that both the sower and the reaper may rejoice together." So shall it be in the day of glory, as the spirit of it is even now true in the Church and the Christian heart. "For in this is the saying true, The sower is one, and the reaper another." But while there are these differences still, it remains that the Apostles are characterised by reaping rather than by sowing, and so, of course, are other labourers also. "I sent (or, have sent) you to reap that on which ye have not toiled: others have toiled, and ye have entered into their toil." How emphatically this was verified at Pentecost and afterwards, all know.

VERSES 39-42.

> "But out of that city many of the Samaritans believed on Him because of the word of the woman as she bore witness, He told me all things that (ever) I did. When therefore the Samaritans came to Him, they asked Him to abide with them. And He abode there two days; and many more believed because of His word. And they said to the woman, No longer on account of thy saying do we believe, for we have ourselves heard and know that this is indeed the° Saviour of the world" (verses 39-42).

It is cheering to see how God honoured the simple testimony of the woman. Many out of that town believed on Him because of her word. Here again she bears witness to the searching of her conscience by His word: "He told me all that ever I did." It is a good guarantee that the work is divine when there is no shrinking from such a scrutiny: otherwise grace is apt to be misused as a cover for sin or a slight dealing with a sinner, instead of judging all in God's light. But faith, whenever it is real, rises from the instrument to Him Who deigns to use it, and God loves to put honour upon the word of Jesus Himself. Hence we are told that, when He graciously acceded to the desire of the Samaritans and abode there two days, "more by a great deal believed because of His word." How sweet to the woman when they said to her, "No longer because of thy saying do we believe, for we have ourselves heard and know that this is indeed the Saviour of the world." God led them, too, in dropping His Messiahship, and the copyists have inserted it without due reason. Ancient authority seems conclusive that the words "the Christ" should disappear. Their confession is much more simple and emphatic when so put. They now knew and confessed the truth—the grace and truth that came by Jesus Christ. (Compare 1 John 4:14.)

Thus without a miracle the Lord has been owned, as we see, in Samaria, first as a prophet by one, finally as Saviour of the world by all who believed on Him there. There the fullest confession of His grace was found where one might have looked for least intelligence; but faith gives new wisdom so different from the old that those who are wise must become fools if they would be wise according to God. How blessed for those who have no wisdom to boast, whom grace forms with all simplicity according to its own power! Such were the

Samaritans among whom the Lord abode for this little while.

VERSES 43-46A.

[Matthew 4:12-17; Mark 1:14-16; Luke 4:14-16.]

"And after the two days He went forth thence[p] into Galilee. For Jesus Himself testified that a prophet hath no honour in his own country" (verses 43-44).

He resumes His place among the despised and lowly. The first Gospel points out that this sphere of His ministry was according to prophecy; for Isaiah, in setting forth the sins and judgment of Israel from first to last, had spoken of the light shining in Galilee when darkness enveloped the favoured seats in the land. All the Evangelists, indeed, for one reason or another, dwell upon His ministry in Galilee, John alone bringing into prominence some characteristic incidents in Jerusalem. Mark speaks much of Galilee, because his office was to describe the Lord's ministry; and there, in fact, we must follow Him if we would trace its details. Luke, again, gives it as illustrating the moral ways of God in the grace of our Lord Jesus, and the activities of One Who went about doing good and healing all that were oppressed of the devil. John, on the other hand, as usual, lays it on a ground that pertains more strictly to His Person.

It was His own testimony that a prophet hath no honour in his own country. He had come down not to seek His own honour, but that of Him Who sent Him. He had riches of grace and truth to dispense; He was sent, He was come, to do His Father's will; content to be nothing, have nothing from men, He goes away into Galilee. But if the Galileans paid Him no honour when He was in their midst,⁹⁶ they were not unmoved by the fame that had gone out, specially by the impression made in the capital.

> "When, therefore, He came into Galilee, the Galileans received Him, having seen all thatᵠ He did in Jerusalem at the feast, for they too went unto the feast" (verse 45).

Galilee was not only the place where He had spent the greater part of His earthly life in humiliation and obedience, but there He had begun to make Himself known to the disciples; and there He had first wrought a sign in witness of His glory.

> "Heʳ came therefore again into Cana of Galilee where He made the water wine" (verse 46a).

That first sign held out the promise, pledge, and earnest of Israel's future joy and blessedness; and He Himself, in the day that is coming, will be there in the land, no longer the guest nor the master of the feast alone, but the Bridegroom. And the barren one shall know her Maker as her husband, Jehovah of hosts His name, and her Redeemer, the Holy One of Israel. The God not merely of the land, but of the whole earth, shall He be called {Isaiah 54:5}.

But it is not yet the day for singing, but of sadness; not yet for enlarging the place of Israel's tent, nor of stretching the curtains of their habitation, nor of strengthening the stakes: no breaking forth yet on the right hand or on the left, no inheriting the Gentiles, or making the desolate cities to be inhabited {Isaiah 54:1-3}. Contrariwise, did not Messiah come to His own things, and His own people received Him not? Nay, they were about to consummate their sin in His cross, and to seal their unbelief in their rejection of the gospel, forbidding His servants to speak to the Gentiles that they might be saved, to fill up their sins always, so that wrath is come upon them to the uttermost, however grace may turn their fall to the salvation and the riches of the Gentiles. Nevertheless, grace is yet to make good every sign which is hung out to Israel, and the Lord adds on this occasion a fresh and suited display of His power for their actual circumstances and present need.

Verses 46b-48.

> "And there was a certain courtier whose son was sick at Capernaum. He, having heard that Jesus was come out of Judæa into Galilee, went away unto Him and asked that He would go down and heal his son, for he was about to die. Jesus therefore said unto him, Except ye see signs and wonders, ye will in nowise believe" (verses 46b-48).

How strikingly in contrast with the simpler souls in Samaria! There was faith in the power of Jesus, but it was of a Jewish sort.[97] The courtier had heard, no doubt, of miracles wrought by Him personally present. His faith rose no higher; yet evidently, if it were the power of God, there could be no limits. Absence or presence could account for nothing—they were but circumstances; and the very essence of a miracle is God rising above all circumstances. It is irrational, as well as unbelieving, to measure a miracle by one's experience. It is solely a question of God's will, power, and glory; and therefore the Lord justly rebukes the unbelief of all such thoughts.

How finely, too, the grace which wrought in the Gentile centurion whose servant was sick contrasts with the limited expectations of this Jewish courtier! There, just to exercise and manifest the power of his faith, the Lord proposed to go with the elders of the Jews who begged Him to come and save his bondman. But even though He was not far from the house, the centurion sent to Him friends expressly not to trouble Him; for he was not worthy that He should come under his roof, any more than he counted himself worthy to come to Him. He had only to say by a word, and his servant should be healed. This accordingly drew out the strong approbation of the Lord, not His censure as here. "Not even in Israel" had He found such great faith.

Verses 49-50.

Nevertheless, the grace of the Lord never fails, and little faith receives its blessing as surely as greater faith its larger answer.

> "The courtier said unto Him, Sir, come down ere my child die" (verse 49).

Here again how scanty the faith, if urgent the appeal! Still faith must have a gracious assurance.

> "Jesus saith to him, Go, thy son liveth" (verse 50a).

It was better for the courtier's soul in every way, and more to the glory of God, that Jesus should bid *him* go, instead of going with him. If it crossed the man's thoughts and words, it was meant to exercise his faith so much the more.

> "(And)⁵ the man believed the word which Jesus had said unto him, and went his way" (verse 50b).

He had not long to wait before he knew the blessing.

Verses 51-54.

"But as he was now going down, his servants met him and brought (him) word, saying, Thy child liveth. He inquired therefore from them the hour at which he got better. They said to him, Yesterday at the seventh hour the fever left him. The father therefore knew that (it was) at that hour in which Jesus said to him, Thy son liveth: and himself believed and his whole house" (verses 51-53).

Thus God took care to arrest the servants, who were all the more interested and responsible because of their master's absence. They would watch the case; they would mark the changes in the malady of the patient; and they, therefore, were the first to see when he began to amend. They could tell the master the precise hour when the fever left the child—the very hour, as he could tell them, when Jesus spoke the word of healing power.

"This second sign again did Jesus on coming out of Judæa into Galilee"[98] (verse 54).

Is it not a sign of what He is to do in the day when, re-animating the dead daughter of Zion, He will also change the water of purification into the wine of joy for God and man? Meanwhile He relieves the one ready to perish in Israel, where there was the faith, however feeble, to seek it from the Christ. It was true even then of His ministry in all its meaning and force. In the chapter which follows we have the rights of His Person asserted still more mightily in effects present and future. Here it is rather arresting the power of death than giving life. Even that He only could do, and did where there was faith.[99]

NOTES ON THE FOURTH CHAPTER

a [*Cf. Lectures Introductory to the Study of the Gospels,* pp. 440-446.][80]

b AB[pm]EΔ, etc. [as Weiss and Blass], omit; ℵCDLMT, 1, 33, 69, and many ancient versions [including Syr^(sin)] insert [as W. and H.].

c ["For ... Samaritans," attested by ℵ^(corr.)ABCL, etc., Orig. Chrys. Cyr. Alex., and read by Lachm., Treg., W. and H. (t), Weiss, but discredited by Tisch., who follows ℵ^(corr.)D. The words are bracketed by Blass[87].]

d It is not merely οὐ μή, nor οὐ μή ... πώποτε, but οὐ μή ... εἰς τὸν αἰῶνα, the strongest possible exclusion of what is in question for eternity.[88a]

e In ℵ^(pm)B and Origen the reading is διέρχωμαι, which Tischendorf and W. and H. [Weiss and Blass] adopt; but the MSS. differ, many giving the indicative, many the subjunctive.

f The imperfect εθαύμαζον is better than the common ἐθαύμασαν, and rests on far better authority; but it is needless to express its continuity in English in such a case as this.

g [Syr^(sin): "was standing and talking," as Blass, ἑστηκὼς ἐλάλει.]

h There is a question between ἄ [Edd.] on the authority of ℵBC^(pm) and some other ancient witnesses, and ὅσα with far more numerous copies, here and in verse 39, the difference in English being that the latter adds "ever."

i The great majority of witnesses [including Syr^(sin)] add δὲ, "and" or "but"; the most ancient omit.

j The best reading [that of Weiss and Blass] and most forcible sense is ποιῶ (אAEGHMSUVΓΔΛ, etc.), not ποιήσω, read by Lachmann, Treg., W. and H., though a manifest assimilation to τελειώσω.

k Tischendorf, etc., sever ἤδη from verse 35 and make it begin verse 36, following some ancient authorities; but the most ancient (א^{pm}BMΠ^{pm}, etc.) leave it open, and most [as Weiss] give as is here done, which seems to be alone in keeping with the context [Blass omits, as Syr^{sin} Chrys. Hil.].

l The common text prefixes καὶ on ample authority [including Syr^{sin}], but the most ancient uncials, and some good cursives, etc., are adverse [so Blass].

m Some good and ancient authorities omit καὶ [as Weiss, but Blass retains it].

n The article before ἀληθινὸς is not read by אBC^{pm}KLT^{b}ΔΠ^{pm}, many good cursives, and some of the Greek fathers [so W. and H., Weiss]. In one passage of Chrysostom which has the article, he has ἀληθὴς after it, and so have a few cursives.

o The Sinai, Vat., Palimpsest of Paris [C^{pm}], and an old St. Petersburg uncial (T^{b}), with almost all the most ancient versions, etc., do not read ὁ Χριστός. [It is in AC^{corr.}DLTΔΛΠ, etc., Syr^{pesch hcl hier (corr)} Chrys. Cyr. Alex.]

p The Received Text, with most uncials and cursives, etc., has also καὶ ἀπῆλθεν, contrary to אBCDT^{b}, 13, 69, and some other excellent authorities.

q There is good authority for ὅσα [Edd.] as well as ἅ, the more widespread, if not ancient, copies inclining to the latter.

r The best witnesses do not read ὁ 'Ι., as do the Received Text and Scholz (though with a slight difference of position), following many MSS.

s ℵBD and a few other authorities omit καὶ, "and."

t ℵD^{gr}L., etc., omit αὐτοῦ, "his."

THE FIFTH CHAPTER [a]

It is one of the peculiarities of our Gospel that in it we see the Lord frequently in Jerusalem, while the Synoptic Gospels are occupied with His Galilean ministry. The miracle at the pool of Bethesda is an instance: only John records it. Both the fact and the discourse which follows eminently bring out His Person. This alone abides, and it is all to the believer, with the infinite work which owes its infiniteness to it. In the other Gospels the process of probation is viewed as still going on; by John all is seen from the first to be closed before God. Hence His moral judgment of Jerusalem is shown us at the beginning by John, as its rejection of Him also. This, to my mind, accounts for the record of the Lord's work there as well as in Galilee in the Gospel of John. If all be regarded as a scene of wreck and ruin morally, it was of no consequence where He wrought. As to trial, all was over; grace could and would work equally anywhere: Galilee and Jerusalem were thus alike. Sin levels all: life from God in the Son was needed by one as much as another. This our Gospel develops.

THE FIFTH CHAPTER

VERSES 1-9.

"After these things was the feast[b] of the Jews, and Jesus went up to Jerusalem" (verse 1).

Here authority is pretty equally divided for and against the insertion of the article. Ten uncials (אCEFHILMΔΠ) insert it, ten (ABDGKSUVΓΛ) omit it. About fifty cursives and the Memphitic and Thebaic versions are with the former; still more with the latter. If the article be received, it can scarcely be any other feast than the Passover, the first and foundation feast of the Jewish holy year. Some have thought that it might be the feast of Purim, but this would not account for Jesus going up to Jerusalem. It had no such divine claim.[100]

"Now there is[101] in Jerusalem at the sheep-gate[c] a pool that is called in Hebrew Bethesda, having five porches. In these lay a[d] multitude of the sick, blind, lame, withered (awaiting the moving of the water. For an angel descended from time to time in the pool and troubled the water. He, therefore, that first went in after the troubling of the water, became well, whatever disease he was affected by). But a certain man was there, for thirty and eight years suffering under his[e] infirmity. Jesus seeing him lying down, and knowing that he was (so) now a long time, saith to him, Desirest thou to become well?

"The infirm (man) answered, Sir,[f] I have no man, when the water is troubled, to put me into the pool; but whilst I am coming, another goeth down before me. Jesus saith to him, Arise, take up thy couch, and walk. And immediately[g] the man became well, and took up his couch and walked. And on that day was Sabbath" (verses 2-9).

A striking picture that scene was of man, of the Jews under law. There they lay without strength, and though the grace of God might interfere at intervals, the greater the need, the less could souls take advantage of His mercy. It was "what the law could not do, in that it was weak through the flesh" [Romans 8:3]. The impotent man was himself the witness of it till Jesus came, and, unsought, sought him. No angel's moving of the water could avail a man unable to step down and without help to plunge him into the pool. He that was stronger could always anticipate the helpless. But now grace, in Jesus the Son of God, looks at him who had been suffering so long; grace speaks to him; grace works for him, in a word, without further delay; for the word was with power. "And immediately the man became well, and took up his couch[102] and walked. And on that day was Sabbath."

But how could Sabbath be kept or enjoined on that day of man's misery? Jesus had come to work, not to rest; whatever Pharisees might urge, He would not seal up man in a rest broken before God by sin and ruin.

Thus the sign wrought on that Sabbath carries out further what the Lord is seen doing throughout these chapters of the Gospel—substituting Himself for every object of trust or means of blessing, of old or in that day, without Israel and within. Even angels bow to the Son; yet was He incarnate, working in humiliation, going on straight to the cross. The law could not deliver from the guilt or power or effects of sin; no extraordinary intervention of God by the highest of creatures could adequately meet the need; nothing and no one but Jesus the Son of God. Yet have we also the clearest proof that the Jews were so self-satisfied in their misery by a misuse of the law, which blinded them to their sin as well as to the Son, that they were content to go on with such a Sabbath, incensed with Him Who wrought a sign that proclaimed not more surely His grace than their ruin. Hopeless, too, it was because of their rejection of the remedy and their self-complacency in their own righteousness.

Observe, however, that the Lord made the infirm feel his powerlessness more than ever before He spoke the word that raised him up. He did awaken the desire to be made whole, as He looked with infinite compassion and knew the case in all its fulness; but the desire then felt expressed itself in the man's conviction of his own wretchedness. It was like the soul's saying, in Romans 7, "O wretched man that I am! *who* shall deliver me," etc. How little he knew Who had deigned to be his "neighbour," and do the part of the good Samaritan—yea, incomparably more here where need is sounded more deeply. The Quickener of the dead is here. "He spake, and it was done," Sabbath as it might be; but what Sabbath acceptable to God can sin and misery keep? Thank God! Jesus wrought; but they felt that if He was right, it was all over with them. Hence they judged Him, not themselves, as we shall see, to God's dishonour and their own perdition.

Undoubtedly to see a man carrying his couch on the Sabbath was a strange thing in Judæa, and especially in Jerusalem. But it was, of course, by a deliberate injunction on the Lord's part. He was raising a question with the Jews which He knew would bring about a breach with their incredulity. It was a blow purposely struck at their self-complacent observance of the Sabbath, when they were blinded, not merely by self-will to violate the law, but by unbelief against their own Messiah, spite of the fullest proofs of His mission and Person. Could God accept the Sabbath-keeping of the people in such a state? Here, then, the Lord commanded an act expressly public on the Sabbath day in Jerusalem.

Verses 10-18.

> "The Jews therefore said to him that was cured, It is Sabbath, and[h] it is not allowed thee to take up thy[i] couch. He answered them, He that made me well, the same said to me, Take up thy couch and walk" (verses 10-11).

The healed man was simple, and his answer bears the stamp of right and truth. The divine power that had wrought beyond even an angel's compass or commission, and without it, was his warrant to act upon the word.

> "They asked him (therefore),[j] Who is the man that said to thee, Take up (thy couch)[j] and walk? But he that was healed[k] knew not Who He was, for Jesus withdrew, a crowd being in the place" (verses 12-13).

The Jews spoke with malice and contempt, "Who is the *man?*" They can scarcely be conceived ignorant that there was more in their midst, and Who He was. They knew His works, if they knew not Himself; and His works as well as ways proclaimed a mission more than human. The very work before them, and they could not deny it, was beyond an angel; yet they asked the healed person, "Who is the man that said to thee, Take up thy couch and walk?" The Lord had ordered things so that the healed man should know no more; He had passed away unnoticed,[103] a crowd being there.

> "After these things Jesus findeth him in the temple, and said to him, Behold, thou art made well.

THE FIFTH CHAPTER

Sin no more, lest some worse thing happen to thee. The man went away, and told the Jews that it was Jesus Who had made him well" (verses 14-15).

It was a gracious, but withal a solemn word. To live now, to enjoy the life that is now, is not the great matter. No cure, however bespeaking the power and goodness of God, could meet man's underlying need, for sin still remained. A cure was only provisional. The man that was cured, though it was Jesus Who cured him, had to be warned, "Sin no more,[104] lest some worse thing happen to thee." He does not appear to have then adequately judged the malice of the Jews. They probably concealed their real feelings. It is often so with men toward Jesus, especially men who have a reputation for religion. They do not believe on Him, neither do they love Him. So the healed man in his simplicity fathomed not their object, but seems rather to have assumed that they were anxious to know his wondrous benefactor. Hence he went off, and brought them word that it was Jesus Who had made him well. There is no ground, I think, to suppose that he shared the feelings of the Jews, or wished to betray Jesus to those who hated Him.

But now they knew, as a fact, what they had, no doubt, suspected from the first, that the sick man had to do with Jesus. I do not say that their informant should not have known better, for they had asked, "Who is the man that said to thee, Take up thy couch and walk?" He told them now that it was Jesus Who had made him well. His heart dwelt on the good and mighty deed that was done; theirs on the word which touched their Sabbath-keeping.

> "And for this the Jews persecuted Jesus,[1] because He did these things on a Sabbath" (verse 16).

It was the blindness of men, who, lost in forms, knew not the reality of God, and consequently knew not themselves in His presence. Sooner or later such men find themselves in collision with Jesus; what will they feel by and by?

> "But Jesus answered them, My Father worketh hitherto, and I work" (verse 17).

It was an overwhelming answer. They knew nothing of fellowship with the Father. He (Jesus), not they, could call God "My Father," and loved to say that He "worketh hitherto." For the Father could not rest in sin, He would not rest in misery. It is not yet God judging. Therefore was He working as Father, and until now, though only now declaring Himself Father in and by the Son. Even before this, however, He had not left Himself without witness in Jerusalem itself, as the crowd of expectant sick round the pool of Bethesda attested. But this was only partial and transient. The Son was here to make Him fully known, and known as One Who could not keep His Sabbath yet, whatever the Jews ignorant of Him might wish to say or do. "My Father worketh hitherto, and I work." Jesus, the Son, had fellowship, unbroken and perfect, with His Father.

Yet the words were still more offensive than the work they had just seen; and the way in which Jesus had openly caused it to be done and seen clashed with all their prejudices and stirred the depths of their unbelief. For in so speaking His personal glory could not but shine forth.

Both the Father and the Son were working, not resting.

> "For this therefore[m] the Jews sought the more to kill Him, because He not only broke[105] the Sabbath, but also said that God was His own Father, making Himself equal with God" (verse 18).

Nor were they mistaken, in this inference at least. For as He did expressly charge the healed man to do what He knew would bring things to a rupture, so He did not deny, but confess, that God was His own Father in a sense that was true of none but Himself. This is the truth; and the truth of all truths most due to God, and the turning-point of all blessing to man. By it the believer knows God, and has life everlasting; without it one is an enemy of God, as the Jews showed themselves that day and ever since. Hardened men, perversely, fatally blinded, who, in presumed zeal for His honour, sought the more to kill Jesus, His own Son, come in infinite love to make the Father known, and to reconcile man to God. But God is wise and infinitely good in His work; for in letting them prove their malice to the uttermost, when the due time was come, in killing Jesus, He proved His own love to the full in atonement, making Christ, "Who knew no sin, to be sin for us, that we might become God's righteousness in Him" [2 Corinthians 5:21].

Verses 19-30.

The Lord takes up the unbelieving rejection of His Person and brings out the truth which puts all in its place.

> "Jesus then answered and said to them, Verily, verily, I say to you, The Son can do nothing of Himself unless He sees the Father doing some-

thing; for whatever things He doeth, these also the Son doeth in like manner" (verse 19).

It is the expression of the entire exclusion of a will separate from God the Father. He speaks of Himself as man on earth, yet God withal: the especial topic of our Gospel. He was here displaying God, Whom otherwise no man had seen or could see; and He displayed Him as Father, however dull even disciples might be to discern it till redemption removed the veil from their eyes and sense of guilt from the conscience, till the love that gave Him to effect it was apprehended by the heart. But He had deigned to take the place of man, without forfeiting for a moment His divine nature and rights: and as such He disclaims the least shade of self-exaltation, or independence of His Father. This flesh cannot understand now more than then; and as then it led the Jews to repudiate the Son, so now in Christendom largely to the open denial of His divine glory or to the practical humanising of Him. Hence the effort of so many to get rid of such a symbol as the Athanasian Creed, and the otiose acquiescence of far more who believe on Him no more than they. The truth is that Scripture goes beyond any creed that ever was framed in the maintenance of His honour; and this not only in the doctrine of His inspired servants, but in their report of His own words as here.

Besides, however, being the Eternal, God all over, blessed for ever, He speaks of Himself as in this world a man, yet the Son, and as such only doing what He sees the Father do: anything else would not be to declare Him. And for this He was here. Yet so truly is He Divine that whatever things the Father does, these also does the Son likewise. He is the image of the invisible God, and alone competent to show the Father. How perfect the conjoint working of the Father and the Son! So we learn here, as in John 10, their unity. It is not only that the Son does whatever the Father may, but in like manner. How blessed their communion!

But the ground the Lord lays is also to be considered.

> "For the Father loveth (φιλεῖ) the Son and showeth Him all things which He Himself doeth; and He will show Him greater works than these that ye may wonder" (verse 20).

Truly the Persons in the Godhead are real, if anything is; and as the divine nature is morally perfect, the affections that reign are not less. The joint working of the Father and the Son our blessed Lord explains by the Father loving the Son and showing Him all that He Himself does; nay, He lets them know, as He knew Himself, that greater works would be shown Him by the Father, as the latter part of this Gospel testifies, "that ye may wonder"—He does not say believe. For He speaks, not of grace, but of power displayed in testimony to the Jews, the effect of which would be, not the faith which honours God, but the amazement which is the frequent and stupid companion of incredulity.

The Lord next singles out the immense miracle of resurrection.

> "For even as the Father raiseth the dead and quickeneth, so the Son also quickeneth whom He will; for not even the Father judgeth any one, but hath given all the judgment to the Son; that all may honour the Son even as they honour the Father. He that honoureth not the Son honoureth not the Father that sent Him" (verses 21-23).

There can be no doubt that giving life to the dead befits and characterises God; but if the Father does so, no less does the Son, and this not as an instrument, but sovereignly: "the Son also quickeneth whom He will." He is a divine Person as truly as the Father, in full right and power. But more: He alone judges.[105a] Judgment as a whole, and in all its forms, is committed to the Son by the Father, Who in this sense judges none, with the express aim that all should honour the Son even as they honour the Father. And so it really is; for they honour not the Father but do Him despite who honour not His Sent One, the Son. It is the Son on Whom, by the Father's pleasure, it devolves to judge; but we shall find that there is a moral reason for this which appears afterward. As it is, we learn that the Son quickens in communion with the Father, and that only He judges. Thus is His honour secured from all men, who are either quickened if they believe, or judged if they do not.

For how can a soul know that he is quickened and shall not be judged? He who reveals the portion that belongs to some and awaits the rest has not left in obscurity or doubt that which is so all-important; He has told out what so deeply concerns every child of man. Only unbelief need or can be uncertain, though it indeed should not be, for its sorrowful end is too plain to others if not to itself. Defying God, it must be judged by Him Whom it can no longer dishonour. What, on the other hand, can be more graciously distinct than the portion our Lord warrants to faith?

> "Verily, verily, I say to you, He that heareth My word and believeth Him that sent Me hath life eternal, and cometh not into judgment, but is passed out of death into life"[n] (verse 24).

THE FIFTH CHAPTER

It was no question of the law, but of hearing Christ's word, of believing (not *in* God in any sense, as the Authorised Version conveys, but) Him that sent Christ, believing His testimony. For this had He sent His Son, that He might give life eternal. He, therefore, that believeth Him "hath life eternal." It is a present gift of God and possession of the believer, to be enjoyed perfectly in heaven doubtless, but none the less truly given now and exercised here where Christ then was.°

But there is more than the actual communication of a new life by faith, a life of which Christ, not Adam, is the source and character; he who has life does not come into judgment (κρίσιν). The Authorised English Version has "condemnation"; but the Lord says more than this: the believer "cometh not into judgment." He will be manifested before Christ's tribunal; he will give account of all done in the body, but he does not, if Christ is to be believed, come into judgment. He will never be put on his trial to see whether he is to be lost or not. Strange notion! after it may be in the separate state departing "to be with Christ, which is far better," certainly after being changed into the likeness of His glory, to be judged. Think of the "beloved disciple," when glorified, put on so awful a trial! It is equally inconsistent for every other believer; for life eternal is the same for all. Salvation does not vary for any, more than Christ does. No! such an idea is theology, the too common doctrine of Christendom, Protestant or Popish, Arminian or Calvinist; but it is directly in collision with the plain and sure words of Christ.

All the great English translations are wrong here, Wiclif, Tyndale, Cranmer, and Geneva, with the Authorised Version. Singular to say, the Rhemish Version alone is right, in this following the Vulgate: a mere accident undoubtedly, for none are so distant from the truth conveyed by their own translation, from the apprehension of exemption from judgment, as Romish doctors. And none are so unfaithful in the next clause, for they actually make the Lord seem to say "shall pass from death into life."[p] He really said ἀλλὰ μεταβέβηκεν ἐκ τ. θ. εἰς τ. ζ., "but is (or, hath) passed (the present result of a past act) out of death into life." Here the Protestant versions are right, Wiclif feeble, the Rhemish false. And there is not even the excuse of the Vulgate, which reads *"transiit"*. Possibly they read *"transiet"*; but if so, it was an error which some copies of the Latin would have corrected, if they ignored the inspired original.

However this be, the truth set forth by our Saviour is of all moment: would that every believer knew it and rejoiced in it with simplicity and in its fulness, as this one verse presents it! It is Christ's word that is heard in divinely given faith, and this quickens the soul: no thought here or anywhere else of any such virtue in an administered ordinance. But faith does not slight His judgment; on the contrary, the believer now bows to it morally in His word, receives God's testimony to His Son, and is passed from death into life.

The Lord has thus answered the question which His solemn words would raise in every soul that fears God. He had shown it to be no question of law or of ordinance, but of hearing His word and believing the Father that sent Him. Such only have eternal life; but he who so believes has it now. How blessed and secure his portion in Christ!

Next He turns to the more general state of things.

"Verily, verily, I say to you, An hour is coming and now is, when the dead shall hear the voice of the Son of God; and they that have heard shall live" (verse 25).

It is indeed the sad truth: men in all the activities of the world are here "the dead." Nor is it a question of a stricter morality or of a holier religion. Either one or other or both they may acquire and yet want life. Dogma cannot give it any more than practice. It flows from the Son of God, Who quickens whom He will; yet is it by faith, and so through the word which the Spirit applies livingly.

Here it is that Evangelicalism is feeble and Sacramentalism is false. If the latter superstitiously gives to a creature ordinance the honour which belongs to a divine Person alone, the former ignores and lowers the truth by talking of a converted character and of devoting to God what was once abandoned to self and sin; but neither has any adequate estimate of the total ruin of man, nor consequently of the absolute need and real power of divine grace. "The dead" are men universally now till born of God. It is no picture of the future resurrection, whether of just or unjust, which follows in verses 28-29, but of the present hour, as the Lord Himself intimates; for it "now is," "when the dead shall hear the voice of the Son of God."[106] His voice goes forth "to every creature" in the gospel; "and those that heard shall live." Such are the means and condition of life. It is of faith that it might be by grace. Man's utter powerlessness is as manifest and certain as His glorious energy.

Those, then, that heard shall live. Alas! the mass of mankind have ears but they hear not; even as to the Jews, when they saw Him, there was no beauty that they should desire Him. Whether it be superstitious or sceptical man, he submits not to the sentence of God on his own estate, nor consequently feels the need of sovereign mercy in Christ, Who alone can give the life man wants for God now or through eternity. But whatever the mercy of God, He will have His Son honoured, and this now by hearing His word and believing the testimony of Him Who sent Him. This tests man thoroughly, which the law only did partially. For never does the sinner trust God for life eternal till grace makes him see his sins and distrust himself utterly. Then how glad is he to learn that the goodness of God gives life eternal in Christ, and has sent Him that he might know it! How willingly he owns himself one of "the dead," which no man does really till he lives of the new life which is in Christ! How heartily he bows to the Son of God, and blesses the God Who sent Him in love and compassion, willing not the death of the sinner, but rather that he might have life through His name!

But the same unbelief, which of old in the Jews violated the law and lusted after idols, now in the Gentiles trusts an ordinance for it, to the exaltation of those that arrogate to themselves its valid and exclusive administration, or openly distrusts God and slights His Son, confiding in themselves without Him. They are the religiously or the profanely infidel. They are "the dead" and have never heard the voice of the Son of God, but only of their priests or of their philosophers. Whatever their boastings, they shall not live, for they have not Christ, but only ideas, imaginative or rational; not the truth which is inseparable from Christ received by faith to the glory of God and the annihilation of human pretensions.

THE FIFTH CHAPTER

It is all-important to see that all truth centres in the Person of Christ, Who, being God from everlasting to everlasting, deigned to become man, without the least forfeiture of divine glory, yet loyally accepting the position proper to humanity. Hence the language of the Lord in what follows, the misapprehension of which has led not a few theologians of eminence to the brink, if not into the pit, of fundamental heterodoxy.[107]

> "For even as the Father hath life in Himself, so He gave to the Son also to have life in Himself; and gave Him authority to execute judgment (also),[q] because he is Son of Man" (verses 26-27).

The Lord evidently speaks here as come below, a man, the Sent of God and Servant of the divine purposes, not as the One Who is over all, God blessed for ever, though both be true of Him in His Person. As the eternal Son, He quickens whom He will; as come in humiliation, it is given Him of the Father to have life in Himself. Born of a woman, He is still Son of God (Luke 1:35). But men despise the man Christ Jesus. Some trust in themselves that they are righteous, all disliking Him Who did not His own will, but the will of Him that sent Him. He Who lived on account of the Father is irksome to all that live to themselves, and odious to such as seek honour one of another. They misuse His humanity to deny His deity. They have no life, for they have no faith. But they cannot escape judgment, and a judgment executed in that very nature of man for which they rejected the Son of God.

It is as Son of Man that the Lord Jesus will sit on the throne. Doubtless He will show His divine knowledge in judging; but, as He says expressly, authority is given Him of the Father to execute judgment, because He is

Son of Man. As Son of God He quickens; as Son of Man He will judge. How solemn! Had He been only Son of God, who would have dared to despise Him? The light of His glory had consumed instantly every proud adversary from before Him. It was His grace, then, in becoming man to save men which exposed Him to contempt in His path of lowly obedience and suffering in love. The archangel is a servant; He stooped to become one (Philippians 2:6-7). But the god of this world blinded them, so that they counted as only man Him Who never more proved Himself God to such as by grace had eyes to see. If they insulted Him in His work of grace, how will it be when He executes judgment, and this as Son of Man? Such is the award of God.

> "Wonder not at this; for an hour is coming, in which all that are in the tombs shall hear His voice, and shall go forth, those that practised good unto a resurrection of life, and those that did evil unto a resurrection of judgment" (verses 28-29).

Thus another hour is announced distinct from what "now is," and only "coming," an hour not of quickening such of the dead as hear the voice of Christ, but of "all that are in the tombs" rising. It is the hour of proper resurrection; and the Lord carefully negatives the popular thought of one general resurrection. Not so; here, as elsewhere, we learn of two resurrections wholly and distinctly contrasted in character, as we find in Revelation 20 they are in time, with the millennium and more between them.

It did not enter into the scope of the Lord's discourse, any more than of the Spirit's design in the Gospel, to reveal in detail the order of events chronologically. This has its suited place in the great prophecy of the New

Testament. But the far deeper difference of their relation to Christ Himself, viewed as Son of God and Son of Man, is laid before us in a few words of the profoundest interest—a difference which would be true if no more than ten minutes intervened, but which is rendered far more distinct and impressive, inasmuch as the Revelation lets us see an interval of more than a thousand years. How great the confusion in the theology of the schools and pulpits, which supposes a single promiscuous rising of just and unjust, and this mainly on an exegesis so absurd as that which applies Matthew 25:31-46 to the resurrection! For it is certainly a judgment of the quick, of "all the nations," before the Son of Man when He comes again in glory; not the judgment of the wicked dead and their works before the great white throne after heaven and earth are fled away, and all question of coming again is closed. There is the further mischief resulting from this interpretation that it tends to insinuate that just and unjust come into judgment, to the destruction of the capital truth of the Gospel, which contrasts life and judgment, as we have seen in our Saviour's words, and may find elsewhere also.

There is this essential difference in the two "hours," that, while in the first some only by grace hear His voice and have life, in the second *all* that are in the tombs shall hear it and shall go forth. But there is no confusion of just and unjust longer. In the world they had been more or less mixed together. In the field where the good seed was sown the enemy sowed darnel; and, spite of the servants, the Lord ruled that both were to grow together until the harvest. But in the coming hour there is no mingling more: the solemn severing of all takes place, "those that practised good unto a resurrection of life, and those that did evil unto a resurrection of judgment." For life eternal in Christ is never inoperative, and the Holy Ghost, Who is given to the believer consequent on the accomplishment of redemption and the ascension of Christ, works in that life, that there may be the fruit of righteousness by Jesus Christ to God's glory and praise. Hence, such as believed are here characterised as those that practised good, and as this had its root in life, so its issue is a resurrection of life; while those who had no life, being rejecters of Him Who is its source, are described as "those that did evil," and their end a resurrection of judgment. In the hour that now is they would not have the Son of God in all His grace; they must be judged by the Son of Man in the hour that is coming. The two resurrections are as distinct as the characters of those who rise in each. But Jesus is Lord of all and raises all, though on a different principle, of a different class, and to a different end.[108]

Nothing can be more definite than the Son's claim of the powers most characteristic of God the Father, quickening and raising the dead; nothing more decided than the Father's resolve to maintain the honour of His incarnate Son. For every tittle and form of judging is committed to the Son of Man, and with the express purpose, which shall surely stand, that all are to honour the Son as they honour the Father. But the giving life is the action of grace in its fullest character, as judgment is the vindication of the Son's honour on those who slighted Him and never had life eternal any more than salvation. To confound the two is the unintelligence of man and his tradition, and is wholly opposed to plain revelation. It is an error of great magnitude.

The Lord still speaks as Son, but as man on earth, and in verse 30 binds together what He had already unfolded with the various witnesses to His glory in what follows. He was equal to the task of judging, though the lowliest of men; and this just because He was in none of His ways or thoughts independent of the Father. It is the perfection of man; He alone was so, Who counted it no object of robbery to be on equality with God. But being God, He had become man for God's glory; and so He says,

> "I cannot do anything of Myself; as I hear I judge, and My judgment is righteous, because I seek not My will, but the will of Him[r] that sent Me" (verse 30).

He saw, He heard, as the perfectly dependent and obedient man, though none could have taken in such a range unless a divine Person. He had a will, but it was used in entire subjection to the Father. He saw whatever the Father does to do the same likewise; He heard with an ear opened and wakened, morning by morning, to hear as the learned, and so He judged; and His judgment was just. There was nothing to distract or mislead, though there was one who sought it with all subtilty. But he was foiled, and failed utterly, for here he was assailing not the first man, but the Second, Who had come to do the will of God. Such a purpose of heart maintains both singleness of eye and unswerving fidelity. Thus did the Sent One ever walk. Who so competent and suited to judge, and this as Man, mankind?[109]

VERSES 31-47.

Next we are introduced to the witnesses who testify to Him.

> "If I bear witness about Myself, My witness is not true.[109a] It is another that beareth witness about

Me, and I know⁵ that the witness which he beareth about Me is true. Ye have sent unto John, and he hath borne witness to the truth. But I do not receive the witness from man; but these things I say that ye may be saved. He was the burning and shining lamp,{110} and ye were willing to rejoice for a season in his light" (verses 31-35).

John the Baptist, then, is the first witness, whom the Lord summons in the ready and everlasting love which said nothing of His own testimony, if by any means they might be convinced and believe the truth. For this had He been born, and for this come into the world. He lived on account of the Father, Who testified about Him. Never was His an interested or an isolated testimony; but He would waive it, and points to His forerunner. For this purpose had John been raised up beyond denial, and no testimony from among men could be conceived more unimpeachable. His birth, his life, his preaching, his death, all bore the stamp of truthfulness; and never had one pointed to another as he to the Lord Jesus. The Jews, too, had sought his death solemnly, and he had not flinched. Who else had ever so testified before and after the coming of the object of testimony? He was not the Christ, as he confessed and denied not, when men were ready to give him the glory due to the Master. Nor, on the other hand, did Christ seek testimony from man; yet to what did He not stoop that souls might be saved? If a man, however, was to be used at all, none greater than John had arisen among those born of women, as the Lord says. The burning and shining lamp had been a source of joy for a while; but men are inconstant, and the testimony of him, who was truly "a voice in the wilderness," was refused.

THE FIFTH CHAPTER

The second and greater witness we see in the works of Christ.

> "But I have the witness greater[110a] than of John; for the works which the Father hath given Me that I should complete them, the works themselves which I do bear witness about Me that the Father hath sent Me" (verse 36).

In every way Christ's works testify not so much of the power displayed as of their character.[110b] What grace and truth shine through them as in Him!

The third witness is the Father's voice.

> "And the Father Who sent Me, Himself[t] hath borne witness about Me. Ye have neither heard His voice at any time nor seen His shape; and His word ye have not abiding in you, because Him whom He sent ye do not believe" (verses 37-38).

This attestation to the relation and glory of the Son rises still higher—we might have thought to the highest, had not our Lord added another[111] and crowning testimony in that which degenerate Christendom is now learning to abandon with contempt, to its own ruin and speedy judgment.

The fourth and crowning witness is that of the Scriptures.

> "Search" (or, "Ye search") "the Scriptures, for ye think that ye have in them life eternal; and it is they that bear witness about Me. And ye are not willing to come unto Me that ye may have life" (verses 39-40).

The practical difference between the indicative and the imperative is not great, because the context decides that it is an appeal, as it has been well remarked, rather than a command. They were not so infatuated as to suppose that they had life eternal in themselves; they looked for it in the Scriptures, and so were in the habit of searching them, as they do, more or less, to this day.[112] But though the Scriptures testify about the Lord Jesus, they have no willingness to come unto Him that they may have the life He alone can give. For the Scriptures cannot give life apart from Him, nor will the Father; yet are the Scriptures the standing witness of Christ, continually holding Him forth as the revealed resource for man and triumph for God, and this in goodness, not merely in judgment, to the utter confusion of the enemy and of all who take their part with him against God. The presence of Christ put to the test, not merely man in his misery and universal departure from God, but those who were intrusted with those oracles of God; and the Saviour Son, despised by the Jews, has but to pronounce the sentence on them thus wilfully slighting their own best witnesses to Him, "Ye will not come unto Me that ye may have life."

Was it, then, that the Lord Jesus sought present honour? His whole life, from His birth to His death, declared the contrary with a plainness which none could mistake. How was it with His adversaries?

> "Glory from men I do not receive; but I know you that ye have not the love of God in yourselves. I am come in My Father's name, and ye receive Me not: if another come in his own name, him ye will receive" (verses 41-43).

"Glory from men" is the moving spring of the world: Jesus not only sought it not, but did not receive it. He always did the things that pleased the Father, Who gave

THE FIFTH CHAPTER

Him commandment what He should say, and what He should speak. He kept His Father's commandments, and abode in His love. In no sense had the Jews the love of God in them: ambitious of human glory, and self-complacent, their soul abhorred Jesus, as His soul was straitened for them. His coming had put them to a fresh and far fuller test. He had brought God too close to them—yea, the Father; but they knew neither Christ nor the Father: if they had known the one, they should have known the other.

But there should be another test yet: not His coming in the Father's name with the simple aim of doing His will and glorifying Him, but *another to come in his own name*. This would suit the Jew—man. Self-exaltation is his bane, and Satan's bait, and therein utterly irremediable ruin under divine judgment. It is the man of sin[113] in contrast with the Son of God, the Man of obedience and righteousness; and, according as we have heard that Antichrist comes, even now there have come many antichrists. But the presence of Antichrist will be "according to the working of Satan, in all power and signs and wonders of falsehood, and in every deceit of unrighteousness, to those that perish, because they have not received the love of the truth that they might be saved" {2 Thessalonians 2:9-10}. They would not have the true God and eternal life in the Son become man and suffering in love for man; they will receive Satan's man when he sets up to be God. This is the great lie of the end, and they will be lost in it who rejected the truth in Christ.

Nor is there anything strange in such a close for those who know the ways of man from the beginning.

"How can ye believe[114] who receive glory one of another, and seek not the glory which (is) from the only God?" (verse 44).

Such is the world, the scene where man walks in a vain show, blessing his soul while he lives, and praised by his fellows when he did well to himself; but such shall never see light. This their way is their folly, let posterity ever so much delight in their mouth. "Like sheep they are laid in Sheol; death feedeth on them, and the upright shall have dominion over them in the morning" [Psalm 49:14]. If God's "children" are told to keep themselves from idols, one cannot wonder that the idolatry of man—of self—should be the death of faith. Any object is welcome rather than the true and only God, "Who shall render to each according to his works; to those who in patience of good work seek for glory, honour, and incorruption, life eternal; but to those that are contentious, and are disobedient to the truth, and obey unrighteousness, (there shall be) wrath and indignation, tribulation and distress" [Romans 2:6-9].

Does the Lord, then, take the place of accusing the Jews? Not so: they boasted of Moses, but will find in him testimony fatal to themselves.

"Think not that I will accuse you unto the Father: there is one that accuseth you, Moses, on whom ye trust [have yet your hope]; for if ye believed Moses, ye would have believed Me, for he wrote of Me. But if ye believe not his writings, how shall ye believe My words?" (verses 45-47).

Never was such honour put on the written word. Jesus had, if any one, God's word abiding in Him. Nobody ever had the Father's words and His word as He; no one gave them out invariably, and at all times, as He; yet does He set the writings of the Bible above His own sayings, as a testimony to Jewish conscience. It was no question of superior claim in themselves, or in the character of truth conveyed; for none of old could compare with the words of Christ. The Father on the holy mount had Himself answered the foolish words of Peter, who would have put Moses, Elias, and the Lord in three tabernacles and co-ordinate glory. Not so. "This is My beloved Son: hear *Him*" [Mark 9:7]. The lawgiver, the prophet, must bow to Jesus. They had their place as servants: He is Son and Lord of all. They retire, leaving Him the one object of the Father's good pleasure, and of our communion with the Father through hearing the Son Jesus Christ our Lord.

Nevertheless, it is the Son Himself Who here gives to the writings of Moses a place in testimony beyond His own words; not because the servant approached the Master, or the Decalogue the Sermon on the Mount, but because the Scripture, as such, has a character of permanence in testimony which can attach only to the written word. And Moses wrote of Christ—necessarily, therefore, by divine power—as a prophet of "the prophet which should come into the world," of the Prophet incomparably more than prophet, the Son of God, Who quickens every believer, and shall judge every despiser, raising from the grave these for a resurrection of judgment, as those for one of life. Had the Jews, then, believed Moses, they would have believed Christ: words which teach us that faith is no such otiose exercise as some would make it; for the Jews in no way questioned, but received his writings as divine. But not to doubt is far from believing; and they saw not in any of his books the great object of testimony in all, Jesus the Messiah, a man, yet far more than man, a divine Saviour of sinners and sacrifice for sins, the Lamb of God which takes away the sin of the world. If they believed Moses, they would have believed Him, for he wrote of Him. But if they believed not his writings, the Saviour did not expect them to believe His own words.

What an estimate of the authority of those very Scriptures which self-sufficient men have assailed as untrustworthy! They dare to tell us that they are neither Mosaic in origin, nor Messianic in testimony, but a mass of legends which do not even cohere in their poor and human reports of early days. On the other hand, the Judge of quick and dead declares that the Scriptures testify of Him, and that Moses wrote of Him, setting the written word in point of authority above even His words. As the Saviour and Rationalism are thus in direct antagonism, the Christian has no hesitation which to receive and which to reject, for one cannot serve both masters. Either he will hate the one and love the other, or he will hold to the one and despise the other. So it is, and must be, and ought to be; for Christ and Rationalism are irreconcilable. Those who pretend to serve both have no principle as to either, and are the most corrupting dogmatically of all men. They not only do not possess the truth, but they make the love of it impossible, enemies alike of God and man.[115]

NOTES ON THE FIFTH CHAPTER

a [*Cf. Lectures Introductory to the Study of the Gospels*, pp. 446-454.]

b ["*The* feast": so אCEFHL, etc., Egypt. Cyr. Alex., followed by Tischendorf; "*a* feast" is read by Lachm., Treg., W. and H., Weiss, Blass, as in ABDG, etc., Chrys. Epiph.]

NOTES ON THE FIFTH CHAPTER

c There is a good deal of confusion in the MSS., even where the text is certain here. Thus, while ἐπὶ τῇ προβατικῇ (at the sheep-*gate*, Nehemiah 3 LXX.) is read by the Vatican, Rescript of Paris, and thirteen more uncials and the great body of cursives, confirmed by most ancient versions [W. and H., Weiss], ℵ^corr. ADGL, etc., have ἐν τῇ π. probably in the sense of the Authorised Version—"sheep-*market*"; whilst ℵ^pm and a few other inferior authorities omit ἐπὶ (or ἐν) τῇ, and hence seem to construe προβατικὴ κολ. a "sheep-pool": so Jerome's *Onomasticon* (ed. Lars. et Parth. p. 112), Theodore of Mopsuestia {*Commentary on the Gospel of John,*} p. 26, and the *Jerusalem Itinerary*, not to speak of the Vulg. Æth. and Slav. Again, for ἡ ἐπιλεγ. [W. and H., Weiss], ℵ^pm gives τὸ λεγόμενον (adopted by Tisch. in his eighth ed.), and ℵ^corr. ἡ ἐπιλεγ.; while DV, eight cursives, etc., read λεγ. [so Blass]. In the same ed. Tisch. exhibits Βηθζαθὰ with ℵL, etc. (D Βελζεθὰ, B, etc. Βηθσαιδὰ, etc., Λ, etc., Βιθεσθὰ).

d In verses 3-4 there are more serious differences. High, if not large, authorities (ℵBCDL, 33, 68, many of the ante-Hier. Latin versions, Theb. Memph. Syr^cu. et hier., etc.) do not read πολὺ, nor (except Dh) παραλυτικῶν, which last is not in T.R. {Textus Receptus}. But the great omission is of the clause ἐκδεχομένων τὴν τοῦ ὕδατος κίνησιν with ℵ^pmBC^pmL, 18, 157, 314 Syr^cu. Theb. Memph^dz. and all verse 4 as in the common text, here strengthened by D (an ancient though erratic copy), but deserted by A^pm. It is certain that the narrative as ordinarily given must have been read by Tertullian (*de Baptismo*, 5); and the answer of the sick man in the critical text, verse 7, implies, if it does not demand, such an explanation. The fact may have been too startling for the copyists to believe, not about themselves or Christian times, but about the days before and up to Christ's ministry. The Romanists found it hard to credit any evidence of God's goodness to the Jews as such, and in the time alleged. Even Lachmann retained the passage. I do not think there is real weight in Alford's argument against its genuineness grounded on the plea that there are seven words used here only, or here only in this sense; for so remarkable and singular a fact would naturally call for words suited to it. There are variations among the MSS. that contain the omitted passage, but not more, perhaps, than usual. [See Westcott, *Additional Note on Chapter V*, and Hort's *Note on Select Readings*, p. 77. Weiss and Blass give up the verse.]

e In verse 5 T.R. omits καί (so BKSVΓΛ., etc.) contrary to ℵACDEFGHILMUΔ and the mass of cursives, versions, etc.; also αὐτοῦ against ℵBC^pmDLΠ^corr., etc., with most ancient versions.

f Several uncials (C^corr.EFGH, with many cursives, etc.) add ναί before κύριε, a few omitting κ. The received reading βάλλῃ is incorrect, and rests on few if any copies.

g ℵ^pmD, the Lat. Cod. Rhedig., and Arm. omit εὐθέως, but all other authorities insert it.

h Καί is omitted in T.R. with at least ten uncials, very many cursives Vulg., Syrr., etc., but read by ℵABC^pmDGLVΓ, forty cursives, most ancient versions and fathers.

i A B and some eleven or twelve other uncials, and most cursives, omit σου, reading "the" [Edd.]. But ℵC^pmDLΔΠ, thirteen cursives, and the body of ancient versions, etc., read the pronoun "thy."

NOTES ON THE FIFTH CHAPTER

j T.R. with most copies, etc., reads οὖν, "therefore"; but it is not found in אBD and several other good authorities. So τὸν κρ. σου is not read by א[pm et corr.]BC[pm]L Sah. Two uncials and six cursives omit the verse, evidently by ὁμοιοτέλευτον. (*Cf.* end of verse 11.)

k For ἰαθεὶς, "healed" (with אABCLΓΔΛΠ, and almost all the rest of the copies and versions and fathers), Tischendorf reads ἀσθενῶν with D and two or three Latin copies—a strange judgment and on light grounds. [Blass accepts neither.]

l T.R. adds καὶ ἐζήτουν αὐτὸν ἀποκτεῖναι with fourteen uncials, most cursives and some versions, contrary to אBCDL, 1, 22, 33, 69, 249, some old Latin, Vulg. Syr[cu. [sin]] Memph. Arm., and early Greeks.

m אD and other authorities, followed by Tischendorf [and Blass] omit οὖν, contrary to the rest [as W. and H., Weiss].

n The contrast of life and judgment here, as of salvation and judgment in Hebrews 9:27-28, is so distinctly revealed, and on ground so solemn as the honour or dishonour of the Son, that one may wonder at the prejudice of the late able Knightsbridge Professor in the University of Cambridge, who opposes Dr. Gr. Guinness where he is as right as he himself was wrong on the judgment in Revelation 20. For the faithful never coming into judgment at all, Mr. T. R. Birks saw "no ground but Alford's altered translation of John 5:24, which I believe to be a mistake" (*Thoughts on the Times and Seasons of Sacred Prophecy*, p. 65, 1880): an astounding utterance, not only in its philological aspect, since the Greek admits of no other sense, but no less certainly as a question of divine grace and truth, and of divine righteousness. It is nothing less than a heterodox or unbelieving offence against the gospel, even against what an Old Testament saint could say before the Saviour came, as in Psalm 143:2. If the manifestation of all absolutely before the judgment-seat of Christ were enfeebled, there had been reason for the gravest warning. But it is agreed, that each of us shall give account of himself to God, and receive the things done through the body accordingly, whether good or evil. This, however, gives no title to deny Christ's word, or the believer's distinctive privilege that he comes not into judgment or needs "acquittal" in that day, after having been already justified. Doctrinally it dishonours the Lord and His work, yet more than the faith of the saint; it replunges into doubt and darkness those whom grace has saved through believing; it would bring back the distress on exercised hearts, which the misrendering of John 5 and of 1 Corinthians 11 introduced. This misrendering in the A.V. is corrected beyond just hesitation by the R.V. As to "Alford's altered translation," be it remarked that the A.V. of John 5:22 and 27 corrects the error in 24 and 29. It is the same word κρίσις all through, which indisputably means "judgment," not damnation or "condemnation" like κατάκριμα, as the verb (22, 30) means "to judge." Nor is it unimportant to notice the ignorance of talking thus of Dean Alford, seeing that the most influential perhaps of all versions, Jerome's Vulgate, is quite right in both John 5 and 1 Corinthians 11, where the A.V. was lamentably and inexcusably wrong. In the Gospel the old Latin MSS., Vercell. Veron. Brix., etc., were right. Many of the Oriental versions are correct; some waver like the A.V., to the ruin of definite truth on what is of great moment. But where the doctrine on everlasting punishment was unsound, it is not surprising to learn that there was lack of faith as to life eternal and its exemption from judgment.

NOTES ON THE FIFTH CHAPTER

o [*Cf. An Exposition of the Epistles of John the Apostle*, {1905,} p. 375.]

p In Nonnus' *Paraphrase* of our Gospel (fifth century, ed. by Passow and Bach, 1834) there is the similar error of rendering ἵξεται ἐκ θανάτοιο. So in the Amiatine and other ancient Vulgate MSS. we have "*transiet*," and in a Munich old Latin copy of the sixth century "*transibit*".

q The majority read καὶ, "also," but not A B L, etc., Memph.

r The received text adds πατρὸς, "Father," with many authorities, but not the most ancient.

s The Sinaitic[pm] and the Cambridge MS. of Beza, with a few other good authorities, read οἴδατε, "ye know" [so Blass], but almost all the rest support the common reading [as Weiss].

t ℵ B L have ἐκεῖνος [Weiss, Blass], D ἐκεῖνος αὐτὸς, for αὐτὸς in the great mass of the authorities, as in T.R.

THE SIXTH CHAPTER [a]

VERSES 1-15.

[Matthew 14:13-21; 15:32-39; Mark 6:32-44; 8:1-10; Luke 9:10-17.]

Our Gospel now gives us the great miracle, or sign rather, common to all the four; and this, as ever here, introductorily to the discourse that follows—Christ, incarnate and in death, the food of eternal life for those who believe on His name. Here it is the Son of Man humbled and ascended, as in chapter 5 the Son of God quickening those that hear, and by and by as Son of Man about to judge those that believe not.

> "After these things Jesus went away beyond the sea of Galilee, of Tiberias; and a great crowd followed Him because they saw the[b] signs which He wrought on the sick. But Jesus went up into the mountain, and there sat with His disciples; and the Passover, the feast of the Jews, was near. Jesus then lifting up His eyes, and seeing that a great crowd cometh unto Him, saith unto Philip, Whence shall we buy loaves that these may eat? But this He said, trying him, for He Himself knew

what He was about to do. Philip answered Him, Loaves for two hundred pence are not sufficient for them, that each of them^c may have some little. One of His disciples, Andrew, the brother of Simon Peter, saith to Him, There is a little boy[116] here that hath five barley-loaves and two fishes; but these, what are they for so many?" (verses 1-9).

The scene is wholly changed from Jerusalem. We see the Lord in Galilee, and in that part of the lake called from the city of Tiberias, as well as from the province bordering on its western side. A great crowd follow Him because of the signs He wrought on the sick. The Lord withdraws to the high land, where He sits with His disciples, the Passover being then at hand. None of the motives mentioned in the Synoptic accounts do we find here: neither the beheading of John Baptist, nor the Apostles' return from their mission, nor the need of rest after toils in teaching or other work. Jesus fills the picture: all is in His hand. It is He Who takes the initiative; not that the disciples may not have previously been perplexed, nor as if John did not know this as well as Matthew and the rest, but because it pleased the Holy Spirit to give us Christ Himself alone master of the situation, as always in his Gospel. The nearness of the Passover is noted as repeatedly in this Gospel. Here, too, there was the reason for it, that the discourse that follows, as well as the sign wrought, is grounded on eating and drinking as the token of communion.

"Jesus then lifting up His eyes, and seeing that a great crowd cometh unto Him, saith unto Philip, Whence shall we buy loaves that these may eat?" The Evangelist, however, is careful of His glory, and loses no time in letting us know that it was out of no uncertainty in His own mind, but in order to test Philip: He knew what He was going to do. Nevertheless, He awaits the despairing words of Philip's fellow-townsman, Andrew, and would teach all now what His gracious power loves to do with the little and despised, were it for the greatest need. The brother of Simon Peter, who was even before his brother in seeing the Messiah, could think of a little boy with five barley-loaves and two fishes, not of Jesus. And where was Peter? where John, the disciple that He loved? Nowhere in faith. Truly flesh cannot glory in His presence.

Let us turn to the One we may and ought to glory in, honouring the Father in honouring Him.

> "Jesus said, Make the people *(ἀνθρώπους)* sit (or, lie) down. Now there was much grass in the place. The men *(ἄνδρες)* then sat down in number about five thousand. Jesus then took the loaves and, having given thanks,[d] distributed[e] to those that were set down, and likewise also of the fishes as much as they would.[117] But when they were filled, He saith to His disciples, Gather the fragments that are over, that nothing be lost. They gathered (them) then, and filled twelve baskets with fragments[117a] of the five barley-loaves which were over to those that had eaten. The people *(οἱ ἄνθρωποι)* then, having seen the sign which Jesus[f] did, said, This is truly the Prophet that is coming into the world. Jesus then, knowing that they would come and seize Him that they might make (Him) king, withdrew (again)[g] to the mountain Himself alone" (verses 10-15).

One is afraid that, poor as was the intelligence of the Galilean crowd, they understood the import of this great sign better than the Christendom of the last seventeen hundred years. They were, no doubt, dull enough as to their deepest need, and they had no appreciation of the Saviour's grace in humiliation and redemption, afterwards fully set forth by Him in the discourse that ensues; but they had some thoughts not wholly untrue, though human and short enough, of the kingdom God is going to set up here below. Now and for many centuries theology indulges in a sort of mystic dream that the gospel or Church is the kingdom of Christ, His kingdom of grace to be at the end His kingdom of glory. But they have no thought of His coming in the kingdom He will have received, that not Israel only but all peoples, nations, and languages should serve Him; and this too an everlasting dominion which shall not pass away, and His kingdom that which shall not be destroyed. A twofold error, which lets slip the oneness of the body of Christ, the Church, with its glorified Head on high, and denies the mercy and faithfulness of God to Israel, who are the destined centre of Jehovah's earthly plans for the kingdom, when we, changed into the likeness of Christ's glory, shall reign together with Him.

The crowd were struck with the fulfilment of this fresh and crowning sign. They had not abandoned as yet their hopes. They knew that Jehovah has chosen Zion; that He has desired it for His habitation; that He will abundantly bless her provision and satisfy her poor with bread (Psalm 132). Was not He Who now displayed this power of Jehovah the promised Son of David Whom Jehovah will set on His throne? Such was their conclusion. "This is truly the Prophet that is coming into the world." They thus bound up the Law,[118] Psalms and Prophets in their testimony to the Messiah; and so far they were quite right. But not so in their desire, which the Lord knew, to force Him to be king.[118a] For this would be in no way the kingdom of God but of man, nor of heaven but of earth. Not so: as He Himself taught afterwards, He was to go into a far country to receive for Himself a kingdom and to return. Not till then shall the kingdom of God appear.

Till then it is a question for us of righteousness and peace and joy in the Holy Ghost, and the kingdom is not in word but in power which is known to faith, not displayed yet. But it will not be always hidden as now, nor the domain of purely spiritual energy. Christ will come in His kingdom and reign till He has put all enemies under His feet, after asking from Jehovah, Who will give Him the heathen for His inheritance and the uttermost parts of the earth for His possession. It will be no question then, as now, of patiently working by the gospel, but of breaking the nations with a rod of iron and of dashing them in pieces like a potter's vessel {Psalm 2:8-9}.

Unbelief either antedates the kingdom, striving to set it up now by man's will, or abandons it for the delusion of human progress, without a thought of God's purpose to establish it by Christ the Second Man when the first is judged. Faith patiently waits for it meanwhile. So the Lord declined then and went up on high—this time Himself alone.[119] It was the figure of what is actually true. Owned as Prophet, He refuses to be man's king, and goes above to exercise His intercession, as He is now doing, the great Priest in the presence of God.

But the Lord vouchsafes another sign to the very people who soon after ask for a sign that they might see and believe (verse 30). So blind is man even when grace is multiplying these helps for those who discern it! Submission to God was the true want, not more signs.

Verses 16-21.

[Matthew 14:22-33; Mark 6:45-52.]

> "But when evening was come, His disciples went down unto the sea, and, having gone on board ship,[h] were crossing the sea unto Capernaum.[120] And darkness had already come on, and Jesus had not yet[i] come to them, and the sea was rough as a strong wind was blowing. Having rowed then about twenty-five or thirty stadia, they behold Jesus walking on the sea[120a] and coming near the ship, and they were affrighted. But He saith to them, It is I: be not afraid. They were willing therefore to receive Him into the ship, and immediately the ship was at the land whither they were going" (verses 16-21).

How striking the contrast with another storm on the same lake, where the waves beat into the ship so that it was now full, and He was on board, but asleep, and the disciples awoke Him with the selfish and unbelieving cry, Master, carest Thou not that we perish? And He arose and rebuked the wind and said to the sea, Peace, and both obeyed the Creator of all, Whom man alone despised because His love made Him the servant of all to God's glory.

Here it is the picture of the Lord's people while Himself is on high, exposed to the storms which the enemy knows how to excite, and after much toil making little progress. So it will be also for those who follow us at the end of the age. They will experience untold trials of the sharpest kind with scanty comfort or even intelligence, save as compared with "the wicked," who shall not understand, least of all (we may perhaps add) in that day. Darkness will have already set in; but in the midst of their increasing troubles Jesus will appear, though they will not even then be delivered from their fears, for the glorious light will rather augment them, till they hear His voice and know that He is indeed their Saviour, long absent, now come back. Received into the ship, He causes it to reach immediately the desired haven. So it will be with the righteous remnant by and by. Whether for them or for ourselves, all turns on Christ; and this it is the peculiar office of our Gospel to illustrate.

Matthew, who alone specifically names the Church as taking the place now of the disowned people after the rejection of the Messiah, alone shows us Peter quitting the ship to walk over the water toward Jesus, to walk where nothing but faith could sustain, and where, therefore, we see him soon sinking through unbelief, as the Church has done still more deplorably: but the Lord, faithful in His care, keeps spite of all. It is only when the ship is entered (the Jewish position properly) that the wind ceases, and He is welcomed with all His beneficent power in the land whence once they had besought Him to depart out of their borders (Matthew 14).

Our Evangelist, however, does not trace these earthly blessings which await "that day," but turns to the circumstances and questions which the Lord makes the occasion of the wonderful discourse that follows. He adheres to his task of unfolding the grace and truth which came by Jesus Christ.

Verses 22-51.

"On the morrow the crowd, that was standing on the other side of the sea, having seen that there was no other boat but one,ʲ and that Jesus went not with His disciples into the ship,ᵏ but that His disciples went off alone (yetˡ (other) boatsᵐ came from Tiberias near the place where they ate the bread after the Lord had given thanks); when the crowd then saw that Jesus was not there nor His disciples, *they* went themselves on board the ships and came to Capernaum seeking for Jesus; and having found Him on the other side of the sea, they said to Him, Rabbi, when camest Thou hither?[121] Jesus answered them and said, Verily, verily, I say to you, Ye seek Me, not because ye saw signs, but because ye ate of the loaves and were filled. Work not for the food that perisheth, but for the foodⁿ that abideth unto life eternal which the Son of Man shall giveº you; for Him the Father sealed, (even) God. They said therefore to Him, What must we do that we may work the works of God? Jesus answered and said to them, This is the work of God that ye believe on Him Whom *He* sent" (verses 22-29).

The particulars related serve to show how the crowd was struck by the mysterious disappearance of the Lord. They knew that He had not accompanied the disciples in their ship, and that there was no other in which He could have crossed the lake when He must have left the mountain. They put forward their curiosity as to His mode of passage as a cover for their desire to profit, as they had done already, by His miraculous supply of their wants. The Lord in reply strips them of their disguise and confronts them with their selfishness. It was this which prompted their search after Him, not their interest in the signs which He had just wrought. He prefaces their exposure with the formula of unusual solemnity which He reserved for the enunciation of great truths. "Rabbi" (said they), "when camest Thou hither?" They had sought after Jesus; they had taken trouble to find Him; when found, they address Him with honour; but they manifest by their inquiry that it was not Himself, nor yet the signs which He had wrought, which attracted them. Faith was not in their hearts, but curiosity about the time and mode of His coming, and at the bottom a desire after present ease through Him. Was the Son of God here to gratify all this?

"Verily, verily, I say to you, Ye seek Me not because ye saw signs, but because ye ate and were filled." Here the Lord searches those who had been in quest of Him and searches them thoroughly, for a single act that looks fair may prove a character hollow and base. And He looked on and listened, and did not trust Himself to them because He knew all men, and needed none to testify of man, for Himself knew what was in man. To make Him a king in order to enjoy His promised earthly favours was nothing in His eyes—nay, called for His most grave detection of them to themselves. It was no question of the Messiah for Israel now, but of a Saviour for sinners. He was rejected as the Christ by those who ought most to have hailed Him with joy, but did not because His coming as He did made nothing of them and their religiousness—that is, of all they valued. And if this poor hungry crowd seemed to feel quite differently and wished to give Him the honour that was due, it was needful to demonstrate that they were not a whit better, but sought their own things, not God's glory in Him. He was really come, into a world of death over which judgment hung, that the poorest of sinners might feed on Him and live for ever: what did they think of or care for His love? They thought only of themselves in their way, just as their rulers and teachers in theirs. God was in none of their thoughts. High or low, they had no sense of their sins or ruin, no knowledge of God or His grace. A Messiah for temporal good was what they wanted, not a Jesus to save His people from their sins. But the Messiah as a divine Person could not but lay bare their alienation and distance from God; and thus He became increasingly odious till their hatred ended in His cross. This made plain the deep purpose of grace in sending Him into the world, not for Israel only, but, if now rejected by them, that we might live by Him and He be a propitiation for our sins.

Hence He adds, "Work not for the food that perisheth, but for the food that abideth unto life eternal, which the Son of Man shall give you; for Him the Father sealed, (even) God." It is no question of Messianic honour or blessing, but of what the Son of Man has to give; and as He gives the food that abides to life eternal, so man needs no less than this. It is as such that God the Father sealed Him. Toil will not suffice, nor any seeming sincerity. The humbled Messiah, the Son of Man, is no less God's object in sealing with the Holy Ghost than He is the Giver of the only food that abides to life everlasting; and nothing less can supply the need of lost man, be he Jew or Gentile.[122]

But the natural man does not receive the things of the Spirit of God, and he cannot know them, because they are spiritually discerned. Hence they misapply the Lord's exhortation, "Work not for the food that perisheth, but for the food that abideth unto life eternal," and infer their own capacity to do something acceptable to God. "They said therefore to Him, What should we do that we may work the works of God? Jesus answered and said to them, This is the work of God that ye believe on Him Whom *He* sent." Jesus is the object of faith. To believe on Him is the only work for a sinful man, if it is to be called a work. It is truly God's work, for man trusts it not, and refuses to confide in Him for eternal life. He would rather trust to his own wretched performance, or his own miserable experience—anything rather than to Jesus only. But God will not allow men to mix up self with Jesus, whether it be a fancied good self or a confessedly evil self. It is the Son of Man Whom the Father sealed, and Him only can He accept as the ground of the sinner's approach to God, Him only does He command as the food that abides to life eternal. For this He sent Him, not for man to make Him a king over a people with their sins unremoved, but to be the true Passover, and the only food that He warrants. Faith, however, is the sole way in which one can feed on Him; not of works, else it must be by the law, and thus be for Jews only. On the contrary; it is by faith that it might be according to grace, and thus be open to Gentile as freely as to Jew. Truly it is not the way of man, but the work of God, that we believe on Him Whom He sent.

The crowd was not so ignorant as not to know that the Lord claimed no insignificant place when He spoke of Himself as the Son of Man. The Psalms and the Prophets had spoken of such a One, and of His wide and exalted glory. Besides, apart and different from the Old Testament testimony, He had just told them that the Son of Man is the Giver of the food that abides unto eternal life, and that the Father, even God, sealed Him. "They said therefore to Him, What should we do that we may work the works of God? Jesus answered and said to them, This is the work of God, that ye believe on Him Whom He sent." Thus, as He spoke clearly, they manifest afresh the inveterate assumption of men in every state and age and country, that fallen man is capable of working the works of God. They ignore their own sin, His holiness and majesty. It was the way of Cain; and professing Christendom is as infected with it as Judaism or heathenism. It is the universal lie of man, till the Holy Spirit brings him to repentance. Then in the new life he feels and judges the old, and finds, as we see in Romans 7, that it is a question not of works but of what he is, and that there is no help for him but deliverance from all, and that in Christ by faith.

So the Lord here answers that the work of God is that they should believe on Him Whom He sent. Similarly the Apostle reasons in Romans 4, that if Abraham were justified by works, he would have had matter for boast, but not before God, from Whom it would detract. Scripture guards against any such misunderstanding, and says plainly that he believed God, which was reckoned to him as righteousness. The principle is thus evident: to him that works the reward is reckoned as not of grace, but of debt; while to him that does not work but believes on Him that justifies the ungodly, his faith is reckoned as righteousness. Man may be fully and securely blest, but it is only of grace, and so by faith, which gives the glory to God, as itself His gift. Faith is thus the work of God, and excludes man's working, not as its effect (for it produces works, and good works abundantly), but as antecedent to it or co-ordinate with it; and justly so, unless it would suit God to be partner with man, and this the believer would be the first to eschew. The Sent One of the Father is the object of faith.

It was at once felt that this was to claim more and more on God's part, although He refused to be made a king by man.

> "They said therefore to Him, What sign doest Thou then that we may see and believe Thee? What dost Thou work? Our fathers ate the manna in the wilderness, according as it is written, Bread out of heaven He gave them to eat. Jesus therefore said to them, Verily, verily, I say to you, Not Moses hath given[p] you the bread out of heaven, but My Father giveth you the True Bread out of heaven. For the Bread of God is He that descendeth out of heaven, and giveth life to the world" (verses 30-33).

Such is unbelief, ever dissatisfied with the admirably suited and magnificent signs of God, refusing perhaps to ask a sign when God offers, despising those He does give. They did not on this occasion say outright what they meant, but it seems to have been some such thought as this: "You ask us to believe; yet, after all, what was the miracle of the loaves to that of the manna? Give us food from heaven, as Moses did, for forty years; and then it will be time enough to speak of believing. Do a work to match his, if You cannot surpass it." The Lord answers that it was not Moses that had given the bread out of heaven, but His Father was giving them the True Bread out of heaven. The Bread of God is Jesus Himself, and these two great characteristics are His alone of all men; He comes down out of heaven, and He gives life to the world. He is a divine Person, yet a man here below, the Bread of God for every one that needs Him. It is no mere question of Israel in the desert: He gives life to the world. Less is not the truth, nor would it suit God.

> "They said therefore to Him, Lord, evermore give us this bread. And (or, Then)[q] Jesus said to them, I am the Bread of life; he that cometh to Me shall in nowise hunger, and he that believeth on Me

shall in nowise ever thirst. But I said to you, that ye have even seen Me, and do not believe" (verses 34-36).

This is their last effort to get what they sought—bread for this world, bread evermore, if not through them in any way, at least from Him. But unbelief is every way wrong. It is life that God is giving, and nothing less meets the true need of man; and this life is in Christ, not from Him. Apart from Him, given out of Him, and thus, so as to be independent of Him, it exists not. In Him was life; in Him only is life found. He is the Bread of life.[123] He is not here viewed as the Son of God, quickening whom He will, even as the Father. Here He is the Son of Man sealed, and the object of faith. "I am the Bread of life; he that cometh to Me shall in nowise hunger, and he that believeth on Me shall in nowise ever thirst." Alas! the crowd that saw Him had no faith in Him. Their privilege in seeing Him but added to their guilty unbelief; and, one must add, that now that the atoning work is done, and He is dead, risen, and glorified, and preached among Gentiles, it is a greater sin still where He is not believed on in the world. Yet men no more believe on Him than those who then followed Him, nor are their motives purer who profess and preach Him than theirs who would have crowned Him in Galilee.

The Lord proceeds to explain what was behind and above this in the words that follow.

> "All that the Father giveth Me shall come unto Me; and him that cometh unto Me I will in nowise cast out. For I am descended from[r] heaven not to do My will, but the will of Him that sent Me" (verses 37-38).

This then is the key, and it is twofold; and only in this largeness do we know the truth. If either side be taken to the exclusion of the other, the teaching is imperfect, and the consequences are apt to be error on this hand or on that. The reprobationist presses the first clause; the Arminian the second. Neither gives its due weight to the clause they respectively omit. The theologian who sees only the divine decrees pays little heed to the encouragement given by the Lord to the individual that comes unto Him. The advocate of what he calls free-will seeks to neutralise, if he does not absolutely ignore, the declaration that all the Father gives to Christ shall come unto Him; and no wonder, for it is an assertion of His sovereignty, which is inexplicable on his own theory. But the hard lines of reprobationism can as little admit cordially the Lord's assurance of a welcome to him that comes unto Him.

The purpose of the Father is as sure as the Son's reception of all that come to Him. The unbelief of Israel, favoured as they were, did not enfeeble the counsels of the Father: and the Son would not refuse the vilest or most hostile that came to Him. The reason given also is most touching. He was thoroughly the servant of God in this. Come to Him who might, He had come down from heaven to serve, not to do His own will. It was for the Father to choose and give. He had descended to serve, and would in nowise cast out even the man who had reviled Himself most. He was the Father's servant in salvation as in all else. The servant would not choose, but receive him that came to Him, as all the Father gives should come. He is come down from heaven to do the Father's will Who sent Him, not His own will.

This is carried out still more fully in verses 39-40, where the Lord says,

"And this is the will of Him Who sent Me, that of all which He hath given Me I should lose nothing, but should raise it up at the last day. For this is the will of My Father, that every one who beholdeth the Son, and believeth on Him, should have life eternal, and I will raise him up at the last day" (verses 39-40).

Thus, on the one hand, He Who sent Christ, and gave Him in His sovereign grace, fails in nothing of His will, for Christ loses nothing of it; on the other hand, Christ abides the test for every soul of man who receives life eternal in Him by faith alone; while in both cases, whether for the whole or for each individual, Christ raises up when man's day is ended for ever. All hope of present deliverance under the Messiah, which they fondly dreamt for men in the flesh or dead as they were, was vain. The Father's will, whether for His children as a whole or individually, shall stand: the whole that He has given to the Son shall be kept, and every believer in Him has life everlasting; as Christ's raising will prove for both when the last day comes.

The Lord is thus contrasting His glory as Messiah on the earth with His raising up the believer at the last day. Unbelief was even then using the former to overlook the latter; but the Lord here brings what was unseen and eternal into prominence, and this, because He had (to God's glory and in love) taken the place of a servant to accomplish purposes yet deeper. Had He sought His own will or His own name, His reign as Messiah would have been still nearer to Him than to the Jews. But no! He sought the glory and the will of His Father, and, as He gave Himself up to suffer, so He should lose nothing, but raise it up at the last day. To the individual all turns on beholding the Son and believing on Him: every one who does should have life eternal, and Christ should raise him up at the last day. Those who look for nothing but the reign of the Messiah inevitably perish. They acknowledge not their sins, they feel not for the violated majesty and holiness of God, they believe not on the Saviour, and, not so believing, have not life. He that believes knows Him to be more than the Messiah, even the Son of the Father; he knows that only in Him has he life eternal, and that he will have his portion with Christ in resurrection at the last day. It is no question of man or the world as they now are, but of Christ then.

This was peculiarly strange to the people of Judæa and Jerusalem, resting as they did in tradition, and so we see next,

> "The Jews therefore murmured about Him, because He said, I am the Bread that came down out of heaven. And they said, Is not this Jesus, the son of Joseph, whose father and mother we know? How then' doth He say, I am come down out of heaven?" (verses 41-42).

Thus they set the circumstances as they knew them (and they knew them ill) against the truth of Christ. It was judging according to appearances, and consequently unrighteous judgment. He was son of Mary—truly and properly man; else His work had not availed for man. He was not son of Joseph save legally; but this He was, in order that He should be Messiah according to the law. Had He been really son of Joseph, as of Mary, He had not been Son of God, or a divine Person; but this was the foundation of all, and without it the Incarnation were a falsehood, and the Atonement a nullity. He was really Son, the Only-begotten Son of the Father, Who deigned to become son of Mary, and by law consequently son of Joseph, who had espoused her (a point of all moment for His Messianic title, for Messiah He could not properly have been unless He were heir of Joseph's rights).[124] But as Son of God, the incarnate Word, He was the Bread which came down out of heaven: thus only could man feed on Him by faith and be blessed for ever.

> "Jesus[t] therefore[u] answered and said to them, Murmur not among yourselves. No one can come unto Me except the Father Who sent Me draw him, and I will raise him up at the last day. It is written in the prophets, And they shall be all taught of God [Isaiah 54:13]. Every one that heard[v] from the Father and learned cometh unto Me. Not that any one hath seen the Father, except He Who is of God, *He* hath seen the Father" (verses 43-46).

Unbelief can only destroy and trouble; it cannot give life or comfort. Man under Satan is the source of unbelief, which ever leads from Christ, not to Him. But as the Father sent Christ, so He draws the believer to Christ, Who raises him up at the last day. It is not man's worth or work or will, therefore, but the Father's grace, by which one comes to Christ. The whole blessing, in short, is of sovereign mercy, and so the prophets have written. All true teaching comes from God, and all are taught of God, Who never forgets what is due to Christ. "Every one that heard from the Father and learned" comes to Christ. Not that the Father has been seen by man. He is known in the Son. "He who is of God, He hath seen the Father"; it is Christ only Who has.

The Lord then solemnly reiterates,

"Verily, verily,[125] I say to you, He that believeth (on Me[w]) hath life eternal. I am the Bread of life" (verses 47-48).

In truth, as the promised One, He was always the object of faith, even as being the eternal Son He had ever quickened the believer. But now He was the Word made flesh; He was the Son of God, and this as man in the world, and, as rejected by Israel, He announces that He is the giver of life eternal. This is the grand point: not the kingdom merely by and by, but life eternal now in the Son and inseparable from Him, but in Him now a man.

Hence the Lord says, following this up,

"Your fathers ate the manna in the wilderness and died. This is the bread that cometh down out of heaven, that one may eat of it and not die. I am the Living Bread that came down out of heaven. If one shall have eaten of this[x] bread, he shall live for ever. Yea, and the bread that I will give is My flesh[y] for the life of the world" (verses 49-51).

Thus, if the Lord was typified by the manna, He went incomparably beyond its virtue. The fathers of the Jews ate the manna in the wilderness; but it could not ward off death, for they died like others. Christ is the bread that comes down out of heaven that a man may eat thereof and not die. Eternal life is in the Son of God, and none the less because He was then the Son of Man. Rather was the grace of God more manifest in Him thus; for, if He were a man, was it not for men to eat thereof and not die? He was the Living Bread that came down out of heaven. If one ate of this bread, he should live for ever.[126]

This, we shall see, involves another truth besides the Incarnation, even His death in atonement; for the bread that He would give is His flesh for the life of the world. Here He hints at what He would open out somewhat further—His atoning death. When His life is given, it is not for the life of Israel only, but of the world. The grace of God which was about to descend so low could not be circumscribed to the Jews alone. "God so loved the world that He gave His Only-begotten Son, that whosoever believeth in Him should not perish, but have life eternal." On this, however, He enlarges more fully afterwards. Did they strive against His words in unbelief? He puts forward the truth, so as still more to offend man's pride and opposition to God, but to feed and strengthen faith in His elect.

Verses 52-59.

Such words from our Lord, His flesh given for the life of the world, were startling enough to those who heard them, but statements yet plainer follow. He insists on the necessity of drinking His blood.

> "The Jews therefore contended among themselves, saying, How can *He* (οὗτος) give us His[z] flesh to eat? Jesus therefore said to them, Verily, verily, I say to you, Unless ye shall have eaten the flesh of the Son of Man and drunk His blood, ye have[aa] no life in yourselves. He that eateth My flesh and drinketh My blood hath life eternal; and I will raise him up at the last day; for My flesh is truly[bb] food, and My blood is truly[bb] drink. He that eateth My flesh and drinketh My blood abideth in Me and I in him. As the living Father sent Me, and I live by reason of the Father, he also that eateth Me, even he shall live by reason of Me. This is the

bread that came down out of heaven. Not as the[cc] fathers ate and died: he that eateth this bread shall live for ever. These things said He in (the) synagogue, as He taught in Capernaum" (verses 52-59).

Thus, as the Lord set forth Himself incarnate under the bread that came down out of heaven to be eaten in faith, so here we have His death under the figure of the flesh[dd] to be eaten, and the blood to be drunk. It is the life given up, the blood drunk as a separate thing, the most emphatic sign of death. Of this faith partakes and finds in it atonement and communion. Without it there is no life. It was the more important, as some professed to receive Him as the Christ but stumbled at His death. The Lord shows that such is not the faith of God's elect; for he who welcomed Him as come down from heaven would glory in His cross; and though none could anticipate His death, all who truly believe would rejoice, once it is made known, and its object and efficacy opened. Those who receive the Incarnation in faith do also with like faith receive His death; and these only have eternal life. For such as accept the former after a human sort are apt to cavil at the latter. Both are objects and tests of faith; and the more decisive of the two is His death.

It may be observed that, as there are two figures in the central part of the chapter, so under the last there are two forms of expression which we distinguish: the act of having eaten [φάγητε] His flesh and drunk [πίητε] His blood, as in verse 53; and the continuous eating [τρώγων] and drinking [πίνων], as in verse 54. This is of moment, as cutting off all occasion from such as either argue for or object against severing eternal life from its source. Scripture leaves no room for the thought. The believer has eternal life, but it is *in* the Son, not apart from Him. The believer eats His flesh and drinks His blood. He is not content that he ate so once: if thus content, can such a one be supposed to have life in him? Assuredly not. If his faith were real, he would be ever eating His flesh and drinking His blood; and he who so does has eternal life, and the Lord will raise him up at the last day. The love that came down from heaven is precious, and the heart receives Christ thus humbled thankfully, not doubting but desiring that it should be the truth. And if that love goes farther, even down to death itself, the death of the cross, the heart is enlarged and well-nigh overwhelmed; but it counts nothing too great, nothing too good, for the Son of God and Son of Man. It bows and blesses God for Christ's dying to accomplish redemption. For the same reason, if it has tasted that the Lord is thus gracious, it perseveres, it can never tire, it feeds on Him again and again. For it is felt that His flesh is truly meat, and His blood is truly drink.

Hence it is added, "he that eateth My flesh and drinketh My blood abideth in Me and I in him." This abiding in Christ and Christ in him is one of the characteristic privileges of the Christian in John. It is not merely security for the Christian, but Christ the home of the soul as it is of Christ. How unspeakable the nearness! And as the life of fellowship is thus blessed, so is the effect in motive and object which accompanies it. "As the living Father sent Me and I live by reason (or, on account) of the Father, he also that eateth Me, even he shall live by reason of Me." As the Father's will and glory were ever before the Lord here below, so is He Himself before the believer. Otherwise one lives to self or the world. "To me to live is Christ" [Philippians 1:21], said the apostle Paul; and this is proper Christian experience. When Christ is the motive, such is the result.

It is well known that many have laboured to prove that the eating the flesh and drinking the blood, on which last our Lord insists as distinct from eating the bread, means His supper. This is groundless, not merely because the Eucharist was not even instituted till long after, but far more because what is affirmed of eating the flesh and drinking the blood here is wholly irreconcilable with participation in the Lord's supper; and this both positively and negatively. For it would follow that the Lord lays down with His most impressive formula of truth, on the one hand the impossibility of life save for those who have so partaken; on the other the certainty of eternal life now and of blissful resurrection at the last day for him who habitually so partakes—yea, the highest privilege of Christianity necessarily attached to the constant celebration of it. Doctrine so absolute as this must be repudiated by all Romanists or Protestants save by such as are utterly blinded by superstition. But it is not a whit too strong when applied to, as it really was spoken of, feeding by faith on Christ's death.[127]

It is not correct to say that the same topic is continued before and after verse 51. There is eating both before and after; and it is conceded on all hands that eating "the bread that came down from heaven" is to be understood of faith. It is harsh in the extreme, therefore, to contend that eating the flesh and drinking the blood means something else than partaking by faith—that it is figurative in the one, and literal in the other. It is at least consistent that, as the eating in the former part of the discourse unquestionably means communion by faith, so it should continue in the latter part. The discourse in both parts clearly refers to what was literal—the eating of the bread miraculously provided for the multitude. But the doctrine, though vitally akin, is not the same in the two parts, for the Lord's incarnation is the topic and object of faith in the former, His death in the latter. It is the way of John on outward facts or miracles to hang some essential truth of Christ's Person or operation; and so it is here. He begins with Himself as the incarnate bread, more immediately answering to the divinely supplied loaves; He goes on, when unbelief cavilled, to bring out the truth of Himself dying, still more repulsive to nature, especially to a Jew.

Thus all hangs simply yet profoundly together. Christ lets the Jews know (for the discourse is to them, not to the disciples)[127a] that He had not come to be a king after the flesh, but to be fed on in humiliation—yea, also in death: the only food of eternal life issuing in resurrection at the last day, not in temporal power and present glory, as the people fondly hoped who wished to crown Him now. To bring in the Eucharist here is to import a foreign element which neither suits the scope of the chapter as a whole, nor a single section of the discourse. And it is the more absurd, when we see that another topic follows the main argument as its fitting conclusion, the ascension of the same Son of Man Whose incarnation and death had been previously presented as the food of faith, and this as a climax for faith when unbelief had stumbled first at His coming down from heaven and yet more at His death. As was said afterwards: "We have heard out of the law that Christ abideth for ever: and how sayest Thou, The Son of Man must be lifted up? Who is *this* Son of Man?" (John 12:34). "Doth this offend you?" said the Lord to the disciples when they too murmured. "What and if ye shall see the Son of Man ascend up where He was before?" It is not an institution which the Lord hints at establishing. Throughout it is Himself the object of faith as the Son of Man incarnate, dead, and ascended.

I am aware that a celebrated controversialist[128] strove to persuade people that the first part closes with verse 47. But this is to the last degree arbitrary. Verse 51 is the true transition where the bread is declared to be Christ's flesh which He should give for the life of the world. This, in answer to their incredulous query in verse 52, the Lord expands in verses 53-58. For the bread as such is still continued in verses 48-50, which ought not to be the case if we had really passed into the second part. The eating of His flesh and drinking of His blood begins properly with verse 53. This is plain and positive in the chapter; and, indeed, it is bold to state differently; but, if so, eating the bread pertains as clearly and certainly to the first part as eating the flesh and drinking the blood to the second. In fact, it is assumed from the beginning (verses 32-35), but definitely affirmed before the end (verses 48-50). Undoubtedly the language is stronger when the necessity of faith in His death is pressed in verse 53 and what follows. But this proves nothing more certainly than the exclusion of the Eucharist, except to such as can conceive our Lord's making His supper more momentous than His work and faith in it. That He would speak more strongly of the giving up of His life than of His coming down from heaven to become man, no Christian could doubt, as well as of the graver danger to man of despising His death, and of the deeper blessing for the believer of communion with it.

Nor, let me add, is it absolutely true that in the first part the Father alone is said to give, in the second the Son of Man; for in the beginning of the first part (verse 33) the Bread of God is said to be He that comes down from heaven and *gives life* to the world, not merely to be given. But so far as it is said, it entirely falls in with the real difference in these two parts. The Father gave the Son to be incarnate; the Son gives Himself to die, and consequently His flesh to be eaten and His blood to be drunk. Further, it is not true that the consequences stand in contrast; for as in the first part eternal life results with resurrection at the last day, so this is carefully repeated in the second part (verse 54).

It is true, as we may readily observe, that more is attached to one's eating His flesh and drinking His blood—namely, his dwelling in Christ and Christ in him (verse 56); but this is as certainly a result of faith in Christ's death as it is nowhere in Scripture attributed to the Eucharist. John 15, where Christ speaks of Himself, and 1 John 4:13-16, where the Apostle speaks of God, approach nearest; neither of these alludes to the Lord's supper, but one sets forth Christ as the only source of fruit-bearing by continual dependence on Him; the other predicates God's dwelling in him and his in God of every soul that confesses Jesus to be the Son of God. These, then, so far confirm the conviction that the Lord is, in John 6:56, describing the privilege enjoyed by him who feeds on His own death by faith. No doubt he that dwells in love dwells in God, and God in him; but all flows from a new life, which comes only through faith in Christ: for without faith it is impossible to please God. This, therefore, shows an advance, not a new and different theme, but the same Christ viewed not in His life but in His death, with its deepening consequences to the believer.[129]

Himself the life eternal which was with the Father before all worlds, He took flesh that He might not only show the Father and be the perfect pattern of obedience as man, but that He might die in grace for us and settle the question of sin for ever, glorifying God absolutely and at all cost in the cross. Except the corn of wheat (as He Himself taught us) fall into the ground and die, it abides alone; dying it brings forth much fruit. His death is not here regarded as an offering to God as elsewhere often, but the appropriation of it by the believer into his own being. Hence, what was comparatively vague in speaking of the bread given from above becomes most precise when He alludes to His death. For this was in the Father's purpose and the Son of Man's heart, not reigning over Israel now, but giving His flesh for the life of the world: for, Jew or Gentile, all are here seen as reprobate, lost, and dead. He only is life, yet this not in living but in dying for us, that we might have it in and with Him, the fruit of His redemption, life eternal as a present thing but only fully seen in resurrection power, already verified and seen in Him ascended up as man where He was before as God, by and by to be seen in us at the last day manifested with Him in glory.

Hence the believer is here said to eat His flesh and drink His blood, and this not once only, when we believed in Him and the efficacy of His death, but continuously taking in its depth and force, as death to the world and man's estate, estranged as they are from God. Drinking His blood gives the more emphasis to the expression of the full reception of His dying by the believer. Had He simply left the world as One ever a stranger to it, we had been left behind for ever, objects of the judgment of God. But, dying to it and for us by the grace of God, He gave us who believe what separated us to God as well as cleansed us from our sins. Had it been simply our death, it had been our judgment and no honour to God, but rather the triumph of the enemy. Blessed be God, it is of His death, and of our entrance by faith into His death in all its reality and value, that He here speaks. It is not His supper; but His supper points as the sign to Christ's death, and these verses speak of the same death. They, however, speak of the efficacious reality, not of its symbol, which, when confounded with the truth, becomes no better than an idolatrous vanity, and when most stript of truth even as a sign is then made openly an object of worship. So we see in Romanism, where the votaries are sentenced *not* to drink the blood. Christ is contained whole and entire, as they say, under the species of bread: so that all is there together, flesh and blood, soul and divinity; but if so, the blood is *not* shed, and the mass is to the Romanist who communicates a too true witness of the non-remission of his sins. Such is the showing of their own formal doctrine and most trusted theologians.

It may be added that, after the rich testimony to His death as the object of faith, which should follow with its consequences, the Lord seems to me in verse 57 to shut out all excuse for overlooking His intention. It was Himself, not a symbolic act, which He here meant, as should be plain from the words "he that eateth *Me*." Further, He unites the two parts of the discourse by the following verse which closes the part about His flesh and His blood by again using the figure of "the bread that came down out of heaven," and "he that eateth this bread shall live for ever": a declaration as true when applied to faith in Himself as it is false of the Eucharist, taken in whatever sense men please.

Verses 60-65.

The Lord had now in the synagogue at Capernaum concluded His discourse, the main topics of which were His incarnation and atonement, as the indispensable food of faith, let men despise them as they might; and let them cry up the manna or aught else, which had neither such a divine and heavenly source nor such an everlasting effect, but must leave men to die after all; for in Him, and none else, was life.

> "Many therefore of His disciples on having heard said, This word is hard: who can hear it? But Jesus, knowing in Himself that His disciples murmur concerning this, said to them, Doth this offend you? If then ye behold the Son of Man ascending where He was before? It is the Spirit that quickeneth: the flesh profiteth nothing. The words which I have spoken[ee] to you are spirit and are life; but there are some of you who do not believe. For Jesus knew from (the) beginning which were they that should believe not, and which was he that should betray Him. And He said, On this account have I said that no one can come unto Me unless it hath been given him from the[ff] Father" (verses 60-65).

A most serious form of unbelief now betrayed itself, not among those of Judæa or elsewhere only, but the disciples, many of whom murmur, stumbling at His words. If they found hard His descent from heaven or His dying, what if they beheld the Son of Man going up where He was before? It was implied in Psalms 8, 80, 110, as well as Daniel 7. But Jewish will had long turned only to Israel's hopes in their land, and liked not a higher aspect, any more than a lower. The cross and heaven were equally out of their field of vision. Hence the Lord here confronts them with His own ascension as a most unpalatable truth. Yet is it one which fitly follows His death, as it falls in with His coming down to be a man in incarnation. He is gone up a Saviour in righteousness, having glorified God to the uttermost about sin, as surely as He came down to serve in love. All hang together here, as, in fact, it is while He is thus ascended on high that faith feeds on Him in life and death here below.[130] But disciples murmuring at His words of humiliation He told of His exaltation, sad to say to still deeper offence. Had they been true, had they known and loved the truth, it had been their joy; but they valued the first man rather than the Second, and were more and more offended.

Such is the flesh even in disciples. It profits nothing. It is the Spirit that quickens, and this by and in Christ, never apart from Him, still less to His dishonour. Hence His words have a character essentially divine and divine efficacy; they are spirit and life, as He says Himself of what He had just spoken in His discourses, stumble as men might; and few words have been more disastrously perverted to this day, idolising the sign to the shame of Him Who was signified to have thus come and died in supreme love, Who blesses faith accordingly. But, alas! "there are some of you who do not believe." Not to believe is fatal to any, most inconsistent withal in a disciple. Christ must be all or nothing. If all, His words are to the believer no reproach but a delight, and have power all through—yea, increasingly as He is thereby better known. Jesus knew their unbelief, not by observation or experience, but from the first. He is God, and none the less because He became man; and this is our Evangelist's constant thesis. Yet did He distinguish between such as did not believe and him who should betray Him; but who ever gathered it save now from His own words? Who had ever seen grace in Him falter in His ways with all? How solemn is the patience of divine love! On the other hand, those who believed had no ground of boasting, for though they did cleave to Jesus, none could come unto Him, except it had been given to him from the Father. It was sovereign grace in God.

Verses 66-71.

> "From that (time) many of[gg] His disciples went away back and walked no more with Him. Jesus therefore said to the twelve,[131] Do ye also wish to go away? Simon Peter[hh] answered Him, Lord, to whom shall we go away? Thou hast words of life eternal; and we have believed and known that Thou art the Holy One[ii] of God. (Jesus)[jj] answered them, Did I not choose you the twelve? And one of you is a devil.[131a] Now He was speaking of Judas (son) of Simon Iscariot;[kk] for *he,* one[ll] of the twelve, was about to betray Him" (verses 66-71).

Thus the warnings of the Lord precipitate the departure of unbelievers, while they knit the faithful more closely to Himself, and bring out their sense of what He is to their souls.[132] The cause lay in their own will, which gave Satan power. Yet the Lord does not hesitate to let the twelve know that, while one confessed for all that He was the Holy One of God, one of themselves should betray Him. What a contrast with all but Himself, unless it be with such as have learned of Him! How different those who seek to draw the disciples after them! Still, His words would confirm His own, even all that were real. The more free, the more are they bound. He only is worthy, He is the Holy One of God.[133]

I am aware that a learned but self-confident German pronounces the "Holy One" not Johannean.[133a] But this was a rash and ignorant judgment. It is a title given to our Lord once in his first Epistle as here once in his Gospel. He is the only writer in the New Testament who ever uses it of the Lord in relation to the saints. It is therefore more characteristic of John than of any other Apostle. Mark and Luke tell us of evil spirits tremblingly owning Him thus. Well might they quail before the Holy One Who is destined to deal with them in judgment. How blessed to hear one saint confess for all their faith in Him in this very character, cleaving to Him and His words of eternal life with confidence! How gracious to hear another comforting the babes of God's family with the reflection that they had received unction from the Holy One and knew all things! Antichrists might go out from among those who bore Christ's name, but they were not of the family of God:[134] if they had been, they would surely have remained as Peter did here, as Judas[135] did not when the last crisis came. First or last, they went out that they might be made manifest that none are "of us"—of the family. For God's children the Holy One is the spring of every joy and of all peace, of repulsion for unbelievers, of terror for demons. The babes rebuke the pride of mere unbelieving human intelligence which denies the Father and the Son, yea, that Jesus is the Christ, and perishes away from Him Who alone has life and gives it to every believer. So it is in the Gospel as in the Epistle.

But we see here also the vast moment of walking with Him, of open identification with Him in this way before men as well as God, the danger and ruin of going away. Faith, however weighty, is not all: one has to walk with Him here below. Where else are words of life eternal? Without may be religion, philosophy, present ease, or honour and power. With Him are those who think of the Father's appreciation of the Son, and act for eternity.

Yet even the apostolate, as the Lord here shows, gives no sure ground to build on—nothing but Himself. So His most honoured servant lets the Corinthians (too enamoured of gifts) know, that he might preach to others, yet, if he kept not his body in subjection, himself must be a reprobate. [1 Corinthians 9:27.] The Son of Man, in life and death appropriated by faith, alone secures life eternal now and resurrection at the last day.

NOTES ON THE SIXTH CHAPTER

a [*Cf. Lectures Introductory to the Study of the Gospels*, pp. 454-456.]

b Without αὐτοῦ ℵABDKLSΛΠ, many cursives, and almost all the ancient versions; with it EFGHMUVΓΔ, etc.

c ℵABLΠ, six cursives, and most versions reject αὐτῶν.

d ℵD, etc., read εὐχαρίστησεν καὶ, "gave thanks and."

e It will be noticed that the vulgar text interpolates the disciples, τοῖς μαθηταῖς, οἱ δὲ μαθηταὶ, while the true text makes it only a question of the Lord. One may add too that ℵDΓ, nine cursive MSS., and other authorities have ἔδωκεν (eight others δέδωκεν), "gave," while ABLΔΛΠ, and most others give διέδωκεν, "distributed" [Edd.].

f Ὁ Ἰησοῦς, the reading of most MSS., is not in ℵBD and some other good authorities [as Syr^{sin}].

g πάλιν is supported by ℵABDKLΛ, many cursives, and some versions. It is omitted by EFGHMSUVΓΔ, more than one hundred cursives, besides versions.

h The article is not in ℵBLΔ, a few cursives, etc., but is in more than a dozen uncials, and most cursives.

i οὔπω is read by ℵBDL, some cursives, and most ancient versions.

j ℵ^cABL, some cursives, and excellent versions, support εἰ μὴ ἕν, but the common text, following at least a dozen uncials, most cursives, etc., has ἐκεῖνο εἰς ὅ ἐνέβησαν οἱ μαθηταὶ αὐτοῦ, "that one whereinto His disciples were entered."

k πλοῖον, ℵABDKLΘ^g, twenty-five cursives, etc.; πλοιάριον, "boat," eleven uncials, most cursives, etc.

l δὲ is omitted by BLΘ^g, etc. It is also a question between ἄλλα, "other," or ἀλλά, " but."

m πλοῖα, "ships," in a few MSS.

n The second τὴν βρῶσιν is omitted by ℵEFGH, etc.

o δίδωσιν, "doth give," is the reading of ℵD, etc. [Blass]; δώσει, "shall give," of ABEFGHKL, etc. [Syr^{sin}, followed by W. and H., Weiss].

p So the majority of uncials with ℵA [Weiss], etc. But BDL, etc., have ἔδωκεν, "gave" [Blass, as W. and H. (text)].

q The witnesses differ, some giving neither.

r ἀπὸ ABLT with cursives, ἐκ ℵDEΔ, etc.

s νῦν, "now" [W. and H., Weiss], is the reading of BCT, the Memph. Goth. and Arm. Syr.^{hiers.}, etc.; οὖν ℵADL and eleven other uncials, all known cursives (Æth. = οὖν νῦν), Theb., etc. Many versions [as Syr^{cu sin}; so Blass] omit both.

t Ἰησοῦς, omitted by most [so Blass], is read by ℵBLT, etc.

u οὖν, "therefore," is read by ℵAD and ten uncials more, most cursives, etc.; but omitted by BCKLTΠ, ten cursives, and several ancient versions [Blass simply, "He said to them"].

v The aorist participle has the preponderance of witnesses in age and number.

w ℵBLT, etc. [so Edd.], omit εἰς ἐμὲ, though given by ACDEΔ, etc., cursives, etc. [Syr^sin, "on God"].

x Instead of τούτου τοῦ, as given by BCLT and twelve other uncials, all cursives, and versions, τοῦ ἐμοῦ, "My," is read by ℵ, some old Latin copies, etc.

y So BCDLT, several cursives [33], ancient versions, and fathers [most Edd., and] so ℵ, etc., putting ἡ σάρξ μου ἐστὶν last [Tisch.]; but twelve inferior uncials [ΓΔΛΠ, etc.] and a mass of other authorities add ἥν ἐγὼ δώσω.

z BT (and the ancient versions apparently) add αὐτοῦ.

aa The Latins read *"habebitis"*, "ye shall have," contrary to all authority.

bb ἀληθὴς ℵ^cBCF^aKLTΠ, many cursives and versions [W. and H., Weiss]; ἀληθῶς ℵ and eleven other uncials, most cursives, etc. [Blass].

cc A dozen uncials and most cursives and versions [including Syr^sin] add ὑμῶν, which is not in ℵBCLT, etc.

dd Dean Alford's notions, that the flesh here is in His resurrection form only, and the world here all the creation form, as said to be held together in Colossians 1:17, are groundless in themselves and contrary to the context.

ee λελάληκα ℵBCDKLTUΠ, many cursives, and most ancient versions; but λαλῶ in the T.R. with ten uncials and most cursives [with Syr^sin].

ff T.R. adds μοῦ, with more than a dozen uncials, etc.

gg BGT, seven cursives, etc., read ἐκ, but the weight of authority is against it.

NOTES ON THE SIXTH CHAPTER

hh The *οὖν* of the T.R. is not in ℵBCGKLUΛΠ, many cursives, and the oldest versions.

ii So ℵBC^pmDL, etc., against the great majority of inferior authorities which support the received reading, *ὁ χριστὸς ὁ υἱός*, many also adding *τοῦ ζῶντος*. There are varieties in copies and versions which point to the most ancient reading, but mixed up with the later ones in different measures and forms. [Syr^sin, with several Old Latt., has "Christ, the Son of God." Syr^cu omits "Christ, " whilst Syr^pesch hier add "living" before "God."]

jj Many omit *ὁ Ἰησοῦς* [so Syr^sin].

kk The T.R. reads *Ἰσκ—ν*, with some good MSS.; but the best have *Ἰσκ—υ*.

ll *ὤν*, "being," is not read by BC^pmDL Syrr.^cu. [sin] et pesch. Æth. [Edd.]., but is found in the great majority.

THE SEVENTH CHAPTER.ᵃ

VERSES 1-13.

The Lord had thus propounded His humiliation and His death, with His ascension to heaven, completely setting aside the carnal expectations then prevalent as to His kingdom. He had done more than this; He had taught the absolute necessity of appropriating Himself, both incarnate and dying, for eternal life. He had pointed forward all hope to resurrection at the last day, however unintelligible to the Jews, and repulsive even to many of His disciples. They looked for present honour and glory through the Messiah; they could not bear death with Him, opening into resurrection life and glory.

"(And)ᵇ after these things Jesus walked in Galilee,[136] for He was unwilling to walk in Judæa, because the Jews[136a] were seeking to kill Him. Now the feast of the Jews, the Tabernacles, was near. His brethren therefore said unto Him, Remove hence, and go into Judæa, that Thy disciples too may behold Thy works which Thou doest; for no one doeth anything in secret, and seeketh himself to be in public. If Thou doest these things, show

Thyself to the world. For not even did His brethren believe on Him" (verses 1-5).

Thus we see the Lord in the despised place the True Light, not in the city of solemnities, where darkness reigned the more, because it was least suspected; and in Galilee He walks about on His errand of love. He does not wait for souls to seek Him; He seeks them, that, believing, they might have life in Him. Judæa He avoids, knowing that the people of that part of the country, identifying themselves with the murderous hatred of their rulers, were seeking to kill Him. He was unwilling, not (one need not say) afraid, to walk about there. He was subject to His Father's will in this. He must complete the work given Him to do. As He said to certain Pharisees who sought to move Him by naming Herod's desire to kill Him, "I cast out demons and accomplish healings to-day and to-morrow, and on the third day I am perfected (that is, reach the end of My course); but I must proceed to-day, and to-morrow, and the next (day), because it cannot be that a prophet perish out of Jerusalem" [Luke 13:32 *f.*]. He knew perfectly the end from the beginning. He feared not man. He goes up at the appointed moment to do and suffer all the will of God, as well as all from man and Satan.

The festival then at hand, the feast of Tabernacles, tests man afresh, or rather our Lord tests by means of it. Those attached to Him by natural kin, His brethren,[c] were impatient at His Galilean sojourn, at His separateness from the centre of religious life and honour. As the Passover closely connected itself with the truth of the last chapter, so the Tabernacles furnished the occasion for what the Lord brings out here. There the blood of the lamb, itself eaten by the Israelites, points to His death, let them hear or forbear. Here the gathering of the people to rejoice was after the harvest and the vintage, types of the various forms of divine judgment at the end of the age when Israel, at rest in the land, will remember their former days of pilgrimage. It was pre-eminently the season of triumph, which proclaimed the promises fulfilled.

But was it really so now? Because Jesus, the Messiah, was there, and working such works as He did, was the time come for the accomplishment of Israel's hopes? So His brethren thought, because they wished it for themselves, though they put forward His disciples, and their need of seeing His works, and this in Judæa. No thought had they of God, not the faintest conception that in the obscurity of Galilee Jesus was glorifying the Father, and manifesting the Father's name to those the Father gave Him. They betrayed their own condition, their ignorance of God, their lack of self-judgment, their unconsciousness not only of their own ruin, but of the world, their unbelief of Him Who deigned to be born of their family: Who He was, and what He had come to do, was in none of their thoughts. They reasoned from self, not from God, and were thus so much the more hopelessly wrong as it concerned the Lord. "No one," said they, "doeth anything in secret, and seeketh to be in public. If Thou doest these things, show Thyself to the world." It was what they would have done. They sought, and conceived that every wise man must seek, present glory. Had they never heard One Who taught even His disciples to do their alms and pray and fast in secret to their Father, Who will render accordingly? If they had, the truth and will of God certainly had left no impression. The real ground of the wish and words was in this, that, as the Evangelist solemnly adds, even His brethren did not believe on Him. Such is man, however nearly related, naturally.

> "Jesus therefore saith to them, My time is not yet come, but your time is always ready. The world cannot hate you; but Me it hateth, because I testify concerning it that its works are evil. Go ye up unto the[d] feast. I go not[e] up unto this feast, for My time is not yet fulfilled" (verses 6-8).

In no sense does flesh profit, and the friendship with the world is enmity with God, Satan taking advantage of both against man as well as God. Jesus abides in perfect dependence (to speak of this only). His movements were invariably in obedience. In everything it was a question to Him of the Father. His single eye saw that His time to show Himself to the world was, and could be, not yet. Death, as He had implied even before His Galilean ministry began (John 2:19-22), and is still more emphatically opened out in John 6, was before being displayed to the world. This will be in its due time; but here, as ever, the order is the sufferings that pertain to Christ, and the glories after these. First must He suffer many things and be rejected of this generation. Man's time, contrariwise, was always ready. They spoke as of the world, and the world heard them. They loved the world, and the things of the world; and the love of the Father was not in them, but, what they valued more, they were loved by the world as its own. Terrible position for His brethren, but not more terrible than true! How could the world hate those who so prized its honours? Jesus it did hate with a deadly hatred, because He bore witness about it that its works are evil; a testimony most of all galling to the religious world, to the men of Judæa and Jerusalem. Hence the Lord bids them go up to this feast, while He tells them that He goes not up, His time not yet being fulfilled.

The significance of this is the more marked by His action in contradistinction from theirs, and, as read above all, in the light of His subsequent testimony on the great day of the feast.

> "ᶠHaving said these things to them,ᵍ He abode in Galilee. But when His brethren had gone up, then He Himself also went up, not manifestly but as in secret. The Jews therefore sought Him at the feast, and said, Where is He? And there was much murmuring about Him among the crowds. Some said, He is good;¹³⁹ others said, No; but He deceiveth the crowd. No one, however, spoke openly about Him because of the fear of the Jews"⁽¹³⁹ᵃ⁾ (verses 9-13).

The seventh chapter of John has this point of view, for the truth taught is based on the sixth; it supposes the Lord not only in death but in ascension. There is a manifest break with the world, and flesh is treated as proved no longer capable of association or communion. It really never was; but now it takes its own way, and the Lord withdraws. His brethren go up to the feast of Tabernacles without Him; He does not go up, but abides in Galilee. Only after they had gone does He go, and then not manifestly, as they desired, but as in secret— more so than ever before. He is content to be, as it were, hidden: type of that which He really is now, and we with Him, as far as our life is concerned, hid in God.

This gives rise to questions and whispers about Him among the crowds, some speaking patronisingly, others with the utmost ill-will and contempt; but even so there was no discourse in public, or plainly. The leaders of Judæa kept men in fear.

That the Lord had a deeper purpose in view was soon apparent. He had refused to go with His brethren; He had affirmed that the fit moment for displaying Himself to the world was not come. But God had a present mission for His Son, and He goes to Jerusalem to fulfil it.

VERSES 14-36.

> "But now in the midst of the feast Jesus went up unto the temple and taught. The Jews therefore[h] wondered, saying, How knoweth this (man) letters, having not learned?[140] Jesus therefore[i] answered them and said, My doctrine is not Mine, but His that sent Me. If one desire to do His will, he shall know about the doctrine whether it is of God or I speak from Myself. He that speaketh from himself seeketh his own glory; but He that seeketh the glory of Him that sent Him—He is true, and no unrighteousness is in Him" (verses 14-18).

There was no secrecy now: Jesus was teaching in the temple. It was His actual work. Soon He would suffer in atonement. Now it was the time for giving out the truth, to the astonishment of those who lived in the region of law and ordinance, who could only ask how He could know since He had not learned. They knew Him not, they rose not above human sources. Jesus was quick and careful to vindicate His Father. What is learned from man man is proud of. His doctrine He would not allow to be His own in the sense of independence, any more than the derivation from human teaching, which they owned to be out of the question. It was not of man but of Him that sent Him. Was this a high claim and easily made? Any one of single eye would soon see its reality. Faith alone gives a single eye. Others speculate and err.

God guides and teaches him who desires to practise His will, as Christ gives the positive assurance that he shall know concerning the doctrine whether it is of God or whether He speaks from Himself. How comforting as well as surely verified! The Son was making known the Father; and God is faithful in this as in every other way. He Who counts every hair of our heads, and apart from Whom not a sparrow falls to the ground, cares for His children.

Every one that is of the truth hears the voice of Christ. Whatever their pretensions, all others are not of the truth: else they would know that His teaching is of God. Where we do not know, we must suspect ourselves, not blame God; if we really desired to do, we should soon learn God's will. Certainly He did not speak from Himself. Yet of all men He was most entitled. But if He is the true God, He is true man, and came to exalt His Father, not Himself. He had no private ends to serve. Lord of all, He became the servant of all—above all, of God. Self is what blinds the race, even the faithful, so far as it is allowed to act. He that speaks from himself seeks his own glory; but Jesus never did so—always served to the glory of Him that sent Him. There is, there can be, no solid guarantee of the truth where God's glory is not sought and secured. Christ in this was perfect; and so He here declares that He is true, and no unrighteousness is in Him. As self is what hinders the truth, so it is just to neither God nor man. Jesus is both true and righteous.

Further, when men boast, they are sure to be wrong, not only in other things, but most where they are haughtiest. Did the Jews pique themselves on the law of Moses? How vain to boast of that law which none of them practised! Yet so it was, as the Lord pressed on their consciences here. They reasoned, but what was their walk?

> "Hath not Moses given you the law? and none of you doeth the law. Why do ye seek to kill Me?" (verse 19).

Jesus is ever the touchstone. One might never have learnt their murderous malice but for Him Who brought God close and convicted them of sin. This they could not bear, and so sought to get rid of Him, in their zeal for the law violating it utterly, and in their dark rebelliousness rejecting Him Who gave it by Moses. But is it now uncommon to glory in the law and hate the truth?

Yet the people in general were not aware how far hatred was impelling the leaders, and had no suspicion that they were bent on the death of Jesus.

> "The crowd answered, Thou hast a demon: who seeketh to kill Thee? Jesus answered and said to them, One work I did, and ye all wonder because of this.[141] Moses hath given you circumcision (not that it is of Moses but of the fathers), and on a Sabbath ye circumcise a man. If a man receiveth circumcision on a Sabbath, that the law of Moses may not be broken, are ye angry at Me because I made a man entirely[141a] sound on a Sabbath?" (verses 20-23).

In their ignorance the crowd spoke with rash irreverence and violence against the Lord, Who stops not to notice it, but draws attention to the absurdity of their quarrelling as well as of wondering at one work of His, the cure of the infirm at Bethesda on the Sabbath. Yet it was a common matter of course to circumcise a male child on the eighth day spite of its being a Sabbath, and this in honour of the law of Moses, though, in fact, circumcision was rather of the fathers. The Lord closes His reproof with an exhortation which touches the root of their cavils,

> "Judge not according to sight, but judge the righteous judgment" (verse 24).

They had not brought in God, and were consequently wrong, not on the surface merely but altogether. If the readings (as in Tischendorf's text) be κρίνετε ... κρίνατε, the first warns against the evil habit in general, the second urges the righteous judgment they should follow on this occasion. It is clear that one wants divine guidance, if we are not to judge according to appearance; but that is what God is so willing to vouchsafe His children, not teaching only, but direction and judgment. Knowing all, He knows also how to communicate what is needed by His own.

The Lord's plain speaking surprised, if the multitude, not such as knew the enmity of the rulers.

> "Some therefore of those of Jerusalem said, Is not this He Whom they seek to kill? And, behold, He speaketh openly, and they say nothing to Him. Did the rulers indeed decide that this is the Christ?[142] Howbeit we know Him whence He is; but when the Christ cometh, no one knoweth whence He is.[143] Jesus therefore cried[144] in the temple, teaching and saying, Ye both know Me and ye know whence I am; and I have not come from Myself, but He that sent Me is true, Whom ye know not. I know Him, for I am from Him, and *He* hath sent Me" (verses 25-29).

THE SEVENTH CHAPTER

The men of Jerusalem, knowing too much of the rulers to accept their decisions absolutely, indulge in irony; but they, too, prove their ignorance like the rest. They did not know whence Jesus was, whilst they ought to have known where and when the Messiah was to be born. Isaiah 7 and Micah 5 taught much more.

Jesus in replying contrasts their assumed knowledge of Him and His origin with their positive ignorance of the Father Who sent Him. He assuredly knew the Father, as He was from Him and sent by Him. And the Father was not only truthful but true, as the Son could attest in all its force, not the Jews, who knew not the Father. This drew on Him the open desire to lay hold of Him with which He had charged them. How little man knows himself any more than God, as Jesus shows!

> "They sought therefore to seize Him, and none laid hand on Him, because His hour had not yet come. But many of the crowd believed on Him, and said, When the Christ cometh, will He do more signs than these[j] which this (man) did?"[j] (verses 30-31).[145]

Those who rejected the Lord for their tradition and will were only the more exasperated by the truth; but they were powerless till His hour came. God abides God, spite of man and Satan. His purpose stands, though the enemies betray and commit themselves; but even when they do their worst, they but fulfil the Scriptures they deny and the will of God they detest. Another effect also appears: "many of the crowd believed on Him." The truth might not enter conscience, and so the result be human; but at least it was felt and owned that from the Messiah none need expect more signs. Still all is vain

Godward but Christ and the faith that receives Himself from the Father that sent Him.

The religious leaders are disturbed at any impression made on the multitude, and show their fear as well as their enmity. They dislike the truth they did not themselves possess and would gladly get rid of Him Who told it out.

> "The Pharisees heard the crowd murmuring these things about Him, and the chief priests and the Pharisees[k] sent officials to seize Him. Then said Jesus,[l] Yet a little while am I with you, and I go unto Him that sent Me. Ye shall seek Me, and shall not find[m]; and where I am,[145a] ye cannot come" (verses 32-34).

The Lord speaks with a solemn calmness. All efforts to apprehend Him would be vain till the appointed moment; nor need they hurry. It was but a little while for Him to be with them: then He is going to His Father. So it is ever in this Gospel. It is no question only of the rejection of men nor of the Jews despising Him, though both were true and fully set out by the Synoptic Evangelists; but here the Spirit shows us One fully conscious of where He was going, and so speaking to all, if any by grace might believe and see God's glory in Him. Soon unbelief would seek and not find Him. What does the world know of the Father? Heaven is to it more dreary than the earth. "Where I am, ye cannot come"; nor would they if they could. Nothing is so repulsive to a sinner as the light, presence, and glory of God.

> "The Jews therefore said unto each other, Where is this (man) about to go that we shall not find Him? Is He about to go unto the dispersion among the Greeks and teach the Greeks? What is

this word which He said, Ye shall seek Me, and shall not find; and where I am, ye cannot come?" (verses 35-36).

It was blindness indeed; nor is any darkness so dense as that of unbelief. But it is striking that what the unbelieving pride of the Jew deemed incredible is what God has made true of Christ exalted to His right hand. It is not more certain that He went on high than that He came and preached peace to the Gentiles that were far off and peace to them that were nigh (Jews), giving both access by one Spirit to the Father {Ephesians 2:17-18}. The dispersed among the Greeks[n] are those that Peter shows to have found in Him the object of their faith, believing on Jesus in the Father's house as they believed on God; and Paul no less clearly shows that he is teaching the Greeks. To those that are called, both Jews and Greeks, Christ is God's power and God's wisdom— Christ crucified, let others count it an offence or foolishness {1 Corinthians 1:23-24}. But He is none the less the Lord of glory, which none of the princes of this age knew: had they known it, they would not have crucified Him {1 Corinthians 2:8}. And so it was that Scripture was verified, man humbled, and God glorified; even as those that dwelt in Jerusalem and their rulers, not knowing Him nor yet the voices of the prophets which are read every Sabbath, fulfilled them by their judgment of Him {Acts 13:27}. And now is God pleased to make known the riches of the glory of this mystery among the Gentiles, "which is Christ among you the hope of glory" {Colossians 1:27}. He is lost meanwhile to the Jew, who, seeking Him not in faith, cannot find Him nor come where He is; for He is in heaven and they given up more and more to an earthly mind, grovelling after filthy lucre.

Verses 37-52.

But the Faithful Witness speaks.

> "Now in the last, the great,[146] day of the feast Jesus stood[147] and cried, saying, If any one thirst, let him come unto Me° and drink. He that believeth on Me, even as the scripture said, Out of his belly shall flow rivers of living water.[148] But this said He of the Spirit, which they that believed[p] on Him were about to receive, for (the) Spirit[q] was not yet,[q] because Jesus was not yet glorified" (verses 37-39).

It is not the new birth, but the Holy Ghost in power of testimony, rather than of worship. Thus is it distinguished not merely from John 3 but also from chapter 4, even though He be given at the same time to be a fountain of living water springing up to life eternal within the believer, and rivers of living water flowing out, which suppose the soul already born afresh. It is not here, however, communion with the Father and the Son in the energy of the Spirit which goes upward in adoration; but the same Spirit going outward to refresh largely the weary and parched in the wilderness from the inmost affections of the believer. Both figures are strikingly true, but they are different, though enjoyed by the same individual. They are the characteristic power and privilege of the Christian, not only the divine life but this in the power of the Spirit going up to its source in praise, or flowing out actually in testimony to Christ in a dry and thirsty land. Here it is the glorified man Who is the object, as in chapter 4 the Son of God is the giver.

Even so there is the most careful guard against coming to the Lord merely for teaching as a scholar or for material as a teacher: both in divine things attitudes of peril to the soul. "If any one *thirst*, let him come unto Me and *drink*." It is the heart met in its own need, not men invited to draw for others, but to drink for themselves; and thus it is they safely and best learn so as to teach others also. "Out of his belly shall flow rivers of living water." Such is the general testimony of Old Testament scriptures; and so the Lord urges even more distinctly. But this follows not only the coming but the glorification of Jesus founded on His work. Only then could the streams flow thus abundantly from "the inward parts," truth being there already and God on His part perfectly glorified in the cross. The Holy Spirit could act freely and in power, on the owned ruin of the first man, to the glory of Him Who is at God's right hand and in those who are His for a little while in a dry and thirsty land where otherwise no water is. But now, to His praise Whom the Spirit is here to glorify, water is given, not alone the fountain to refresh within, but rivers to flow out. The Israelites never rose to this even in figure. They drank of water from the smitten rock; and after, when the rod of priestly power had budded, the rock was but to be spoken to in order to yield abundantly. But no Israelite, not even a Moses or an Aaron, could be the channel of living water, as every believer now; and this, let it be repeated, no premium on the Christian, but solely in witness of God's delight in Christ and appreciation of His work, wherein as He is, so are we in this world.

The feast, and the day of it so noted, are not without deep significance. It was not Pentecost as might be thought natural in view of the gift of the Spirit, but Tabernacles. Indeed, if the feast of Weeks was ever the epoch of any acts or discourses of our Lord in the fourth Gospel, it is carefully kept out of sight; and this because it falls within the province of Paul, rather than of John, whose characteristic truth is the revelation of God and of the Father in the man Christ Jesus on earth, not the Head of the body on high. It is not therefore the Spirit baptizing into one body which is here treated, but power of testimony, and this from the most intimate enjoyment of the soul, through that Spirit Who comes from Jesus glorified.

We are not in heaven yet, but passing through the wilderness. The day of glory is not come; but He Who died in atonement is in glory, and thence sends down the Spirit on us who are here that we may have a divine association with Him there. What could give such force to testimony? There is more than the brightest hope; for the Spirit is a present link with Him Who is on high; yet is there all the power of hope bearing us onward and above surrounding circumstances. For the glory itself does not yet appear, though He Who will introduce it is already in it, its centre and in its highest sphere. His hour will come to show Himself to the world. Meanwhile we are in the secret of His exaltation and waiting for His display; while we have the Holy Ghost sent down by Him from that glory which He gives us to know and so much the more to feel the dreary desert through which we pass. This is not our rest; it is polluted; and here we have no continuing city, but we seek the one to come {Hebrews 13:14}. But we are awaiting, not righteousness nor the Spirit of glory, but through the Spirit by faith the hope of righteousness (that is, the glory of God) {Galatians 5:5}. And He Who is not only in the glory, the Head and Heir of all things, but will shortly come to bring us like Himself there, gives us the Spirit as rivers of living water to fill us inwardly and to flow abroad, let the wilderness be ever so parched.

I do not know a stronger expression of the intimacy of the Spirit's indwelling in us as contrasted with His working of old even though by saints. But here there is supposed such a deep intermingling with the inner man's affections and thoughts as is eminently characteristic of the Christian's possession of the Spirit, and the more remarkably because it is in view of a rich outflow of testimony to Christ on high. Hence there could be no such privilege till Jesus was glorified consequent on His glorifying of God morally by the death of the cross.

The phraseology of verse 39, though at first it may sound strange, is strictly accurate and suitable. The Spirit is beyond doubt a person, but He is viewed here as the characterising fact of a state not yet in being. Hence it is πνεῦμα without the article. Again it is ἦν, not ἐγένετο. He never began to exist, for His being was Divine and eternal. But it was not yet a fact for man on earth. At Pentecost He was sent down from heaven. Compare Acts 19, where the question was, Did ye receive the Holy Spirit when ye believed? and the answer is, We did not even hear if the Holy Spirit was (*literally*, is). The meaning is not at all as to His existence but His baptism, of which John the Baptist had testified to his disciples.[149]

We have had, then, the Lord's anticipative declaration of the power of the Spirit that the believer was about to receive, which he did receive at Pentecost and thenceforward: not the quickening of the unbeliever; nor yet power rising up in worship, but flowing forth abundantly from the inner man in testimony, both eminently characteristic of Christianity. How painful that Christendom should now, and for ages, show itself incredulous and hostile! But thus it is that God's warnings must be verified in every tittle. In man's hands each dispensation makes manifest nothing so much as faithlessness to its own special privileges and responsibility. Thus Israel not only rebelled against the law but renounced Jehovah for heathen vanities, the returned even rejecting their own Messiah. Is the Spirit now sent down and present since Jesus was glorified? Christendom, since the apostolic days, ran greedily after law and forms, reinstating thus the first man, to the denial of the cross on earth and of the Second Man in heaven about to come again. It opposes itself to no truth so expressly as that to which it is called above all to testify in word and deed.

The words of our Lord made a certain impression;[150] but all is in vain unless conscience be reached before God.

> "(Some)[r] of the crowd, therefore, when they heard these sayings,[s] said: This is truly the Prophet; others said, This is the Christ; others[t] said, Doth the Christ then come out of Galilee? Did not the scripture say that the Christ cometh of the seed of David, and from Bethlehem, the village where David was? A division therefore took place in the crowd on account of Him; and some of them wished to seize Him, but none laid his hands on Him" (verses 40-44).

Men do not only join what God separates, but separate what God joins. Some called Him the Prophet, others the Christ, as we have seen from the beginning of this Gospel: a distinction then prevalent but unfounded. The objections which lack of knowledge makes expose an ignorance which the least conscientious inquiry must have dispelled. With faith too there may be, and often is, want of light; but, spite of obstacles, it holds on to what it discerns to be of God, instead of being stumbled by a difficulty which further knowledge would have shown to be unreal. Bartimæus, when he heard that Jesus of Nazareth was at hand, did not fail to cry, "Son of David, have mercy on me"; and his faith reaped the blessing immediately. None the less was He the Messiah from Bethlehem,[151] and of David's line, because He was the despised prophet of Galilee. But unbelief is blind to His glory, and finds but an occasion of division[152] in the only centre of union. Yet, whatever the hostility of men, they could not take Him till the hour was come, little as they thought it, for God to accomplish the reconciliation in His cross.

There were darker traits, however, in the religious leaders than in the crowd; and this the Spirit next brings before us.

> "The officials therefore came unto the chief priests[153] and Pharisees, and these said to them, Why did ye not bring Him? The officials answered, Never man so spake as this man.[u] The Pharisees therefore[v] answered them, Are ye also deceived? Did any one of the rulers believe on Him, or of the Pharisees? But this crowd that knoweth not the law, they are accursed" (verses 45-49).

Here conscience answered to the words of the Lord in such a manner at least as to draw out before their masters an involuntary confession of the power with which He spoke. It was not as the scribes. But the Pharisees, with invincible hardness, retort on their weakness, challenge them to produce any of the rulers or of the Pharisees that believed, and betray their contempt for the mass of their countrymen. Boasting in law, they by transgression of the law and far worse were then dishonouring God. But God brings forward an unexpected, even if feeble, witness from among themselves, not only a Pharisee but a ruler.

> "Nicodemus[w] saith unto them, being one of them, Doth our law judge the man, unless it have first heard from him, and know what he doeth? They answered and said to him, Art thou also of Galilee? Search and see that no prophet ariseth[x] out of Galilee" (verses 50-52).

Unable to resist the righteous requirement of their own law, they proved that their insubjection had a deeper root by their haughty contempt, not now of the ignorant rabble, but of not the least of their own chiefs; and, as usual, they manifest that men are never so sure to err as when most confident in an arm of flesh. Indeed, it is the fatality of tradition-mongers to be always astray, whether in Judaism or in Christendom. Scripture alone is reliable; and those who profess to be ruled by Scripture as interpreted by tradition will be found, like all who serve two masters, to hold to tradition and its uncertainty, and to despise Scripture spite of its divine authority, with a blindness to their own state which is truly pitiable, though not less censurable also. Thus Eusebius of Cæsarea, though by no means the least able or the most superstitious of the Fathers, makes the grossest mistakes in reporting ecclesiastical facts from the Acts of the Apostles, or elsewhere.

So here the Pharisees assume that no prophet arises out of Galilee. They were wrong in every possible way. Were they prophets to speak for God at that time? Had they never heard of Jonah or Nahum? The greatest of the prophets who wrote not—the mysterious Tishbite—who had arisen, and will yet again arise, was of Gilead, and so even more severed than Galilee from the seat of religious pride, being on the east of the Jordan. But the truth is, that the One their soul abhorred, on Whom the poor of the flock waited, had come forth out of Bethlehem-Ephratah, Whose goings forth are from of old, from the days of eternity [Micah 5:2]. Of Him they were profoundly ignorant, though Law and Prophets everywhere testified to Him; but the pillar of the cloud which encompassed Him gave no light to the proud men of Jerusalem. Their darkness comprehended not the True Light.

NOTES ON THE SEVENTH CHAPTER

a [Cf. *Lectures Introductory to the Study of the Gospels*, pp. 456-460.]

b καί is read by most uncials and cursives, but not ℵ^{pm} D, etc.

c ["*His brethren* were sons of Mary after His own birth. Of course, we can understand that Romanists have been anxious to make out that they were sons of Joseph, and not of Mary; but they were sons of Mary and of Joseph. They would like to make it out, sons of a former marriage of Joseph. We do not know anything of a former marriage, nor do they. We do know that Scripture is quite plain."—From *Lectures on Jude*.][137]

d ταύτην is added here in T.R., in the ℵ^{pm} and eleven other uncials and many ancient versions [as Syr^{sin}], but not in B and some of the best. It was probably taken from the next clause.

e οὐκ ℵDKMΠ and the most ancient versions [including Syrr.] and fathers [Epiphanius, Chrysostom, Cyril]; οὔπω in BLT and eleven other uncials, etc. [Lachm.,

W. and H., Weiss; but Blass adopts οὐκ, as did the American Revisers for their text.]¹³⁸

f δὲ is added in many uncials.

g For αὐτὸς ℵDKLXΠ, etc., excellent authority gives αὐτοῖς, "to them." [So W. and H. and Weiss; but Blass accepts neither.]

h οὖν ℵBDLTX, some cursives, etc.; καὶ, as in T.R., most uncials cursives, and versions.

i T.R., with DLX and few cursives, etc., omits οὖν.

j ἐποίησεν, the common reading, is supported by ℵ^corr.BLT and the body of the uncials and cursives, save ℵ^pmD, 13, 69, and a few versions, which read ποιεῖ, "doeth." [So Blass. Syr^sin has "showeth."] The best witnesses omit τούτων, "these" also.

k There is high authority for the transposition here as compared with the T.R.

l There is little authority for adding αὐτοῖς, "to them," as in T.R.

m BTX with a few cursives and ancient versions [as Syr^sin] add με, which Lachmann edits here, and in verse 36 too.

n The late Dr. Alford says (*The Greek Testament, in loco*): "The διασπ. τ. Ἑλλ. must not be interpreted 'the Hellenistic Jews,' for the Ἕλληνες are always distinguished from the Jews; and this would convey hardly any meaning. The sense of διασπορὰ is—see reff. James, 1 Peter—'the country where Jews lay scattered,' as qualified by the succeeding genitive, where one occurs, as here. So here ἡ δ. τ. Ἑλ. means 'the dispersed in the Gentile world.' " This seems a singular mystification of plain Greek. The meaning unquestionably is the Jews dispersed among the Greeks as representative of Gentiles in general. The country is in no way expressed, but at most implied. The Dean further confused the meaning in his "Prolegomena" to 1 Peter (*The Greek Testament*, iv., third edition, p. 123) by saying that δ. "may well designate the engrafting of Gentile (!) converts into dispersed Israel."

o Tischendorf omits πρός με (or ἐμὲ), "unto Me," on the testimony of ℵ^{pm}D and a few other witnesses contrary to the great mass [as Syr^{sin}, and so the other Edd.].

p πιστεύοντες the vast majority, πιστεύσαντες BLT, etc. [Syr^{sin}].

q ἅγιον and δεδομένον are evident additions, contrary to the best authorities. [ℵKTΠ, etc., followed by most Edd., as Blass. The Vatican has the added words, which Weiss accepts.]

r πόλλοι is added by some eleven uncials and most cursives, etc., as in T.R., contrary to ℵBDLTX and some other of the most ancient authorities.

s τῶν λόγων ℵBDEGHKLMTUΓΔ^{pm}Π and many more witnesses, many of which give τούτων also, contrary to T.R., which on inferior authority has τὸν λ.

t T.R. adds δὲ with some cursives [and Syr^{sin}].

u Besides a difference in collocation, ℵ, etc., add λαλεῖ; others omit the clause, perhaps by ὁμοιοτέλευτον, or through love of brevity.

v ℵD, twelve cursives, etc., omit οὖν.

w T.R. adds ὁ ἐλθὼν νυκτὸς πρὸς αὐτόν, with EGHM SΓΔ, most cursives (probably from 19:39), some, as KUΔΠ, putting v. after π. αὐ., and others, as ℵ$^{corr.}$BLT, etc., omitting v. and adding πρότερον [W. and H.,

Weiss], and others giving both, as X and some cursives and ancient versions. Tischendorf omits the clause with ℵ^{pm}, etc. [so Blass].

x ἐγείρεται ℵBDKS^{mg}TΓΔΠ, many cursives, Latin and other ancient versions [as Syr^{sin}, and followed by Edd.]; ἐγήγερται, "is risen," T.R. following many uncials, cursives, etc.

THE EIGHTH CHAPTER [a]

CHAPTER 7:53 TO CHAPTER 8:11.

We are now arrived at a section of our Gospel, the external condition of which is to the reflecting mind a solemn evidence of human unbelief, here as daring as usually it appears to hesitate. No Evangelist has suffered as much in this way, not even Mark, whose close disappears from two of the most ancient manuscripts. But as we saw that the angel's visit to trouble the waters of Bethesda was unwelcome to not a few copyists of John 5, so here again incredulity indisposed some to reproduce the story of the adulteress. This is plain from some copies (as LΔ), which leave a blank—a fact wholly inexplicable, if the scribe had not been aware of a paragraph which he knew to exist, but for reasons of his own thought fit to omit. Others, again, transposed it to another place, as the cursives 1, 19, 20, 129, 135, 207, 215, 301, 347, 478, etc., to the end of the Gospel (and 225 after chapter 7:36), and even to another Evangelist, as 13, 69, 124, 346, and 556, though alien in tone from all but John, and suiting no place in John but here, where the mass of authority gives it. אA (probably) BC (probably) TX, with many cursives and ancient versions [as Syr^{sin pesch}], simply omit the passage; DF (defective) GHKUΓ (defective), more than 330 cursives, and many versions have it. It is marked by an asterisk, or obelus, in EMSΛΠ, etc. The variations of the copies which do give it are considerable. This brief view of the evidence may suffice for the general reader, as it is more than enough to prove the peculiarity of the case externally.

As regards the internal evidence, some have alleged against the passage its entire diversity from the style of the Gospel elsewhere; and this, not merely in words and idioms which John never uses, but in its whole cast and character, which is said to savour more of the Synoptic Gospels.

All this, however, fails to meet the positive weight of truth in the passage; and its fitness at this very point of the Gospel is utterly unaccountable in a forgery or a tradition. The Lord is displaying the true light in His Person, as contrasted with others who boasted in the law. We have seen their conscienceless discussion in the preceding chapter.[154]

> "And they went each to his home, but Jesus went to the mount of Olives" (7:53; 8:1).

Afar from man's uncertainty and contempt, the Son of God retired to enjoy the fellowship of the Father. Thence He returns for service.

> "And early in the morning He came again to the temple, and all the people were coming unto Him; and He sat down, and was teaching them" (verse 2).

The Lord's habit in this respect, recorded by Luke (21:37-38; 22:39), is a strange reason for discrediting

John's mention of this particular instance. Nor does any reason appear to question that it was not merely "the crowd" (ὄχλος), but "the people" in a large sense (λαὸς), which here flocked to the Lord's teaching in the temple.

> "And the scribes[155] and the Pharisees bring to Him a woman taken in adultery, and having set her in (the) midst, they say to Him, Teacher, this woman was taken in the very act of adultery. Now in the law Moses charged us to stone such:[156] Thou, therefore, what sayest Thou? But this they said proving Him, that they might have (whereof) to accuse Him. But Jesus stooped down, and with His finger was writing on the ground" (verses 3-6).

Such is man at his best estate when he sees and hears Jesus, but refuses the grace and truth which came by Him. They were not ignorant men, but learned in the Scriptures; they were not the crowd that knew not the law, but possessed of the highest reputation for religion. Nor could there be a question as to the guilt and degradation of the woman. Why they brought her, and not her paramour, does not appear. But her they brought in the hope, not only of perplexing, but of finding ground of accusation against, the Lord. It seemed to them a dilemma which allowed of no escape. Moses, said they, bade the Jews stone such as she. What did Jesus say? If He only confirmed the decree of the law, where was the grace so much boasted of? If He let her off, did He not evidently set Himself in opposition not only to Moses but to Jehovah? What profound iniquity theirs! No horror at sin, even of the darkest dye, but an unfeeling perversion of the exposed adulteress to entrap the Holy One of God.

But if the Lord wrote on the ground, it was in no way as if He heard them not. Rather was it to give them time to weigh their guilty question, and guiltier motive, while their hope of entrapping Him betrayed them more and more to commit themselves as He stooped to the ground.

> "And when they continued asking Him, He lifted Himself up and said to them, Let him that is without sin among you first cast the stone at her;[156a] and, again stooping down, He was writing on the ground. But they, having heard (it),[b] kept going out one by one, beginning from the elder ones until the last; and Jesus was left alone, and the woman standing in (the) midst" (verses 7-9).

Thus did the Lord show Himself the True Light which lightens every man. Occupied with the law in its condemnation of the adulteress, and, indeed, far more essaying to condemn the Lord Himself, their darkness is laid bare by these few solemn words. God judges sin, not gross sins, but all sin, be it what it may be; and the Judge of quick and dead was He Who thus searched them through and through. It was no question of the law for either now: they shrank abashed from the light, even though Jesus stooped down again, and was writing on the ground. Assuredly He heard their question, and discerned their iniquitous aim, veiled as it was; and now they heard Him, and cowered before His all-scathing words of light. Convicted by their consciences, but in no way repentant, they sought to flee, ashamed to see His face Who stooped once more and thus gave them time to retire, if they refused to bow with broken spirit and heartfelt confession.

THE EIGHTH CHAPTER

This, however, is not the object of the passage to illustrate, but the supremacy of divine light in Jesus, let Him be ever so lowly, and in presence of the proudest. And they were going off, one by one, beginning at the elder until the last, beginning at those who dreaded most their own exposure—an exposure which the youngest could not bear, only less ashamed of their fellows than of Jesus, Who had awakened the feeling. How awful the contrast with their own sweet singer, who, spite of his sins, could say by grace, "*Thou* art my hiding-place!" [Psalm 32:7]—hiding in God, not from Him, and having before him One Who could and would cover all his iniquities, and impute nothing. Vain, indeed, is our effort to cover our sins, or to escape from His presence. But unbelief trusts itself, not Him, and betrays the will to get away from His light, as it may for a little season, till judgment come. How will it be then? It will be theirs to stoop in shame and everlasting contempt, when evasion cannot be even for a moment, and all is fixed for ever.

Jesus then was left alone, as far as the tempting scribes and Pharisees were concerned, and the woman in the midst; for "all the people" appear to have been around, and He addresses them in a subsequent discourse, which seems to be founded on this very incident, as giving occasion to it (see verse 12 and following).

> "And Jesus lifting Himself up, and beholding no one but the woman, said to her, Woman, where are they, thine accusers? Did no one condemn thee? And she said, No one, Sir. And Jesus said to her, Neither do I condemn thee: go and sin no more" (verses 10-11).

It is the mistake of Augustine, as of others in modern no less than ancient times, that we have here "misera" in the presence of "Misericordia," which is much more true of the scene at the end of Luke 7.

Here the Lord acts as light, not only in the detection of His self-righteous and sinful adversaries, but throughout. There was no need, however, for His exposure of the woman caught in the very act of sin. Hence the ignorance of the scribes who left out the tale was as glaring as their impiety was without excuse. There is not the least semblance of levity in dealing with her evil. The Lord simply brings out the fact that her accusers retreat from the light which convicted their conscience, when the law had utterly failed to reach it; and as they could not condemn her, because they were sinners no less truly than herself, so He would not. It was not His work to deal with causes criminal any more than civil. But if grace and truth came by Him, He is none the less the True Light; and so He abides here. As we do not hear of repentance or faith in the woman, so we have no such words from Him as, "Thy sins are forgiven thee," "Thy faith hath saved thee," "Go in peace." He is the light still, and goes not beyond "Go and sin no more." By and by He will act as a king, and judge righteously; on their own showing, He speaks as a "teacher," not a magistrate. And it was a question of sin, but most unexpectedly of theirs as well as of hers, if they face the light of God.[157]

The words of our Lord are utterly lowered by such as infer that, either to the accusers or to the accused, He restrains sin to that offence against purity of which the woman was guilty. He means any and all sin as intolerable to God, Who is light, and in Whom is no darkness at all.[158]

The Eighth Chapter

The Lord continues His teaching of the people, but not without allusion to the incident which had just occurred, or rather to the character in which He had dealt with it. Nothing can be more evident than the True Light which was then shining and lightening every man. It is the more striking because the word "light" does not occur in that transaction; but the fact is thoroughly in harmony with what immediately follows.

Verses 12-20.

> "Again[159] therefore Jesus spoke to them, saying, I am the Light of the world: he that followeth Me shall in no wise walk in darkness, but shall have the light of life" (verse 12).

His rejection by the Jews always brings Him out in a still larger character of blessing and glory to others. In our Gospel, however, the Spirit speaks of what He is personally or independently of all circumstances and above all dispensations. He is "the Light of the world." His glory, His grace, could not be confined to Israel. He is come to deliver from Satan's power and to give the enjoyment of God and the Father. Hence, whatever be the darkness of men—and it was now profound among the Jews—"He that followeth Me shall in no wise walk in darkness, but shall have the light of life." The Christian is not only called out of darkness into God's wonderful light, but he becomes light in the Lord, a child of light, and he walks in the light, being brought to God Who is light; and in the light, as John says, we have fellowship one with another, for in Him is life as well as light; or, as He says here, His follower has "the light of life." He has Christ, Who is both.[159a]

So energetic a testimony rouses the pride and enmity of those who listened. They could not but feel that He spoke of a privilege and blessing which they did not enjoy.

> "The Pharisees therefore said to Him, Thou bearest witness of Thyself; Thy witness is not true" (verse 13).[160]

They turn His own words in chapter 5:31 against Himself, but most unfairly. For there He was speaking of testimony alone and human, such as vanity gives itself; here, as He proceeds to show, He has the very highest support in God Himself.

> "Jesus answered and said to them, Even though I bear witness of Myself, My witness is true; for I know whence I came, and where I go, (but)[c] ye know not whence I come or[d] where I go" (verse 14).

They were wholly ignorant of the Father as of the Son. They never thought of heaven. The Lord had the constant consciousness of the truth of His Person and mission; and His witness was inseparable from the Father's. As He says elsewhere, "I and My Father are one"—not more true in divine nature than in testimony to man. He never lost the sense for a moment whence He came and whither He was going away, whereas they had no true idea of either. They were in utter darkness, though the light was there shining in Him.[160a] How truly then He could say,

> "Ye judge according to the flesh, I judge no one. And if also I judge, My judgment is true,[e] because I am not alone, but I and the Father[f] that sent Me" (verses 15-16).

Self is the source and object of all the activity of the flesh, according to which the Jews were judging. Christ

THE EIGHTH CHAPTER

brought love as well as light into the world. He was judging none; He was serving all. This made Him intolerable to the self-complacent. Yet is He to be the Judge of all. In His resurrection God has given the pledge that He is to judge the world; even as in His own Person He is the fitting one to do so, being Son of Man as well as Son of God. "And if also I judge, My judgment is true, because I am not alone, but I and the Father that sent Me." It was an admitted principle that by the mouth of two or three witnesses every word should be established. To this the Lord here appeals,

> "And in your law too it is written that the witness of two men is true" (verse 17).[161]

How much more, then, the testimony of the Father and the Son!

> "I am He that testifieth concerning Myself, and the Father that sent Me testifieth concerning Me" (verse 18).

Of this, too, the Lord had spoken before in chapter 5, but they had not heard to receive it, only to despise Him.[161a]

> "They said to Him then, Where is Thy Father? Jesus answered, Ye know neither Me nor My Father. If ye had known Me, ye should have known My Father also" (verse 19).[162]

Such ignorance of the only true God and of Jesus Whom He sent is death, eternal death; and the more solemn, because it was said not to the heathen but to Jews who had the oracles of God. These things they were saying because they knew not the Father nor the Son; as the hour would come when they would think to render God service by killing Christ's disciples. Their sayings and doings betrayed their state of utter alienation from and ignorance of the Father. All that followed of persecution and hatred, whether for Christ or for the Church, was but the consequence.

> "These words He spoke in the treasury, teaching in the temple; and no one seized Him, because His hour was not yet come" (verse 20).[163]

Their malice was as manifest as it was deadly; and it was against the Father as much as the Son.

But, spite of will, they were powerless till the time was come. Then was He given up to their murderous iniquity; then, too, still deeper counsels were in accomplishment through the sacrifice of Himself. If on the one hand He was cut off and had nothing of His Messianic rights in the midst of the Jews in the land, He was on the other to suffer for sins, Just for the unjust, to bring all who believe to God, to be glorified on high, and to have a bride given Him associated with Himself in His supremacy over all things. But this would carry us into the apostle Paul's teaching. Let us pursue the line given to St. John, where we behold the Word become flesh, and His divine glory shining through the veil of humiliation, and in this chapter particularly, first as light convicting, then as the light of life possessed by His followers; but if His word were rejected, no less was He the Son Who alone can make free—yea, the I AM—let men avail themselves of His manhood to scorn and stone and crucify Him as they may.

The next discourse turns on our Lord's announcement of His departure—a truth of the most solemn import, especially for Israel responsible to receive Him as their Messiah.

THE EIGHTH CHAPTER

VERSES 21-30.

> "He[g] said therefore again to them, I go away, and ye shall seek Me and shall die in your sin:[h] where I go away, ye cannot come. The Jews therefore said, Will He kill Himself because He saith, Where I go away, ye cannot come? And He said to them, Ye are of the things beneath, I am of those above; ye are of this world, I am not of this world. I said therefore to you that ye shall die in your sins; for, unless ye believe that I am (He),[164] ye shall die in your sins" (verses 21-24).

The departure of Jesus after His coming is the overthrow of Judaism and the necessary condition of Christianity. We must not be surprised, then, if our Lord again and again recurs to it, to its moral associations and consequences, and, above all, to its bearing on Himself personally, ever the uppermost thought of our Evangelist. He was going, and they should seek Him and die in their sin. They sought amiss, and found Him not. They sought a Messiah that they might gratify their ambition and worldly lusts; and such is not the Messiah of God, Who is now found of those that sought Him not, after having spread out His hands all the day to a rebellious people that walked in a way anything but good, after their own thoughts. But God is not mocked, and he who sows to the flesh reaps corruption: if it be not public judgment, it is none the less the recompense of evil into the guilty bosom. "Ye shall die in your sin." They were rejecting Christ and cleaving to their own will and way. There was no fellowship between them and Him. "My soul loathed them, and their soul also abhorred Me" [Zechariah 11:8]. The issue would make it still more apparent: "Where I go away, ye cannot come." They could not follow Him.

The Lord was going to heaven, to His Father. Their treasure was not there, nor therefore their heart, as both were on His part. So, too, as grace attracts the heart of the believer to Christ, faith follows Him where He is; and He will come and bring us there in due time, that where He is there we may be also. Unbelief clings to self, to the earth, to present things; and so it was and is with the Jews: "Where I go away, ye cannot come." They were rejecting the only One Who could wean from earth or fit for heaven, meeting them in their sin that they might not die in it, but live through Him. But Him they would not have and are lost, and proved it by their utterly false estimate of Him and of themselves, present or future, as we see in what follows. "The Jews therefore said, Will He kill Himself because He saith, Where I go away, ye cannot come?" There was nothing too evil to impute to Him Whom they more and more hated.

But He tells them out more. "And He said to them, Ye are of the things beneath, I am of those above; ye are of this world, I am not of this world. I said therefore to you, that ye shall die in your sins." Here the Lord solemnly unveils the sources of things. To be of this world now is to be not merely of earth, but from beneath. Such is the Jew that rejects Jesus, Who is not of this world, but of the things above. Therefore should they die in their sins: their nature evil as their works, and they refusing the only light of life, how else could they end? "For, unless ye believe that I am (He), ye shall die in your sins." The truth shines out fully from a rejected Christ—not only His personal glory, but their subjection to Satan, who employs them to dishonour Him. But His rejection is their everlasting ruin. They die in their sins, and have as their judge Him Whom they refused to believe on for life eternal.

THE EIGHTH CHAPTER

> "They said therefore to Him, Who art Thou? Jesus said to them, Absolutely[i] that which I am also speaking to you" (verse 25).

Jesus is not merely the Way and the Life, but the Truth. He is, in the principle of His being, what also He speaks. A less expected answer could not be, nor one more withering to the thoughts of themselves and of Him. He alone of all men could say as much; yet was He the lowliest of men. His way and words were in perfect accord; and all expressed the mind of God. It is not merely that He does what He says, but He *is* thoroughly and essentially what also He sets out in speech. The truth is the reality of things spoken. We cannot know God but by Him; nor can we but by Him know man. Good and evil are displayed and detected only by Him, and He identifies Himself with His speech.

Such was the One the Jews were then rejecting. They have then and there lost the truth. Impossible to have the truth apart from Jesus, Who adds,

> "I have many things to speak and to judge concerning you; but He that sent Me is true, and I, what I heard from Him, speak these things unto the world" (verse 26).

He was a servant though Son, and uttered what the Father pleased as needed truth, not according to the affluence of what He had to say and judge respecting the Jews.

It is impossible to know the Father but by receiving the Son; and Him they rejected, as they did even to the cross.

> "They knew not that He was speaking to them of the Father. Then said Jesus (to them),[j] When ye

shall have lifted up the Son of Man, then ye shall know that I am[164] (He) and from Myself do nothing, but, even as the Father taught Me, these things I speak. And He that sent Me is with Me: He[k] left Me not alone, because the things pleasing to Him I do always" (verses 27-29).[165]

It is the actual truth presented by God which tests the soul. A former testimony, however true, does not provoke opposition in the same way. Often, indeed, unbelief avails itself of the past to strengthen its present antagonism to what God is doing. Thus the Jews avail themselves of the unity of God to deny the Son and the Father, for they knew not of Whom Jesus was speaking. His cross might not convince them divinely or win their heart to God; but it would convict them of deliberate and wilful rejection of the Messiah, and prove that what He spoke was spoken from the highest authority. As He was sent, so was He taught. The Father was with Him too, for Christ was doing always the things that pleased Him. If we know this in our measure, how much more fully and unwaveringly was it true of Him Who did not sin, neither was guile found in His mouth!

How solemn it is to weigh the force of "When ye shall have lifted up the Son of Man, then ye shall know that I am (He) and from Myself do nothing, but just as My Father taught Me, these things I speak"! For the Son of Man is alike His title as the rejected Messiah, and as the appointed Judge of living and dead. So He was crucified, and so returns for the kingdom of universal glory as in Psalm 8 and Daniel 7. How terrible to know this too late, when pride shuts out repentance to the acknowledgment of the truth!

THE EIGHTH CHAPTER

It is an encouraging fact that a time of unbelieving detraction may be used of God to work extensively in souls.

"While He was speaking these things, many believed on Him" (verse 30).

But faith, where divinely given, is inseparable from life, exercises itself in liberty, and is subject to the Son of God; where it is human, it soon wearies of His presence, and abandons Him Whom it never truly appreciated, for licence either of mind or of ways in rebellion against Him. Hence the urgency of the Lord's solemn appeal. Continuance in and with Him is of God.

VERSES 31-59.

"Jesus therefore said to the Jews that had believed Him, If ye abide in My word, ye are truly My disciples; and ye shall know the truth, and the truth shall make you free.[165a] They answered Him, We are Abraham's seed, and have never been in bondage to anyone: how sayest Thou, Ye shall become free? Jesus answered them, Verily, verily, I say to you, Every one that practiseth sin is a bondman of sin. Now the bondman abideth not in the house for ever; the son abideth for ever. If therefore the Son shall make you free, ye shall be free indeed. I know that ye are Abraham's seed, but ye seek to kill Me because My word maketh no way[166] in you. I speak what I have seen with My Father, and ye therefore practise what ye have seen[l] with your[m] father. They answered and said to Him, Our father is Abraham. Jesus saith to them, If ye are[n] Abraham's children, ye would practise the works of Abraham; but now ye seek to kill Me, a man[167] who hath spoken to you the truth which I heard from God: this Abraham did not practise. Ye practise the works of your father. They said (therefore)° to Him, We were not born of fornication; we have one father, God.[167a] Jesus said[p] to them, If God were your Father, ye would have loved Me, for I came forth from God and am come; for neither have I come of Myself, but He sent Me. Why do ye not know My speech? Because ye cannot hear My word. Ye are of your[q] father, the devil, and ye desire to practise the lusts of your father. He was a murderer from (the) beginning, and standeth[169] not in the truth, because there is no truth in him: whenever he speaketh the lie, he speaketh out of his own things, because he is a liar, and the father of it. But because I speak the truth, ye believe Me not. Which of you convinceth Me of sin? If[r] I speak truth, why do ye not believe Me? He that is of God heareth the words of God; for this cause ye hear (them) not, because ye are not of God" (verses 31-47).

To abide in His word, then, is the condition of being in truth Christ's disciple. Others may be interested greatly, but they soon grow weary, or turn ere long to other objects. Christ's disciple cleaves to His word, and finds fresh springs in what first attracted. His word proves itself thus divine, as it is faith which abides in it, and the truth is thus not only learned but known. Vagueness and uncertainty disappear, while the truth, instead of gendering bondage, like the law, makes the soul free, whatever its previous slavery. There is growth in the truth and liberty by it. Law deals with the corrupt and proud will of man to condemn it on God's part, as is right; the truth communicates the knowledge of

Himself as revealed in His word, and thus gives life and liberty: privileges unintelligible to the natural man, who hates the sovereign grace of God as much as he exalts and loves himself, while he despises and distrusts others. Man's only thought, therefore, of obtaining righteousness is through the law. They know not the virtue of the truth, and dread liberty as though it must end in licence; while at the same time they are proud of their own position, as if it were inalienable, and God were their servant, not they bound to be His. Hence the Jews answered Jesus, "We are Abraham's seed, and have never been in bondage to anyone: how sayest Thou, Ye shall become free?"

Far from this was the truth. Even outwardly, not to speak of the soul, the Jews were, and had long been, in servitude to the Gentiles. So Ezra (chapter 9) confessed at the evening sacrifice: "Since the days of our fathers we have been in great trespass to this day; and for our iniquities we, our kings, our priests, have been given into the hand of the kings of the lands, to the sword, and to captivity, and to spoil, and to confusion of face, as it is this day. And now for a little space there hath been favour from Jehovah our God, to leave us a remnant to escape, and to give us a nail in His holy place, that our God may lighten our eyes, and give us a little reviving in our bondage. For we are bondmen; yet our God has not forsaken us in our bondage, but has extended mercy unto us before the kings of Persia," {verses 7-9} etc. So, again, Nehemiah (chapter 9): "Yet many years didst Thou forbear with them, and testifiedst against them by Thy Spirit through Thy prophets; but they would not give ear: and Thou gavest them into the hand of the peoples of the lands. ... Behold, we are bondmen this day, and the land that Thou gavest unto our fathers to eat the fruit thereof and the good thereof, behold, we are bondmen in it. And it yieldeth much increase unto the kings whom Thou hast set over us because of our sins: and they have dominion over our bodies, and over our cattle, at their pleasure; and we are in great distress" {verses 30, 36-37}.

Thus men of conscience felt when they lay under conquerors milder far than the Romans who now ruled. It was not that the Jews to-day were lightened, but that they had grown so used to the yoke as to forget and deny it altogether. And if it were because of God's righteous government externally, much less did they estimate aright their true state before God, as the Lord Jesus was bringing it out now. Their haughty spirit was nettled at His word, which lay bare their thraldom to the enemy. "We are Abraham's seed, and have never been in bondage to anyone: how sayest Thou, Ye shall become free?" Jesus in His answer brought in the light of God, for eternity indeed, but also for the present. "Verily, verily, I say to you, Every one that practiseth sin is a bondman of sin." How true, solemn, and humiliating! No bondage so real, none so degrading, as that of sin: could they seriously deny it to be theirs? Truly unbelief blinds to moral state, and even to plain facts. Only grace delivers, and through the truth believed.

But the Lord intimates more. None under sin is entitled to speak of permanence. Such an one exists only on sufferance till judgment. Bondage there was none when God created and made according to His mind; nor will there be when He shall make all things new. The bondman, in every sense, belongs only to the transitory reign of sin and sorrow. So says the Lord: "Now the bondman abideth not in the house for ever." Another and contrasted relationship suits God's will; "the son abideth for ever." But there is infinitely more in Christ. He is not merely Son, but "*the* Son." He is the Son in His own right and title, as God and when man, in time and in eternity. He is therefore not "free" only, as all sons are, but such is His glory that He can and does make free in virtue of the grace which pertains to Him alone. Thus it is not only the truth which sets free, where law could only condemn, but the Son also gives and confirms the same character of liberty according to His own fulness. It is a question of what suits not them merely but Him. He could make free those who hear Him and abide in His word, and nothing else but free. It is worthy of Him to deliver from sin and Satan; and "if the Son shall make you free, ye shall be free indeed." He frees after a divine sort. He brings into His own character of relationship out of the bondage to sin, which the first man made our sad inheritance. The last Adam is a quickening spirit and a Deliverer. Let us stand fast in His liberty, and be not entangled again with any yoke of bondage, as the Apostle exhorts the Galatians against that misuse of the law, whatever its shape [Galatians 5:1].

To be Abraham's seed, as the Lord lets the Jews know, is a sorry safeguard. One might be of Abraham, and be the worst enemy of God. Such were the Jews then, who were seeking to kill Christ because His word had no hold in them. Every one acts according to his source; character follows it. So our Lord deigns to say, "I speak what I have seen with My Father; and ye therefore practise what ye have seen with your father." To be of Abraham does not save from Satan. To hear the Son, to believe on Him, is to derive one's nature from God and have life eternal. They boasted most of Abraham who were still in the darkness of unbelief and the enemy's power. Hence "they answered and said to Him, Our father is

Abraham. Jesus saith to them, If ye were Abraham's children, ye would practise the works of Abraham; but now ye seek to kill Me, a man Who hath spoken to you the truth which I heard from God: this Abraham did not practise. Ye practise the works of your father." It was allowed already that they were descended from the father of the faithful; but did they bear the family likeness? Was it not an aggravation of their evil that they stood in contrast with him from whom they vaunted themselves sprung? Abraham believed, and it was counted to him for righteousness. They believed not, but sought to kill the man, albeit the Son of God, Who spoke to them the truth which He heard from God the Father. Whose works were these? Certainly not those of Abraham, but of a very different father. They were corrupt and violent.

The Jews felt what was implied and at once take the highest ground. "They said therefore to Him, We were not born of fornication; we have one Father, God. Jesus said to them, If God were your Father, ye would have loved Me, for I came forth from God and am come; for neither have I come of Myself, but He sent Me. Why do ye not know My speech? Because ye cannot hear My word. Ye are of your father, the devil, and ye desire to practise the lusts of your father. He was a murderer from the beginning, and standeth not in the truth, because there is no truth in him: whenever he speaketh the lie, he speaketh out of his own things, because he is a liar, and the father of it. But because I speak the truth, ye believe Me not. Which of you convinceth Me of sin? If I speak truth, why do ye not believe Me? He that is of God heareth the words of God; for this cause ye hear (them) not, because ye are not of God."

THE EIGHTH CHAPTER

The case is thus closed as regards the Jews. They were of the devil beyond all doubt, as this solemn controversy proved. It is really the conviction of man as against Christ, in every land, tongue, age. He turns out no other when tested by the truth, by the Son; however circumstances differ, this is the issue, and it comes out worst where things look fairest. If there was a family on earth which might have seemed farthest removed from impurity, it was the Jews; if any could claim to have God as their father, they most of all. But Jesus is the touchstone; and they are thereby proved to be God's enemies, not His children; else they would have loved Him Who came out from God, and was then present in their midst, Who had not come of His own mere motion but at God's sending. He came and was sent in love beyond man's thought or measure; and they rose against Him in hatred, seeking to kill Him.

The Jews did not even know His speech {λαλιά}; such utter strangers were they to Him, and the God Who spoke by Him. The reason is most grave: they could not hear His word {λόγος}. It is through understanding the thought, the scope, the mind of the person speaking that one knows the phraseology; and not the inverse.[168] If the inner purpose is not received, the outer form is unknown. So it was with Jesus speaking to the Jews; so it is pre-eminently with the testimony in John's writings now. Men complain of mysticism in the expression, because they have no notion of the truth intended. The hindrance is in the blinding power of the devil, who is the source of their thoughts and feelings, as surely as he is the adversary of Christ. Men's judgments flow from their will and affections, and these are under the sway of His enemy. And as he pushes on men, especially those who are most of all responsible to bow to Christ as the

Jews then were, to practise the lusts of their father, so violence follows as naturally as falsehood. For Satan was a murderer from the beginning, and stands not in the truth, because there is no truth in him, the great personal antagonist of the Son.

Jesus alone of men is the Truth; He is not only God, but the One Who reveals God to man. In Him is no sin, nor did He sin, neither was guile found in His mouth.[170] He was the manifest opposite, in all respects, of the devil, who, whenever he speaks falsehood, speaks out of his own store, because he is a liar and the father of it. Jesus is the Truth, and makes it known to those who otherwise cannot know it. "But because I speak the truth, ye believe Me not." How awful, yet how just, God's judgment of such! For we are sure that the judgment of God is according to truth; and what can be the end of these things but death and judgment?

Finally, the Lord proceeds to challenge them, in order to lay bare their groundless malice. "Which of you convinceth Me of sin? If I speak truth, why do ye not believe Me? He that is of God heareth the words of God: for this cause ye hear them not, because ye are not of God." He was the Holy One, no less than the Truth, and surely both go together. And thus were they convicted of being, in word and deed, in thought and feeling, wholly alienated from, and rebellious against, God. They were not of God, save in haughty pretension, which only made their distance from Him, and opposition to Him, more glaring. Instead of convincing Christ of sin, they were themselves slaves of sin; instead of speaking truth, they rejected Him Who is the Truth; instead of hearing the words of God, they hated Him Who spoke them, because they were not of God but of the devil. Terrible picture, which the unerring light failed not to draw and leave, never to be effaced, of His adversaries! To be not of God is to be wholly without good, and left in evil, exposed to its consequences, according to the judgment of Him Who will not, cannot, change in His abhorrence of it. Such were and are the rejecters of Jesus.

There is nothing a man so reluctantly allows {*i.e.,* admits} as evil in himself; there is nothing he so much resents as another's saying evil of him, and leaving him no loophole of escape. So was it now with the Jews whom the Lord denied to be of God, as they heard not His words. Never had their self-complacency been thus disturbed before. The scorn of the heathen was as nothing compared with such a libel, which was severe in proportion to its self-evident truth. For the ground taken was indisputable. Who could doubt that he who is of God heareth the words of God? How solemn, then, to face the fact that One Who spoke as none ever did declared with holy calmness that therefore they did not hear, because they were not of God! Conscience might wince, but refused to bow. Will, ill-will, alone declared itself, save, indeed, that it was animated from beneath.

> "The Jews[s] answered and said to Him, Say we not well that Thou art a Samaritan, and hast a demon? Jesus answered, I have not a demon, but honour My Father, and ye dishonour Me. But I seek not My glory: there is One that seeketh and judgeth. Verily, verily, I say to you, If any one keep My word, death he shall in no wise behold for ever" (verses 48-51).

Thenceforth the Jews, unable to refute, and unwilling to confess, the truth, betake themselves to insolent retort and railing. They justify and openly repeat their application of "Samaritan" to Him; for what could more prove enmity in their eyes than to refuse their claim to be pre-eminently God's people? If He declared them to be of their father, the devil, they did not scruple to rejoin that He had a demon. He was, they dared to imply, outside the Israel of God and the God of Israel. Yet was He the true Israel and the true God.

No Christian, then, has ever suffered worse in this way of dishonour than Christ. The disciple is not above his Lord, and can expect no exemption. And none are so prone to reproach others falsely as those who are themselves really slaves of the enemy. But let us learn of Him Who was meek and lowly of heart, and now calmly repudiates their taxing Him with a demon. Not so, but He was honouring His Father, they dishonouring Him. Yet was there no personal resentment as on his part who courts his own honour now, or seeks to injure when he can such as insult him.[171] "But I seek not My glory: there is One that seeketh and judgeth." He leaves all with His Father, Himself content to serve, able and ready to save. "Verily, verily, I say to you, If any one"—let him be the vilest of His foes—"keep My word, death he shall in no wise behold for ever." Such an utterance was worthy of all solemnity on His part, of all acceptation on theirs.

> "The Jews therefore[t] said to Him, Now we know [learn, perceive] that Thou hast a demon. Abraham died, and the prophets; and Thou sayest, If anyone keep My word, he shall never taste of death. Art Thou greater than our father Abraham who died, and the prophets died? Whom makest Thou Thyself? Jesus answered, If I glorify Myself, My glory is nothing; it is My Father that glorifieth Me, of Whom ye say, He is our[u] God, and ye have not known Him, but I know Him; and if I should say, I know Him not, I shall be like you a liar; but

I know Him, and keep His word. Abraham your father exulted to see My day, and he saw and rejoiced. The Jews therefore said to Him, Thou art not yet fifty years old,¹⁷² and hast Thou seen Abraham?ᵛ Jesus said to them, Verily, verily, I say to you, Before Abraham was, I am. They took up therefore stones to cast at Him; but Jesus hid Himself, and went out from the temple,ʷ going through the midst of them, and so passed by" (verses 52-59).

Unbelief reasons from its own thoughts, and is never so confident as when completely wrong. So the Jews, misinterpreting the faithful sayings of the Lord Jesus, avail themselves of it triumphantly as the proof that Abraham and the prophets could not be of His school; for they, beyond controversy, were already dead. He must be possessed, therefore, to speak thus. Did He set up to be greater than they? Whom did He make Himself? Alas! it is here that man, Jew or Gentile, is blind. Jesus made Himself nothing, emptied Himself, taking a bondman's form, becoming a man though being God over all blessed for ever, and as the humbled man exalted by God the Father. If the eye be single, the whole body is full of light. So it was with Him Who came here and became man to do the will of God, in Whom He could and did confide to glorify Him. His path was one of unbroken fellowship as of obedience. He never sought His own glory, He always kept His Father's word; He could say, from first to last, I know Him; in all leaving us an example that we should follow His steps. We may learn of Him that, if it be the grossest presumption for men of the world to affect the knowledge of God the Father, it is the greatest wrong in a child of His to deny it. "If I should say, I know Him not, I shall be like you a liar." But He that claims to know Him keeps His word, and herein gives the testimony of reality along with that claim. The Spirit of truth is the Holy Spirit, and where He communicates the truth, He also effectually works in holiness according to God's will.

But the Lord did not hesitate to meet their challenge of Abraham, and lets the Jews know that the father of the faithful exulted to see His day (as ever, I presume, His appearing in glory),[x] and saw and rejoiced. It was, of course, by faith, like the not seeing or tasting death in the context; but the Jews took all in a mere physical way, and on their arguing from His comparative youth to the denial of Abraham's seeing Him, the still deeper utterance comes forth, "Verily, verily, I say to you, Before Abraham was, I am," the ever-subsisting One.[173]

It was said: the good confession before the Jews, the truth of truths, the infinite mystery of His Person, which to know is to know the true God and eternal life, as He is both. Such He was, such He is, from everlasting to everlasting. Incarnation in no way impeached it, but rather gave occasion for its revelation in man to men. He Who was God is become man, and as He cannot cease to be God, so He will not cease to be man. He is the Eternal, though also a man, and has taken manhood into union with Himself, the Son, the Word, not with God only, but God too. "Before Abraham was (γενέσθαι), I am" (εἰμί). Abraham came into being. Jesus is God, and God *is*. "I am" is the expression of eternal subsistence, of Godhead. He could as truly have said, Before Adam was, I am; but the question was about Abraham, and with that calm dignity which never goes beyond the needed truth, He asserts it, and no more; but what He asserts could not be true, were He not the ever present and unchanging One, the I AM before Adam, angels, and all things; as, indeed, He it was Who created them. All things were made by Him, and without Him was not anything made that has been made.

Not to know Him is the fatal ignorance of the world; to deny Him, the unbelieving lie of the Jews, as of all who assume to know God independently, and to the exclusion, of His divine glory. And it is death while they live, eternal death, soon to be the second death, not extinction but punishment in the lake of fire. Meanwhile unbelief can with impunity show its spite. "Then took they up stones to cast at Him; but Jesus hid Himself, and went out of the temple." The remaining words are probably taken from Luke 4:30, though many witnesses (ACELXΔ, etc., with some very ancient versions)[y] insert them.

NOTES ON THE EIGHTH CHAPTER

a [*Cf. Lectures Introductory to the Study of the Gospels*, pp. 461-477.]

b The clause translated, "and being convicted by their conscience," in the T.R., and supported by EGHKS, etc., is omitted by still better authority.

c ℵFHK, many cursives, etc., omit δέ.

d ἤ BD^gr KTUXΛ, very many cursives and ancient versions [as Syr[sin]], instead of καί with the rest and T.R.

e ἀληθής ℵ and eleven other uncials, most cursives, etc.; ἀληθινή BDLTX, etc.

f ℵ[pm]D omit πατήρ [as Weiss and Blass; W. and H. bracket].

g Eleven uncials, and the cursives, versions, etc., insert ὁ Ἰησοῦς, contrary to ℵBDLTX, etc. [Syr[sin]], Orig. Cyr.

h All the old English versions, too, are wrong, save the Rhemish, which has "your sinne."

i The Authorised Version is here faulty like many others ancient and modern. It is true that ἀρχήν, with or without the article, may be used in ordinary Greek for "at the first," or "formerly." So in the Septuagint of Genesis 13:4; 43:18, 20, etc.; and thus Nonnus understood the language of our Evangelist in this place. Not the temporal sense, however, of the word is meant in the present remarkable phrase, but that of archetypal character or first principle. Thus, Tyndale (1534): "Even the very same thinge that I saye unto you"; and Cranmer (1539), only changing "saye" into "speake." After them the Rhemish followed the strange and ungrammatical rendering of the Vulgate, "Principium qui et loquor vobis." It is hard, if not impossible, to understand "qui" here; yet "principium" is not so far from the truth, as if the phrase had been confounded with "ab initio." Indeed, the old Cod. Verc. has "Initium quod loquor vobis," as Cod. Brix. "Principium quod et loquor vobis." The Geneva Version misled the translators of 1611 into a sort of double rendering, "Even the very same," which would be a good enough version of τὴν ἀρχήν, but they added also "from the beginning," which necessitated a false representation of λαλῶ as if it were ἐλάλησα or ἔλεξα.

As the fourth Gospel pointedly employs ἐν ἀρχῇ, ἀπ' ἀρχῆς (and in two cases ἐξ ἀρχῆς), there is the less reason for confounding the single occurrence of τὴν ἀρχήν with any of them. The Lord uses the phrase prominently in answer to the question, "Who art Thou?" raised by the contemptuous unbelief of the Pharisees. He had already declared Himself the Light of the world, but that they knew neither Him nor His Father, and should die in their sin because of their unbelief. He had not yet in terms disclosed His eternal Being as in verse 58, but is gradually rising to this from the incident which so fittingly opens the chapter. The law of death in man's hand is powerless before the Light of Life, Who is from above, and not of this world. He is the Word of God. He, and He alone, when challenged, could say, "I am absolutely [Kuinoel][164a], altogether, what I speak also to you." His speech thoroughly expresses Himself. Essentially [Alford], precisely [Godet], What He is, He also speaks. These alternatives, suggested by various interpreters, differ no doubt in degrees of accuracy; but substantially they agree in identifying the Lord with His utterance also; for He is the Truth. They seem better than "originally," which means little more than "at first" or "at the beginning," and, though often legitimate, looks quite out of place when applied to Christ, the Faithful Witness, Who is "the same yesterday and to-day and for ever." He alone could say that He was wholly what He also speaks. Mr. McClellan is right in holding that Christ's speech reveals His eternal Being; but does not "originally" fail to convey it?

If the Sanscrit root helps us, it implies "worth, merit, fitness, dignity, and worship"; and "beginning" is secondary. Certainly ἀρχή appears in philosophic usage as "a principle," whether of being or of thought; and in ordinary application as a "first place," estate, or office, and even materially as in Acts {10:11; 11:5}. Thus, "at the first," or "originally," is the sense in Herodotus (i. 86, 140; ii. 28, 148; iv. 59; viii. 128, 132), when contrast with the present is intended. But an exclusive force appears with the negative even more frequently still (as in i. 192; ii. 95; iii. 16, 39; iv. 25, 28; vi. 33; vii. 26; ix. 57). On its very first occurrence (i. 9), how could "originally" assure Gyges? Did not the king mean that his own contrivance was to screen him absolutely? So Larcher understood in his learned version (i. 8, note *a*, ed. 1802). Dean Blakesley's view was "to begin with," which would be almost absurd, and certainly inadequate, for our text. To assume that only in negative sentences the absolute sense occurs is mistaken, at any rate, in later Greek; as the reader may see in the following references to Dion Cassius (vol. i. 96 [Fr. Peir. ci.], ii. 342 [xlv. 34], iii. 688 [lix. 19], iv. 52, [lxii. 4] ed. Sturz. Two cases, at least, might be added of ἀρχὴν without τὴν.

We may dismiss, then, among many untenable proposals, the renderings of Wiclif and the Wiclifites (iv. 260, Oxford, 1850), following the Vulgate, with which go Syr.[hcl.] and the Gothic; and with slight variations Augustine of old, and Fritzsche and Wordsworth of late. Not so held Cod. Veron. but "Imprimis," as Cod. Corb. "de superioribus," though it is hard to say what they meant. Nor can the interrogation stand with "at all," as Chrysostom, Cyril. Alex. (and so Lücke and Ewald), and the R.V. margin [as Westcott]; nor with "from the beginning," as Meyer. The more prevalent construction of the A. and R.Vv., like the Sah. Memph. Syr.[pesch.], slights both the sense and the tense of λαλῶ, with the place and force of καὶ, through the first fault of misrendering τὴν ἀρχὴν. The Æth. Arab. Arm. differ from these and from one another, but afford no help, as far as I can judge. "Absolutely (or, In principle) what also I speak to you," reflects justly the language, the order of the words, the grammar, and above all the bearing of the context and of this sentence in particular. There is no need, therefore, of connecting the end of verse 25 with the beginning of 26, as Bengel, Raphelius, and Wakefield suggested, who otherwise rather confirm the true import, as does the ὅλως of Euthymius Zigabenus.

j BLT, etc., omit αὐτοῖς, which is read by the great body of the witnesses [and so Blass].

k Some good authorities [and so Blass] prefix καὶ, "and," others add ὁ πατήρ, "the Father," at the end of the clause, and so T.R.

l ἑω(ο)ράκατε ℵ^pmDEFGHMSTUΓΔΛ, etc., T.R.; ἠκούσατε ℵ^corr.BCKLX, etc. [W. and H., Weiss, Blass].

m The great majority read ὑμῶν, but not BLT, etc.

n ἐστε ℵBDLT, etc.; ἦτε T.R. following the great mass [as Syr^sin].

o T.R. adds οὖν with fifteen uncials, but not the oldest.

p The authorities are pretty equal for and against reading οὖν, "therefore," as given in T.R. [W. and H., Weiss, Blass omit].

q T.R. omits τοῦ, contrary to all good witnesses.

r δὲ is added by many uncials, etc., and followed by T.R., contrary to the best MSS. and versions. [Syr^sin has it.]

s A dozen uncials and most cursives, etc. (and so T.R.) add οὖν, "therefore," contrary to the oldest, ℵBCDLX, many cursives and versions.

t Fifteen uncials and most cursives, etc., read οὖν, "therefore," but not ℵBC, etc., with some very old versions [as Syr^sin].

u ℵB^pmDFX, etc., ὑμῶν (and so T.R.), contrary to the rest.

v [Syr^sin shows "has Abraham seen Thee?" so ℵ^corr.B^pm.]

w Here end ℵBD and some of the oldest versions [as Syr^sin], the rest adding substantially as in T.R.

x ["It was the day when the promises would be accomplished, and very naturally he who had the promises looked for the time when they are to be made good in Christ."—*Lectures Introductory to the Study of the Gospels*, p. 476, note.]

y [But not Syr^{sin}.]

THE NINTH CHAPTER [a]

The light of God had shone in Jesus (light, not of Jews only, but of the world); yet was He rejected, increasingly and utterly, and with deadly hatred. There was no miracle wrought; it was emphatically His words that we hear, but asserting at length the divine glory of His Person. This roused, as it always does, the rancour of unbelief. They believe not on Him, because they bow neither to their own ruin nor to the grace of God, which thus comes down to meet man, revealing the God Who is unknown. But Jesus pursues His way of love, and unfolds it in a new and suited form, only to meet with similar rejection afresh, as our chapter and the next will show.

VERSES 1-12.

"And passing along He saw a man blind from birth.[174] And His disciples asked Him, saying, Rabbi, which sinned, this (man) or his parents, that he should be born blind? Jesus[b] answered, Neither this (man) sinned nor his parents, but that the works of God might be manifested in him. I[c] must work the works of Him that sent Me[c] while it is day: night cometh, when no one can work. When I am in the world, I am the world's light" (verses 1-5).

It was an act of pure grace which the Lord was about to do. Nobody had appealed to Him, not even the blind man or his parents. The disciples only raised a question, one of those curious speculations in which the later Jews delighted:[175] was it the man's sin, or his parents', which had involved him in congenital blindness? Certainly no such Pythagorean fancy prevailed then in Judæa as that a man might have sinned in a previous existence on earth, and be punished for it in an after-state also on earth. Nor is there any sufficient reason to endorse a pious and learned author's view, that the disciples might have entertained—what rabbis afterwards drew from Genesis 25:22—the notion of sin before birth.

It seems easy to understand that they conceived, however strangely, of punishment inflicted anticipatively on one whose eventual sin was foreseen by God. Doubtless it was unsound; but this need be no difficulty in the way; for what question or assertion of the disciples did not betray error enough to draw out the unerring correction, so precious to them and us, of our Lord? He now puts the case on its real purpose in the divine mind—that the works of God might be manifested in him. It is the day of grace now: therefore was Jesus come; and this was just an opportunity for the display of His gracious power. Yet man understands not grace but by faith, and even believers only so far as faith is in exercise. Government is the natural thought when one sees God's cognisance of every thing and every one here below. But it was not then, nor is it now, the time for His government of the world. Here lay the mistake of the disciples then, as of Job's friends of old: a mistake which leads souls, not only to censoriousness and misjudgment, but to forget their own sins and need of repentance in occupying themselves with what they count God's vengeance on others.

Here, however, it is not the side of uncharitable self-righteousness which the Lord exposes. He speaks of the activity and purpose of grace as the key. It was no question of sin, either in the blind man or in his parents, but of God's manifesting His works in man's grievous need and sorrow. In the world He was the world's light. He was the Sent One and Servant in doing His work, as in speaking His word. Perfect God, He was perfect man, never swerving from the place He had taken here below.

Further, the pressure of His rejection was felt by our Lord, whatever the holy calm which could so quickly turn from man's murderous hatred to a work of divine love. "I must work the works of Him that sent Me while it is day: night cometh, when no one can work." He was the "light" of the "day" which was then shining for Him to do the will and manifest the love of the One Who sent Him—yea, to declare God (see chapter 1:18), Whom man otherwise was incapable of seeing. Truly the need was great; for man, like the one in question, was utterly blind. But Jesus was the Creator, though man amongst men. Let Him be in the world, He is its light. It attaches alike to His mission, and to His Person, in virtue of His divine nature.

> "Having said these things, He spat on the ground, and made clay of the spittle, and spread the clay over his eyes,[176] and said to him, Go, wash in the pool of Siloam, which is interpreted Sent. He went away therefore, and washed, and came seeing" (verses 6-7).

This was no unmeaning act on Christ's part, no mere test of obedience on the man's. It was a sign of the truth which the chapter reveals, or, at least, in harmony with it. For He Who was there manifesting the works of God was Himself a man, and had deigned to take the body prepared for Him; most holy, beyond all doubt, as became the Son of God Who knew no sin, about to be made sin for us on the cross, but none the less really of the woman, of blood and flesh, as the children partake. But Incarnation, precious as is the grace of the Lord in it, of itself is quite insufficient for man's need; yea, it seems rather to add at first to the difficulty, as did the clay on the man's eyes. The Spirit must work by the word, as well as the Son sent into the world, Jesus Christ come in flesh. Without the effectual work of the Holy Spirit in man he cannot see. Compare chapter 3. So it is here: the man must go to the pool of Siloam, and wash there. Attention is the more fixed on this by the appended interpretation or meaning of the word.[177] It signifies the soul's recognition that Jesus was the Sent One of God, sent to do His will and finish His work, the Son yet servant withal, to accomplish the great salvation of God. The heart is thus purified by faith. Now the man has eyes and can see, not when the clay was laid on, but when he washed in the pool of Siloam. Christ must be here, and a man too, in contact with men in all their darkness; but only when the Holy Ghost applies the word to the conscience do they, owning Him to be the Sent of God, receive sight. Not Incarnation only but the efficacious work of the Spirit is needed that man may see according to God. "According to His own mercy He saved us through the washing of regeneration and renewal of the Holy Ghost, which He shed on us richly through Jesus Christ our Saviour, that, being justified by

His grace, we might become heirs according to the hope of eternal life" [Titus 3:5-7].

> "The neighbours therefore, and those who used to see him before that he was a beggar,ᵈ said, Is not this he that sitteth and beggeth? Some said, It is he; othersᵉ said, No, but he is like him; butᵉ he said, It is I. They said therefore to him, How thenᶠ were thine eyes opened? He answered, The manᵍ that is called Jesus made clay, and anointed mine eyes, and said to me, Go untoʰ Siloam, and wash. Having gone away thenⁱ and washed I received sight. Andʲ they said to him, Where is He? He saith,ᵏ I do not know" (verses 8-12).

Those accustomed to the blind beggar could not conceal their surprise and perplexity; for as the sightless eyes are a prime disfigurement of the human face, so their presence thus unexpectedly changed the man's entire expression. No wonder that they wondered; yet was the fact certain, and the evidence incontestable. God took care that there should be many witnesses, and would make the testimony felt the more it was discussed and weighed. Had they known Who Jesus was, and for what He was sent, they would have understood the fitness of the work done that day. But he on whom the work was wrought gave out no uncertain sound. *He* was the man whom they were used to see sitting and begging. His witness to Jesus is most explicit. He does not know much yet, but what he knows he declares with plain decision. How could he doubt whose eyes were opened? Did they ask how it was? His answer was ready and unreserved: "The (or, A) man that is called Jesus made clay, and anointed mine eyes, and said to me, Go to Siloam and wash." The mighty effect followed at once: "And having gone away and washed, I received sight."

They are curious to know where Jesus is; but the man is as frank in acknowledging his ignorance of this as before in confessing the reality of what He had done. It might not be to his own praise that he did not return to Jesus in thanksgiving for God's grace; but God would use it to show how wholly the worker and the object of the work were above collusion. How few have the honesty to say "I do not know" when they know as little as he who here owns it! Yet is it no light condition of learning more.

On the other hand, we see that the Lord not only would draw attention by men's debate, and by the man's distinct testimony, but leaves the man for the present, that, by his own reflection on what was done and answering their questions, he might be prepared both for trial that was coming, and for still better blessing from and in Himself. The agitation among the neighbours was to be followed quickly by the more serious inquisition of the religious chiefs. These, as we shall see, readily find matter in the good deed for their usual malevolence toward that which brought honour to God independently of them. Worldly religion, whatever its profession, is really and always a systematic effort to make God the servant of man's pride and selfishness. It knows not love, and values not holiness; it is offended by the faith that, feeding on the word, serves by the Spirit of God, glories in Christ Jesus, and has no confidence in the flesh. It hates walking in the light as a constant thing, for it only wants religion at its fit times and seasons as a shield against the day of death and the hour of judgment. Hence, for the Son of God to be here on earth, a man presented to men's eyes, blind as they are, and sending them where they can wash and see, outside the regular established religion of the land and without the medium of the accredited guides, is intolerable. It comes out plainly in what follows, a most weighty, and, I doubt not, intended lesson in this instructive narrative: God's witness in work, as before (chapter 8) in word.

Whenever God acts, the men of religion set up to judge, and the neighbours fear their displeasure more than they pitied the blind man or rejoiced in his healing. Such men are accredited of the world, and count it their province to decide such questions, while others love to have it so. What, then, will the Pharisees say? They had cavilled before.

Verses 13-34.

> "They bring unto the Pharisees him that was once blind" (verse 13).

Nor are the Pharisees slow to detect a flaw, as they supposed. Not that the man had not been blind, nor that Jesus had failed to give him sight; but had they not both, Jesus especially, broken the law?

> "Now it was Sabbath (on the day)[1] when Jesus made the clay, and opened his eyes" (verse 14).

How little men, particularly those whom public opinion regards as pillars, are apt to suspect that their will exposes them to Satan! But so it is, and, above all, where the Son of God is concerned, Who was manifested that He might destroy the works of the devil, and give us an understanding that we should know Him that is true. Yet those who, confident in their traditions, dare to arraign the Saviour, commit themselves the more to the enemy, because they flatter themselves that they are upholding the cause of God. Thus are they ensnared to the destruction of themselves and of all who heed them.

"He that honoureth not the Son honoureth not the Father that sent Him" (chapter 5:23).

> "Again therefore the Pharisees also asked him how he received sight. And he said to them, He put clay upon mine eyes, and I washed and do see. Some of the Pharisees then said, This man is not of God, because He keepeth not the Sabbath. ᵐOthers said, How can a sinful man do such signs? And there was a division among them" (verses 15-16).

They are uneasy, whatever may be their affectation of superior sanctity and zeal for God's honour. The power which gave sight, where blindness had hitherto ever rested, startled them, and excited their curiosity, with the desire of discovering an evil source, if not of alarming the man. But grace wrought in him, and gave him quiet courage to confess the good deed wrought, albeit on a Sabbath and without a word about it. "He put clay upon mine eyes, and I washed and do see." God calls us, when blessed through Christ, all to be confessors, though not all martyrs; and surely it is the least we owe Him in praise and our fellow-men in love.

But all true confession is odious to the religious world and its leaders. "Therefore said some of the Pharisees, This man is not of God, because He keepeth not the Sabbath." This malicious plea had been already refuted; but Pharisaism has no heart for, no subjection to, the truth. It had never entered their consciences, or they had forgotten it in their zeal for forms and traditions. But how sad the self-deceit of men destitute of true holiness, or of real obedience, daring to arraign the Holy One of God!

THE NINTH CHAPTER

Yet others there were among them not so blinded by party passion or personal envy who ventured to say a word, if they took no further step. "Others said, How can a sinful man do such signs?" All they meant was that He Who wrought thus could be no such deceiver or impostor as the rest conceived. They had no right view of Himself, of His Person, or His relation to God. They had not the faintest idea that He was God manifest in flesh; but they questioned whether He must not be "of God," since He did such signs.[178] "And there was a division among them." Thus, as they were not yet of one mind, there was a delay for Satan's design.

But in their restlessness they examine once more the man, and are used unwittingly by the God of grace to help him on in the apprehension and acknowledgment of the truth which is according to piety.

> "They say therefore[n] to the blind (man) again, Thou,[o] what sayest thou of Him, because He opened thine eyes? And he said, He is a prophet" (verse 17).

The first examination was as to the fact and the manner. Now they want to force out of the man his thoughts of his benefactor, in their malice wishing to find a plea for condemning both. On the other hand, the grace of God is as manifest as it is sweet in using the painful trial and exercise of soul to His own glory, through the man led on and blessed only the more. He knew their hatred of Jesus, yet he answers their challenge boldly, "He is a prophet": a decided advance on his previous confession, though far from the truth he is soon to learn. He owns that Jesus has the mind of God as well as His power.

Baffled by his quiet firmness, the religious inquisitors turned to another and accustomed means of assault. As the neighbours in their perplexity appeal to the Pharisees, so these work on and by natural relationships too. They would try whether some disproof could not be made out of the parents. Clearly unbelief lies at the bottom of all. Man, being fallen and evil, is unwilling to believe in the goodness of God—above all, in His grace to himself. Had the neighbours bowed to the clear evidence of God's intervention, they would not have brought the man to the Pharisees; had the Pharisees, they would not have persisted in sifting again and again beyond the ascertainment of the fact; still less would they have awakened the fears of the family.

> "The Jews therefore did not believe concerning him that he was blind, and received sight, until they called the parents of him that received sight, and asked them, saying, Is this your son who, ye say, was born blind? how then doth he now see? His parents therefore[p] answered and said, We know that this is our son, and that he was born blind; but how he now seeth we know not, or who opened his eyes we know not; ask himself: he is of age, he will speak for himself. These things said his parents because they feared the Jews; for the Jews had already agreed that, if any one should confess Him (to be) Christ, he should be put out of the synagogue. On this account his parents said, He is of age: ask him" (verses 18-23).

The matter of fact is thus again the cardinal question, as it really was; and as to this the parents answered conclusively. That the man now saw was undeniable, and this through Jesus, as he declared; that he was their son and born blind, the parents maintained unhesitatingly. The conclusion was irresistible, if unbelief did not resist everything where God is concerned. The parents answer only where they are concerned. It was not that they, or any reasonable person, doubted that Jesus had wrought the miracle; but they dreaded the consequence, from Pharisaic enmity, of going beyond their own circle of natural knowledge, and pleaded ignorance of how it was done, or of Whom it was that did it. Overborne by fear of the Pharisees, they forget even the affection that would otherwise have sheltered their offspring from the impending blow; and they throw all the burden on their own son. "Ask him: he is of age, he will speak concerning himself." Thus their very fears, on which the Pharisees reckoned for a denial of the facts, God used to make it solely a controversy between the Pharisees and the man himself, when they were compelled by the evidence of the parents to accept as a certain fact that he who now saw had been ever blind, and blind till just now.

Another thing also comes out very plainly, that the enmity of the Jews to the Lord Jesus was known ere this to have gone so far as to threaten with excommunication every one that confessed Him to be the Christ.[179] The will of man is blind to proofs; and as this flows from corruption, it issues in destruction.

Hence the man is once more appealed to, and all question of the miracle is dropped.

> "Therefore they called a second time the man who was blind, and said to him, Give glory to God: *we* know that this man is a sinner. He therefore answered,[q] If He is a sinner I know not. One thing I know, that, blind as I was, now I see" (verses 24-25).

They now assume the highest ground; they at least hold to the divine side, if others are carried away by the apparent good done to man. Accordingly they call on him to give glory to God,[180] whilst they assert their unqualified assurance that Jesus was a sinner. Nor has it been an uncommon thing, from that day to this, for men to profess to honour God at the expense of His Son; as the Lord warned His disciples to expect to the uttermost, where the Father and the Son are unknown. But the man in his simplicity puts forward the fact which he deeply felt and they would fain hide. "If He is a sinner I know not. One thing I know, that, blind as I was, now I see." No argument can stand against the logic of reality—above all, of such a reality as this. He certainly did not know what they pretended to know; but that Jesus was a sinner could not be: he alleges the most distinct and irrefragable proof; and this on their own ground of what was before all. If reasoning be unseasonable and powerless, what is religious antipathy in presence of an undeniable fact which proves the mighty power and goodness of God? Their efforts proved their ill-will to Him Who had thus wrought: the blessed reality remained, whatever the insinuations or the assaults of unbelief.

It is well also to remark that with faith goes a mighty operation of God, with its own characteristic effects, and more important in every soul that believes the gospel than even that of which the man, once blind but now seeing, was so sensible. Those who believe are quickened from death in trespasses and sins {Ephesians 2:1, 5}, and they henceforth live to God. Crucified with Christ, they nevertheless live, yet not they themselves properly, but Christ lives in them {Galatians 2:19-20}. They are thereby partakers of a divine nature {2 Peter 1:4}, being born of God {1 John 5:1}. It is no improvement of their old nature as men. They are born of water and Spirit; they are begotten by the word of truth. With faith goes this new life, which shows itself in wholly different thoughts and affections, as well as ways or walk. Of its gradual progress in the midst of opposition and persecution, the story of this blind man, who now saw, is no unapt illustration.

The pertinacity of the Pharisees finds in the man a quiet courage, which stands out in contrast with the fears of his parents, and even urges the claims of Him Who had wrought so good and great a deed on His adversaries in a way they could not resist. If they ply the man with the question, *How?* he answers with the question, *Why?*

> "They said therefore[r] to him (again),[s] What did He to thee? how opened He thine eyes? He answered them, I told you already, and ye did not hear: why do ye wish to hear again? Do ye also wish to become His disciples? They railed[t] at him, and said, Thou art His disciple, but we are disciples of Moses. We know that God hath spoken to Moses, but this man we know not whence He is" (verses 26-29).

It was unbelieving scorn, not real ignorance.[181]

He who was once blind, but now saw, discerned the true state of the case, as those did not who had never experienced His gracious power. He felt satisfied that their opposition was invincible. The Apostle of grace none the less, but the more, warns the despisers of their self-willed unbelief and danger of perishing {Acts 13:41}. The same spirit of faith expresses itself in him who just now was but a blind beggar, even as from those that had not should be taken away what they seemed to have. Christ is a rock of strength to the one, and of offence to the other. They thus expose themselves to the sharp rebuke of their folly by the man they affected to despise. Zealous for the servant whom they set up as master, they confessed their ignorance of Him Who is Lord of all.

> "The man answered and said to them, Why in this is the[u] wonderful thing, that *ye* know not whence He is, and He opened mine eyes! [v]We know that God heareth not sinners, but if anyone be God-fearing, and do His will, him He heareth. Since time (began) it was not heard that anyone opened a born blind man's eyes. If this man were not of God, He could do nothing. They answered and said to him, In sins *thou* wast born wholly, and dost *thou* teach us? And they cast him out" (verses 30-34).

The man's answer was as solid as to the point. He discards the attack on himself personally, and treats it as a question between the religious leaders, who avowedly could not tell whence He was Who had wrought a work wholly unexampled as a display of God's power. It was hard, if not impossible, to believe that such a one could be evil, as they had imputed. "We know that God heareth not sinners; but if anyone be God-fearing and do His will, him He heareth." For what can be surer, as a general principle, than that "them that honour Me I will honour, and they that despise Me shall be lightly esteemed" [1 Samuel 2:30[182]]? Indeed, this was plain as between Jesus (to take the lowest ground) and the Pharisees, whose moral incapacity astonishes the man. What then remained for his adversaries? Nothing but contemptuous rage, and the extreme blow of the ecclesiastical arm. "They cast him out," but not before they unwittingly testified to the force of his words. "In sins *thou* wast born wholly,¹⁸²ᵃ and dost *thou* teach us?" They were too proud to learn.

Verses 35-41.

But they cast him out into the arms and bosom of the Lord. For, as we are next told,

> "Jesus heard that they had cast him out, and, having found him, He said, Believest *thou* on the Son of God (or, Man)? He answered,ʷ and said, Andˣ who is He, Sir [Lord], that I may believe on Him? ʸJesus said to him, Thou hast both seen Him, and He that speaketh with thee is He. And he said, I believe, Lord; and he did Him homage" (verses 35-38).

Such is the final step of God's grace in working with the blind man. He is thrust outside Judaism for the truth's sake, consequent on the work wrought on his person; he there is found by Christ, and led to know and believe on Him, far beyond any thought, however true, he had previously conceived. It was faith in His own testimony and Person.

It is really the history of a soul that goes onward under the guidance of God, Who makes the grace of the Lord and His glory shine the more fully after one is outside the world's religion, whether cast or going out. And such is the character of Christianity, as the believers had at length to learn from the Epistle to the Hebrews, especially from its final chapter. So patient was the Spirit of grace with those of the ancient people of God, dull to learn the new thing which God has introduced through and in our Lord Jesus. But, late as it may be, the breach with earthly religion must come. "Let us go forth therefore unto Him without the camp, bearing His reproach"

{Hebrews 13:13}; and this so much the more, because we have boldness to enter into the holies by the blood of Jesus, the new and living way which He has dedicated for us through the veil—that is, His flesh {Hebrews 10:19-20}. But the work was not yet done which opened this way, nor the Spirit shed to give souls the consciousness of righteous title. We have one, therefore, not yet going forth thus, but cast out by hatred far more against the name of Jesus than against the man—yea, we may say against the man solely for Jesus' sake, Who had heard of, and felt for, and found the sheep thus worried of men.

But a perplexing difference of reading follows, which claims more than a bare critical notice. "Dost thou believe on the Son *of Man?*" say the Sinaitic, the Vatican, and the Cambridge (of Beza) manuscripts, supported by the [Syr^sin], Sahidic, Roman edition of the Æthiopic, etc., though more than a dozen uncials [A, L, etc.], all the cursives, and the rest of the ancient versions, etc., give us τοῦ θεοῦ, "of God" [Lachmann and Tregelles]. But Tischendorf in his eighth edition, and Westcott and Hort [Weiss and Blass] adopt τοῦ ἀνθρώπου. Nor can it be denied that, as the rule, the Lord habitually and graciously loved to present Himself in relation to man; as, again, it is plain that this chapter in particular sets Him forth, not only as the Light, Word, and God, like the preceding one, but as the Incarnate One Who was sent to manifest the works of God, the rejected Messiah about to suffer, but to be exalted over all. On the other hand, that the Son of God is the great distinctive testimony of our Gospel none can overlook; and we can well understand how the light of this glorious truth (bursting on the soul gradually led on, spite of, and in a certain sense through, the blind hostility of the Pharisees)

THE NINTH CHAPTER

draws him out in homage to the Lord. It was, at any rate, the Son of God in grace, a man on earth, Who had been seen by, and was talking with, one who had experienced His light-giving power.[183]

> "And Jesus said, For judgment I came into this world, that they that see not may see, and they that see may become blind. ᶻAnd some of the Pharisees that were with Him heard these things,ᶻ and said to Him, Are we blind also? Jesus said to them, If ye were blind, ye would not have sin; but now ye say, We see,ᵃᵃ your sin remaineth" (verses 39-41).

The Lord thereon shows how His coming acted, and was meant to act, on souls. It had a higher purpose and more permanent result than any energy, however mighty and benign, that dealt with the body. He was the life to those, however dark, who received Him: those who rejected Him sealed their own ruin everlastingly, whatever their estimate of themselves or in the mind of others.[184] The Jew, especially the Pharisee, might be ever so confident that he himself was a guide of the blind, a light of those in darkness; but the coming of the only True Light brought to evident nothingness all such haughty pretensions as surely as it gave eyes to such as owned their blindness. No flesh therefore shall glory: he that glorieth, let him glory in the Lord Who was come a man, but God on earth, for this reversal of fallen man's thoughts, and display of His own grace. Pharisaic pride refuses to bow to Jesus imputing blindness, as they thought; but if it speaks, it is obliged to hear its most withering sentence from the Judge of all mankind. For blindness there is all grace and power in Christ; but what can be the portion of those who, stone-blind, say they see? Their sin remains, as well as blindness, which of itself is not sin, though its consequence.[185]

NOTES ON THE NINTH CHAPTER

a [*Cf. Lectures Introductory to the Study of the Gospels*, pp. 477-485.]

b Some authorities insert ὁ, "the," contrary to the great mass.

c Tischendorf, in his eighth edition, reads ἡμᾶς, "us," in both occurrences, following ℵ^pmBDL, several ancient versions, etc.; but Alford, Green, Griesbach, Scholz, Lachmann, etc., adhere to ἐμὲ and με, with AC and the great majority of uncials, cursives, and many ancient versions. BD give με in the second place, followed by Tregelles, as by Westcott and Hort also [and Weiss], with the Sahidic and the Syriac of Jerusalem, etc. This goes far to explode the "we" [Syr^sin] must work; still more is the internal evidence against it.

d The common and largely supported reading is τυφλὸς, "blind"; but the more ancient is προσαίτης, "a beggar." [So Syr^sin, Weiss, Blass.]

e So read ℵBCLX with many old versions; T.R. ἄλλοι δὲ ὅτι, with more than a dozen uncials, etc., as δὲ also.

f οὖν ℵCDLX, etc.

g ὁ ... ὁ ℵB, etc., but omitting the first καὶ εἶπεν, as the mass [so Blass, etc.] omit the articles.

h ℵBDLX, etc., omit τὴν κολυμβήθραν τοῦ, and read τὸν Σ. [W. and H., Weiss, Blass].

i οὖν ℵBDLX, etc. [Weiss, Blass], δὲ the mass.

j καὶ ℵBLX, etc., οὖν majority, but A and some old versions omit both [as Blass].

NOTES ON THE NINTH CHAPTER

k D, etc., with ancient versions, add αὐτοῖς, "to them."

l ἐν ᾗ ἡμέρᾳ ℵBLX, etc, but the great mass give ὅτε, "when."

m ℵBD and some cursives and versions [Syr^{sin}] add δὲ, "but."

n οὖν ℵABDLX, many cursives and versions [W. and H., Weiss, Blass]; but most, followed by T.R., omit.

o σὺ τί T.R. with most; τί σὺ ℵBLX, etc.

p οὖν ℵB, etc.; most δὲ; many [as Blass] omit, and so T.R., which adds αὐτοῖς with most, contrary to ℵBLX, etc.

q καὶ εἶπεν is the addition of T.R., following most uncials and cursives, but not of ℵABDL, some good cursives, and the best ancient versions.

r T.R. has δὲ, "and," with many good authorities, but not ℵ$^{corr.}$ (ℵ^{pm} omitting) BDKLX, many cursives and versions.

s πάλιν, T.R., with most uncials, cursives, etc., but not ℵBD, etc., and many ancient versions.

t οὖν is added in T.R., with little support; καὶ ℵB, etc., but the most read neither.

u τὸ θ., "the," in ℵBL, a few cursives, etc., omitted in the great majority.

v T.R. adds δὲ, "now," with most [as Syr^{sin}], against ℵBDGL.

w B and Theb. omit ἀπεκρίθη ἐκεῖνος, "he answered." Memph. omits "said."

x T.R. omits καὶ, "and," with AL and a few others, but good versions.

291

y T.R. adds δὲ with many good authorities, but ℵBDX, etc., omit.

z ℵBLK, three cursives, Theb. or Sah. Memph. Arm., etc., do not read καὶ, as in T.R. with most uncials, cursives, and versions, which also add ταῦτα, "these things," save ℵ^{pm}D, etc., with several versions [as Syr^{sin}].

aa T.R., adds οὖν with ten uncials and most cursives [with Syr^{sin}], contrary to ℵBDKLX, etc., and the bulk of the ancient versions.

THE TENTH CHAPTER[a]

VERSES 1-6.

The Lord proceeds to set forth the consequences of His rejection, spite of His dignity, under a variety of forms. It is the disclosure of His grace to and for the sheep (from His humiliation as man and servant, even to the laying down His life in all its intrinsic excellency), and of His glory as one with the Father. The bright side of the truth comes to view.[186]

> "Verily, verily, I say to you, He that entereth not through the door into the fold of the sheep but climbeth up otherwise, *he* is a thief and a robber; but he that entereth through the door is shepherd of the sheep. To him the porter openeth, and the sheep hear his voice; and he calleth[b] his own sheep by name, and leadeth them out.[187] [c]When he hath put forth all[d] his own, he goeth before them, and the sheep follow him because they know his voice; but a stranger they will in no wise follow, but will flee from him, because they know not the voice of strangers. This proverb said Jesus to them; but they knew not what things they were which He was speaking to them" (verses 1-6).

The mode of speech is allegorical, departing so far from ordinary language, but adopting a figure very familiar to the Law, the Psalms, and the Prophets (Genesis 49; Psalm 80; Isaiah 40; Ezekiel 34; Zechariah 11, 13). The application to pastors of the church is ridiculously out of place and time. It is the Shepherd of Israel in contrast with those who claimed to guide the ancient people of God. Even He, albeit a divine Person, entered in the appointed way. Others who had no competency were no less destitute of title or commission. The woman's Seed, the virgin's Son, the Seed of Abraham, the Son of David, the mighty God, the Father of the age to come, coming forth out of Bethlehem, from of old, from everlasting, yet to be cut off after sixty-nine of Daniel's seventy weeks, the righteous Servant abased beyond all yet to be exalted above all, what did not meet to point Him out and exclude every rival? Yes, the rejected Christ is He that entered through the door, Shepherd of the sheep—none but He.

All others sought to mount some other way. Theudas might boast to be somebody, Judas of Galilee draw away people after him, Pharisees love the first seats, scribes and doctors of law lay heavy burdens on men. But the sheep, taught of God, hear His voice, not theirs; even as the Spirit, in His care for God's glory, was pleased to do the porter's work, opening the door to Him only, as we see from the beginning in the Simeons and Annas and all who waited for redemption in Jerusalem. The others, small or great, orderly or revolutionary, had no right to the sheep; they were nothing better than thieves or robbers, if they claimed as they did the sheep that were His. He only is Shepherd, and the sheep hear His voice. They are His own, and He calls them as such by name. Who could, who would, but Himself? He knows and loves them, making them feel that He has an interest in them, such as God alone could feel, and such a right to them as God alone had and gave.

Again, Christ entered in, but He leads out. Judaism is doomed. The Israel of God follow Him outside. It was no question now of gathering back into the land the outcasts of Israel, or the dispersed of Judah; this must await another day. Now He calleth His own sheep by name, and leadeth them out. "When He shall have put forth all His own"—for if such were the principle of His action now, still it was to be the necessary effect of His death on the cross—He goes before them, and the sheep follow Him because they know His voice. It is the wisdom of God for the simple.[188]

Precious word of God, the hearing of His voice! It is due to His Person, it is the fruit of His grace, it is their true and best safeguard. "And a stranger will they in no wise follow, but will flee from him, because they know not the voice of strangers." The "stranger," or alien, has nothing to do with them; however he might seek it, what have they to do with him? Their wisdom is to follow Jesus, Whose they are, Whose voice they hear and know. How simple, were we but simple! How honouring to the Son! This, too, best pleases the Father. It is through faith we are kept, not by discerning shades of scepticism or superstition, though this may be for some a duty or call of love for others, but by adhering to the truth.

Yet such words are powerless to the men of either reason or tradition. For they seek their own honour, they give or receive it one of another. Jesus came in the Father's name, and Him they receive not. They avow themselves strangers to Him; they deny that any can know His voice. Had they heard it themselves, they would not doubt it could be known. They prefer and follow a stranger. The superstitious exalt their church; were it God's church, it would repudiate such exaltation at the expense of Christ. The sceptical exalt man as he is. But both agree in ignoring the Shepherd's voice. So it is now, and so it was then.

"This proverb[e] said Jesus to them, but *they* knew not what things they were which He was speaking to them." His sayings are as Himself: if He is valued, so are they; if He is not believed on, neither are they understood.[188a] He is the Light and the Truth. All that He says depends on faith in Him for its apprehension. And therefore it is that in 1 John 2 the very babes of the family of God are said to know all things. Knowing Christ, they have an unction from the Holy One. It is not by learning or by logic, any more than by sentiment, enthusiasm, or bigotry, but by the possession of Christ, that they refuse errors which have ensnared unnumbered doctors of divinity. They are thus kept bright and fresh, simple and secure, because dependent on Him. Those who count themselves wise venture to judge for themselves, and perish in their unbelieving presumption. To hear His voice is the humblest place in the world, yet has it the power and wisdom of God with it. What they heard from the beginning abides in them, but for the stranger they have no ear or heart. They are satisfied with Christ's voice. They know the truth in Him, and that no lie is of the truth. They are glad of every help which reminds them of His words, and brings them home to their souls. A stranger's voice they distrust, and flee from him. They are right: God would have us value no other voice.

THE TENTH CHAPTER

VERSES 7-21.

> "Therefore said Jesus again to them,[f] Verily, verily, I say to you, I am the Door of the sheep. All as many as came (before Me)[g] are thieves and robbers, but the sheep did not hear them. I am the Door; through Me if anyone have entered, he shall be saved, and shall go in and shall go out, and shall find pasture. The thief cometh not unless that he may steal and slaughter and destroy; I came that they might have life, and have abundantly" (verses 7-10).

In the former allegory the Lord speaks of Himself generally as Shepherd of the sheep, and this to put them forth, going at the head of them as they follow Him. Now He employs a different figure of Himself in direct terms, and with no less solemnity, "Verily, verily, I say to you, I am the Door of the sheep." There is no confusion with the former relation. It is not a question now of the sheepfold. This He had entered with every proof suited to man by God—proofs personal, moral, ministerial, miraculous, and prophetic; but the carnal mind is invincible in its unbelief, and withal being enmity against God, it is, if possible, less subject to His grace (which it understands not, but suspects) than to His law, which conscience feels to be just and right. When bowed or broken in the sense of sin against God, how sweet to hear the voice of Jesus! "I am the Door of the sheep," not of the fold but of such as are of God, who yearn after the knowledge of Him and deliverance from self. "All, as many as came ... are thieves and robbers, but the sheep did not hear them." They were not sent, but came without warrant; they sought their own things, not those of Jesus Christ, not of others, therefore. Corrupt or violent, how could they avail, either for the sheep, or for God's glory? To them the porter did not open, and if the adversary deceived, the sheep listened not; these were guarded, however tried.

But quite another was here. "I am the Door; through Me, if any shall have entered, he shall be saved, and shall go in and shall go out, and shall find pasture." How striking, yet perfectly simple, the fulness of grace touched in His words! It is no longer the narrow enclosure, but in principle for "anyone" to enter; and if one shall have entered through Christ, there is salvation, liberty, and food[190]—the sure, free, and rich blessing of Christianity. All turns on His glorious Person. Grace bringing salvation to any, to all, has appeared. When law shut up a people from the depravities of a rebellious and idolatrous race, when it schooled those who heeded it, we can see why the wisdom of God chose a single nation for this great moral experiment. But when the fulness of the time was come, God sent forth His Son, come of woman, come under law, to redeem those under law, that *we* (the sheep of the fold) might receive sonship. But because *ye* are sons (the Gentiles that believe the gospel) God sent forth the Spirit of His Son into our hearts, crying Abba, Father (Galatians 4). The gift was too precious, the boon too efficacious, to be pent up in the strait limits of Israel, especially as the Light manifested the darkness universal around.

Whoever, then, has entered through Christ shall be saved, shall go in and shall go out, and shall find all he lacks. God "that spared not His own Son, but delivered Him up for us all, how shall He not also with Him freely give us all things?" [Romans 8:32]. The law condemned the sinner, placed him in bondage, and sentenced him to die. The unchanging One changes all for the believer, be he who he may. This is grace as well as truth, and

THE TENTH CHAPTER

both came through and in Christ the Lord. What a Saviour! How worthy of the God Who gave and sent Him, His Only-begotten Son, into the world, that we might live through Him!

Outside Christ is sin and misery. Such is the world; and of all the world no part so delusive, so selfish, so fatal to itself and all governed by it, as the religious world and its leaders, the leaders now of infidelity as well as of superstition. Here is the testimony of Christ, of Him Who is the truth; "the thief cometh not unless that he may steal, and slaughter, and destroy." No creature can rise above his level; what, then, can the creature do that is steeped in unremoved evil and selfishness? It may sink indefinitely; it cannot possibly rise above itself. The world's hatred may become more deadly, its darkness more dense; yet no ideas nor feelings, no helps nor ordinances, can change its nature. But the pretension to be of God, when one is not, may and does precipitate into the depths of avarice and cruelty. It is the more destructive because the false claim of His name shuts up every avenue of ordinary human pity; and the reality of what is of God provokes in the unreal the determination to get rid of what condemns itself.

How blessed the contrast of Christ! "I came that they might have life, and have abundantly." He was the life, and life was in Him—not light only but life. All outside Him lay in darkness and death. He not only was sent of the Father but came, and came that the sheep might have life; and He would give it abundantly,[191] as was most due to His personal glory and His work—a work ever before Him here. Hence it was only in resurrection that He breathed into the disciples. As Jehovah God breathed on Adam, and the man became a living soul, after a different sort from every other living thing on earth; so did He, Who was alike the risen Man and true God, breathe a better life into those who believed on Him. It is life eternal, and this after all question of sin and law was settled for faith by His death.

The Lord next presents Himself in the beautiful character of the good Shepherd; a most affecting and expressive proof of His lowly love, when we think Who He is, and what we are.

> "I am the good Shepherd. The good Shepherd layeth down his life [soul][192] for the sheep. (But)[h] he that is a hireling, and not a shepherd, whose own the sheep are[i] not, beholdeth the wolf coming, and leaveth the sheep, and fleeth, and the wolf snatcheth them, and scattereth; and the hireling fleeth[j] because he is a hireling, and no care hath he for the sheep" (verses 11-13).

This indeed is love; not that we loved Him, but that He loved us, and died as propitiation for our sins. The giving up of life, in any case, for others would have been the fullest manifestation of love: how much more in His, to Whom the sheep belonged, Who had been from of old promised to stand and feed in the strength of Jehovah, in the majesty of the name of Jehovah His God! Greatness to the ends of the earth is a little thing compared with the good Shepherd's laying down His life for the sheep. It is the same Messiah; but how incalculably greater the testimony to His love in thus dying than in reigning ever so gloriously, however suitable and due to Himself, as well as to God's glory, and blessed for man when the kingdom comes![193]

Another phase of human pretension in divine things next appears, not thieves and robbers as before, but the "hireling," the man who meddles with the sheep, without higher motive than his own pelf {*i.e.*, wealth} or greed. "The hungry sheep look up, and are not fed," as sung one of our own poets,[193a] and not untruly. Here, then, the Lord first describes not their trials, but his character who claims what is not his own but Christ's, and so deserts them openly in the hour of danger. He "beholdeth the wolf coming, and leaveth the sheep, and fleeth." It is the adversary, by whatever means or instruments he may work. Then follows the peril they incur, and the actual injury done. "And the wolf snatcheth them, and scattereth; because he is a hireling, and no care hath he for the sheep." As divine love wrought in God's purpose and will, so in Christ's death; nor is there anything good or acceptable where love is not the motive. It is the true and only right spring of service; even as the Lord intimated to the servant, now fully restored and reinstated, after his denial of Himself, "Feed My lambs—My sheep." Not that He does not propose rewards the most glorious to encourage the servant who is already in the path of Christ and apt to be cast down by its difficulties; but love alone is recognised as that which constrains him to serve. Christ was the perfection of self-sacrificing love; and it is Satan who, as the wolf, seizes and scatters what is so precious to Him, through the selfishness of such as abandon the sheep in their greatest peril, the mercenary having no care for the sheep. The character of man and Satan is as plain as that of Christ, which last comes out for other traits in the next verses. From Him self-seeking was wholly absent; love only was there.

> "I am the good Shepherd, and know Mine, and Mine know Me,[k] even as the Father knoweth Me, and I know the Father, and My life I lay down for the sheep" (verses 14-15).

Here it is in the mutual knowledge of the Shepherd and the sheep that His goodness is shown; and this, wondrous to say, after the pattern of the Father's knowledge of the Son, and the Son's of the Father. It is a knowledge after a divine sort, and as true in His absence as in His presence. It was not such sheltering care as the Messiah might and will extend to His people, however tender; for "He will feed His flock like a shepherd; He will gather the lambs with His arms, and carry them in His bosom; He will gently lead those that give suck" [Isaiah 40:11]. But there had never been such transparent intimacy as between Him while on earth and His Father; and after this pattern, and none other, was it to be between Him on high and the sheep here below. This mutuality of knowledge disappears almost entirely in the Authorised Version through the unhappy full stop between verses 14 and 15, and the consequent mistranslation of the earlier clause of verse 15.

The Lord returns to His laying down His life for the sheep. Nor can we wonder; for as He could give no greater proof of love, so there is nothing which is so strengthening, as well as humbling, to our souls, nothing that so glorifies God, and no other turning-point for the blessing of the universe. At this point, however, it is the good Shepherd's love for the sheep.

Here the Lord can speak distinctly for the first time of other objects of His love. He might come minister of the circumcision for the lost sheep of the house of Israel [Matthew 15:24]. But His love could not be so circumscribed, when His death opens the floodgates. The mention of His death leads Him to speak of what was quite outside Israel.

THE TENTH CHAPTER

"And other sheep I have which are not of this fold"

—not of the Jewish people within their enclosure of law and ordinance;

"them also I must lead, and they shall hear My voice; and there shall be¹ one flock, one Shepherd" (verse 16).

It is not, as in the English Bible and others, following the Vulgate, "one *fold*," but "one flock." God owns no such thing now as a fold. It is exclusively Jewish; and the idea came in among Christians through the Judaizing of the Church, while the truth of the Church, when seen, makes such a thought or word, as applied to itself, intolerable. The truth is, as we have heard, that the Lord was to put forth all His own, He going before them, and the sheep following. So it was out of the Jewish fold. But other sheep He had which were not of it. "Them also I must lead, and they shall hear My voice." It was to be from among the Gentiles; and the believers there hear His voice, believing the gospel. But they form no new enclosure, fenced in by law, like the fold of Israel. The liberty of Christ is of the essence of Christianity, not only life and pardon, but freedom as well as food. For if Christ be all, what lack can there be? The Jewish sheep have been led out, the Gentile sheep are gathered, and both compose one flock, as truly as there is one Shepherd.[194]

One cause that has done as much as anything to dull the saints to the perception of the truth here is the fact of so many denominational enclosures in which they find themselves. Does it seem harsh to say that such a state of things, built up by Reformers and others of peculiar energy since the Reformation, is unauthorised? But what saith the Scripture, our only standard? "One flock, one Shepherd." How painful to find persons so prejudiced as to teach, "Many folds, but one flock"! But this is to pervert rather than to expound the word of God, which admits of no fold now that spirit and letter refuse the plea.

Another element which has wrought powerfully in favour of "one fold" is the mischievous confusion of the Church with Israel, Zion, etc., which runs through not only common theology, but even the headings of the Authorised Version, and constantly, therefore, is before all eyes. Hence, if we are now so identified with the ancient people of God that we are warranted to interpret all that is said of them in the Old Testament as our present portion, one cannot be surprised that this should tend to a similar result in the New.

But Christ's death has an aspect towards His Father of the deepest delight and complacency, besides being the basis of redemption and of Christianity.

> "On this account the Father loveth Me, because I lay down My life (soul) that I may take it again. No one taketh it from Me, but I lay it down of Myself. I have authority to lay it down, and I have authority to take it again: this commandment I received from My Father" (verses 17-18).

The Lord does not add here "for the sheep," nor should we limit His death to ourselves. He lets us see the value His own laying down His life had in itself. It was a fresh motive for the Father's love; and no wonder, if it were only as the unfathomable depth to which His own devotedness could go down. But, indeed, none but the Father knows what He found in it of love, confidence in Him, self-abandonment, and moral excellence in every way, crowned by the personal dignity of Him Who, standing in ineffably near relationship to the Father Himself, was thus pleased to die. Hence it could not but be that the Son would take His life again, not now in connection with the earth and man living on it, but risen from the dead, and so the power and pattern of Christianity.[195]

In this profound humiliation, to which the Lord submitted in grace, there is the utmost care to guard against the least suspicion that could lower His glory as the Son and God. It is not, as in Matthew (where He is viewed as the rejected Messiah, the Son of Man, not merely the destined head of all nations and tribes and tongues, but in command of the holy angels—His angels): He had only to call on His Father, Who would furnish Him more than twelve legions of angels. And what would have availed all Rome's legions against those heavenly beings, mighty in strength, that do His word? But how, then, He blessedly adds, could the Scriptures be fulfilled that thus it must be?

Divine Person though He was, He had come to die; the Life Eternal which was with the Father before there was either man or earth, He had deigned to become man, that He might thus lay down His life and take it again. But here He speaks not more in lowly love than as consciously God, "No one taketh it [away][195a] from Me, but I lay it down of Myself. I have authority to lay it down, and I have authority to take it again: this commandment I received from My Father." On the one hand there is the calm assertion of the right as well as power to lay down His life and to take it again. As none but the Creator could do the latter, so no creature is entitled to do the former. None but God has power and title to do both; and the Word, without, of course, ceasing to be Divine (which, indeed, could not be), became flesh that He might thus die and rise. On the other hand, even in this, which might have been justly deemed the most strictly personal of all acts, He abides the obedient man, and would do only the will of His Father. He was come to do the will of God. This is perfection, and found in Jesus alone.[195b] Well may we adore Him with the Father Who gave Him. He is worthy.

These wondrous words were not without effect even then among the Jews. Love unknown before, the lowliness of a servant, the dignity of One consciously Divine, wrought in some consciences, while they roused others to a deeper hatred. So it is, and must be, in a world of sinful men, where God and Satan are both at work in the momentous conflict of good and evil.

> "There was a division[m] again among the Jews because of these words; but[n] many of them said, He hath a demon and is mad: why hear ye Him? Others said, These are not the sayings of one possessed by a demon: can a demon open blind (men's) eyes?" (verses 19-21).

The greater the grace, and the deeper the truth, the less does the natural mind appreciate Christ. He is, indeed, the test of every soul that hears His word. But if some imputed what was infinitely above man to a demon, and to the raving consequent on such a possession, others there were who felt how far the words were from those of a demoniac, and who bowed to the divine power which sealed them. The words and the works to their consciences had another character and import.[196]

Verses 22-38.

> "Now[o] it was the feast of the dedication at Jerusalem, (and) it was winter; and Jesus was walking in the temple in the porch of Solomon. The Jews therefore surrounded Him, and said to Him, How long dost Thou hold our soul in suspense? If Thou art the Christ, tell us openly. Jesus answered, I told you, and ye believe not. The works which I do in the name of My Father, these bear witness of Me; but ye believe not, because ye are not of My sheep.[p] My sheep hear My voice, and *I* know them, and they follow Me; and *I* give them life eternal, and they shall in no wise ever perish, and no one shall seize them out of My hand. My Father[q] Who[q] hath given Me (them) is greater than all; and no one is able to seize out of the hand of My[q] Father. I and the Father are one" (verses 22-30).

We are many of us familiar with the effort to sustain tradition and human authority in divine things by such a passage as the opening of verse 22. But it is really futile. For here we learn nothing of our Lord's participation in any observances of men,[197] whatever they may have been, but of His being then in Jerusalem, winter as it was, and walking in Solomon's porch, when the Jews came round, and kept saying to Him, "Till when (or, How long) dost Thou excite our soul (or, keep it in suspense)?" Wretched and guilty as their unbelief was, the Jews drew no such inference from His presence then and there. They were uneasy, spite of their opposition to Him. "If Thou art the Christ, tell us openly."[198] But the fatal hour was at hand, and the power of darkness; and the light was about to pass away from them after its full manifestation in their midst. "Jesus answered, I told you, and ye believe not." Take only His words recorded in John 5, 6, and 8. A plainer and richer testimony could not be. But testimony does not always last. It is given freely, fully, patiently, and may then be turned aside from those who reject to such as hear. Thus is God wont to act, and so does the Lord answer on this occasion. "I told you, and ye believe not."

But there was more than words, however truly divine—words of grace and truth according to His Person. There were works of similar character; and the Jews were accustomed to look for a sign. If they sought honestly, they might see signs beyond man's numbering or estimate. "The works which I do in the name of My Father, they bear witness of Me." What could account for such hardness in any heart? "But ye believe not, because ye are not of My sheep." Solemn solution of a difficulty, of a resistance to truth, of a rejection of Christ, as true now as ever!

Men trust to themselves, to their own feelings, to their own judgments. Have these never played them false? Have they ever been true before God? What suicidal folly not to distrust themselves, and look to God, cry to God, ask of God, what is His way, His truth, His Son! But no: this were to believe and be saved; and they will not. They are too proud. They will not bow to the word that arraigns them as sinners, even though it sends them the message of remission of sins on their faith. They feel that such grace on God's part supposes utter guilt and ruin on theirs, and this they are too hard, too proud, to own. They believe not; they are not of the Saviour's sheep. Criminals, heathen, perhaps, may need a Saviour; not decent, moral, religious men like themselves! They do not, will not, believe, and are lost, not because they are too great sinners for Christ, but because they refuse Christ as the Saviour, and deny their ruin as sinners. They prefer to go on as they are, like the great mass of men: God, they think, is too merciful; and they hope to improve some day if they feel not quite right to-day. Thus are they lost. Such is the way and end of many an unbeliever now, as of the Jews then.

How, then, are Christ's sheep characterised? We need not hesitate to receive the answer, for here is His own account of them. "My sheep hear My voice": a quality incomparably better than doing this, or that, or all things without it. It is the obedience of faith, the holy parent of all holy issues. Without faith it is impossible to please God; and this is the present characteristic of those who are of faith: they hear the voice of Christ, and are truly humble, yet firm. It is not self-assertion, nor the forgetfulness of their own sinfulness and of His glory. It is the simple owning of His grace, and of their own need; and thus only are souls blessed through Christ to God's glory.

This, however, is not their only privilege. "And *I* know them," says the Saviour. It is not here said that they know Christ, however true by grace. But He knows them, all their thoughts and feelings, their words and ways, their dangers and difficulties, their past, present, and future. He knows themselves, in short, perfectly, and in perfect love. How infinite the favour and the blessing! What a resource and a joy!

But there is more. The sheep not only hear Christ's voice, but, says He, "They follow Me." For faith is living and practical, or worse than useless. And as it is due to Christ that His own should follow Him, so they need it, exposed as they are to countless foes, seen and unseen. It is their security, whatever the circumstances they pass through: Christ Who leads the sheep cannot fail, and, as He knows them, so they follow Him. Thus He keeps them by the way, which He is.{198a}

"And *I* give them life eternal, and they shall never perish, and no one shall seize them out of My hand." Thus the Lord guarantees His own life to them, not the life of Adam, who brought in death, and died, and left the sad inheritance to all his offspring; whereas the Second Man and last Adam, being Son of God, quickens whom He will, and quickens with and to life everlasting. Is it said, however, that the sheep are weak? Unquestionably; but here He excludes fear and anxiety for all who believe in Him, for He immediately adds that "they shall in no wise ever be lost." No intrinsic weakness, therefore, shall compromise their safety for a moment. Nor shall hostile force or wiles jeopard them; for "no one shall seize them out of My hand."[199]

Could love assure its objects of more? His love would impart to them the certainty of His own deepest joy, His Father's love as sure as His own; and so He closes His communication with it. "My Father Who hath given to Me is greater than all, and no one is able to seize out of the hand of My Father. I and the Father are one." Here we rise into that height of holy love and infinite power of which none could speak but the Son; and He speaks of the secrets of Godhead with the intimate familiarity proper to the Only-begotten Who is in the Father's bosom. He needed none to testify of man, for He knew what was in man, being Himself God; and He knew what was in God for the self-same reason. Heaven or earth made no difference, time or eternity. Not a creature is unapparent before Him, but all things are naked and laid bare in His eyes with Whom we have to do. And He declares that the Father Who had made the gift resists all that can threaten harm, and as He has given to Christ, so He is greater than all, and none can seize out of His hand. Indeed, the Son and the Father are one, not one Person (which ἐσμεν, with every other scripture bearing on it, refutes), but one thing, ἕν, one divine nature or essence (as other scriptures equally prove). The lowliest of men, the Shepherd of the sheep, He is the Son of the Father, true God and eternal life. And He and the Father are not more truly one in divine essence than in the fellowship of divine love for the sheep.

Thus did the Lord assume and imply divine glory as His, no less than the Father's, spite of the place of man He had taken in the humiliation of love, in order to undo the works of the devil, and deliver guilty sinners who hear His voice from the bondage of sin and God's most righteous judgment. This roused again the murderous hatred of His hearers.

> "The Jews (therefore)[r] again took up stones, that they might stone Him. Jesus answered them, Many good works I showed you from the (or, My)[s] Father: on account of which work of them do ye stone Me? The Jews answered Him,[t] For a good work we stone Thee not, but for blasphemy, and because Thou, being a man, makest Thyself God" (verses 31-33).

Alas for the will and self-confidence of man! They were right in saying that Jesus was a man; they were not wrong in understanding that He claimed to be God. But it was the insinuation of Satan working on man's unbelief of all beyond his senses and mind, that He Who was God would not deign, in love to men and for the divine glory, to become man in order to accomplish redemption. Was it incredible that God should stoop so low for these most worthy ends? And had not Jesus given adequate evidence of His glory and relation to the Father, in power and goodness, as well as truth? A life of purity unknown, of dependence on God beyond parallel, of active goodness untiring, of humility and of suffering the more surprising, because in evident command of power unlimited in testimony to the Father, and this in accomplishment of the entire chain of Scripture types and prophecy, combine to hurl back the imputation of imposture on the old serpent, the liar and father of it; whose great lie is to oust God from being the object of man's faith and service and worship for false objects, or no object but self, which, however little suspected, is really Satan's service.

Nothing, therefore, so rouses Satan as God thus presented in and by the Lord Jesus, Who displays His own perfect meekness and man's enmity by no intervention of power to save Him from insult and injury. "First He must suffer many things, and be rejected of this generation" [Luke 17:25]—a generation which goes on still morally, and will, till He returns in glory to judge. They therefore took up stones to stone Him; for Satan is a murderer as well as a liar, and nothing so awakens violence, even to death, as the truth which condemns men pretending to religion. To their blinded and infuriated minds it was blasphemy[200] for Him to say that He gave His followers eternal life beyond the weakness or the power of the creature—blasphemy to assert that He and the Father were one; whereas it is the truth, so vital and necessary that none who reject it can be saved. His words were as good as His works, and even more momentous to man; while both were of the Father.[201] He Whom God sent, as John testified, spoke the words of God. It was they who blasphemed, denying Him to be

THE TENTH CHAPTER

God Who, in grace to them, condescended to become man.{201a}

But He meets them on their own ground by an *a fortiori* argument, which left His personal glory untouched.

> "Jesus answered them, Is it not written in your law, I said, Ye are gods? If He called them gods to whom the word of God came²⁰² (and the Scripture cannot be broken), say ye of Him Whom the Father sanctified and sent into the world, Thou blasphemest, because I said, I am Son of God?" (verses 34-36).²⁰³

Thus does He reason most conclusively from the less to the greater; for every Jew knew that their inspired books, as for instance, Psalm 82, calls judges *elohim* (gods), as commissioned by God and responsible to judge in His name. If such a title could be used of a mere magistrate in Scripture (and its authority is indissoluble), how unreasonable to tax with blasphemy Him Whom the Father set apart,ᵘ and sent into the world, because He said He was God's Son! He is not affirming or demonstrating what He is in this, but simply convicting them of their perverseness on the ground of their law. They had not the least excuse whilst they claimed adherence to their law of divine authority. If God called the judges by His name as being His representatives, how much more was it due to Him Who had a place so unique?

> "If I do not the works of My Father, believe Me not; but if I do, even if ye believe not Me, believeᵛ the works, that ye may perceive and know [or, believe]ᵛ that the Father (is) in Me, and I in the Father"ʷ (verses 37-38).

There was no denying the irresistible force of this appeal. The character of the works bore testimony, not only to divine power, but to this in the fulness of love. Think as they might of Him, the works were unmistakable, that they might learn and come to know the unity of the Father and the Son. It is not that He enfeebles the dignity of His Person, or the truth of His words; but He was pleading with them, and dealing with their consciences, by those works which attested not more the power than the grace of God, and consequently His glory Who wrote them. But self-will holds out against all proofs.

Verses 39-42.

> "They sought therefore again to seize Him, and He departed out of their hand. And He went away again beyond the Jordan[204] to the place where John was at first baptizing, and abode there. And many came unto Him and said, John did no sign, but all things whatsoever John said about Him were true. And many believed on Him there" (verses 39-42).

Thus it was not that their unbelief was incomplete, but that His time was not yet come. The Lord therefore retires till the moment appointed of God, and meanwhile goes to the scene of John's work at the first, and there abode, where grace wins many a soul that recognised in Him the truth of John's testimony.

NOTES ON THE TENTH CHAPTER

a [Cf. *Lectures Introductory to the Study of the Gospels*, pp. 485-495.]

b καλεῖ T.R. with eleven uncials and most cursives, etc.; φωνεῖ ℵABDLX, some cursives, etc. Either means "calleth."

c Most [as Syr^{sin}] insert καὶ (as T.R.), or δὲ; but the most ancient omit.

d Most uncials, etc., read πρόβατα, "sheep," as T.R., but very ancient ones have either πάντα, "all," or [as Blass] nothing more than τὰ ἴδια, "his own."

e The Gospel of John does not use the ordinary word "parable," as the Synoptics do frequently, and no other, for our Lord's narrative likenesses in illustration of truth. John was led to employ the word [παροιμία] given in the Septuagint [Proverbs 1:1] for a "proverb," in the sense of an "allegory," or a divergence from the common way of speech, as parable means a comparison.[187a]

f Some omit πάλιν and others αὐτοῖς.

g Authorities are about equally for and against [Syr^{sin}, Blass] πρὸ ἐμοῦ, as in T.R.[189]

h The copulative particle δὲ is not in BGL and a few other good witnesses.

i ἐστὶν ℵABLX, etc.; εἰσὶν most uncials and cursives.

j This clause ὁ δὲ μισθωτὸς φεύγει, "and the hireling fleeth," is not given in ℵ (A is somewhat uncertain) BDL, some cursives, ancient versions [as Syr^{sin}], etc., but a dozen uncials of inferior age and weight, with most cursives and some of the old versions, insert as in T.R.

k The T.R., with thirteen uncials and perhaps all cursives, etc., has γινώσκομαι ὑπὸ τῶν ἐμῶν, "I am known of Mine"; אBDL, with the oldest versions [as Syr^{sin}, Weiss, Blass], γινώσκουσί με τὰ ἐμά.

l א^{corr}BDLX, etc., support the plural form, γενήσονται, "they shall be," the rest have the singular, γενήσεται [Weiss, Blass], which might bear the same meaning.

m "Therefore" in the T.R. has considerable support of MSS., but the older omit it.

n Here, again, some give "therefore" instead of "but."

o BL, 33, Memph. have "then," as they and more omit "and." [Text as אADX—adopted by Blass—Latt., Syrr., Chrys.]

p The weightiest authorities omit "as I told you."

q Some MSS. say "the" for "My" [Blass]; others, not "Who," but "as to what He."—אBL [Syr^{sin}] omit last μου, "My" [Weiss, Blass].

r אBL, 33, etc., omit; the rest add.

s א^{pm}BD omit μου, "My."

t The bulk of witnesses omits, "saying."

u It is well to note that the Lord predicates sanctification of Himself in chapter 17:19 as set apart now in heaven, the model Man in glory, and here by the Father for His mission into the world, quite distinct from the application of the word to us who were sinners, and even dead in sins. Sanctification, in the case of the Holy One, resolves itself into its pure and abstract sense of setting apart.

v The weight of testimony is for πιστεύετε [אA, etc., so Weiss] rather than πιστεύσατε [Blass]. Then, as γινώσκητε [know, come to know] seemed difficult after γνῶτε [perceive, learn], many read πιστεύσητε [believe] as the T.R. has it.

w "The Father" is in ℵBDLX, two cursives, several It. Vulg. Syrr. Sah. Arm. Arab. Anglo-Sax. Pers. (Memph. Æth. reversing order[—as Weiss]); "Him," as in T.R., AΓΔ and nine uncials more, mass of cursives, some It. Gothic, Syrr.[txt] Slav [Blass].

THE ELEVENTH CHAPTER[a]
VERSES 1-16.

The Lord was rejected, rejected in His words, rejected in His works. Both were perfect, but man felt that God was brought near to him by both; and, an enemy of God, he increasingly musters hatred against His Son, His image.

But the grace of God still waits on guilty man, and would give a fresh, full, and final testimony to Jesus. And here we begin with that which was most of all characteristic of our Gospel—His divine Sonship displayed in resurrection power. All is public now; all near or in Jerusalem. The design of God governs here, as everywhere. All the Evangelists present the testimony to His Messianic glory, the second of these three testimonies, though none with such fulness of detail as Matthew, whose function it was pre-eminently to show Him as the Son of David according to prophecy, but rejected now, and about to return in power and glory. It was John's place, above all, to mark Him out as Son of God, and this the Holy Spirit does by giving us through his Gospel the resurrection of Lazarus. Christ is in resurrection the life-giving spirit, as contrasted with Adam {1 Corinthians 15:45}; but He is the Son eternally, and the Son quickens whom He will {John 5:21}, before death no less than after resurrection; and this is here exhibited with all fulness of detail as was due to it.[205]

> "Now there was a certain (man) sick, Lazarus, from Bethany, of the village of Mary and Martha her sister. But Mary was she that anointed the Lord with unguent, and wiped His feet with her hair, whose brother Lazarus was sick.[206] The sisters then sent unto Him, saying, Lord, behold, he whom Thou lovest (φιλεῖς) is sick" (verses 1-3).

Thus does John introduce the account. It puts us at once in presence of all concerned—the household whither He used to retire from the sterile but guilty parties of Jerusalem. Who had not heard of the woman that anointed the Lord with unguent, and wiped His feet with her hair [12:3]? Wherever the gospel was preached in the whole world, this was told for a memorial of her. But her name had been withheld till now. It was John's place to mention what so closely touched the Person of the Lord. John names others, if he conceals his own name. It was Mary; and she, with her sister, sent a message to the Lord, reckoning on the promptness of His love. They were not disappointed. His love exceeded all their thought, as His glory was beyond their faith, however real it might be. But their faith was tried, as it always is.

> "But when Jesus heard, He said, This sickness is not unto death but for the glory of God, that the Son of God may be glorified by it. Now Jesus loved (ἠγάπα) Martha and her sister and Lazarus. When therefore He heard that he was sick, He then remained two days in the place where He was; then after this He saith to His[b] (or, the) disci-

ples, Let us go into Judæa again. The disciples say to Him, Rabbi, the Jews were just now seeking to stone Thee, and goest Thou thither again? Jesus answered, Are there not twelve hours of the day? If one walk in the day, he doth not stumble, because he seeth the light of this world; but if one walk in the night, he stumbleth, because the light is not in him" (verses 4-10).

First appearances are ever in this world against the good and holy and true. Those who seek occasion against what is according to God can easily find excuse for their own evil. And the moral object of God, as of His word, tests every soul that comes into contact. So here the Lord knew the end from the beginning when He said, This sickness is not unto death; but he who was quick to judge by the beginning must inevitably misjudge. What would he have judged who heard Him say, Lazarus, come forth, and saw the dead man come forth from the cave of burial?

Resurrection displays the glorious power of God beyond all else. It arrests, and is intended to arrest, man, who knows too well what sickness is and how hopelessly death severs him from all his activities. The sickness of Lazarus then, just because it ran up into death, was about to furnish a meet occasion for God's glory, and this, too, in the glorifying of His Son thereby.

There are those who delight in what they call "the reign of law"; but what is the sense of such thoughts or words when brought to the touchstone of resurrection? Does not the raising of the dead prove the supremacy of God's power over that which is a law, if there be an invariable lot appointed to sinful man here below, the law of death? For certainly death is not the cause of resurrection; but the Son is He Who wields the power of life. He quickens whom He will, for He is God, but as the Sent One, the dependent and obedient Servant, for He is man. Such was Jesus here in this world, and this manifested most fully a short time before He laid down His life for the sheep.

But man is a poor judge of divine love, and even saints learn it only by faith. Jesus will have us confide in His love. For this is love, not that we loved Him, but that He loved us, and proved it in His dying a propitiation for us {1 John 4:10}. Even here, too, how significantly the Evangelist says that Jesus loved Martha and her sister and Lazarus, just before the mention of His staying two days in the place where He was after the message came. If a mere man, with power to heal, loved another that was sick, how soon he would have healed the patient! And Jesus had already shown His power to heal in the same hour. No matter what the intervening distance, or how unconscious the sufferer, why not speak the word on behalf of Lazarus? Did He love the nobleman of Capernaum and his boy, did He love the Gentile centurion and his servant, better than Lazarus? Assuredly nothing of the sort; but it was for the glory of God that the Son of God might be glorified by that very sickness, not arrested but allowed to work its way.

The Lord was about to raise the dead Lazarus; and this when it had not the appearance of a law, but rather by grace the exemption of one from the law of death. How truly for the glory of God was the result! Not so was the way man would have wrought at once if he could. He Who was God, and loved as no man ever did, abode two days where He was, and then calmly said to the disciples, Let us go into Judæa again. They wonder. Did He not know better than they the murderous rancour of the

Jews? Had He forgotten their repeated efforts to stone Him? Why then, did He propose to go thither again? He was here to do the will of His Father; and here was a work to do for His glory. His eye certainly was ever single, His body full of light.

"Jesus answered, Are there not twelve hours of the day? If one walk in the day, he stumbleth not, because he seeth the light of the world; but if one walk in the night, he stumbleth, because the light is not in him." If it was the will of the Father, it was day; and as Jesus was not only sent by the living Father, but lived on account of Him, so for the disciple He is the light and the food and the motive. The known will and word of God is the light of day; to be without it is to walk in the night, and stumbling is the sure consequence. If Christ be before us, the light will be in us, and we stumble not. May we evermore heed His word!

The Lord would exercise the hearts of His own. As His tarrying in the same place for two days was not the impulse of human feeling, so His going to the place of deadly hatred was according to the light He walked in and was. He has more to say which they had to ponder. He abides in dependence; He awaits His Father's will. This given decides His movements at once.

> "These things said He, and after this He saith to them, Lazarus our friend is fallen asleep; but I go that I may awake him. Therefore said the disciples to Him,^{c} Lord, if he is fallen asleep, he will recover. But Jesus had spoken of his death, but they thought that He was speaking (*literally*, speaketh) of the rest of sleep. Then therefore said Jesus to them plainly, Lazarus is dead; and I rejoice on your account that I was not there, that ye may

believe. But let us go unto him.²⁰⁷ Thomas therefore, that is called Didymus, said to his fellow-disciples, Let *us* also go, that we may die with him" (verses 11-16).²⁰⁸

The Lord begins to disclose what He was about to do; but they were dull to think of death on the one hand, or of His resurrection power on the other. The prevention of death, the healing of disease, is far short of triumph over death. The disciples were to be strengthened by the sight of resurrection before He died on the cross and rose again.

It is important to note that here, as everywhere, sleep is said of the body. It is the suited word of faith for death: how dark the unbelief that perverts it, as some do, to materialise the soul! He Who is the Truth speaks as the thing really is. He knew that He was about to raise Lazarus.

But the Lord Who tries faith meets the weakness of His disciples, and clears up the difficulty. He tells them plainly "Lazarus is dead," and expresses His joy on their account that He was not there (that is, merely to heal), in order that they might believe, when they knew better His power to quicken and raise the dead. Gloomy Thomas can see only His rushing into death when He proposed to go to Judæa, though his love to the Lord prompts him to say, Let *us* also go that we may die with Him. How poor are the thoughts of a disciple, even where affection was true to the Master, Who was indeed about to die in willing grace for them—yea, for their sins—that they might live for ever, justified from all things; but Who would prove before He died a sacrifice that He could not only live but give life to the dead as He would, yet in obedience to, and in communion with, His Father! Such is our Saviour.

Verses 17-44.

"Jesus therefore, on coming, found that he was four days in the tomb. Now Bethany was[209] near Jerusalem, about fifteen furlongs off; and many of the Jews had come unto Martha and Mary[d] that they might comfort them concerning their brother. Martha then, when she heard Jesus is coming, met Him; but Mary was sitting in the house. Martha then said unto Jesus, Lord, if Thou hadst been here, my brother had not died. And now I know that, whatsoever Thou mayest ask of God, God will give Thee. Jesus saith to her, Thy brother shall rise again. Martha saith to Him, I know that he shall rise in the resurrection at the last day.[210] Jesus said to her, I am the Resurrection and the Life: he that believeth on Me, though he have died, shall live; and every one that liveth and believeth on Me shall never die (*literally*, shall in no wise die for ever). Believest thou this? She saith to Him, Yea, Lord, I do believe (I have believed, and do) that Thou art the Christ, the Son of God, that should come into the world.[211] And having said this she went away, and called Mary her sister secretly, saying, The Teacher is here, and calleth thee. When she heard (it), she riseth quickly, and cometh unto Him" (verses 17-29).

The interval since death and burial is carefully stated, as well as the contiguity of the spot to Jerusalem, and the number of Jews who at the moment had joined the company of Martha and Mary, with a view to console them in their sorrow. God was ordering all for a bright testimony to His Son. For Æschylus (*Eumenides*, {line} 647) but expressed the universal mind of the heathen, himself a religious heathen, that man, once dead, has no resurrection. What had God for such as believe on Jesus? What had Jesus? What is He but the Resurrection and the Life? It was no question of the last day only. Jesus was there then, the conqueror of death as of Satan.

Again Martha, prompt as ever when she heard of Jesus approaching, went to meet Him, while Mary kept sitting in the house with a deeper sense of death, but at least as ready to go when summoned. Meanwhile she waits, as the Lord knew well and appreciated. When Martha did meet the Lord, she confesses His power to have warded off death by His presence. She owns Him as the Messiah; and as such she is confident that even now, whatever He may "ask" of God will be given Him. No doubt she meant this as a strong expression of her faith. But it was to correct this error, to give an incomparably fuller apprehension, that the Lord came now to raise Lazarus. Hence she applies to the Lord language far below His true relation to the Father: ὅσα ἂν αἰτήσῃ τὸν θεόν. Had she said ἐρωτήσῃ τὸν πατέρα, it would have been more becoming. It is all right to use αἰτέω of us, for the place of a suppliant or petitioner becomes us; but the word of more familiar demand, ἐρωτάω, is suitable to Him. This, however, she, though a believer, had to learn.

When Jesus tells Martha that her brother shall rise again, she replies at once, "I know that he shall rise again in the resurrection at the last day." But the Lord was here, not to teach truths known already, but to give what was unknown, and this in the glory of His own Person. Therefore said Jesus to Martha, "I am the Resurrection and the Life," and in this order as strictly applicable to the case in hand, Lazarus being dead and buried. He is the Resurrection no less than the Life, and this in fulness of power. "He that believeth on Me, though he should die, shall live; and every one that liveth and believeth in Me shall never die: believest thou this?" It is the superiority of life in Christ over all impediments, to be displayed at His coming. "For we shall not all sleep, but we shall all be changed in an instant, in the twinkling of an eye, at the last trumpet; for the trumpet shall sound, and the dead shall be raised incorruptible, and we shall be changed" [1 Corinthians 15:51 *f.*]. Thus, at the coming of the Lord "the dead in Christ shall rise first; then we the living that remain," without passing through death, "shall be caught up together with them to meet the Lord in the air, and so shall we ever be with the Lord" [1 Thessalonians 4:16 *f.*]. Thus will He be proved the Resurrection and the Life: the Resurrection, because the dead believers immediately arise, obedient to His voice; the Life, because every one that lives and believes on Him has mortality swallowed up of life at the same moment.

This tests Martha. To the Lord's inquiry, "Believest thou this?" she can only give the vague reply, "Yea, Lord, I have believed, and do believe [πεπίστευκα] that Thou art the Christ, the Son of God, that should come into the world:" a word containing truth doubtless, but no real answer to the question. She felt the uneasiness usual even to saints who hear what is beyond their depth; and she thinks of her sister as one that would understand incomparably better than herself; and so, without staying to learn, she hurried off, and called Mary secretly, saying, "The Teacher is here, and calleth thee." Mary, when she heard, quickly rises and comes. How sweet the call to her heart!

THE ELEVENTH CHAPTER

There was not the smallest haste in the movements of our Lord. Indeed, we may rather note His calm bearing in presence of the one sister, so quick to go before she was called, and of the other when she was. Jesus abides the same, a man yet in the quiet dignity of the Son of God.

> "Now Jesus had not yet come into the village, but was in the place where Martha came to meet Him. The Jews therefore who were with her in the house and consoling her, having seen Mary that she quickly rose up and went out, followed her,ᵉ thinking she goeth unto the tomb, that she may weep there" (verses 30-31).

It was not so, however; but the grace of Christ meant that there He should meet Mary, soon about to behold a bright outshining of the glory of God in her beloved Lord. What strangers to Jesus were those who would console her in vain in the presence of death!

Not that Mary was above the pressure of death more than others. She repeats what Martha said; but she was of a different spirit in repeating it.

> "Mary therefore when she came where Jesus was, having seen Him, fell at His feet, saying to Him, Lord, if Thou hadst been here, my brother had not died" (verse 32).

But if she saw in Him as yet only power to preserve, if she had to learn that He is the Resurrection and the Life, at least she fell at His feet, as Martha did not; and the Lord, if He says nothing, will soon answer in deed and in truth. But the consciousness of divine glory, and this about to manifest itself superior to death in presence of all, in no way detracted from the sensibilities of His spirit. On the contrary, the very next verses let us know how deep were the emotions of our blessed Lord at this moment.

> "Jesus therefore, when He saw her weeping, and the Jews that came with her weeping, was deeply moved in spirit, and troubled Himself, and said, Where have ye laid Him?[212] They say to Him, Lord, come and see. ᶠJesus wept. The Jews therefore said, Behold, how He loved (ἐφ.) him! And some of them said, Could not this (man) that opened the eyes of the blind, have caused that this (man) also should not have died?" (verses 33-37).

The word translated "deeply moved" occurs elsewhere for a "strict" or stern "charge," as in Matthew 9:30, Mark 1:43; or an angry speech, as in Mark 14:5. Here it is rather the inward feeling than the expression, approached rather nearly by such use as that in Lucian (*Necyomantia*, 20), of (it would seem) groaning. It means the strong, and it may be indignant, affection the Lord experienced at the power of death over not the Jews only but Mary, wielded as it still was by the enemy. This is still farther expressed by the phrase that follows, as well as by verse 38. His tender sympathy appears rather in His weeping (verse 35), after asking where they had laid Lazarus, and the invitation to come and see. His indignant sense of Satan's power through sin did not interfere in the least with His deep compassion; and what we see here is but the counterpart of His habitual bearing the diseases and taking the infirmities, which the first Gospel applies from Isaiah 53:4 [Matthew 8:17]. Never was it mere power, nor was it only sympathy, but the entrance of His spirit into every case He cured, the bearing of the weight on His heart before God of all that oppressed sin-stricken man. Here it was the still greater ravage of death in the family He loved.

But we may note that in our Lord's case, profound as was His grief, it was His servant. "He troubled Himself." It did not gain the mastery, as our affections are apt to do with us. Every feeling in Christ was perfect in kind and measure as well as season. His groaning, His trouble, His weeping—what were they not in God's sight! How precious should they not be to us! Even the Jews could not but say, "Behold, how He loved him!" What had they thought had they known He was just going to raise the dead man? If they did not recall His power, it was only the unavailing regret that He Who healed the blind had not forefended death in the case of Lazarus. They were utterly at fault about this sickness, as blind to the glory of God as to the way of it, that the Son of God would be glorified thereby. Faith in the glory of His Person alone rightly interprets and appreciates in its measure the depth of His love. "Jesus wept." What a difference these words convey to him who sees nothing but a man, and to him who knows Him to be the mighty God, the Only-begotten Son! Even the unbeliever could not in this case fail to own His love; but how immensely that love is enhanced by His divine dignity, and the consciousness that He was about to act in the power of divine life above death![212a]

Now it is of all consequence that we should believe and know, without doubt, that all which Jesus showed Himself that day on behalf of Lazarus He is, and far more, for His own, and that He will prove it for every one of us at His coming. For there is now also the fruit of the travail of His soul, and the power of His resurrection, after the fullest judgment of sin in the cross. Hence all His love and power can act unhinderedly on our behalf, as they surely will to the glory of God, that the Son of God may be glorified thereby. What men then beheld was but a testimony, however truly divine; but at His coming the truth will be fully out in power. Now is the time to believe and confess the truth in the midst of a crooked and perverted generation. May we be enabled in lowliness of mind to appear as lights in the world, holding forth the word of life!

> "Jesus therefore again, deeply moved in Himself, cometh unto the tomb. Now it was a cave,[213] and a stone lay upon it. Jesus saith, Take away the stone.[214] Martha, the sister of the deceased,[g] saith to Him, Lord, he already stinketh, for he is four days (dead). Jesus saith to her, Said I not to thee that if thou wouldest believe, thou shouldest see the glory of God? They took away therefore the stone;[h] and Jesus lifted His eyes upward, and said, Father, I thank Thee that Thou heardest Me. And I knew that Thou hearest Me always; but on account of the crowd that standeth around I said (it), that they may believe that Thou didst send Me.[215] And having said this, He cried with a loud voice, Lazarus, come forth. And[i] the dead came forth,[215a] having the feet and the hands bound with graveclothes, and his face was bound round with a handkerchief. Jesus saith to them, Loose him, and let him[i] go" (verses 38-44).

It was no longer the time for words, and Jesus, again realising for Himself the power which shut out God's glory from man, comes to the cave with a stone laid on it, which served for a tomb. There the unbelief of Martha ventured (what does it not?) to oppose the Lord's word to remove the stone: He, that all might be clear; she, because His words disappointed her haste, if, indeed, she expected anything. But if Martha could not rise above the humbling effects of death, which she would shut out from others, Jesus would not hide what was due to God in grace to man. How quickly the word of the Lord is forgotten in presence of the sad circumstances of human ruin! Faith gives the word heed, and reaps the blessing in due time. Listen to Jesus. He is heard already. He knows beforehand that He has what He asks, heard now as always before. The Father was concerned no less than the Son, and it was said that those who heard might believe that the Father sent Him forth.

Thereon comes the word of power: "Lazarus, come forth." He had prayed to the Father, jealous above all for His glory, and never forgetful of the place He had Himself come down to as man. But He was the Son, He could quicken whom He would, and so He does. Yet even in the majesty of this divine display, He intermingles after, as well as before, what drew men's attention, that they might not be faithless but believing. What difficulty was there in the stone? For Himself He needed to remove nothing. It was for their sakes. Behold, man in the loathsomeness of death before he was raised! And so now what for Him mattered the binding of the graveclothes, or of the handkerchief? The grace of the Lord by both would only give them the better confirmation of what He had wrought. He could have loosed Lazarus as easily as He could have caused the stone to disappear; He could have willed all without crying with a loud voice; but He, Who would that we should confide in the power of His word, would have us note the corruption that precedes quickening and the bondage which may follow it now. Liberty is needed as well as life; but it is unnatural that one who is made to live should be longer bound.

Mighty as was the work of thus raising Lazarus, we see here, as everywhere, how dependent man is on grace. Sin makes him the slave of Satan, little as he suspects it. His will is against God, in His goodness or in His judgment, in His word or His works; and the greater the mercy, the less he likes what is so contrary to his thoughts, and so humbling to his pride. If many were impressed and believed, some went mischievously to the enemy with their information.

VERSES 45-54.

"Many of the Jews therefore that came to Mary, and beheld what He did, believed on Him; but some of them went away unto the Pharisees, and told them what Jesus did.[215b] The chief priests therefore and the Pharisees gathered together a council, and said, What do we, for this man doeth many signs? (and)[j] if we leave Him thus, all will believe on Him, and the Romans will come and take away both our place and nation. But a certain one of them, Caiaphas, being high priest of that year, said to them, Ye know nothing, nor reckon[k] that it is profitable for you[l] that one man should die for the people, and not the whole nation perish. Now this he said not from himself, but, being high priest of that year, he prophesied that Jesus was about to die for the nation, and not for the nation only, but that also He should gather together into one the children of God that were scattered abroad. From that day therefore they consulted[m] that they might kill Him. Jesus therefore walked no more openly among the Jews, but went away thence into the country near the desert, unto a city called Ephraim, and there He abode^n with the° disciples" (verses 45-54).

The chief priests and the Pharisees are immediately on the alert. They assemble a council; they wonder at their own inactivity in presence of the many signs done by Jesus; they fear that, if left alone, He may become universally acceptable, and that they may provoke the Romans to destroy them, "Church and State", as men now say. How affecting to see the power of Satan blinding those most who take the highest place in zeal for God after the flesh! It was their desperately wicked purpose to put Him to death—a purpose as desperately effected, which led to the cross, in which He did become the attractive centre to men of every class and nation and moral condition; and it was their guilt in this especially, though not this alone, which drew on them the wrath of "the king," who sent his forces, destroyed those murderers, and burnt their city. All righteous blood came upon them, and their house is left desolate unto this day, and this, too, by the dreaded hand of the Romans, whom they professed to propitiate by the death of Jesus. Such is the way and end of unbelief.

Yes, most solemn it is to see that God at the last hardens those who have long hardened themselves against the truth. So He is by and by to send men "a working of error, that they should believe what is false, that all might be judged who have not believed the truth, but found pleasure in unrighteousness;" and this most justly, "because they received not the love of the truth that they might be saved" [2 Thessalonians 2:10-12].[216] It was He Who spoke by Balaam against his will to bless His people, though hired of Balak to curse them, and proving afterwards, not only by his corrupting wiles but to his own destruction, how little the prophecies then were from himself. It is He Who now speaks by Caiaphas, whose high-priesthood in that year gave his words the more official weight. Not that it was an orderly condition that there should be such shiftings of the high priest.[217] But so it was total confusion when the Son of God came here; so most of all when He was to die. No wonder that God, long silent, should speak by the high priest of that year.[217a] He is Sovereign. He can employ evil as well as good—these heartily, those spite of themselves, and if their will be in it, with a sense as wicked as themselves.

So it was here, when Caiaphas[217b] said, "Ye know nothing, nor reckon that it is profitable for you that one man die for the people, and not the whole nation perish." God was not in his thoughts but self without conscience. The Evangelist comments on this, that he said it not from himself, but, being high priest of that year, *prophesied* that Jesus was about to die for the nation,[218] and not for the nation only, but that He should also gather together into one the children of God that were scattered abroad. In the heart of Caiaphas it was an unprincipled sentiment; in the mind of the Spirit it was not only most holy, but expressed the foundation of God's righteousness in Christ. On His death is based the future hope of Israel, and the actual gathering of God's scattered children, the Church.[p] From that day measures were taken in concert to compass the death of our Lord,[219] Who retired to the northern wilderness of Judæa, and there abode awhile with the disciples in the city called Ephraim.[220] The hour was coming.

The Eleventh Chapter

Verses 55-57.

"But the Passover of the Jews was near; and many went up unto Jerusalem out of the country before the Passover, that they might purify themselves. They were seeking therefore Jesus, and said among themselves, standing in the temple, What think ye? that He will not at all come unto the feast? Now the high priest and the Pharisees had given commandment that if any one knew where He was, he should inform, that they might seize Him" (verses 55-57).

Thus the closing scene is at hand; and Jesus pursues His service in retirement during the little interval before the Passover, the last so soon to be fulfilled in His death. They went up to purify themselves before the feast, which gives rise to their seeking Him and to surmises as to His not coming. For orders had been given to inform them of His whereabouts, in order to His apprehension. Little did any, friends or foes, anticipate that one would be found among the chosen twelve to indicate the spot whither the Lord was wont to resort; but He knew all that should come upon Him. How far is man from suspecting that it is all a question between Satan and God, and that, if evil seems to gain the upper hand, good triumphs even now to faith, as it will in the judgment of evil to every eye ere long!

But if the Lord retired from the machinations of men hardened in their enmity toward Himself because of their false pretension to feel and act for God, He had His own death on the cross to God's glory ever before Him. It was not to be done in a corner, nor on mere secret information. It must be at that feast, and no other, at the approaching Passover, when all the religious chiefs should thoroughly commit themselves, the elders, chief priests, and scribes; when the whole nation save the little remnant that believed should also play their blinded part; when they all should deliver Him to the Gentiles to mock and scourge and crucify. Oh, how little did any of them think of Him as in all this guilt and faithlessness of theirs the Son of God, and the Son of Man come not to be served, but to serve, and to give His life a ransom for many! Then should He quickly, but in measured, predicted time, rise in resurrection power, transcending that of Lazarus beyond all comparison; thenceforward to work spiritually in all that believe, quickened with Him and raised up together, and made to sit down together in the heavenlies in Him (as another Apostle was given to teach) [Ephesians 2:5-6], before the bright moment of His coming for us, when we shall all be changed.

NOTES ON THE ELEVENTH CHAPTER

a [*Cf. Lectures Introductory to the Study of the Gospels*, pp. 495-502.]

b ℵBELX, etc., read τοῖς [Weiss, Blass], but the weight favours αὐτοῦ also.

c αὐτῷ οἱ μ., ℵDKΠ, etc., some adding αὐτοῦ with Syrr., etc.; BC^{pm}X, etc., οἱ μ. αὐτῷ (the latter only is in A, etc.), while the T.R. with most gives οἱ μ. αὐτου.

d The Received Text {T.R.} with [AC$^{corr.}$ΓΔ] Syr^{hcl} implies "and their company" [Blass, conflate reading]; but the more ancient copies and versions do not allow this.

e δόξαντες ℵBC^{pm}DLX, some cursives, and most ancient versions etc.; λέγοντες, "saying" (T.R.), AC$^{corr.}$ and a dozen uncials, most cursives and versions.

f ℵD, etc., with most of the ancient versions, add the copula καὶ, "and."

g For the received reading τεθνηκότος, "dead," supported by a good many uncials and most cursives, the highest authorities give τετελευτηκότος, "deceased."[214a]

h T.R., with the great majority of MSS., adds οὗ ἦν ὁ τεθνηκὼς κείμενος, AKΠ, etc., only οὗ ἦν, but the best (ℵBC^{pm}DLX, some cursives, and the oldest versions) omit.

i The Received Text with most authorities begins with the copula καὶ, "and," but omits the last αὐτὸν, "him," contrary to a few of the best authorities.

j D, 255, with Syrr., Memph.^{wi}, Æth.^{r}, add καὶ, "and."

k λογίζεσθε ℵABDL, some cursives, etc., instead of the T.R. διαλ., "consider," supported by most uncials, cursives, etc.

l ὑμῖν, "you," BDLMXΓ, many cursives, etc., ἡμῖν, "us," still more witnesses; ℵ, etc., omitting either [Blass].

m ἐβ. ℵBD, etc.; συνεβ. much the most.

n Instead of διέτριβεν, "tarried," as most [so Blass]; ℵBL ἔμεινεν, "abode" [W. and H., Weiss].

o ℵBDILΓΔ, etc., do not read αὐτοῦ, "His," as in the rest.

p [*Cf. Lectures on the Church of God*, pp. 82-84 {pp. 84-87, 2007 edition, Scripture Truth Publications}.]

THE TWELFTH CHAPTER [a]

Such was the testimony God gave to the Lord Jesus as the Son in resurrection power, with the plain result of deadly hatred in those that bowed not by faith. Here,[220a] before a fresh witness is given, we are permitted to see Him in the home of those He loved at Bethany, where the Spirit gives us a fresh proof of grace in the recognition of His glory, and this in view of His death. There reclined the man so recently raised from the dead with Him Who raised him!

VERSES 1-11.

[Matthew 26:6-13; Mark 14:3-9.]

"Jesus therefore, six days before the Passover, came unto Bethany, where was Lazarus,[b] whom Jesus[b] raised from (the) dead. They made there for Him a supper, and Martha served; but Lazarus was one of those at table with Him. Mary then, having taken a pound of unguent of costly pure[c] nard, anointed the feet of Jesus, and wiped His feet with her hair; and the house was filled with the odour of the unguent. And[d] Judas Iscariot,[e] one of His disciples that was about to give Him up, saith,

Why was this unguent not sold for three hundred denaries, and given to poor (persons)? And this he said, not because he cared for the poor, but because he was a thief, and, having[f] the bag,[f] used to bear what was deposited. Jesus then said, Leave her to have kept it[g] for the day of My preparation for burial: for the poor ye have always with you, but Me ye have not always" (verses 1-8).

In presence of the Lord each comes out in his true colours. Jesus personally, as everywhere, is the object of God, the light which makes all manifest. But He does more. As He had brought life into the scene of death, the witnesses of His power and grace are there in their due place, according to their measure, one only having that special discernment which the love that is of God imparts, though grace may interpret it according to its own power. They[221] made for Him a supper there, Martha serving, Lazarus at the table with Him, Mary anointing His feet with the precious spikenard; and the house filled with the odour of the unguent.[222] The Lord felt and explained its meaning, according to His own wisdom and love.

But if one of the blessed family was led by a wisdom above her own, in single-eyed devotedness, to an act most fitting and significant at that time, one of His disciples was not found wanting for the work of the enemy, which makes nothing of Jesus. All of good or evil turns at bottom into a true or false estimate of Him. We may be, and are, slow to learn the lesson, albeit of greater moment than any other; but it is the object of the Spirit in all Scripture to teach us it, and nowhere so conspicuously, or so profoundly too, as in this Gospel. So Judas Iscariot, one of His disciples that was about to give Him up, says, Why was this ointment not sold for three hundred denaries, and given to poor people? He never thought of Jesus! Yet Mary's act might naturally have awakened affection. What was He not to her? Judas coolly calculates the lowest selling price of the nard[223]; he falsely puts poor persons forward for whom he had no real care; he would have liked that sum added to his unlawful gains.[224] Nothing can be more thoroughly withering, more calmly true, than the comment of the Holy Ghost in verse 6. But what said Jesus? "Leave her to have kept it[225] for the day of My preparation for burial: for the poor ye have always, but Me ye have not always."

Here is the truth said in divine love. Not, indeed, that Mary had received any prophetic intimation. It was the spiritual instinct of a heart that had found the Son of God in Jesus, of a heart that felt the danger that hung over Him as man. Others might think of His miracles, and hope that murderous intents might pass away at Jerusalem as at Nazareth. Mary was not so easily satisfied, though she had witnessed His resurrection power with as deep feelings as any soul on earth. And she was led of God to do what had a weightier import by far in the Lord's eyes than in her own. The love that had prompted it was of God, and this is above all price. "If a man would give all the substance of his house for love, it would utterly be contemned" [Song of Solomon 8:7]. So said he who knew above the sons of men the vanity of human love, with the amplest means ever vouchsafed to the head of any house. But what was Mary's unguent, or the love that brought it out (kept as it had been, and now she knew why at that critical moment), compared with His Who vindicated her, and was about to die for all, even for Judas?

It is, indeed, a scene to dwell on, most instructive and affecting, whether one contemplates the family as a whole, or Mary in particular, whether one may think of the disciples (for Matthew and Mark show that all were unappreciative, some even angry), or of the one whose dark influence acted so ill on the rest, and, above all, when one looks and listens to Him Whose grace formed Mary's heart according to its own nature and ways.

> "A (or, The)[h] great crowd[226] of the Jews therefore knew [learned] that He was (*literally*, is) there, and came not on account of Jesus only but that they might see Lazarus also whom He raised from (the) dead. But the chief priests consulted that they might kill Lazarus also, because on his account many of the Jews were going away and believing on Jesus" (verses 9-11).

"The Jews," as often remarked, are not merely Israelites but men of Judæa, and greatly under the influence of the rulers in their hostility to Jesus, as in other things. But they are not the rulers, and one sees the difference marked in these verses. The great crowd, however, seemed influenced quite as much by curiosity as by better motive. To see Lazarus who was raised from the dead is a very different thing from believing God. Still, there was reality among some; and hence the deeper and deliberate malice of the chief priests, because many of the Jews were deserting them and believing on Jesus.

Mary had not at all misread the position of the Lord. The crisis was at hand. Perfectly did He understand to what point every current was flowing; He knew what was in man, in Satan, and in God, and that as the malice of the creature would thus push to the uttermost in rebellious hatred, God would go farther still in redeeming love, but withal in His most solemn judgment of sin. Of this moral glory how little as yet could any heart conceive! Yet Mary's affection was led of God to divine the enmity growing up rapidly and ruthlessly against the One Who more than ever possessed her heart's homage and love.

But the final testimony must be full. Jesus had already shown Himself Son of God in power by raising Lazarus from the grave wherein he had lain a dead man: a testimony characteristic of John's Gospel, and peculiar to it. Men have raised objections, which only prove their own spiritual incapacity; for here it exactly suits, as it would nowhere else, and it was the right place and time too. All was divinely ordered.

Verses 12-19.

[Matthew 21:1-11; Mark 11:1-10; Luke 19:29-40.]

The next testimony is to His Messianic title, and fittingly, therefore, given in every one of the Gospels. It could be wanting to none, and we find it as the next fact recorded by our Evangelist.

> "On the morrow,[227] a great crowd that came unto the feast, having heard that Jesus is coming into Jerusalem, took branches of palm, and went out to meet Him, and cried, Hosanna, blessed (is) He that cometh in Jehovah's name, (even) the King of Israel. And Jesus, having found a young ass, sat upon it, as it is written [Zechariah 9:9], Fear not, daughter of Zion; behold, thy King cometh, sitting upon an ass's colt.[228] ⁱThese things His disciples knew not at the first; but when Jesus was glorified, then they remembered that these things were written of Him, and they did these things to Him. The crowd therefore that was with Him bore witness, because[j] He called Lazarus out of the tomb,

and raised him from (the) dead. Therefore also the crowd met Him, because they heard that He had done this sign. The Pharisees therefore said among themselves, Ye behold[230] that ye profit nothing: behold, the world is gone away after Him" (verses 12-19).

Thus did the crowd welcome Him as Messiah, applying to Him very justly the language of Psalm 118, which the Lord, in Matthew 23, declares shall be said by the repentant remnant who shall see Him when He returns to reign. Till then the house, once hallowed by Jehovah and bearing His name, is but *their* house, and left unto them desolate; as, indeed, they had made it a house of merchandise and a den of robbers. Nor was it mere enthusiasm in the crowd, but God at work; and the Lord Himself sat on the young ass according to the prophecy of Zechariah 9. It is remarkable how both Matthew and John omit the clause of the prophet which did not then apply, however sure by and by; for He knew well that He was to suffer then, in order to bring salvation when He comes again in glory. It was but a testimony at the time, and in the word to faith; when He comes, having salvation for His own, it will be in destructive judgment of all that oppose.

Here again it is notified for us that even His disciples knew not these things at the first; but when Jesus was glorified, then they remembered that these things were written of Him, and that they did these things to Him. *He* needed not that any should testify either of man or of Himself. Past, present, future, earth, and heaven, were open to His gaze. He Who made all knew all; as John constantly shows in harmony with the glory of His Person, which is everywhere prominent, save what He was pleased, in His capacity of servant, not to know, leaving it in the authority of the Father (Mark 13). In the light of His glorification the disciples learnt the import of the word and of the facts. It was His resurrection power which impressed the crowd so mightily. They did not draw the full lesson of faith, but concluded that He must be the promised Son of David, and met Him as such; while the Pharisees could not but own among themselves that obviously their stand and opposition were in vain, and the world, the prize of unbelief, gone after Him. Little knew they what is proclaimed just afterwards: "Now is the judgment of this world." In misjudging Him, its own doom was sealed; He sought its salvation, not popularity, but God's will.

Verses 20-36a.

But another scene completes the circle of the testimony here given before the close.

> "And there were certain Greeks of[231] those coming up to worship at the feast; these therefore came to Philip, who was from Bethsaida of Galilee,[232] and asked him, saying, Sir, we desire to see Jesus. Philip cometh and telleth Andrew, and[k] Andrew cometh and Philip, and they tell Jesus. But Jesus answered[l] them, saying, The hour is come that the Son of Man should be glorified. Verily, verily, I say to you, Except the grain of wheat falling into the ground die, it abideth alone; but, if it die, it beareth much fruit. He that loveth his life (soul) shall lose it,[m] and he that hateth his life in this world shall keep it unto life eternal. If anyone serve Me, let him follow Me, and where *I* am, there also My servant shall be;[n] if anyone serve Me, him will My Father honour" (verses 20-26).

These were Gentiles, Greeks and not merely Hellenists, who desired to see the Lord; and Philip and Andrew name it to Him. It was enough. The Lord opens the great truth. It is not now the Son of God quickening or raising the dead, nor the Son of David coming to Zion according to prophecy, but the *Son of Man* glorified. This He explains after the solemn asseveration, so often found in our Gospel, under the well-known figure of death and resurrection in nature: "Verily, verily, ... Except the corn of wheat falling into the ground die, it abideth alone; but, if it die, it beareth much fruit." He Himself was the true corn thus to produce fruit abundantly, yet even so only by death and resurrection.[232a] This was not, could not be, from defect of power in Him. It was from man's estate that it could not righteously be otherwise before God. Death only can meet the evil, or fill the void, and His death alone. Of all others death were vain—yea, fatal. Death to them must be for themselves to perish. He only could save, but through His death and resurrection; for as He would die, so He could rise, and by the infinite value of His death avail for others so as to raise them righteously. Living, He, even He must abide alone; dying, He bears much fruit in the energy of His resurrection.

Thus was He the Son of Man glorified.[233] It was for sin that God at length might be glorified; and now He was. Sin brought in death; His dying for it, by God's grace and to God's glory, laid the basis for the change of all things, even for the new heavens and earth in the eternal state; how much more for all that believe to be meanwhile blessed in a new life before they are changed into the likeness of His glory, when He comes for them! "He shall see a seed, He shall prolong [His] days, and the pleasure of Jehovah shall prosper in His hand. He shall see of [the fruit of] the travail of His soul, [and] shall be satisfied" [Isaiah 53:10 *f.*]. So said the first of prophets, and this founded on His death—"when Thou shalt make His soul an offering for sin," in accordance with His own words here seven centuries after, when approached that wondrous hour and act of man's guilt where he meant pain and ignominy, and God inflicted incomparably worse in His unsparing and unfathomable judgment. To Him the hour was come that the Son of Man should be glorified. What perfect self-sacrifice! What devotedness to God! What love to man, even to His bitterest enemies! Such was Jesus going down to death—yea, death of the cross; and such the fruit unfailing.

The principle, too, becomes a primary one thenceforth, not ease and honour and advancement for self (which is truly the greatest loss), but suffering and shame, and, if need be, death, now in this world for Christ's sake. Such is practical Christianity. "He that loveth his life [soul] loseth it, and he that hateth his life in this world shall keep it unto life eternal.[234] If any man serve Me, let him follow Me, and where *I* am, there shall also My servant be; if any man serve Me, him will My Father honour." And what an honour! He assuredly knows what it is, and how to give it. But it is not in self-devised and self-imposed abasements; neither in flagellations of the back, nor in lickings of the dust, nor in like heathenish effort that dishonours the body to the satisfying of the flesh. It is in what the Holy Spirit alone can guide and sustain, in serving Christ—a service inseparable from following Him, its beginning life eternal in the Son, its end the same life in glory with Him; for such as serve and follow Him will the Father honour. May we be strengthened to discern and do the truth!

THE TWELFTH CHAPTER

The Lord reverts to thoughts of His approaching death. There is no avoidance of contemplating that which it was part of His perfection to feel, as no man ever did. He estimates it rightly and fully as before, instead of braving it as men do who cannot escape. To Him it was no inevitable doom, but divine love, that God might be glorified in a guilty world, that sinners might be saved righteously, that the entire creation of heaven and earth (I say not those under the earth, the infernal beings of Philippians 2) might be reconciled and blessed for ever. He, and He only, had authority to lay down His life ($\psi υ χ \grave{η} ν$), as He had authority to take it again. As He is the Resurrection and the Life ($ζ ω \grave{η}$), so no one takes the life He had in this world from Him, but He lays it down of Himself, though also in obedience to His Father, and to the everlasting glory of God, as the fulness of His Person enabled Him to do. None the less but the more did He feel the gravity, humiliation, and suffering of what was before Him. There was the deepest sense of death, not only as man and Messiah but of its import from man's hand and from God's judgment. Not an element of grief and pain and shame and horror was absent from His heart, compatible with the perfection of His Person and His relationship to God.

> "Now is my soul troubled, and what shall I say? Father, save Me from this hour; but on account of this came I unto this hour. Father, glorify Thy° name" (verses 27-28a).

He was the life, yet came to die; He was light and love, yet rejected and hated as man never knew before, nor will again. The reality of His manhood, the glory of His Godhead, in no way hindered His sorrow; His being Who and what He was, and perfect in all, only gave Him infinite capacity to feel and fathom what He endured, none the less because He came to endure it all, and had it now before Him in immediate prospect, though none of men saw it but Himself. He had not been perfect man if His soul had not been troubled, so as to feel, "What am I to say?" He had not been Son of God as man had He not in His soul-trouble prayed, "Father, save Me from this hour," and quite as little, "but on this account came I unto this hour," crowned with, "Father, glorify Thy name." To have felt and expressed the first petition perfectly suited Him Who was man in such circumstances; to have added the second was worthy of Him Who is God no less than man in one undivided Person; to have said both was perfection in both, in sorrow as in joy, as to death no less than life.[235]

The Father appreciates and answers accordingly.

> "There came therefore a voice out of heaven, I both have glorified and will glorify (it) again. The crowd then[p] that stood and heard said that it thundered; others said, An angel hath spoken to Him" (verses 28b-29).

Augustine and Jerome confound this[q] with chapter 17:5, from which it is wholly and demonstrably distinct; but we must never expect spiritual intelligence, sometimes not even common orthodoxy, from the Fathers so-called. The later passage in our Gospel is the Son requesting the Father that He as the risen Man should be glorified, on the completion of His work, as well as consonantly with the rights of His Person, along with the Father Himself in the glory which the Son had along with Him before the world was.

The passage before us refers to what had just been, and what was going to be, done in this world; for as the Father had glorified His name in the resurrection of

Lazarus, so yet more infinitely would He in the rising from the dead of His own Son. The moderns, such as Dean Alford, fail, in meagre, vague, and even erroneous thought, to reach the mark as much as, or more than, the ancients. For how poor it is to tell us that διὰ τοῦτο = ἵνα σωθῶ ἐκ τῆς ὥρας ταύτης, that I might be safe from this hour!—that is, the going into and exhausting this hour, this cup, is the very appointed way of My glorification, or, as Meyer says, that Thy name may be glorified, which is to anticipate what follows. It was really to die, though undoubtedly to the glory of the Father by the Son. So, again, ἐδόξασα points to something much more definite than "in the manifestation hitherto made of the Son of God, imperfect as it was (see Matthew 16:16-17); in all Old Testament type and prophecy; in creation, and, indeed, (Augustine in Joan. lii. 4 {*In Ioannis Evangelium Tractatus CXXIV*, 52, 4}) *antequam facerem mundum* {before I made the world}". Lastly, it is losing the exact force to treat πάλιν as a mere intensification of the δοξάζειν, instead of seeing a distinct and higher display of that resurrection power which marked out the Son of God.

As to the question why some said the voice from heaven was thunder, others the speaking of an angel to the Lord, it seems vain to seek an answer. It was merely speculation on the part of the crowd, who all fell short of the truth. Unbelief of Him can weaken or get rid of all testimony till He come in judgment. Yet was it really in grace to them, for

> "Jesus answered and said, Not on Mine account hath this voice come, but on yours. Now is judgment of this world; now shall the prince of this world be cast out: and I, if I be lifted up out of the earth, will draw all[r] to Myself. But this He said sig-

nifying by what death He was about to die. The crowd thenˢ answered Him, *We* heard out of the law that the Christ abideth for ever; and how sayest *Thou* that the Son of Man must be lifted up? Who is this Son of Man? Jesus then said to them, Yet a little time the light is amongᵗ you. Walk while ye have the light, that the darkness may not overtake you; and he that walketh in darkness knoweth not where he goeth. While ye have the light, believe in the light, that ye may become sons of light" (verses 30-36a).

These words, if any, are surely of the most solemn import, and the more, as Christendom now as ever ignores their truth. For men, Christian men, believe nothing less than that "now is the judgment of this world," even while some of them look for the casting out of its prince in due time.[236] The glory of the Son of Man is founded on death. The rejection of the Messiah gives occasion for what is thus incomparably larger and more profound; and thus is God's glory immutably secured, and much fruit borne, even the blessing of those otherwise lost, now blessed with and in Christ, not merely by Him. But if heaven be thereby opened (for the cross and heaven answer to each other),[237] the world is judged. Before God and to faith now is its judgment, and not only when execution takes place publicly and in power. But now it is judged for him who has the mind of Christ, who shares His rejection and awaits glory with Him on high. What does His cross mean morally?

A living Messiah should have gathered the twelve tribes of Israel round Himself as their Chief, raised up of God according to promise; but He was to be lifted up out of the earth, crucified, Satan's seeming victory but his real and everlasting defeat, and so known to faith, while we wait for the day which shall declare it beyond contradiction. Christ on the cross is a very different object from reigning over His people in grace, and abiding for ever; yet they should have read it also out of the law, for there it is, if dimly. But grace makes Him manifest thus lifted up, the attractive centre for all, Gentile or Jew, spite of their sins, which He was to bear in His own body. A suffering Son of Man was, and is, no article of Jewish faith, though certainly revealed in their Scriptures.[238] To their expression of ignorance the Lord replies by telling them how brief was the stay of the light, by warning them of the darkness about to seize on them, and by exhorting them to faith in the light, if they, escaping the darkness, would have the light to characterise themselves.

Verses 36b-43.

The close was at hand, and a token even then was given that the light would not be always there.

> "Jesus spoke these things, and, going away, hid Himself from them. But though He had done so many signs before them, they did not believe on Him, that the word of Isaiah the prophet which He said might be fulfilled. Jehovah, who believed our report? and to whom was Jehovah's arm revealed? [Isaiah 53:1]. On this account they could not believe because Isaiah said again, He hath blinded their eyes, and He hardened[u] their heart that they may not see with their eyes and understand with their heart, and be converted [turn], and I heal them. These things said Isaiah, because (or, when[v]) he saw His glory, and spoke concerning Him [Isaiah 6:10]. Still, however, from among the rulers also many believed on Him, but

on account of the Pharisees did not confess, that they might not be put out of the synagogue; for they loved the glory of men more than the glory of God" (verses 36b-43).

Such was the result of the only absolutely perfect testimony ever rendered in this world, the words, and ways, and signs of the Son of God; and this, not where blank ignorance might be pleaded in extenuation, but where God had done all possible to prepare the way by prophecy, and to arouse attention by sign, grace, and truth in the midst of a people used to divine intervention. But man's unbelief, left to itself and Satan, can shut out every sight and sound from God. So it was among the Jews of our Lord's day, and so it continues till this day. It is still "this generation," which shall not pass away till all God's threats be fulfilled. Of the outward judgments, however, John does not speak, but the Synoptic Evangelists; John of having no more Him Who is all. For what is it to lose the light, to be abandoned to that darkness where he who walks in it knows not where he goes? And this is precisely the state of the Jews; the more aggravated because they had the light for a little among them, and did not believe, so that they failed to become children of light, and the darkness seized on them.[239] Thus was the prince of prophets fulfilled by their unbelief in their own ruin, and this in both the parts of his prophecy, early and late, which speculation vainly seeks to divorce. But we believe the inspired Evangelist, not the presumptuous professor, and are as assured that both prophecies are Isaiah's, as that they were divinely given and now fulfilled in the Jew so long incredulous.

But as the first citation proves the guilt of rejecting God's testimony, so the second, though really earlier, points to the solemn fact of judicial blindness, never pronounced, still less executed, of God, till patience has had its perfect work and man has filled up the measure of his guilt beyond measure. Under such a sentence of hardening, no doubt, they could not believe;[240] but the sentence came because of wickedness consummated in wilful rejection of God and His will when they did not believe, in spite of the fullest appeals to their hearts and consciences. As the first citation shows utter unbelief when Christ came in humiliation and suffering to do the work of atonement, so the latter conveys the dread word which shut them up in blindness before the light they had so long despised, followed up by the inspired comment that these things said Isaiah when he saw Christ's glory and spoke of Him.[241] It is Jehovah in the prophecy, Christ in the Gospel; but they are one—as, indeed, Acts 28:25-27 enables us to include the Holy Spirit. How thoroughly confirmed and confirming the still older oracle in Deuteronomy 6:4, "Jehovah our God is one Jehovah!" John 12 and Acts 28 weaken it in nothing, but add to its force and expressiveness, as they show out more and more the patience of God and the darkness of the Jew after ages of trifling with His mercy and His menaces alike. And the darkness increased as the light shone out.

But ungodliness betrays itself not only in the insubjection of the heart to believe, but in the cowardliness of the soul to confess the Lord (Revelation 21:8); as we see here that "many from among the chief rulers believed on Him, but on account of the Pharisees did not confess, that they might not be put out of the synagogue." And the motive or moral reason is given: they loved glory from men rather than glory from God. They feared the religious world, being keenly sensible of human glory, but dull to that which is from God.[242] But we must not forget that, if "with the heart man believes to righteousness, with the mouth confession is made to salvation" [Romans 10:10]. God makes much of confession of His Son, nor can we safely own salvation otherwise.

Verses 44-50.

Next, comes the final public testimony of our Lord, given in this Gospel.

> "But Jesus cried and said, He that believeth on Me believeth not on Me but on Him that sent Me; and he that beholdeth Me beholdeth Him that sent Me. *I* am come a light into the world, that every one that believeth on Me may not abide in darkness. And if anyone have heard My words and not kept[w] (them), *I* judge him not, for I came not to judge the world, but to save the world. He that slighteth Me and receiveth not My words hath one that judgeth him; the word which I did speak, that will judge him in the last day, because I did not speak from Myself, but the Father Who sent Me hath Himself given[x] Me commandment, what I should say, and what I should speak; and I know that His commandment is life eternal. What things then I speak, as the Father hath said to Me, so I speak" (verses 44-50).

The Lord spoke with earnestness, as elsewhere and always;[243] and it was due to men in His grace, considering the solemn issues at stake, and the divine glory concerned. It was a question of His Father Who sent Him, no less than of Himself. To believe on the Son, to behold Him, was to behold and believe on the Father. They were inseparably one, as He had already declared; and he who had the Son had the Father also. Further, the Lord was come as light into the world (for it was no question of Israel only) that every believer on Him might not abide in darkness.²⁴⁴ He has the light of life, and not life only; He is light in the Lord. It was therefore ruin to have heard and not kept His words; but such was the grace in which He came, that He could add, "*I* judge him not, for I came not that I might judge the world, but that I might save the world." How, then, would His glory be vindicated in his case who slights²⁴⁵ Him and receives not His words? He has that which judges him—the word. "The word which I have spoken, that shall judge him in the last day"; and the more surely, because Jesus spoke not from Himself, as if He sought His own will or glory, but was simply and uniformly subject to the Father, Who not only sent Him but enjoined what He was to say and speak; the Father's commandment He knew to be life eternal [Psalm 133:3²⁴⁶]. Jesus was as subject to Him in His utterances as in His doings, being here to declare Him and do His will.

NOTES ON THE TWELFTH CHAPTER

a [*Cf. Lectures Introductory to the Study of the Gospels*, pp. 502-507.]

b T.R. adds ὁ τεθνηκὼς, with large consent of uncials, cursives, and versions [as Syr^sin], contrary to ℵBLX, Syr.^pesch, Sah., Æth., etc.; as it omits Ἰησοῦς at the end, spite of the best witnesses inserting it. [Blass, πρὸς Λάζαρον, omitting the rest of the words.]

c πιστικὸς perplexes the critics, some taking it as *liquid*, others as *genuine*, or *pure*, according to its supposed source.

d δὲ ℵB, Memph., Goth., [Syr^sin,] and probably Syr^pesch, Æth., etc.; T.R., οὖν, with most uncials and cursives, etc., a few omitting.

e T.R. Σίμωνος without ὁ, on the authority of many MSS., etc.

f εἶχεν καὶ T.R. with most; ἔχων ℵBDLQ, a few good cursives and versions. The ancient versions generally render γλ. "chest."

g τετήρηκεν T.R., with a dozen uncials, most cursives, and many versions, but ἵνα ... τηρήσῃ ℵBDKLQXΠ, several cursives [33], and most ancient versions.

h A few witnesses of the highest antiquity and character (ℵB^pmL) read the article, as to which some of the old versions are ambiguous [W. and H. insert, Weiss and Blass omit].

i The copula of T.R., with fourteen uncials and most cursives, is not in ℵBLQ and some of the more ancient versions.

j ὅτι DE^pmKLΠ and some of the oldest versions [old Latin, Chrys., followed by Blass]; ὅτε, "when" (Steph., not Elz.), ℵAB, and most of the other uncials, many cursives, etc. [Weiss].[229]

k So a few of the oldest MSS., with a slight variation, while T.R. with most has καὶ πάλιν, Ἀ. κ. Φ. λ., as in the Authorised Version.

l ἀποκρίνεται, "answereth," ℵBLX, etc. [Blass]; ἀπεκρίνατο, "answered," T.R., with the mass of uncials, cursives, and versions [Weiss].

m ἀπολλύει, "loseth," ℵBL, 33, etc. [Weiss, Blass].

n καὶ, "and," is added in T.R., with thirteen uncials, and most other authorities, but not the oldest.

o B, by an evident slip, reads μου for σου, to the grievous detriment of the sense.

NOTES ON THE TWELFTH CHAPTER

p B omits οὖν [so Blass], while ℵADLX, etc., have it [Weiss].

q So does the venerable but gloss-loving Codex Bezae (conventionally called D), for it actually adds to the text ἐν τῇ δόξῃ ᾗ εἶχον παρά σοι πρὸ τοῦ τὸν κόσμον γενέσθαι.

r For πάντας with the great mass [Weiss] ℵ^pmD, and some ancient versions [Latt., Syr^hcl], read [as Blass] πάντα, "every one," or "all things," as Augustine *in loc.* expressly says. But there is the strongest internal reason to stand by the weight of external testimony.

s Most omit οὖν, but not ℵBLX, etc.

t ἐν ℵBDKLMXΠ, etc., instead of T.R. μεθ' AEFGH SUΓΔΛ, etc.

u ἐπώρ. AB^pmKLX, etc. (ℵΠ in a corrupt form); πεπ. T.R., following very many.

v ὅτι, ℵABLMX, etc.; ὅτε, T.R., most uncials [DIΔΛΠ, etc.] and cursives, etc.

w φυλάξῃ [*cf.* Luke 11:28], ℵABDKLXΠ, etc.; πιστεύσῃ, "believed," EFGHMSUΓΔΛ, etc.

x δέδ., ℵABMX, many cursives, etc.; ἔδ., T.R., DLΓΔΛΠ, etc.

357

THE THIRTEENTH CHAPTER [a]

We enter now on a new section of our Gospel: the last communications of the Lord to His disciples, closing with His heart opened out to the Father about them. The entire drift is in all points and ways to lead His own into a true spiritual understanding of their new place before God the Father, in consequent contrast with that of Israel in the world. It is not as the Church, but most fully and distinctively the Christian position in virtue of Christ, Who sets aside Israel in all respects. He was going to His Father on high, and here reveals what He in that glory would do for them while here below. His love must take a fresh shape; but it is faithful, unchanging, and perfect.

VERSES 1-11.

> "Now, before the feast of the Passover,[247] Jesus, knowing that His hour was come that He should depart out of this world unto the Father, having loved His own that (were) in the world, loved them unto (the) end" (verse 1).

He was the only man whom nothing took by surprise. All was read and known and felt in the presence of God

His Father. Not only was He aware throughout that He was to die, and of its form, character, and object in God's purpose, as well as in man's and Satan's malice, but we see here that its immediate proximity was before His mind with its immense consequences. Yet in John it is not man's or God's forsaking Him in that bitter crisis; but the hour came for His departure out of this world to His Father, instead of staying here as Jews expected according to the Old Testament for their Messiah. As the other Gospels bring out the evidence of His rejection by the people, our Evangelist sees Him from the first rejected, and at the end preparing the disciples for the unlooked-for change at hand, when the Christ should be in heaven, and the Holy Spirit sent down to be in and with His own on earth, the Father, too, being the relation of God, not to Him only, but in due time and way to them also.

Further, He would show His love in fresh and suited forms. "Having loved His own that were in the world," He loved not merely till the end, as a question of time, however true this may be, but taking up each need, and incurring all labour for them, whatever the draught on it, unremittingly and without wavering. Such is the love of Jesus to His own in the world, where it is constantly wanted. We know what love He expressed to them at that last Passover (Luke 22:15), and how infinitely it was proved in His blood and death for them as a lamb without blemish and without spot, foreordained before the foundation of the world, but manifested at the end of the times for their sakes who believed {1 Peter 1:19-21}. But now He would show them a love as active for them day by day, when He should depart to His Father, as when He fulfilled the Passover in dying for them.

"And, supper being come,[b] the devil having already put (it) into the heart of Judas, Simon's (son), Iscariot, that he should deliver Him up, (Jesus, or)[c] He, knowing that the Father had given all things into His hands, and that He came out from God and goeth unto God, riseth from supper and layeth aside His garments, and, having taken a towel, girded Himself" (verses 2-4).

The Authorised Version regards the phrase $\delta.\ \gamma.$ as implying the end of the repast; but I agree with those who take it to mean the arrival of the time for supper, which is confirmed by the wondrous action we are about to hear of. It cannot be doubted that it was usual to have the feet washed before, not after, supper.

But if Jesus had ways of infinite love before His heart, the devil had already planted in that of Judas Iscariot the awful treachery to his divine Master, which no rolling ages can erase. So it was with Jesus: the enemy's hate came out most, as the love of God manifested itself in and by Him; but how withering to human pretension it was that the devil wrought by a man and a disciple, the close personal honoured follower of the Lord Jesus! "It was thou, a man mine equal, my guide, and mine acquaintance" [Psalm 55:13]. In that holy companionship he had trifled with sin, with his besetting covetousness; and now the devil prompted the gratification of it by betraying the Son of God. The Lord, as we shall later see, deeply felt it, but here He pursues the design of love with the consciousness of the Father's purposes and plans, with the consciousness, too, that He was going back to God with the same absolute purity in which He had come out from Him. It was no merely Messianic sphere, not even that of Son of Man. The Father had given all things into the hands of His Son, and He was going back a man with not a shade over that intrinsic holiness which marked His coming out from God to become a man. He abode ever the Holy One of God, yet rises from supper, lays aside His garments, takes a towel and girds Himself.

Jesus occupies Himself with a new service, which their nearness to God as His children called for, the removal of the defilements of His own in their walk as saints through the world. This is the meaning of what follows.

> "Then He poureth water into the basin, and began to wash the feet of the disciples, and to wipe them with the towel with which He was girded" (verse 5).[249]

Be it carefully observed that it is a question here of water, not of blood. The reader of John's Gospel will not have overlooked that He makes much of "water" as well as "blood." So did the Lord in presenting the truth to His own, and no one shows this more than John. His first epistle also characterises the Lord as "He that came by (δι') water and blood; not in (ἐν) water only, but in water and blood" [1 John 5:6]. He purifies as well as atones. He employs the word to cleanse those who are washed from their sins in His blood. The apostles Paul, Peter and James insist on this effect of the word, as John does. It is disastrous and dangerous in the highest degree to overlook purification by the washing of water by the word. If "the blood" is Godward, though for us, "the water" is saintward to remove impurity in practice,[250] as well as to give a new nature which judges evil according to God and His word, of which it is the sign, adding to it the death of Christ, which gives its measure and force. Out of His pierced side came blood and water (chapter 19).

As to this grave and blessed truth Christendom remains, one fears, as dark as Peter, when he declined the gracious action of the Lord. Nor did Peter enter into the truth conveyed by His most significant dealing till afterwards—that is, when the Holy Spirit came to show them the things of Christ. On the occasion itself he was wrong throughout. And so are men apt to be now, even though light divine has been fully afforded. They still perversely limit its extent to teaching humility. *This* only Peter saw, and hence his mistake; for he thought it stooping down excessively, that the Lord should wash his feet; and, when alarmed by the Lord's warning, he fell into an opposite error. We are only safe when subject to His word in distrust of ourselves.

The fact is that, since apostolic times, the truth (save as to the foundation, perhaps) has been either misapprehended, or perverted often to lifeless ordinances. Evangelicals, as the rule, ignore it, or merge it in the blood of Christ. Catholics (Greek, Oriental, Roman, or Anglican) misapply it to baptism. Hence not only do they miss the Lord's special lesson of washing in water, but they enfeeble propitiation. Consequently, non-imputation of sin is all but unknown from the earliest Fathers till our own day. The Reformers wrought no deliverance in this respect; and the Puritans increased the confusion and darkness by pressing, not ordinances, but the law as the rule of life, instead of recalling by the Spirit of the Lord to Christ as the object according to which the Christian is being transformed here below. The Lord suffered once for sins, Just for unjust. The efficacy is as perfect for the believer as is His Person; and the unity of His sacrifice is, therefore, the great argument of Hebrews 9-10, as contrasted with the repetition of Jewish ones. By His one offering we are not only sanctified but perfected in perpetuity. Is there no failure in the saint afterwards? Too often there may be. What, then, is the provision for such? It is the washing of water by the word which the Spirit applies in answer to the Son's advocacy with the Father. Of this Christ was here giving the sign.

The Lord proceeds to the work in hand.

> "He cometh then unto Simon Peter. He saith to Him, Lord, dost *Thou* wash my feet? Jesus answered and said to him, What I am doing thou knowest not just now, but shalt know [understand] afterwards. Peter saith to Him, In no wise shalt Thou wash *my* feet for ever. Jesus answered him, If I wash thee not, thou hast no part with Me. Simon Peter saith to Him, Lord, not my feet only, but also my hands and my head. Jesus saith to him, He that is washed (bathed) hath no need to wash (other) than his feet,[d] but is wholly clean; and ye are clean, but not all. For He knew him that was delivering Him up: on this account He said, Ye are not all clean" (verses 6-11).

In divine things the wisdom of the believer is subjection to Christ and confidence in Him. What He does we are called to accept with thankfulness of heart, and as Mary said to the servants at the marriage feast, "whatsoever He saith unto you, do it." This Simon Peter did not. For when the Lord approached him "in the form of a servant," or bondman, he demurred. Was there not faith, working by love in Peter's heart? Both, undoubtedly, yet not then in action, but buried under superabundant feeling of a human sort: else he had not allowed his mind to question what the Lord saw fit to do. He had rather bowed to Christ's love and sought to learn, as He might teach, what deep need must be in him and his fellows to draw forth such a lowly yet requisite service from his Master. Ah! he knew not yet that Jesus must go lower down far than stooping to wash the disciples' feet, even to the death of the cross, if God were to be glorified and sinful man to be justified and delivered with an indisputable title. But the grace which was undertaking that infinite work of propitiation (the groundwork for meeting every exigency of the divine nature and majesty and righteousness in view of our guilt, and unto the glory of God) would provide for every step of the way where defilement abounds. Thus might we enjoy communion, spite of Satan's power and wiles and our own weakness—yea, spite of failure be restored to communion with Him in the light and glory of God to which He was going back, and into which we shall in due time follow Him.

Peter did believe, but he did not yet believe "all that the prophets spoke" (Luke 24:25). He feebly entered into what he himself afterwards called the sufferings as to Christ, and the glories that should follow them {1 Peter 1:11}. He continued to regard the Lord too exclusively as Messiah, little estimating till afterwards the depths involved in the Son of the living God, though his own lips had thus confessed His glory before. Nature was too little judged in Peter, so that he did not yet appreciate its meaning and application and results as subsequently under divine teaching when the cross manifested its worth, or rather worthlessness, before God and man. Too self-confident and, indeed, ignorant not only of himself and the defiling scene around but of the depths and constancy of Christ's love, Peter says to Him, "Lord, dost *Thou* wash my feet?" We grant that he could not know what was not yet revealed; but was it comely in him, was it reverent, to question what the Lord was doing? He may have thought it humility in himself, and honour to the Lord, to decline a service so menial at His hands. But Peter should never have forgotten that as Jesus never said a word, so He never did an act, save worthy of God and demonstrative of the Father; and now more than ever were His words and ways an exhibition of divine grace, when human evil set on by Satan, not only in those outside, but within the innermost circle of His own, called for increased distinctness and intensity in view of His departure.

The truth is that we need to learn from God how to honour Him, and learn to love according to His mind. And if any man thinks that he knoweth anything, he knoweth nothing yet as he ought to know {1 Corinthians 8:2}. This, too, was Peter's mistake. He should have suspected his thoughts, and waited in all submissiveness on Him Who, as many confessed that knew far less than Peter, "hath done all things well," and was absolutely what He was speaking, truth and love in the same blessed Person. The thoughts of man are never as ours; and saints slip into those of man, unless they are taught of God by faith, in detail too as well as in the main; for we cannot, ought not, to trust ourselves in anything. God the Father will have the Son honoured; and He is honoured most when believed and followed in His humiliation. Peter, therefore, was equally astray when he once ventured to rebuke the Lord for speaking of His suffering and death, as now when he asks, "Dost *Thou* wash my feet?"

But the meek Lord answered in fulness of grace and said to him, "What I am doing thou knowest (οἶδας) not just now, but shalt know (γνώσῃ)[251] afterwards." Was not this a grave but compassionate intimation to Peter, had he been in the mood to learn? He ought to have gathered from the Lord's words, if he did not at once bow to His act, that there was a meaning worthy of Him Who deemed it due to the Father in truest, lowliest love to the children to wash their feet; he ought to have gathered more than this, that what he did not *know of himself* then, he was to *learn* afterwards: I presume, after the things now in progress, His rejection and death, resurrection and ascension, when the Holy Spirit should be given guiding them into all the truth.

But Peter was not yet of those who are guided with the Lord's eye; he did not feel the need of being instructed and taught the way in which he should go. There was too much of the horse or of the mule in him, too much need of being held with bit and bridle [Psalm 32:9]; and failing to receive of the Lord that he should submit now and learn later, he plunges farther and more boldly into error with himself. "In no wise shalt Thou wash my feet for ever": the strongest repudiation of it, and this not merely in this life, but for that to come—for ever.

It was feeling, it was ignorance, no doubt; but should he have trusted himself to utter words so strong of the gracious way and act of his Master? How blessed that he had, that we have, to do with One Who does not hold His peace so as to bind the soul with a bond, Who knows when and how to disallow the foolish and even God-dishonouring word, so that it shall not stand and the soul be forgiven! (See Numbers 30.) The Lord made Peter's words utterly void the moment He heard them, as we shall see, in the grace which corrects every fault, and bore all our iniquity.

"Jesus answered him, If I wash thee not, thou hast no part with Me." Solemn assurance, not for Peter only, but for all who slight the same gracious provision on His part, who forget or have never apprehended their own need of it. It is a question not so much of life as of fellowship, of a part *with* Christ rather than in Him, though not really separable. Christ was going on high to God, Peter and the rest still on earth and surrounded by defilements in the way. Christ would neither abate His love to His own, nor would He make light of their failures. Hence the need of washing the disciples' feet, apt to be soiled in walking through the world. And this is carried on by the word applied to the conscience by the Spirit. The believer bows, judges himself, and is practically cleansed. His communion is restored, and he can enjoy the things of Christ. He has part with Him.

Alarmed by the Lord's warning, His servant instantly flies to the opposite extreme: "Lord, not my feet only, but also my hands and my head." Now Peter cannot have too much. He seeks to be bathed all over, as if all the value of his previous washing could evaporate, and he needed it afresh no less than if it had never been. But it is never so. To see and enter the kingdom of God one must be born afresh, born of water and of the Spirit. But this is never repeated. The new birth admits of no such repetition. It was wrong to suppose that, born of God, one needs nothing else, that defilements either cannot befall a believer, or that, if they do, they are of no consequence.

What Simon thus thought and said in his ignorance, a certain school of divinity has formulated in its presumption. But this is not true knowledge of God. If law punishes transgression, grace condemns sin still more deeply. Impossible that any system of religious dogma could be of God which slurs over or ignores evil. But Simon Peter, convicted of danger on this side, falls into another on that side, and, roused to own the needful washing to have part with Christ, claims it all even for the believer as for the natural man. And here, too, an opposite school presents its corresponding dogma, denies the standing of the believer if unhappily he may get defiled, and insists that he must begin over again, perhaps many times in his life. Thus life eternal as a present possession in Christ is done away, and the constant responsibility which flows from the constant relationship of a child of God. One might be thus often lost, often saved spiritually!

The Lord corrects by anticipation both schools in correcting Peter. "He that is washed (λελουμένος) hath no need to wash (νίψασθαι) (other) than his feet, but is wholly clean; and ye are clean, but not all. For He knew him that was delivering Him up: on this account He said, Ye are not all clean." Thus simply, but perfectly, does He put each truth in its place and in relation to all the rest. Grace is maintained, but so is righteousness. Not a sin is passed over lightly. Not a believer has reason for discouragement; his every failure is an object of fresh concern to the Lord, a fresh proof of love that will not let him go but bless him, spite of the carelessness which let the Lord go. But He will not go; He washes the feet of him that is already washed all over, that he may be wholly clean. Thus the new birth holds and is never renewed, because it abides true and good; while the failure of him who is born again comes under Christ's active love and advocacy, and the soul is brought to judge himself in order to restored communion. Again, the case of Judas is not one of losing life, but of manifesting that he never had been born of God, as, indeed, no scripture ever affirms it. It was not a sheep of Christ becoming unclean, but a dog returning to his vomit—

yea, far worse, because of such proximity to Him Whose intimacy he abused for lucre to betray Him to His enemies.

It is of capital moment to hold fast along with atonement the washing of water by the word. Else the blood of Christ is diverted from its true aim and effect before God, and practically used as the resource in case of failure.

Let us hear Calvin as an influential witness of the error it involves, where he teaches from the word of reconciliation in 2 Corinthians 5:20 ("Be reconciled to God"), that Paul is here addressing himself to believers, instead of illustrating the message of grace to the world. "He declares, {that he brings} to them every day this embassy. Christ therefore, did not suffer, merely that He might once expiate our sins, nor was the gospel appointed merely with a view to the pardon of those sins which we committed previously to baptism, but that, as we daily sin, so we might, also, by a daily remission, be received by God into His favour. For this is a continued embassy, which must be assiduously sounded forth in the Church, till the end of the world; and the gospel cannot be preached unless remission of sins is promised. We have here an express and suitable declaration for refuting the impious tenet of Papists, which calls upon us to seek the remission of sins after baptism from some other source, than from the expiation that was effected through the death of Christ. Now this doctrine is commonly held in all the schools of Popery—that, after baptism, we merit the remission of sins by penitence through the aid of the *keys* (Matthew 16:19)—as if baptism itself could confer this upon us without penitence. By the term *penitence*, however, they mean *satisfaction*. But what does Paul say here? He calls us to go, not less *after* baptism, than *before* it, to the one expiation made by Christ, that we may know that we always obtain it gratuitously. Farther, all their prating as to the administration of the *keys* is to no purpose, inasmuch as they conceive of *keys* apart from the gospel, while they are nothing else than that testimony of a gratuitous reconciliation, which is made to us in the gospel" (*Commentary on the Epistles of Paul the Apostle to the Corinthians*, ii. 240-241, The Calvin Translation Society, 1849).

Clearly this teaching is erroneous, not only founded on a misapplication to saints of the gospel ministry to sinners, but consequently unsettling their reconciliation as a great finished fact. It is not true that the Apostle declares this embassy to believers every day.[252] He declares, on the contrary, that the work is done, and the worshippers once purged so as to have no longer any conscience of sins [Hebrews 10:2]. There is no question of imputing sins or errors, nor of God's judgment of them by and by. The error undermines or excludes the constant relationship of the Christian on the ground of peace made by the blood of Christ's cross, and present and permanent fitness for sharing the inheritance of the saints in light (Colossians 1:12).

The one offering of Christ does not merely once expiate our sins, but has perfected in perpetuity the sanctified [Hebrews 10:14]. The Romanist meets the need created by failure after baptism by penitence aided by the keys; the Protestant by fresh approach to the sacrifice of Christ, the one being as ignorant as the other of the washing of the defiled feet by the word in answer to the advocacy of Christ with the Father. The continued embassy is by the Lord's servants in proclaiming the gospel to the world. There is no such thing as God's receiving the believer by a daily remission into His favour. There may be the necessity of removing the uncleanness of flesh or spirit which hinders communion; but this supposes the groundwork of propitiation undisturbed and of the favour in which we stand. That the Christian requires to be reconciled afresh, that the call "Be reconciled to God" goes out to failing believers, proves that Calvin, able as he was and a saint himself, was ignorant even of the elementary and distinctive truth of the gospel. This opened the door to the opposed error of Arminianism, which takes its stand more consistently on the same mistake, that the failing believer has to start afresh, as if eternal life had no meaning, and the blood of Christ lacked everlasting efficacy. Both systems are faulty.

The truth puts everything in its place. The blood of Christ abides in its unchangeable value before God sacrificially and judicially; but the failing believer is inexcusable, and needs to wash his feet. The word must deal with him morally, producing self-judgment and confession; and the Lord looks to it in His ever-watchful grace by taking up his cause in living love with the Father. The Spirit, too, has His own suited function in producing, not the joy of fellowship with Christ in the things of Christ, but here grief and shame, pain and humiliation, in recalling the man's own ways—haste, levity, pride, vanity, and perhaps corruption or violence; for of what is the flesh unjudged not capable? By that word of truth he was begotten of God, awakened to self-judgment in His sight; by the same word is each defilement judged day by day, making it so much the more painful because the Spirit reminds the soul what Christ suffered for the sins which the flesh feels so lightly.

But far from dissolving the relationship, the sense of inconsistency with it, and with the grace which at so much cost and sovereign love withal conferred it on us, is that which most of all tries and humbles the erring one. Flesh would like exceedingly to have its way and indulge its pleasures, and the soul begin again; but God holds the believer to a relationship, which, if real, is everlasting, and makes every delinquency, therefore, to be so much the deeper sin, because it is against not conscience and righteousness only but the richest grace God could show in Christ. We were reconciled to God through the death of His Son {Romans 5:10}. There is no repetition of reconciliation any more than of the new birth. There is complete remission of sins through His blood, and hence no longer an offering for sin {Hebrews 10:17-18}. The one and only offering which could avail is made and accepted. But there is, whenever needful, a fresh application of "water by the word." And this ever deals with the soul. The word detects whilst it removes the defilement, applying the death of Christ thus to man, as the blood dealt with the sins before God. Thus is the work carried on holily without weakening the sole foundation for a sinful man's peace as well as for divine glory.

VERSES 12-30.

> "When then He washed their feet and took His garments and reclined again, He said to them, Know ye what I have done to you? Ye call Me the Teacher and the Lord, and ye say well, for I am. If I then, the Lord and the Teacher, washed your feet, ye also ought to wash one another's feet; for I have given you an example, that even as I did to you, ye should also do. Verily, verily I say to you, A bondman is not greater than his lord, nor yet an

apostle greater than He that sent him. If ye know these things, happy are ye if ye do (or, practise) them" (verses 12-17).

Undoubtedly the humility of the Lord was beyond question in His washing the disciples' feet, and that He would have them cultivate it He had solemnly urged on them in the plainest terms, as we see in all the Synoptic Gospels. But then there is another and deeper instruction. It is the renewal of their defilements in walking through the world which is before His mind, now that He is about to leave them; and about this He would exercise their hearts by the question, "Know ye what I have done to you?" It is His way indeed to teach us afterwards the good He has already done us; and as we grow up to Him in the truth, we appreciate better what we understood[253] but slightly at first. Grace instructs us, as well as acts on our behalf; and it is humbling to find out how little we have understood while its activity has never staid. But how good and strengthening it is to learn its ways and lessons!

The Lord next enforces what He had done by appealing to the titles they habitually gave Him. "Ye call Me the Teacher and the Lord; and ye say well, for I am:"[254] One to obey as well as to instruct, as could not but be where His personal glory is known. If He then stooped in love to wash their feet, what did they not owe one another? It is not only that we should serve the Lord in the gospel. "By this shall all men know," He says later on in this very chapter, "that ye are My disciples, if ye have love one to another." Here, however, it is a definite call, where we are apt most to fail, to share His grace in seeking the restoration of each other where failure has come in. On the one hand, it needs faith and self-denial and divine affections. Indifference about it detects our own failure.

But, on the other hand, the righteousness that censures another is as far as possible from washing the feet, resembling rather the scourge than the service of the towel and basin. And assuredly, if grace be needed to bear the washing, a far larger measure must be in action to wash the feet. Hence says the Apostle, "Brethren, even if a man be overtaken in any fault, ye that are spiritual restore such an one in a spirit of meekness" [Galatians 6:1]. Where flesh was judged, love could act more powerfully, and with deeper sense that all is of grace. Self is the greatest hindrance in dealing with another's trespass.

The service of love in every form is the mind which was in Christ. Hence He calls them here to weigh what they had first seen. "For I have given you an example that ye also should do even as I did to you. Verily, verily, I say to you, A bondman is not greater than his lord, nor an apostle greater than He that sent him. If ye know these things, happy are ye if ye do them."[255] The Lord knew the end from the beginning, and how soon His ministry would degenerate into a worldly institution, and become a title of pride, instead of being a work of faith and labour of love. Hence the need for His solemn formula, as a standing witness to all His own so prone in a world of vain show and selfishness to forget His word and wander from His way. But there His warning abides; to decline His service in washing the feet of His own is to set oneself above the Lord, and to claim a greater place than His Who sends even an apostle. Oh, for the blessedness of doing as well as knowing these things! It is the fellowship of His love in one of its most intimate forms; and "love is of God, and every one that loveth hath been begotten of God and knoweth God" [1 John 4:7].

THE THIRTEENTH CHAPTER

The hint which closed verse 10 is now expanded into the growingly solemn intimations in word and deed that follow. It is no longer Christ's love caring for His own, either once for all in atoning self-sacrifice to God for them, everlasting in its efficacy; or in unintermittent cleansing by the word, as for whom He died on earth, living for them in heaven, that they might be practically in unison with the relationship of grace into which they had been brought, spite of the defilements of the way. Here it is the faithless indifference of nature, with a conscience increasingly seared by indulgence in a besetting sin, which Satan was about to lure and blind to high treason against Christ, availing itself of the closest intimacy to sell the Master and Lord, the Son of God, for the paltriest price of a slave—to sell Him into the hands of enemies thirsting for His blood. It may not be the hatred of these; it is utter lovelessness, betraying Him Who was at this time more than ever showing and proving His love, not only up to and in death, but in life beyond it evermore. Now the unbelief which, having eyes and heart, sees not nor feels such love, precipitates above all into Satan's deceit and power. This we sorrowfully behold in Judas; and no one felt the sorrow as the Lord.

> "I speak not of you all: I know whom[e] I chose out, but that the scripture may be fulfilled, He that eateth bread with Me hath[f] lifted up his heel against Me.[255a] Henceforth (or, From this present time) I tell you before it come to pass, that, when it hath come to pass, ye may believe that I am (He).[256] Verily, verily, I say to you, He that receiveth whomsoever I shall send receiveth Me; and he that receiveth Me receiveth Him that sent Me" (verses 18-20).

[*Cf.* Matthew 26:21 *ff.*; Mark 14:18 *ff.*; Luke 22:21 *ff.*]

"Having said these things Jesus was troubled in His spirit and testified and said, Verily, verily, I say to you, One of you shall give Me up. The disciples (then)ᵍ looked one on another, doubting of whom He spoke (*literally*, speaketh)" (verses 21-22).

The Lord then did, and does, look for activity of love among His own. If they were objects of a love which could never fail, He would have them instruments or channels of it one toward another, and this in respect of evil to remove it, whereas legality could only condemn. Himself the Son yet the Servant in love, He would exercise them in the service of love, where defilement otherwise would repel. But as He came to suffer for our sins, so also He was going away to form us while on earth into His own mind and affections, through the truth, and in doing so to cleanse from every way which might grieve the Holy Spirit, whereby we are sealed till the day of redemption {Ephesians 4:30}. For it is not a question of removing the guilt of a sinner only, but of restoring the communion of a saint, whenever interrupted by allowed evil. And in this last dealing of love, He would have His own caring one for another. But He did not speak of all the disciples then present: sad presage of what was to be far more common in afterdays! He knew whom He chose out: Judas was not among such, though called to be an apostle. He had never known the Lord, knew nothing truly of His grace or of His mind, and was not born of God. Why then had he been selected for that place of honour, the apostolate, in immediate and constant attendance on the Lord here below?

THE THIRTEENTH CHAPTER

It was not that the Lord was unconscious of his character, conduct, or coming catastrophe, but that the scripture might be fulfilled, He that eateth bread hath lifted up his heel against Me [Psalm 41:9]. "Jeshurun grew fat and kicked" of old; "he gave up God Who made him, and lightly esteemed the Rock of his salvation" [Deuteronomy 32:15]. Judas went incomparably farther in his guilty indifference to the Son of God come down in love and humiliation, and in his eagerness to serve himself at all cost, betraying his gracious Master for the merest trifle. Never was such love, never such slight and abuse of it, and this in one of those specially responsible to be faithful. Doubtless it would be through Satan's power; but to this flesh exposes, and so much the more because of nearness outwardly to the Lord Who is not believed on to salvation. Thereby comes out, most palpably and fatally, the hard baseness of the unrenewed heart, and this against the grace of the Lord above all. Thus, if the disciples were in danger of being stumbled by such a one's defection, the evident fulfilment of Scripture was meant to strengthen their faith in every written word of God. By this man lives Godward: bread, money, anything here below, may be the occasion of his ruin. How wondrous the patience which, knowing all from the beginning, bore all to the end, without a frown or sign of shrinking from the traitor! But so much the more withering must be the sentence of judgment when it comes from His lips, the Lord of glory, the hated and despised of man.

The Lord gives precision to ancient oracles, hitherto applied only to others, as here to David suffering from Ahithophel. But the Holy Spirit wrote of Him pre-eminently; and He too, before the event, cites the word about to be verified in the treachery toward Himself.

Thus did the Lord prove alike His perfect and divine knowledge of what lay yet in the future, while He taught the inestimable worth of Scripture, and, not least, of prediction not yet fulfilled, meeting in every form the incredulity of believers as well as of unbelievers. For who knows not the accepted maxims which assume the dark and doubtful character of unfulfilled prophecy, which denies prophecy even to the Prophets, still more to the Psalms and to the Law? At least men should fear to give the lie to Him Who declares Himself the truth, and spoke as never man did. They have reason to fear, if they turn away from Him to lying vanities which, far from being able to save their votaries in the day of need, shall assuredly be as stubble to burn themselves and all who trust them. Jesus, on the contrary, is never so transparently the Messiah as when beforehand He points to the word of Scripture about to be accomplished in His own rejection and death of the cross, and affords in it a firmer ground of blessing for the poorest of sinners than in all the glories of the kingdom to be fulfilled in their seasons.

Then, with His usual mark of profound solemnity, the Lord binds the reception of His sent ones with Himself and His Father. "Verily, verily, I say to you, He that receiveth whomsoever I may send receiveth Me; and he that receiveth Me receiveth Him that sent Me." This was the more important to be added here, for some might question their standing before God because of the awful doom of Judas, when and where known. The Lord comforts such, and turns from occupation with the fallen servant to the Master Who abides for ever the same, as does the Father. Did Judas betray the Lord? This sealed his own doom, but touched not the authority any more than the grace of Christ, as of God Himself. If they received one whom Christ sent, be his end even what it might, they received the Son, and so the Father, instead of sharing in the guilt or danger of the servant's punishment who dishonoured his Master to his perdition.

The Lord then, manifesting the deepest emotion, proceeds to urge the sin home, limiting its worst form to one only of the disciples. "Having said these things, Jesus was troubled in His spirit, and testified and said, Verily, verily, I say to you, One of you shall deliver Me up." It was holiness, it was love, which took thus to heart the impending iniquity of Judas. In every point of view the Lord felt it[257]—in itself, in its contrariety to God, in its bearing on others as well as on Himself, and in its awfulness for the wretched guilty one. It is not self, but love, which is associated with the truest sensibility; and the Lord expresses it as a testimony also, "Verily, verily, I say to you, One of you shall give Me up." They were all faulty; but one, and only one, was thus about to become a prey to Satan, and the tool of his malice against the Lord. Their doubts were as honest as his place in their midst was now a lie against the truth. If he joined the rest in looking one on another, it was hypocrisy; for he could not really doubt of whom Jesus was speaking. Yet no blush, no paleness, betrayed Judas. The disciples must have recourse to other means of learning the sad truth.

The announcement of a traitor among the twelve troubled the disciples and led to anxious thought,[258] as they looked one on another. What a testimony to His perfect grace Who had known it all along, and had given no sign of distrust or aversion! How solemn for the saints who have to do with the same unchanging Christ day by day! Nothing precipitates into the enemy's hands more than grace abused and sin indulged, while outwardly he is in the presence of the only One Whose life rebukes it absolutely. Let us look a little into the scene.

> "(Now)[h] there was at table[259] one of [h]His disciples in the bosom of Jesus whom Jesus loved.[260] Simon Peter then beckoneth to this one and saith to him, [i]Tell who it is of whom He speaketh. He then[j] having thus[j] fallen back[j] on the breast of Jesus saith to Him, Lord, who is it? Jesus (then)[j] answereth, That one it is to whom I, having dipped the morsel, shall give (it). Having then dipped He (taketh and) giveth the morsel to Judas (son) of Simon, Iscariot. And after the morsel, Satan then entered into him. Jesus therefore saith to him, What thou doest do more quickly. But no one of those at table knew why He said this to him; for some supposed because Judas had the bag that Jesus saith to him, Buy the things that we have need of for the feast, or that he should give something to the poor. He therefore having received the morsel went out immediately; and it was night" (verses 23-30).

Peter and John are often seen together. So here in their perplexity Simon Peter beckons to John as he reclined at table in the bosom of Jesus; for that John and no other was this favoured disciple cannot be doubted from chapters 19:26; 20:2; 21:7, 20, 24. And how truly of the Spirit that one enjoying such favour should describe himself, not as loving Jesus, though indeed he did, but as beloved by Him; and this, too, as the disciple whom Jesus loved, withholding his name as here and elsewhere of small account, though plainly described at the close where needed, and named where men might deny the authorship, as they have done![260] It is intimacy with Jesus that gathers secrets, but imparts them for others' good.

THE THIRTEENTH CHAPTER

Falling back just as he was on the breast of Jesus, John asks who it is; and the Lord answers, not in word only, but with a sign strikingly according to Psalm 41:9, though an even more special mark of intimacy.{262}

In Judas' state that token of love only hardened the conscience long seared by secret sin, which shut out from the heart all sense of love. His very familiarity with Christ's passing through the snares and dangers of a hostile world may have suggested that so it would be now with his Master, while he himself might reap the reward of his treachery; and the knowledge of His grace, without heart for it, may have led him to hope for mercy he had never known refused to the most guilty. The moment comes when holy love becomes unbearable to him who never relished it; and the sin he preferred blinded his mind and hardened his heart to that which had otherwise touched the most callous. "After the morsel, Satan then entered into him." The devil had already put it into his heart to deliver the Lord up; now, after receiving without horror or self-judgment the last token of his Master's love, the enemy entered. At being thus designated there may have been irritation, which if retained gives room for the devil even in ordinary cases; much more in his who had trifled with unfailing grace, and thus forgot wholly His glory, as he had ever been insensible to God's nature and his own sin. "Jesus therefore saith to him, What thou art doing do more quickly"—that is, sooner than was indicated by his pretension to share the doubts of the disciples or to join in what was before their hearts.

Never does God thus abandon to Satan poor man, however wretched and sinful, till he rejects His love and holiness and truth, above all shown in the Lord Jesus and in this Gospel. There He may and does judicially harden, and this to irretrievable ruin, but only after the heart has steeled itself to the appeals of His most patient goodness. Still, judicial hardening is a real thing on God's part, whatever may be argued by those who seem unwilling to allow frankly and fully the activity of God on the one hand and of Satan on the other. Not a whit better is the opposite school which seems to banish from conscience the solemn fact of responsibility, whether in a man or in a Christian, or, as here, in one who, though in the unremoved darkness of a man, drew so near the Son of God, the personal expression in man of all God's light and love.

We have heard already how deeply our Lord felt the sin of Judas as the moment approached and the design was allowed in his heart. Now the sentence goes forth, which closed the door of life for the earth on the Saviour—of everlasting wrath on Judas. Yet did the disciples look on and listen without knowing the awfulness of the issues then pending. Not even John penetrated the meaning of words soon to be clear to all. It was not to buy things needful but to sell their Lord and Master; it was no preparation for the feast[263] but that to which it, not they, had ever looked onward, the fulfilment of God's mind and purpose in it, though it were the Jews crucifying their own Messiah, by the hand of lawless men; it was not that Judas should give to the poor, the last thing which would occupy his mind, but that He should Who was rich yet for our sakes became poor, that we through His poverty might be made rich [2 Corinthians 8:9]. It was a man's, a disciple's, worst sin; it was God's infinite love, both meeting in the death of the Lord on the cross; but where sin abounded, grace exceeded much more {Romans 5:20}.

Judas "therefore having received the morsel immediately went out." What darkness rested thenceforward on that soul! "It was night," says our Evangelist.⁽²⁶³ᵃ⁾ And that night deepened in its horrors on the faithless man, given to see his irreparable evil only when done, till it closed on his going to his own place.

VERSES 31-38.

The Lord felt the gravity of the moment, and saw the way and end from the beginning. All the wondrous and everlasting consequences of His death were stretched out before Him; and now that Judas is gone, He gives free expression to the truth in divinely perfect words.

> "When therefore he was gone out, Jesus saith, Now is (*literally,* was) the Son of Man glorified, and God is glorified in Him"ᵏ (verse 31).²⁶⁴

His own cross is fully in view, and there was laid the basis for all true abiding glory, not for God only (though assuredly for God, for there can be none really unless He be foremost) but for man also in the person of the Lord, the Son of Man, Who alone had shown what man should be for God, as He had shown what God is, even the Father, in Himself the Son.

It is indeed a theme of incomparable depth, the Son of Man glorified, and God glorified in Him; and no statement elsewhere, though from the same lips, was meant so to present and fathom it, though each was perfect for its own object, as the one before us.

In chapter 12, when certain Greeks came to Philip the apostle, desiring to see Jesus, and Andrew and Philip tell Jesus, He answered them saying, "The hour is come that the Son of Man should be glorified;" and forthwith, with His most solemn emphasis, He speaks of His death as the condition of blessing to others. So only should He bear much fruit. Otherwise the grain of wheat abode alone. A living Messiah is the crown of glory to Israel; a rejected One, the Son of Man, by death opened the door, for the Gentile even, into heavenly things, and is the pattern thenceforth. So true is it that to love life in this world is to lose it, to hate it here is to keep it to life eternal; and hence following Him Who died is the way to serve Him, secure the Father's honour, and be with the heavenly Master and Lord. It is by death that He takes the place, not of Son of David, according to promise (though this in grace He does also, according to Paul's gospel), but of Son of Man, and thus have all things and all men, Greeks no less than Jews, according to the counsels of God, heirs of God, and joint-heirs with Christ. There was no other way for guilt to be effaced, for heaven to be opened and enjoyed by those who were once lost sinners. Thus the heavenly glory follows the moral glory; and every hope, for the Gentile most manifestly, turns on Christ's obedience even unto death, wherein Satan's power was utterly broken, and the judgment of God perfectly satisfied. For if the world was therein judged, and its prince to be cast out, Christ lifted up on the cross becomes the attractive centre of grace for all, spite of degradation, darkness, and death.

In chapter 17 the Son looks to the Father Whom He had glorified, that the Father might glorify Him in heaven. He was Son before time began; He had therefore of course glory with the Father before the world was. But He had taken the place of servant in manhood on earth, and now asks that the Father should glorify Him along with Himself with the glory which He had along with Him eternally. A man to everlasting, He would receive all from the Father, albeit Son from everlasting; and when glorified, it is that He may glorify the Father. Such is perfect love and devotedness.

Here, in chapter 13, He speaks of the Son of *Man* glorified, and of *God* glorified in Him. This has its own peculiar force. The first man was an object of shame and judgment through sin; the Second Man, Jesus Christ the righteous, was glorified, and God was glorified in Him. He sees it all summed up in the cross, and so speaks to the disciples, now that the traitor's departure left His heart free to communicate all that filled it. It is not the Father, as such, glorified livingly by His Son in an obedience which knew no limit but His Father's will, but a man, the rejected Messiah, the Son of Man, devoting Himself at all costs to the glory of God. This was indeed the Son of Man's glory, that God should be, as He was, glorified in Him. Blessed Saviour! what a thought, and now a fact and a truth, the truth made known to us, that we might know not merely God come to us but ourselves brought to God, and this in peace and joy, because man is glorified in the Person of Christ, and God is glorified in Him a Man, the man Christ Jesus.

For in deed and in truth God is glorified in the cross as nowhere else—His love, His truth, His majesty, His righteousness. "Herein was manifested the love of God in our case, that God hath sent His Only-begotten Son, that we might live through Him. Herein is love, not that we loved God, but that He loved us, and sent His Son as propitiation for our sins" (1 John 4:9-10). And His truth, majesty, and righteousness have been maintained, no less than His love; for if God threatened guilty man with death and judgment, Jesus bore all, as man never could, that His word might be vindicated fully. Never did man prove his enmity to God, never did Satan prove his power over man, as in that cross where the Son of Man gave Himself up in supreme devotedness and self-sacrificing love to the glory of God. Nowhere was so demonstrated the holiness of God, the impossibility of His tolerating sin; nowhere such love to God, and such love to the sinner. The Son of Man was glorified, and God was glorified in Him.

When, where, was Jesus so glorified as in stooping to the uttermost when God "made sin Him Who knew no sin, that we might become the righteousness of God in Him" [2 Corinthians 5:21]; where Jesus, feeling the truth of death and judgment as none else ever could, bowed His head, not merely to man's contemptuous hatred and to Satan's wily malice, but to God's indignation against sin—despised of man, abhorred of the nation, abandoned of the disciples, forsaken of God, when most of all needing comfort, doing and suffering His will perfectly in the only unstormed fortress of the enemy's power—to God's glory and in His grace? No, there is nothing like it, even where, and where alone, all was perfection, in the life of Christ. *This* was glorifying the Father as to good in a devotedness and dependence with which none can compare; *that*, a glorifying God as to evil by the endurance of all that the Holy One of God could suffer from all that God could and did inflict in unsparing judgment—both the one and the other in absolute obedience and love and self-renunciation to His glory. And all this, and more than this, blessed be God! we see in man, the Son of Man; that in Him, in that nature which had wrought foul dishonour and rebellion against God from first to last, God might be glorified. "Now is the Son of Man glorified, and God is glorified in Him."[265]

In that Person, and by that work, all was reversed. The foundation was laid, the seed was sown, for an entirely new order of things. Previously God forbore, not only with man, but even with the saints, looking unto Him Who should come; and sins were not remitted exactly but prætermitted (Romans 3:25), if we would speak with dogmatic propriety. Man was simply and solely a debtor to God's mercy. Nor would we weaken for a moment that man is still a debtor to His mercy, and must ever be. But there is a revelation now in virtue of Christ's death, a new and different and infinite truth, that God is a debtor to the Son of Man for glorifying Him as to evil no less than good; not only fulfilling all righteousness, but suffering for all unrighteousness. This is alone in the cross, which constitutes its specific glory, ever fading away from feeble man's eyes unless filled with light from Christ in glory, never forgotten of God the Father, Who, in answer to the cry, "Glorify Thy name," said, "I have both glorified and will glorify it again." And so He does and ever will, whatever appearances may for a little while say to the contrary.

His righteousness, once so dreaded a sound, armed (as it could not be without Christ) against us, is now by His death as distinctly for us, as is its spring, the grace which reigns through it unto eternal life. And we boast in hope of His glory, which, without Christ's death, had been instant and everlasting destruction to us; as surely as we have an access by faith into His favour, in which we stand as a present thing. Oh, what has not the death of Christ done for God and for us?

Hence the Lord adds,

> "If God is (*literally*, was) glorified in Him,[1] God also shall glorify Him in Himself, and shall glorify Him immediately" (verse 32).

If we may reverently so speak, it is God now Who has become debtor for the vindication of His glory to the Man Who suffered on the cross. Was He not God from everlasting to everlasting, no less than the Father? yet did He become most truly man, and as man the Son of Man—which Adam was not—He brought glory to God, even in the matter of sin. Therefore it is that God, having been glorified in Him, could not but also glorify Him in Himself. This He has done by setting Him (not on David's, but) on His own throne in heaven, the only adequate answer to the cross. There He alone is set down, the Son but a man, on God's throne; and this "immediately." God could not, would not, did not, wait for the kingdom, which will surely come, and Christ in it, when the due time arrives. But the work of Christ was too precious to admit of delay, and God had long hidden counsels to bring out meanwhile. Thus should He glorify Christ immediately; and so it is, as we all know now, however strange to Jewish expectation then.

Not only was His death before the Lord, but His departure from the world—a notion absolutely new to a Jewish mind in connection with the Messiah. The more such a soul believed Him to be the promised One, the less could it be conceived that He should quit the scene which He had come to bless. "We have heard out of the law," answered the people not long before, "that Christ abideth for ever; and how sayest Thou, The Son of Man must be lifted up? Who is this Son of Man?" There too He had intimated to the Jews not only His death but what death He should die, and His retirement from their midst. A new creation and heavenly glory were beyond their field of vision. But here the Lord prepares His disciples more fully for what was then coming and is now come: facts simple enough for us who have to do with them every day, but wholly unlooked for in Israel, who expected the kingdom immediately to appear, not the things unseen and eternal, with which our faith is called to be conversant.

> "Little children,[266] yet a little I am with you. Ye will seek Me; and, even as I said to the Jews, where I go away [back] ye cannot come, also to you I say now" (verse 33).

None had passed this way heretofore. It must be a new and living way, and only His death could make it possible, consistently with God or with man. But to His own there is a title of endearment; and if He was to be but a little with them, they were to seek Him. Heaven, however, was in no way accessible to man like the earth, of whose dust his body was made. Christ came from God, and went to God, as He will come by and by and receive us to Himself, that where He is, there we may be also. But no more is the Christian able to go there than any other man; Christ alone can bring any therein, as He will surely do with His own at His coming.

But He meanwhile lays a characteristic injunction on them here below.

> "A new commandment I give to you, that ye love one another; even as I loved you, that ye also love one another. By this shall all know that ye are My disciples, if ye have love among one another" (verses 34-35).

The nation disappears. It is no question of loving one's neighbour, but of Christ's disciples and of their mutual love according to His love. New relationships would come out with increasing plainness when He rose from the dead, and sent down the Holy Spirit; and this new duty, loving one another, would flow out of the new relationship: a convincing proof to all men Whose they were, for He alone had shown this throughout His life and death, as also alive again—love unfailing. How far were the Jews from such love? The Gentiles had not even the thought of it. And no wonder. Love is of God, *not* of man, which accounts for the blank till He came Who, though God, manifested love in man and to man, and was thus, through His death and resurrection, to bear much fruit. Their love was to be, if we may so say, of His own material and mould—to abide, if it did not begin, when He went away. For, as is written in 1 John 2:8, the new commandment now "is true in Him and in you; because the darkness passeth and the true light already shineth." While He was here, it was true perfectly, but only in Him; when He gave them redemption in Him through His death and resurrection, it was true in them also. The darkness was passing ("is past" being too strong to say), and the true light already shines. It is not here activity of zeal in quest of sinners, however precious, but the unselfish seeking of the good of saints as such, in lowliness of mind and in Christ's love.[m] [267]

[Matthew 26:33-35; Mark 14:29-31; Luke 22:31-34.]

An irrepressible disciple, with a curiosity habitual in him, turns from what the Lord was enjoining to the words before:

> "Simon Peter saith to Him, Lord, where goest Thou? Jesus answered (him),[n] Where I go, thou canst not follow Me now, but thou shalt follow Me afterwards. Peter saith to Him, Lord, why cannot I follow Thee now? My life [soul] for Thee I will lay down. Jesus answereth° (him),[p] Thy life [soul] for Me wilt thou lay down? Verily, verily, I say to

thee, In no wise shall a cock crow till thou shalt have denied Me thrice" (verses 36-38).

Peter knew and really loved the Lord, but how little he as yet knew himself! It was right to feel the Lord's absence; but he should have heeded better the mild yet grave admonition, that where Christ was going away he was not able to follow Him now; he should have valued the comforting assurance that he should follow Him later. Alas, how much we lose at once, how much we suffer afterwards, through not laying to heart the deep truth of Christ's words! We soon see the bitter consequences in Peter's history; but we know, from the further words of our Lord in the close of this Gospel, how grace would ensure in the end the favour compromised by that self-confidence at the beginning, which he is here warned against.

But we are apt to think most highly of ourselves, of our love, wisdom, power, moral courage, and every other good quality, when we least know and judge ourselves in God's presence; as here we see in Peter, who, impatient of the hint already given, breaks forth into the self-confident question, "Lord, why cannot I follow Thee now? I will lay down my life for Thy sake." Peter therefore must learn, as we also, by painful experience what he might in faith have understood even better by subjection of heart to the Lord's words. Where He warns, it is rash and wrong for us to question; and rashness of spirit is but the precursor of a fall in fact, whereby we must be taught, if we refuse it otherwise. He that slighted the warning when Christ spoke it, lied through fear of a servant-maid. True Christian courage is never presumptuous, but well consorts with fear and trembling; for its confidence is not in the resources of self, or in the circumstances of others, but in God, with a due sense of the power of Satan and of our own weakness.

When ignorance slips, as it often does, into presumption, the Lord does not spare rebuke. "Wilt thou lay down thy life for My sake?" Was this Peter's resolve? Soon would that stout heart quail at the shadow of death. Yet what was death itself for any saint to compare with Christ's death, when tasting rejection as none ever did, and bearing our sins in His own body on the tree, as it was His alone to suffer for them from God! It was judgment as well as death, but endured as only He could.

But ignorance works often in another way. They will not believe their own utter weakness, spite of Christ's plain warning, and want light to prove His truth and their folly. Nor is this all. They assume that if a believer fail once, he must immediately repent in dust and ashes. How little they know themselves, or have profited by Scripture! "Verily, verily," said the all-patient Master, "In no wise shall a cock crow till thou shalt have denied Me thrice."[268] We recall Peter's repeated denial of his Lord, and with oaths, too, under the most solemn circumstances, not to lower him but for the profit of our own souls, and to exalt Him Who alone is worthy. How infinite the grace which made the measure of his sin to be the signal and means of his repentance, under the Lord's use of His own word, and in His wonder-working mercy! And what He was to Peter, He is to us, and nothing less.

NOTES ON THE THIRTEENTH CHAPTER

a [*Cf. Lectures Introductory to the Study of the Gospels*, pp. 507-511.]

b γινομένου, BLX, Æth. [and Origen, Tisch., Treg., W. and H., Weiss]; γενομένου, AD^gr·ΕΓΔΛΠ, etc., the cursives, Chrys. Cyr., Ital. and Vulg. [Lachmann and Blass, as above]; ℵ reads γειν. and gives γεν. as correction.[248]

c ℵBDLX, and a few cursives, etc., omit, though most insert.

d ℵ, though the only MS. that omits ἢ (or εἰ) μὴ τοὺς πόδας, is followed by Tisch., ed. 8. The words are bracketed by W. and H. [Retained by Weiss, after Lachm. and Treg., but omitted by Blass, after Origen.]

e τίνας, ℵBCLM, etc. [Edd.]; οὕς, AD, and eleven more uncials, etc.

f ἐπῆρκεν, ℵAUΠ,etc. [Tisch.], the mass followed by T.R. ἐπῆρεν [most Edd.].

g οὖν, ℵ^pm, and most uncials, cursives, and versions, and so T.R. [Weiss]; but ℵ^corr·BC, etc., omit [as Blass, after Tisch.].

h BC^pmL, etc., have no copula, but it appears in the other uncials, etc., and T.R., which omits ἐκ, with some of the uncials and most cursives, contrary to the more ancient authorities.

i ℵ exhibits both readings which divide the other MSS.; πύθεσθαι τίς ἂν εἴη περὶ οὗ ἔλεγεν· καὶ λέγει αὐτῷ· εἶπε τίς ἐστιν περὶ οὗ λέγει. [Blass omits "and ... speaketh."]

j Tischendorf abandons ἀναπεσών [so W. and H., Weiss], with some good and old uncials (the usual phrase for the position), for ἐπιπ., with most MSS., and some ancient, which express the change of action [Blass, πεσὼν].²⁶¹—It is a question of οὖν and δὲ in connection with it.—οὕτως, "thus," [just as he was] seems pretty sure, though omitted by T.R.

k It is not that the aorist, as here, ever means the present or the future, but that in the Greek the act is spoken of as complete, summed up from the commencing fact to its completion. See chapter 15:6 also, and Revelation 10:7.

l The oldest and best MSS. omit this clause, ℵᵖᵐBCᵖᵐDLXII, a dozen cursives, some of the good Latin [Syrˢⁱⁿ], etc. Hence, Lachmann and Tregelles bracket the clause, and W. and H. go so far as to omit it altogether. Before them, Schulz remarks on the omission: "Recte, nam inepta videtur iteratio eiusdem dicti" {"Rightly, the repetition of the same statement seems absurd"}. This is bolder than man should say and simply proves his own spiritual incapacity. It was worthy, if anything was, of repetition, and most impressive. Twelve uncials, besides the correction of the Sinai MS., and the Rescript of Paris, the mass of cursives, much the weightier of the versions, not to speak of the fathers who commented on the passage, cite the passage as unquestionable Scripture. [Weiss, here uninfluenced by B, and Blass retain "if God," etc.]

m [*Cf. An Exposition of the Epistles of John the Apostle*, p. 96.]

n Omitted by BCᵖᵐL [Edd.], but supported by ℵACᶜᵒʳʳ·D, etc.

o The best sustain the present tense.

p The oldest omit "him."

THE FOURTEENTH CHAPTER^a

VERSES 1-14.

The way was now opened to bring out the Christian's hope. Death, in its most solemn and most blessed aspect, had been put before the disciples, however little able as yet to follow their Master in thought, impossible then, indeed, in any way, as the Lord let the too confident hear, though Peter learnt it not till he proved his own utter powerlessness by the basest denial of Him he loved. How much we have to learn by most painful and humbling experience of ourselves, because we fail in sustained subjection to, and dependence on, our Lord! But now, this cleared, the Saviour turns to what is unfailingly bright, because it centres in Himself. It is no coming as Son of Man to judge, no appearing in glory to set all that is crooked straight and to govern all righteously. It is His own coming for His beloved ones, that they may be with Him where He is, in the Father's house on high.

"Let not your heart be troubled:[269] ye believe[270] on God, believe on Me also. In My Father's house are many mansions: if not so, I would have told you, because^b I go to prepare a place for you. And if I go and[c] prepare a place for you, I am coming again, and will receive you unto Myself, that where I am ye also may be. And where I[d] go ye know the way" (verses 1-4).

A greater break with Jewish feeling could not be than such a hope, a shock assuredly as wholly changing all they had expected, but only as supplanting an earthly prospect, however blessed, by a heavenly one incomparably more blessed. If His going away by death, not yet understood, either in its depth of suffering or in its efficacy, but as departure from them on earth, might naturally disturb their heart, He begins to explain its all-importance as making way for faith. He was no longer to be, according to prophetic intimation, as the Messiah of Israel on earth, still less displayed there in indisputable glory and resistless power. He is about to go a man yet to heaven, and there to be an object of faith as no longer seen, even as God is. "Ye believe in God, believe also in Me." This was a quite new thought about the Messiah, rejected here, glorified in heaven, believed on in earth: simple enough now, but then a strange sound, and an entirely new order of associations, which set aside for a time all that saints and prophets looked for. Not that these things were more than postponed, but that those, altogether unprecedented and unexpected, were to come in by the Lord's going on high after redemption, with just enough in the Old Testament (as, for instance, in Psalm 110:1) to stop the mouth of a Jew who might pervert the law to deny the gospel.

This, then, is the central fact for the Christian as for the Church—Christ not reigning over the earth, but glorified on high as the fruit of His rejection here below. But it is far from all, though all else be but consequences in divine grace or righteousness. The next thing He proceeds to unfold is that there is room above where He is for the saints who follow their rejected Lord. "In My Father's house are many mansions: if not so, I would have told you, because I go to prepare a place for you." He would not have raised a hope incapable of realisation for these saints. If He discloses His own bright abode with the Father, there is ample room for them as for Him; and His love, which was giving Himself for them, would keep back nothing else. His love and the Father's love—for indeed they were one in purpose as in nature—would have them near Himself there. There are many abodes in the Father's house. It is no question of crowns, or cities, or place in the kingdom. There will be reward according to walk, though grace will secure its own sovereign rights. But here differences vanish before the infinite love that will have us with Himself before His Father. Were it too much, or not so, He would have told us, because He goes to prepare a place for us. Love never could, nor does, wittingly disappoint its object.

There is another thing of deep moment contingent on this, but plainly revealed, instead of being left for us to infer. He is coming to fetch His own to heaven.[271] And this was meant to be ever acting on the heart, as we see by the subsequent teaching of the Holy Ghost throughout the rest of the New Testament. Our new place and home is where Christ is, and whither He is to translate us, we know not how soon. Times, dates, signs, circumstances, are purposely excluded. The Christian understands them by a sound intelligence of the word which takes cognizance of all things, but knows nothing of them for his own hope. He reads them about the Jew or the Gentile for the earth; but his are heavenly things, where such measures do not govern. He looks above sun, moon, and stars, where Christ sits at God's right hand, and knows that Christ is coming again, as surely as He went, and this to prepare a place for us. And mark, He is not sending angels to gather us above. This were a great thing, but how immeasurably more the love as well as honour, since He, the Son of God, is coming again, and will receive us to Himself, that, where He is, we also may be! He came for us to die for our sins to God's glory; He is coming again, to have us with Himself in the same home of divine love and nearness to the Father where He is. He could not do more, He would not do less. There is no love like that of our Lord Jesus; nor is the predicted exaltation for Israel, still less for others, to be compared with it, any more than earth is with heaven.

"And where I go ye know the way."[272] His own Person, the Son of the Father, in grace and truth, presented to man, and revealing the Father, is the way which could not but lead to heaven. He came from God, and was going to God. No earthly blessedness could adequately express His glory: He might, and would, take it, and glorify God in glory as in humiliation; but the saint constantly feels there is, and must be, more and higher. Heaven is His Who could communicate with His Father, and command its resources, though never whilst here abandoning the place of the lowliest of men and servant of all need. Yet, as He was the conscious Son, so the saints knew He must be going to the Father, as He was and is the way there.

The Lord had laid down the inward conscious knowledge of the disciples according to God, and the glory of His own Person Whom they confessed, soon by redemption and the gift of the Spirit to bloom in full intelligence. But in this they were as yet dull to apprehend His meaning; and he who was remarkable among

THE FOURTEENTH CHAPTER

them for his gloomy thoughts expresses this difficulty of his for all.

> "Thomas saith to Him, Lord, we know not whither Thou goest; (and)^e how know we (or, can we know)^e the way? Jesus said to him, I am the Way, and the Truth, and the Life: no one cometh unto the Father but by Me. If ye had known^f Me, ye would have known^f My Father also; and^f from henceforth ye know Him, and have seen Him^f" (verses 5-7).

No! the thoughts of Thomas limited the Lord to that earthly horizon which formed the boundary of his own hopes of Israel clustering around their Messiah. He could not conceive, any more than the rest, whither the Lord was retiring, now that He had come to the people and the land which, he knew, He was pledged to bless richly and for ever. How then know the way? His mind was yet earthly. As he had no thought of heaven for the Lord Jesus, so he overlooked the way. But this furnished the opportunity for the Lord to announce in words as simple as profound, "I am the Way, and the Truth, and the Life." Much conveyed in them might have been gleaned from testimonies to Him, most from His own previous discourses as given in this very Gospel, but nowhere so much combined with so brief an expression as here. It was worthy of Him, and at that moment above all.

A way is a great boon, especially through a wilderness which characteristically has no way. Neither had Eden, or unfallen creation, a way; but then it needed none. For all things everywhere were good, and as long as man ate not of the forbidden tree, there was no straying. All else it was for him to enjoy, giving thanks to God. But sin came in, and death, the harbinger of judgment; and all was changed into a wilderness, and men wandered in all directions, alas! all of them away from God and irreparably wrong: a wilderness-world truly, a void place, where there is no way. Not that promise did not, less or more, hold out the hope of better things; not that law did not in due time thunder and lighten; but God's way was not known, as His grace alone could show it. Now it is; for Christ is the Way, the only sure way, for the most erring of sinners, avowedly for the lost, whom He is come to seek and to save; and He is the way to the Father, not to God displayed in power and glory on the earth, as the Jew should expect for the day that is coming, when the rejected Messiah returns as the glorious Son of Man. But He is much more, and above all time or change, the deepest rejection only forcing out what was there always, His own personal glory as Son of God superior to every dispensation. And in the fullest consciousness of it He says to dimly-seeing Thomas, "I am the Way."

Why should one wait for the time when the wilderness shall be gladdened by His presence and power? Then doubtless "the mirage shall become a pool, and the thirsty land springs of water"; "and a highway shall be there, and a way, and it shall be called, The way of holiness; the unclean shall not pass over it, but it shall be for these: the wayfaring men, even fools, shall not err [therein]" [Isaiah 35:7-8]. But He is this and more now to all that believe in Him; and faith delights to own, as God to make known, all He is, when unbelief disowns and slights and casts Him out. He is accordingly the one divine way; and as there is none other, so is He all-sufficing for him who has no strength or wisdom or worth in any sort. But Christ is the way now for the steps of such as know Him, the wisdom of God in an evil world—Himself the highest and perfect expression of that wisdom, and thus open to the babe in faith no less than to an apostle.

Further, He is the Truth, the full expression of every one and of every thing as they are. He tells us in His own Person what God is; He shows us the Father, being Himself the Son. But He, not Adam, shows us man. Adam, no doubt, shows us falling or fallen man; Christ alone is man according to God, both morally, as once here below, and in counsel, as now risen and in heaven. Moreover, as He shows us holiness and righteousness, so also He brings out sin in its true colours; as He says Himself, "If I had not come and spoken unto them, they had not had sin, but now they have no cloak for their sin. He that hateth Me hateth My Father also. If I had not done among them the works which none other man did, they had not had sin; but now have they both seen and hated both Me and My Father" {John 15:22-24}. Hence He, and He only, brings out His adversary the devil personally, the prince of this world, but the constant enemy of the Son.

Even the law, holy, just, and good as the commandment may be, is not the truth; for it is rather on God's part the demand of what a man should do; but Christ tells out, not merely what he ought to be, but what he is. The law claims his duty; Christ declares that all is over, and he is lost. But Christ also shows us a Saviour in His own Person, and this from God and with God. Not that He is not the Judge, for He will judge living and dead, as surely as He will appear and set up His kingdom; but He is Saviour now and to the uttermost. Indeed, it would be impossible to say what of good and glorious He is not, nor from what evil He does not deliver. He is the Truth, the exhibition of the true relation of all things with God, and consequently of the departure of any from God. He, and He only, to the challenge, Who art thou? could answer, "Absolutely that which I am also speaking to you." He is what He also speaks; He is, as no other man was, the Truth; and this, as He intimates in the same chapter 8 of our Gospel, because He is not man alone but God.

But He is more than the Way and the Truth; He is Life, and this because He is the Son. In communion with the Father, He quickens. It is not so in judgment; for the Father judges none, but has given every kind of judgment to the Son, and this because He is the Son of Man; and as men dishonoured Him because He deigned in love to become man, so the Father will have Him honoured not only as God but as man in judgment. Believers honour Him in a very different and far more excellent way. They bow to Him now; willingly, gladly, they exalt Him while rejected by the world. They are thus by grace in communion with God, Who has set Him on high at His own right hand, and will by and by compel every creature to bow and own Him Lord to His own glory. But those that believe have now in Him life, which issues by the Spirit's power in the practice of good; and hence they will enjoy life-resurrection at His coming, as those that have done evil must be raised to a resurrection of judgment in its day.

Thus the believer has Christ for all possible need, and all the blessing that our God and Father can bestow. One cannot have Him as the Way and the Truth without having Him as the Life also, for indeed He is the Resurrection and the Life; and this life, which we have in Him the Son, the Holy Spirit strengthens and exercises, as His word nourishes it, revealing Him ever afresh to our souls. The gift of God is eternal life through Jesus Christ our Lord; and as the way in Christ is a path of love and liberty and holiness, so the end also is life everlasting.

Nor is there any other means of blessing: "No one cometh unto the Father but by Me," says the Lord. There is the surest guarantee, the amplest and the highest good, but it is absolutely exclusive. By none but the Son can one come to the Father; by Him can come any, the proudest Jew, the most debased Gentile. Through Him we both have access by one Spirit unto the Father, as the Apostle says expressly [Ephesians 2:18], when showing the nature of that Church which now takes the place of the ancient people of God. And be it observed that it is not to God only in sovereign grace above sin, saving the most guilty and wretched, but to the Father as such; in it is that relationship of grace which the Son knew eternally in His own right and title, and none the less but the more to His Father's honour, when He glorified Him on earth as the perfectly dependent and obedient man. How wondrous that we should come to the Father, His Father and ours, His God and ours! All glory to Him and His work of redemption, through which alone it could be to us who believe!

Next the Saviour lets them know that the knowledge of the Father is inseparable from that of the Son. "If ye knew Me, ye would know My Father also; and henceforth ye know Him, and have seen Him." He is the image of the invisible God; in the Son is the Father known; and this the disciples are given to learn now objectively.

But there is no capacity in the bright and active-minded disciple to enter into divine things, any more than in the most reserved or sombre one.

"Philip saith to Him, Lord, show us the Father, and it sufficeth us" (verse 8):

an excellent wish, it might seem, to many who read his words, for one who had both seen Jesus and helped others in their desires to see Jesus. But it was sad unbelief in Philip, especially after the patient gracious words just uttered to lead them on.

"Jesus saith to him, Am I so long a time with you, and hast thou not known Me, Philip? He that hath seen Me hath seen the Father; (and)[g] how sayest thou, Show us the Father? Believest thou not[h] that I (am) in the Father, and the Father is in Me?[273] The words which I say[i] to you, I do not speak from Myself; but the Father that abideth in Me, He doeth the works.[i] Believe Me that I (am) in the Father, and the Father in Me; but, if not, believe Me[j] for the very works' sake.[274] Verily, verily, I say to you, He that believeth on Me, the works which I do shall he do also; and greater things than these shall he do; because I go unto the Father"[k] (verses 9-12).[275]

The Lord thus poured a flood of light on the perplexity of the disciples. The Messiah Himself was not a mere man, however endowed and honoured of God. He was true man, and the lowliest of men; but Who was He that was pleased to be born of the virgin? He was the Son— He was God, no less than the Father, and in Him the Father was displaying Himself as such. It was God in grace, forming and fashioning His children by the manifestation of His affections and thoughts and ways in

Christ the Son, a man on earth. This they had known, and yet had not known. They were familiar with Him, and the facts of His everyday works and words, little feeling as yet that they were words and works for eternity of the Creator displaying Himself in incomparably deeper fashion than in the wonders of His creation, or of His government in Israel.

"No one hath seen God at any time: the Only-begotten Son, Who is in the bosom of the Father, He hath declared Him" {John 1:18}. It was for this He came, not only to annul sin by the sacrifice of Himself, but to manifest the eternal life which was with the Father, and this as the Son revealing the Father. How new the order of being, how strange the range of thought, to the disciples! Yet this had Jesus been ever doing here below, occupied with His Father's business long before the beginning of His ministry.

"Believest thou not that I (am) in the Father, and the Father is in Me?" All turned on the glory of His Person; and the very unity of the Godhead, the cardinal truth Israel had to testify, made a difficulty to the reasoning mind of man, unable to rise above its own experience. Not only had law and prophets prepared the way, and John the Baptist's witness, but the words that Jesus said were not as any other man spoke. They were no mere human things, nor independently of His Father. He had been made flesh, but never ceased to be the Word, the Son; and the works He did bore the unmistakable imprint of the same gracious One—the Father. It was He that did the works (or, His works). The disciples were therefore called to believe that He was in the Father, and the Father in Him; a state of being only possible in the divine nature, to which the works themselves gave a witness that left the incredulous without excuse.

And this the Lord follows up with His formula of special solemnity in verse 12, wherein He intimates the testimony that would be rendered to the glory of His Person when, and because, He was going to the Father; the power which should invest the believer, and enable him to do not only what they had seen Jesus do but things greater still in honour of His name. And this was to the letter fulfilled. For never do we hear of the Lord's shadow healing the sick, nor were napkins taken from His body (save in lying legends) to cure disease, or expel demons, not to speak of the multitudes which were brought in far and wide by apostolic preaching. What greater proof of divine power than to work as He Himself did, and yet more by His servants! and more again, when He went on high, than when He sent them out from His presence on earth! But if the power displayed—if the works were to be greater, who could compare himself with the Lord in self-renouncing love, dependence, and obedience? Certainly none that believed on Him, none that through Him wrought so mightily.

Thus had the Lord guaranteed the solemn and withal cheering promise, that His proceeding to the Father was in no way to stem and dry up the mighty stream of gracious power in which He had wrought here below. The believer on Him was to do what He did, and yet greater things. This He now follows up and explains by the place given to that exercise of faith which issues in prayer, henceforth to have its fullest character in His name Who had glorified the Father to the uttermost.

> "And whatsoever ye shall ask (or beg, $\alpha i\tau.$) in My name, this I will do, that the Father may be glorified in the Son. If ye shall ask[1] anything in My name, I will do it" (verses 13-14).

THE FOURTEENTH CHAPTER

The disciples were thus to count on power that could not fail, if sought in His name; for Jesus was no mere man, whose departure must terminate what He used to do when present. Absent He would prove Himself divine, and none the less interested in their petitions because He was risen from the dead. Whatever they might ask He would do, that the Father might be glorified in the Son. And not content with a broad assurance in verse 13, no matter what the difficulty, He repeats it in verse 14 as to any particular petition on their part with a yet more emphatic pledge of His personal action.

Verses 15-24.

But the Lord adds a great deal more, and of the deepest moment.

> "If ye love Me, keep (or, ye will keep)[m] My commandments[276]; and I will request[n] the Father, and He will give you another Paraclete, that He may be with you for ever, the Spirit of truth, Whom the world cannot receive, because it beholdeth Him not, nor knoweth Him; but ye know Him, because He abideth with you, and shall be in you. I will not leave you orphans, I am coming unto you. Yet a little, and the world beholdeth Me no more; but ye behold Me: because I live, ye also shall live" (verses 15-19).

The way to show their affection and devotedness to their Master would be by obedience; for, whatever His grace, He does not disguise from them His authority. To obey His commandments, then, would prove their love far better than zeal in work or in sorrow for His absence; for His absence, however serious in itself, is turned by God's goodness and wisdom to better blessings and deeper ways for the saints, even as it furnishes the occasion for bringing out the hidden counsels of God to His own infinite glory in Christ. Their place was to obey His commandments, as they loved Him; whilst He would pray the Father, Who would send them another,[277a] a Paraclete or Advocate, as He Himself had been, One Who would undertake and carry through their cause, as a Roman patron of old did for his clients or a modern solicitor does now in his little measure. "Comforter"[o] seems too narrow a word, and separates the Spirit unduly from our Lord, Who could hardly be so styled in 1 John 2:1, where Paraclete is applied to His action on high, as here to the Holy Ghost's on earth.

Further, this other Paraclete, given by the Father in answer to Christ, was not to be for a brief season, like the Saviour here below. "He will give you another Paraclete, that He may be with you for ever." This is a truth of the deepest consolation, but most solemn for Christendom. Who believes it? Certainly not those who boast of evangelical views, yet proclaim their unconscious unbelief by regular prayers at the beginning of every year that God would pour out afresh His Holy Spirit on His children in their low estate. Is it meant that the self-complacent mass in Christendom (which utters no such special petitions, but assumes that the Holy Ghost acts, necessarily and infallibly, through popes, or patriarchs, or kindred officials) are more really believing? Far from it. They are inflated with pride, as if God sustains and sanctions their position; and utter blindness holds their eyes, so that they cannot see their state to be one of departure from God's will and truth and grace. But the opposite pole of an error may be also an error; and the assumption that the Holy Spirit directs Babylon, in her confusion of the world and the Church, is not remedied by the practical denial of the abiding presence of the Spirit in the periodical petitions for a fresh outpouring on us.

It were well to ask for a single eye and a spirit of humiliation, that we might cease to do evil, and learn to do well, and this with a truly contrite heart, and a deep sense of whence we have fallen, and of Christ's speedy coming. It were well to judge ourselves by the word of God, not only in our individual walk, but in our corporate ways and worship, to see to it that we neither grieve nor quench the Spirit, to desire earnestly that we "be strengthened with power by the Spirit in the inner man," if, indeed, we do not also need first to be "enlightened of Him," so that we should " know what is the hope of God's calling, and what the riches of the glory of His inheritance in the saints, and what the surpassing greatness of His power toward us who believe" [Ephesians 3:16; 1:18 *f*.]. These are the true wants, even where peace with God is enjoyed individually; for there is nothing in general so little known to the Christian or the Church, as what the Christian and the Church really are; and how can the functions or duties be discharged where the relationship is ignored or mistaken?

Now, all this turns on the great truths before us in these chapters of our Gospel, the absence of Christ from the world to take His place as the risen Man in heaven on the footing of redemption, and the presence of the Holy Ghost sent down to be with the saints for ever. Faith, then, shows itself, not, surely, in imputing to Him failure in abiding, spite of our failure, and praying for a fresh outpouring, as if He had fled in disgust and needed to be sent down again, but in separating from every evil condemned by the word, and doing the will of God as far as we learn it, counting on the assured presence of the Spirit according to the Saviour's promise. Blessing and power follow obedience, even as the Lord puts it here. Nothing can be conceived more false morally than to abide in what we know to be wrong, waiting for power, and then obeying. Not so; more especially, too, as even this hollow excuse denies the distinctive privilege of the Christian, that he has the Spirit already in being a Christian. And so has the Church of God: if not, it is some other church, not His; for only by the presence of the Spirit is the Church really such, always and in all things responsible to be guided of Him, even "the Spirit of truth, Whom the world cannot receive, because it beholdeth Him not, nor knoweth Him; but ye know Him, because He abideth with you, and shall be in you."

The Lord herein looked onward to the presence of the Holy Ghost with the saints, not only assuring them that it should be perpetual, but explaining why the world could have no portion in Him; whereas men might behold and know the Messiah objectively, though externally and in vain for eternal life. But with the Spirit as now given, what could the world have in common? He could but, by His presence with the saints outside the world, prove sin, righteousness, and judgment. But He is no object of sight or knowledge, and the world has no faith, or it would not be the world; whereas the saints, the Christians henceforth, would be characterised by knowing Him, invisible as He is, "because He abideth with you, and shall be in you." Not that one thinks with Euthymius Zigabenus, followed by many a believer from his day to ours, that His abiding in Jesus Who was among them is the meaning; but that when given, He was to abide with them, instead of making a brief sojourn like the Lord's; yea, that He should not only abide, but be *in* them, which Messiah, as such, could not be, however companying with them. It was to be a new, special, intimate presence of God in and with the saints, in contrast with the world which had rejected Christ. And there is no surer sign of, or preparation for, the final apostasy, in its complete form, than that unbelieving departure from God which binds together the saints and the world: whether in a popish assumption of the Spirit's sanction, or in a Protestant unbelief of His presence. One can understand this last, because of their experience of a name to live with death around and within {Revelation 3:1}; which prompts them to cry for the Spirit as if He were gone, instead of quitting all that grieves Him, and hinders the manifestation of His gracious action.

But, said the Lord, "I will not leave you orphans: I am coming to you." It is not here by His future advent, but by the gift of the Spirit.[278] Thus would He comfort them in His own absence. "Yet a little, and the world beholdeth Me no more, but ye behold Me: because I live, ye also shall live." Nothing could be more opposed to their thoughts of, and expectations from, the Messiah of Israel seen by every eye, though in special nearness to His own people on earth. Now they were by the Holy Ghost to see Him Whom the world had rejected and lost, and should see no more save in judgment. And the saints should not behold Him only, but live of the selfsame life, having Christ living in them, as says the apostle Paul [Ephesians 3:17], or, as the Lord here, "Because I live, ye also shall live." Christ is their life, and this in resurrection-power, to which the future tense may point.

But there is more than life, blessed as it is, living because Christ lives, Himself their life, not as Son simply, but as risen and gone to heaven. The Spirit is power to see and know, in contrast with flesh and world. And here He is supposed to be given, known, abiding with them and in them. A most solemn thing is His power, where Christ is not the life: unspeakably blessed, where we live of His life.

> "In that day ye shall know that I (am) in My Father, and ye in Me, and I in you" (verse 20).

It is not here simply the glory of His Person, as in verses 10-11. This was true and an object of faith then. "Believest thou not," said the Lord to Philip, "that I (am) in the Father and the Father is in Me?" Words and works both attested it. "Believe Me," He said to all, "that I (am) in the Father and the Father^p in Me." His being man in no way hindered or lowered His dignity, nor His essential oneness with the Father; and it was and is of all moment to believers unwaveringly to hold it and adoringly. The Son is God, even as the Father. But now more was to be, and to be known; impossible without His personal glory, but dependent on His work and the gift of the Spirit. This we have now, for that day *is* come. It is not the future glory, but present grace putting us in the closest vital association with Him Who has gone into heavenly glory, and yet is one with us here, as we with Him there, by the Spirit given that we might know it all.

In this knowledge saints—true saints of God—are painfully dull, not merely to their privation in countless ways of the utmost moment, but to His dishonour Who cannot be duly served or worshipped now but in Spirit and in truth. The day of forms and shadows is closed; the true light now shines in Christ only, of Whom His saints are the responsible light-bearers as they hold forth the word of life. But there is more here, though all is bound up with Him. It is not Christ present in the world, and reigning over the land or even all the earth.

He is here the despised and rejected of men, but glorified on high. "In that day ye shall know that I (am) in My Father"—a relationship and sphere incomparably more glorious than the throne of His father David. It is not only heavenly, but also expressive of infinite nearness to the Father; and this gives its character to Christianity. All its blessedness turns on Who and what and where Christ is. Unbelief in saints, walking with the world and numbed by tradition, treats all as lifeless fact, not as truth which by the Spirit forms and guides the soul; unbelief in men learns fast to deny and deride even the fact. So much the more urgent call is there on those who believe by grace to walk on in the heavenly light; and the more so, as we know not only that He is in the Father, but that we are in Him and He in us, as the Lord proceeded to say in the words already cited.

There can scarce be conceived a more striking contrast in position and relationship than of Christ and His own as here described with the Messiah and His people, which those then present had gathered, not from the tradition of the elders, but from the ancient oracles of God. But God is sovereign, though ever wise and never arbitrary. All His ways are good and glorious, as they all turn on Christ His image and their centre, the prime object before Him for heaven and earth. On earth government was and will be the aim; for heaven grace reigns, first, however, suffering to His glory, yet morally and infinitely superior to evil, by and by supreme when evil is dealt with and disappears by divine judgment. Between the humiliation of the cross and the coming again is the place of the Son as now known in the Father, as of us in Him and of Him in us.

No Old Testament saint knew or could speak thus; nor did an expectation of it ever dawn on a single heart of old. No millennial saint will ever know such a relationship of Christ or of those then on earth. It is wholly and necessarily a part of what God is now intermediately working for the glory of the Lord; and as faith beholds Him in such a height of divine intimacy, so it owns the incomparable grace which has put us in Christ, and gives us to feel the grave responsibility of Christ in us. What can tell out our nearness more than such an identification of new life and nature, and this in power by the Spirit? Truly, "he that is joined to the Lord is one spirit" [1 Corinthians 6:17]; and the union is just so much more real and permanent than natural oneness, as the Spirit is mightier and closer and more abiding than the flesh. But if thus one with Him and in Him by the Spirit, He is in us by the same Spirit. There is thus alike the highest privilege and the strongest obligation; and we must beware of sundering what the Lord here joins together. If we have life in the Son, we need to remind our souls that Christ lives in us, and that we are to show out Him, not ourselves. Doubtless this demands true and deep and constant self-judgment, and the faith that always bears about in the body the dying of Jesus; and God helps us by trials of all sorts, that the life also of Jesus may be manifest in our mortal flesh {2 Corinthians 4:10-11}. Thus only does Christian practice flow from Christian principle and privilege; and all is of Christ by the Holy Ghost in us. How comforting that our duty as Christians supposes our blessedness! How humbling that the gift of the Spirit makes our failure inexcusable![278a]

But there is meanwhile, and especially connected with Christ being in us, not yet government of the earth by Christ reigning righteously and in power, but moral government of our souls in obedience, which assumes a twofold shape.

> "He that hath My commandments and keepeth them, he it is that loveth Me; but he that loveth Me shall be loved of My Father, and I will love him and will manifest Myself to him" (verse 21).

To the superficial mind of man it may seem strange that our Lord should speak of having His commandments, not only keeping them, as a proof of loving Him; but it is profoundly true. The wicked, the disobedient, the careless, do not understand but the wise, even those whose wisdom ends not, though it begins, with the fear of the Lord. The single eye is full of light. The desire to do His will finds and knows what it is. Thus the loving heart has and keeps His commandments; and, loving Him, draws down His Father's love, Who honours the Son and will not be exalted at His expense. Obedience springing from love is thus the condition of the disciples, which ensures the love of Jesus and the manifestation of Himself to us here below.

Such a manifestation took the disciples by surprise; and one of them, Judas, carefully distinguished from the betrayer, could not but ask for explanation.

> "Judas, not the Iscariot, saith to Him, Lord, (and)^q how is it that Thou wilt manifest Thyself to us and not to the world? Jesus answered and said to him, If anyone love Me, he will keep My word, and My Father will love him, and We will come unto him, and make^r Our abode with him. He that loveth Me not keepeth not My words; and the word which ye hear is not Mine, but the Father's that sent Me" (verses 22-24).

When Messiah manifests Himself to the world as He will when the world-kingdom of our Lord and of His Anointed is come, there will be a feigned obedience rendered by many kept in check by the display of His power and glory. Obedience now that He is absent must be more put to the proof, and is precious to Him as being real; and it should grow as being of life in the Spirit, as the knowledge of His will becomes better known. Compare Colossians 1: 9-10. Hence it deepens from His commandments to His word. His commandments were not grievous; His word is treasured because He Himself is loved. So it is the Lord counts it; and fuller manifestation is enjoyed of the Father and the Son, and more abidingly.

It will be noticed that in verse 23 it is "My word," not, as in the Authorised Version, "My words." He that loves the Lord will keep His word as one whole, because it is His; as He adds in verse 24, that he who loves Him not does not keep His words or sayings. It is not his habit or way to keep any of them in detail. Disobedience betrays absence of love for Jesus; and this is the more serious, because it is not simply the Son Who is in question, but the Father that sent Him, Whose word is slighted. There is nothing so characteristic of a saint now as obedience. It was so perfectly with our Lord Himself. He came to do the will of God; He did and suffered it to the uttermost. Thus only is God known growingly by His children, and most intimately, as the Lord here declares. We must know Him to do His will, which can only be through knowing Jesus Christ Whom He sent; but keeping His word (as the expression not of His authority alone, though this is dear to us from the first, but of His will), we grow by the knowledge of God, and this indefinitely while here below, though ever in unsparing judgment of ourselves and in confiding dependence on Him. And how cheering to the heart the abiding sense of the presence of the Father and the Son with us as thus walking! Would that we knew it better! A manifestation is much, an abode is more.[278b]

Verses 25-31.

The value of what directs the life, of which it was also the revealing means, cannot be exaggerated; and this we have seen in the commands and words of our Lord Jesus, by which He exercises the life He has given to the believer, as, indeed, He is their life. But now He adds fresh consolation and blessing in the relation borne by the Advocate or Paraclete (for so now the Spirit is not only characterised but called).

> "These things I have spoken to you, while abiding with you; but the Paraclete, the Holy Spirit, Whom the Father will send in My name, He shall teach you all things, and bring to your remembrance all things which I said to you" (verses 25-26).[279]

How blessed that the same Holy Spirit Who anointed and abode in Him, while ministering here below, was to teach the disciples all things, and to give them back all the words of Jesus! And so it was fulfilled, and more, as became a divine Person Who deigned to serve in love, sent by the Father in the name of the Son. It is not here the Son requesting the Father and the Father giving, as in verse 16, but the Father sending in the name of the Son the One Who could and would teach all things, besides recalling all that Jesus said to them. Room is thus left, not only for His reviving in their memory all the injunctions of Christ, but also for His own unlimited teaching.

But there is more than doctrine.

> "Peace I leave with you, My peace I give to you, not as the world giveth give I to you. Let not your heart be troubled, neither let it be afraid" (verse 27).

Throughout the Lord supposes His death. This was necessary to peace; His own peace goes farther still. It was the peace He enjoyed while here—a peace unruffled by circumstances, and in unbroken communion with His Father; a peace as far as possible from man's heart, in such a world as this, ignorant of the Father, and on all points at issue with Him. But it characterised the Second Man Who gives it to us. In the faith of Him Who loves us perfectly and to the end, Who has accomplished all to God's glory and for us, we are entitled to it; and the Holy Ghost would have us enjoy it according to His word. He Who gives it gave it not away, and had it not the less because we were to receive it. Like all else that He gives, it is enjoyed unimpaired in its own divine fulness, every one that shares rather adding to it than taking from it. The question is not merely of reality, but of its course and character. "Not as the world giveth, give I unto you. Let not your heart be troubled, neither let it be afraid." Why, indeed, with His peace, should the heart be confounded or fearful?

But the Lord looks now for hearts purified by faith to delight in His glory.

> "Ye heard that I said to you, I go away, and come unto you; if ye loved Me, ye would have rejoiced that[s] I go unto the Father, because the[s] Father is greater than I. And now I have told you before it come to pass, that when it is come to pass ye may believe" (verses 28-29).

THE FOURTEENTH CHAPTER

Thus, whatever His essential and personal glory, He never forgets that He is man on earth. As such He goes away, and comes back to the disciples. As such He calls upon them to rejoice in His proceeding to the Father.[280] It was no small thing that man in His Person should thus enter into glory; and there is almost as much unbelief in Christendom's taking it as a matter of course, utterly indifferent to its value, as in Jewish rejection of it as incredible, if not impossible. The Jew, as such, looked for man—that is, for himself—to be blessed in the highest degree by God on the earth; and so, doubtless, beyond his thought, it will be in the kingdom by and by. But the Lord would have the Christian rejoice in the Second Man, gone up even now into the paradise of God, the sure pledge of our own following Him there when He comes back again for us. And therefore does He the more impressively call attention, not to the fact only, but to His mention of it then before it came to pass, that when it did, they should believe. Himself in glory is the living object of faith, full of weighty and fruitful consequence for us. It is well to give His death the deepest value. Never can we lose sight of His profound humiliation in self-sacrificing love to glorify God and to bear our burden of sins and judgment, without incalculable loss to our souls; but we do well to have our eye fixed on Him "received up in glory," and ever to wait for Him as about to come and have us there with Himself in the Father's house.

> "No longer shall I talk much with you, for the prince of the[t] world cometh, and hath nothing in Me. But that the world may know that I love the Father, and as the Father commanded[u] Me, so I do. Arise, let us go hence" (verses 30-31).

The Lord thus intimates that He has not much more to talk with them. He had another task on hand; for the enemy was coming, characterised now as the prince of the world which had rejected the Son of God, proving thereby its opposition to the Father and its subjection to Satan; but, come when he might, he had no more in Christ at the end than at the beginning.[281] Then he would gladly have enticed the Saviour out of the path of obedience by offering gratification; now he strives to fill Him in that path with fear and horror of the death which was before Him. It was in vain: "The cup which My Father giveth Me, shall I not drink it?" In us naturally there is everything which can afford a handle to Satan; in Christ he had nothing. So it could not but be because of the glory and unsullied perfectness of His Person, true God and unblemished Man; and so it must be for us, if we were to have eternal life in Him, and He to take away our sins, and all this in obedience and to the glory of God His Father. Therefore does He add, "but that the world may know that I love the Father, and as the Father commanded Me, even so I do." It was indeed the Son's love to the uttermost; it was also unqualified obedience.

Here the Lord ends this part of His communications, and marks it by the closing words, "Arise, let us go hence."[282]

NOTES ON THE FOURTEENTH CHAPTER

a [*Cf. Lectures Introductory to the Study of the Gospels,* pp. 511-518.]

b ὅτι, ℵABC^{pm} DKLXΠ, twenty cursives, and most ancient versions [as Syr^{sin}], etc.; but T.R. [as Blass] omits, with some ten or eleven uncials, most cursives, the Gothic, Æth., etc.

c DM, with more than sixty cursives, read ἑτοιμάσαι; others, like AEGKΓΔ, and forty cursives, with the Gothic and Pesch. Syr., simply ἑτοιμάσω, without καὶ [as Blass], but ℵBCLNSUXΛΠ, and versions [Syr^{sin}], καὶ ἐτ.

d Some authorities omit ἐγώ, and most [as A C^{corr}D, Syr^{sin pesch hier}], with T.R., add καὶ ... οἴδατε, "and ... ye know."

e BC^{pm}L, etc., omit καὶ; whilst BC^{pm}D, Lat. MSS., Æth., etc., read οἴδαμεν, "know we." T.R., with sixteen uncials, perhaps all the cursives, and the versions generally, has δυνάμεθα τ. ὁδ. εἰδέναι, "can we know," etc.

f ἐγνώκατε ... γνώσεσθε, ℵD^{pm}, instead of ἐγνώκειτε ... ἐγν. ἄν, as in all the other uncials, save that BC^{pm}, etc., give for the last ἄν ᾔδειτε. Some of these uncials, etc., omit καὶ before ἀπ' [as Blass], and ℵ reads after it γνώσεσθε, not without some support from Latin; BC^{pm} omitting αὐτὸν at the end. [Blass read ἐγνώκατε ... γνώσεσθε, but with μὴ before the one, οὐ before the other.]

g Most MSS. read καὶ π., but the copulative is omitted by ℵBQ, etc.

h B^{pm} strangely reads οὐ πιστεύσεις, "wilt thou not believe?"

i λέγω, B^{corr.} (pm om.) LNX, etc., instead of the first λαλῶ, as in most [so Blass], as BL, etc., omit ὁ after the second πατήρ [which Blass retains]. ℵBD read αὐτοῦ ("His works") at the end, instead of αὐτός either there or before as ordinarily.

j ℵDL, etc., omit [as Edd.] final μοι, read by the mass of authorities.

k The weight of authority (ℵABDLQXΠ, many cursives, almost all the ancient versions, and the fathers) is against the addition of μου after πατέρα.

l [Edd. here adds με ("Me") after ℵB, etc., 33, etc. Blass omits the whole verse, as Syr[cu sin], Nonnus, and Chrysostom.]

m BL, etc. (ℵ, 33, 69[pm] τηρήσητε) τηρήσετε, "ye will keep." So W. and H. [Weiss and Blass] edit. [Syr[sin] has "keep."]

n It is of interest, and even of importance, to mark the distinctness of ἐρωτάω, as used of Christ with the Father, and αἰτέω of the disciples. Scripture nowhere predicates of Him the last or supplicatory expression, save in Martha's mouth [11: 22], whose faith, though real, was low. Christ uses ἐρ. in speaking to the Father, as the disciples use αἰτ. to Him, and both words to Christ. The word ἐρ. is also employed in the sense of "interrogating," or "questioning."[277]

o Philologically it is hard, not to say impossible, to conceive the Greek term meaning "Comforter." Its structure and usage alike point to one "called to aid," as a cognate but different form signifies a comforter. This a paraclete may well be; but He is far more, and summoned for every difficulty and need. So is the Paraclete, and in an infinite way, as a divine Person. To comfort is but a small part of His functions. "Advocate" might do, as in

NOTES ON THE FOURTEENTH CHAPTER

1 John 2:1. [See, further, *An Exposition of the Epistles of John the Apostle*, p. 56 *ff.*]

p In the Elz. of 1624 and 1633, ἐστὶν, with the slenderest support; Steph. rejects it in his edd. of 1546, 1549, and 1550, as Beza in all his.

q καὶ ℵGHKMQSUΓΔΛΠ, and many cursives; but ABDELX, etc., with almost all the other versions, omit.

r ποιησόμεθα ℵBLXΠ², some cursives, and many fathers [W. and H., Blass]; instead of the T.R. ποιήσομεν (or -ωμεν), as in most uncials and cursives and many fathers [Weiss]. D. [Syr^sin], etc., strangely read ποιήσομαι, "I will make." The middle voice gives the force of "Our" in the strongest way, which the T.R. loses.

s T.R., following the later uncials and most cursives, adds εἶπον, "I said"; but the best give the text preferred. There is rather better authority for adding μου to ὁ Π. (= "My F.").

t ℵABD^gr LXΓ, and seven more uncials, 150 cursives, the Syriac, etc., omit τούτου, which appears in the T.R. supported by a few cursives and the versions in general, etc.

u ἐνετείλατό μοι ℵADΓ, with ten other uncials and most cursives and versions [Weiss]; Lachmann, Treg., with W. and H. [and Blass], edit ἐντολὴν ἔδ. (or δέδ.) μοι. after BLX, etc., with the It. and Vulg.

THE FIFTEENTH CHAPTER [a]

VERSES 1-17.

The change of subject having been made thus apparent, the Lord now proceeds to set forth His mind for the disciples in one of the allegories peculiar to our Gospel.

> "I am the True Vine, and My Father is the husbandman. Every branch in Me not bearing fruit, He taketh it away; and every one that beareth fruit, He cleanseth it, that it may bring forth more fruit. Already *ye* are clean, because of the word which I have spoken to you. Abide in Me, and I in you: as the branch cannot bear fruit from itself, unless it abide in the vine; so neither (can) ye, unless ye abide in Me" (verses 1-4).

Thus the Lord sets aside Israel as any source of fruit-bearing for God. Long since had the prophets denounced the nation as bearing wild grapes, as an empty vine, or as only fit for the burning. But the Lord brings to light Himself as the true and only stock acceptable unto God. This was an immense truth for Jews to learn. In Israel was all that they trusted for religion. There was the temple, there the priesthood, there the sacrifices, there the feasts; there every ordinance, public or private, great or small, instituted of God. Outside Israel were the heathen who knew not God. *Now* the Lord does not merely strip the veil from the elect people's hollow state, but make known the secret. He is the Vine—the True Vine. He is not merely a fruitful branch, where all others were unfruitful; He is Himself the True Vine. Thus we have the positive object before us, the one source of fruit-bearing.

"And My Father," He adds, "is the husbandman." But there is another truth needed, the revelation of His Father (not yet fully revealed as theirs, though soon to be in His resurrection), no longer of Jehovah as once in the vineyard of the nation, nor as the Almighty known to their fathers. As Father, He deals with the branches of the Vine, which is Christ Himself on earth, object of all the active and watchful interest of His Father Who looks for fruit. But it is not Himself alone; there are branches in Him. It is here their responsibility enters: for they are the Lord's disciples, once but Jews in their natural condition, henceforth called to bear fruit unto God.[283]

And what, then, are the terms laid down? "Every branch in Me not bearing fruit, He taketh it away; and every one that beareth fruit, He cleanseth it, that it may bring forth more fruit." Clearly it is the Father's government of those who bear the name of the Lord. The fruitless professor He removes; the fruitful one He cleanses, that more fruit may be borne. It is the Father judging according to every man's work. The disciples were primarily in view; but the principle, of course, applies to us, now that Israel is still more manifestly set aside. As the Apostle teaches us in Hebrews 12, He chastens us for our profit, that we might be partakers of His holiness. Here, if not taken away, we are cleansed in order to bear more fruit.

It is a wholly different state of things from a Messiah reigning in power, and His people in nothing but prosperity, Satan shut up, and the desert rejoicing and blossoming as the rose. Doubtless, it is not union with Christ in heaven, nor even the privileges of grace generally in Him, but the call to make Him everything on earth in daily ways, if we would indeed bear fruit. He, not the law, is the rule of life, and the source of fruitfulness; nor is there any other for the Christian, not even the Spirit Who uses the word to glorify Christ, but Himself.[284]

The disciples had already proved the purging power of the word. "Already *ye* are clean because of the word which I have spoken to you."[285] They had received it, and knew that He came from God, though they knew the Father imperfectly, if at all. Yet Christ's word had wrought in their souls; it had cleansed their ways, it had judged their worldly thoughts, it had laid bare their carnal desires: the effect was real in their consciences. Judas was now gone, so that the Lord does not need to say, "Ye are clean, but not all"; but, on the contrary, "*Ye* are clean already," even before the Holy Ghost was given as power from on high. The cleansing efficacy of the word is a cardinal truth of Scripture apt to be forgotten, not merely by the Romanist who trusts in ordinances, but by the Protestant who speaks exclusively of the Saviour's blood "that cleanseth from all sin." God forbid that a word should be said to obscure that blood, or to turn a soul from its justifying value. But out of the Lord's side flowed water and blood; and we need both. The blood atones, the water purifies; and as the blood abides shed and efficacious once for all, in contrast with the ineffectual and many sacrifices of the Jews, the washing of water by the word is not only applied at the first but is needed to purge all through. Where this is not seen, confusion follows, and the enfeebling, if not destruction, of fundamental truth.

But here the Lord insists on more—the necessity and the importance of dependence on Him, of intimacy with Himself. This is to abide in Christ; and His word is, "Abide in Me, and I in you." It is not sovereign grace to the sinner, but His call to the disciple; and hence His abiding in us, as a matter of daily communion, depends on our abiding in Him. "As the branch cannot bear fruit from itself, unless it abide in the vine; so neither (can) ye, unless ye abide in Me." Nothing simpler than the fact outwardly, nothing surer in our experience than that so it is inwardly. He, and He only, is the dwelling-place for the soul in this world of snare and danger, in this desert where no water is. Make Him the resource, make Him the object; and the sap, as it were, flows without hindrance, and fruit is borne. Without Him no teaching avails, and all religious excitement fails; bring Him in, confide in Him, and, no matter what the difficulty or the pain or the shame, no matter what the opposition or the detraction, He sustains the heart, and fruit-bearing follows.[286] Apart from Him we can do nothing; with Him, all things. So said one who had learnt it well, "I have strength for all things in Him that giveth me power" (Philippians 4:13).

It seems scarcely needful to remark that the relation of head and body serves quite another purpose in Scripture, and must be kept wholly distinct. Heavenly grace forms that one body by the one Spirit united to the glorified Head; and therein we do not hear of rending, maiming, or cutting off. It is the Church viewed as the object of Christ's unfailing love, till He present it to Himself in glory. Responsibility on earth under divine government is another thing; and this, not the unfailing heavenly relationship of the Church, is taught by the Vine and its branches. Hence Calvinistic devices are as uncalled for as the Arminian assaults they are meant to avert. No one doubts that profession may fail. Life is eternal for all that; and in Christ there is nothing short of eternal life; but this is not the teaching of the Vine, any more than the unity of the body. It is a pity that learned commentators do not read with faith and care the scriptures they essay to comment on.

The opening words had laid down the principle of Christ as the source of fruit, in contrast with Israel, and under the living watchful care of the Father. It was wholly distinct from government of the flesh by the law before Jehovah, as in the chosen nation to which all the branches belonged. Christ here displaces the old associations. He had shown fruit to be so indispensable in the Father's eyes that not to bear it involves the removal of the branch, whilst that which bears fruit is cleansed in order to bear more. He had pronounced the disciples already clean by reason of His word, and had urged them to abide in Him, as He in them; and this because they could not bear fruit except they abode in Christ, any more than the branch itself except it abide in the vine.

Next, He sums up and applies this weighty truth of communion with Him, in its great positive elements, and in strong contradistinction from abandonment of Him.

> "I am the Vine, ye are the branches. He that abideth in Me, and I in him, he beareth much fruit; because apart from Me ye can do nothing" (verse 5).

THE FIFTEENTH CHAPTER

Nothing more precise. The Lord leaves no uncertainty in a matter so nearly affecting both Himself and them. As surely as He was the Vine, they were the branches. There is, and could be, no failure on His part. It is easy for us to fail in dependence, and to lack confidence in Him. To abide in Him supposes, not merely distrust of ourselves, but cleaving to Him and counting on Him. Every influence around us is adverse to this; every natural feeling not less so. Faith working by love alone secures it, for self and the world are then alike judged in the light of God. It is not only that we need and cannot do without Him for the least things as truly as the greatest, but He attracts us by His positive excellency. If He is the one source of fruit agreeable to the Father, He cannot be slighted with impunity, least of all by those who confess Him. It is not the grace which gives eternal life in Him of which the Lord speaks, but throughout these verses the responsibility of the disciples. Hence, as we shall see presently, there is danger of ruin, no less than fruitlessness, where one does not abide in Him.

This, then, is the secret of fruit-bearing. It is not in saints any more than in self, but by abiding in Christ and Christ in us. Then there is more than promising blossom; fruit follows. Where He is intercepted from our view, or we look elsewhere, there is no such power: we manifest our nature, not Christ. Nor does the character of the circumstances affect the result: He is superior to all, spite of our weakness. Abiding in Christ, we may safely face the most hostile; and if traps be laid and provocation given, what matters it, if according to His word we are found abiding in Christ, and Christ abides in us, as He then does? For that the two are correlative, He guarantees, and we know. Again, does fruit follow because we are with dear children of God? Alas!

how often the very reverse is proved, and the levity, if not the bitterness, in the heart comes out so much the more because we are saints not abiding in Christ. For gossip about saints to saints is even more painful than among the sons of this age, not a few of whom seem above it, though on grounds of nature—of course, not of Christ. Trials, again, cannot shake off spiritual fruit, nor blighting influences enter, if we abide in Christ and Christ in us; but the greater the pressure, the more fruit where we thus abide. And the heart feels that so it should be, as it is. For, as ordinances fail, and law is the strength of sin (not of holiness, flesh being what it is), Christ here, as everywhere, has the glory by faith and to faith; "because apart from Me ye can do nothing."

On the other hand, the peril is proportionately greater.

> "If one abide[b] not in Me, he is cast out[287] as the branch, and is dried up: and they gather it,[c] and cast (it) into the fire, and it burneth" (verse 6).

Christ being the sole source of fruit, to abandon Him is fatal; and so much the worse, if so at the last, when He should be the more precious, as the worthlessness of all else is learnt practically, and His excellency better known to faith. So it was with Judas, so in general with those not born of God who essay to follow Jesus. Not only their lusts but His words may give the occasion, as we see in John 6. It is vain and mischievous to distinguish between the person and the work, as theologians and others do who reason on either side of the equation of truth. The Calvinist fears to compromise his doctrines of grace; the Arminian is anxious to push his advantage on the side of falling away. Hence the former is apt to evade the solemn warning of personal ruin and final judgment conveyed here, as the latter argues that

THE FIFTEENTH CHAPTER

the passage implies that a saved soul may be lost after all. They both confound the figure of the Vine with the body in Ephesians 2-4, and hence are alike wrong, and of course unable to expound these scriptures satisfactorily, so as to hold all the truth without sacrificing one part to another.

The error comes out plainly in the Anglican Baptismal Service: "Seeing now that this child is regenerated, and grafted into the body of Christ's Church." To be grafted into the olive of Romans 11 is equivalent, in this teaching, to being made a member of Christ's body; and the results of such confusion are ever favourable to the adversaries of the truth. The answer is that the body is the expression of unity by the Holy Ghost; the Vine insists on communion as the condition of bearing fruit. In no case do such trees necessarily imply life, but the possession of privilege, as the olive, and the responsibility of bearing fruit, as the vine. To leave Christ, therefore, is utter ruin, not only to be fruitless, but to burn. It is not merely suffering loss as in 1 Corinthians 3:15, but to be manifestly lost as in 1 Corinthians 9:27. Thus each scripture renders its own testimony, and has its own value, while none can be broken, though men may stumble at the word, being disobedient, as another Apostle warns {1 Peter 2:8}.[288]

But now, from the sad case of the man that quits Him, the Lord returns to the disciples, and with divine simplicity and fulness gives the way of blessing and abundant fruit.

> "If ye abide in Me, and My words abide in you, ask (or, ye shall ask)[d] what ye will, and it shall come to pass for you. In this is (*literally*, was)[e] My Father

glorified, that ye bear much fruit, and (ye shall) become[f] My disciples" (verses 7-8).

Thus is each thing put in its place. The first need for the Christian is to abide in Christ; the next, to have Christ's words abiding in Him; then he is emboldened to ask with the assurance that the resources of divine power effect accordingly. For thus Christ Himself has the first place, and the saint is kept in dependence as well as confidence. Then His words direct as well as correct; and we need and have both, though doubtless in so abiding direction would here be the characteristic, rather than that holy correction which we deeply want in our walk through this unclean and slippery world. If so led, prayer is encouraged to expect the surest answer, for the heart is in fellowship with Him Who prompts the desire, in order to accomplish it in His love and faithfulness. Further, in this is the Father glorified, that we bear much fruit, and become disciples of His. What enlargement of heart that so it should be in the midst of what, apart from Him, would be but a grief and worry to the saint, if not worse! With Christ all is changed, and even the most distracting cares turn to fruit; so that to live in flesh, instead of being with Him in glory, becomes worth the while, but only when to live is Christ. Thus was His Father glorified even now, and we became Christ's disciples in deed and in truth.[289]

Another element of incalculable value in the disciple's path is the consciousness of the Saviour's love. This is next set before them.

> "As the Father loved Me, I also loved you: abide in My love. If ye keep My commandments, ye shall abide in My love; even as I have kept My Father's commandments and abide in His love. These

things have I spoken to you that My joy may be[g] in you, and your joy may be fulfilled" (verses 9-11).

We must bear in mind that the subject is fruit-bearing during the disciple's passage through this world. It is not eternal purpose, nor is it that love in relationship which secures unfailingly from first to last, but Christ's love toward each in His path of daily walk and trial. He knew what this was on His Father's part to Himself as man, though never ceasing to be Son here below. Such was His own love to the disciples; and now He calls on them to abide in it, not in Him only, but, what is more, in His love; an immense and unfailing spring of comfort in the necessarily painful and otherwise disappointing current of earthly circumstances so strongly opposed to them for His sake. "Give wine," says the Book of Proverbs, "unto those that be of heavy hearts" [Proverbs 31:6]. But His love is better than wine, cheering and strengthening without fleshly excitement. There is thus not only dependence on Him, but that confidence in Him which His love is meant to inspire.[290]

But there is more that follows, even obedience. "If ye keep My commandments, ye shall abide in My love; even as I have kept My Father's commandments and abide in His love." It is manifest that we have nothing here to do with the sovereign mercy of God which goes out to the lost and reconciles enemies by the death of His Son. "For as by the disobedience of the one man (Adam) the many were constituted sinners, so also by the obedience of the one (Christ) shall the many be constituted righteous" {Romans 5:19}. Grace in Christ surmounts every hindrance, and reigns righteously above all evil, whether of the individual or of the race. Here not the sinner's ruin or deliverance, but the disciple's path, is in question; and his obedience is the condition of abiding in his Master's love. He Who in all things has and must have the pre-eminence trod the same path and accepted the same condition as man here below; though He counted it no robbery to be on equality with God, He became obedient, and this to the lowest point, for the glory of God the Father. He in unwavering perfection did the will of Him that sent Him, and enjoyed its fruit in a like perfection; we follow Him, though with unequal steps; and assuredly "he that says he abides in Him ought himself also so to walk even as He walked" {1 John 2:6}. And obedience is the way. None other morally befits us; as this but verifies our love to Him and sense of relationship to God. Nothing is so lowly, nothing so firm, as obedience. It delivers from self-assertion on the one hand, and on the other from subjection to the opinions or traditions of men. It brings us face to face with God's word, and tests our desire to please Him in the midst of present ease, honour, lust, or passion. Here, too, it is a question of keeping Christ's commandments, as that which secures His love, as in chapter 14 we saw that it proved their love to Him.

The last motive the Lord brings to bear on the disciples as to this is contained in the next verse. "These things have I spoken to you that My joy may be in you, and your joy may be fulfilled." Nor is there a better criterion of our state, and consequently of our failure or success in entering into His mind. For if we take up the words of this chapter legally, scarce any words in the Bible are surer to plunge an upright soul into sorrow and depression; but if we understand them as He intended, they are expressly given to impart His joy to us and make our joy full. His joy when here was in pleasing His Father; to obey His commandments was not burdensome. This joy of His, unbroken in His path, He would now make ours.

What a contrast with the unfruitful groaning of a soul under law, even though quickened, as in the close of Romans 7! What a mercy, if we have tasted such bitterness, now to know our joy in obedience fulfilled! The latter part of Romans 7 is a wholesome process for us to pass through, but a miserable ground of standing: for this God never intended it. Chapter 8 shows us the Christian delivered, holy, and abounding in good fruit. Can we be on both grounds at the same time? Only he would assert this who is not yet set free. Look to it, theologians; and you who believe them, and taste not Christ's joy.

This is clearly His desire concerning us. Those who ignore or deny it would deprive us of His joy, as no doubt they lack it themselves. Nor need we wonder; for as philosophy never can conceive divine love, so theology, pandering as it does to human science, ever misses the Saviour's joy, seeking pleasure and applause in the schools of the world, which knows the Father no more now than of old. "O righteous Father," said He a little later, "the world knew Thee not; but I knew Thee, and these (the disciples) knew that Thou didst send Me; and I made known to them Thy name, and will make it known; that the love wherewith Thou didst love Me may be in them, and I in them."

What ineffable goodness! Does not every thought, feeling, word, prove itself divine? Settled peace is a great thing as the soul's foundation, never to be moved, and God would have us know it simply and immutably; but we must not forget the joy of obedience and the favour of the Lord as a present thing in our daily ways. This has been too much overlooked by the children of God, and scarcely more through the slipshod laxity of evangelicalism than by the morose hardness of the legalists, ignorant alike of the full ground of grace, and of the true character of God's government which is bound up with it as a present thing.

The Lord now specifies one special character of fruit, ever precious, but here in the disciples' relation one to another, as before we had the relation of Christ and the Father to them.

> "This is My commandment, that ye love one another, as I loved you. Greater love no one hath than this, that one[h] lay down his life for his friends. Ye are My friends if ye do what (ever)[i] I command you. No longer do I call you bondmen, for the bondman knoweth not what his lord doeth; but you I have called friends, because all things which I heard from My Father I made known to you. Not ye chose Me, but I chose you and appointed you that ye should go and bear fruit, and your fruit abide; that whatsoever ye shall ask the Father in My name He may give you. These things I command you, that ye love one another" (verses 12-17).

Love is emphatically the Lord's injunction on His disciples, the love of each other. It is not the general moral duty of loving one's neighbour, but the mutual love of Christians, of which His own love to them is the standard. The nature of the case excludes the love of God which went out to them in their guilt, enmity, and weakness, when objects of sovereign grace. They were now born of God, and hence love; for love, as it is of God Who is love, is the energy of the new nature.[290a] Hence, whatever else the Lord may enjoin, this is His commandment: He loved them, and would have them love one another accordingly. So Paul tells the Thessalonians that he needed not to write about it to them, for, young as they were in divine things, they were taught of God to love one another [1 Thessalonians 4:9]. This, too, was the more excellent way he would show the Corinthian saints, preoccupied to their hurt with power rather than love, at best the display of the Lord's victory in His creation over Satan rather than the inward energy which enjoys His grace toward our own souls or others to God's glory [1 Corinthians 13]. On the Roman saints, again, love is repeatedly urged, as that which should be unfeigned, and also which, wherever it is, has fulfilled the law practically without thinking of it [Romans 12:9; 13:10]. It is needless to go over all the Epistles where the Holy Spirit unfolds its immense place and power.

But every believer acquainted with the New Testament will remember how large a part it fills in the First Epistle of our Evangelist. Not that love is God, but God is love as He is light; and he that loves is born of Him and knows Him. For men as then made knowledge all, as before some made power; but it is a question of life in the Son of God, and the Holy Ghost works in that life by virtue of redemption, and those who have life, as they walk in the light, so also walk in love. And even as to knowledge, there is none true save in Him that is true, in His Son Jesus Christ. He is the true God and eternal life: every object outside Him is an idol, from which we have to keep ourselves, be it knowledge, power, position, love, truth, or anything or anyone else. For whoever denies the Son has not the Father; he who confesses the Son has the Father also. And as the Father has bestowed on us love beyond all measure, giving us even now to be children of God, so loving the brethren marks those who have passed from death unto life. The old commandment is the word of Christ that we should love one another, but it is also a new commandment as being true in Him and in us. If Christ lives in me, I live by faith of the Son of God Who loved me and gave Himself for me: and this life is characterised not only by obedience, but by love according to its source.

And so here. The Lord had laid it down as a new and distinguishing commandment He was giving them in chapter 13. Here He repeats love to one another according to the pattern of His love to them. How pure and unbounded it was! Do we believe this as His will about us? Do we love as if we believed Him and appreciated His love? Can anything be more hollow, or dangerous, or nauseous than the highest words with low and inconsistent ways? Gnosticism ate out the heart of early Christendom, where it fell not into superstition and formality, ever growing more dark and cold; and the same spirit is yet more destructive now, because it has more abundant materials, and hardens itself in unbelief even to Agnosticism. Loving one another, not merely those who think alike, least of all those who think alike on some comparatively small and external point, but loving those who are Christ's spite of ten thousand things trying to our nature, is of all moment along with the truth, and guarded as it is here, loving one another as He loved us. He delights in love up to death.

Greater love none has than to lay down his life for his friends.[290b] The love of God in Jesus went infinitely beyond this; but then necessarily it stands alone, and it is meet that it should. *We* ought to lay down our lives for the brethren, as we are taught elsewhere. But where is the worth of such a theory if we fail in everyday going out of heart to common wants and sufferings of God's children (1 John 3:17-18)? The Lord at once binds love up with obedience, without which it is but self-pleasing, not having Him in it or before the soul. "Ye are My friends if ye do what (ever) I command you." It is not reconciling enemies He speaks of, but why He calls us His friends. Obedience is the character and condition. Nor does He here indicate how He stood as our friend when we were enemies, but He calls us His friends if we practise what He enjoins on His disciples.[291]

Is this all? Far from it. He treats us as friends according to His perfect love, for He lets us into His secrets, instead of merely pressing our duty. "No longer do I call you bondmen, for the bondman knoweth not what his Lord doeth; but you I have called friends, because all things whatsoever I heard from My Father I made known to you." He who of old was called "the friend of God" enjoyed this intimacy with his Almighty protector in the midst of the doomed races he lived amongst, a separated and circumcised pilgrim; and so it is with His own now that the Lord deals in still more lavish grace; for what did He keep back? In another sense it is our boast to be His bondmen, as one said who was pre-eminently separated to the gospel of God. But none the less—indeed, very much more truly—do we enter in, and value and act on the free communication of His love if we are habitually obedient, as we may see in Joseph of old or in Daniel later. It ought to be, it is in principle, the cherished privilege of the Church thus to know His mind, and by it to interpret the tangled web of human life or even the world's changing fortunes; but practically we must be exercised and constant in obedience if the privilege is to be a living reality and not a bare title. Christendom has given it up, counting it nothing but presumption, and content to walk by sight, not by faith, in denial of its privilege.

But God is faithful, and there are those who, walking obedient to His word, enter into what He has made known, and find the blessing. Doubtless the responsibility is great no less than the privilege; and therefore do His own need to be cheered with the grace that underlies all. Hence it is that He adds, "Not ye chose Me, but I chose you and appointed (or, set) you that ye should go and bear fruit, and your fruit abide; that whatever ye may ask the Father in My name He may give you. These things I command, that ye love one another."

Blessing ever comes from the Lord Jesus and the grace that is in Him. Obedience follows, and ought to follow, such unmerited favour, as in obedience there is surely fresh blessing. But the heart needs to turn from our obedience or its blessing to the Blesser, if it would escape fresh dangers and positive evil; the spring of power is never known save in Him, and the grace that sought and found, saves and blesses. Hence it was of the greatest moment, in pressing the divine government of the saints, that they should ever remember Him and His sovereign will, as the source of all that distinguished them. Not they chose Christ, but He chose them. Nor was it only to know and follow their Master. He appointed,[j] or set, them that they should go and bear fruit, and their fruit should abide. Though apostles, they were His friends to obey Him all the more.

Thus, while responsibility is maintained intact, grace is shown to be the fountain of all that is looked for and made good; and, further, the connection of both with dependence on the Father, Who alone brings to a successful issue whatever they should have asked in the name of Jesus. The deeper and higher the blessing, the more need of prayer; but then the character and confidence of prayer should rise with the sense of grace in

THE FIFTEENTH CHAPTER

Christ, and the Father's unwavering purpose to put honour on His name in which they draw near with their petitions. His name by faith in it can make the weakest strong, and the Father is thus glorified in the Son Who glorifies Him. Distrust or negligence is equally precluded.

It is hardly necessary to say many words in disproof of Calvin's exposition, and of others, who make this a question of choosing and ordaining to the apostolate, and, consequently, who take the fruit abiding to mean that the Church will last to the very end of the world as the fruit of apostolic labour continued also in their successors. The love enjoined here is, accordingly, restricted to mutual affection among ministers. Undoubtedly a free and unsuspicious flow of loving confidence is essential to a good state, and among those who labour especially, as the lack of it here is most deplorable; but the Lord does not limit His words to the apostles, or even to such as follow them in the public service of His name.

To love one another, then, is the new and repeated commandment of Christ to His own. To love is the positive and proper and constant exercise of the new nature, as acted on by the Spirit's ministration of Christ, not always brotherly kindness in exercise, but love never failing. But this very affection, strange here below, exposes those in whom it is found to the direct counter-working of Satan—a murderer and liar from the beginning. Conscious that unselfishness in affection according to God is an impossibility to nature, men regard any evidence of it as mere hypocrisy, to be scorned and detested in the Christian. For how could he be different from others?[291a]

Verses 18-27.

"If the world hateth you, know (or, ye know) that Me it hath hated before you. If ye were of the world, the world would love (ἐφ.) its own; but because ye are not of the world, but *I* chose you out of the world[291b], on this account doth the world hate you. Call to mind the word which I told you, A bondman is not greater than his lord. If they persecuted Me, they will persecute you also; if they kept My word, they will keep yours also; but all these things they will do unto you on account of My name, because they know not Him that sent Me" (verses 18-21).

To be Christ's is enough to rouse the world's rancour. Circumstances may be needed to call it forth, but there it is. The world hates those who, being His, are no longer of the world. But the Lord would have us know that, not more surely does it hate us, than it had hated Himself before us. Is it not sweet and consoling to us that so it is, however awful in itself, to have such a conviction of the world? For it hates us because of Him, not Him because of us. It is not our faults, therefore, which are the true cause, but His grace and moral excellence, His divine nature and glory; it is the world's repugnance and enmity to what is of God, and to Him Who is God. The world hates the Father shown in the Son; hence it hates the children who were the Father's and then were given to the Son. Christ was hated first, they next, and for His sake.

Not that the world does not love in its own way those who are of it, in most pointed contrast with the grace that goes out to the stranger and the wretched and the lost, to such as have wronged and have despitefully treated us. But grace is of all things most offensive to the world, which can love nature in its fallen state. Even righteousness, with its necessary condemnation of the sinner, is not so repugnant as the grace which can rise above the sins it condemns in compassion toward the sinner to save him by and in Christ; and this because it treats man as nothing, giving the entire glory to God: indignity intolerable to the flesh, the mind of which is enmity against God. Hence the world's hatred and rejection of Christ, Who had revealed God perfectly, and perfectly glorified Him in all His nature and ways. Hence, also, the world's hatred of us who confess Christ, not only because we are not of the world, but as chosen out of it by Christ, which implies its utter worthlessness and condemnation. Divine love is as odious as divine light.

The Lord then recalls to their mind His word that no bondman is greater than his lord. They must rather expect His position, Who was despised and rejected of men. They themselves and their teaching would be equally odious for His sake. If they persecuted Me, they will persecute you also; if they kept My word, they will keep yours also. His Person and His word brought God too near their souls, which drew back, unwilling either to own their sins or to be debtors to nothing but grace for pardon and deliverance. But this aversion assumes a stronger form where religion is honoured and men have a character to lose; and as these things were true in the highest measure among the Jews, they broke out to the last degree in resentment which claimed to persecute, as a duty to God, the Master first and then the disciples. And here the Lord graciously forewarned them that no sorrow might befall them unawares.

But He does more. He gives His own the comfort of knowing in such hours, it might be of bitter woe, as beforehand also, that all the contempt and suffering they might endure from the world was for His sake, because of the world's ignorance of Him that sent Himself, ignorance of the Father. How profoundly true! Impossible that a professing religion could persecute if it really knew Him that sent Christ.

There might be discipline according to His word; and there must be in that which bears the name of the Lord: else the very grace it knows would tend to sink it below the world's level if there were not vigilant, constant, and holy discipline. But discipline is never holy, but worldly, when it takes the shape of persecution. What can one think, then, when that which arrogates the loftiest name invoked the civil arm to enforce the punishment of men's bodies for the pretended good of their souls? What, when it sought and found means to inaugurate ecclesiastical tribunals with torments up to the bitter end in congenial secrecy with an unrelenting cruelty which never had a match even in this dark world? Truly it was the self-same spirit of worldly hatred which first animated the Jews against the Lord and His disciples, and later wrought in the world-church, when it exchanged its pagan for its papal garb, and baptism was more easily adopted than circumcision. "But all these things they will do unto you on account of My name, because they know not Him that sent Me."

No! forms avail not: God will have reality, and never more plainly and stringently than since Christ and His cross, which proved the vanity of religious man and of a worldly sanctuary. Christianity came into being and manifestation when it was demonstrated that man in his best estate was not only worthless before God, but would not have God at any price, even in the Person and mission of His own Son come in grace. "O righteous Father, the world did not know Thee." Yet is there no life eternal for man save in the knowledge of the only true God, the Father, and of Jesus Christ Whom He sent. The world is lost, and nowhere more evidently and guiltily than when, in religious pride, it hates Christ and those who are His.

The presence and testimony of the Son of God had the gravest possible results. It was not only an infinite blessing in itself, and for God's glory, but it left men, and Israel especially, reprobate. Law had proved man's weakness and sin, as it put under curse all who took their stand on the legal principle. There was none righteous, none that sought after God, none that did good, no, not one {Romans 3:10-12}. The heathen were manifestly wicked, the Jews proved so by the incontestable sentence of the law. Thus every mouth was stopped, and all the world obnoxious to God's judgment. But the presence of Christ brought out, not merely failure to meet obligation as under law, but hatred of divine goodness come down to man in perfect grace. God was in Christ, as the Apostle says, reconciling the world to Himself, not reckoning to them their offences. How immense the change! How worthy of God when revealed in His Son, as Man amongst men! But they could not endure His words and His works, and this increasingly, till the cross demonstrated that it was absolute rejection of God's love without bounds. It is not here the place or time, as with the apostle Paul, to show how divine love rose in complete victory over man's evil and hatred as attested in the ministry of reconciliation which is founded on the cross [2 Corinthians 5:19]. Here the Lord is affirming the solemn position and state of the world in antagonism to the disciples, after preparing them for persecution: from its hating them as Him, and its ignorance of Him Who sent their Master.

> "If I had not come and spoken to them, they had not had sin;[292] but now they have no excuse for their sin. He that hateth Me hateth My Father also" (verses 22-23).

Sin before or otherwise was swallowed up in this surpassing sin of rejecting the Son come in love and speaking not merely as man never spoke but as God never spoke; for by whom should He speak as in a Son? It was meet that He Who is the image of the invisible God, the Only-begotten in the bosom of the Father, should speak above all, as He is above all, God blessed for ever. Servants had been sent, prophets had spoken; and their messages had divine authority; but they were partial. The law had made nothing perfect. *Now* He Who had thus spoken of old πολυμερῶς καὶ πολυτρόπως (in many measures and in many manners) spoke to us ἐν υἱῷ (in a Son) [Hebrews 1:1 f.]. He was their Messiah, the Son of David, born where and when they expected, attested not only by the signs and vouchers of prophecy but by the powers of the world to come; but He was more, infinitely more; He was the Son of God, unapproachable in His own glory, yet here on earth the most accessible of men, giving out the words of the Father, as none had ever spoken since the world began. There never had been an adequate object on earth to draw out such communications; now there was in both dignity of person, intimacy of relationship, and moral perfection as man. And the disciples were reaping the benefit; as the Jews, the world, which had Him before their eyes and ears, had the responsibility. Flaws, failure, there had been in all others who had spoken for and from God (though not in the inspired Scripture), so as to weaken the effect of their testimony where men thought of men and forgot the God Who sent them.

But now the Father had sent the Son, Who had come and spoken not in law, but in love, the True Light shining in a world of darkness which apprehended it not, and sin appeared as never before. What pretext could be pleaded now? It was no question of man or his weakness; no requirement of his duty as measured by the ten words, or any statutes or judgments whatsoever. There was the Son, the Word become flesh dwelling among men, full of grace and truth, in divine love that rose above every fault and all evil, to give what is of God for eternity, only met by increasing hatred till it could go no farther. Their ignorance of Him Who sent Christ was no doubt at the bottom of their hating Him, but it was inexcusable. For He was God as well as Son of the Father, and so perfectly able to present the truth and render man thoroughly and evidently guilty if he bowed not. What then did their not bowing prove but sin, without excuse for it, and hatred of the Father also in hating the Son?

And there was this further aggravation of their sin, the works that He had wrought. For some men are affected powerfully by suited words, others yet more deeply by works which express not power only but goodness, holiness and love. Here they had in perfect harmony and mutual confirmation such words and works as never were save in Jesus the Son of God. But what was the effect?

> "If I did not among them the works which no other did, they had not had sin; but now have they both seen and hated both Me and My Father. But

(it is) that the word might be fulfilled that is written in their law, They hated Me without a cause [Psalm 69:4]" (verses 24-25).

Such was man's gratuitousness in presence of divine grace. Full manifestation of grace can have no other issue. The mind of the flesh is enmity against God. Not only is there insubjection to His law, but hatred of His love; and this was proved now. Anything short of Jesus thus present, speaking and working among men as He did, would have fallen short of the demonstration. The testimony was complete; the One Who is the sum and substance, the subject and object of all divine testimony, was there; and they had seen Him, as well as the Father in Him; and they had hated both! They, the people of God once, had nothing but sin—they were lost. So they were then, and so they abide still, whatever grace may do another day to save the generation to come. But hatred of the Father and the Son is in itself irreparable, complete, and final.

Nor did the law in which they boasted to the rejection of their Messiah speak otherwise; on the contrary, it was fulfilled in the word there written of Him, long suspended over them, now applied by His own lips to His own Person, They hated Me for nothing—gratuitously. How true and how solemn! "O Jerusalem, Jerusalem!" O Israel, what have you not lost in the rejected Messiah, in the Father and the Son alike seen and hated? And what have not we gained, once poor sinners of the Gentiles? Life eternal in the knowledge of a God no longer dwelling in thick darkness, but fully revealed in Christ, and in the utmost nearness to the believer, His Father and our Father, His God and our God. Truly Israel's fall has proved the world's wealth, and their loss the true wealth of nations. But the nations so blessed boast and

THE FIFTEENTH CHAPTER

are high-minded, and will be spared no more than the Jews, who, no longer abiding in unbelief, shall be grafted in again, and so all Israel shall be saved [Romans 11:23-26]. Meanwhile they have lost their Messiah to their ruin, and their sin cannot be hid.

Thus had the Lord prepared His own for the world's hatred, not only because He had known it before them, but because it had fallen on Him with an intensity and groundlessness beyond all experience. As even their law had forewarned of it, they were the more inexcusable. But nothing is so blind as unbelief, nor so cruel as its will irritated by the light of God, which treats it as sin, and sin refusing God in sovereign grace, the Father and the Son.[292a] For they that dwell at Jerusalem and their rulers, as Paul could say elsewhere, because they knew Him not, nor yet the voices of the prophets which are read every Sabbath day, they have fulfilled them in condemning Him {Acts 13:27}. Therefore came the wrath on them to the utmost.

It might seem, then, all must be swept away by the murderous rancour of man, and especially religious man. But not so. It is not that the Lord was not to die as well as suffer; nor that His feeble followers should escape the lot of their Master, as far as God was pleased to let them taste it; but that He was about to leave the world for glory on high, and to send down the Holy Ghost thence, as a new, divine, and heavenly witness here below.

> "(But)[k] when the Paraclete shall have come, whom *I* will send to you from the Father, the Spirit of truth who proceedeth out from (παρὰ) the Father,[293] He shall testify concerning Me; and *ye* too testify, because ye are with Me from (the) beginning" (verses 26-27).

Here the Holy Spirit is viewed as sent by the ascended Christ from the Father, and consequently as witness of His heavenly glory. This is an advance on what we saw in the preceding chapter, where Christ asks and the Father gives the Paraclete to be with them for ever, sending Him in the Son's name. Here the Son Himself sends, though of course from the Father. The Spirit of truth is thus the suited testifier of Christ as He is above; the disciples also testify, as His companions and so chosen from the beginning. For the first time it is said, "When the Paraclete is come," not merely given or sent. He is a divine Person in the fullest sense, not only to abide, teach, and recall to remembrance, but to testify concerning Christ, and that which the chosen companions, the apostles, of the Lord could not testify. For they as such could not go beyond what they had seen and heard—at any rate, what fell within the range of their being with Him from the beginning. The Spirit of truth which proceeds out from the Father would not merely strengthen them to do perfectly that task, but add quite another testimony of hitherto unknown blessedness, as sent by Christ personally from the Father.

Thus is clearly defined the position of the disciples, henceforward in due time called Christians: not of the world, but chosen by Christ out of it, commanded to love one another as loved of Christ, and hated of the world, with the Paraclete the Spirit of truth sent by Christ to testify of Him, of Whom they too were bearing witness as being with Him from the beginning. Who so competent to tell of Christ's glory with the Father as the Spirit proceeding forth from the Father, and sent by the exalted Christ? Thus was secured full testimony to His glory morally on earth by the disciples (though not without the Spirit's power already assured), and actually in heaven as the glorified Man by the One Who in every way could make it best known.

It is evident that those who personally followed the Lord had a special place in the testimony to His manifestation on earth; and this testimony we have in the Gospels as fully as God saw fit to preserve it permanently for all saints. So the Holy Ghost's testimony to His heavenly glory was pre-eminently presented in the inspired Epistles of Paul for like permanent use, though doubtless in no way limited to him or them.

And assuredly in principle the place of testimony abides for those who are Christ's, whatever the change of circumstances, and, alas! of state. As certainly as Christ abides on high and the Holy Ghost is come, never to leave us, it is not only that we know by faith the Son's relationship to the Father, and our blessedness by virtue of it, and in Him Who is in the Father as He is in us, but we have all the profit of His place as the True Vine on earth, as we know Him gone on high exalted as man, a quite new thing. And as we have the joy of His relationship to the Father and to us, we are called to bear witness to Him in every way. Wonderful comfort in our weakness! He, the Spirit of truth, was to testify of Jesus, and especially of Jesus where none could be with Him, none but the Paraclete Himself competent. It was not necessary to repeat here or later that He abides: this had been said at first in relation to us (chapter 14), where His guaranteed presence with us was most graciously named, lest we might feel orphans indeed. But if we have the comfortable pledge of His being with us for ever, it is without doubt not less but more for testifying of Christ's glory than for our consolation. Of this, however, we shall hear more in what is to follow, where the Lord renews the subject most fully.

NOTES ON THE FIFTEENTH CHAPTER

a [*Cf. Lectures Introductory to the Study of the Gospels*, pp. 519-543.]

b μένῃ ℵ^pm ABD [W. and H., Weiss], μείνῃ the mass [Blass].

c αὐτὸ ℵDLXΔΠ, many cursives, and some ancient versions [as Syr^sin]; αὐτὰ ("them") the great majority, the Alex. and Vat. among them [Edd.].

d αἰτήσασθε (-θαι ADΓ, etc.) ABDLMXΓ, many cursives, and the oldest versions; αἰτήσεσθε T.R., with ℵ and most MSS.

e [See appended note on 13:31.]

f γένησθε BDLMX, etc. [Treg., W. and H., Blass]; ℵ and the rest support the future [Weiss, after Tisch.].

g ᾖ ABD, many cursives, It. Vulg. Goth., the Syrr. Arm. and Æth. [Edd.]; μείνῃ T.R., ℵL and twelve uncials more, most cursives, but scarcely any ancient version, unless the Georgian.

h ℵ^pm D^pm, etc., omit τις, contrary to the rest.

i ἅ ℵDLX, some cursives, and versions, etc. ὅ B, etc. ὅσα the mass, as also T.R.

j "Ordained" suggests another line of things foreign to the passage and connection. In Acts 1:22 the same word, as is commonly known, is foisted into the Authorised Version, for it has no counterpart implied in the Greek.

k ℵBΔ and some other good authorities omit the copula, which the great mass support.

THE SIXTEENTH CHAPTER [a]

VERSES 1-15.

The Lord proceeds to explain why He had now and not before spoken of the things which were then occupying His heart and being made known to the disciples.

> "These things I have spoken to you that ye should not be stumbled. They will put you out of the synagogue; nay, an hour is coming that every one who hath killed you will think that he is offering service to God. And these things will they do to you[b] because they knew not the Father nor Me. But I have said these things to you, that when the (or, their)[c] hour shall have come, ye may remember them that I told you; but these things I told you not from (the) beginning, because I was with you. But now I go (ὑπάγω) unto Him that sent Me, and none of you asketh Me, Whither goest Thou? But because I have said these things to you, sorrow hath filled your heart" (verses 1-6).

Many were to be stumbled among the Jews who looked for anything but sorrow, shame, and groundless hatred to be the portion of those who follow the Messiah. But the Lord graciously considers His own; and while He uses trial for the blessing of the strong, He would shield and strengthen the weak, both by warning them of the world's undying ill-will and of the Holy Ghost's coming to add His testimony to theirs in the face of the persecution of the servants as of their Master. How precious what He has thus spoken!

Two forms should be taken to get rid of Christians and their testimony: one in common when men affect the utmost zeal for divine authority and holiness; the other open to individuals even to the extreme point of death to extinguish malefactors not fit to live. "They will put you out of the synagogue; nay, an hour cometh that every one that hath killed you will think that he is offering service to God." Impossible to conceive rancour more deadly, yet sanctioned by all, than that anyone who liked might take on himself (though not without the seal and law of authority) to kill a follower of Christ, not only with impunity, but claiming therein to do a religious service to God.[294] Saul of Tarsus furnishes a notable example of this till sovereign grace chose him to bear the Lord's name before all and to suffer great things for His sake.

Doubtless there is a disposition in men generally to fight for their religion, whatever it be. But a special reason gives intensity to the world's, and in particular to the Jews', enmity to Christians. Any measure of truth possessed is to the flesh the most powerful motive for disliking and resenting that which claims fuller light; and Christianity cannot but confess the truth in all its fulness in Christ by the Holy Ghost sent down from heaven. He who confesses the Son has the Father also; as he is the antichrist who denies both (1 John 2:22-23). And this is what the proud unbelief of Judaism ever tends to when confronted with the testimony of Christ. They set their partial and preparatory knowledge against that complete revelation which could not be till He came Who shows the Father, and accomplished everlasting redemption. How blessed for the babes of God's family that, if what they heard from the beginning abides in them, they too shall abide in the Son and in the Father!

And as it was with the Jew, so it is with every ecclesiastical system of Christendom itself, which in order to embrace the greatest possible number contents itself with the least and lowest confession, and hence is exposed to the snare of the devil in setting itself against all that go beyond the Christian alphabet. So even the Reformed bodies settled themselves on what their founders learnt on emerging from Popery, and oppose as innovation all that working of the Spirit which recalls to the fulness of Christ in the written word that was long before either the Reformation or Popery. They, too, persecuted when they had any confidence in their own Confessions; till of late they have become so honeycombed with the indifference or the activity of scepticism that they care too little for anything to persecute anybody.[294a] But where there is a real holding fast of such a measure of traditional truth as arrogates the name of orthodoxy, there is always a jealousy of the action of the Spirit which insists on Christ more richly known with fresh power to men's hearts, and, consequently, claiming exercise of faith.

So the Jew set the unity of the Godhead to deny the Father and the Son and the Spirit; so men now resist the truth of the one body and one Spirit, devoted to the fleshly unity of Rome or boasting of the active rivalry of Protestant societies. But the more they hold even truth itself in a measure as a form, the less willing are they to allow the activity of the Spirit by God's word as a whole. "And these things will they do, because they knew not the Father nor Me." Yet to know both is eternal life, which every Christian characteristically has by the gospel, though the most advanced is marked by deepening acquaintance with Him that is from the beginning. When and where idols reigned, it needed the energy of grace to turn to God, the living and true; where God was making Himself known in the Son, flesh might avail itself of old truth no longer contested nor costing any sacrifice, and have its tongue set on fire of hell to blaspheme the full revelation which tests actual faith and faithfulness, and seek to exterminate those who testified it. The principle holds good in small things as well as in the greatest, and now as ever.

But as the Lord thus prepared the disciples for harsher things from the professing people of God than from men wholly ignorant, so now He lets them know what they must suffer, that they might gather comfort even in that hour by remembering His words. As the trial that came to pass was known to Him and made known to them, now they could trust His assurance of love and blessing, of deliverance and glory. Besides, He explains why He had not told of these things before. He was with them, their shield and Paraclete; and what need was there to say a word? But as He was about to leave them, it was well, and would help all to work for good.

"But now I go unto Him that sent Me, and none of you asketh Me, Whither goest Thou [back]? But because I have said these things to you, sorrow hath filled your heart." This sorrow was more of nature than of faith. No wonder it surprised them to hear of their divine Master leaving them with such a prospect before them, with so little manifestation of the effects of His coming in the world or even in Israel. And they had forsaken their all and followed Him: what could it mean? He had already assured them that He would not leave them orphans, but was coming to them. Had faith been simpler, they would have not only counted on His loving care of them, but have asked whither He was going, and have learnt its bearing on His glory and their blessing. It is ignorance of His mind which fills the heart with sorrow at His words, for they are spirit and life, though we may need to wait on God in order to lay hold on them intelligently.[295] But the Lord proceeds to bring out all clearly in what follows.

This leads the way to the main distinctive truth the Lord is intimating, the presence and action of the Holy Ghost when sent down from heaven. The Son would send Him.

> "Nevertheless, *I* tell you the truth: it is profitable for you that I go away; for if I go not away, the Paraclete will not come unto you; but if I depart, I will send Him unto you" (verse 7).

The Lord had told them before, that had they loved Him, they would have rejoiced because He said, I go unto the Father. What was it not for the humbled, holy, and suffering Son of Man to quit the scene of His unequalled sorrows for His Father's presence on high? Now He shows the connection of His departure with their fresh and deeper blessing. It might seem, to them especially, strange to say that the loss of His bodily presence should be their gain. But so it was to be. The truth is not what seems but the manifestation of what really is; nor is it found in the first man but in the Second; nor can we know it but by the Spirit. Now it was to be established and enjoyed more than ever. For Christ was going to heaven on the ground of accomplished redemption, thence to send the Holy Spirit to the saints on earth. It was profitable for them, then, that Christ should go away. He Who alone effectuates any spiritual good would not otherwise come. God's will must first be done (Hebrews 10:5-10).

And now that the Lord was going above, having obtained eternal redemption, the Holy Spirit was not only to work as He had never before wrought in the children of men or in the children of God, but was to come personally[296] and undertake the entire charge and business of the disciples. For this is the meaning of παράκλητος, which our "Comforter"[d] imperfectly represents. He had come in person to abide in Jesus; He had sealed the Son of Man; He had anointed Him with power. None else could have Him thus till God's judgment of sin had taken its course in the cross. Not that compassion or fidelity of goodness, or any other form or way of divine love had been lacking in times past; but this presence of the Spirit could not be till then. Jesus at His baptism had the Spirit thus descending and abiding on Him, and this as the perfect Man without bloodshedding, for He knew no sin. But others were sinners, and those who believed had a sinful nature, notwithstanding their believing. The flesh still remained, and they are contrary to each other. Here comes in the efficacy of Christ's work. God was then and there glorified even as to sin in His cross. His blood cleanses from all sin. God "made Him to be sin for us, that we might become the righteousness of God in Him" {2 Corinthians 5:21}. "What the law could not do in that it was weak through the flesh, God, sending His own Son in the likeness of sinful flesh and for sin, condemned sin in the flesh" {Romans 8:3}. Not only were the bad fruits gone but the evil root that bore them was judged and sentence executed. Hence could the Spirit come and dwell in us as never before, not as if we were better than the saints of past ages, but in virtue of Christ's death and its infinite value in God's eyes, and in pursuance of divine counsel.

This, then, is the distinctive character of Christianity. It is not the kingdom, Christ reigning in Jehovah power and glory, and the Spirit poured out upon all flesh; but Christ departing to be in heaven, and the Spirit as Paraclete sent and abiding with the saints on earth.

> "And when come, He will convince (or, afford proof to) the world of sin, and of righteousness, and of judgment: of sin, because they believe not on Me; of righteousness, because I go unto My (or, the)^e Father, and ye behold Me no more; of judgment, because the prince of this world is (or, hath been) judged" (verses 8-11).

The world cannot receive the Spirit of truth, because it seeth Him not, neither knoweth Him. He is the object of neither sense nor intellect. Whatever the effects or displays of His energy, He abides invisible in Himself and outside the ken of the world. But the saints know Him, and that their bodies are His temple; even as they by Him know all else that they really know. God has revealed to us by His Spirit what is beyond human intelligence as such; for the Spirit searches all things, yea, His depths; and just as the spirit of man knows the things of a man, even so the things of God none knows but the Spirit of God [1 Corinthians 2:10-11]. And Him we as Christians have received, not the spirit of the world, but the Spirit of God, that we might know the things that are freely given us of God. And not only so; but they are communicated in words by Him, and received by His power in the believer, as truly as they are by Him revealed: all is by the Holy Spirit of God.

Here we have His present relation, not to the saints, but to that world which is outside. And the Lord tells us that, when come, He ἐλέγξει the world. It is difficult to convey justly the force of this. "Reprove," as in the Authorised Version, is too narrow a meaning, if not false. "Rebuke" is here out of the question. "Convict" hardly applies, even to the first, not at all to the second and third clauses; and supposes an effect produced which may not really be in any case. Nor is one satisfied with "convince," save in the sense of affording proof by His presence, rather than by His action. For by His coming and abiding in the saints, apart from the world, He gives it demonstrative proof of sin, of righteousness, and of judgment.

The law dealt with Israel as those under it. But now it is the Spirit Who demonstrates the "sin" of the world; and this not because they violate that divine measure of a man's duty, but because they reject the Son of God: "of sin, because they believe not on Me." He had come in grace; to reject this was fatal. It is not merely failure in obligation, but despite of God's love. Such is the true and actual gauge of the world before God, Who tests and proves the guilt of the whole system which opposes Him by its unbelieving ignorance and refusal of His Son, spite of the fullest testimony. This is the sin demonstrated.[297]

Further, He affords demonstration of "righteousness." Where is this? In the race or first man? On the contrary, there is none righteous, no, not one. And as for the

Righteous One, even Jesus, He, as we have seen, was despised and rejected of men, by none so keenly as by the Jews, but in fact and to the uttermost by the world. Where, then, is the Spirit's proof of righteousness? "Because I go to My (or, the) Father, and ye behold Me no more." Righteousness is on God's part only. Man condemned and killed the Just One; God raised Him from the dead and set Him at His own right hand. The Son "going to the Father" is the standing witness of righteousness there, and not here. For man He Who came into the world in love is clean gone. They would not have Him, and "ye behold Me no more." He returns for the world as Judge; but this is a wholly different and most solemn affair. But He is lost to men according to His presence in grace as at His first Advent; all is closed with His mission to the world as He came. And the Spirit testifies and demonstrates only divine righteousness in Him on high, and man lost in casting out Him no longer to be seen as before here below.[298]

But, again, the Spirit gives proof of "judgment"; and this, "because the prince of this world is (or, hath been) judged." Here again it is not a question of the kingdom in power and glory when Jehovah shall punish the host of the high ones on high, as well as put down the kings of the earth upon the earth, and slay the dragon that is in the sea [Isaiah 24:21; 27:1]. The Christian knows what will be for the earthly people's deliverance and the joy of all nations, but he sees already by faith that Satan is judged in Christ's death and resurrection and ascension. The Holy Ghost sums up all in Christ's Person; and this is the grand demonstration for the world. Its ruler is already judged in rejecting Him Who made known the Father, glorified God, and is glorified of God. All is closed for the world in Him Who came in love, and is gone up in righteousness. The ruler of the world is judged in His cross.

Men are apt to err doubly in their estimate of the Holy Spirit's relation to us. They either overlook the immense effect of His presence and teaching, or they attribute to Him what may be the mere fruit of natural conscience and diffused information. Our Lord here puts in His own perfect way what the Spirit would do as sent down from heaven, not now in external demonstration to the world, but in the positive blessing and help of the disciples.

> "I have yet many things to say to you, but ye cannot bear (them) now. Howbeit when He, the Spirit of truth, shall have come, He will guide you in[f] (or, into) all the truth; for He will not speak from Himself, but whatever[g] He shall hear[h] He will speak; and He will announce to you the things to come. He will glorify Me, for He will receive of Mine, and will announce (it) to you. All things that the Father hath are Mine: on this account I said, that He receiveth[i] of Mine and will announce (it) to you" (verses 12-15).

It has been repeatedly shown—and in this chapter most expressly—that the presence of the Spirit depended on the departure of Christ to heaven, consequent on accomplished redemption. This changed the entire groundwork, besides morally fitting the saints for the new truth, work, character, and hope of Christianity. The disciples were not ignorant of the promise that the Spirit should be given to inaugurate the reign of the Messiah. They knew the judgment under which the chosen people abide "until the Spirit be poured upon us from on high, and the wilderness be a fruitful field, and

THE SIXTEENTH CHAPTER

the fruitful field be counted for a forest" [Isaiah 32:15]; so vast outwardly, no less than inwardly, the change when God puts forth His power for the kingdom of His Son. They knew that He will pour out His Spirit upon all flesh; not only the sons and daughters, the old and young of Israel, enjoying a blessing far beyond all temporal favours, but the servants and the handmaidens—in short, all flesh, and not the Jews alone, sharing it [Joel 2:28-29].

But here it is the sound heard when the great High Priest enters into the Sanctuary before Jehovah, and not only when He comes out for the deliverance and joy of repentant Israel in the last days. It is the Spirit given when the Lord Jesus went on high, and by Him thus gone. For this they were wholly unprepared, as, indeed, it is one of the most essential characteristics of God's testimony between the rejection and the reception of the Jews; and the Spirit, when given, was to supply what the then state of the disciples could not bear. For the Spirit searches all things, even the depths of God (and He is a spirit, not of fear, but of power and of love and of a sound mind), besides the incalculable facts of Christ's work in death, resurrection, and ascension, to which He testifies. Truly the Lord had many things to say reserved for the Holy Ghost, when the disciples had their consciences purged and could draw near boldly into the holies, and a Man glorified in heaven furnished the meet occasion for the display of all that is in God, even for the secret hid in God before all worlds, of which not John or any other than the apostle Paul was to be the administrator.

But be the instrument who it might, when the Spirit of truth is come, as the Lord intimates here, "He will guide you into all the truth," or "in" it all as the Sinaitic,

Cambridge (D), and Parisian (L) uncials with other authorities have it. For this two main grounds are given, besides His necessary competency as a divine Person. First, He does not act independently, but fulfilling the mission on which He is sent expressly. "For He will not speak from Himself, but whatever He shall hear, He will speak; and He will announce to you the things to come." Secondly, His prime object is to exalt the Lord Jesus, and therefore He will assuredly make this good in testimony to the disciples. "Me He will glorify, for He will receive of Mine and announce (it) to you."

The reader must guard against the popular error, easily suggested by the Authorised Version of verse 13, as if the sense meant were that the Spirit shall not speak *about* Himself. For it is neither true as a fact, nor is it of course intended here. The Spirit largely speaks concerning Himself in this Gospel, and particularly in the section we are examining. So He does in Romans 8; in 1 Corinthians 2, 12; in 2 Corinthians 3; in Ephesians 1, 2, 3, 4, and many other parts of Scripture. This makes it the more strange that even the simplest have not learnt the meaning here to be, that He shall not speak *from* Himself, but, as the next clause explains, whatever He shall hear He will speak. As the Son came not to act independently, whatever might be His glory, but to serve His Father; so the Spirit is come to serve the Son, and whatever He shall hear, He will speak.[299]

But there is more. Not only can He speak of the Son in heaven as Himself sent down by Him, and thus bear the highest testimony to His intrinsic dignity and the new position Christ is in there, but He has not ceased to be the Spirit of prophecy. On the contrary, He would thus work abundantly in view of the world's total ruin and the blessing that waits on the Lord's return. "And He will announce to you the things to come." The prophetic word is found largely in the New Testament, not only in the Gospels, but also in the Epistles, but most of all in the wonderful book of Revelation. And the effect was immense in detaching the saints from the world as under judgment, however this might tarry. They knew these things before, and thus held fast their own steadfastness. Nevertheless prophecy as occupied with the earth, even though it go on to the kingdom of God there, is but a small and even inferior part of the Spirit's testimony, however astonishing in man's eyes and precious in itself.

Christ's own glory, now on high, is the direct object; and this in every way. "Me He will glorify, for He will receive of Mine and will announce (it) to you." And here also all is in contrast with Messianic light or earthly dominion, however just and great. "All things that the Father hath are Mine: on this account I said that He receiveth of Mine and will announce (it) to you." He is sent down to glorify not the Church but Christ, and this by receiving and reporting what is Christ's (and all the Father has is His), not by exaggerating man's importance or allowing the will of man. Thus it was not only the universe which God had created, but the new creation also in relationship with the Father, and this even specifically.

But there is another intimation needful to press the "little while" with its issues of sorrow and joy.

Verses 16-24.

"A little while and ye behold Me not:[j] and again a little while and ye shall see[300] Me (because I go away unto the Father).[j] (Some) therefore of His disciples said one to another, What is this which He saith to us, A little while and ye behold Me not:

and again a little while and ye shall see Me, and because I go away [back] to the Father. They said therefore, What is this that He saith, the[k] little while? We know not what He speaketh. Jesus knew (therefore[l]) that they wished to ask (ἐρωτᾶν) Him, and said to them, Do ye inquire of this one with another, because I said, A little while, and ye behold Me not; and again a little while, and ye shall see Me? Verily, verily, I say to you, *Ye* shall weep and lament, but the world shall rejoice; [m]*ye* shall be grieved, but your grief shall be turned into joy. The woman, when she bringeth forth, hath grief because her hour is come; but when she shall give birth to the child, she no longer remembereth the affliction for the joy that a man was born into the world. And *ye* therefore now have grief, but I will see you again, and your heart shall rejoice, and your joy no one taketh from you" (verses 16-22).

The "little while" in any and every sense was a strange sound to Jewish ears; so was His going away to the Father. It is no question here of their lost Messiah, the suffering Son of Man. This of course is true and important in its place, and fully treated in the closing scenes of the Synoptic Gospels. But here we see and hear the conscious Son of God, a man, but a divine Person Who had come from, and was now going *back* to, the Father. We need especially to be in the spirit of this to estimate the "little while," and indeed Christianity, in contradistinction to what was and what will be. The Resurrection brought the disciples into the intelligence of this "little while," though it may not be all out till He comes again. The Jew thought nothing more certain than that the Christ when He came would abide for ever.

THE SIXTEENTH CHAPTER

The "little while" was therefore another enigma which His death and ascension cleared up, and the Spirit subsequently showed to be bound up with all that is characteristic of the present work of God for the glory of Christ. We anticipate by faith what will come, and manifestly at His appearing.[300b]

Nothing can be more marked than the Lord's avoidance here of introducing His death as such; and it is all the more striking because it is so prominent in chapters 1, 2, 3, 6, 8, 10, 12. Here no doubt it underlies all, and poor indeed had been the joy without His infinite sorrow on the cross. But that solemn hour is here passed over thus: "A little while, and ye behold Me not; and again, a little while, and ye shall see Me. Verily, verily, I say to you, Ye shall weep and lament, but the world shall rejoice; ye shall be grieved, but your grief shall be turned into joy." This was surely true when He rose after His brief absence, as it will be fully verified when He comes for them never to part more.[301] And this He illustrates by the most familiar of all figures of sorrow issuing in joy (verses 21-22). The absence of the Lord is to the world getting rid of Him; but even now His resurrection is a joy which none takes away. What will it be when He comes to receive us to Himself?

The Lord proceeds to set forth yet more fully the blessing and privilege which should flow from His going to heaven, and so bringing out the Father's love to them.

> "And in that day ye shall ask[302] Me nothing; verily, verily, I say to you,[n] Whatsoever ye shall ask the Father, He will give you in My name.[o] Hitherto ye asked nothing in My name: ask, and ye shall receive, that your joy may be full" (verses 23-24).

It is well known that the Greek words we are well-nigh obliged to translate "ask" in verse 23 are not the same, the first (ἐρωτάω) being expressive rather of familiar entreaty, the second (αἰτέω) of lowly petition. Hence, while our Lord often in this Gospel employs the former in His requesting the Father on behalf of the disciples, never does He use the latter. However low He may go down in grace, He is ever the conscious Son of God in flesh, but none the less a divine Person; whilst Martha shows her slight appreciation of His glory by supposing that He might fitly and successfully appeal to God after a suppliant sort (chapter 11:22).[302a]

But it seems too strong to say that every competent judge admits that "ye shall ask" of the first half of the verse has nothing to do with "ye shall ask" of the second; or that in the first Christ is referring back to the desire of the disciples in verse 19 to question Him. So Euthymius Zigabenus, as well as the Vulgate, and a crowd of moderns from Beza to Trench, including many German and British theologians. But though the word ἐρωτάω occurs often in the New Testament, and even in this chapter, with the ordinary classical sense of "question" *(interrogo)*, it is used quite as often or more so for "requesting" or "beseeching," etc. *(rogo)*, as in the LXX., and thus like our English "ask," which means "to request" no less than "to question" or "inquire." Inquiring of God in Old Testament phrase approaches, in fact, nearer to prayer for any one or thing than to a question. It seems, then, that varying the English word is not the true solution, though obvious enough on the surface, and that the earlier Greek commentators were nearer the truth, save Origen, who, like later errorists, perverted the passage to deny the propriety of praying to our Lord, thus flatly contradicting the early disciples

(Acts 1:24), Stephen (Acts 7:59), and the apostle Paul (2 Corinthians 12:8). In matters which concern His service and His Church it is even more proper, according to Scripture, to pray to Him than to the Father, to Whom we instinctively turn for all that concerns the family of God in general.

The Lord is really signifying the great change from recourse to Him as their Messiah on earth for every difficulty, not for questions only but for all they might want day by day, to that access unto the Father into which He would introduce them as the accepted Man and glorified Saviour on high. Till redemption is known, and the soul by grace is set in righteousness, even believers are afraid of God and hide, as it were, behind Christ. They draw near in spirit, as the disciples did actually, to Him Who in love came down from heaven to bless and reconcile them to God. But they do not really know what it is to come boldly to the throne of grace to obtain mercy and find grace. They are not in the distinct consciousness of children before their Father, enjoying liberty in Christ by the Spirit of adoption.

This, then, appears to me what the Lord gives the disciples to know should follow His resurrection and departure "in that day": a day already come, the day of grace, not of glory, save so far as we enter in by virtue of Him Who is gone above and sent the Spirit thence to be in us. He had already and fully told them what the Spirit of truth would do in guiding them into all the truth (verses 12-15); here He substitutes access to the Father for everything in prayer, instead of personal requests to Himself as their Master ever ready to help on earth. It is not a question, then, of a declaration of being so taught of the Spirit as to have nothing further to inquire, but of no longer having One at hand to Whom they had been in the habit of appealing for each difficulty as it rose. The departing Son of God would draw out confidence of heart in the Father.

Hence the solemnity of making known their new resource. "Verily, verily, I say to you, Whatsoever (or, If) ye shall ask the Father in My name, He will give you (in My name)." The text differs in the manuscripts and other authorities; but the best of them place "in My name" after the assurance that the Father will give, not after the saints asking the Father as in the common text, which, however, is best supported by the ancient versions.[p] There can be no doubt, as we shall see presently, that the saints are encouraged and entitled in the value of the revelation of Christ to prefer their requests to the Father; but, if the more ancient reading holds in verse 23,[q] we have the collateral truth that He gives in virtue of that name whatsoever they shall ask Him. How blessed and cheering to the saints! What pleasure to the Father and honour to the Son! The rejection of the Messiah only turns to His greater glory and better blessings for His own.

And this is followed up in verse 24: "Hitherto ye asked nothing in My name: ask, and ye shall receive, that your joy may be fulfilled." The importance of this can hardly be exaggerated: I do not mean as bearing merely on the use of the blessed prayer given long before to the disciples, but on the broader question of their approaching new relationship and standing by redemption and the gift of the Spirit. On the face of the words, however, it is plain that to use that prayer is not to ask the Father in Christ's name. The disciples were, no doubt, in the habit of using it day by day; yet up to the present they had asked nothing in His name. Now, so to ask the Father in the Son's name is alone Christian prayer in the true and full sense. Those, therefore, who insist on going back to the prayer of the disciples fail to enter into the new place on which the Lord here sets all that are His. It may be reverently meant; but is it the faith which really enters into God's mind and honours the Master? I trow not. As a prayer to be used when the disciples knew not how to pray, it was perfection; as a model, it abides ever full of depths of instruction. But the Lord, now at the end of His career here below, lets them know the shortcoming in ground and object of their previous petitions, and tells them what should be their appropriate character in future through their new blessing at hand through redemption and ascension.

It would have been out of season and presumptuous for the disciples in the past to have drawn near to the Father as the Son did, Who, in His wisdom and goodness, gave them a prayer perfectly suited to their then state when the atoning work was not yet done and the Holy Ghost accordingly not given. But now, as we have already seen so often in this context, consequent on Christ's glorifying God on earth by death and going up on high, the Holy Ghost would come to be in and with them. And this is the great result Godward, as we have already seen much saintward: they should ask in Christ's name; and they are called to ask and receive, that their joy might be full. Life in Christ would go forth in suited desires, to which the Holy Ghost would impart power as well as intelligence; and assuredly, with such a ground and motive before Him as the Son of Man Who had devoted Himself at all cost to His glory, the Father would fail in nothing on His part. Their joy would indeed be at the full.

Verses 25-33.

"These things have I spoken to you in proverbs (allegories): an hour[303] cometh when I shall speak no longer to you in proverbs, but openly report[r] to you about the Father. In that day ye shall ask (αἰτήσεσθε) in My name, and I say not to you that I will request (ἐρωτήσω) the Father for you; for the Father Himself dearly loveth you because ye have dearly loved Me and have believed that I came out from (παρὰ) God.[s] I came out from[t] the Father and am come into the world; again I leave the world and proceed unto the Father" (verses 25-28).

It is owing, I presume, to the large and various meaning of the Hebrew מָשָׁל that we have in Greek παροιμία as well as παραβολή used correspondingly not only in the LXX. but in the New Testament, the Synoptic Gospels always using the latter, John only the former, as in chapter 10 and here. Perhaps "allegory" might be more appropriate, or even a "dark saying" in our chapter where parable or allegory can scarcely apply. A close examination of the usage will prove that both Greek words are employed with considerable latitude in the four Gospels, as elsewhere.

Here the Lord was conscious that what He uttered fell like enigmas on the ears of the disciples. His plain declaration or report about the Father would clear up all in due time. What did not His resurrection? and His appearances and converse from the first to the last of His forty days' intercourse, as well as His ascension? Take alone the message through Mary of Magdala on the first day of the week. Did He not plainly declare about the Father, His and theirs? Was not His God and

THE SIXTEENTH CHAPTER

their God a deep intimation of blessing? But, above all, when He testified by the Holy Ghost sent down from heaven, did not the truth shine out more than ever? He made known to them His Father's name then; He was to make it known when gone above (chapter 17:26), and did so only more effectively from thence.

This also turned (as was intended) to their increasing sense of the value of Christ's own name. "In that day ye shall ask ($αἰτ.$) in My name." Asking in His name is not merely for Christ's sake as a motive, but in the value of Himself and His acceptance. His worth goes in its fulness to the account of those who thus plead; and how precious and all-prevailing it is in the Father's eyes! How glorifying to both the Father and the Son! How humbling and no less strengthening to the saints themselves! It is the title of every Christian now; none ever enjoyed it before. Never was there a soul blessed on earth apart from Him and His work foreseen; but this is known nearness and acceptance applied even to our petitions in virtue of Himself fully revealed when His work was done and accepted in infinite efficacy.

"And I say not that I will request ($ἐρωτ.$) the Father for you, for the Father Himself loveth you dearly, because ye have loved Me dearly, and have believed that I came out from God." This is another of those sentences over which not men and scholars but saints also stumble, because many a believer even is not enjoying the truth of it; and what John's Gospel and Epistles treat of must be really entered into to be understood. This verse 26 not more denies Christ's intercession for us than verse 23 forbids the servant praying to His Lord about His work or His house. It is not an absolute statement, nor is there the smallest need to apply the technical device of Præteritio, as it is called, so as to convey not a negation but a strong affirmation. Thus it would mean, "I need not assure you that I will request the Father for you." But it is simply an ellipse, which the words following explain: I do not say that I will request the Father for you, as if He did not love you; for the Father Himself (*proprio motu* {"of His own accord"}) does love you dearly, etc. This, too, accounts for the words of special affection, φιλεῖ and πεφιλ., which follow. It was grace, the Father's drawing, which brought them to hear the voice of the Son and believe on Him; yet does the Lord speak of the Father's dearly loving them and of their having dearly loved Him, to Whom they clung truly, however feebly.[304] They had believed that He came out from God. They truly believed that He was the Christ of God, and was born of God. It was divine teaching and grace as far as it went.[305]

But this was far short of the full truth which He proceeds to reveal: "I came out from the Father and am come into the world; again I leave the world and proceed unto the Father." Here they were altogether short. They realised as yet little or nothing of His full, divine, and eternal glory as the Son of the Father. God the Father was fully revealed, no doubt, in the Son; but the presence and power of the Spirit, personally sent down, was needed to give them communion with Him thus made known. It is this which, when the conscience is purged, brings into happy liberty. Here, then, is what so many saints are still ignorant of, in the state of their souls pretty much where the disciples then were; for though they may see rather better the glory of the Son, they fail to see in Him and His work their title to rest in the Father's love.

It is striking to remark the contrast throughout this series of discourses with the Synoptic Gospels. In these

Christ's death is made most prominent; here it is going away to the Father. How true to the design the Holy Spirit impressed on the narrative of John!

It would be difficult to find a verse of John which presents more tersely and completely, too, the character of his Gospel than the one we have just had before us; nor one less really apprehended now as then by the disciples. His divine relationship and mission from the Father stand clearly revealed on earth before they join Him on high. His presence as man in the world, no less than His quitting the world, and going to the Father, none the less the Son now become man, with the immense results of all this for God and more especially for the saints. These great truths wholly transcend all Messianic glory which as yet filled the minds of His followers, who proved how little they knew by the very fact that they thought they knew all clearly.

> "His disciples say (to Him)," Behold, now Thou talkest with openness and speakest no parable. Now we know that Thou knowest all things and hast no need that one ask Thee: herein we believe that Thou didst come out from God" (verses 29-30).

Their own language bewrayed them. Simple as His words were, they had not taken in their depth. They had no conception of the mighty change from all they had gathered of the kingdom as revealed in the Old Testament to the new state of things that would follow His absence with the Father on high and the presence of the Spirit here below. It sounded plain to their ears; but even up to the Ascension they feebly, if at all, caught a glimpse of it. They to the last clung to the hopes of Israel, and these surely remain to be fulfilled another day. But they understood not this day, during which, if the Jews are treated as reprobate, even as He was rejected of them, those born of God should in virtue of Christ and His work be placed in immediate relationship with the Father. His return to the Father was a parable still, though the Lord does not correct their error, as, indeed, it was useless: they would soon enough learn how little they knew. But at least even then they had the inward consciousness that He knew all, and, as He penetrated their thoughts, had no need that any should ask Him. "Herein we believe that Thou camest out from God." Undoubtedly: yet how far below the truth He had uttered is that which they were thus confessing! The Spirit of His Son sent into their hearts would give them in due time to know the Father; as redemption accomplished and accepted could alone lay the needful ground for it.[306]

> "Jesus answered them, Just now do ye believe? (or, ye believe).[307] Behold, an hour cometh, and[v] is come, that ye should be scattered, each unto his own,[308] and leave Me alone; and I am not alone, because the Father is with Me. These things have I spoken to you that in Me ye may have peace. In the world ye have[w] tribulation; but be of good courage: I have overcome the world" (verses 31-33).

Their faith was real, but they were shortly to show how small it would be proved to be in the hour of trial already come. If doubt is never justifiable, it is good in our weakness to live in constant dependence. When strong in our own eyes, we are weak indeed; when weak, we are strong in the grace of our Lord Jesus. But oh, what a Saviour! and what disciples! They scattered to their own, and He left alone in the hour of His deepest need! Would any heart but His own have hastened to add, after such desertion on their part, "and I am not alone, because the Father is with Me"? Could any but Himself have added, especially to such saints and under such circumstances, "These things have I spoken to you that in Me ye may have peace"? or have given such solid ground for it, at the very moment of contemplating their present portion of trouble in the world? "Be of good courage: I have overcome the world." As Christ alone could so feel and bless, so are these words worthy of Him; and one knows not whether to admire most their divine authority, or their matchless grace and suitability to our need here below. As He is absolutely what He also speaks, so He speaks what He is to the unfailing comfort of the believer.

Strikingly characteristic of our Gospel is the omission of the sorrows of Gethsemane,[308a] and yet more of God's abandoning Him on the cross. Neither fell in with that account of Him which sets forth the glory of His Person, Whose it was to do the will of Him Who sent Him and to finish His work. Others bring out His complete rejection and humiliation, the service He rendered, and the depth of His sympathy as the perfect Man. John sees, hears, and records the Son above all circumstances, the object and the revealer of the Father, even when that sorrow came which scattered them, and that forsaking of God which was unfathomable save to Himself.

With all before Him He spoke what He did here, that in Him they might have peace; and so He walked Himself. In the world tribulation was to be their portion, not as for the Jew retributively at a specified and measured hour (Jeremiah 30:7; Daniel 12:1; Matthew 24:21; Mark 13:19) at the time of the end, or even preparatorily meanwhile (Luke 21:22-24), but habitually for those not of the world, and hence a prey in it. Yet are they called to courage, as knowing Him Whom they have believed, His glory and His grace Who has overcome the world. What a spring and cheer, that we have to overcome a foe already overcome! He indeed alone; we looking to Him Who gives power for all things. And this is the victory that overcometh the world, our faith. Who is he that overcometh the world but he that believeth that Jesus is the Son of God? [1 John 5:4-5[309]].

NOTES ON THE SIXTEENTH CHAPTER

a [*Cf. Lectures Introductory to the Study of the Gospels*, pp. 543-556.]

b T.R. ὑμῖν, "to you," with אDL, etc., a few cursives [33 in the form πρὸς ὑμᾶς (*cf.* 15:21)] and versions, but the mass of manuscripts and oldest versions omit.

c αὐτῶν, "their," ΑΒΠ[pm], etc., but the great majority [including אDΓ] reject.

d It is striking to see how almost all the ancient translators felt compelled to adopt rather than to render the Greek word; for so it is in languages different as the Syriac, the Sahidic, and the Memphitic, the Latin (old Itala as well as Vulgate), the Æthiopic, the Arabic, the Gothic, and the Persian. The Armenian gives "Comforter," followed by Georgian and the Sclavonic, and, it would seem, by the Anglo-Saxon in its own way, and certainly by Wiclif and his disciple-translator; but they have "Advocate," like the Vulgate, Syrr., etc., in 1 John 2:1.

e אBDL, some cursives and versions, omit μου, "My," which the rest add.

f ἐν ℵ (om. πάσῃ) DL [1], etc. [Tisch.], but ABY, etc., εἰς τ. ἀ. π., [Treg. and later Edd.], while the mass [ΓΔΛΠ, etc.] have, with T.R., εἰς π. τ. ἀ.

g Many add ἄν, some ἐάν.

h T.R. ἀκούσῃ with most, ἀκούσει BDE^pm HY [Treg.]; ἀκούει ℵL, etc. [most Edd.].

i λήψεται T.R., but λαμβάνει the best and most numerous.

j οὐκέτι, "no more," is read by ℵBD^gr, etc. [W. and H., Weiss, etc.]; but οὐ T.R., with most [as Blass], ℵBDL, and other good authorities, omitting the last clause, although it is added by some fourteen uncials, most cursives, and many ancient versions [Syr^sin pesch jer, Cod. Brix, and other old Latt.].[300a]

k BLY, etc. [Treg., W. and H.], omit the article, contrary to the mass [Weiss, Blass, after Tisch.].

l ℵBDL, etc. [Edd.], omit οὖν, contrary to most.

m T.R., with most, adds δὲ, "and."

n ὅτι (T.R. after very many) is not in some of the best, and for ὅσα ἄν, "whatsoever," T.R., supported by most; ἄν, or ἐάν τι BCDLY, etc.; or ὅ ἄν ℵ; ὅ ἐὰν ΧΠ, etc.

o ἐν τῷ ὀν. μου, after "the Father," AC^corr.D, etc., and T.R.; but at the end ℵBC^pmLXYΔ, etc. [Edd.].

p [ℵBC^pmLXYΔ, Orig., Cyr., place the words after "give," whilst ℵC^corr.D, Syrr., old Latt., have "them" after "Father." Blass follows other Edd. in reading, as in ℵ, etc.]

q [The words ἄν τι, instead of ὅτι ὅσα ἄν of T.R.]

r ℵABC^pmDKL MNXYΠ [Edd.], ἀπαγγ., "report", others ἀναγγ. "announce," as in verses 13, 14, 15.

s θεοῦ ℵ^{pm}A and most MSS. and versions [as Syr^{sin}]; πατρὸς BC^{pm}DLX, etc. How singularly biassed was Tregelles to edit the latter, being plainly inconsistent with the context! The edition of W. and H. follows Tregelles. [Weiss and Blass follow Tisch., θεοῦ.]

t ἐκ BC^{pm}LX, etc., παρὰ AC$^{corr.}$ΕΓΔ, etc.

u αὐτῷ T.R. [Blass], with most MSS. [ℵ^{pm}, etc.], vv., etc.; but not the most ancient [ℵ$^{corr.}$B, etc.], some of which add ἐν before παρρησίᾳ [W. and H., Weiss].

v T.R. adds νῦν, "now," with some old MSS. and versions; but ℵABC^{pm}D^{pm}LX, etc., have it not.

w ἕξετε, "ye shall have," is the error of D and many cursives [67, etc.], with most of the Latin copies, etc., followed by Elzevir, but not Stephens, for though it appears in the text of his edition of 1550, it is corrected at the end according to his editions of 1546, 1549; ἔχετε, "ye have," ℵABCL and a dozen more uncials, etc. [Tisch., W. and H., Weiss]. Here many of the ancient versions are wrong, but not the Syrr., Memph., some old Latin, etc. It is strange that Lachmann edited ἕξετε, not only in his small edition of 1831, but in his larger and more mature one of 1842, actually giving B with D *abc* as authority. [Blass follows Lachm.]

THE SEVENTEENTH CHAPTER [a]

Next follows a chapter which one may perhaps characterise truly as unequalled for depth and scope in all the Scriptures. Holiness, devotedness, truth, love, glory reign throughout. Who can wonder, seeing that it is unique in this respect, as it is the Son opening His heart to the Father when just about to die and leave His own for heaven? Yet, profoundly interesting and momentous as the case was, it is the Son addressing Him thus which is so wondrous a privilege for us to hear. But all this may well fill our hearts with the sense of utter insufficiency to speak of such communications suitably. Nevertheless, as the Saviour uttered all within the hearing of the disciples, so the Holy Spirit has been pleased to reproduce His words with divine precision.[310] They are therefore for us now, as then for His favoured followers. Encouraged by this grace, we would count on the Lord's real and living interest in us and on His faithfulness Who still abides with us to glorify Him by taking of His things and showing them to us.

Verses 1-19.

"These things[310a] spake Jesus, and lifting up His eyes unto heaven, said, Father, the hour is come:

glorify Thy Son, that Thy[b] (or, the) Son[b] may glorify Thee,[311] according as Thou gavest Him authority over all flesh, that, everything which Thou hast given Him, He should give them life eternal. And this is the eternal life,[312] that they know[312a] Thee, the only true[312b] God, and Him Whom Thou didst send, Jesus Christ.[312c] I glorified Thee on the earth, having[c] finished the work which Thou hast given Me to do; and now do Thou, Father, glorify Me along with ($παρά$) Thyself with the glory which I had along with Thee before the world was" (verses 1-5).

The Lord had closed His parting instructions to the disciples, who had now to testify of and for Him; and so much the more because He was just about to leave them, His own personal testimony being already complete. To them not only had He spoken with fulness, but promised the Holy Spirit from heaven on His departure that there might be power as well as truth. Unto heaven, therefore, did the Saviour lift up His eyes in addressing His Father. He Who even as Son of Man is in heaven as a divine Person was going there in bodily presence, when the work of redemption was effected. In virtue of this work accomplished in death, proved in resurrection, He would take His seat there, the witness of its infinite acceptance. His proper ministry on earth, not merely to men but to the disciples, had been fully rendered. To the Father He turns as ever, but now in the hearing of His own, as indeed He would open His heart, if about Himself and His work, about them yet more, always the Sent One and Servant in divine love, though Lord of all. He looked to heaven when He blessed and brake the five loaves to feed the five thousand. He looked there and groaned as He made the deaf stammerer to hear and speak. Upward He lifted His eyes when at the grave of Lazarus He said, "Father, I thank Thee that Thou hast heard Me." To heaven He, raising them once more, said, "Father, the hour is come: glorify Thy Son, that Thy Son may glorify Thee." He is ever a divine Person, the Son, but in flesh; not here as in the other Gospels the rejected and agonized sufferer, but the perfect executor of God's purposes, heavenly and everlasting, and the manifestation as Son of the Father.

Hence, whatever the necessary and all-important intervention of His death, without which all else had been in vain for God's glory in presence of sin and ruin, He nowhere speaks of it here, nor does He ask for resurrection but glorification. Further, the Father's name, so prominent in this Gospel, and particularly in these closing discourses to the disciples, is manifestly and more than in this chapter. It is indeed the characteristic of the Christian; even in the simplest form of His blessedness, the youngest, the babe, is described by our Apostle as having the Father known (1 John 2:13): a wondrous privilege, only possible through the Son of God come and redemption wrought, only enjoyable by the Holy Spirit given, the Spirit of adoption. But as at the beginning zeal for His Father's house devoured Him, so here His heart is set on glorifying His Father in that heaven to which His eyes were lifted. "Father, the hour is come: glorify Thy Son;" but, even so, it is "that Thy Son may glorify Thee." Become man, He asks the Father to glorify Him; He is Son, and when there glorified, it is still to glorify the Father. "According as Thou gavest Him authority over all flesh, that, everything which Thou hast given Him, He should give them eternal life." Though God, He exerts no power in His own right; He is true to the place into which He was pleased to come, and as man receives authority from the Father, but authority inconceivable either in its universality of sphere or in its speciality of object, were He not God. For the authority given is over "all flesh"; and the special aim now, as to whatsoever the Father had given Him, is to give them eternal life. Thus the right of our Lord extends without limit, the Gentile being no more outside His title than the Jew; whilst eternal life is the portion of none beyond what is given of the Father to the Son, as elsewhere it is said to belong to the believer only.

This leads to the explanation of "the eternal life" in question. Life for evermore, life to eternity, is the blessing commanded by Jehovah on the mountains of Zion (Psalm 133); and of the many Jews that sleep in the dust of the earth, some shall wake to everlasting life, as others to shame and everlasting contempt (Daniel 12). But both these scriptures contemplate that great turning-point for the earth, the kingdom when it comes in manifest power and glory. The Lord speaks of life as given in Himself to faith now. "And this is the eternal life, that they know Thee, the only true God, and Him Whom Thou didst send, Jesus Christ." If it be distinguished from that which is to be enjoyed in the displayed kingdom by and by, it stands as to its character in the knowledge not of the Most High, Possessor of heaven and earth, with the true Melchisedec a Priest on His throne, but of the Father and of His Sent One, the only true God now plainly revealed in the Son, the one Mediator between God and man. If distinguished from the past, it is no longer the Creator-God giving promises to the fathers protected and lodging as under the shadow of the Almighty; nor yet the sons of Israel in relationship with the name of Jehovah, the moral

THE SEVENTEENTH CHAPTER

governor of that chosen nation. But the children of God now possess the revelation of the Father and of Jesus Christ Whom He sent; and this knowledge is identified, not with promises nor government, but with "eternal life," as a present thing in Christ, the portion of every believer. A deeper blessing it is impossible for God to bestow or for man to receive; for it is exactly what characterised the Lord Himself, Who is the eternal life which was with the Father and was manifested unto us. Only Christ could be said to *be* that life; we as believers are not, but we *have* it in Him; and as by faith alone it is received, so in faith it is exercised, sustained, and strengthened.

It may be noticed further that, as eternal life is bound up with the knowledge of the Father, the only true God, in contrast with the gods many and false of the Gentiles,[313] so it can only be where Christ is known Whom the Father sent, in contrast with His rejection by the Jews to their own deeper guilt and ruin. Neither the Son nor the Holy Ghost is excluded from the deity, which is elsewhere predicated or assumed of both equally with the Father. The object in hand is to assert it of the Father and to state the place taken here below by Him Who did not regard it as a prize (act or object of plunder) to be on equality with God, but emptied Himself, taking the form of a bondman [Philippians 2:7]. He was here to obey, to do the will of the Father that sent Him. But that He took such a place in lowly love is the strongest if indirect proof of His proper and eternal Godhead; for even the archangel *is* a servant and can never rise out of the position or relation of a servant. Whereas the Son was pleased to take it in order to make good the full blessing of redemption unto the glory of God the Father. So life was in Him, and He was eternal life before all ages; but here He is viewed as coming down to impart it in a scene departed from God, and to a creature, which otherwise must know death in its most terrible shape of judgment as now of guilt.

Next, the Lord presents His work: we have seen His Person as already pleaded. But now He urges what He had done here below. "I glorified Thee on the earth, having finished the work which Thou hast given Me to do. And now, Father, glorify Thou Me along with Thyself with the glory which I had along with Thee before the world was." The language here is more of sustained relationship than in chapter 13:31-32, where it is a question of glorifying *God*, before Whom sin comes into unsparing judgment. Here it is glorifying His Father, and so there is no special contemplation of that final dealing where all that God is and feels came out against evil imputatively laid on the head of the Son of Man.[313a] Here the entire path of Christ on earth in giving Himself up to obey and please His Father is summed up. Therefore it was the more needful to specify its completion, "having finished the work which Thou hast given Me to do." He speaks not more as the faithful servant than as the conscious Son of God Who sees all completed to the Father's glory, Who had given Him the work that He should do it Who alone could. And thereon does He ask the Father to glorify Him, not because of His personal glory and relationship only but in virtue of the work completed to His glory here below, that He might thus lay a valid and sure title for us to join Him in the same heavenly blessedness.

It is not that He ever did or could cease to be God, any more than after becoming incarnate He will ever cease to be man; but, having in divine love come down to be a servant and a man to glorify God the Father and make a righteous channel for all the purposes of divine grace, He asks to be glorified by the Father along with Himself with the glory which He had along with Him before the world was. There He had been from everlasting as the Son; there He asks to be as the Son but now also man, the Word made flesh but risen, to everlasting. It was His perfection as man to ask for this glorification. Not even as risen does He glorify Himself. He had emptied and humbled Himself for the Father's glory; He asks the Father to glorify Him, though He states His eternal and divine competency by asking to be glorified with the glory He had with the Father before the world was.[313b] Never so weighty a plea, never so solid a ground of righteousness, never such exquisite and infinite grace.

The Lord then explains how souls were brought into such nearness of relationship to Him before the Father; as He had already laid the basis in His Person and work.

> "I manifested Thy name to the men whom Thou gavest Me out of the world. Thine they were, and to Me Thou gavest them, and they have kept Thy word. Now have they known that all things as many as Thou hast given Me are of (παρὰ) Thee; because the words which Thou gavest Me I have given to them, and they received (them), and knew truly that I came out from Thee, and believed that Thou didst send Me" (verses 6-8).

Thus the manifestation of the Father's name is first laid down. It was a characteristic and most influential truth, the Son being the only one competent, though none of course could enter in even so but by the Spirit, as we know and as is taught elsewhere. But as the Son could manifest His Father's name, so this He did in unjealous love, that the disciples, the men whom the Father gave

Him out of the world, might know what He is as the Son knew Him; not, it need hardly be said, infinitely as was proper to the Only-begotten, but after that manner, as children of God, to whom the Son would impart that which was wholly outside and above man, and intrinsically of God for the family of God.[314]

For though the Lord had come to the Jews as their promised Messiah on earth, Him they would not have but even rejected, as they were just about to do even to the death of the cross. Hence, whatever may be the divine retribution another day when God makes inquisition for blood, and above all for His blood which they had blindly imprecated on themselves and their children, it became wholly a question of sovereign and heavenly grace, which, coming in the Person of the Son, manifested His Father's name as no saint had ever enjoyed, no prophet so much as predicted, save, perhaps, in such a sort as to fall in with and confirm this most precious privilege when communicated. But even Hosea 1:10 is comparatively vague. Here all is as full as it is precise. It was the positive side of what the Lord undertook with His own here below, and its highest character: not the meeting sin and misery in grace, nor even the display of excellency as the righteous One, the Servant and Man, and as such Son of God; but the manifestation of what His Father was and is as He knew Him, and as they were learning who were given to the Son by the Father out of the world. For the world is now defined and judged as alien and opposed to the Father. How blessed for the disciples to hear themselves thus singled out and designated as His by the Son to the Father!

Nor is this all. "Thine they were, and to Me Thou gavest them, and they have kept Thy word" (λόγον). It appears to me that they err who refer the Lord's description to His followers as formerly of Israel merely, and as walking in all the commandments and ordinances of Jehovah blameless. These were His elect out of the elect nation, His enemies now yet to be restored another day. The Father had a purpose about these, and thus they belonged to Him Who gave them to the Son, the object of His love and effectuator of His counsels, as He is also the accomplisher of redemption, to His own glory. And as the men given out of the world are thus viewed on a divine ground outside Jewish ties, so that which formed their souls and their ways was quite distinct; they had kept, says the Son, His Father's word, made known by Himself when with them on earth hitherto. This we have, speaking generally, in the Gospels, with not a little they could not then bear in the Epistles. Everything refers to the Father: the Son, a man on earth, is always exalting Him, and in view of His own departure would endear them to Him and give them the assurance of it.

This is developed yet more in what follows. "Now have they known that all things as many as Thou hast given Me are of Thee." They had entered into the secret of which the world knew nothing: the Father was the source of all that was given to the Son. Some wondered at His works and His words; others in their enmity blasphemously attributed what was beyond man to Satan. The disciples had learnt that they were all of the Father, as the Son desired that they should. It was not only that He came out from the Father, nor that He had finished the work the Father had given Him to do, as their title to blessing with the Son before Him; but the means for bringing them into the blessing were also of the Father; "because the words which Thou gavest Me I have given them, and they received (them), and knew truly that I came out from Thee, and believed that Thou didst send Me."[314a] Thus the Lord handed over to His disciples those intimate communications of grace which the Father gave to Himself. It was no longer a question of the ten words given by Moses, the measure of man's responsibility to prove his sin and ruin which he neither owned nor felt.

The words ($ῥήματα$) which the Father gave the Son were the expression of divine grace and love according to that blessed relationship in which the Son stood, though man; and the disciples, once mere men, but now born of God, have life eternal in Him and are given these words by the Son, that they might know and enjoy the new relationship which grace had conferred on them. Nor was it in vain, however slow of heart they might be in believing all. For if He had given to them the words the Father gave to Him, the disciples received the truth really, though no doubt imperfectly. The result was that they came to know truly that Christ the Son came out from the Father, and believed also that the Father sent Him. This is all the reckoning of grace here, not measuring degrees, but making much of reality, as He can well do Whose love gives, deepens, and secures from first to last. Even for them to know assuredly that the Son came out from the Father does not suffice His heart, for this would not necessarily prove more than His own love in so coming; but the disciples believed the further truth that the Father sent Him, the proof of His own love to them. How rich, how needful, is every word of His grace!

> "*I* request for[315] them: not for the world do I request, but for those whom Thou hast given Me, for they are Thine (and all My things are Thine, and Thy things Mine), and I am glorified in them.

THE SEVENTEENTH CHAPTER

And I am no longer in the world, and these[d] (or, they) are in the world, and I come to Thee" (verses 9-11a).

It is concerning the disciples He makes request, not for Israel nor the nations, not for the land nor the earth at large, but concerning those whom the Father had given Him. It is no question of taking up the world for government or blessing now: He is occupied with the joint-heirs, not with the inheritance as yet. By and by, as Psalm 2 lets us know, Jehovah will say, "Ask of Me, and I will give (Thee) nations for an inheritance, and the ends of the earth for Thy possession."[315] But then the Son will reign on His holy hill of Zion, instead of being rejected on earth and received up on high. Then, instead of sustaining the suffering family of God who bear His reproach here below and wait for heavenly glory with Him, He will break the nations "with a sceptre of iron, and dash them in pieces as a potter's vessel." It will be, not the interval of the gospel as now, but the day of the kingdom in power and glory. Here the Lord is praying for His own as the precious gift of the Father to Himself, while cut off and having nothing that was promised Him here below; and He asks the more, because they were the Father's.

But it may be well to say that this gives occasion for a parenthetic statement which lets out much of the light of His personal glory: "And all My things are Thine, and Thy things Mine."[e] As the Son of David, the Messiah, could this reciprocity have been so expressed? Is it not evidently and only in virtue of His being the Eternal Son, one with the Father, that they have rights and interests no less boundless than common? After this, however, He returns to the saints as those in whom He was glorified as a fact, not past but abiding, urging their care on the Father, because He sees both Himself no longer with them in the world and themselves so much the more exposed in it, as He was going back to the Father. Hence arises a fresh appeal.

> "Holy Father, keep them in Thy name which[f] Thou hast given Me, that they may be one even as (also)[f] We[316] (are). When I was with them,[f] *I* was keeping them in Thy name which Thou hast given Me, and I guarded (them), and not one of them perished but the son of perdition, that the scripture might be fulfilled. And now unto Thee I come, and these things I speak in the world that they may have My joy fulfilled in themselves" (verses 11b-13).

The Lord asks His Father, as the Holy Father, to keep the disciples in His name that they might be one, even as also the Father and the Son are. And this was accomplished by the power of the Holy Ghost in those very men who then stood around Him. Never before or since was such unity produced in human beings on earth. Yet the Gospels are the plainest proof that they were far from it whilst our Lord was here below with them. It was to be the fruit of His grace through redemption after He went on high and sent down the Holy Ghost to effect it. And it was essential as a practical basis for Christianity. For doctrine is not enough without reality in life, and this most of all in those who were raised up of God to lay down the foundation. Their work and their written words were all during one generation in striking contrast with those of the Old Testament.

Granted that they were men of like passions with ourselves or any; granted that they displayed varied and not slight infirmities even under their Master's eyes and ministry on earth; granted that they then from first to last betrayed petty prejudices and narrow hearts and no small jealousy of each other, even in presence of the deepest love and lowliness, and of words and ways which made their contrasted jars (and the selfishness which gave rise to all) most humbling and painful: all this, with more, only adds to the blessedness of what God wrought in these very men by His Spirit in answer to the Lord's demand. The power of the Father's name, which the Lord here below knew so well, was manifest in them; and the twelve were one even as the Father and the Son. None would have ventured so to describe but Christ; but if He did, He is the Truth; and, in fact, with whom or what else could their unity as witnessed in the Acts and Epistles of the Apostles be compared? Never elsewhere was seen such rising above egotism in the aims, measures, objects, in the life and service, of men on earth; never such common devotedness to, and absorption in, the will of God for the magnifying of the risen and glorified Jesus.

The Lord, then, in committing to the Father His own whom in that name He was keeping whilst here, speaks of having kept them safe, save that one who was doomed to destruction. Awful lesson! that even the constant presence of Jesus fails to win where the Spirit brings not the truth home to the conscience. Does this enfeeble Scripture? On the contrary, the scripture was thereby fulfilled. Chapter 13 referred to Judas that none should be stumbled by such an end of His ministry. Here it is rather that none should therefore doubt the Lord's care or the scripture. He was not one of those given to Christ by the Father,[317] though called to be an apostle: of those so given He had lost none. Judas was an apparent, not a real, exception, as he was not a child of

God but the son of perdition. To see the awful end of so heartless a course would only give more force to His works of grace Who, if He left the world for the Father, was bringing them into His own associations before the Father. Judas may never have meant the worst, as Satan did who entered him; but he did mean at all cost to gratify his love of money, trusting that He who had heretofore baffled His enemies would be able to extricate Himself. But he trusted his own thoughts to the death of his Master, and to his own eternal ruin; as Jesus carrying out His love in obedience to His Father would bring His own by His death to glory on high and His own place there, and expressed it here that even now they might have His joy fulfilled in themselves. For now that the Lord was going to the Father He speaks these things in the world to that end. The Father would prove the value of His name when the Son was not here in person to watch over them; and the very ruin of Judas rightly read should make the scripture still more solemn and sure to their souls.

From verse 14 the Lord pleads for another object on behalf of the disciples. He had entreated for them to be set in His love in presence of the Father; He now asks that they may have His place in presence of the world. As He had sought their association with Himself in the one case, so in the other He would have no less an association. There it was for His joy to be fulfilled in them; here it is for the Father's testimony in and by them. It was His own place on earth, as in heaven.

> "*I* have given them Thy word; and the world hated them because they are not of the world, as I am not of the world. I do not ask that Thou shouldest take them out of the world, but that Thou shouldest keep them out of[317a] the evil. Of the

world they are not, as I am not of the world" (verses 14-16).

It is not here, as in verse 8, "the words" (ῥήματα) given of the Father to the Son which the Son had given to the disciples, the communications of love, whence they knew truly that He came from the Father, and believed to their joy that the Father sent Him. It is here (as in verse 6) the Father's "word" (λόγος), the expression of His mind. This, it was said already, they had kept. But the Lord resumes the notice of it in connection with testimony in the world which for Him was closed. In the world they were to be witnesses of Him, and the Father's word He has given them, and the world hated them, not for that word only, offensive as it is to the world, but because they, the disciples who had it, were not of the world even as their Master is not. This is the true measure of unworldliness, and it is intolerable in the world's eyes, and nowhere so much as in the religious world. For men on earth to know themselves possessors of life eternal sounds presumptuous to such as know not Christ and His work. But to add that they are not of the world, the world will have to be the worst intolerance.

Yet nothing is so lowly as faith, and faith works by love, the very reverse of despising others or trusting in themselves that they are righteous. Christ is all to the believer, as He is to the Father; and as He is not of the world, so they are not. That they are not of the world depends on the former truth, that they are the Father's and given to the Son, Who manifested the Father's name to them and kept them in that name; as He besought that the Father would keep them still during His absence from the world. Christ in John is from the outset unknown to the world and rejected; they know not the Father and the Son. So it is with the children of God.

"Therefore the world knoweth us not because it knew Him not" [1 John 3:1]. The breach is complete. "The world hatedᵍ them," as it hated both the Father and the Son.

Never had there been such a breach before. It was not so during God's dealings with Israel of old; nor yet in their ruin during the ensuing times of the Gentiles. Man was still under trial; and even while the Lord was here below, the character of His ministry was God in Him reconciling the world to Himself. But the world would none of Him, and is judged in its prince. And as man is now in the light of the cross pronounced lost, so is the saint crucified to the world and the world to him. They are not of the world, as Christ is not of the world. It is a fact, and not merely an obligation, though the firmest ground of obligation. They *are* not of the world, not merely they ought not to be; whilst if they are not, it is grievous inconsistency even to seem to be of the world. It is to be false to our relationship, for we are the Father's and given to the rejected Son, Who has done with the world. But if it be said that this is to bring in everlasting and heavenly relationships now, be it so; this is exactly what Christianity means in principle and practice. It is faith possessing Christ, Who gives the believer His own place of relationship and acceptance on high as well as of testimony apart from and rejected by the world below; which he has to make good in words and ways, in spirit and conversation, whilst waiting for the Lord.

Hence, if going back to law or flesh, as in Galatia, was to fall from grace, no less thorough is the departure of the Christian when he seeks the world of which he is not. That the world improves for Christ or His own is as false as that the flesh can ameliorate. It is the light become darkness, and how great is that darkness! There may not

THE SEVENTEENTH CHAPTER

be the reflex of the latter part of Romans 1, but it answers to the beginning of 2 Timothy 3. It is the natural man knowing enough to forego what is shameless, and to invest all with a religious veil; it is the world essentially, occupying itself with the things of God in profession but in reality of the world, where common sense suffices for its service and its worship, and the mind of Christ would be altogether inapplicable. What a triumph to the enemy! It is just what we see in Christendom; and nothing irritates so much as the refusal so to walk, worship, or serve. It does not matter how loudly you denounce or protest; if you join the world, they will not mind your words, and you are faithless to Christ. Nor does it matter how much grace and patience you show; if you keep apart as not of the world, you incur enmity and hatred and contempt. A disciple is not above his Master; but every one that is perfected shall be as his Master. To act as not of the world is felt to be its strongest condemnation; and no meekness or love can make it palatable. Nor does God intend that it should, for He means it as part of the testimony to His Son. And as the world neither receives nor understands the Father's word, so it hates those who have that word and act on it.

Doubtless there is a moment when the dead in Christ shall rise first; then we the living who remain shall be caught up together with them in clouds to meet the Lord in the air, when He shall Himself with a shout, with archangel's voice, and with trump of God, descend from heaven; and thus we shall ever be with Him. But the Lord did not ask yet that the Father should thus take His own out of the world, but that He should keep them out of the evil. This He does by His grace through His word, as we shall see presently. Only the Lord, before He explains how the Father keeps the saints, reiterates in a new form so as to give greater emphasis, "Of the world they are not, even as I am not of the world." Nor is anything more speedily forgotten, unless the eye be fixed on Christ above with continual vigilance as to our motives, ways, and ends, as well as unsparing self-judgment. It was of all moment to have it firm and clear that the world and the Christian have no common ground, and that Christ Himself, according to Whose grace and for Whose glory in communion with the Father we are here, is the pattern of our unworldliness. What separateness so absolute? or dependent on relationship to the Father so near, save only His Who is in the highest way its pattern? For the world in the sense here conveyed is that vast system which man has built up away from God in independence and self-reliance, and to the exclusion, not of His nominal honour but of any real submission to His righteousness, His will, word, or glory. This fully came out in the rejection and cross of His Son, Who thereon reveals as wholly distinct in source, nature, character, and aim, those that the Father owns as His in the world, whose fellowship is indeed with the Father and with His Son Jesus Christ. Of the world they are not, as He is not. They are Christ's.

Now comes the formative power, as wholly new as above man, and not of God merely but of the Father.

> "Sanctify them by (or, in) the truth;[318] Thy word is truth. As Thou didst send Me into the world, I also sent[318a] them into the world. And for their sakes *I* sanctify Myself that they also may be sanctified in truth" (verses 17-19).

It is impossible to overrate the importance of the Saviour's words for His disciples; it is easy for men to misapprehend them, as those do who lower and narrow the word to separation for ministerial service.[h] But He had at heart a more personal and intimate want, that the disciples should themselves be imbued with, formed and fashioned by, the truth. The law now sufficed not; not even in the most comprehensive sense, as embracing the Prophets and the Psalms. For Christ was come, the Only-begotten Who declared God otherwise unseen of anyone. He revealed the Father, Who would make a fresh and full yet permanent revelation, as we have it not only in Him but in the Scriptures as a whole. The sanctification or setting apart was therefore as new as complete. It was to the Father that the Son spread His request for men who were none of them heathen but of the holy seed.[319] Yet for such does He say, "Sanctify them by the truth." The truth was revealed as it never was before. "Thy word," the Father's word, "is truth." Truths had been made known, never the Truth till Jesus Who is it. For He first, He only as an objective display, showed out every one, God, man, Satan even, and every thing, heaven, earth, hell, and all things in them, as they really are; for His Person (the Word made flesh) alone was competent to do it. His advent and redemption gave the suited occasion and needed object for the full revelation, as being Son of Man and withal true God and eternal life. By the truth, then, the Father's word, were the disciples to be sanctified. The Father revealed, not only in the Son personally but in His word detailedly, changed all for the soul. None but the Son, and the Son a man on earth, glorifying the Father perfectly in His life, glorifying God as such in His death, could furnish the adequate motive for the Father's love, object for His ways, centre of His counsels, and manifestation of His glory. Hence all is out and in perfection: testimony higher, deeper, fuller, is looked for in vain; as those know who, acknowledging the Son, have the Father also, and are not of the world.

Then comes their mission, which is drawn from the same unworldly source and is characterised by it. "As thou didst send Me into the world, I also sent them into the world." Moses disappears even as a pattern; so do the prophets. Even John the Baptist (and among those born of women was no prophet greater) was but man in mission from God; but he that is least in the kingdom is greater than John. He that cometh from above—from heaven—is above all. Such was Jesus; and as the Father sent forth Him, so He too sent those who then surrounded Him, their mission as new as the word which formed and furnished their souls. It flowed from One apart from the world and above it, Who had been sent into it on an errand of infinite love to the Father's glory, and was in spirit no more here but in heaven, whither He was actually going soon. It was thus the Son sent the disciples associated with Himself in heaven and charged with the Father's testimony to the world. Not of the world as He was not, they could be and were sent into it. Had they been of the world, they could not be sent into it; but, as taken out of it by grace in Christ, they were not of it, and could be sent.

This is fitly followed by another and crowning means of sanctification of which the Lord speaks. "And for their sakes *I* sanctify Myself that they also may be sanctified in truth." It is not the Father's word now as given to them here and revealing Him in every detail as the disciples needed, though inseparable from Christ's Person as come into the world, where they too were sent. This was essential both for themselves and their work. But grace does more; and the Lord goes on to show how He is setting Himself apart on high, the Son as ever but model Man before the Father in heaven, so as to complete their sanctification in seeing Him thus in glory.

Thus it is not only the truth brought out here in all its application, but the truth also in the glorified Christ as the suited object to animate and strengthen as well as transform, while we behold Him with unveiled face: God revealed in man, the Son of Man; the Son of Man now glorified by God in Himself, and this straightway, that the disciples might be sanctified "in truth," both bearing on their nature and walk. For, without such an object above, the fullest demonstration of God's righteousness and power were lacking; and so too one might add, of the Father's love and glory, as well as what was due to His own Person, not only as divine but as man, and man glorified according to the counsels of God. And the disciples also needed His blessed Person thus before them at God's right hand in order to fix and fill their affections, beside the word which perfectly reveals all the mind of God in grace. For it is not simply as incarnate that the Lord sanctifies Himself on their behalf; nor yet as dying sacrificially, according to Chrysostom and Cyril of Alexandria, with a crowd of followers since their day. For on the cross for us God made Him sin Who knew no sin {2 Corinthians 5:21}. It is as glorified, consequent on death and resurrection, that He becomes the pattern of His own. Beholding Him they are transformed into His image from glory to glory even as by the Lord the Spirit {2 Corinthians 3:18}; and, when He shall be manifested, they are to be like Him, seeing Him as He is {1 John 3:2}, and conformed to the image of the Son in resurrection glory. God Himself could give no other portion so blessed, when Christ shall be the Firstborn among many brethren {Romans 8:29}.

The Lord now proceeds to plead for those to be brought into faith in Him by apostolic testimony that they too might form a unity according to God and bear witness before the world to His mission of the Son. Verse 11 had contemplated only those disciples who were then surrounding Him in view of special grace and the consequent responsibility which attached to them. Those to follow have their new vested interest.

Verses 20-26.

> "And not for these only do I request, but also for those that believe[i] on Me through their word, that they may all be one,[319a] even as Thou, Father, in Me and I in Thee, that they also may be one[j] in us, that the world may believe that Thou didst send Me" (verses 20-21).

There was to be, as we have seen, an astonishing exhibition of unity in the Apostles. But there is another and larger unity here. Those believing on Him through their word are now presented to the Father, "that they may all be one." Room is thus left for multitudes of believers, for confessors of His name, Jew or Greek, barbarian, Scythian, bond or free; for those that had hitherto clung tenaciously to legal forms, the substance of which they refused through their unbelief of Him; for those that had been well-nigh as obstinate in cleaving to the dreams of heathenism and its debasing immorality, in utter ignorance of the only true God truly known through Him Whom He sent. The gospel was about to go forth to every land and in every tongue, as the Holy Ghost bore witness on the day of Pentecost; and the most strikingly on that day, because they as yet were Jews only from Gentile countries as well as Palestine. For the miracle was not the senseless and comparatively

THE SEVENTEENTH CHAPTER

easy one of enabling all, home or foreign sons of Israel, to understand the wonderful works of God in the Hebrew tongue, but conversely that they, every man in his own dialect in which he had been born, should hear the disciples speak. God had of old smitten men's pride and divided them into ever so many differing tongues. Grace now rose above judgment, not reducing them all to one lip and the same words, but meeting each where thus confounded and scattered.

Nor was this by any means all; but the power of the Spirit baptized all the believers into one body, the Church. The unity here, however, though produced of course by the same Spirit in those who compose that body, is not that which fell to the apostle Paul to set out. Of a spiritual nature it nevertheless displays itself in that which the world can see and appreciate in measure. It is not precisely "one as we," that is, as the Father and the Son, which verse 11 had predicated of the disciples. As the Father and the Son had but one mind and affection, purpose and way, so was this oneness desired for the Apostles in their work and life; and wondrously was it realised in them as we have already noticed. Here the saints at large, those who believe through their word, are in view; and the thing sought is that they should "all be one," "even as Thou, Father, in Me, and I in Thee, that they also may be one in us"—not "*as* we" but "*in* us," in the Father and the Son. It is communion in virtue of the Father made known in the Son, and of the Son the object of the Father's love and delight, into which we are brought by the Holy Ghost. With the Father we share the Son; with the Son we share the Father. Into this blessedness the saints were now for the first time to be introduced, and in such sort that they should all be one, even as the Father in the Son, and the Son in the Father, so they also one in the Father and the Son.

This was to be a testimony to the world, not preaching only, but this oneness so unearthly, so unprecedented among men, oneness in the joy of divine grace which drew together souls so diverse and by the power of divine objects, motives, and affections, those who had been once utterly indifferent or bitterly opposed, hating and hated. What a call for the world to believe that the Father sent the Son! For this, and this only, but this adequately, accounted for it, when the Holy Ghost sent down from heaven gave the truth energy in hearts purified by faith. For as flesh tends to scatter by the assertion of its own will, so the Spirit operates to unite in the Father and the Son; and when the world sees the fruits of such gracious and holy power in the oneness of men otherwise alienated, and by nothing so keenly and permanently as by their varying religions, what a demonstration that the Father sent the Son! For here at least was no power of the sword, here no pandering to lust, here no inducement of wealth or worldly honour, here no allowance any more of sin than of human righteousness, no pride of philosophy any more than religious show or ritualism. None can deny that as built upon the foundation of the Apostles and prophets there was constant and unresisting exposure to the world's scorn and violence. Self-sacrificing love reigned, grace we may say through righteousness in devotedness to the name of Jesus; and a heavenly separateness to Him for Whom they avowedly waited from heaven. What then accounted for so astonishing a change from all that had previously characterised mankind, not merely among the Gentiles but in Israel even in its most flourishing estate? What did it attest but that the Father sent the

Son? What of grace and truth, of perfect and eternal redemption, of near and heavenly relationship, does not this involve?

For if the Father sent the Son, it could not but be for ends impossible otherwise and worthy of the true God revealing Himself in sovereign grace, yea, in intimate love as well as in the light which makes everything manifest. Nor was the Son only to make the truth known and to impart the divine nature, the eternal life capable of receiving and enjoying light, and walking in it by the Spirit of God. There was an incomparably solemn yet blessed work to be wrought to God's glory as well as for man's deep need and everlasting salvation: sin had to be borne in judgment, a propitiation made for our sins so complete that God should be righteous in justifying the believer, and that believers should become God's righteousness in Christ. Thus washed, sanctified, justified, children of God consciously, the Holy Ghost given, they find others in the communion of the same blessing. They are all one, as the Father in the Son and the Son in the Father, and brought out as they were of the strongest prejudices into a mutuality of enjoyed blessedness, into oneness in the Father and the Son. What could more powerfully bear witness to the world that the Father sent the Son?

There is yet another unity of the deepest interest which our Lord next spreads before the Father: not discipular or apostolic, which was so marvellously sustained; nor of testimony in the grace that would embrace all Christians, which after a bright display at first has long painfully broken down; but unity in glory where all is to be stable and according to God perfectly.

"And the glory which Thou hast given Me I have given them, that they may be one as We (are) one, I in them and Thou in Me, that they may be perfected into one, (and)[k] that the world may know that Thou didst send Me and lovedst them as Thou lovedst Me" (verses 22-23).

This is wholly distinct from what we have seen, though all be to the praise of Christ. It is an exclusively future unity, though the glory be given to our faith now, and grace would have us apprehend it and feel and walk accordingly.[320] For all is revealed to act now on our souls. But this unity will be in glory when we shall be one as the Father and the Son are. Hence failure here is impossible. The weakness of man, the power of Satan, can damage no more.

The manner of this unity is to be noted also. It is not the mutuality which we had described in verse 21, that we should be one in the Father and the Son, as the Father in the Son and the Son in the Father. Such is the admirable way in which the Saviour set out what we are called to now by the Spirit, that the world may believe the Father sent the Son. But by and by, when the glory is revealed, there will be this new character, that, while the saints are to be one even as the Father and the Son are one, it will be Christ the Son in them and the Father in Him. And this as exactly agrees with Revelation 21 as the former answers to 1 John 1:3.

For as the holy city—new Jerusalem—is the bride, the Lamb's wife, the symbol of ourselves glorified in that day, so we are shown that the city had "the glory of God," and the Lamb its lamp, while the nations walk in its light (Revelation 21:11, 23-24). Thus are the blessed on earth to enjoy the heavenly glory, not directly like the glorified on high who have the Lord God Almighty and the Lamb as their temple, and need none other; whereas those on earth have it but mediately. Yet how constant and impressive the proof before them that the Father sent the Son! For how else could there have grown up such a holy temple in the Lord? And what adequately could account for men thus called out of the earth and glorified on high? Sovereign grace had given them that heavenly portion as the fruit of His mission Who at all cost to Himself had glorified God on the earth. And now they share His glory above, and are so displayed before the wondering world.

The salvation-bearing grace, which had appeared to all and had done its suited and appointed work in redeeming and purifying these to God as a people of possession, will then have given place to the appearing of the glory of our great God and Saviour Jesus Christ; but this through the Church reigning over the earth, at any rate as the ordinary or normal method of its manifestation during the kingdom. As we by faith saw the Father in the Son to eternal life, they in that day will behold and learn them in the Church, the glorious vessel of the light of Christ in Whom God's glory shines. For then the false glory of man is for ever judged, never more to mislead the heart; and Satan will never regain his bad eminence in the heavenlies whereby he found means most effectively to misrepresent God, oppose Christ, accuse the saints, and deceive the world. It is thenceforward the glory of God that is established before all eyes, so that men "know" it in and by the glorified saints, instead of being objects of testimony that they might "believe." For the earth shall be full of the glory of Jehovah (Numbers 14:21) and of the knowledge of Jehovah (Isaiah 11:9) and of the knowledge of the glory of Jehovah (Habakkuk 2:14), as the waters cover the sea. Then Christ shall have "come to be glorified in His saints, and to be admired in all them that believed, in that day" {2 Thessalonians 1:10}.

Therefore do we hear for the first time of being "perfected into one." The apostolic unity first spoken of, unity in counsel and action as the Father and the Son gave pattern, was as blessed as it was all-important for the place they had to fill and the work to be done in the testimony of Christ. Still it was comparatively partial, at least necessarily on a small scale. Far wider was the second unity of fellowship in the Father and the Son exhibited in the Pentecostal assembly at large, when thousands of souls walked together superior to selfish influence, and great grace was upon them all, and of the rest durst no man join himself to them, but the people magnified them, and believers were the more added to the Lord, multitudes both of men and women [Acts 5:14]. But this was only transient. The third will be perfect in glory, and thus permanent as well as complete.[321]

And the effect will be immense and immediate, as indeed one could not conceive it otherwise. The world will contemplate with amazement the Church in the glory and the glory of God in the Church, or (as the Lord says) the Father in Him, and He in them glorified. It is unity perfect both in connection with its source and in manifestation of the divine glory. And what a demonstration that the Father sent the Son and loved the saints as He loved Him! For how should the Son be there as the glorified Man unless previously sent here in love? and how should we be manifested together with Him in glory, unless loved with the same love? It is no question of "believing" then, but of undeniable fact. The world will "know" it. We may know now what is only revealed in the word to our faith; but in that day will be a display of divine glory.

The closing section of our Lord's words is quite distinct in its character, and yet more intimate, as is marked by His use of θέλω, "I will" (or "desire"), for the first and only time throughout His prayer.

> "Father, that what[1] Thou hast given Me, I desire that, where I am, they also may be with Me, that they may behold My glory which Thou hast given Me, because Thou lovedst Me before (the) world's foundation. Righteous Father, though[m] the world knew Thee not, but I knew Thee, and these knew that Thou didst send Me. And I made Thy name known to them and will make (it) known, that the love wherewith Thou lovedst Me may be in them and I in them" (verses 24-26).

First, the Lord desires of the Father that those whom He had given Him should be with Him where He is. He is in spirit on high before the Father, and would have His own with Himself there. It is no question of display in glory before the world, even though in the closest association with Him; it is to be with Himself where no stranger can (I do not say merely, intermeddle with the joy, but) look on Him or them, in the hidden scene which divine love forms for its deepest satisfaction. There the Father has the Son after glorifying Himself perfectly in the face of all possible difficulty, and the suffering entailed not only by creature opposition and malice, but by divine judgment of God on that evil, the consequences of which must be borne unsparingly by Him, Who would vindicate God on the one hand, and on the other deliver to the uttermost the guilty, so far as suited the gracious purpose of God. And this Jesus did in absolute obedience, as became Himself a man in grace beyond measure and at all cost; this He did in infinite suffering to His Father's praise, Who acquired fresh and everlasting glory and could thenceforward act as freely as righteously according to His nature and His love.

And now, as we have seen at the beginning of the chapter, going to heaven on the ground not of His personal title only but of His work, He expresses His desire that His own also, the disciples whom the Father had given Him, should be with Him above, "that they may behold My glory." It is not, on the one hand, that which is personal from everlasting to everlasting, beyond creature ken, that in the Son which I presume none really knows nor can, save the Father Who is not said to reveal Him (Matthew 11:27). Neither is it, on the other hand, the glory given to the blessed Lord which is to be manifested even to the world in that day, in which glory we are to be manifested along with Him (Colossians 3:4). Here it is proper to Himself on high, yet given Him by the Father, as we are in His perfect favour to behold it: a far higher thing than any glory shared along with us, and which the Lord, reckoning on unselfish affections divinely formed in us, looks for our valuing accordingly, as more blessed in beholding Him thus than in aught conferred on ourselves. It is a joy for us alone, wholly outside and above the world, and given because the Father loved Him before its foundation. None but the Eternal could be thus glorified, but it is the secret glory which none but His own are permitted to contemplate, "blest answer to reproach and shame," not the public glory in which every eye shall see Him. Nothing less than that meets His desire for us. How truly even now our hearts can say that He is worthy![322]

THE SEVENTEENTH CHAPTER

Next, the Lord draws the line definitely between the world and His own, and makes it turn not on rejecting Himself, but on ignoring His Father. Here, therefore, it is a question of judgment in result, however grace may tarry and entreat; and therefore He says, "Righteous Father," not "Holy Father" as in verse 11, where He asks Him to keep them in His name, as He Himself had done whilst with them. Now He sets forth not the lawlessness of the world, not its murderous hatred of Himself or of His disciples, nor yet of the grace and truth revealed in the gospel, nor of the corruptions of Christianity and the Church (which we are sure lay naked and opened before His all-seeing eyes), but that on the one side the world knew not the Father, and on the other that the Son did, as the disciples that the Father sent the Son: words simple and briefly said, but how solemn in character and issues!

Never was so competent a witness of anyone or anything, as Christ of the Father. Yet the world knew Him not, nor received His testimony for a moment, but rose up more and more against it till all closed in the cross. Thenceforward He is hid in heaven, and those who believe on Him are heavenly. False pretension to it is salt that has lost its savour. And all those who are true are the first to own that all turns for them on the Son's knowledge of the Father, as they themselves knew the Father sent Him. It is no question of themselves at all but of the Father; and He is only known in the Son Whom He sent; and this is eternal life, whether now had in Christ or enjoyed without alloy when we behold His glory on high; as ignorance of the Father implies the guilty rejection of the Son, to the everlasting loss, and not merely passing judgment, of the world.

But lastly, where Christ is known as the Father's Sent One, the deepest blessing and the highest privileges are even now given, and not merely what awaits the saints at Christ's coming. "And I made known to them Thy name, and will make known, that the love wherewith Thou lovedst Me may be in them, and I in them." If ever there was one capable of estimating another, it was the Son in respect of the Father; and His name, the expression of what He was, with equal competency He made known to us. He had done it on earth to the disciples; He would do so from heaven whither He was going; and this that He might give them, and give us, the consciousness of the same love of the Father which rested ever on Himself here below. As if to cut off the not unnatural hesitation of the disciples, He adds the blessed guarantee of His own being in them, their life. For they could understand that, if they lived of His life, and could be somehow as He before the Father, the Father might love them as Him. This is just what He does give and secure by identification with them, or, rather, as He puts it, "and I in them." Christ is all and in all.

NOTES ON THE SEVENTEENTH CHAPTER

a [*Cf. Lectures Introductory to the Study of the Gospels*, pp. 556-558.]

b Treg. and Tisch., with W. and H. [and others], omit σοῦ, "Thy," following אBC^{pm}, etc. T.R. has καὶ, "also," but the best do not accredit it.

c So אABCLΠ, etc.; but the finite verb in DEXYΔΛ, etc.

d אB, two cursives, DF (not the other Ita. nor Vulg.) Memph., Æth., Arm., Goth. read αὐτοὶ, "they," in which they are followed by Tisch. in his last ed. and by W. and H. [and Blass, but Weiss adheres to οὗτοι].

e It is surprising that the editors and commentators have not noticed the natural if not necessary parenthesis of all but the last clause of verse 10. As to the universe, it would not be true to say yet δεδόξασμαι ἐν αὐτοῖς. It is precisely true of the saints.

f The T.R. has οὕς, "whom," but the better authorities support ᾧ, "which" (verse 11); and so in 12, though not so many.—The best also omit "in the world" (12), as some of them καὶ, "also" (11).

g The verb ἐμίσησεν is to be explained as meaning, neither the *future* as Kuinöl, nor the *present* as Bloomfield. It is the most emphatic preterite possible, the whole being summed up in its conclusion, though no doubt it was the fact then, and was about to be yet more and more manifest by and by.

h Hence Joseph Mede regarded ἐν τῇ ἀλ. as meaning εἰς τὴν ἀλ., and Bishop Pearce followed, as did Tittmann and Kuinöl, in the same wake. So Dr. Bloomfield (*Recensio Synoptica Annotationis Sacræ*, iii. 634). "From this verse He speaks of the evangelical office to be committed to their charge, and expresses His wish that they should be 'wholly dedicated and given up to it.' " He consequently would take ἐν τῇ ἀλ. as for ὑπὲρ τῆς ἀλ. How little these commentators believe that every word of Scripture is from God!

i T.R. reads the future with some cursives, but against the great authorities.

j ἕν ℵAC^{corr}ELXYΓΔΠ, etc., and good versions; but BC^{pm}D, some old Latin and other versions, omit, followed strangely by Treg., Tisch., Alford, W. and H., and the Revisers [Weiss and Blass]. The homœoteleuton plainly accounts for this.

k BCDLX, some cursives, etc., omit καὶ, "and" [Edd.], which is read by A and a dozen more uncials, most cursives, and good ancient versions.

l ὅ, "what," ℵBD, etc. [most Edd.], instead of οὕς, "whom" [Lachmann], as in the mass of authorities [ACL, Syr^{sin}, etc.].

m It has been suggested, in order to make it smoother English, "though the world knew Thee not, yet," etc., to translate thus, "Righteous Father! and the world knew Thee not! But," etc. I prefer simply to follow the words faithfully, "but I knew Thee," in a sort of parenthesis, contrasted with the world, and introductory of His own, who at least knew Him as the Sent One.

THE EIGHTEENTH CHAPTER [a]

The Lord had concluded His words to the disciples and to His Father. His work on earth, now about to close, had been before Him, as well as His departure on high, and contingent on both the approaching mission of the Holy Spirit to abide with His own apart from the world. That rejection of the Saviour which has been in view throughout our Gospel was now to reach its extreme in the cross; but its dark shadow, far from obscuring, only serves to bring out the True Light more distinctly. He is man, but a divine Person, the Son throughout wherever He moves.

VERSES 1-11.

[*Cf.* Matthew 26:36, 47-56; Mark 14:32, 43-52; Luke 22:39, 47-53.]

> "Having said these things Jesus went out with His disciples beyond the torrent-bed of Kedron,[b] where was a garden, into which He entered, Himself and His disciples. And Judas also that was delivering Him up knew the place, because Jesus often met there with His disciples.[323] Judas then, having received the band and officials from the

high priests and from (the) Pharisees, cometh there with lanterns and torches and weapons. Jesus then, knowing all things that were coming on Him, went out and saith to them, Whom seek ye? They answered Him, Jesus the Nazarean. Jesus[c] saith to them, I am (He). And Judas that was delivering Him up was standing with them. When then He said to them, I am (He), they went away backward and fell to the ground. Again then He asked them, Whom seek ye? And they said, Jesus the Nazarean. Jesus answered, I told you that I am (He): if then ye seek Me, leave these to go away; that the word might be fulfilled which He said, Of those whom Thou hast given Me, I have lost not one of them. Simon Peter then, having a sword, drew it, and smote the bondman of the high priest, and cut off his right ear. Now the bondman's name was Malchus. Jesus said then to Peter, Put the[d] sword into the scabbard: the cup which the Father hath given Me, shall I not drink it?" [*Cf.* Matthew 26:39] (verses 1-11).

It was the same orchard or garden which in the other Gospels is called Gethsemane (a word formed from the Hebrew words meaning "a winepress" and "oil"), but giving no real ground to say,[e] as some after the patristic and mediæval style, that here emphatically were fulfilled those dark words, "I have trodden the winepress alone," as Isaiah [63:3] has foretold, and as the name imports. For the treading of the winefat is when the Lord comes to judge, not to suffer, as the connected text (Revelation 14:20) ought to have made plain. Indeed, no reader save one perverted by theological tradition could mistake the earlier prophet any more than the latest. For what is described in these prophecies is not agony but vengeance, not His bloody sweat with strong crying and tears, but His treading the peoples in His anger and their blood sprinkled on His garments.

But an intelligent and thoughtful reader would remark the striking absence of that wondrous scene where even those who loved the Lord—yea, Peter, James, and John—could not watch with Him one hour. For His soul was exceeding sorrowful even unto death, and though He asked them to tarry and watch whilst He went a little farther to pray, He found them sleeping for sorrow, and this repeatedly. It is notorious that some left out of their copies of Luke [Luke 22:43 *f.*] the verses which record the angel which appeared from heaven strengthening Him, and the conflict such that His sweat became as great drops of blood falling down on the earth; as if the Lord were lowered by such an expression of real humanity and unspeakable grief, instead of seeing how characteristic the facts are of that Evangelist, and of adoring Himself Who could so love and suffer as there portrayed. Yet John, who alone of all four writers of the Gospels was near the Lord, nearer than Matthew—John is the only one who does not describe that conflict at all: and this, not because it was not infinitely precious to his spirit, nor because the others had given it to us, but because what he gave, as they also, was by inspiration and in no way a question of human judgment or feeling. John records, no less than Matthew and Mark and Luke, the miracle of the five barley loaves; and this because it was as essential to the work given him to do as for the others in theirs. For the same reason he, led by the Holy Spirit, does not give the agony in the garden, as not falling within his assigned province. He knew it of course, and must have often dwelt on it in his spirit deeply meditative beyond all the others, yet he is silent.[235]

Can anything more attest the overruling wisdom and power of the inspiring Spirit! Yes, in every part and every detail, one as much as another, and almost as self-evident were we not so dull of hearing; nor only in what is omitted, but in what is inserted by infinite grace. Witness what our Evangelist tells us next. He brings before us the no doubt appalling spectacle of Judas availing himself of his intimate knowledge of the Saviour's habit and haunt to guide those who wished to take and slay Him. With the band and officers from His enemies, Judas guides them to the spot of nightly prayer, with lanterns and torches and weapons to make sure of their prey, though full moon shone and He had never struck a blow in self-defence. But Judas really knew not Him any more than his companions did. How terrible the sight of a soul blinded to the deadly malice at work, no less than to the Saviour's glory and His love! How surely Satan had entered when we look at him as he stood with them to betray Him!

Jesus, knowing all that was coming on Him, goes out to them, saying, Whom seek ye? And at His confession of Himself in reply to their answer of Jesus the Nazarean,[f] they went backward and fell to the ground. How manifest the proof of His intrinsic divine glory! A Man sent and come in love yet the true God, this was the constant and special testimony of John, the true key to what he does not say no less than to what he does say. Yet is there no effort, but the most charming simplicity along with this deep and divine undercurrent. Not all the treachery of Judas, not all the hatred and enmity of the Jews, not all the power of Rome could have seized the Lord had not the time arrived to give Himself up. His hour was

THE EIGHTEENTH CHAPTER

now come. He could have destroyed the company which sought to apprehend Him as easily as He caused them to fall prostrate before His name; as by and by in virtue of His name every knee shall bow, of beings in heaven and beings on earth and beings under the earth, and every tongue confess that Jesus Christ is Lord to the glory of God the Father (Philippians 2:10-11).[324]

But when He asked them again, Whom seek ye? and they said, Jesus the Nazarean, grace shone out, not power: the former now, as the latter before, expressing the true God Who was now manifesting Himself on earth in His own Person. "If then ye seek Me, leave these to go away; that the word might be fulfilled which He said, Of those whom Thou hast given Me, I have lost not one of them." Like the ark in Jordan He would go alone into the waters of death, and His own pass over dryshod. He gives Himself up freely for them[325]. The great salvation which is infallible includes every lesser one which suits and serves the glory of God meanwhile. And blessed it is to trace to the same spring of gracious power in Christ all the passing mercies we experience where His hand shields us from the enemy's malice. He puts Himself forward to endure all. His people go free; His word is fulfilled in every way. Where the Father gives, the Son loses none. What comfort and assurance before a hostile world!

But even His most honoured servants fail, and are apt to fail most where they push forward in natural zeal and their own wisdom, too self-confident to watch His ways and heed His word and thus learn of Him. So Simon Peter then displays his haste in total discord with the grace of Christ; for, having a sword, he drew it and struck Malchus,[326] the servitor of the high priest, maiming him of his right ear. Had Peter watched and prayed instead of sleeping, it might have been otherwise; when we fail to pray, we enter into temptation.

Luke alone, true to his testimony to God's grace, tells us of the Lord's answer, "Suffer ye thus far," and of His touching the ear to heal the wounded man. Matthew alone, in harmony with the rejected Messiah but true King of Israel, gives the reproof which warned His servant of what it is for saints to resist carnally. Mark mentions the fact, but no more. John, agreeably to the purpose of God in his province, presents the Lord in unfaltering obedience to His Father, as before in divine power and grace. Nothing more calm than His correction of Peter's energy; nothing more distinct than His submission to the Father's will, whatever it cost. "The cup which the Father hath given Me, shall I not drink it?"

It is the same Jesus as in Luke and the other Gospels, yet what a difference! Everywhere worthy, never a word or way beneath the Holy One of God, but here above all the Son with perfect dignity and withal entire subjection of heart in suffering as in work. May we think it was His drink now in enduring His will, as before His meat in doing it? Certainly the inward trial, to say nothing of all the outward suffering, was far deeper; yet His heart bowed to all, where to bow in obedience was infinite perfection. As the living Father sent Him, and He lived on account of the Father, so He lays down His life that He may take it again; but if He says, I have authority to lay it down and I have authority to take it again, He adds, This commandment I received of My Father. Never was such deep and holy conflict as the Second Man knew in the garden; but none of this appears in John.[327] Here it is all the power and grace and calm of the

Son with no motive but the Father's will. Never was there an approach to such glorifying of God the Father.

The believer will note the bearing of our Lord throughout these closing scenes, His lowliness and dignity, His infinite superiority to all who surrounded Him, friends or foes, His entire submission and withal His power intact. He is a man, the Sent One but Son of God throughout. It is He Who shelters and secures the disciples; it is He Who offers Himself freely. The traitor and the band, the torches and the weapons, had all failed, if He had not been pleased in letting His own go to give Himself up. For this indeed had He entered the world, and His hour was now come. But it was His own doing and according to the will of His Father, whatever man's wickedness and Satan's malicious wiles. Not more surely was it the power of His name which overwhelmed the armed crowd of His would-be captors than that His grace alone accounts for His subsequent subjection to their will.

Verses 12-27.

[Matthew 26:57-75; Mark 14:53-72; Luke 22:54-71.]

"The band therefore and the commander (chiliarch), and the officials of the Jews, took Jesus and bound Him and led (Him away)[g] unto Annas first;[328] for he was father-in-law of Caiaphas who was high priest of that year.[329] But it was Caiaphas who counselled the Jews that it was expedient (or, profitable) that one man should die[h] for the people. Now Simon Peter was following Jesus, and the[i] other disciple. And that disciple was known to the high priest,[330] and went in with Jesus into the palace of the high priest, but Peter was standing at the door outside. The other disciple therefore, that was known to the high priest, went out and spoke to the porteress and brought in Peter. The maid therefore, the porteress, saith to Peter, Art thou also of this man's disciples? He saith, I am not. But the bondmen and the officials were standing, having made a coal-fire because it was cold, and were warming themselves; and there was[j] with them Peter standing and warming himself. The high priest then asked Jesus about His disciples and about His doctrine. Jesus answered, I have openly spoken in the world, I always taught in (the)[k] synagogue and in the temple, where all[k] the Jews assemble, and in secret I spoke nothing: why askest thou Me? Ask those that have heard, what I spoke to them: behold, these know what I said. But when He said these things, one of the officials as he stood by gave Jesus a slap on the face, saying, Thus answerest Thou the high priest? Jesus answered him, If I spoke ill, testify of the ill; but if well, why smitest thou Me? Annas (therefore)[l] sent him bound unto Caiaphas the high priest. Now Simon Peter was standing and warming himself. They said therefore to him, Art thou also of His disciples? He denied and said, I am not. One of the bondmen of the high priest, being kinsman of him whose ear Peter cut off, saith, Did I not see thee in the garden with Him? Peter therefore denied again, and immediately a cock crew" (verses 12-27).

Our Evangelist notices the fact that the band led off our Lord, not only to Caiaphas the high priest, but before that to Annas his father-in-law, who had preceded him in that office, but was succeeded by Caiaphas before his death. All things were out of course, and in nothing was

THE EIGHTEENTH CHAPTER

this more evident than in the closing scenes of the Saviour. And therefore does the Gospel recall what was already recorded in chapter 11, where the highest religious office blended with the lowest expediency, and the prophetic Spirit wrought in the wicked high priest, as of old in the unprincipled prophet of Pethor. As the rule the Holy Spirit actuated holy men for God's will and glory; but exceptionally He could and did use for that glory those whom Satan was employing to thwart it as much as possible. Nothing can be more striking in Caiaphas' case than the way in which his heartless sentiment is turned by grace into the expression of a great truth wholly outside his ken.

Again we see Simon Peter following the Lord, but not in the Spirit, nor was the other disciple there to his own honour, still less to the Lord's. For he finds access to the high priest's palace, as known to that functionary, and in no way as a follower of Jesus. And how he must have soon grieved over the kindly influence he exerted to get Peter let in, who had been obliged to stay without! Little did he think that his word to the porteress would give occasion to the terrible and repeated fall of his beloved fellow-servant! But every word of the Lord must be fulfilled. It would seem that the maid who kept the door was not ignorant of John's discipleship, for she says to Peter, "Art *thou* also of this man's disciples?" But the trying question was put not to John, but to Peter; and Peter, in the garden so bold, now utterly quails before this woman. Such is man, though a saint: what is he to be accounted of? Nor is fleshly energy better really in Christ's eyes than fleshly weakness, which not only lied but denied his Master in denying his relationship to Him as a disciple. And this was warm-hearted, fervent, courageous Peter! Yes, but it was Peter tried under the shadow of the coming cross. Death is an overwhelming trial to the disciple till he knows what it is to have died with Christ to sin and law, crucified to the world which crucified Him, and able therefore to glory in the cross. It was not so yet with Peter, and he fell; nor can we say more of John and the rest than that they were not so tried. That they would have stood the test better is more than any can accept who believe what God says of them and of man in general.

The high priest pursues his investigation; Peter renews his sin. And no wonder. For he had slept when he ought to have watched and prayed, and he had ventured into the scene of temptation instead of heeding the warning of the Lord. "But the bondmen and the officials were standing, having made a coal-fire, for it was cold, and were warming themselves; and there was with them Peter standing and warming himself." Evil communications corrupt good manners; and the confession of Jesus before friends is very different from confession before bloodthirsty enemies; and Peter must learn by painful experience what he was too unspiritual to realise from the words of Christ. It is blessed to learn our nothingness and worse in His presence Who keeps from falling; but every saint, and specially every servant, must learn himself, if not there, in the bitter humiliation of what we are when we forget Him. May we abide in Him, and have His words abiding in us, and so ask what we will and have it done unto us! Peter had not thus failed before men if he had not failed before with his Master. Doubtless it is by the power of God we are kept, but this is through faith.

"The high priest[331] then asked Jesus about His disciples and about His doctrine." He desired grounds against the Lord. Was this the procedure of—one will not ask the grace which should characterise a priest, but—ordinary painstaking righteousness? It was not to screen Himself that the Lord points to His open and constant testimony. Others unlike Him might cultivate private coteries and secret instructions, not to speak of darker counsels inciting to deeds that shunned all light of day. "Jesus answered, I have openly spoken in the world, I always taught in synagogue,^m and in the temple, where all the Jews assemble; and in secret I spoke nothing:[332] why askest thou Me? Ask those that have heard what I spoke to them: behold, these know what I said." It was unanswerably true and right. The only reply was a brutal insult from a Jewish underling who would thus, as he could not otherwise, sustain the high priest.[333] But the Lord answered the low as the high with a righteous dignity immeasurably above them all: "If I spoke ill, testify of the ill; but if well, why smitest thou Me?"

So fared the Lord with the high priest: how painful the contrast of the disciple warming himself with the slaves! More than one assailed him with the crucial question, "Art thou also of His disciples?" Again the fear of man prevailed; and he who truly believed on Him did not confess but denied and said, I am not. But this was not all. For "one of the bondmen of the high priest, being kinsman of him whose ear Peter cut off, saith, Did I not see thee in the garden with Him? Peter therefore denied again, and immediately a cock crew." Oh, what fear of man bringing a snare! What blinding power of the enemy thus to involve a saint in direct and daring falsehood, and this to shame Him Who was his life and salvation! But of what is not the heart capable when the Lord is not before it, but fear or lust or aught else by which Satan beguiles? God, however, took care that the dread of man to His dishonour should cover the guilty disciple with self-reproach and contempt and utter humiliation when an eyewitness could brand him before all with his reiterated lying in denial of his Master.

It will be noticed that we have in this Gospel neither the Lord's antecedent praying for Peter and assurance of restoration, nor His turning and looking on Peter after his last denial, when he, remembering the word of the Lord, went out and wept bitterly. These are given explicitly in the only Gospel whose character they suit and sustain (see Luke 22:31-32 and 61-62). Here all turns, not on the discovery of what man's heart is, and the grace of the Lord, but on the Person of Christ as the one central object, not so much the Second Man despised by man, and the energy of His love acting on a disciple spite of utter failure in himself, but the Son of God glorifying the Father in the midst of complete and universal ruin, with friends or foes.

The Lord has been before the religious authority;[334] He is now to appear before the civil power. It was a mockery everywhere; and so it must be shown out against His Person Who will one day cut off him that privily slanders his neighbour, and will not suffer the man that has a high look and a proud heart, any more than the liar and deceiver, early destroying all the wicked of the land, and especially from the city of Jehovah {Psalm 101:5, 7-8}. Yet His glory they wist not, nor consequently His grace; yet they should not have been blind to His holy and righteous ways; but man, religious or profane, was filling up the cup of his iniquity, and the more so because of God's longsuffering.

THE EIGHTEENTH CHAPTER

VERSES 28-40.

[Matthew 27:2, 11-30; Mark 15:1-19; Luke 23:1-25.]

"They led then Jesus from Caiaphas to the prætorium;[335] and it was early; and they entered not into the prætorium that they might not be defiled but eat the Passover. Pilate then went out unto them, and saith,[n] What accusation do ye bring against this man? They answered and said to him, If this (man) were not an evil-doer, we should not have delivered Him up to thee. Pilate therefore said to them, Take ye Him, and judge Him according to your law. The Jews said to him, It is not allowed to us to put any one to death; that the word of Jesus might be fulfilled which He said signifying by what death He should die. Pilate then again entered into the prætorium, and called Jesus and said to Him, Art thou the King of the Jews? Jesus answered, Of thyself sayest thou this, or did others say (it) to thee about Me? Pilate answered, Am I a Jew? Thy nation and the chief priests delivered Thee up to me: what didst Thou? Jesus answered, My kingdom is not of this world: if My kingdom were of this world, My servants (ὑπηρ.) would fight that I might not be delivered up to the Jews; but now My kingdom is not from hence. Pilate then said to Him, Art Thou then a king? Jesus answered, Thou sayest that I am a king. I have been born for this, and for this I have come into the world, that I might bear witness to the truth. Every one that is of the truth heareth My voice. Pilate saith to Him, What is truth? And having said this, he again went out unto the Jews, and saith to them, I find no fault in Him; but ye have a custom that I should release one to you at the Passover: will ye therefore that I release to you the King of the Jews? They all cried then again, saying, Not this (man) but Barabbas. Now Barabbas was a robber" (verses 28-40).

The activity of hostile will marked the Jews, whose zeal was as great as their punctiliousness and their lack of conscience. Late and early were they at work, from one high priest to another, pushing on to the Roman governor. Bent on the blood of the Messiah, they scrupled to enter the prætorium; they must not be defiled, as they would eat the Passover and had not yet done so (verse 28).[336] Little thought they that they were but bringing about the death of the true Paschal Lamb, and so in guilty unbelief fulfilling the voice of the law to their own destruction, whatever God's purpose in His death. The hard-hearted pagan seems at first fair and just compared with the chosen nation: we shall see how at last Satan found the way to excite his unrighteousness and fix him, as them, in hopeless evil through rejecting Christ. Pilate felt that there was no proper case for him, and asks a tangible accusation (verse 29). The want of this they evade by an affected or real affront at his question, as if they could not be unjust (verse 30). The governor would gladly have thrown the responsibility on the Jews, who betray their own foregone conclusion: Jesus must die; and as death could not be lawfully at their hands, it must be by the hand of lawless men. He must die the death of the cross.

Thus was the word of Jesus to be fulfilled, signifying by what death He should die (verse 32). Compare John 3:14, 8:28, 12:32-33, (Peter) 21:18-19; also Matthew 16:21, 17:12, 22-23. Stephen might be stoned by the Jews in an outburst of religious fury, James be slain with the sword by Herod; but the Son of Man must be condemned by the Jewish chief priests and scribes, and be crucified by the Gentiles.[337] "For in truth against Thy holy servant Jesus Whom Thou anointedst, both Herod and Pontius Pilate with the nations and people of Israel were gathered together in this city to do whatsoever Thy hand and Thy counsel pre-determined should come to pass" (Acts 4:27-28). *Man* universally must prove his guilt to the last degree and the divine word be fulfilled to the letter, God Himself (we may say in the Person of His Son) being cast out in shame from His own earth; for all this and more was involved in the deliberate and fatal act. Yet was it the deepest moral glory. Now was the Son of Man glorified, and God was glorified in Him. Obedience unto death, absolute devotedness, suffering beyond measure both for righteousness and for sin, met there on the one hand; and on the other the truth, the justice, the grace and the majesty of God, were not vindicated only but glorified. Therein too Satan's power and claims were for ever annulled, and a perfect everlasting basis to God's glory was laid for the blessing of man and creation in general. Such were the fruits of Christ's death on the cross. How dense the blindness of its instruments! how dim the intelligence even of its favoured objects! How blessed the Father and the Son in love and holiness, spite of all accomplishing all!

Again the Roman (whose characteristic common sense saw through the envy and malice of the Jews, and repudiated all anxiety as to the honour or security of Cæsar) entered into the prætorium, called the Lord, and said, Art Thou the King of the Jews? He Who was silent before the high priest till adjured by the living God answered Pilate by the question, Of thyself sayest thou this; or did others say it to thee about Me? (verses 33-34). This was the turning-point. If the governor were uneasy as to the rights and interests of Cæsar, the Lord could have pointed to His uniform life as in John 6:15, and to His invariable teaching as in Luke 20:25, for a perfect disproof and reassurance. But if the question originated, as it really did, with the Jews (Luke 23:2), the Lord had nothing to say but the truth in the face of Israel's unbelief and gainsaying, nothing to do but witness the "good confession" before Pontius Pilate [1 Timothy 6:13]; and this He does with all simplicity.

The governor's answer made plain what was already sure, that the true Son of David was rejected by the Jew definitively false to the one divine hope of the nation. "Am I a Jew?" said he. "Thy nation and the chief priests delivered Thee up to me: what didst Thou?" Not one thing against which there is any law: every word, every way, testified of God. He spoke, He was, the truth, which not only detected man but presented the Father; and both were intolerable. They would have none of Him; not because He did not give every possible proof of His Messiahship, but because He put them in presence of God and of their sins, from which testimony there was no escape but the rejection of Himself. Hence the all-importance of what was in question. People and priests alike refused their own Messiah; and He bowed to it. Deeper things were meanwhile in accomplishment; and the infinite glory of His Person, already confessed by the disciples, as well as His work of eternal redemption, were about to be proclaimed in the gospel and to supersede Jewish hopes. For the gathering together in one of the scattered children of God should replace the disowned nation, till at the end of the age they shall say, Blessed is He that cometh in the name of Jehovah. Then shall the long-rejected Jesus once more and for ever recall them as His own, and bless them unchangingly, and make them a blessing to all the families of the earth.

Hence Jesus answered, "My kingdom is not of this world: if My kingdom were of this world, My servants would fight that I might not be delivered up to the Jews; but now My kingdom is not from hence" (verse 36). When the Jews repent and the Lord returns in power and glory, not only will He be revealed from heaven in flaming fire taking vengeance [2 Thessalonians 1:8], but Jerusalem be made a burdensome stone for all peoples {Zechariah 12:3}, as He bends Judah for Him and fills the bow with Ephraim [Zechariah 9:13]. But here we have Christianity, which has come in before that day with His kingdom not of this world, nor from hence but from above, where all savours of the rejected but glorified Christ, and according to the revealed knowledge of the Father, the Jews being as such outside and manifest enemies.

The governor, while satisfied that there was nothing to fear politically, could not but perceive a claim incomprehensible to his mind. "Art Thou then a king?" This the Lord could not deny. It was the truth, and He confessed it, whatever it might cost. But having done so, He set forth that which applies now. "Thou sayest I am a king. I have been born for this, and for this I have come into the world, that I might bear witness to the truth."[338] The law was given by Moses, and Jesus was the born King of the Jews. But He was conscious of another and higher glory bound up with His Person as Son of God: grace and truth came through Jesus Christ. "Every one that is of the truth heareth My voice." How solemn and unwavering the testimony! The Jews were zealous for the law, not because it was of God, but because it was theirs; the Romans sought this world and its power.

They were both blind to the eternal and unseen. Jesus was the Truth, as well as the Faithful and True Witness to it.

It may help some to remark here that "King of His Church," the favourite idea of Puritan theology, is not only unfounded but opposed to all the testimony of Scripture. Even "King of saints," as in the Textus Receptus of Revelation 15:3, must be abandoned by all who know the best reading. It should be "of the nations," though "of the ages" has excellent authority. Whichever of these may be adopted, it is certain that "of the saints" has scarce any support, as it is also foreign to Scripture and to the mind of Christ in it. "Of the nations" seems plainly drawn from, or in full accordance with, Jeremiah 10:7. Christ is King of Israel in Zion; as Son of Man all the peoples and nations and languages shall serve Him; and as Jehovah He shall be King over all the earth. But even as Head, it is written that He is so given "*to* the Church," His body, "and *over* all things" {Ephesians 1:22}; never over the Church, as men have said, who misunderstood His revealed relationships.

He adds, strange to the ears of man, not least to Roman ears: "Every one that is of the truth heareth My voice." If a man did not hear Him, he was not of the truth. How could it be otherwise if He was the Only-begotten Son, yet man on earth? What could such a One come for but for this, if He came in grace, not in judgment? And Pilate, with a "What is truth?" returns to the Jews. He did not seriously seek an answer: an awakened conscience alone does; and grace, as it produces the desire in the sinner, gives the answer of good from God. Not so Pilate, who having said this went out again to the Jews, saying: "I find no fault in Him";[339] and suggesting as a solution of the difficulty the customary release of a prisoner at the feast, he offers to let go their King. But this only draws out the depth of their hatred, and they all cry out: ... "Not this man, but Barabbas." Now Barabbas, as the Evangelist adds, was a robber. So the Jews chose Satan's "son of the father" (for so the word means). How evident that man rejecting Jesus is Satan's slave![339a]

But the Jews in their unbelief are more daringly evil than the dark heathen procurator. He, like the rest of the world, did not know anything of "truth"; they had abundant speculations, one as little satisfactory as another, no certain truth, least of all about God. The Jews knew better; and the Lord compelled them to hear what they could not deny, but would not receive. Therefore, all ended for the present in their hatred of Him up to the cross, and their avowed preference of a robber and a murderer. No flesh shall glory in His presence.

NOTES ON THE EIGHTEENTH CHAPTER

a [*Cf. Lectures Introductory to the Study of the Gospels*, pp. 558-560.]

b The variations are strange: τῶν κέδρων ℵ[corr]BCL, etc. [Treg., W. and H.], the most uncials and cursives, τοῦ κέδρου ℵ[pm]D, etc. [Tisch.], τοῦ κεδρὼν ASΔ, etc. [Lachm., Weiss, Blass]; others κένδρων, or even δένδρων.

c A few witnesses [BD, etc.] omit [as W. and H., Blass], but the most and best read ὁ Ἰησοῦς [so Tisch., Weiss: "He ... I am Jesus"].

d The best MSS. and versions omit σοῦ, "thy."

e So Mr. Ffoulkes in Smith's *Dictionary of the Bible*, i. 684.

f It seems desirable to note that the term "Nazarean" in verses 5, 7, and in chapter 19:19, is Ναζωραῖος. So it is in Matthew 2:23, 26:71; Mark 10:47; and Luke 18:37 (though both questioned); and in Acts 2:22, 3:6, 4:10, 6:14, 9:5 (though the best omit), 22:8, 24:5, and 26:9. It is the name of shame and scorn. Ναζαρηνὸς, like ἐκ Ναζαρὲτ, is an inhabitant of Nazareth, reproached or not, and occurs in Mark 1:24, 14:67, 16:6; Luke 4:34; and our Lord we have characterised as τὸν ἀπὸ Ν. in John 1:46 and in Acts 10:38.

g The oldest authorities omit.

h The bulk of MSS. support ἀπόλεσθαι, "to perish" (T.R.), but the best ἀποθανεῖν [Edd.].

i The article is omitted by some of the best witnesses [ℵ^{pm}AB; so Tisch., W. and H., Weiss].

j ℵBCLX, several cursives; Theb. Memph. Syrr.$^{pesch\ et\ hcl}$ Arm. Æth. add "also" [as W. and H., Weiss, Blass], which the rest omit.

k The article, added in T.R., with many, is omitted by the best and most; also πάντοτε, "always," the more common reading (πάντοθεν, Elz.) is inferior to πάντες, "all."

l οὖν, Elz., with BC^{pm}L, etc. [1. 33], δὲ ℵ, etc. Steph. omits, following most [AC^{corr}, etc.].

m "In synagogue," without the article, for there were many; "in the temple," with the article, for there was but one.

n ℵBC^{pm}LX, cursives, Cyr., for the T.R. "said" with most.

THE NINETEENTH CHAPTER [a]

Hard-heartedness and insult took their course, for His hour was come. Pilate took and scourged Jesus the Lord of glory; the soldiers treated their meek prisoner with the unfeeling scorn, natural in such towards One Who resisted not; yet we must look to the Jews for extreme and unrelenting hatred.

Verses 1-15.

> "Then Pilate therefore took Jesus and scourged (Him). And the soldiers platted a crown of thorns and put (it) on His head, and clothed Him with a purple garment,[340] and were coming to Him[b] and saying, Hail, King of the Jews! and gave Him slaps on the face. And Pilate went out again and saith to them, Behold, I bring Him out to you, that ye may know that I find no fault (in Him). Jesus therefore came out wearing the crown of thorns and the purple garment, and he saith to them, Behold, the man!" (verses 1-5).[341]

The Roman saw through the baseness of the people, through the craft and deadly malice of the religious chiefs; and he seems to have resorted to the unjust policy of scourging the Lord, followed up by the allowed, if not prescribed, derision of the soldiers, as a means of satisfying the Jews and letting Jesus go. Contrary to truth and righteousness, he would humour their feelings against Jesus, but he would save an innocent man if possible without loss to himself. Such is man in authority here below—at least, where Christ is concerned, or even those that are Christ's. It was the place of judgment, but wickedness was there; and the place of righteousness, but iniquity was there. There was not one spark of conscience in the judge, any more than in the accusers, or the crowd now quite carried away. There was man deceived by Satan; and God was in none of their thoughts. Pilate probably hoped that the uncomplaining endurance of such cruel mockery and scourging in their sight might perchance move the multitude and its leaders to compassion, whilst the exposed futility of the royal claims of Jesus would naturally awaken their contempt, and so in both ways further his own desire to dismiss the captive, in Whom he avowedly saw no guilt whatever. But, no! all must come out in their true colours—priests and people, learned and unlearned, civilians and soldiers, judge and prisoner. It was their hour and the power of darkness. But if man and Satan were there, so was God morally judging them all by the One they misjudged.

Still in that blind and hardened throng the Roman, unjust as he was, shines in comparison with the Jews of all ranks; and as the difficulty grew of delivering the Guiltless from their will set on destruction, we see a man in spite of himself growingly impressed with the unaccountable dignity of Him Who appeared to be at his mercy. Elsewhere, indeed, we read of his wife's dream sent to warn him on the judgment-seat; but here it is His Person, with His silence and His words alike, which increased the desire to extricate Him from unscrupulous and murderous adversaries, always despised in Pilate's eyes, never so despicable as now.

Pilate's effort, however, was vain. "Behold, the man!" had for its effect neither the pity nor the contempt intended to divert the crowd from their fell purpose, but rather to whet their rage afresh in clamouring for the Lord's death. In the ways of God He will not allow iniquity to prosper, least of all where Christ is in question. The unjust judge might abuse and insult the Lord, hoping to gratify the Jews thus far and to turn them from an aim from which even his stern and callous mind revolted as useless crime. But God, Who abhorred the horrible iniquity of them all, lets Satan ensnare them all in the consequences of their utter unbelief, and their habitually evil state—deaf to every warning and blind to the fullest testimony of moral goodness, and divine glory, and perfect grace in the holy Sufferer before them. As the judge acknowledged His innocence, yet would risk nothing on His behalf, so all commit and condemn themselves to their own ruin, stumbling over the precious Corner-stone and sure foundation as a stone disallowed by the builders [Psalm 118:22].

> "When then the chief priests and the officials saw Him, they cried, Crucify, crucify.[342] Pilate saith to them, Take ye Him, and crucify; for *I* find no fault in Him. The Jews answered, We have a law, and according to the^c law He ought to die, because He made Himself Son of God.[343] When Pilate therefore heard this word, he was the more afraid, and entered into the prætorium again, and saith to Jesus, Whence art Thou? But Jesus gave him no

answer. Pilate saith to Him, Speakest Thou not to me? Knowest Thou not that I have authority to release Thee, and I have authority to crucify Thee? Jesus answered, Thou hadst[d] no authority at all against Me except it were given thee from above: on this account he[344] that delivered Me up to thee hath greater sin" (verses 6-11).

The charge failing against the Lord as hostile to the powers of the world, His accusers now betake themselves to the still more solemn cry, He ought to die because He made Himself Son of God. And Pilate was the more afraid, but not more ready to fall in with their design, though he were a heathen and they the blasphemers of the Hope of Israel, the Holy One of God! Yes, He is going to die, but not for the lies some swore falsely against Him, but for the truth of God, the capital truth for man, the object of faith and the one source of eternal life. Having emptied Himself, He humbled Himself; but Son of God He was and is from all eternity to all eternity. Not more sure is it that man is a sinner dead to God than that Jesus is His Son; and eternal life is in Him only, yet for every soul to have that believes on Him. "He that believeth hath everlasting life." Neither is there salvation in any but Jesus, nor another name under heaven which is given among men whereby we must be saved {Acts 4:12}. But those who ought most to have welcomed Him, and most to have set forth His glory, were those who feared not to say, According to our law He ought to die, because He made Himself Son of God! Oh, how real, how darkening the power of Satan, when Jews blasphemed Him boldly, and the heathen procurator "was afraid" before Him!

Fear, however, is not faith; and in Pilate it was not more than undefined dread of the mysterious Man then on

His trial, and a strong sense that the enmity to Him was without a cause save in their ravenous will. So, entering his palace again, he inquires, Whence art Thou? and, mortified at receiving no answer, he vaunts his authority to release or to crucify Him. The Lord did not answer the one query, which had no better motive than curiosity apart from the fear of God or His love; but He replied to the second in terms worthy of His Person, in fulness of grace and truth. Truly the hour was come that the Son of Man should be glorified, and God be glorified in Him. What was the authority of a Roman governor without the will of God to sanction it? His ways, His nature, must be made good; the words were now, for the deepest of purposes, just about to be accomplished to His own glory for ever; and Jesus bowed absolutely to all.

Nevertheless, the accomplishing of divine counsels in Christ does not consecrate the will of man that cast Him out and slew Him; and God is righteous in judging the evil. "On this account he that delivered Me up to thee hath greater sin." The Gentile was wicked, the Jew worse; if Pontius Pilate were inexcusably unrighteous, how much more awful the position of Caiaphas or Judas Iscariot and of all they represented that day! If God sent His Son in infinite grace, He did not fail to present adequate proofs of Who and what He is, to leave all inexcusable for not perceiving and receiving Him; not only those who had God's outward authority in this world, but yet more those who had His living oracles that testified of His Son, Who was the centre and object of them all. Were they not witnesses of such works and words and ways as never had been known on earth, proportionately measuring the guilt of those who after such grace rejected One so glorious?

"From this (time) Pilate sought to release Him; but the Jews kept crying, saying, If thou wilt release this (man), thou art not a friend of Cæsar: every one that maketh himself a king speaketh against Cæsar. Pilate then, having heard these words, led Jesus out and sat down on (the) judgment seat[345] at a place called Pavement,[e] but in Hebrew Gabbatha. Now it was (the) preparation[f] of the Passover; it was about sixth[g] hour. And he saith to the Jews, Behold, your King. They cried therefore, Away with (Him), away with (Him); crucify Him. Pilate saith to them, Shall I crucify your King? The chief priests answered, We have no king but Cæsar" (verses 12-15).[347]

How powerless is the struggle to do right, where the world is loved, one's sins are unjudged, and grace unknown! The Jews saw through Pilate as he through them. How wretched not to have Christ for eternal life! Pilate preferred the friendship of the world to the Son of God, as the Jews saw no beauty in Him that they should admire Him; and both played their part in crucifying Him. Pilate may seek to release Jesus, may go in and out, may speak to Jesus and pour scorn on the Jews. But the last word of apostate unbelief passes their lips and closes Pilate's mouth, who will not be behind the Jews in allegiance to Cæsar. All is over now. The prince of the world comes, and though he has nothing in Christ, Christ dies rejected of man, forsaken of God, the Righteous One for our sins; never such hatred and unrighteousness as on the world's part toward Him; never such love and righteousness as on God's part toward the world in virtue of Him.

The Christ-rejecting word was passed. Their allegiance to the Roman was a lie, their mad guilt manifest in getting rid of Messiah and God Himself and all their faith and hope. The Jews abhorred subjection to Cæsar; they owned neither his right nor their own sin, which was the occasion of his supremacy. But they abhorred the Messiah more,[h] not their idea, but the reality according to God. They had not a thought nor a feeling, not a word nor a way nor a purpose, in common with Jesus; and this because He brought God near to them in grace, because He manifested man in perfect dependence and obedience to God, and their will with a bad conscience rejected both. Hence the cross was to them most repulsive. "We have heard out of the law that Christ abideth for ever; and how sayest Thou, the Son of Man must be lifted up? Who is this Son of Man?" Yet was the law plain enough that the Messiah should be rejected by man, especially by the Jew, and die that death of curse, the terrible sin of man, yet God's atoning sacrifice for sin. But will, governed by Satan to serve a present purpose in pursuance of man's lusts and passions, blinded them to His word and to their own suicidal wickedness; as ere long they were about to prove their rebelliousness to Cæsar, and have the Romans come and take away their place and nation, but not before they had filled Jerusalem with the spectacle of their own penalty till there was no room left for more crosses, and wood failed to make them: so Josephus.

Verses 16-30.

[Matthew 27:31-50; Mark 15:20-37; Luke 23:26-46.]

Verses 16-27.

"Then therefore he delivered Him up to them that He might be crucified. They took then Jesus[i] (and led (Him) away); and bearing for Himself the cross He went out[348] unto the place called of a

Skull, which is called in Hebrew Golgotha, where they crucified Him, and with Him two others, on this side and on that, and Jesus in the middle. And also Pilate wrote a title and put (it) on the cross; and there was written, Jesus the Nazarean, the King of the Jews.³⁴⁹ This title therefore many of the Jews read, because the place where Jesus was crucified was near the city; and it was written in Hebrew, in Greek, in Latin. Therefore said the high priest of the Jews to Pilate, Write not, The King of the Jews, but that He said, I am King of the Jews. Pilate answered, What I have written I have written" (verses 16-22).

Faith alone preserves from the power and wiles of the devil. Pilate and the Jews were wholly opposed in their thoughts and wishes; but God was not in the thoughts of the one more than of the others. They had each his own way, but all astray; and now they show themselves the open enemies of righteousness as well as of grace, incapable of discerning the clearest ways, marks, and proofs of God present in love to man, no matter how low He might come down. The cross of Christ makes all and every one manifest. Pilate under pressure of fear for his own worldly interests gave up Jesus to their malice, though knowing Him innocent; and He bearing His cross went forth to the place of a Skull, Golgotha, in Latin "Calvary." There was He crucified with peculiar indignity, a robber also on either hand, as a robber had been preferred to Him. Yet God took care that even there a fitting testimony, from whatever motive in Pilate's breast, should be rendered to Him in the inscription on the cross; the despised man of Nazareth was the Messiah. Where were the Jews if He was their King? The keenest adversaries of the true God, blindly fulfilling

His terrible prophecies of their unbelief and wickedness under a self-complacent zeal for His name and law. There stood His title, read by many; for the place was near the city, written in the tongues not of the officials only, nor of the polite world, but of the Jews too; and all the efforts of their high priests but riveted it to the cross under the pertinacious and irritated and scornful spirit of the procurator.

But the lowest played their part at the cross as well as the highest, men used to arms no less than the ministers of the sanctuary; and every class, every man, showed out there what each was in selfish indifference to the grace and glory of the Son of God, Who suffered Himself to be numbered with the transgressors.

> "The soldiers therefore, when they crucified Jesus, took His garments and made four parts, to each soldier a part, and the vest; but the vest was seamless from the top woven through the whole.[350] They said therefore unto one another, Let us not rend it, but let us draw lots for it whose it shall be; that the scripture might be fulfilled that saith, They parted My garments for themselves, and for My vesture they cast lots. The soldiers therefore did these things" (verses 23-24).

Little thought the soldiers who had charge of the execution beyond their poor perquisites. But God's eye was now as ever on His Son, and He had taken care in His word to mark it. For in one of the most manifestly Messianic psalms (Psalm 22:18) stands written, a thousand years beforehand, the minute prediction of the soldiers' appropriating the garments of the Saviour in a way unmistakably applicable to Him. He is the object of Scripture, though unbelief sees it not and has a will against it, because His Person is as unknown as our own need of divine mercy in the cross. With what interest the Holy Spirit contemplated, as we should, every detail of His suffering, and of man's behaviour at that hour! God counted Him not less worthy because He was made the object of such indignities. To make them known beforehand was of all moment. The very minuteness of what is mentioned bears witness to the accurate reality of the prophecy. He is the demonstrated as well as rejected Messiah. His glory made it due to Him to name the particulars, which also bear witness to the depth of His grace in humiliation, that God and man might be fully shown out, and that the words of the Psalmist be proved His word in the face of every gainsayer.

But faith and love gathered near the dying Saviour some of very different mind.

> "Now by the cross of Jesus stood His mother, and the sister of His mother, Mary the (wife) of Clopas, and Mary of Magdala.[351] Jesus therefore, seeing His mother and the disciple standing by whom He loved, saith to His mother, Woman, behold, thy son. Next He saith to the disciple, Behold, thy mother;[351a] and from that hour the disciple took her unto his own (home)" (verses 25-27).

These were among the women who had followed Him in His ministry and had ministered to Him in life. There they stood in His rejection by the cross, where the Lord shows how little asceticism rises to the truth. He had been absorbed in the work for which He was sent by the Father; no honey mingled with the offering, any more than leaven: salt was never absent, nor the unction of the Holy Ghost. All had been in the consecrating power

THE NINETEENTH CHAPTER

of the word and Spirit of God, and to God. But perfect human affections were there, though the work undertaken in communion with the Father had filled heart and lips and hands with the higher object to the glory of God. Yet eternal interests, when thus taken up, do not efface or dishonour nature or its relationships according to God; and the Lord here marks this by commending in the most solemn and touching way John to His mother as son, and Mary to John as mother: a loving trust honoured from that hour. How sweet for the loved disciple to remember and record! And how strong the contrast with superstition, no less than as we have seen with asceticism! And what a testimony in all to His own entire superiority to overwhelming circumstances!

Verses 28-30.

> "After this Jesus, knowing that all things were now finished, that the scripture might be accomplished, saith, I thirst [Psalm 69:21]. A vessel (therefore) was standing there full of vinegar; and they, having filled a sponge with vinegar and put hyssop round (it), put (it) up to His mouth. When therefore Jesus received the vinegar, He said, It is finished, and bowing His head delivered up His spirit" (verses 28-30).

It is not only that in human tenderness He provides for all left behind in that supreme moment, but He thinks of Scripture in spirit or in terms not yet fulfilled. No doubt there is the distressing physical effect expressed of all that mind and heart and body had endured till then; but His last request is here bound up, not with His want only, but with His undying zeal for the word if only a single thing lacked to make it honourable. Every word that proceeds through God's mouth must be fulfilled;

and had He not said of Messiah, "My tongue cleaveth to My jaws," and "In My thirst they gave Me vinegar to drink"? Then, having drunk, the Saviour says, "It is finished," with a divine calm as perfect here as His expression is given elsewhere of His unfathomable suffering.

Of none but Jesus is it or could it be said that He gave up (παρέδωκεν) the spirit, which is wholly distinct from the "expired" (ἐξέπνευσεν) of Mark and Luke, confounded with the former by our translators. To expire could apply to any one's death, the blessed Lord being man as truly as any other; to give the spirit up, as said in John, expresses His divine glory though a dying man, as the One Who had title to lay down His life no less than to take it again. So Matthew implies Who the dying Messiah was in "He dismissed the spirit" (ἀφῆκε τὸ πν.). Nor can words be more characteristic of Luke than "Father, into Thy hands I commit My spirit," nor of John than "It is finished." He was man, though God; He was God though man; and both in one Person.

The reader will remark how perfectly the account of the Lord's death suits the general character and special design of John's Gospel and of no other. Here Jesus is the conscious Son, the divine Person Who made all things, but became flesh that He might not only give eternal life but die as a propitiation for our sins. And here, therefore, here only, He said, "It is finished, and bowing His head delivered up His spirit." There are witnesses, as we shall see, but they are of God, not of man or the creature, and they intimately flow from His own Person. No darkness is mentioned, no cry that His God had forsaken Him, no rending of the veil, no earthquake, no centurion's confession; all of which meet to proclaim the rejected Messiah (Matthew 27). So substantially, save the earthquake, the Servant Son of God obedient to death in Mark 15. Luke 23 adds the testimony to His grace in the crucified robber, His firstfruits in Paradise, and the centurion's witness to "Jesus Christ the righteous," after He had committed His spirit into His Father's hands. It was reserved for John to set forth His death Who was God not less surely than man, and as such. The Creator but man lifted up from the earth could say, in dying for sin to God's glory, "It is finished." The work, the infinite work, was done for the putting away of sin by His sacrifice. Thereon hangs not only the blessing of every soul that is to be justified by faith but of new heavens and new earth wherein dwelleth righteousness. "It is finished," τετέλεσται: one word! yet what word ever contained so much?

But no heathen were more blinded and obdurate than God's ancient people who take the lead against Jesus in an unbelieving religiousness without true fear of God, and who, consequently, saw not that they were but accomplishing His word in their guilty rejection of His and their Messiah.

Verses 31-37.

> "The Jews therefore, since it was the preparation, that the bodies might not remain on the cross on the Sabbath (for the day of that Sabbath[j] was great),[352] asked of Pilate that their legs might be broken, and they be taken away. The soldiers therefore came and broke the legs of the first and of the other that was crucified with Him; but coming to Jesus, when they saw that He was already dead, they broke not His legs, but one of the soldiers with a spear thrust His side, and there came out immediately blood and water. And he

that hath seen hath borne witness, and his witness is true, and he knoweth[353] that he saith true, that ye also[k] may believe. For these things came to pass that the scripture might be fulfilled, Not a bone of Him shall be crushed; and again another scripture saith, They shall look on Him[354] Whom they pierced" (verses 31-37).

In the Law, the Psalms, and the Prophets the Spirit of God had Christ before Him, and in the sufferings to come on Him, as well as in the glories that should follow. But the fleshly mind, as it shrinks from sufferings, is disposed to overlook and get rid of testimony; especially so if the sufferings be the effect and the proof of man's evil estate, for this is of all things most unpalatable. Thus was the Jew dull to see what condemned himself and levelled him morally to the condition of any other sinner; and rejecting the fullest evidences and Christ's own presence in divine grace and truth and the gospel at last, he was given over to judicial hardening when wrath came on them to the uttermost. Christ alone gives the key to the paschal lamb; Christ is the main object in the Psalms. No reasoning of sceptics, even if theologians, can efface the truth, though it exposes their own unbelief; and assuredly if the heart were made right by grace, it would desire that to be true which is the truth, instead of stumbling at the word being disobedient, or neglecting it because of indifference. In vain, then, do the Rosenmüllers and the like hesitate or avow their dislike of the type and the allusion. To faith it is food and strength and joy; for if God's word is instinct with His delight in Christ giving Himself to die, He also expresses it in every sort of form beforehand that the very facts of His atoning death, the great stumbling-block, might render the most irrefragable testimony to its truth and His glory, when thus manifested here below in shame, to man's shame and everlasting contempt.

How marvellously meet in Christ's cross the proud enmity of the Jew, the lawless hand of the Gentiles, the determinate counsel and foreknowledge of God, and this in perfect grace to the guiltiest of Jews and Gentiles! For out of Christ's pierced side came forthwith blood and water.[l] And John was not so preoccupied with the Saviour's dying charge concerning Mary as not to mark the sight. In the strongest form he lets us know that what we saw and testified was no mere transient fact but before the mind as present, of permanent interest and importance. In his First Epistle (5:6) he characterises the Lord accordingly. "This is He that came through (διὰ) water and blood, Jesus Christ; not in (ἐν) the power of water only, but in the power of water and blood. And it is the Spirit that beareth witness, because the Spirit is truth." Moral purification, however needed and precious, is not enough; there must be expiation of sins also; and both are found by faith in the death of Christ, not otherwise nor elsewhere. As a fact, in the Gospel the order is blood and water; as applied to us in the Epistle it is the water and the blood, and the Spirit as One personally given follows.[m] Nothing but death flows to man from Adam: Christ, the Second Man Who died for sin and sinners, is the source alike of purification and of atonement to the believer, who needs both and is dead before God without both. For though the Son of God with life in Himself, He stands alone till He dies; dying He bears much fruit. He quickens, purifies, and expiates; and the Holy Ghost consequently given brings us into the import of His death as well as blessing resulting from it. For it is judgment pronounced and executed by

God in His cross on the flesh, but in our favour, because in Him Who was a sin-offering.

No wonder, then, that John was inspired to record the fact, not more wondrous in itself than in its consequences now made known to the believer. The salvation must be suited to and worthy of the Saviour. If He was eternal, it was everlasting; if divine judgment fell on such a Victim, it was that they believing Him should not come into judgment but have life, being forgiven all their offences and made meet for the inheritance of the saints in light {Colossians 1:12}. Such is the declared standing of every true Christian, but it is in virtue of Christ, Who is all and in all. Creeds and theological systems enfeeble and hinder its enjoyment; but all this, and more than one could here develop, is clearly and plainly revealed to faith in Scripture, as it is indeed due to Christ's glory in Person and work.

Hence the care with which the word of God is cited and shown to be punctually fulfilled. "For these things came to pass that the scripture might be fulfilled, Not a bone of Him shall be crushed [Exodus 12:46]; and again another scripture saith, They shall look on Him Whom they pierced [Zechariah 12:10]."[n] The natural circumstances of the crucifixion, more especially on a Friday, and that Friday the eve of Sabbath in the paschal week, would have called for the breaking of the legs as a *coup de grâce*. And, in fact, such was the portion of the two malefactors. But Jesus, as He had proved Himself in the preceding chapter the willing Captive, was now the willing Victim; and this was made manifest in His dying as and when He did die. For it surprised not only the Jews and the soldiers, but Pilate, as we learn elsewhere; and it superseded all need of the *crurifragium* in His case. But it marked the separated Lamb of God, the Righteous

One, all Whose bones Jehovah keeps, not one of them broken.

Yet this very exemption led as a fact, doubtless, to the deed of the soldier, whose lance pierced not the malefactors but only the dead body of the Saviour, wholly ignorant that so it must be, for God had said it by His prophet. All was ordered and measured; even these minute differences were revealed beforehand; yet were men and Satan indulging freely their enmity against the Son of God. And in the face of such love and light men combine their ignorance° with their learning to escape from the truth into the dark once more. But we need not here dwell on such things. It is the same spirit that surrounded the cross:

> "Thy love, by man so sorely tried,
>   Proved stronger than the grave;
>   The very spear that pierced Thy side
>   Drew forth the blood to save."

Verses 38-42.

[Matthew 27:57-61; Mark 15:42-47; Luke 23:50-55.]

"And after these things Joseph from Arimathea, being a disciple of Jesus[354a] but a secret one for fear of the Jews, asked Pilate that he might take away the body of Jesus; and Pilate gave leave. He[p] came therefore and took His body away. And there came also Nicodemus, that came at first to Him[p] by night, bringing a mixture of myrrh and aloes about a hundred pound (weight). They took therefore the body of Jesus and bound it in linen swathes with the spices, as it is the Jews' custom to prepare for burial.[q] Now there was in the place where He was crucified a garden, and in the garden a new tomb in which no one was ever yet laid."³⁵⁴ᵇ There then on account of the preparation of the Jews, because the tomb was near, they put Jesus"³⁵⁵ (verses 38-42).

God uses a perilous time to call forth His own hidden ones. Joseph of Arimathea can be a secret disciple no longer. He was a rich man (Matthew 27) and an honourable counsellor (Mark 15); but wealth and position make the confession of Christ only the harder. Fear of the Jews had hitherto prevailed. The death of Jesus, which caused others to fear, made Joseph bold. He had not consented, indeed, to the counsel and deed of the Jews. Now he goes to Pilate and besought the Lord's body. Nor was he alone: Nicodemus, longer known, but with no happy reputation for moral courage at the first, though afterwards venturing a remonstrance to the haughty yet unjust Pharisees, joins in the last offices of love with an abundant offering of myrrh and aloes. The cross of Christ, so stumbling to unbelief, exercises and manifests his faith; and the twain, waxing valiant by grace, fulfil the lack of service of the twelve. They take the body of Jesus and bind it in linen swathes with the spices, in the manner of the Jews to prepare for burial. Egypt had its custom of embalming; so in a measure had the Jews in hope of the resurrection of the just. No prophecy is cited here; but who can forget Isaiah's words: "He made His grave with the wicked (men) and with the rich (man) in His death"? He was "appointed His grave with the lawless, and was with the rich man in His death" [Isaiah 53:9]—that is, after being slain: a strange combination, yet verified in Him; and who could wonder, seeing that He had done no violence and no deceit was in His mouth? And now we see in Joseph's garden, hard by the fatal scene, a new tomb which had never known an inmate. So had God provided, in honour for the body of His Son and in jealous wisdom for the truth, hewn out in the rock (as Matthew, Mark, and Luke tell us). There the Lord was put meanwhile in view of more formal burial when the Sabbath should pass. So little did the disciples anticipate what the glory of the Father had at heart, though the Lord had so often plainly revealed it, till the Resurrection was a fact in its own predicted time.

NOTES ON THE NINETEENTH CHAPTER

a [*Cf. Lectures Introductory to the Study of the Gospels*, pp. 561-563.]

b Such is the reading of אBLUXΛΠ, more than twenty cursives, and nearly all the ancient versions, followed by the chief editors. The clause [through homœoteleuton] is omitted in T.R., with most uncials and cursives.

c אBD^{suppl}LΔ, most It. Vulg., etc., omit ἡμῶν, which the rest give.

d So in BΓΔ and six more uncials, most cursives, etc. [most Edd.]. But ἔχεις, "hast" [Tisch.], in אAD^{suppl}LXYΛΠ, a dozen cursives, etc.

e In later Greek τὸ λιθόστρωτον was said for tessellated work or mosaic used for the floors of buildings, public or domestic, and very particularly for the tribunal of a Roman in the execution of his office. So Julius Cæsar, on his military expeditions, regularly carried such a mosaic with him, as Suetonius tells us (cap. 46). The Chaldee word גַּבְּתָא seems to be from a Hebrew root, גָּבַה, "to be high" (*cf.* Geba, Gibeah, Gibeon, etc.). The one apparently refers to the flooring, the other to the elevated platform, unless Lightfoot's idea be well founded, who derives G. from גַּב, "a surface," and hence regards the Greek and Hebrew words as equivalents.

f No matter of fact in the Gospel has been debated more keenly or with wider differences among men of piety and learning than this of παρασκευὴ τοῦ πάσχα in connection with chapter 18:28, which doubtless disposes a modern or Gentile reader at first sight to conceive that the Lord must have observed the Passover and instituted His own Supper on the day before the time followed by the Jews. On the other hand, it is no less plain that according to the three Synoptic Gospels the Lord partook of the Passover with the disciples at the regular season, 14th Nisan. Hence there have not been wanting those who have dared to reject the narrative of John, whilst a still greater number have fallen into the opposite error and treated the earlier Evangelists as confounding the meal with the Passover. Not a few, like the late Dean of Canterbury, Dean Alford, give up the question in despair as to us insoluble. The truth is, that all these contending parties start with the error of forgetting the obvious and certain fact that the Jews reckon the day from evening to evening; and that hence *it is all a mistake to suppose that the Lord took the Passover with the disciples on one day and suffered the next* [Neander, Meyer, Godet, Weiss, Ellicott, Westcott, Sanday]. So it would be to our Western habit of thought, but not so according to the Jews nurtured in the law. It was on our Thursday they ate, and on our Friday He suffered; but to the Jews it was one and the same day. Hence there was still time for such Jews as had been too much occupied with the mock trial and condemnation of our Lord to eat the Passover if they did not legally defile themselves meanwhile. The preparation of the Passover does not mean the 13th but the 14th Nisan. It was the day before the Paschal Sabbath, which was on this occasion a double one, and so of peculiar sanctity. Hence Matthew {27:62}, speaking of this Sabbath, says, ἥτις ἐστὶν μετὰ

NOTES ON THE NINETEENTH CHAPTER

τὴν παρασκευήν, as Mark {15:42} explains παρασκευὴ ὅ ἐστιν προσάββατον, or Sabbath eve. This seems conclusive in reconciling the statements of the fourth Gospel with those of the other three. The painful fact is the unbelief that exposed so many persons eminent for erudition and even for godliness to such hasty and careless discussion of Scripture. Had they held firmly the inspired character of the holy writings, they would at least have avoided error and irreverence if they could not clear up the difficulty.

g It is well known that not Nonnus only in his poetical paraphrase of our Gospel gives "third" hour, but also five uncials and four cursives, either in the original text or in a correction, not to speak of less direct authorities. Still, the weight of witnesses is overwhelming for ἕκτη, "sixth." It would seem that *our Evangelist adopted a different reckoning of hours, from midnight to noon, as we do.* Certainly the Romans did for their civil day (see Pliny, *Naturalis Historia*, ii. 79; Censorinus, *De Die Natali*, xxiii; Aulus Gellius, *Noctes Atticae*, iii. 2; and Macrobius, *Saturnalia*, i. 3). And it suits all the mentions of hours in the Gospel of John excellently, besides falling in with Mark's third, sixth, and ninth hours of the natural day from the sun. This serves to explain the otherwise singular message of Pilate's wife (Matthew 27:19), in which she spoke of suffering much "to-day in a dream because of Him." To Procula, as a Roman, the day was reckoned from midnight; as the hours appear to be throughout our Gospel, but not in the Synoptists.

It is singular, as showing the perplexity in minds of old as now, that Jerome says in his breviary on Psalm 77: "Sic scriptum est in Matthæo et Ioanne quod Dominus noster hora sexta crucifixus sit. Rursus scriptum est in

Marco: quid hora tertia crucifixus sit. Error scriptorum fuit; sed multi episemum Græcum ϛ putaverunt esse γ: sicut et ibi error fuit scriptorum: ut pro Asaph, Isaiam scriberent" (Hieronymus, *Opera Omnia*, vii., 1046, ed. Migne). Jerome's remedy was thus to correct the text, not of John [as Wesley, into "third"], but of Mark—a correction of but one known cursive manuscript of the eleventh century, the margin of the later Syriac, and the Æth., on which last says Bode (*Pseudocritica Millio-Bengeliana*, 265): " Habet omnino Æth. *sexta hora*, idque ex Io. 19, 14. Nimirum Interpres Ioanni contradicere noluit." But it is the just retribution of these tamperings with Scripture that they do *not* satisfy the desired aim; for John connects *his* sixth hour with what was before—possibly hours before—the hours specified by Mark, be it sixth or even third. Thus the violence done to the surest authority in Mark would no more reconcile the statements than the similar violence offered to the witnesses of John 19:14; for Mark specifies the time when our Lord was crucified as the *third* hour, John speaks of the time when Pilate took his seat on the tribunal to give sentence as *about the sixth* hour. To change the latter to the third, or the former to the sixth, if admissible in the face of the gravest adverse evidence, would not clear the truth, but only give birth to fresh confusion. [Cf. Westcott and Hort's *Select Readings*, p. 90.]

The true state of the readings also thoroughly overthrows the efforts of some eminent Greeks and Latins, who try to explain the earlier hour as applicable to the Jewish outcry for the crucifixion, the later hour as the actual moment when the soldiers carried it into effect. But this is only neglect of Scripture; for John predicates "about the sixth hour" of the outcry, Mark "the third hour" of the actual crucifixion. As there is no sufficient reason to doubt the accuracy of the seemingly conflicting texts of the second and fourth Gospels (in itself no mean evidence that the apparent discrepancy exhibits the genuine readings of both), and as the very slight variation of readings is easily accounted for by the desire thus to reduce them to harmony, the natural solution is that John's reckoning of time differs from that of the other Evangelists. It will be found by comparing the various hours named in John 1:39, 4:6, 52, that the hours of the civil day suit as well after all as those of the natural (the last occasion apparently better), so as to confirm the different computation of John throughout. John 11:9 in no way opposes this, as being a general way of describing a working day, whatever the mode of computation—as, for instance, *we* can say so, who follow the style of the civil day from midnight. [*Cf.* Edersheim, *The Temple*, etc., p. 245, and note appended below, No. 346.]

h "Jesum negant usque eo ut omnino Christum negent." {"They deny Jesus, until they deny the Christ completely."} (Bengel, *Gnomon Novi Testamenti, in loco.*)

i Thus end BLX, etc. [Edd. in general]. But most with DE, etc., add "and led." [Blass brackets the words.] A, etc., support T.R. ℵ supports the same sense in a peculiar form.

j ἐκείνου Stephens, ℵABD[suppl]LXY, nine more uncials, the great bulk of cursives, etc.; ἐκείνη Elz. with a late uncial (H) and a few cursives, Vulg., etc.

k The oldest read καὶ, which T.R. [as Blass] omits, with seven uncials and most cursives.

l Euthymius Zigabenus (*Commentarius in quatuor Evangelia*, III. 619, ed. C. F. Matthaei) thus writes; Ὑπερφυὲς τὸ πρᾶγμα, καὶ τρανῶς διδάσκον, ὅτι ὑπὲρ ἄνθρωπον ὁ νυγείς, ἐκ νεκροῦ γὰρ ἀνθρώπου, κἂν μυριάκις νύξῃ τίς, οὐκ ἐξελεύσεται αἷμα. "The fact was supernatural, and clearly teaches that He Who was pierced was more than man. For from a dead man, if one should pierce him ten thousand times, no blood would come out." What follows is a poor effort to connect with it Genesis 2, or even false doctrine when he speaks of two baptisms: one by blood, martyrdom; the other by water, regeneration, by whose stream the stream of sin is overwhelmed. How constant is one's disappointment in these Greek and Latin ecclesiastics! Like the Galatians, if they begin by the Spirit, how quickly they pass into a vain effort after perfection by flesh! Not one even of the ablest and most orthodox adheres simply and thoroughly to the delivering gospel of God's grace, though many of them loved the Lord and hated known error. But the full efficacy of redemption was unknown to anyone, so far as I can speak.

It is curious, by the way, that a modern work of reputation like Dr. Smith's *Dictionary of Greek and Roman Biography* should continue to repeat that "the Greek original (? of this work on the four Gospels) has never been printed" (vol. ii. 125, col. 1). So one understands the writer. Matthaei's work appeared at Leipzig in 1792, and is familiar to students.

m [*Cf. An Exposition of the Epistles of John the Apostle*, p. 62.]

n Dr. Thomas Randolph, in his little work on *The Prophecies and other Texts, cited in the New Testament, compared with the Hebrew Original, and the Septuagint*

NOTES ON THE NINETEENTH CHAPTER

Version (4to., Oxford, 1782), remarks (p. 32) that "the Evangelist here plainly reads אליו instead of אלי in the Hebrew: but so also read forty Hebrew MSS. And that this is the true reading appears by what follows—'and they shall mourn for Him.' The Syriac renders it, 'they shall look on Me through Him, whom they have pierced.' The Sept. I cannot make sense of."

Now there is really no serious doubt that the true reading is the latter ("to Me"), not the former ("to Him"), and that the best and most MSS. and versions are justified. It was in fact originally nothing but a marginal correction, due to the desire partly of eliminating so strong a testimony to the deity or Jehovah title of the Lord Jesus, partly of easing the flow of the context from the concurrence of "Me" and "Him." Even the Targum and the Talmud, like the more ancient MSS., and all the Greek early versions, refute the idea. So even most of the better Jewish expositors, notwithstanding their controversy with Christians and in the course of it. De Rossi suggests that "to Him" may have entered by accident through the scribe having Psalm 34:6 in mind. Much better and wiser, therefore, would it have been to have adhered to ancient and good authority, spite of seeming difficulty, than to have adopted this Jewish *keri* like Newcome and Boothroyd, and so to help on such a humaniser as Ewald. Even R. Isaac, in his *Chizzuk Emunah*, when controverting those whom he calls the Narazines, admits the reading אֵלַי, though he tries to weaken its force by interpreting אֵת אֲשֶׁר as "because of him whom they pierced" and applying it to the war of Gog and Magog. Now it is true that אֵת אֲשֶׁר may and does sometimes mean "because" (and so the LXX took the words, probably also confounding דָּקַר with רָקַד which might originate κατωρχήσαντο); but the meaning cannot possibly be "because of Him Whom," for this would leave the verb without an object contrary to invariable Hebrew idiom. Hence also Radak's (or R. D. Kimchi's) translation fails, "because they have pierced," though less objectionable, perhaps, as not foisting in an expressly false object. But they both divert from the true object; and therefore Abarbanel, Aben Ezra, Alshech, etc., condemn it, and so far confirm our Authorised Version. Rashi (*i.e.*, R. Solomon) is no bad proof of the perplexity the clause presents to the Jewish mind; for he inconsistently applies it to Messiah ben-Joseph in his comment on the Talmud, whereas in his *Commentary on the Bible* he gets rid of this, applying it to some of the Jews pierced and killed by the Gentiles. It is the more surprising in the face of all, that these exploded mistakes should be reproduced in modern Jewish versions; as when Dr. A. Benisch, like D. Kimchi, omits the object in his *School and Family Bible*, and Mr. J. Leeser, in his *Holy Scriptures* supplies "every one," to the manifest falsification of the sense like R. Isaac. There is really an emphatic object in the Hebrew text, which accounts for (if it does not require) the change of construction in the foregoing clause. The conclusion, then, is that the Evangelist read no otherwise than we do in the ordinary Hebrew, and that the Holy Spirit in the Gospel and the Revelation does not cite but suppose that text, which is distinctly applied to the fact carefully recorded in the history, and doctrinally employed in John's First Epistle.

o It may be worth mentioning as a singular instance of the importance of knowing the original that Euthymius Zigabenus, in his comment on verse 37, speaks of the scripture as probably got rid of by the Jews since the Gospel. "For nowhere is it found now; or he means another scripture of the books called Apocryphal" (vol. iii., 621). This sounds strong with Zechariah 12:10 in view. How is it to be accounted for? This Greek monk read the prophet in the Septuagint, where the clause as to the piercing is miserably mistaken, ἀνθ' ὧν κατωρχήσαντο, "because they insulted (Me)," while the later Jewish rendering of Aquila evades the truth by giving σὺν ᾧ. Theodotion has rendered the passage rightly on the whole. Hence the Spirit of God (both in John's Gospel and in the Revelation) does not cite the Septuagint, but alludes to it in terms which accurately represent the clause.

p Tischendorf now [followed by Blass] adopts the plural "they" with ℵ^pm, etc.; also αὐτὸν, "Him," instead of τὸ σῶμα αὐτοῦ as in ℵ^corr.BLXΛ, ten cursives, etc. [Treg., W. and H., Weiss], or τ. σ. τοῦ Ἰ. with a dozen uncials and most cursives, etc., and in T.R.; so in verse 39, the best give "to Him," the majority "to Jesus."

q The word is not θάπτειν but ἐνταφιάζειν, which is used for embalming, or at least preparing for burial as in the case before us.

THE TWENTIETH CHAPTER [a]

As no created eye beheld what was deepest in the cross of Christ, so it was not for man to look on the Lord rising from among the dead. This was as it should be. Darkness veiled Him giving Himself for us in atonement. Man saw not that infinite work in His death; yet was it not only to glorify God thereby, but that our sins might be borne away righteously. We have seen the activity of the world, and especially of the Jew, in crucifying Him; high and low, religious and profane, all played their part; even one apostle denied Him, as another betrayed Him to the murderous priests and elders. But Jehovah laid on Him the iniquity of us all; Jehovah bruised and put Him to grief; Jehovah made His soul an offering for sin [Isaiah 53:6, 10]; and as this was Godward, so was it invisible to human eyes, and God alone could rightly bear witness, by whom He would, of the eternal redemption thus obtained, which left divine love free to act even in a lost and ungodly world.

So with the resurrection of Christ. He was raised up from the dead by the glory of the Father; God raised up Jesus Whom the Jews slew and hanged on a tree; He had laid down His life that He might take it again, in three days raising the temple of His body which they destroyed. But if no man was given to see the act of His rising from the dead, it was to be testified in all the world as well as His atoning death. "Preach the gospel," said He risen, "to every creature" [Mark 16:15]. And assuredly he who withholds His resurrection maims the glad tidings of its triumphant proof and character, and compromises the believer's liberty and introduction into the new creation, as he immensely clouds the Lord's glory: even as the denial of resurrection virtually charges God's witnesses with falsehood, and makes faith vain. So the Apostle insists in 1 Corinthians 15. Had death held the Saviour fast, all were lost; had it been only His spirit winning its way into the presence of God, would it be even a half-deliverance? His resurrection is, in truth, a complete deliverance, of which the Holy Spirit is to us the seal.

Hence we find it is the grand foundation truth of the gospel. To be a witness of His resurrection was the main requirement for an apostle (Acts 1); and that God had raised up Jesus Whom the Jews had crucified was the truth most pressed by Peter (Acts 2). So it was urged by him in Solomon's porch subsequently (Acts 3) and before the Jewish council once and again (Acts 4, 5). Just so it was in preaching to the Gentiles (Acts 10); and by Paul yet more than by Peter (Acts 13). This witness especially grieved the Sadducean chiefs (Acts 4); this is what rouses the undying scorn or opposition of unbelief all the world over. And no wonder; for if the Resurrection be the spring of joy and ground of assured salvation to the believer, if it be the secret of his holy walk as the expression of the life he has in Christ risen, and the power of a living hope, it is also the measure of the real estate of man as dead in sins; as it is the present, fixed, and constant pledge that judgment hangs over the habitable earth, for God has raised from among the dead as its appointed Judge the Man Whom the world slew [Acts 17:31]. The Resurrection, therefore, is as repulsive to man as it is apt to be slighted by the fleshly mind even of Christians who seek earthly things.

As the Resurrection is thus manifestly a truth of capital moment, the Spirit of God has taken care that the testimony to it should be as precise as it is full. Hence Matthew, who from the design of his Gospel omits the Ascension, does not fail to bring out the proof of Christ's resurrection most clearly; and so does Mark; and Luke, with more detail than either, shows us the Lord in resurrection with all His loving interest in His own. He is a man as truly as ever, with flesh and bones, capable of eating with them, but risen. John, as usual, presents the conscious Son of God, the Word become flesh, but now in resurrection. Here the proofs are characteristically inward and personal, where the others as fittingly present what was outward but no less necessary.

As a bulwark against philosophic scepticism the Resurrection stands firm and impregnable; for it resists and refutes unanswerably the sophistry which ignores God and reduces the idea of causes to an invariable antecedence of constantly observed phenomena as in sequence—a theory quietly assumed and diligently instilled, so as to set aside the very possibility of divine intervention whether in grace or judgment, in miracles or prophecy, or in any relationship beyond nature with God. With God did I say? Why, according to this system logically carried out, He is, and must be, unknown; but if unknown, who can tell if He exist? or if all do not end in a mere deification of nature? Now the resurrection of

THE TWENTIETH CHAPTER

Christ rests, as has been often shown, on far fuller evidence and surer and better grounds than any event in history; and this because it was sifted at the time by friends and foes as nothing else ever was, and because God Himself gave a multiplicity of testimony, proportioned to its incalculable moment, not to us merely but to His own glory. Now as a fact without argumentation, it overthrows of itself and instantly every opposition to the truth of science or knowledge falsely so called; for it would be the depth of absurdity to suppose that the death of Jesus was the cause of His resurrection. What then was its cause? Of what antecedent was it the sequence? If anything points to the power of God, it is resurrection no less than creation.

The truth is that the effort to reduce cause and effect to a mere antecedent and consequent springs from the desire to get rid of God altogether; for cause really implies will, design, and power in activity, though we must distinguish between the *causa causans* {causing cause} and the *causæ causatæ* {caused causes}. These causes are in nature by God's constitution, but He lives, wills, acts. Hence the resurrection of Christ stands in the midst of this world's history to judge all unbelief, viewed now as a simple fact most fully proved. We may see its consequences, as far as our chapter presents them, later on. The Lord had distinctly and often spoken of His death and resurrection during His life. He had died and was buried; and here we learn that no power or precaution prevailed against His word. The grave had lost its inmate; and this was all Mary's heart took in—the loss of the dead body of the Lord. Deplorable forgetfulness, but of a heart absorbed in that one sad treasure here below, and it was gone!

Thus, even here the proof was in the wisdom of God gradual, and the growth of the Apostles themselves slow in the truth. There was afforded the most evident demonstration that, as the power in itself was of Him only and immediately, above the entire course of nature and human experience, so those who were afterwards its most competent, strenuous, and suffering witnesses only yielded to its certainty by such degrees as let us see that no men were more surprised than the Apostles. Even the enemies of the Lord had an undefined dread or uneasiness, which led to Pilate's allowance of a military guard with the seal of the great stone to make the sepulchre sure. Not a disciple, so far as we know, looked for His rising.

Nevertheless, Christ did rise the third day according to the Scriptures. In this very thing—the teaching of God's word—were the disciples weak; not the uninstructed Magdalene only but all, as we shall see, senseless and slow of heart to believe in all that the prophets spoke; all as quick to forget the plain words in which the Lord Himself repeatedly announced not only His death but His resurrection on the third day.

Accordingly, the opening verses have for their object to show us how the truth first began to dawn on any heart. Not only was there no collusion in feigning the resurrection of their Master, there was not so much as a hopeful anticipation in a single heart of which one can speak. The gloom of the cross had shrouded every heart; the fear of man pressed on the men yet more than on the women. Even where the fact should have been patent, she who saw the fact misunderstood its import and was more distressed than ever.[356]

THE TWENTIETH CHAPTER

Verses 1-18.

[Matthew 28:1-10; Mark 16:1-11; Luke 24:1-12.]

"Now on the first (day) of the week Mary of Magdala cometh early while it was yet dark unto the tomb and seeth the stone taken away from the tomb.[357] She runneth therefore and cometh unto Simon Peter and unto the other disciple whom Jesus dearly loved (ἐφ.), and saith to them, They took away the Lord out of the tomb, and we know not where they laid Him" (verses 1-2).

Mary of Magdala seems to be alone on the first day; certainly, if other women were with or near her, as other testimonies may imply[358] (not to speak of the plural form here, "we know," which may be merely general), she alone attracts the notice of the Spirit of God. He portrays a heart, first attracted irresistibly to a scene so overwhelming and withal sacred by her love to Him Whose body had been laid in the tomb; then at length met and blessed by the Lord when the best resources among the saints had failed, as will come before us in due time.

Before His death Mary, the sister of Lazarus, had anointed the Lord, His head and His feet, out of the fulness of her affection, which lavished what she had most precious on Him, just at that time when she instinctively felt danger impending, and hears, in answer to heartless indifference only thence hurrying on to the deadliest ungodliness, the vindication of His love which gave a meaning to her act beyond her thoughts. Oh, how satisfying to her heart till with Himself! It was a deep and true affection met by the affection of Jesus, not perfect only but divine.

And here, too, it was not in vain that Mary of Magdala was drawn thus early, dark as it was, to the grave, the empty grave, of Jesus. She had been there, though not alone, after Sabbath had closed, when it was growing dark (not "dawning," though the word applies to either) toward the first day of the week, for this is the true meaning of Matthew 28. With this compare Mark 16; as Luke 23:54 shows they had been on the preceding evening when Friday was closing and Sabbath was drawing on.

It is remarkable that this Mary runs to tell the fact of the stone's removal, and what she inferred as to the Lord's body, not to John only but to Peter also. The latter had notoriously and grievously dishonoured the Lord just before His death; but doubtless his repentance was well known to the saints at least. Still, there is the record of her unhesitating appeal. Mary's heart judged who among the disciples would most heartily answer to the anxious inquiry which filled her own soul. For assuredly it was not lack of love but of self-judgment which had exposed that ardent disciple to deny his Master. On the contrary, it was confidence in his own love for Him with utter ignorance of himself, and without due dependence on God, in the face of a hostile world with the shadow of death before his eyes. And the Master in the next chapter manifests His own grace toward His servant to the utmost, even while laying bare the sinful root which had betrayed him to such shameful failure. In fact, Mary was far more justified in reckoning on the sympathy of Peter and John in that which troubled her, than in the ignorance which concluded that men had carried off the Lord's body on the resurrection-day. Even the warmest love cannot without the word conceive a right thought of Him Who died for us. Her notion was wholly unwor-

THE TWENTIETH CHAPTER

thy of Christ or of God's care for Him. But unbelief in the saint is no better than in the sinner; and the very strength of her love to the Lord only brings out the more into evidence how faith is needed in order rightly to understand in divine things. He, however, "giveth more grace."

As to the accounts of the Resurrection, let none believe that it is fruitless to compare them, any more than to accept the perfect accuracy of each one. Whether one attempt or despise a harmony, the result must be utterly wrong if he start with interpreting Matthew 28 of the dawn of Sunday morning instead of the dusk of Sabbath evening, which last to the Jew (and Matthew, above all, has the Jews in view) was, and is, the true beginning of the first day, however Western prejudice may incline to the Gentile sense of the day. This error must vitiate all right understanding for the student as much as for the harmonist. Let us read as believers.

It has been said to be "impossible that so astounding an event, coming upon various portions of the body of disciples from various quarters and in various forms, should not have been related, by four independent witnesses, in the 'scattered and fragmentary' way in which we now find it" {Alford, *The Greek Testament*, Volume I, page 905}. Certainly it would be impossible if there were no God securing perfect truth by all His chosen witnesses, and in each of their accounts. The remark is, therefore, mere unbelief, and quite unworthy of any intelligent Christian. "Scattered and fragmentary" is *not* the way of the Holy Ghost, Who does not employ the four like men giving evidence in a court of justice, each of what he saw and heard. Not only is this inapplicable to Mark and Luke, but it does not fall in with the facts in John and Matthew. For He leads each of them to omit what both saw and heard, and to insert only such a selection as illustrates the scope and design of each particular Gospel. Was not Matthew a riveted spectator of the Lord in the midst of the disciples at Jerusalem on the evening of the day He rose from the dead? Was not John with the rest at the appointed mountain in Galilee?

It is not merely true, then, that in the depth beneath their varied surface of narrative the great central fact of the Resurrection itself rests unmoved and immoveable (for this might be in merely human accounts of facts), but that every one of the four had a special object or aim in the mind of the inspiring Spirit, which is carried out unerringly in general plan and in minute detail. The objection admits the honesty of the Christian witnesses, but leaves God out of their writing, which is the essence of infidelity: the more painful, as the objector [Alford, "Prolegomena," Ch. I, Sect. V.] is really a believer, but with a wholly inadequate and dangerous theory of inspiration. The fact is that no man, who had the material, or knew what each Evangelist had before him, would ever have written as any one of them did; and that nothing accounts for their peculiar form but God giving a testimony in perfect keeping with each Gospel, so as by them all to furnish a complete whole. Where men of God only are seen, with nothing more than such guidance of the Spirit as in ordinary preaching or the like, what a blight such unbelief entails! Calling it inspiration only adds to the delusion. Are they *God's* word?

Confessedly the Resurrection was that, above all other things, to which the Apostles bore their testimony; but it is, as we have seen and might show yet more fully, neglect of the evidence to suppose that each elaborated faithfully into narrative those particular facts which came under his own eye or were reported to himself by those concerned. This is a poor and misleading *à priori* hypothesis. Their diversity springs not from human infirmity, but from divine wisdom.

But we turn for a few moments more to the effect of the empty tomb on those who first noticed it. And certainly one cannot speak of spiritual intelligence in Mary of Magdala; but she clung in deep affection to the Lord's Person; and He was not unmindful of it. She was the first, as we shall see, to have joy in Him, and He puts honour on her. Yet what could be less worthy of Christ than her hasty conclusion from the empty tomb! "They took away the Lord out of the tomb, and we know not where they laid Him." She can think of Him only as under the power of death. She judges by the sight of her eyes; and to her mind as yet man has the upper hand. His assurance of resurrection had left no trace, as if on the barren sand. Who can glory in man thus overwhelmed before the undiscerned yet glorious power of God which had already raised Him from among the dead? Nevertheless, her heart was true to Him, and she shows it, if only now by her visit to such a scene while it was yet dark, and by her extreme agitation when she saw the stone taken away, and the body gone from the tomb. What can she do but run with the news to break it to congenial hearts?

> "Peter therefore went forth, and the other disciple, and were coming unto the tomb. And the two were running together, and the other disciple ran forward more quickly than Peter, and came first

unto the tomb, and stooping down seeth the linen clothes as they lay; nevertheless he went not in. Simon Peter therefore cometh following him, and entered into the tomb, and beholdeth the linen clothes lying, and the handkerchief which was upon His head, not lying with the linen clothes but folded up in a place apart. Then entered therefore also the other disciple that came first unto the tomb, and he saw [εἶδεν] and believed; for as yet they knew not the scripture that He must rise from (the) dead. The disciples therefore went away again unto their own (home)" (verses 3-10).

It was not John only who went forth at the tidings of Mary. Love, roused by words which sounded strange to their ears, led Peter to run along with John,[359] with no less desire, if not so fast. He had slumbered, when he ought to have watched and prayed; and, when the crisis came, he had denied his Master with no small aggravation after His solemn warning. But he was not a Judas: very far indeed from it. He loved the Lord Who Himself knew that he loved Him; and therefore, notwithstanding his deep and shameful sin, his heart was moved by the news so unaccountable to him of the disappearance of the body from the tomb. So the two disciples (who were for other reasons often seen together) strove which should reach the spot soonest. Not the most distant hope of what the fact was had as yet crossed their minds; yet were they as far as possible from indifference to any little circumstance which concerned even His body. That it was no longer where it had been laid, especially with such a safeguard against conceivable hazards, is enough to stir both deeply; and they are on the scene forthwith, John outrunning Peter. And as he came first to the tomb, so did he stoop down[360] and see the linen clothes as they lay;[b] yet went he not in. Peter, though less agile, went farther when he reached the place, for he went into the tomb, and inspected the linen clothes as they lay, and the napkin which was on His head, not lying with them but wrapped up in one place by itself.

So also reports Luke (24:12), though not in such detail as John does, who describes not only the twofold examination on his own part, but an added feature in Peter's intent gaze [θεωρεῖ], observing the peculiarity of the napkin wrapt up by itself. What clear presumptive proof that the body had not been taken away by enemies any more than by friends! for why should either leave the linen swathes behind? Who but one arising from sleep would dispose of the habiliments in this calm and orderly fashion? It must be His own doing as He rose from among the dead,[361] and laid aside what was unsuited to, as well as needless for, His new estate.[362] For here we may contrast the very different way in which Lazarus appeared when raised by the Lord, indicative of the different character of the Resurrection. Still, there was no depth in the conviction Peter could not but form; for he returned home, the true rendering, wondering at what had come to pass. Wonder is in no way the expression of the intelligence which faith gives; it implies rather the distinct lack of it. It does seem surprising that such men as Bengel and Stier should follow Erasmus and Grotius in the idea that John merely went as far as Mary's idea in verse 2.

"Then entered, therefore, also the other disciple that came first unto the tomb, and he saw[362a] and believed." It was faith, but founded on evidence, not on the written word. Mary's inference was upset by the indications John as well as Peter observed. Theirs was a sound conclusion, based on a reasonable judgment of the facts observed; but this in itself is only a human deduction, however right in itself, instead of being the subjection of the heart to the testimony of God. And it is John himself who, here as elsewhere, teaches us to draw this most momentous distinction. But Peter seems, though amazed, to have taken in the import of what he observed as well as John. They both went beyond Mary of Magdala and inferred that He must have risen; not that either Joseph and Nicodemus on the one hand, nor that the Jews or Romans on the other, had taken away the Lord's body[362b]. On ground of the apparent facts, they rightly accounted for the disappearance of His body. But in neither was there that character of faith in His resurrection which springs from laying hold of God's word. The former was human, the latter divine, because in this alone is *God* believed, which gives Him His true place and puts us in ours. Thus is the soul purged by virtue of the word, which is no less needful than cleansing by blood; and hence repentance ever accompanies faith. We could not be made meet for the inheritance of the saints in light did we not know experimentally the washing of water by the word as well as cleansing from our sins by Christ's blood.

Now it is not too much to say that, as far as the truth of resurrection, soon to be the characteristic testimony of the apostles John or Peter, it was not yet taught them of God. They did not as yet with the fact connect God's testimony in the Law, the Psalms, or the Prophets, nor even the plain and recent words of our Lord Jesus. So little is there of truth in Lampe's judgment that from this moment in the very darkness of the tomb the mind of John was enlightened with the saving faith of the resurrection of Jesus as with a certain new ray of the risen "Sun of Righteousness." There is nothing in divine things beautiful which is not true; and this is not only not true, but the reversal of the truth inculcated by John himself in his inspired comment on the fact. They both believed in Christ, on the ground, not of facts only, but of God's word; they neither of them believed in His resurrection beyond the seen facts that so it must be. "For as yet they knew not the scripture that He must rise from[363] (the) dead."

We have had a fair sample of Protestant (I do not say Reformation) theology, which shows their loose and human idea of faith. Romanist, and perhaps one might add Catholic, views are no better. Hence the Tridentine depreciation of faith; hence the effort to bring in love and obedience and holiness in order to justification. They feel that there must be a moral element, and their reducing faith to an intellectual reception of propositions excludes it; so that they are driven to add other things to faith in order to satisfy themselves. All this turns on the great fundamental error that the thorough-going Papist makes faith in the Church the resting-place of his soul and the rule of faith, not the Scriptures, nor God revealed in Christ by them. If they carried out the error to its results, no Romanist could be saved; for he believes not God's word on God's authority, but Scripture and tradition on the Church's word. *By his own principle* he excludes faith in God, and could not truly believe unto life at all. Only through grace men may be better than their principle, as many, alas! are worse when the principle is of God. Believing Scripture as *God's* word, believing God in it, is of vital moment.[363a]

Facts are of high interest and real importance; and as the Israelite could point to them as the basis of his religion, to the call of Abram by God, and the deliverance of the chosen people from Egypt and through the desert and into Canaan, so can the Christian to the incomparably deeper and more enduring ones of the incarnation, death, resurrection, and ascension of the Son of God, with the consequent presence of the Holy Ghost sent down from heaven. But faith to have moral value, to deal with the conscience, to purify and draw out the heart, is not the pure and simple acceptance of facts on reasonable grounds, but the heart's welcoming God's testimony in His word. This tests the soul beyond all else, as spiritual intelligence consists in the growing up to Christ in an increasing perception and enjoyment of all that God's word has revealed, which separates the saint practically to Himself and His will in judgment of self and the world. One has put off the old man and put on the new, being renewed into full knowledge according to the image of Him that created him {Colossians 3:9-10}.

To "see and believe," therefore, is wholly short of what the operation of God gives; as traditional faith or evidence answers to it now in Christendom. It is human, and leaves the conscience unpurged and the heart without communion. It may be found in him who is in no way born of God (compare chapter 2:23-25), but also in the believer as here: if so, it is not what the Spirit seals, and it in no way delivers from present things. And this it seems to be the divine object to let us know in the account before us. Faith, to be of value and have power, rests not on sight or inference but on Scripture.[363b] Thus, as the disciples show the most treacherous memory as to the words of the Lord till He was raised up from the dead (chapter 2:22), so were they insensible to the force and application of the written word: after that they believed both, they entered into abiding and enlarging blessing from above. This, as Peter tells us in his First

Epistle (chapter 1:8), is characteristically the faith of a Christian, who, having not seen Christ, loves Him; and on Whom though not now seeing Him but believing, he exults with joy unspeakable and full of glory. The faith that is founded on evidences may strengthen against Deism, Pantheism, or Atheism; but it never gave remission of sins, never led one to cry, "Abba, Father," never filled the heart with His grace and glory Who is the object of God's everlasting satisfaction and delight.

Here, also, we have the further and marked testimony of its powerlessness; for we are told (verse 10), "The disciples therefore went away again unto their own (home)." The fact was known on grounds indisputable to their minds, but not yet appreciated in God's sight as revealed in His word; and hence they return to their old unbroken associations.

Mary did not, could not, take things so quietly as the two disciples. What was "home" now to her? What was the world? Nothing but an empty tomb where Jesus had lain. Others might depart again to their own home. For her heart it was impossible.

> "But Mary stood at the tomb without {*i.e.*, outside} weeping. While then she was weeping, she stooped into the tomb, and beholdeth two angels in white sitting, one at the head, and one at the feet, where had lain the body of Jesus. And they say to her, Woman, why weepest thou? She saith to them, Because they took away my Lord, and I know not where they laid Him. Having said thus, she turned back, and beholdeth Jesus standing, and knew not that it was Jesus. Jesus saith to her, Woman, why weepest thou? Whom dost thou seek? She, thinking that it was the gardener, saith

to Him, Sir, if thou didst carry Him off, tell me where thou laidest Him, and I will take Him away. Jesus saith to her, Mary. She, turning, saith to Him in Hebrew,[c] Rabboni, which meaneth (or, is to say) Teacher" (verses 11-16).[364]

The sorrow of love for Jesus, that which mourns His absence, or which feels wrong done to Him in any way, is far different from the sorrow of the world that worketh death. It soon passes into life and peace through the grace of Jesus. Mary's sorrow was not fruitless, nor was it long. Other servants of the Lord, and the Lord Himself, Whom she saw not, looked upon her. While she wept outside, she stooped into the tomb and beheld two angels in white. But He was not there; they were sitting one at the head and one at the feet where the body of Jesus had lain. Yet we hear of no alarm, no amazement on her part: so absorbed was her heart with that one Person, to all appearance lost to her, even His body gone so that she could not weep over it. Nor does she speak to them, but they say to her, "Woman, why weepest thou?" They were in the secret. She had not read as yet aright the signs of the grave. Her sorrowing heart would ere long receive better and clearer tidings still. Meanwhile she explains to them why she wept: "Because they took away my Lord, and I know not[365] where they laid Him." She wholly overlooks the strangeness of the angelic apparition within the tomb, and takes for granted that every one must know Who He was Whose body was gone. But not even yet has the thought of His resurrection crossed her mind. The Lord was her Lord; she loved Him exceedingly, but to her apprehension men had taken Him and laid Him where she knew not. A soul may love the Lord, yet be dark indeed as to His risen glory, as we cannot fail to read here.

THE TWENTIETH CHAPTER

Grace would now intervene. "On saying this she turned round[366] and beholdeth Jesus standing, and knew not that it was Jesus." How often the like may be for our dull hearts! But He never acts beneath His name, and speaks that we may know Him. "Jesus saith to her, Woman, why weepest thou? Whom dost thou seek?" This last was a leading question. Till He is known, however, there is still darkness, though there may be love. "She, thinking that He was the gardener, saith to Him, Sir, if thou didst carry Him off, tell me where thou laidest Him, and *I* will take Him away." One word dispels all the difficulty and doubt, the expression, not of our love to Him, but of His love to us. "Jesus saith to her, Mary." The work was done, the great discovery made. He had died, He was now risen, and He appeared first to Mary of Magdala. She that had sown in tears reaps now in joy. The Lord appreciated her abiding at the tomb in sorrow, even though but an empty tomb. Her heart was now filled with joy; and, as we shall see, the joy would run over to gladden other hearts, the hearts of all that believed.

It was the good Shepherd calling His own sheep by name. She was the same to Him as ever; He stood in resurrection power; but His love was the same to her, certainly no less than when He cast seven demons out of her. Doubtless there was a sameness in the expression of her name which went straight home to her heart and recalled her from her dream about His Person, once dead but now in truth alive again for evermore. Soon she would learn that, as He lived, so did she also, alive to God in Jesus Christ her Lord. But for the moment to know Himself alive, Himself uttering her name with unutterable love, was the fruit of divine grace that touched and best satisfied her heart.

Mary had known Christ according to the flesh, and evidently thought that she was thus to know Him still. But it is not so. Henceforth we know none after this sort. Christ was dead and risen, and about to take His place in heaven according to the counsels of God. The Christian is called to know Him as Man in heaven, always the Son, but now Man glorified on high. Hence the force of that which follows. Mary must learn to regard the Lord in an entirely new light, not in bodily presence here below, but for an object of faith as received up in glory. She is thus delivered from all her former associations, and is the given ensample of the Jewish remnant henceforward to become Christian.

> "Jesus saith to her, Touch Me not, for I have not yet ascended[367] unto the (or, My)[d] Father; but go unto My brethren and say to them, I ascend unto My Father and your Father, and My God and your God. Mary of Magdala cometh bringing word to the disciples, I have seen[e] the Lord, and that He said these things to her" (verses 17-18).

It is the more striking if we compare Matthew 28:9 with the Lord's prohibition of Mary in our Gospel. Both incidents happened very nearly about the same time. Yet the Lord permitted the other women to come and hold Him by the feet, and pay Him homage, whereas only a very little while before He forbade Mary of Magdala to touch Him. *We know* that He was divinely perfect on both occasions, as, indeed, always, that though man and the Son of Man it was not His to repent, for He is the Truth. But we may be permitted, and I think ought, to inquire why ways so different and so rapidly following one another could be each absolutely right in its own place. The difference of design in the two Gospels helps much to clear the matter.

THE TWENTIETH CHAPTER

In Matthew the risen Lord resumes His relations with the Jewish remnant, and gives these women, as a sample of that remnant, to enjoy His presence on earth. For this reason, too, there is not only no ascension scene in the end of Matthew, but no allusion to the fact there; indeed, it would mar the perfection of the picture, which shows us the Lord present with His own until the consummation of the age. In John, on the other hand, Jewish feeling is immediately corrected; new relations are announced, and ascension to the Father takes the place of all expectations for the nations on the earth with the Jews as the Lord's centre and witnesses. "Touch Me not," says Jesus to Mary, "for I have not yet ascended unto the Father." Henceforth the Lord is to be known characteristically by the Christian as in heaven. The Jew had looked for Him on earth, and rightly so; as by and by the Jew will have Him reigning over the earth, when He comes again in power and great glory. Between the broken and restored hopes of Israel, we find our place as Christians. We are baptized unto His death, and we show forth His death until He come, remembering Him in the breaking of the bread; but we know Him above, no longer dead but risen and glorified.

Yea, though we had known Christ according to flesh, yet now we know Him thus no more. Indeed, without boasting, in sober truth but all-surpassing grace, we can say, and as believers are bound to say, that we are in Him. "In that day ye shall know that I am in My Father, and ye in Me, and I in you." "That day" of the New Testament is this day, being already come, the day of grace to the world in the gospel; the day of grace to the saints in their union with Christ. "So if anyone be in Christ, it is a new creation; the old things have passed away, behold, all things are become new; and all things are of the God Who reconciled us to Himself by Jesus Christ" [2 Corinthians 5:17 *f.*]. Such is Christianity; and this undeveloped was implied in our Lord's dealing and words with Mary of Magdala. "Touch Me not" was a saying of eminent significance, and still more when interpreted by the words that accompany it. It is not, as in Colossians 2:21, μή ἄψῃ (a single transient action), but μή μου ἅπτου, "Do not go on touching Me"; it is a general and continuous prohibition, and this to represent the remnant taken out of their associations as Jews and put into new relations, not only with Christ in heaven, but through Him with His Father and God; as contradistinguished from those who represent the remnant allowed to lay hold of Him as a sign of His return in bodily presence for the kingdom.

But there is more. "Go unto My brethren." He is not ashamed to call the disciples His brethren. He had prepared the way for this; He had said on Israel's rebellious rejection of their Messiah, "Whosoever shall do the will of My Father which is in heaven, the same is My brother, and sister, and mother" [Matthew 12:50]. Now, on the accomplishment of His atoning work He acknowledges definitely this blessed fruit of it, not only sins forgiven to faith by virtue of His shed blood, but believers in the most intimate way related to Himself, the risen Man and Son of God. They are His brethren; to whom, according to Psalm 22:22, He proceeds to make known the name, not merely of Jehovah, but of the Father. For now they were not quickened only, but quickened with Christ. They stood in Him risen from the dead, forgiven all trespasses. And they learn that thus related to Christ in His new place as in the condition of Man according to divine counsels for eternity, all question of sin being closed triumphantly on the cross, not for Him Who had

THE TWENTIETH CHAPTER

no need, but for the believer who had all possible need in guilt and an evil nature and an accusing enemy and a holy, righteous Judge, they enter into His own blessed and everlasting relationship with His Father and God. "And say to them, I ascend unto My Father and your Father, My God and your God."

It was a moment of unequalled depth: the Son risen again after having borne the judgment of our sins in His own body on the tree and glorified God in respect, not of obedience in life only but up to death for sin, on the resurrection morning sending, through one from whom He had formerly expelled seven demons, to His disciples (desponding through unbelief) a message of the new and incomparable blessedness He had acquired for them by His death and resurrection. Doubtless He is the risen Messiah of the seed of David, and the mercies of David are made sure by His resurrection, as will be proved in the kingdom restored to Israel in due time. But this must be postponed in God's wisdom and yield to the far deeper purpose meanwhile coming into evidence, the calling out of God's children, heirs of God and joint-heirs with Christ, into the knowledge and enjoyment and testimony of Himself and His Son by the Holy Ghost, which is usually styled "Christianity." It could not be before, nor only because He had relations after flesh and by promise with Israel, until they had thoroughly despised and rejected deliberately through unbelief, but guiltily and inexcusably, their infinitely blessed King; but because solely on the ground of redemption by His death could God be free to form and gather into one those children of His freed from their sins and quickened together with Him, whether Jew or Gentile. Now, having died, He could bear much fruit; and here He announces the fact as worthy of Himself as of the God Who sent Him in love beyond all thought of man. "I ascend unto My Father and your Father, My God and your God."

How poor and pale are the dreams of men even in their highest aspirations, compared with the simple truth spoken by the Lord and sent to His own! Yet nothing less could satisfy His love, which must demonstrate its power, first by going down with our sins to suffer for them from God, and next by ascending into glory and giving us as far as possible His own position as sons and saints, with all evil and guilt for ever gone before God, purged worshippers having no more conscience of sins. This was not merely a hope to be made good when He comes again to receive us to Himself, but the truth of a really existing relationship announced now on the resurrection day, sent to His disciples that they might know and enjoy it to the full, as pledged in His own ascension to the presence of the Father in heaven. It is for all saints till He come again: would that all knew it as their only true place in Him! Still, grace has given the truth fresh power in our day, though by messengers who have no more reason to boast than Mary of Magdala that came then with the tidings to the disciples (verse 18), I have seen the Lord; or, as it is more commonly read, that she had seen the Lord, and He had spoken these things to her. But we may and ought to glory in our risen Lord, and of such a place for the believer in Him. "Of such a one will I glory," said a greater than any of us; "yet of myself I will not glory, but in mine infirmities" [2 Corinthians 12:5]. Of a man in Christ it is well to glory: only we cannot expect those to do so who do not even conceive what it means, and who are so depraved by a jargon of Jewish and Gentile notions, commonly called systematic divinity, that they are slow indeed to learn. If we know the truth, may we have grace not only to walk in it, but to wait on such as know it not, if peradventure grace and truth may at length win their way and the saints learn their true blessedness in Christ.

The Lord's message was not in vain. The disciples gathered on that resurrection-day with the world shut out; and Jesus stood in the midst. It is the beautiful anticipative picture of *the assembly,* as may be seen more fully when details are entered into.

Verses 19-23.

[Mark 16:14-18; Luke 24:36-49.]

> "When it was evening then, on that day which was the first of the week,[368] and the doors were shut where the disciples[369] were by reason of the fear of the Jews, came Jesus and stood [took His stand] in the midst, and saith to them, Peace to you. And having said this He showed them His hands and His side. The disciples then rejoiced when they saw the Lord. He (or, Jesus)[f] said therefore to them again, Peace to you: according as the Father hath sent Me forth, I also send you. And having said this, He breathed into and saith to them, Receive the Holy Spirit: whose soever sins ye remit, they are remitted to them; whose soever ye retain, they are retained" (verses 19-23).

How many things of spiritual weight were here brought into the smallest compass and conveyed in the simplest form! That day which in due time was to receive its appropriate designation of "the Lord's day" (Revelation 1:10), as characteristic of the Christian as the Sabbath of the Jew, was marked off, not only by the gathering together of the saints, but by the presence of the Lord in their midst. So it was at the beginning of the following week (verse 26); and so afterwards does the Holy Spirit distinguish it as the day when the *breaking of the bread* is observed (Acts 20:7), and the wants of the holy poor rise up in remembrance before Him and them (1 Corinthians 16:2). It was indeed divine guidance, though it did not take the shape of a command; but none the less precious or obligatory on all who value His special presence in communion with His own and the showing forth of His death till He come. It was the day, not of creation rest nor of law imposed, but of resurrection and of the grace which associated the believer with its rich and enduring results; on which all thus blessed come together to enjoy in common that death of the Lord which is the righteous ground of these privileges and of all others.

On that day the Lord gave the assembled disciples a signal witness of the power of life in resurrection; for where they were, the doors having been shut for fear of the Jews, Jesus came and stood in the midst. Weakness attaches to the natural body, which, unless a miracle be wrought, is stopped by a wall or a closed door or a chain or a thousand other checks. Not so the body which is raised in power, as the Lord here silently shows them. It appears to be the object of the statement here, and again lower down, to intimate that the risen body can thus enter, not by miracle (however wonderful it may seem to us, who view and measure things by the actual condition of this life) but normally as in the power of resurrection, wherein all indeed is supernatural. There is no ground here to suppose, but rather the contrary, that the doors were caused to open of themselves. So it was (Acts 5:19), when the angel led the apostles Peter and John out of prison; so, again, when Peter was a second time set free (Acts 12:10), and the iron gate opened of itself, not to let in the angel, who needed it not, but to let Peter out. It is no question of omnipotence but of the risen body, which has no more need of an open door than an angel. The ancients seem to have had far simpler faith as to this than most moderns who betray the growing materialism[g] of the day. To talk of philosophical difficulties is puerile pretension: what does philosophy know of the Resurrection? It is a question of God and His Son, not of mere causes and effects, still less of experience. The Christian believes the word and knows what God reveals. Let philosophy confess, not boast of, its nescience: if dumb before creation, resurrection is to it still more confounding.

Jesus then and thus came and stood in the midst, saying to the disciples, "Peace to you." This He had left as His legacy before the cross; now alive again from the dead He announces it to His own: how sweet the sound in a world at war with God! Doubly so where earnest souls have striven ineffectually to make it for themselves with God, whatever their sighs and tears and groans, whatever their prayers, yearnings, and agony, whatever their efforts to eschew the evil and cleave to the good. For such best know that conscience and heart can find no solid peace in self-judgment or in self-denial, in contemplation of God or in labours for Him; on the contrary, the more sincere, the less have they peace. They are on a wholly wrong road. Peace for a sinful man can only be made by the blood of Christ's cross, which faith receives on His word. And so the Lord spoke it to the disciples that day, the mighty work on which it is grounded being finished and accepted of God, as His resurrection declares. "And having said this He showed them His hands and His side. The disciples then rejoiced when they saw the Lord."

Some have conceived that the second "Peace to you" was a sort of farewell or *valete,* as the first a *salvete*.[h] As the former was far otherwise, even the deep blessing which characterises those who are justified by faith, and ever recurring in one form or another throughout the New Testament, so the second is in connection with the mission the Lord proceeds to confer on the disciples. They first received peace for themselves; they are next charged to go forth with the gospel of peace to others. "According as the Father hath sent (ἀπέστ.) Me forth, I also send (π.) you." These are Christ's true legates *à latere:* others are but thieves and robbers whom the sheep do well not to hear. Strangers to peace themselves, as their own tongue cannot but confess, how can they tell others of a peace which poor sinners might trust with assurance?

But the Lord next proceeds to another highly significant token of new and lasting privilege. "And having said this, He breathed into and saith to them, Receive [(]the[)] Holy Spirit:[i] whose soever sins ye remit, they are remitted to them; whose soever ye retain, they are retained." It was He Who before He took flesh had breathed into Adam's nostrils the breath of life; and now He breathed into the disciples the breath of a better and everlasting life, His own life, as being both now—that is, Jehovah-God and the risen Second Man—in one Person. Never had He so done before.[370] The right moment was come. He had been delivered for their offences and was raised for their justification. The risen life is deliverance from the law of sin and death, as well as the bright witness of a complete remission of sins; and this not as an abstract truth for all believers, but

THE TWENTIETH CHAPTER

intended to be known and enjoyed by each. "There is therefore now no condemnation to them which are in Christ Jesus. For the law of the Spirit of life in Christ Jesus hath delivered *me* from the law of sin and death" [Romans 8:1-2]. In Romans 7 before, from verse 7, we read how tried and sifted and wretched the *"I"* was, till it dropped self to find grace in Christ, not only for the past but for the present and, of course, for ever.

What can be more intensely personal than this deliverance from misery? and what more evident also that it was not only a new and divine life, but this after judgment of sin and the curse of the law had fallen on Christ, and He risen victoriously dispensing a life beyond sin, law, or judgment, and this as having borne all and borne all away for the believer righteously? Of this His inbreathing was the sign; and He says: "Receive [(]the[)] Holy Spirit": not yet the Spirit sent down from the ascended Lord and Christ to baptize into one body and to give power and testimony, but the energy of His own risen life. For the Spirit ever in the closest way takes His part in every blessing; and as for the kingdom of God every one is born of water and Spirit, and none else can see or enter that kingdom, so here with life in resurrection to deal with souls that heard and believed the gospel.

For this is not all. The disciples thus delivered are invested with a blessed privilege and a solemn responsibility as regards others. Those without are now viewed as sinners, the old distinction of Jews and Gentiles for the time disappearing in the true light. But if it be the judgment of the world, it is the day of grace; and the disciples have the administration, the Spirit of life in Christ giving them capacity. Hence the word of the Lord is, "Whose soever sins ye remit, they are remitted; whose soever ye retain, they are retained." So repentant souls were baptized for the remission of sins, whilst a Simon Magus was pronounced in the gall of bitterness and bond of iniquity. So the wicked person was put away from among the saints, and the same man after the judgment of his evil and his own deep grief over his sin was to be assured of love by the assembly's receiving him back, obedient, yet taking the initiative in the act that it might be conscience work and not of bare authority or influence. It was the assembly's doing. "To whom ye forgive anything, I also; for also what I have forgiven, if I have forgiven anything, (it is) for your sakes in Christ's person" [2 Corinthians 2:10]. Paul would have nothing forced, but fellowship unbroken in discipline: not he dictating and they blindly or in dread following, as in the church-world; but they following Christ's authority and he also in a communion truly of the Spirit.[371]

VERSES 24-29.

On the resurrection-day the Apostles were not all present.

> "But Thomas, one of the twelve, called Didymus,[372] was not with them when Jesus came. The other disciples said [began to say] therefore to him, We have seen the Lord. But he said to them, Except I see in His hands the print of the nails, and put my finger into the print of the nails, and put my hand into His side, I will in nowise believe" (verses 24-25).

His state of soul coincided with his absence on that day. He resisted the blessed news of the Resurrection, and did not join the gathering of the disciples to share the joy of the Master's presence in their midst. Slow of heart to believe, he missed the early taste of the blessing, and abode in the darkness of his own unbelief, whilst the rest were filled with gladness. He becomes, therefore, no unmeet type of the Jew, not of the ungodly mass who receive another coming in his own name, but of the poor sorrow-stricken remnant who cleave to the hope of the Messiah in the latter day, and will enter into rest and joy only when they see Him appearing for their deliverance.

> "And after eight days again His disciples were within, and Thomas with them. Jesus cometh, the doors being shut, and stood in the midst, and said, Peace to you. Then He saith to Thomas, Reach hither thy finger, and see My hands, and reach thy hand, and put (it) into My side, and be not unbelieving but believing. Thomas answered and said to Him, My Lord and my God. Jesus saith to him, Because thou hast seen Me, thou hast believed; blessed are those that saw not and believed" (verses 26-29).

It is a blessed picture of the fruit of Christ's resurrection in the latter day: not the Church but "the great congregation" [Psalm 22:25], brought in infinite grace to know and praise the Lord, when He is no longer hidden but visibly reigning. Those before will have had the good portion, which shall not be taken from them—they saw not, yet believed.[373] Israel will see and believe: blest indeed, but not after the same high measure of blessing. There will be no such revelation of the Father to them, no such association with the Son, no conscious link by His ascension with the heavens. The rejected One will have returned to reign in power and glory; and the heart of Israel, long withered and dark, is to be lighted up at length with the brightness of their hope accomplished in the presence of the Lord to make good every promise, when they on their part boast no more of their own righteousness, but take their stand on the mercy that endureth for ever. They recognise the Judge of Israel that was smitten with a rod upon the cheek, and themselves given up by Him, until the birth of God's great final purpose in their favour, when He shall be great to the ends of the earth, and they as a dew of blessing from Jehovah in the midst of the nations, and all their enemies shall be cut off. "They shall look upon Me Whom they pierced, and they shall mourn for Him," in bitterness of self-reproach, but with a spirit of grace and supplication poured upon them. For truly He was wounded in the house of His friends, but wounded (as they learn afterwards) for their transgressions, bruised for their iniquities, stricken for the transgression of Jehovah's people (see Micah 5, Zechariah 12, {13,} and Isaiah 53).

Hence we hear nothing now of not touching the Lord because of His ascension to His Father, nor of going to His brethren, and saying to them, "I ascend unto My Father and your Father, and My God and your God." On the contrary, grace will condescend to those who demanded signs and tokens ere they would believe; and they will stand overwhelmed and abashed at the fulness of visible proof when Messiah returns here below. There is peace to them; "for this man shall be the peace" in that day also, whatever the pride and power of the foe. But there will not be the same mission of peace in the power of His risen life; all their iniquities forgiven, all their diseases healed, but not the place of the Church to forgive or retain sins in the name of the Lord.

Accordingly, there is the characteristic exclamation and confession withal of Thomas, "My Lord and my God."[j] So will Israel say in the kingdom. "And it shall be said in that day, Lo, this is our God; we have waited for Him, and He will save us: this is Jehovah; we have waited for Him, we will be glad, and rejoice in His salvation" [Isaiah 25:9]. It is the truth, and true blessing for Israel to possess and blessedly acknowledge, especially for those who had so long despised Him to their own shame and ruin; but it has not the intimacy of that fellowship into which the Christian is now called. "For truly our fellowship is with the Father, and with His Son Jesus Christ"[1 John 1:3]. "We walk by faith, not by sight" [2 Corinthians 5:7]; and having not seen Christ, we love Him; "on Whom, though now we see Him not, yet believing, we rejoice with joy unspeakable and full of glory" [1 Peter 1:8].

Here the Evangelist, as on occasion is his manner, interrupts for a moment the thread of the divine tale to say a few words on the gracious way of the Saviour in the affluence of signs or significant miracles which studded His ministry here below, as well as on the purpose of blessing the Holy Ghost had in view, in selecting from that countless crowd such as were most suitable for permanent testimony to God's grace. Two objects are set out: first and pre-eminently, the glory of the Lord's Person, that Jesus is the Christ, the Son of God; secondly, that the believer may have life in His name.

VERSES 30-31.

> "Many other[k] signs therefore did Jesus in the presence of the[l] disciples, which are not written in this book; but these are written, that ye may believe that Jesus is the Christ, the Son of God; and that believing ye may have life in His name" (verses 30-31).

No doubt this was a fitting moment here to pause and thus to speak. The unbelief of a believer, yea, of an apostle, furnished the material where the Lord had stooped to meet and receive His erring servant by the visible tokens and the tangible proofs he had insisted on in his folly, and to his hurt irreparable, if grace had not intervened as we have seen. It was a priceless favour to have seen the things the disciples saw. It is better still to believe without seeing. And grace would provide for those who in the nature of things could not see, that they might hear and live. Hence the writing of this precious book. It was to be in witness of Jesus; it was to be known and read of all men. Not that Scripture ever exhausts its wondrous theme, whatever it may be; and here, above all, it is as infinite in the Person described, as the blessing is eternal for those who believe. God graciously selects some signs out of many, in the considerate goodness which knows precisely what we can bear. For if Scripture be His word, it is given to man, even to us who believe, to the end of our enjoying that blessing in His Son—indeed, the deepest which He could bestow—the communication of that nature which, as it comes from God, ever goes to Him, yea, yields fellowship with the Father and with His Son, Jesus Christ our Lord.[374]

But as the supreme and crucial test now is the Person of Jesus Christ come in flesh (1 John 4:2-3), so connected with it is the divinely given and guarded testimony to God's grace and Christ's glory, by which the family of God, weak as they are, overcome the adverse might of the world and its prince; because greater is He that is in them than he that is in the world. And those who are of God turn a deaf ear to such as are of the world and speak as of the world whom the world hears; but have

THE TWENTIETH CHAPTER

they none especially to hear? Thanks be to God, they know God and hear those who are of God, His chosen witnesses, whom the Holy Ghost was to lead, and did lead, into all the truth, and who in due time wrote "this book," as did others no less inspired for the work than John. On the other hand, those who are not of God do not hear the Apostles, preferring the thoughts of themselves or of other men to their irremediable ruin. "By this we know the Spirit of truth and the spirit of error" [1 John 4:6].

After this brief but worthy and gracious interruption the Evangelist turns to "the third" (21:14) of the great manifestations of the risen Jesus which it was his task to describe, before he closes with the respective and peculiar places the Lord would give Peter and John in their service here below. How any men of intelligence could say that our two verses which conclude chapter 20 are a formal close of the Gospel might have been viewed as inconceivable, if it was not positive fact. Grotius[375] seems to have been the first man of mark who gave expression and currency to a supposition irreconcilable with the plain connection of the two first days of the week in chapter 20, and with the scene which follows in chapter 21: irreconcilable just in proportion to one's real understanding of the Gospel as a whole. Modern Germany took up this and other injurious notions of that learned Dutchman, not only Ewald, Lücke, and Tholuck, but even Meyer, Neander, and Stier. It is painful to add that Alford, Scrivener, Westcott, etc., have yielded to the uncalled-for theory that John 20 originally ended the Gospel, and that chapter 21 is a later appendix from the Apostle's own hand, though many go farther and deny it to him altogether.[375a]

When we enter on the details of the concluding chapter, we may be enabled to show yet more how unfounded is this thought. Meanwhile it suffices here to point out briefly the mistake of regarding as a true end the two verses which have been now occupying us. In fact, they are an instructive comment by the way, not without a glance at the signs wrought by the Lord all through, but with special declaration of God's aim for the glory of Christ and the blessing of the faithful, suggested by the case of Thomas, yet delicately avoiding any needlessly direct allusion to one so honoured of the Lord. It would, indeed, be as true to say that the Evangelist began more than once in chapter 1 as to admit more than one ending in chapters 20, 21. In fact, if men are to reason thus from superficial appearances, it would be more plausible to infer at least two, if not three, supplements to the Epistle to the Romans. Nor is authority wanting which transports the doxology from the end of chapter 16 to that of chapter 14. Yet it is to be doubted if the hypothesis there be so unnatural as it would be here to sever the third manifestation of the Lord in resurrection from the two which preceded it, or even to admit the former as a later addition, since it is necessary to the completeness of the picture. It is the true complement. In no way is it, as men have thought, a mere supplement, since it forms an essential part of one organic whole; just as chapter 2:1-22 pertains as a sequel to chapter 1 and never could be justly dislocated from it, as an afterthought supplied at a later date even by the same hand.

Mr. J. B. McClellan, in his *New Testament* (I. 744-747), is an honourable exception to the fashion of the day, which subordinates sound criticism to subjective ideas. On the one hand, the external authority is full and unimpeachable; on the other, the peculiarity of the

Evangelist's manner has not been fairly taken into account by any who have indulged in the hypothetical Appendix. John was led of the Spirit to intervene from time to time with the expression of his heart at what affected his divine Master for good or ill, or at the testimony rendered in His words, in His ways, and in the signs that accompanied all as here. More than this is a spurious inference, which severs chapter 21 from its due place. How discreditable to the self-vaunting "modern critics" that they allow their own thoughts to run away with them in the face of overwhelming authority and consentient witnesses! Nor is this all. For the true internal evidence is conclusive for the continuity of the text as it stands, as it demands the chapter which follows to complete the scope of this Gospel in general, and especially the bearing of what was begun in the latter part of chapter 20.

NOTES ON THE TWENTIETH CHAPTER

a [*Cf. Lectures Introductory to the Study of the Gospels*, pp. 563-566.]

b The careful reader will notice the emphatic place given to the lying of the grave-clothes as seen by John, compared with Peter's contemplating them as they lay, and the kerchief or napkin for the head, not with them but apart and wrapped up. I reject the irreverent thought of Wetstein that John shrank from going in "ne pollueretur, Numbers 19:16"; for this would have operated to hinder John afterwards (verse 8) as well as Peter's entrance. It was Peter's ardour, not burning less now but more from the sense of his recent wrong, which impelled him not merely to take a glance but to enter and survey all more closely.

c The T.R. [as Blass] omits Ἑβραϊστί with twelve uncials [AE, etc.], most cursive MSS., and a few versions. But the Sinaitic, the Vatican, Beza's of Cambridge, the Parisian 62 [L], the Moscow [V] of cent. ix., the Munich or Landshut [X] of a later date, those of St. Gall [Δ] and of St. Petersburg [Π], both of the ninth century, with some excellent cursives [as 33], and most of the ancient versions [Syr^{pesch hier}], give the reading [most Edd.].

d T.R. adds μου with most uncials, cursives, and versions [Syr^{sin pesch}, etc.], but not אBD and some few other authorities [Edd.].

e The oldest manuscripts give the uncompounded form of the participle, and also the direct style, "I have seen," etc., not as in T.R.

f T.R. and Lachmann [with Weiss] follow AB and eleven other uncials, most cursives, etc., in reading ὁ Ἰ., but אDLCX and most ancient versions omit [as Tisch. and Blass; W. and H. bracket].

g Even Calvin was led into misunderstanding of this scripture, through his dread of Popery and its effort to prove the dogma of a real presence everywhere in the Mass. His faith in, or at least intelligence of, the Resurrection was small.

h It will hardly be credited that Calvin saw no more than a desire for prosperity in these words of our risen Lord.

i That character of the Holy Spirit's action, which consists of life in resurrection; and hence expressed without the article. It was not yet the Holy Spirit given personally, the baptism of the Spirit, as at Pentecost.

j That Gilbert Wakefield should deny the confession and merge all in a mere exclamation, or rather in two, "O! my Lord! and O! my God!" was to have been expected from his heterodoxy. But such a notion is as inconsistent with the context as it is irreverent, and of course misses all the force of the truth. For it will be observed that the Gospel says, not merely that Thomas said these words, but that they were said *to his Master*. It is true that, if a mere assertion, the article would be absent, as being simply predicative. The emphatic form of the sentence is due to its combining exclamation in the vocative according to the New Testament usage with confession, and this said to the Lord Jesus; which also accounts for the twofold occurrence of the personal pronoun, the first of which assuredly could not have been used had it been an address to Jehovah as such.

k It may be that the Authorised Version has led some into, or confirmed in, the mistake of a possible conclusion here. "And many," etc., is not a quite correct rendering. It is literally the familiar "Many and other signs," that is, "Many other signs," etc.

l αὐτοῦ, "His," is added by many copies, but not the oldest or best.

THE TWENTY-FIRST CHAPTER [a] [376]

It is impossible fairly to sever the manifestation of Jesus at the lake of Tiberias from the two previous scenes of which it is the complement; as, indeed, verse 14 warrants us to say with decision. It is therefore quite improper to speak of the chapter as an appendix, still more so to speculate on its being written at an interval of some length after the rest of the Gospel: an inference due chiefly, if not altogether, to a misunderstanding of the two closing verses of chapter 20, as has been already pointed out.

The reader will notice that the connection is immediate and marked with the two previous manifestations of the risen Lord. First, we have seen Him (after making Himself known to Mary of Magdala and sending by her a most characteristic message to His disciples) standing in their midst when gathered together, without seeing Him enter, on the first or resurrection day of the week, in their enjoyment of peace and the mission of peace in the power of the Spirit to remit and retain sins in His name. Secondly, we have seen Him eight days after meeting His disciples again when Thomas was there, representing saved Israel of the latter day who only

THE TWENTY-FIRST CHAPTER

believe by the sight of Him risen. Now we have the beautiful picture of the millennial ingathering from the sea of Gentiles, which follows the Jews returning as such to the Lord, as all prophecy leads us to expect. The third scene follows in due order the second, on which the future truth conveyed by it hangs as a consequence, as here said to be "after these things."

VERSES 1-14.

"After these things Jesus manifested Himself[377] again to the disciples at the sea of Tiberias; and He manifested (Himself) thus. There were together Simon Peter, and Thomas called Didymus (that is, Twin), and Nathaniel from Cana in Galilee, and the (sons) of Zebedee,[378] and two others of His disciples.[379] Simon Peter saith to them, I go away to fish. They say to him, We also come with thee.[379a] They went forth, and entered[b] into the boat, and that night took nothing. But when early morn was now breaking,[c] Jesus stood on[c] the shore: however the disciples did not know that it was (*literally*, is) Jesus. Jesus therefore saith to them, Children [Lads], have ye anything to eat? They answered Him, No. And He said to them, Cast the net on the right side of the boat, and ye will find. They cast therefore, and were no longer able[d] to draw it from the multitude of fishes" (verses 1-6).[380]

Peter, with his usual energy, proposes to go a-fishing, and six others accompany him. But the result is no better than when some of the same disciples with the same Peter essayed to catch fish before his call and theirs. Even in the days of the kingdom the power must be manifestly of the Lord, not of man nor of the saints themselves; and Peter must, and would, learn the lesson, if the Roman Catholic sect falsely claiming Peter refuse it in pride. It is not yet the kingdom manifested in power and glory, but in mystery for such as have ears to hear. And although grace works its wonders, the nets break, and the boats threaten to sink, even when their partners come to share in taking the great multitude of fishes.

Here Jesus is not aboard, and there is no putting out into the deep, but with the early morn just breaking He stood on the beach, and still unknown put a question which brought out their confessed lack of success. Then comes the word, "Cast the net on the right side of the boat, and ye will find." And so it was; for so casting they were now unable to draw the net for the multitude of fishes. It is the figure of the great millennial haul from among the nations, when the salvation of all Israel will prove to be incomparably blessed to the Gentiles. If their "fall" has been so fraught with good in divine grace, how much more their "fulness" (Romans 11:12), of which these seven Israelites may be the pledge?[380a] The once rejected but now risen Christ is to be the head of the heathen, not only of the Church now on high, but by and by of the nations on the earth, owned by previously unbelieving Israel to be their Lord and their God. Then will the Jew sing, "God shall bless us; and all the ends of the earth shall fear Him" [Psalm 67:6 *ff.*]; and again, "Princes shall come out of Egypt: Ethiopia shall soon stretch out her hands unto God, Sing unto God, ye kingdoms of the earth; O sing praises unto Jehovah" [Psalm 68:31 *ff.*]. In the figure of that day the nets do not break, nor is there any thought of putting the fishes into the boat, still less of gathering the good into vessels and casting the bad away. The weakness of man and of earthly circumstances wanes before the present power of the Lord Who directs all.

Augustine may be safely regarded as the ablest and most enlightened of the early writers on this sign, which he compares with that which preceded the call of Simon Peter and the sons of Zebedee. He is right in distinguishing the take of fish which followed the Resurrection from the miraculous draught before it. Nor does any other among the ancients add to the truth of his observations, Gregory the Great rather darkening the force of our scripture by his effort to make much of Peter's part in order to help on the Papal pretensions then in course of rapid growth. The earlier miracle he regards as significant of the good and evil in the Church as it is now; the later, of the good only which it is to have for ever when the resurrection of the just is accomplished in the end of this age (*Sermons on the Liturgical Seasons*, ccxlviii.-cclii., etc.).

Enough, perhaps, has been said already which anticipatively corrects so erroneous an interpretation of the sign before us. There is no thought of a fishing scene in the resurrection either of just or unjust, no truth in the employing of Jews or men for gathering in the risen righteous to their heavenly and eternal rest. The Fathers saw nothing of the future restoring of the kingdom to Israel, nor of the general blessedness of all nations as such under the reign of the Lord in the age to come. The moderns are in general no less uninstructed; for though some see and allow the restoration of Israel to their land and the accomplishment of the glory promised so largely throughout the Old Testament, they somehow, with strange inconsistency, merge all into this age. They do not perceive that these are among the constituents of the age to come, before the eternal state when there will be no difference between Jew and Gentile absolutely, as there is none even now for the Christian and the Church.

But here is another source of this deep, long-lasting, and widespread misconception. Men, and even good men, fail to see the true nature of the Church, as they do not believe in the special features of the millennial age. How much error would be avoided if they discerned the peculiar character and unexampled privilege of the body of Christ in union with its heavenly head, since redemption, while He sits at God's right hand! How much more, if they looked for His return with His bride, already complete and caught up to be with Him on high, to make His foes His footstool, and Judah His goodly horse in the battle which introduces Jehovah-Jesus King over all the earth—one Jehovah, and His name one in that day {Zechariah 10:3, 14:9}! It is as egregious to confound with the Church wherein is neither Jew nor Greek all this distinctive blessing of Israel and the nations on the earth under the reign of the Lord, as it is to merge both in the end of the age or in the eternity which, they assume, is to follow. They blot out the new age to come, which is to be characterised by the reign of the Second Man, the Lord Jesus, the absence of Satan, the exaltation of the glorified saints in power on high, and the blessedness of all the families of the earth here below.

But these all stand indelibly written in the Scriptures; and no strugglings of unbelief can get rid of a truth which may be, and is, offensive to the pride of nature and the worldly mind, as it would prove full of help and value to Christian men often perplexed by their own misreading of revelation and their misconception, consequently, of what is to be sought or expected at this present time. For there is no error which does not bear

THE TWENTY-FIRST CHAPTER

its own baneful fruits; and the error in question, though not assailing fundamental truth, affects most extensively the right understanding of the past, the present, and the future. Thus are the chief characteristic differences blurred, and an undistinguishable vague is presented; whereas the word of God affords the fullest light on the various dispensations, as well as on that mystery in regard of Christ and of the Church which comes in between and is superior to either.

The love which is of God makes the eye single, and thereby the whole body is full of light. John was quick to discern the Lord.

> "Therefore that disciple whom Jesus loved saith to Peter, It is the Lord. Then Simon Peter, hearing that it was (*literally*, is) the Lord, girt his over-coat about (him)—for he was naked—and cast himself into the sea. But the other disciples came in the little boat (for they were not far from the land, but about two hundred cubits off), dragging the net of the fishes. So when they had got off to the land, they see a coal-fire laid, and fish laid thereon, and bread. Jesus saith to them, Bring of the fish which ye took just now. Simon Peter (therefore)[e] went up and drew the net to land[f] full of great fishes, a hundred (and) fifty-three: and, many as they were, the net was not rent. Jesus saith to them, Come, dine. And none of the disciples durst inquire of Him, Who art Thou? knowing that it was (*literally*, is) the Lord. Jesus[g] cometh and taketh the bread and giveth to them, and the fish likewise. This already (was the) third (time) Jesus was manifested to the disciples[h] after having risen from (the) dead" (verses 7-14).

But if John was the first to perceive Who He was that spoke to them,[381] Peter, with characteristic promptness, is the first to act so as to reach His presence, yet not naked but in seemly guise. He had failed miserably and profoundly and repeatedly, but not his faith; even as the Saviour had prayed for him that *it* should not fail. Despair because of the gravest failure is no more of faith than the indifference which hears not the Saviour's voice, and, never knowing His glory or His grace, never has the consciousness of its own guilt. In the Lord he thus learns experimentally to confide, after having too much trusted his own love for his Master; and Christ must be all to the heart of him who is to strengthen his brethren.

The Lord, however, despises none, and the other disciples follow in the small boat, dragging the net full of the fishes; for He had not given such a haul to leave it behind. Grace makes to differ, never to behave oneself unseemly. Peter carried himself suitably toward the Lord; so did they in their place; for, indeed, they all had one heart and purpose to please the Lord.

Thus will it be when the abundance of the sea shall be converted to Zion. What will not be the effect of all Israel being saved? "If their fall is the riches of the world, and their loss the riches of the Gentiles, how much more their fulness? What shall the receiving of them be but life from the dead?" [Romans 11:12, 15]. Jehovah will destroy the veil that is spread over all nations; and Israel will not only be the instrument of divine vengeance on their enemies but of God's mercy and blessing to all the families of the earth. "And the remnant of Jacob shall be in the midst of many peoples as dew from Jehovah, as the showers upon the grass, that tarrieth not for man, nor waiteth for the sons of men. And the remnant of

Jacob shall be among the nations in the midst of many peoples as a lion among the beasts of the forest, as a young lion among the flocks of sheep: who, if he go through, both treadeth down, and teareth in pieces, and there is none to deliver" (Micah 5:7-8).

It is remarked and remarkable that, when the disciples landed, they see a fire laid and fish thereon and bread. The Lord had wrought before them and without them, though He would give them communion with the fruits of the activity of His grace. He will have got ready a Gentile remnant Himself before He employs His people to gather the great millennial catch out of the sea of Gentiles. The grace of God will work after a far more varied and vigorous sort than men think; and while He deigns to use His people, it is good for them at that very time to learn that He can, and does, work independently. "Oh, the depth of the riches of the wisdom and the knowledge of God! How unsearchable are His judgments, and His ways past finding out!" {Romans 11:33}. How verified both in Israel and in the Gentile!

Yet the Lord would have His own enter into the fellowship of what He has wrought as well as enjoy their own work. "Jesus saith to them, Bring of the fish which ye just now took. Simon Peter therefore went up and drew the net to land, full of great fishes, a hundred and fifty-three;[382] and, as many as there were, the net was not rent. Jesus saith to them, Come, dine."

The contrast with all that characterises the actual work of His servants is very plain. The parable in Matthew 13 [verse 47] shows us that even up to the close of the age good and bad fish are contained in the net, and that it is the marked call of the fishermen just then to put the good into vessels as well as to cast the bad away; whilst the angels, as we know, do the converse work, when judgment comes at the Lord's appearing, of severing the wicked from among the righteous. The miraculous draught in Luke 5 [verses 4-9], descriptive of present service, shows us the nets breaking and the boats into which the fishes were put beginning to sink. Nothing of this appears here where the days of the kingdom are set forth, when the Lord is with His own on earth. There are many great fishes named but none bad; the net is expressly said to be unrent; there is no thought of the boat sinking, and the net was dragged along instead of the boat being filled. Thus a wholly different and future state of things is pictured after this age closes and before eternity begins.

The Lord will surely yet and thenceforward renew His associations with His people on earth: I speak not of the Father's house on high and its heavenly relations, but of those to be blessed and a blessing on earth. It is an unquestionably scriptural prospect, and most cheering, that this very earth is to be delivered from its present corruption and thraldom into "the liberty of the glory of the children of God" [Romans 8:21]. For the revelation of His sons the earnest expectation of the creation waits, though, as we know, the whole of it groans and travails in pain till now {Romans 8:19, 22}. But it will not be so always. The Lord Himself is coming, and the day of His appearing will see creation delivered, not, of course, as we who have the firstfruits of the Spirit are now into the liberty of grace by faith, but the creation itself also by power shall be freed into the liberty of glory. It will be the kingdom of God, no longer a secret to faith, but displayed in power and in all its extent of blessing, with its earthly things and its heavenly, as the Lord intimated to Nicodemus and as we are taught in Ephesians 1 and

THE TWENTY-FIRST CHAPTER

Colossians 1 in connection with the headship of Christ and His reconciliation.

Here the Lord on that day was giving the pledge of the future widespread blessing, when the Gentile world will afford common joy, and the occasion of the manifestation of His risen power and presence, to His people. None but He could or would act after such a sort. His grace is unmistakable. "And none of the disciples durst inquire of Him, Who art Thou? knowing that it was the Lord. Jesus cometh and taketh the bread and giveth to them, and the fish likewise.[383] This already (was the) third (time) Jesus was manifested to the disciples,[384] after being risen from the dead." It is the day, prefigured in prophecy and awaited by the saints from of old, when they shall all know Him from the least of them to the greatest of them, none more needing to say, Know the Lord. "At that time they shall call Jerusalem the throne of Jehovah; and all the nations shall be gathered unto it, to the name of Jehovah, to Jerusalem; and they shall no more walk after the stubbornness of their evil heart. In those days the house of Judah shall walk with the house of Israel; and they shall come together out of the land of the north to the land that I caused your fathers to inherit" (Jeremiah 3:17-18).

There would be an utter gap for this world and God's glory in it, a gap which nothing else could fill up for him who takes a large and observant view of God's dealings with the world, if there were not a period of divine blessedness here below for Israel and the nations through the grace and to the praise of the risen Lord Jesus. This does not in the least interfere with the deeper and higher things above the world to which the Christian and the Church are now called. On the contrary, when the reality and the true character of the kingdom at Christ's appearing are not seen, there is a confusion of it with the proper hopes of the Church, which is ruinous to the distinctive blessedness of the Church on the one hand and of Israel with the Gentiles on the other.

{VERSES 15-25.}

But our Gospel, while fully revealing God in Christ on earth, and in these closing chapters tracing His ways in Christ risen, first for the Christian and the Assembly, next for Israel, and lastly for the Gentiles, never loses sight of grace working with the individual soul. Thus Peter must be thoroughly restored and publicly reinstated: so would the Lord have it. He had been already singled out specially (Mark 16:7) at a moment when such a distinction was of all moment, both to himself and before his brethren, who would naturally have regarded with deep distrust the man who had so grievously, and spite of full warning, denied his Master. And before the eleven had the Lord standing in their midst, He had appeared to Simon (Luke 24:34; 1 Corinthians 15:5). But He would carry on the gracious work profoundly in Peter's heart, and let us into the secrets of this truly divine discipline.

> "When therefore they had dined, Jesus saith to Simon Peter, Simon (son) of Jonah (or, John),[i] lovest thou Me more than these? He saith to Him, Yea, Lord; Thou knowest that I dearly love Thee. He saith to him, Feed My lambs. He saith to him again a second time, Simon (son) of Jonah,[i] lovest thou Me? He saith to Him, Yea, Lord; Thou knowest that I dearly love Thee. He saith to him, Tend My sheep. He saith to him the third time, Simon (son) of Jonah,[i] dost thou dearly love Me?

Peter was grieved because He said to him the third time, Dost thou dearly love Me? and he said to Him, Lord, Thou knowest all things, Thou knowest that I dearly love Thee. Jesus saith to him, Feed My sheep (or, little sheep)" (verses 15-17).[385]

The Lord goes to the root of the matter. He does not speak of Peter's denying Him, but penetrates to its cause. Peter fell through confidence in himself, at least in his love to his Master. He judged that he might go where others could not safely, and that he would stand to the confession of His name in the face of prison and death. The result we all know too well. The greatest of the twelve denied the Lord repeatedly and swore to it, notwithstanding fresh and solemn warning. But restoration is not complete though we own the fruit ever so fully. In order to thorough blessing the Lord would have us, like Peter here, to discern the hidden spring. This he had not reached yet: the Lord makes it known to His servant. There is no haste; He waits till they had broken their fast, and then He says to Simon Peter: "Simon (son) of John, lovest thou (ἀγαπᾷς) Me more than these?" He calls him by his natural name; for well He knew wherein lay the secret which gave a handle to the enemy; and He would awaken a true sense of it in the Apostle's soul. Through assurance of his own superior affection he had not merely trusted in himself, in comparison with others, but slighted the word of the Lord. Had he laid His words to heart with prayer, he had not fallen when tried, but endured the temptation and suffered. But it was not so. He was sure that he loved the Lord more than all the rest; and if they could not stand such a sifting, he would; and this confidence in his own surpassing love to Christ was precisely the cause, as the interrogation of the bystanders was the occasion, of his fall. And now the Lord lays the root bare to Peter, who had already wept over the open fruit.

Yet at first Peter does not discover the aim of the Lord. He does avoid unwise comparison with others; he simply appeals to the Lord's inward conscious knowledge: "Yea, Lord, Thou knowest that I dearly love (φιλῶ) Thee." Far from denying his profession of tender affection, the Lord proves His own value for it, and His confidence in Peter. For He, the good Shepherd, about to quit the world, entrusts to His servant that which was unspeakably precious in His eyes and most of all needed His care: "Feed My lambs." Thus does He prove our love by answering to His love for the weakest of saints. "Whosoever loveth Him that begat, loveth him also that is begotten of Him." "We love because He first loved us"; but it is not that we love Him only, but those that are His, not those that love us naturally, but those that He loves as divinely. "He that saith, I know Him and keepeth not His commandments, is a liar, and the truth is not in him"; and "If a man say, I love God, and hateth his brother, he is a liar; for he that loveth not his brother whom he hath seen, how can he love God Whom he hath not seen? And this commandment have we from Him, that he who loveth God love his brother also" {1 John 5:1, 4:19, 2:4, 4:20-21}.

Did not Peter deeply and increasingly feel the Lord's loving trust thus reposed in him, more than even before he fell? The administration of the kingdom of the heavens, the keys (not of the Church nor of heaven, but) of the kingdom, had been promised to Peter, and made good in due time. Here it is more tender and intimate, though there is no ground to extend the flock here committed to him beyond those of the circumcision (*cf.* Galatians 2). Did he not remember Isaiah 40:11, in communion with the blessed Messiah in His work of feeding that flock like a shepherd, gathering the lambs with His arm, and carrying them in His bosom, while gently leading the nursing ewes?

The Lord appeals once more, but drops all reference to others. "He saith to him again a second time, Simon (son) of John, lovest thou Me? He saith to Him, Yea, Lord; Thou knowest that I dearly love Thee. He saith to him, Feed My sheep." It is painfully instructive that even such a ripe scholar as Grotius should commit himself to an opinion so unworthy as that these marked changes of expression represent no weighty distinctions of truth.[j] But Peter, though he no longer thinks disparagingly of others, cannot give up his assurance that the Lord was inwardly aware of his true affection for Himself. And the Lord now bids him tend or rule His sheep, as before feed His lambs.[386] So Peter at a later day impresses the same on the elders among the Jewish Christians he was addressing, sojourners of the dispersion in Pontus and other districts of Asia Minor: "Tend the flock of God which is among you, overseeing not of constraint, but willingly; nor yet for filthy lucre, but readily; nor as lording it over your possessions, but making yourselves ensamples to the flock" (1 Peter 5:2-3).

In the Lord's words, as in the Apostle's, it will be noticed to our profit how carefully the lambs and the sheep are said to be Christ's, not the elders' nor even the Apostle's. The flock is God's flock. He who treats Christians as *his* congregation is guilty of the same forgetfulness of divine grace and divine authority as the congregation in regarding the minister as *their* minister, instead of Christ's. If any think these to be slight distinctions, it is clear that they have no right apprehension of a difference which is as deep in truth as it is fraught with the most momentous consequences for good and ill in practice. Only this gives moral elevation, as it alone springs from faith; this alone delivers from self and gives the true relation and character, even Christ, whether to those that minister or to those ministered to.

But the Lord speaks to him yet again. "He saith to him the third time, Simon (son) of John, dost thou dearly love Me?" Here the probe reached the bottom. Not a word of blame or reproach; but the Lord for the third time questions him, and for the first time takes up his own word of special affection. Did not his threefold denial appear in the light of the threefold appeal, and, above all, of that word expressive of endearing love? "Peter was grieved, because He said to him the third time, Dost thou dearly love Me? and he said to Him, Lord, Thou knowest all things; Thou knowest that I dearly love Thee. Jesus saith to him, Feed My sheep," or, if the reading of the Alexandrian, the Vatican, and the Paris palimpsest, etc., be preferred, My "little sheep,"[k] a diminutive of tenderness and endearment.

The work of restoration was now fully done. Peter abandons every thought of self and can find refuge only in grace. Only He Who of Himself knows all without an effort, only He could give credit to Peter's heart, spite of his mouth and all appearances; yet did not He know that His poor denying servant dearly loved Him? The answer of the Lord, committing afresh what was dearest to Him on earth—the gift of the Father's love to Himself—seals Peter's restoration, not in soul only but in his relation to the sheep of His pasture. *Feed* them, says the Lord. To tend or rule pastorally is not forgotten; but positive nourishment, as of the lambs at the beginning, remains to the last, the abiding task of the shepherd, the habitual need of the sheep; but it demands enduring and deep love, not to scold, perhaps, or govern, but to feed, and not least of all the least of all Christ's sheep. Only the love of Christ can carry one through it.

But this is not all. It is not enough for the Lord to restore fully the soul of Peter and to more than reinstate him in his relation to the sheep which might have seemed otherwise compromised. Grace would give him in God's due time what he had not only lost but turned to his own shame and his Master's dishonour, the confession of His name even to prison and death.

> "Verily, verily, I say to thee, When thou wast young, thou girdedst thyself and walkedst whither thou wouldest; but when thou shalt be old, thou shalt stretch forth thy hands, and another shall gird thee, and carry thee whither thou wouldest not. And this He said, signifying by what death he should glorify God. And having said this, He saith to him, Follow Me" (verses 18-19).[387-389]

In this, as in what precedes and in what follows, actions and words are veiled yet significant. There was the intention to convey important and interesting truth, but only to such as weighed all and went not beyond the just bearing of the Lord's sayings or doings. Peter was then in his prime of natural vigour. In his youth (and he was still far from being an old man) he was ready for energetic action, and disposed to use his liberty with too little distrust of himself. He had just ventured to go whither he would, into the high priest's house; and as far as doughty words promised, one might have thought he had girded up his loins like a man to do great feats of valour, or to endure a great fight of afflictions for his betrayed and insulted Master. The issue we all know too well; and Peter had been led more and more to see and feel it, till he had now got down to the root and judged it thoroughly before God. But now also the Lord lets him know that grace would give him back what had seemed for ever lost to him, the fellowship of Christ's sufferings and conformity to His death, far more, in fact, than Peter in his own too confident love and strength had proffered before he miserably broke down.

See how grace shuts out all ground for boasting, while it secures honour beyond what we in our most sanguine desires ever anticipated. Is not this worthy of God and suited to His saints? When Peter went forward according to his own words, he came to worse than nothing; he a most favoured servant denying the Holy and Righteous One, his own most gracious Master. It was the deepest humiliation, yet was he a true saint and a loving disciple; but so it was because he entered into temptation at his own charges, instead of enduring it, when tried by it, according to God. Thus his fall was inevitable; for none can endure save in faith and self-judgment. To be a believer and fervently to love the Lord will not preserve in the least under such circumstances, however strange this may sound to many, who little think how often and deeply they deny the Lord practically, in great matters and small to which He attaches His name. We must be put to shame in whatever thing we are proud; and how much better is even this gain, than to be let go on in unrebuked self-complacency?

But the Lord promises Peter that, when he should be old, he should stretch forth his hands, and another gird and carry him whither he would not. Thus, when it was no longer possible to boast of his own strength or courage, as a helpless old man, Peter would enjoy from

THE TWENTY-FIRST CHAPTER

God the singular privilege, not only of death for Christ's sake which in younger days he had essayed to face and most ignominiously failed in, but of that very death which the Lord had suffered with its prolonged agony and shame. For the Lord, as we are expressly told, said as He did, signifying not death so much as "by what" sort of death Peter was to glorify God; and after saying this, He saith to him, Follow Me.

The allusion was scarcely mistakable. In those days, when such a punishment was common enough for the lowest slaves and guiltiest criminals, everyone understood the meaning of being "lifted up," or outstretching the arms by the force of another. Again, the illustrative act of calling Peter to follow Him as He walked some paces on the shore made plain its grave intent. Yet even then and thus, another carrying him whither he would not proves how little of self was to be in Peter's death on the cross in contrast with those who, at a later day and a day lower incomparably, sought a martyr's death to win this crown. No! Peter's close on earth was to be suffering and death for Christ, Who would give him to endure at the fit moment. Not heroism nor asceticism is the Christian badge, but obedience.

The lesson of its surpassing grace abides for us who love the same Saviour, and have a nature no better than the disciple's. Have we been taught it? Can one learn it safely and surely, save as following Christ? "If any man serve Me, let him follow Me; and where I am, there shall also My servant be; if any man serve Me, him will My Father honour" {John 12:26}. Peter when called should follow the Master; and so he did. May the same grace strengthen and guide us in the same path for life or death! To follow Christ as He calls is our best service.

The ardent mind of Peter, kindled by the solemn intimation of the Lord, seizes the opportunity to inquire about one so closely linked with him as the beloved disciple. It is hard in this question to discern the jealousy of the active for the contemplative life, of which early and mediæval writers say much. But the Lord gives him the correction he needed.

> "Peter[l] turning round seeth the disciple whom Jesus loved following (who also at the supper leaned on His breast and said, Lord, who is he that delivereth Thee up?); Peter therefore[m] seeing him saith to Jesus, Lord, and what (of) this man? Jesus saith to him, If I will that he abide till I come, what (is it) unto thee? Follow *thou* Me. This saying therefore went forth among the brethren that that disciple doth not die; yet Jesus said not to him, that he doth not die; but, If I will that he abide till I come, what (is it) to thee?"[n] (verses 20-23).[390-392]

It was really loving interest concerning one more closely associated with himself than his own brother Andrew by the bond of a common affection for Jesus and of Jesus. This made Peter curious to learn about John now that his own earthly destiny was just revealed. But the gracious Lord, if He reproved in His own gentleness the prying spirit of His servant, did furnish ample matter for thought in the riddle He sets before Peter. One can readily see how shallow is the notion of Augustine and many since his day, that the Lord meant no more than John's living to a protracted and placid age, in contrast with Peter slain violently in old age, as with his own brother James in youth. Peter emphatically was to follow the Lord even in His death as far as this could be. Not so John, who was to abide hanging on the will of the Lord till He came. "If I will that he abide," etc.

THE TWENTY-FIRST CHAPTER

Needless to say that there is evident and intentional mystery in the manner it was spoken of; and some have supposed that the destruction of Jerusalem and the judgment of the Jewish polity are here alluded to; as there is certainly more in such a thought than a merely peaceful death in advanced age. For death is in no true sense the Lord's coming, but rather the converse, our going to Him.[393] We know, at any rate, that to John it was given to see the Son of Man judging the churches, and to have visions not only of God's providential dealings with the world whether Jews or Gentiles, but of the Lord's return in judgment of the apostate powers of the earth and of the man of sin, in order to the establishment of the long-predicted kingdom of God and the times of the restitution of all things, with the still higher glory in the New Jerusalem.

Out of the Lord's words, perverted as they speedily were, the synagogue seems to have had its fable of the wandering Jew, and Christendom its Prester John, to entertain minds which had lost the truth either through rejecting Christ or by turning to superstition.

But this we learn of great practical moment from verse 23, how dangerous it is to trust tradition, even the earliest, and how blessed to have the unerring standard of God's written word. The saying that went forth among the brethren in apostolic times seemed a most natural, if not necessary, inference from the words of our Lord. But we do not well to accept unreservedly an inferential statement, still less to be drawn into a system built on such deductions. We have the word of the Lord, and faith bows to it for its joy and rest to God's glory. Error easily insinuates itself into the first remove from what He says, as the Apostle instructs us here that the Lord did not affirm that that disciple was not to die, but "If I will that he abide till I come." Yet those who let in this primitive mistake were not enemies, were not grievous wolves, or men speaking perverse things to draw away the disciples after them. It was "among the brethren" that the tradition, unfounded and misleading, got spread. Miracles did not hinder, nor gifts, nor power, nor unity. The mistake arose from reasoning, instead of cleaving to the word of the Lord. The brethren, through lack of subjection to God and of distrust in themselves, gave the words a meaning, instead of simply receiving from them their true import. No wonder another great apostle commends us to God and to the word of His grace {Acts 20:32}; for if we may fully profit by His word in simple dependence on Himself, we cannot duly honour Him if we slight His word. And though it is by the Holy Spirit that we are thus kept and blest, even He is in no sort the standard of truth (while He is power in every way), but Christ as revealed in the written word.[394]

Last of all comes the personal seal or attestation of the writer.

> "This is the disciple that beareth witness of these things, and wrote these things: and we know that his witness is true. And there are also many other things which Jesus did, the which, if they were written one by one, I suppose that not even the world itself would contain the books that should be written" (verses 24-25).°

It was John, and no other.[394a] Every inspired writer preserves none the less his own style and manner, and none more unmistakably than he who wrote the fourth Gospel. Yet what was written is but a sample, selected in divine wisdom, and with a specific plan subserving the grand scope and purpose of divine revelation. If everything which Jesus did were written out, well might the adoring Evangelist suppose that the world itself would be too small for the needed books.[395]

It may be noticed how strikingly the close of the Gospel answers to the beginning, or at least the latter part of chapters 1 and 2. For though the subject be the Person of the Son manifested on earth, and then sending the Holy Spirit on His going to the Father, while thus beyond all others consisting of eternal truth and the highest privilege, yet is there care, before and after this is done historically, to show that the dispensational ways of God are in no way slighted. The latter part of chapter 20 and the beginning of chapter 21 are the counterpart of the early notice. We may add that the Epistles of John are, of course, devoted to the deeper task of tracing eternal life and the fellowship it gives with the Father and the Son, of which the word, through the Apostles, is the revelation, and the Holy Spirit is the power. The book of the Apocalypse, on the other hand, is the full and final unfolding of the dispensational ways of God; but it also reveals that which is above them all, and their connection with heaven and eternity brought before us far more completely and vividly than anywhere else in the testimony of God.

NOTES ON THE TWENTY-FIRST CHAPTER

a [*Cf. Lectures Introductory to the Study of the Gospels*, p. 566 *ff.*]

b The Compl. rightly gives ἐν-, Erasmus wrongly ἀν-, with Steph., Be., and Elz., though not without uncials (ΔΛ) and other support; but the Compl. is as wrong as the rest in adding εὐθὺς with many more MSS.

c γεν. T.R., [Blass] early read in uncials, and most copies; γιν. ABC^(pm)EL, ten cursives, etc. [Tisch., W. and H., Weiss]. The MSS. also differ as to ἐπὶ [Tisch., Blass] and εἰς [W. and H., Weiss].

d The more correct form ἴσχυον is given by ℵBCDLΛΠ, more than ten cursives, many Latin copies, Syriac, etc.

e ℵBCL{X}Π^(pm), etc., add οὖν [W. and H.], contrary to most uncials and cursives [Tisch., Weiss, Blass].

f Most, with T.R., read ἐπὶ τῆς γ., but the best εἰς τὴν γ., a few ἐπὶ τὴν γ.

g οὖν is added by most, but ℵBCDLX, etc., do not warrant it.

h T.R., against ℵABCL, etc., adds αὐτοῦ, "His."

i "John" is supported by a few of the oldest authorities [Edd.], "Jonah" or Jonas, too, being perhaps only an abridged form of the name Johanan or Jehohanan.

j "Promiscue hic usurpavit Iohannes ἀγαπᾶν et φιλεῖν, ut mox βόσκειν et ποιμαίνειν. Neque hic quaerendæ subtilitates." {"Here John has used ἀγαπᾶν and φιλεῖν indiscriminately, as presently βόσκειν and ποιμαίνειν. Nor should subtle distinctions be looked for in these instances."}

NOTES ON THE TWENTY-FIRST CHAPTER

k [So W. and H., but Blass follows Syr^{sin} reading πρόβατα.]

l T.R., which ℵDXΓΔΠ² and others support, adds δὲ, "but," not the other ancient manuscripts.

m The highest authorities add οὖν, "therefore," but most oppose.

n ℵ^{pm} is alone in omitting τί πρός σε, "what is it to thee?" [so Cod. Vercellensis of Old Lat., and Syr$^{\text{sin hier}}$].

o Verse 25 is omitted in Tischendorf's eighth edition on the slender omission of the Sinaitic copy [*prima manu*], supposed to be confirmed by "Scholia," edited by Matthæi. The Ἀμήν at the end (T.R.) is not in ℵABCD, etc. [Blass brackets the verse; see W. and H., *Select Readings*, p. 90 *f.*].[396]

AN EXPOSITION OF THE GOSPEL OF JOHN

Indexes to the Exposition

Index of Scripture Quotations 627

Index of Greek and Hebrew Words 632

Index of Subjects 633

References in these indexes are to page numbers in the Exposition.

AN EXPOSITION OF THE GOSPEL OF JOHN

Index of Scripture Quotations

Genesis
1:1-2. 28
2 558
13:4. 268
20:7. 128
25:22. 274
43:18, 20. 268
49 294

Exodus
12:46. 550

Numbers
14:21. 507
19:16. 597
30 366

Deuteronomy
6:4. 353
18 41
32:15. 377

1 Samuel
2:30. 286

Ezra
9:7-9. 257

Nehemiah
9:30, 36 f. 257

Psalms
2 22, 55, 491; 8-9. 186
8 22, 56, 210, 254
22:18. 543; 22. 582; 25. 591
32 54; 7. 245; 9. 366
34:6. 559
40:6 f. 92
41:9. 377, 381
43 84
49:14. 174
55:6 ff. 84; 13. 360
67:6 ff. 602
68:31 ff. 602
69:4. 448; 9. 71; 21. 545
73 84
77 555
80 210, 294
82 313
85:10 f. 94
101:5, 7-8. 526
105:15. 128
110 210; 1. 396
118 343; 22. 537
132 185
133:3. 355, 484
143:2. 180

Proverbs
1:1. 315
8 29
30:4. 90
31:6. 433
Isaiah
6:10. 351
7 227
9:7. 105
11:2-4. 88; 9. 507
24:21. 461
25:9. 593
27:1. 461
32:15. 463
35:7 f. 400
40 294; 11. 302, 612; 29-31. 138
44:3. 79
52:7. 120
53:1. 351; 4. 328; 5. 592; 6. 562; 9. 552; 10. 562; 10 f. 345 f.
54:1-3. 143; 5. 143; 13. 199
55:1. 80
63:3. 516
Jeremiah
3:17 f. 609
10:7. 532
30:7. 477
Song of Solomon
8:7. 340
Ezekiel
34 294
36:23-36. 85 f.; 25-28. 79
Daniel
7 210, 254
12:1. 477; 2. 484
Hosea
1:10. 488
Joel
2:28 f. 463

Micah
5:2. 54, 227, 237, 592; 7 f. 607
Habakkuk
2:14. 508
Zechariah
9:9. 343; 13. 531
10:3. 604
11 294; 8. 251
12:3. 531; 10. 550, 561, 592
13 294; 6. 592
14:9. 604
Malachi
4 41
Matthew
2:23. 534
4:12. 117
6:10. 87; 22. 52
8:17. 328
9:30. 328
11:14. 40; 27. 510
12:50. 582
13 140; 41-43. 87; 47. 607
14 188
15:24. 302
16:16 f. 349; 19. 369; 21. 528
17:11 f. 40; 12., 22 f. 528
23 66; 39. 343
24 66; 21.477
25:31-46. 167
26:39. 516; 71. 534
27 546, 552; 19. 555
28 568, 569; 9. 580
Mark
1:14. 117; 24. 534; 43. 328
2:18. 58
9:7. 175
10:47. 534
13:19. 477; 32. 344
14:5. 328; 67. 534

INDEX OF SCRIPTURE QUOTATIONS IN THE EXPOSITION

15 547, 552; 42. 555
16 568; 6. 534; 7. 610; 15. 563

Luke
1:35. 165
3:15. 55
4:30. 267; 34. 534
5:4-9. 608
11:13. 123; 28. 357
13:32 f. 219
17:25. 312
18:37. 534
20:25. 530
21:22-24. 477; 37 f. 242
22:15. 359; 31 f. 526; 39. 242;
   43 f. 517; 61 f. 526
23 547; 2. 530; 54. 568
24:12. 537; 25. 364; 34. 610

Acts
1 – 5 563
1:22. 452; 24. 469
2:22. 534
3 41; 6. 534
4:10. 534; 12. 538; 27 f. 529
5:14. 508; 19. 586
6:14. 534
7:59. 469
9:5. 534
10:11. 269; 38. 534; 40. 563
11:5. 269
12:10. 587
13 563; 27. 229, 449; 41. 285
17:31. 564
19:1-7. 42; 2. 233
20:7. 586; 32. 620
22:8. 534
24:5. 534
26:9. 534
28:25-27. 353

Romans
1:18 ff. 497; 20. 26
2:6-9. 174; 12-16. 98; 24. 84
3:10 ff. 445; 25. 387
4:2. 193
5:10. 372; 19. 433; 20. 382
6 76; 3. 76
7 435; 7 f. 193, 589; 24. 153
8 33, 435, 464; 1-3. 121;
   1 f. 589; 3. 152, 459; 7 f. 68;
   19. 608; 21. 608; 22. 608;
   29. 501; 32. 298
9:4 f. 131
10:9 f. 110; 10. 354
11:12. 602, 606; 15. 606;
   17. 431; 23 ff. 449; 33. 607
12:9. 437
13:10. 437

1 Corinthians
1:23 f. 229
2 464; 8. 229; 10 f. 459;
   11, 14. 83
3:15. 431
4:15. 77
6:17. 414
8:2. 365
9:27. 214, 431
11 180
12 464
13 437
14:24 f. 128; 37. 111
15 56, 563; 5. 610; 45. 318;
   47. 77; 51 f. 326
16:2. 586

2 Corinthians
2:10. 590
3 464; 18. 501
4:10 f. 414
5:7. 593; 17 f. 581 f.; 19. 445;
   20. 369;

21. 157, 386, 458, 501
8:9. 382
12:5. 584; 8. 469

Galatians
2 612; 19 *f*. 284; 20. 77
4:4. 47; 6. 298
5:1. 259; 5. 232
6:1. 374

Ephesians
1 – 4 464
1 56, 608; 10. 50, 87; 18 *f*. 409; 22. 532
2 – 4 431
2:1, 5. 284; 5 *f*. 336; 17 *f*. 229; 18. 403
3:16. 409; 17. 411
4:9 *f*. 90; 30. 376
5:26. 77

Philippians
1:21. 203
2:6 *f*. 166; 7. 485; 10. 347; 10 *f*. 519
3:3. 133
4:13. 427

Colossians
1 609; 15. 30; 9 *f*. 416; 12. 370, 550; 16 *f*. 28; 17. 216; 18. 82; 20. 87; 27. 229
2 76; 9. 26; 21. 582
3:4. 34, 510; 9 *f*. 576

1 Thessalonians
4:9. 437; 16 *f*. 326

2 Thessalonians
1:3. 63; 8. 531; 10. 508
2:9 *f*. 173; 10-12. 333

1 Timothy
6:13. 530; 16. 30

2 Timothy
3 497

Titus
3:5-7. 277

Hebrews
1:1 *f*. 446; 3. 82
2 56
9 362; 27 *f*. 179
10 362; 2. 370; 5-7. 92; 5-10. 458; 14. 370; 17 *f*. 372; 19 *f*. 288
12:10. 425; 22-24. 87
13:13. 287 *f*.; 14. 232

James
1:18. 77, 135

1 Peter
1:8. 577, 593; 11. 364; 12. 82; 19 *ff*. 359; 23. 77, 135
2:8. 431
3 76
5:2 *f*. 613

2 Peter
1:4. 33, 77, 284

1 John
1:1-4. 31; 2. 34; 3. 506, 593; 5. 30
2:1. 24, 408, 423, 478; 4. 612; 6. 434; 8. 31, 390; 13. 483; 14. 31; 17. 104; 18. 18; 20. 296; 21. 37; 22 *f*. 454; 27. 37
3:1. 33, 49, 496; 2. 501; 17 *f*. 438
4:2-3. 594; 6. 595; 7. 374; 9 *f*. 91, 385; 10. 321; 13-16. 207; 14. 141; 19. 612; 20 *f*. 612
5:1. 78, 284, 612; 4 f. 478; 6. 77, 361, 549; 20. 28

INDEX OF SCRIPTURE QUOTATIONS IN THE EXPOSITION

Revelation
1:10. 585
3:1. 411
4 19
10:7. 394
13 43
14:20. 516
15:3. 532
20 179, 166; 14. 267
21:8. 353; 11. 506; 23 *f.* 506

Index of Greek and Hebrew Words

ἀγαπᾶν, φιλεῖν, 611 ff.
αἰτέω, 325, 422, 468
ἀμνός, ἀρνίον, 43
ἀναβέβηκεν, proleptic perfect, 90, 114
ἅπτου, ἅψῃ, 582

ἐλέγχειν, force of, 460
ἐρωτάω, 325. See under αἰτέω

ἴδια, ἴδιοι, 32

κατάκριμα, 180
κρίσις, 161 f., 179 f.

ἐνδιάθετος, προφορικός, 56

מָשָׁל, meaning of, 472

παῖς, used of JESUS, 33
παράκλητος, meaning of, 458, 478
παραβολή, παροιμία, 296, 315, 472
φιλεῖν, 474, 612 ff., 622

ῥῆμα, 490, 495

τέκνον, not used of JESUS, 33
τετέλεσται, 547
θειότης, θεότης, 26
θέλω, use of, 509

υἱός, use of, 33

Index of Subjects

Abarbanel, 560
Aben Ezra, 560
Abiding in Christ, 203, 432
Æschylus, reference to, 325
Agnosticism, 438
Alford (Dean), 58, 178 *ff.*, 216, 238, 269, 290, 349, 513, 554, 569 *f.*, 595
Allegories, 294, 297, 315, 424, 472
Alshech, 560
Andreas, 19
Annas, trial before, 522
Antichrist, coming in his own name, 173
Antinomianism, 196, 367 *f.*
Aorist, force of, 394, 513
Aquila, 561
Arminianism, 371, 428, 430 *f.*
Ascension, none in the fourth Gospel, 20;
 of Son of man, climax for faith, 210
Asceticism, 544
Athanasian Creed, 158
Augustine, 19, 246, 270, 348 *f.*, 357, 603, 618

Baptism, John's, 39, 76;
 Christian, 42, 76 *ff.*, 112 *f.*;
 of the Holy Ghost, 47 *f.*;
 sign of death, 76;
 misapplication of, 362

Baptismal service, the, 76 f., 431
Bar Abba, 533
Basilides, 59
Believer, gives account, 96
Bengel (J. A.), 114, 270, 557, 573
Benisch (Dr. A.), 560
Beza, 468
Birks, (T. R.), 179
Blakesley, 270
Blass, 11
Blindness, spiritual, arising from sin, 289 f.
Blood and water, 361, 549
Bloomfield, 513
Bode, 556
Body of Christ, the Vine and the, 428 f., 430 f.
Boothroyd, 559
Brethren of the Lord, 219, 237
Burial of JESUS, prophecy fulfilled in, 552

Cain, the way of, 193
Calvin, 42, 369 ff., 428, 430, 441, 598
Cartwright, 112
Causes and effects, philosophical, 564 f.
Censorius, 555
Censure of others, 374
Christ, the Person of, 17, 26 ff., 404 f.;
   pivot of everything, 19, 25;
   sole centre for His people on earth, 48 ff.;
   not detached from "Jesus" before death, 59;
   in contrast with law, 98, 152 f.;
   His heavenly intercession as Priest, 186;
   as glorified known by the Christian, 580;
   abiding fellowship with, eating His flesh, 203;
   confession of, 353 f.;
   Advocate with the Father, 370 f.;
   glorification of, central fact for Christian, 396;
   absent, would prove Himself Divine, 407;
   obedience to words of, 415 f.;
   dwelling-place of the soul, 427;
   His death, and going to the Father, 475;

INDEX OF SUBJECTS IN THE EXPOSITION

sanctifying Himself, 500 *f.*
Christendom, 69, 108, 113, 129, 158, 161, 171, 185, 193, 233 *f.*, 236, 350, 362, 408, 438 *f.*, 455, 497, 576, 619
Christianity, characteristics of, 581 *f.*;
    that usually styled, 584
Chrysostom, 270, 501
Church, always distinct from Israel, 185, 304;
    heavenly relationship of the, 427 *f.*
Communion, in one kind, 209;
    as condition of fruit-bearing, 431;
    maintenance of, 364
Congregation, the great, 591
Conscience, awakened for sense of grace, 127;
    purged, 132
Conversion, constituents of, 69
Copyists, ignorance of, 246
Courage, true Christian, 391 *f.*
Cranmer, 161, 268
Creation, by the WORD, 28
Cross, necessary for eternal life, 91 *ff.*;
    God glorified in the, 385 *f.*
Cyril of Alexandria, 270, 501

Darkness, 29, 99
Death, words used by Evangelists of the Lord, 546;
    JESUS Divine in His, 546 *f.*;
    the second, 100
Demiurge, 29, 59
Denominations as folds, 303 *f.*
Dependence, living in constant, 476
De Rossi, 559
Development, excluded, 46
Dion Cassius, 270
Discipleship, 256
Dispensational ways of God, 24 *f.*, 476;
    design in the Evangelist's omissions, 517 *f.*
Dispersion, Jewish, 229, 238 *f.*
Divine, Sonship displayed in resurrection power, 318;
    nature needed by man, 21, 74 *f.*
Divinity, systematic, a jargon of Jewish and Gentile notions, 584

Dove, the baptismal, 46

Edersheim (Dr. A.), 557
Ellicott (Bp.), 554
Emanation, 27, 59
Erasmus, 573
Error, possession of Christ arms against, 296
Eternal life, 305, 310, 484 *f.*;
   connected with Cross, 93;
   connection with Kingdom, 484;
   manifestation in man, 19;
   present gift of, 161, 208. See also under Life
Eucharist, not in Chapter 6, 204 *ff.*, 209
Eusebius, 236
Euthymius Zigabenus, 270, 410, 468, 558, 560
Evangelists, not to be regarded as forensic witnesses, 569 *f.*;
   à priori hypothesis as to their method, 570 *f.*
Evidence, belief on, 68 *ff.*
Evil, whether made by the Word, 57
Ewald (H.), 270, 559, 595

Faith, not logical inference, 73, 573 *f.*, 576;
   not a natural growth, 107;
   accompanied by repentance, 108, 127;
   essentials of, 110;
   from the heart, 110;
   certainty attaching to, 110;
   Christ glorified the living object of, 419;
   working by love, 429;
   Tridentine treatment of, 575;
   Romanist rule of, 575;
   in Scripture vital, alone of moral value, 576;
   love and joy the elements of, 577
Father, declared by Christ, 38;
   known in the Son, 403;
   access to, for prayer, 469 *ff.*;
   known through the Spirit, 476;
   glorified by Christ, 486;
   His name manifested, 487;
   submission of JESUS to the will of the, 520 *f.*

Fathers, spiritual intelligence of so-called, 348;
  ignorant of future restoration of Israel, 603
Ffoulkes (E.), 533
Fig-tree as symbol, 54 *f.*
Flesh, relationship in, abolished, 19;
  self the source and object of activity of the, 248
Flock, one, 303 *f.*
Fold, the Jewish, 303;
  none now, 303
Free-will, 196
"Friend of God", 439
Fritzsche, 270
Fruit-bearing, secret of, 429;
  believer appointed for, 425, 440

Galilee, ministry in, preceded by Judæan, 142 *ff.*
Gellius, Aulus, 555
Genealogy, none in Fourth Gospel, 21
Generation, this, 312, 352
Gentiles, millennial ingathering of, 601
Gethsemane, not fulfilment of Isaiah's winepress, 516 *f.*
Gnosticism, 59, 101, 438
God, the Truth not coextensive with, 38;
  unknown under modern philosophy, 564;
  made known as Father, not merely Jehovah, 582
Godet (F.), 269, 554
Godhead, Persons of, 26
Good confession of JESUS, 266, 530 *f.*
GOSPEL OF JOHN, exhibits God on earth, 17, 20 *f.*;
  manifests the Father in the Son, 18;
  written when Christ's Person was being undermined, 18;
  authorship, 620 *f.*;
  compared with Synoptists, 474 *f.*;
  real close of, 595
  Doctrine:
    Blood and water, 361
    Centre, Christ His people's, 48 *ff.*
    Communion with Christ, 202 *f.*, 431
    Cross, truth of the, 91 *ff.*, 385 *f.*
    Darkness, light, 30 *f.*, 99

Flock, fold, 303
Glorified Christ, the Christian concerned with, 580
Gnosticism, bearing on, 59, 438
Judgment, 97, 160, 179, 461
Kingdom of God, 74, 86
Oil and blood, 47
Person of Christ, the, 17 *ff.*, 26 *ff.*, 404 *f.*
Prayer, 470 *f.*
Vine, Christ as the, 428, 430
Doctrine (see main index entries):
Ascension of Son of man; Blindness, spiritual; CHRIST; Christianity, characteristics of; Church, heavenly relationship of; Conscience; Conversion; Creation; Discipleship; Eternal life; Eucharist; Faith; FATHER, the; Free-will; GOD, GODHEAD; Grace; Heavenly things; HOLY SPIRIT, the; Paraclete, the; Incarnation; Israel and the Church; JESUS; Judaism, overthrow of; Judge, Christ the; Knowledge; Lamb of God; Law; Life; Love; Messiah; Miracles; New birth; Obedience; Profession, Christian; Prophetic Word, the; Religion; Remission of sins; "Remnant", the Jewish; Responsibility; Restoration, mutual; Resurrection; Righteousness of God; Sabbath, the; Sanctification; Scripture, interpretation of; Second Coming of Christ; Shepherd, Christ as; Sin; Son of God; Son of man; Testimony to Christ; Truth; Unity; Water, figurative use of; Word; World; Worship

Government, Divine, 274 *f.*, 427 *f.*;
communion and God's moral, 431
Grace, activity of love in midst of evil, 35;
without limit, 36;
precedes truth, 35;
produces confidence, 123:
relieves where Law powerless, 152;
abused, 379
Gregory (the Great), 603
Grotius, 573, 613
Guinness (Gr.), 179
Gyges, 269

Hardening, judicial, 381 *f.*
Hatred of the Father and the Son, 132, 447 *f.*

Heavenly things, and Son of Man, 86 *f.*
Hegelianism, 57
Hellenistic Jews, 238
Herodotus, 269
"Holy One of God", Jesus the, whether Johannean, 212
Holy Spirit, blessedness of presence of, 19;
    operation in conversion, 75 *ff.*;
    not given in measure to Christ, 110;
    communion with Father and Son in the energy of the, 130 *f.*, 230;
    living water, 123;
    in power of testimony, 230 *ff.*;
    Advocate, 408;
    the "porter", 294;
    abiding presence, 408 *f.*;
    in Church, the spirit of truth, 450;
    proceeding from the Father, 450;
    jealousy of action of the, 455;
    inaugurating Messianic reign, 462;
    serves and glorifies the Son, 464 *f.*;
    as energy of Christ's risen life, 589
Homœoteleuton, 514, 553
Hooker (R.), 76, 113
Hours, in the Fourth Gospel, 555 *ff.*;
    essential difference in two, of Chapter 5, 167
Humanitarianism, now substituted for Kingdom, 186
Humility, misuse of, 362

Incarnation, 34, 90;
    and Death, 201;
    to save, needs regeneration, 276 *f.*
Inquisition, 444
Irenæus, 19
Isaac (Rabbi), 559 *f.*
Israel, the Church not to be confounded with, 185, 304

Jerome, 348, 555
Jerusalem, moral Judgment of, 150
JESUS, no record of childhood in fourth Gospel, 21;
    manifestation to Israel, 45;

following, 52;
Prophet, 54, 175, 185, 234, 281;
omniscience of, 54;
omnipotence of, 61;
sinlessness, 92, 262;
making Himself equal to GOD, 157;
no self-exaltation, 158;
identifying Himself with His speech, 253;
the Truth, 262;
pre-existence of, 266 *f.*;
bearing reproach of, 287;
Divine in His death, 546

Jews, those specially so called in fourth Gospel, 341;
ungodly future, 84;
darkness falling on the, 352

John the Apostle, writer of the Gospel 18, 620 *f.*;
an eye-witness, 18

John the Baptist, the lamp, 31;
testimony of, 31, 36, 102 *f.*

Joseph, of Nazareth, 53, 64, 198

Josephus, 541

Judaism, overthrow through departure of Jesus, 251

Judas Iscariot, treason of, 375;
why chosen apostle, 376 *f.*
character of, 493 *f.*

Judæan ministry, the early, 103, 117

Judge, Christ to be, 249

Judgment, exemption of believer from, 96, 160;
the Spirit's demonstration of, 461

Kimchi (David), 560
"King of the Church", unscriptural, 532
Kingdom of God, 73 *f.*;
new birth needed for, 74;
earthly department of, 80, 86;
of the Father, 87;
of the Son, 87;
mystical idea that gospel or Church is the, 185;
antedated by unbelief, 186;
in mystery, misapplied by Roman Catholic sect, 601 *f.*

INDEX OF SUBJECTS IN THE EXPOSITION

Knowledge, Jewish and Christian, 87
Kuinöl, 269, 513

Lamb of God, 43 *ff.*
Lampe, 574
Larcher, 270
Law, misuse of, by Puritans, 98;
    the Person of Christ in contrast with, 98 *f.*, 152 *f.*;
    not rule of life, 362
Legates *à latere*, true, 588
Leeser (J.), 560
Liberty, comes from Truth, 259
Life, in John's writings, 33 *f.*;
    as possessed by Old Testament saints, 77 *f.*;
    Christ the, 402;
    abundant, 299;
    of Christ regarded as redemptive, 485 *f.*
Light, 30 *f.*;
    Quaker inward, 58;
    no excuse for lack of, 99
Lightfoot (Dr. John), 553
"Little while", the, 466 *f.*
Liturgies and the Word of God, 44 *f.*
Logic of facts, 284
Lord's Day, the, 585 *f.*
"Lord's Prayer", the, 470 *f.*
Lord's supper, the, 113, 204, 207
Love, of Jesus to His own, 359;
    disciples' mutual, the badge of Christians, 389 *f.*, 436;
    consciousness of the Saviour's, 432;
    resting in the Father's, 474
Lucian, reference to, 328
Lücke (G. C. F.), 58, 270, 595

Macrobius, 555
Magistrate, Christ did not act as, 246
McClellan, 269, 596
Man, ruin of, 68;
    pride in what is learnt from, 223
Manichees, 31

Mariolatry, 62
Mary, mother of the Lord, 545
Mede (J.), 513
Men of God, not God's Word, 570
Messiah, Death of Son of man in contrast with reign of, 388 *f.*
Meyer (H. A. W.), 270, 349, 554, 595
Millennium, net not breaking, 602, 607 *f.*
Ministry, degenerated into worldly institution, 374;
    Galilæan, 142
Miracles, in general, 67 *f.*, 144;
    feeding the Five Thousand, 182 *ff.*;
    resurrection of Lazarus, 318 *ff.*
Moses, honour put by Christ on writings of, 175 *f.*
Mythology, Indo-Aryan, 27

"Nazarean", force of, 518
Neander (A.), 554, 595
New birth, 74
Newcome, 559
Nonnus, 268, 555

Obedience, of faith, 309;
    to words of Christ, 415 *f.*;
    characteristic of saint, 416, 433 *f.*;
    the Christian badge, 617
Oil, not preceded by blood, in case of JESUS, 47
Olive-tree, sets forth privilege, 431
Omissions in fourth Gospel, 477, 517, 526, 570
Ordinances, lifeless, 362
Origen, 147, 393, 468

Pantheism, 27
Paraclete, the, 408, 422, 450 *f.*;
    sent by Christ from the Father, 450
Peace, settled, 435
Pearce (Bp.), 513
Penitence, Romish, 370
Persecution, out of fashion, 455
Pharisees, jealous of Christ, 118, 228, 247 *f.*
Philonism, 31
Pilate, policy as judge, 535 *ff.*

Platonism, 31
Pliny, 555
Prayer in Christ's name, 470 *f.*
Preparation, the Paschal, 554 *f.*
Priest, Christ as, 186
Probability, faith does not draw conclusion from, 108
Profession, Christian, 428
Prolepsis, 114
Prophecy, vicious maxims as to, 378;
    fulfilment in burial of JESUS, 552
Prophet, functions of a, 128
Prophetic Word, the, 465
Purim, Feast of, 151

Quotation, Septuagint disregarded, 560 *f.*

Randolph (Dr. T.), 558
Raphelius, 114, 270
Rashi, 560
Rationalism, Christ irreconcilable with, 176
Reaping, day of grace characterised by, 140
Reception of Christ's sent ones, 378 *f.*
Reconciliation, Calvin on, 369
"Reign of Law", 320
Religion, worldly, 278;
    traditional, 69, 278 *f.*;
    breach with earthly, 287
Remission of sins, administrative, 558 *ff.*
Remnant, the Jewish becoming the Christian, 580, 582;
    the future, 187 *f.*, 582
Repentance, faith worthless without, 127
Reproach, bearing Christ's, 287
Reprobation, 196
Responsibility, 427 *f.*
Restoration, mutual, 373
Resurrection, fundamental truth of Gospel, 67, 563;
    opposition of unbelief to, 563;
    bulwark against philosophic scepticism, 564, 587;
    slighted by fleshly-minded Christians, 564;
    points to power of God, 565, 586;

how treated by Evangelists, 569 *f.*;
attitude of Apostles towards, 570 *f.*;
popular idea of general, 166 *ff.*
Righteousness of God, 460 *f.*
Ruin of man, 68

Sabbath, alleged desecration by JESUS, 152 *ff.*
Saint, obedience characterises a, 416
Sanctification, by truth, 498 *f.*
Sanday (Prof.), 554
Scripture, as interpreted by tradition, 236
Scrivener, 595
Second Coming of Christ, 397 *f.*, 619
Self-judgment, 371, 414, 498, 568, 587
Shepherd, the rejected Christ, 294;
    voice of the good, 295 *f.*;
    mutual knowledge of himself and sheep, 302;
    lays down His life, 302
Simon Peter, self-confidence of, 391, 611;
    natural zeal, 519
Sin, of the world, 44;
    before birth, 274;
    non-imputation of, 362;
    Spirit's demonstration of, 460
Sleep, not used of soul, 323
Son of God, heavenly origin of, 90 *ff.*;
    given, 93 *f.*;
    rejected by the Jews, 95;
    gives life, 96;
    disobeying the, 97 *ff.*;
    conjoint working of Father and, 158 *f.*;
    alone judges, 160;
    Christ quickens as, 163, 165 *f.*;
    in connection with Son of man, 288 *f.*
Son of man, 56, 87 *f.*;
    lifted up, 91 *f.*;
    suffering, 94;
    glorified, 345 *f.*, 383 *f.*;
    as Judge, 95, 165 *f.*;
    sealed of the Father, 191 *f.*;

INDEX OF SUBJECTS IN THE EXPOSITION

rejected Messiah, 254, 350, 384
Spiritual understanding, conditioned by desire to do God's will, 224
Standing in grace, 436 *f.*
Stier, 573, 595
Superstition, 545;
    exalts its church, 296
Synoptic Gospels, Contrast of fourth Gospel with, 474 *f.*

Tabernacles, Feast of, 219, 231
Teaching of Christ, given Him by the Father, 223
Temple, desecration of the, 65
Tense, the historical: see under "Aorist"
Tertullian, 115, 177
Testimony, none receiving Christ's, 107;
    to Christ fourfold, 169 *ff.*
Theodotion, 561
Theology, panders to human science, 435
"Third day", typical of millennial day, 61 *ff.*
Tholuck (A), 595
Thomas, type of remnant believing when seeing, 591
Tittmann, 513
Touchstone, Jesus the, 225, 261
Tradition, danger of trusting, 619
Trench (Archbp.), 468
Triad, Hindoo, 27
Truth, revelation, 35;
    God not said to be the, 38;
    Christ is the, 38, 253, 262, 401;
    the Spirit guiding into, 463;
    twofoldness of Divine, 195 *f.*;
    apprehension of, dependent on faith, 296
Tyndale, 161, 268
Types, German dislike of, 548

Unbelief, already judged, 96;
    not as being under law, 98;
    in condemnation, not a question merely of, 99;
    of the brethren of the Lord, 220 *f.*;
    clings to earth and self, 252;

exalts man, 296;
in saint no better than in sinner, 569
Unity, 431;
discipular (apostolic), 492 *f.*;
present, 502 *ff.*
future, 505

"Verily, verily", significance of, 189 *f.*
Victorinus, 19
Vine, the body of Christ and the, 427 *f.*, 431

Wakefield (G.), 270, 598
Washing of feet by Jesus, 361 *ff.*;
self hindrance to, 374
Water, figurative use of the word, 76, 361;
does not quicken, 78;
living, 123 *ff.*
Way, Christ the, 124, 399 *ff.*
Weiss (Prof. B.), 11, 554
Wesley (J.), 556
Westcott (Bp.), 270, 554, 595
Wetstein, 597
Wiclif, 161, 270, 478
Williams (I.), 19
Witness, of God in His Word, 171 *f.*;
in His work, 279
WORD, the, 17 *f.*, 26
Word, cleansing effects of God's, 361, 426;
cleaving to God's, 129;
of Christ, as distinct from His commandments, 416
Words, Christ's λόγος explains His λαλιά, 261
Wordsworth (Bp. Chr.), 270
Works of Christ, 171
World, the, its hatred for those confessing Christ, 443, 495;
Christians' mission to, 500;
no amelioration of the, 496 *f.*;
meaning in this Gospel, 498;
the religious, 299;
judgment of the, 350
Worldliness, 221, 496

INDEX OF SUBJECTS IN THE EXPOSITION

Worship, Christian, 130 *ff.*;
   national, a delusion, 133;
   in millennium, 134;
   the Father the object of, 133 *f.*
Worshippers, true, 133 *f.*

AN EXPOSITION OF THE GOSPEL OF JOHN

Appendix of Additional Notes by Edward Elihu Whitfield

AN EXPOSITION OF THE GOSPEL OF JOHN

Editions of Authors Used

N.B.—Foreign works existing in English translations are recorded under the titles of such; all are cited in the notes by English titles. An asterisk (*) is attached to the name of any Roman Catholic writer, a dagger (†) to that of any professed Unitarian.

BRITISH.

ABBOTT, DR. E. A.:
    Article "Gospels" in Encyclopædia Britannica, 9th ed., vol. x. (1879).
    Article "Gospels" in Encyclopædia Biblica, §§ 8-107.
    From Letter to Spirit (1903).
    Johannine Vocabulary (1905).
    Johannine Grammar (1906).

ANGUS, J.:
    Bible Handbook, revised by S. G. Green (second impression, 1907).

ARNOLD, M.:
    Literature and Dogma (1873; cheap reprint, 1903).
    God and the Bible (1875; cheap reprint, 1906).

*BARRY, DR. W.:
    The Tradition of Scripture (1906).

BELLETT, J. G.:
    The Evangelists: On the Gospel according to St. John (ed. of 1900).

BENN, A. W.:
The History of English Rationalism in the Nineteenth Century (1906).

BERNARD, T. D.:
The Central Teaching of Jesus Christ (1892).

BRUCE, A. B.:
The Kingdom of God (1899).

BURKITT, PROFESSOR:
The Gospel History and its Transmission (1906).

CARPENTER, BISHOP:
Introduction to the Scriptures (1903).

†CARPENTER, PROFESSOR:
The Bible in the Nineteenth Century (1903).

CASSELS, W. R.:
Supernatural Religion, 7th ed. (1889).

*CLARKE, R. F.:
The Pope and the Bible (1889).

DARBY, J. N.:
Irrationalism of Infidelity (1853; reissued, abridged, 1890).

DODS, DR. M.:
The Expositor's Greek Testament: The Gospel of St. John (1897).

†DRUMMOND, PRINCIPAL:
Inquiry into the Character and Authorship of the Fourth Gospel (1903).

EDERSHEIM, DR.:
Life and Times of Jesus the Messiah (eleventh impression, 1901).

FIELD, DR. F.:
Notes on the Translation of the New Testament (1899).

GARDNER, PROFESSOR:
Exploratio Evangelica (1899).

GARVIE, PRINCIPAL:
Studies in the Inner Life of Jesus (1907).

GLOAG, DR. P.:
Introduction to the Johannine Writings (1891).

EDITIONS OF AUTHORS USED

GORE, BISHOP:
Bampton Lectures—On the Incarnation (1903).
The Creed of the Christian (1905).
GOVETT, R.:
Exposition of the Gospel of St. John (1884).
GREEN, T. H.:
Works, ed. by Nettleship (1885-1888).
HORTON, DR. R. F.:
The Teaching of Jesus (1895).
Inspiration and the Bible (1888).
The Commandments of Jesus (1898).
ILLINGWORTH, J. R.:
Christian Character (1904; cheap reprint, 1907).
Doctrine of the Trinity (1907).
INGE, PROFESSOR:
Bampton Lectures—Christian Mysticism (1899).
Studies of Christian Mystics (1906).
KINNEAR, J. B.:
The Foundations of Religion (1905).
KNOWLING, PROFESSOR:
Literary Criticism and the New Testament (1907).
LATHAM, H.:
The Risen Master (1901).
LIDDON, DR. H. P.:
Bampton Lectures—On the Divinity of Our Lord (1867).
Elements of Religion, 7th ed. (1890).
LIGHTFOOT, BISHOP:
Biblical Essays (1893).
LOCK, DR. W.:
History and Character of the Fourth Gospel (*Interpreter*, July, 1907).
MACLAREN, DR. A.:
Exposition of the Gospel of St. John (1907).
MCCLELLAN, J. B.:
The New Testament—vol. i., The Gospels (1875).
*MCRORY, PROFESSOR:
The Gospel of St. John, with Notes (1897).

MANSEL, DEAN:
: The Gnostic Heresies of the First and Second Centuries (1875).

†MARTINEAU, DR. J.:
: The Seat of Authority in Religion (1890).

MEYER, F. B.:
: Exposition of John: Love to the Uttermost (1898).

MILLIGAN, DR. W., and MOULTON, DR. W. F.:
: Commentary on the Gospel of John (reprint, 1898).

MOULE, BISHOP:
: The High-priestly Prayer (1907).

NEWMAN, F. W.:
: Phases of Faith (1850).

NORRIS, ARCHDEACON:
: The New Testament, with Notes (1880).

ORR, PROFESSOR:
: The Christian View of God and the World (Kerr Lectures, 1897).

*PALEY, F. A.:
: The Gospel of St. John, from the Vatican MS., with Notes (1887).

PLUMMER, DR. A.:
: The Gospel according to St. John (ed. of 1900).

REYNOLDS, DR. H. R.:
: Exposition of Gospel of St. John (Pulpit Commentary, 1888).

ROBINSON, DEAN:
: Advent Lectures on the Historical Character of the Fourth Gospel, reported in *Guardian* (December, 1907).

RYLE, BISHOP J. C.:
: Expository Thoughts on the Gospel of St. John (1873).

SADLER, M. F.:
: The Gospel according to St. John, with Notes (1883).

SALMON, DR. G.:
: Historical Introduction to the Study of the Books of the New Testament (1885).
: The Human Element in the Gospels (1907).

SANDAY, PROFESSOR:
   The Gospels in the Second Century (1876).
   Criticism of the Fourth Gospel (1905).
   Article "Son of God" in Hastings' Dictionary of the Bible.
SCOTT, E. F.:
   The Fourth Gospel: its Purpose and Theology (1906).
STANTON, PROFESSOR:
   The Gospels as Historical Documents (1903).
STRONG, DEAN:
   Article "John the Apostle" in Hastings' Dictionary of the Bible.
TRENCH, ARCHBISHOP:
   On the Miracles, 13th ed. (1886).
   Synonyms of the New Testament, 7th ed. (1871).
   Studies in the Gospels (1867).
TURTON, COLONEL:
   The Truth of Christianity, 6th ed. (1907).
WATKINS, ARCHDEACON:
   Bampton Lectures—On Modern Criticism in its Relation to the Fourth Gospel (1890).
WATSON, DR. F.:
   Inspiration (1906).
WESTCOTT, BISHOP:
   Introduction to the Study of the Gospels, 6th ed. (1872).
   Commentary on the Gospel of St. John (1882).
   The Historic Faith (1883; cheap reprint, 1904).
WILLIAMS, I.:
   The Gospel Narrative of our Lord's Ministry (second year, 1848).

AMERICAN.

†ABBOT, DR. E.:
   Authorship of the Fourth Gospel (1880).
ANDREWS, S. J.:
   The Life of Our Lord upon Earth (1892).
BACON, PROFESSOR:
   Introduction to the New Testament (1900).

The Johannine Problem (*Hibbert Journal,* 1903-1905).
The Defence of the Fourth Gospel *(Hibbert Journal,* 1907).
The Beloved Disciple *(Expositor,* October, 1907).

BRIGGS, PROFESSOR:
New Light on the Life of Jesus (1904).

DU BOSE, PROFESSOR:
The Soteriology of the New Testament (1892).
The Gospel in the Gospels (1906).

GREGORY, PROFESSOR (at Leipzig):
Canon and Text of the New Testament (1907).

JAMES, PROFESSOR:
The Varieties of Religious Experience (1902).

*KENRICK, ARCHBISHOP:
The New Testament, with Notes, 2nd ed. (1862).

McGIFFERT, PROFESSOR:
A History of Christianity in the Apostolic Age (1897).

NASH, PROFESSOR:
A History of the Higher Criticism (1901).

STEVENS, PROFESSOR:
Johannine Theology (1894).

GERMAN.

ACHELIS, DR. T.:
Sketch of Science of Comparative Religion (1904).
Ethics (1904).

BEYSCHLAG, W.:
The Johannine Question (1876).
Theology of the New Testament, 2nd ed. (1895).

BLASS, F.:
The Gospel according to John (1902).
Grammar of New Testament Greek (1905).
Philology of the Gospels (1898).
Paper in *Expository Times,* "St. John" (July, 1907).
Papias in Eusebius (1907).

BOUSSET, PROFESSOR:
Commentary (Meyer's) on the Apocalypse (1896).

EDITIONS OF AUTHORS USED

Article "Anti-Christ" in Encyclopædia Biblica.
The Jewish Religion, etc. (1903).

CLEMEN, PROFESSOR:
The Origin of the New Testament (1906).

DELFF, H.:
Rabbi Jesus of Nazareth (1889).
The Fourth Gospel (1890).

DELITZSCH, FRANZ:
Article "Passover" in Riehm's Handbook of Biblical Antiquities, 2nd ed. (1893).

EWALD, H.:
The Johannine Writings (1861).

GERDTELL, L. VON:
Is the Doctrine of Christ's Atonement still Tenable? 2nd ed. (1905).
Are the Miracles of Primitive Christianity sufficiently Attested? 2nd ed. (1907).
The Christian Miracles before the Forum of Modern Thought, 2nd ed. (1907).

HARNACK, PROFESSOR:
History of Dogma, 3rd ed. (1894); (English translation, 1899).
History of Old Christian Literature. Two Parts (1893-1904).

HEITMÜLLER, W.:
Exposition of the Gospel of John (1907).

HERRMANN, PROFESSOR J. W.:
Faith and Morals (1904).

HOLTZMANN, PROFESSOR H.:
Manual Commentary on the New Testament, 2nd ed. (1893).

HOLTZMANN, PROFESSOR O.:
The Gospel of John (1887).
Life of Jesus (English translation, 1904).

JÜLICHER, PROFESSOR:
Introduction to the New Testament (English translation, 1904; 6th German ed., 1906).

LOTZE, H.:
Outlines of a Philosophy of Religion (English translation, 1892).

LUTHARDT, PROFESSOR:
The Johannine Origin of the Fourth Gospel (1874).
Exposition of the Gospel of John (1886).

NEANDER, A.:
Life of Christ (American translation, 1871).

PFLEIDERER, PROFESSOR:
Primitive Christianity (2nd German ed., 1902).

REUSS E.:
History of the Sacred Scriptures of the New Testament (English translation of 5th ed., 1884).

*SCHANZ, PROFESSOR:
Commentary on the Gospel of St. John (1885).

SCHÜRER, PROFESSOR:
The Fourth Gospel *(Contemporary Review,* 1891).

STAERK, DR. W.:
The New Testament Period (1907).

VON SODEN, PROFESSOR THE BARON:
History of Early Christian Literature (English translation, 1906).

WEISS, PROFESSOR B.:
Introduction to the New Testament (English translation, 1887, 1888).
Ninth Edition of Meyer's Commentary on the New Testament (1902).
Manual Commentary on the New Testament (1902; American translation, 1906).
Life of Christ (English translation, 1885).
Theology of the New Testament (English translation of 3rd ed., 1882, 1883).

WEIZSÄCKER, C.:
Investigations respecting the Gospel History (2nd German ed., 1901; English translation, 1905).
The Apostolic Age of the Christian Church (from 2nd ed., 1894).

WELLHAUSEN, PROFESSOR:
Interpolations and Alterations in the Fourth Gospel (1907).

WENDT, PROFESSOR:
The Gospel of John (ed. of 1900; English translation, 1902).

WENTSCHER, PROFESSOR:
Introduction to Philosophy (1907).

ZAHN, PROFESSOR:
Introduction to the New Testament (1899).
Article "John the Apostle" in Hauck's Encyclopædia for Protestant Theology, etc. (1901).
The Gospel of John Expounded (1908).

DUTCH.

SCHOLTEN, PROFESSOR:
The Gospel according to John (1864-1866).

FRENCH.

D'ALMA:
The Fourth Gospel Controversy (1907).

*LEPIN:
Origin of the Fourth Gospel (1907).

*LOISY, A.:
The Fourth Gospel (1903).

RENAN, E.:
Life of Jesus (1863).
The Gospels (1877).

RÉVILLE, PROFESSOR A.:
Jesus of Nazareth, 2nd ed. (1906).

RÉVILLE, PROFESSOR J.:
The Fourth Gospel (1901).

SABATIER, A.:
Article in Lichtenberger's Encyclopædia of Religious Knowledge, vol. vii., pp. 181-193 (1880).

SWISS.

BARTH, PROFESSOR:
The Chief Problems of the Life of Jesus, 2nd ed. (1903).
The Gospel of John and the Synoptic Gospels (1905).

GODET, F.:
Commentary on the Gospel of John (English translation, 1886; 4th ed. of French, 1905).

SCHMEIDEL, PROFESSOR:
Article "Son of Zebedee" in Encyclopædia Biblica.
Jesus in Modern Criticism (English translation, 1907).

WERNLE, PROFESSOR:
Sources of the Gospels (English translation, 1907).

NOTES ON THE INTRODUCTION

1 The traditional writer of the fourth Gospel was John the Apostle. Of the two oldest manuscripts of the original text, the *Vatican* (B) has simply "According to John" as both columnar title and subscription, whilst the *Sinaitic* (א) shows this as subscription (so also the Old Latin copies). "Gospel according to John" is found in ACEFGL, etc. Manuscripts of the Apocalypse bear the superscription of "John the divine (θεόλογος)," which refers to his λόγος doctrine (Reuss, p. 21), but, Weiss and Zahn think, was not so used before the third century. Dr. Barry has described him as "last of Apostles and first of divines" (p. 264).

Most manuscripts assign to it the last place among the Gospels, but in D it is placed next to Matthew's, as being both by Apostles.

This John was, it would seem, the younger of the two sons of Zebedee and Salome (*cf.* Matthew 27:56 with Mark 15:40). The Gospels "according to" Matthew and Mark both always name James first; and so Luke generally, but twice the third Evangelist writes "John and James" (8:51, 9:28).

The Synoptic Gospels would lead us to suppose that theirs was a Galilean family, and probably of Bethsaida (*cf.* John 1:44 with Luke 5:10), in easy circumstances (Mark 1:20). Until the brothers became permanently attached to JESUS they followed the calling of fishermen (see, further, notes on 1:35 and 18:15 {and notes on 19:25 and 21:2}).

John's definite call to discipleship is recorded in Matthew 4:21 *f.* and Luke 5:1-11. The Lord gave to him and his brother the joint name of "Boanerges" (Mark 3:17); so that writers concerned with the question of the authorship of the Apocalypse have to consider the fitness of the designation of a son "of thunder" in that connection, as also when investigating the authorship of the Epistles which go under John's name.

The "disciple whom Jesus loved," spoken of in the Gospel attributed to John the Apostle, is generally supposed to be a designation of himself (see, further, note on 13:23). To the disciple so described our Lord when dying bequeathed the care of His mother (19:26). This Apostle is, besides, spoken of as one of the "pillars" of the Church at Jerusalem (Galatians 2:9; *cf.* Acts 15, A.D. 51). The last glimpse we have of him in the New Testament is as an exile in the island of Patmos during the reign, Eusebius (iii. 18) states, of Domitian. Before that time, according to Tertullian (*De Præscriptione Hæreticorum*), while the Apostle was in Rome, he was cast into a cauldron of boiling oil, from which he emerged unhurt. Ecclesiastical tradition carries on the story of his life, when released from Patmos, by representing him as prominently connected with the churches of Asia Minor, with Ephesus in particular (Irenæus). Zahn supposes that he removed from Palestine during the fatal Jewish war of the year 69,

NOTES ON THE INTRODUCTION

whilst Blass, comparing Acts 15 with chapter 21 there, considers that he must have finally left Jerusalem by at least the year 54. His residence in Asia Minor has been questioned, on insufficient grounds, by Keim, Scholten, H. Holtzmann, Harnack, Bousset, and Schmiedel, from its not suiting their theory as to the authorship. Amongst other familiar incidents related of that period of his life are the stories of his reclaiming a notable backslider (Eusebius iii. 23), and of his meeting a Gnostic in a public bath, when he at once rushed out of the place. Irenæus's account (iii. 3, 9) gives Cerinthus as the name, but Epiphanius (xxx. 24) says that it was Ebion. The last-named writer states that the Apostle remained unmarried. John is generally reported to have passed away in Ephesus by a natural death soon after the year 98—*i.e.*, after the accession of Trajan (so Irenæus, ii. 22, 5). Eusebius (iii. 31) states that his grave was shown there; another account is that two graves were shown at Ephesus connected with the name John {Eusebius (iii. 39; vii. 25)} (see, further, note on 21:22 *f.*).

1a Indications of authorship present themselves in the Gospel itself at 1:14, 19:35, 21:24. So much of the tradition as concerns the Apostle's connection with it is pieced together from the *Church History* of Eusebius (iii., chapter xxiv.), who has preserved the Preface to comments on *Logia* of the Lord, by Papias, Bishop of Hierapolis (see Colossians 4:13) about A.D. 130 or 140 (see Sanday, *Gospels in the Second Century*, pp. 145-160, or Stanton, pp. 166-168), from the Muratorian Fragment, about A.D. 170 (see Westcott on the Canon), and from Irenæus in his treatise *Against Heresies* (A.D. 180), whose statement in (iii. 11) Weizsäcker acknowledges as documentary evidence, not mere tradition. The language of Papias is too vague to be of any help as to this Gospel and its authorship. Justin Martyr came in between this Papias and Irenæus. He seems to quote from the Gospel in both his *Apology* and his *Dialogue with Trypho*, but does not name the author. The Muratorian Fragment, however, is distinct in its evidence, not only for the Apostolic authorship, but for the supreme value it attached to the fourth Gospel. By the time of Irenæus acceptance of the Johannine authorship is clear; of him Jülicher candidly says that "he was not the man to spin tradition out of his own brain" (p. 405). Indeed, the late Dr. Ezra Abbot, an American Unitarian, was convinced that we need not travel lower down for recognition of John's authorship than the time of Justin Martyr—*i.e.*, in the middle of the second century (p. 80, *cf.* Stanton, pp. 181-191). Justin's adherent, Tatian (A.D. 160), seems to have used this Gospel for his *Diatessaron*, which begins with "In the beginning was the Word" (*cf.* testimony of Theodoret, in Zahn). As far as is known, recognised opponents of Christianity, such as Celsus and Porphyry, did not attempt to disturb the received opinion. It is true that so-called *Alogi* (see note on 1:1) attributed the authorship to Cerinthus, and the acceptance of the Johannine claim in the second century was retarded by the circumstance that the Gnostic heretic did actually appeal to this Gospel (see notes on 1:1, 4, 14, etc.). So according to Origen, Heracleon in Italy (170-180), whilst the Alexandrian Basilides, "about the year 175," as wrote Matthew Arnold (*God and the Bible*, p. 268 *f.*), "had before him the fourth Gospel." Zahn (ii. 459 note) gives ample references for such writers, as well as to Theophilus of Antioch, who died in 186, the first of the orthodox distinctly naming the author. Stanton well says: "That this Gospel, unlike as it is to the Synoptics, should have overborne the resistance offered to its acceptance is, humanly, only to be

NOTES ON THE INTRODUCTION

explained by its Apostolic authorship" (p. 277; cf. Sadler, Introduction to Commentary, xxv.).

In the early years of the third century we find Clement of Alexandria (according to Eusebius, vi. 14) affirming that he had heard from men of Asia Minor that John the Apostle wrote this Gospel after being "urged by his friends and divinely moved by the Spirit." Origen's acceptance, soon after Clement's, of the received opinion is no less clear; the great Christian scholar does not even hint at any diversity of opinion about it. All down the centuries such was the belief, until in 1792 an English clergyman named Evanson questioned it (*The Dissonance of the Evangelists*). In 1820 a German professor, Bretschneider, followed, and, again, Strauss in 1835, as Baur of Tübingen in 1844. But for some thirty years after the appearance of Strauss's famous *Life of Jesus* most German theologians, including independent workers like Neander, De Wette, and Ewald, followed the lead of Schleiermacher in adhering to the old view, and resisting the ideas of the "Tübingen school." So also Renan in his *Life of Jesus*, belonging to the sixties; but by the time he wrote his *Evangiles* this famous French writer's opinion had changed (p. 428; cf. the *Life*, etc., 13th ed., p. 10 f.).

In 1864 appeared a work by Weizsäcker (Baur's successor), entitled *Investigations respecting the Gospel History*, and also the Dutch theologian Scholten's *The Gospel according to John*, which may together be taken as marking increased academical acceptance of the "modern" view, now largely held in Protestant circles on the Continent, especially since the publication of Keim's *Jesus of Nazara*. Weizsäcker's position in his later work, *The Apostolic Age*, is that the Apostle was the indirect, a confidential disciple of his the direct author

665

(*cf.* Harnack's *The Gospel of John the Elder according to John the son of Zebedee*). Such, likewise, was essentially the view of the late Auguste Sabatier, of the French "Liberal" school, as it is of Loisy, his counterpart among French Romanists, to whom Nouvelle has replied. Schürer (see English edition of his pamphlet) is of the same opinion, which was adopted also by Matthew Arnold (*God and the Bible*, p. 256 *f.*).

Amongst Germans the names of Lücke, Bleek, Meyer, Hengstenberg, Credner, Luthardt, Bunsen, Ritschl, B. Weiss, Schanz, Beyschlag, Zahn (as Haussleiter and Blass, regarding the "Elder" as none other than the Apostle), and Goebel stand for defence of the Johannine authorship; but those of the two Holtzmanns, Pfleiderer, Schürer, Jülicher, Bousset, Clemen, and the Swiss professors Wernle and Schmiedel, rank as opponents. In this country Dr. S. Davidson, Dr. Jas. Martineau, and Dr. E. A. Abbott, as, of course, the now disclosed author of *Supernatural Religion*, support the negative position; whilst Bishops Lightfoot and Westcott, with Professors Sanday and Stanton, Dr. Plummer, Dr. Salmon and Dr. Gloag, besides Dr. Jas. Drummond among Unitarian scholars, uphold the older view. So also the Swiss scholar, Professor Barth, and the late F. Godet. French and American writers are likewise in different camps.

The literary question has been complicated by the fact that Eusebius (book iii.) evidently understood Papias as saying that there were two Johns of Ephesus—John the Apostle and John the Elder (see Stanton, pp. 168-171); the passage would be found in Routh's *Reliquiæ Sacræ*, vol. i., p. 8. The tendency now is to discredit the existence of two such contemporaries at the same place: so Harnack (*Chronology*, i., pp. 409, 662 note, 674), for whom it is merely "a third-century idea," with Schürer,

Loisy, etc. The distinguished professor of Berlin holds that whilst the Apostle's influence lies behind (p. 677), the Evangelist was the Elder, to whom he ascribes all the Johannine writings (*op. cit.*, i., p. 659 *f.*). On the other hand, conservative scholars, by specially "critical" Germans called "Apologists," generally regard "the Elder" as identical with the Apostle (*cf.* 2 John 1, 3 John 1, with 1 Peter 5:1). Even Hilgenfeld (of the Tübingen school) thought the existence of a distinct Elder (still held by H. J. Holtzmann and others) very shadowy; so also Drummond.

Wendt (reviving an idea of Weisse) takes a mediating position; he analyses the book into a "Source" (the Evangelist, John the Apostle) and an Editor ("redactor"). The American professor, Briggs, is of the same mind. His countryman, Bacon of Yale, sets up a triple authorship, although disclaiming classification with the writers last-named (for him the "redactor" was "Theologos," the teacher of Justin Martyr). But most scholars, as Pfleiderer (ii., p. 480 *f.*) and Martineau (*Seat of Authority*, p. 189), decide for a single writer. There are, accordingly, three main views—that the writer was (*a*) the Apostle; (*b*) a distinct Elder; (*c*) a disciple, whether of the Apostle or of this Elder (as Bousset and von Soden think). The last takes the form in the hands of Dr. Salmon (see his posthumous work, p. 436) of a *hermeneutes*, or interpreter acting as amanuensis.

The third view is akin to the idea of a "Second (Third) Isaiah" in Old Testament criticism. "That the author of this Gospel," writes Sir R. Anderson, "should not have left even a tradition of his personality or name is a supposition which tries even a trained capacity for misbelief" (p. 142 of 2nd ed. of "Christianized Rationalism" in *Twentieth Century Papers*).

Opinion differs amongst the "advanced" writers as to whether the Evangelist was of Jewish or of Gentile descent. Keim and Scholten thought that he was a Gentile Christian; others, as O. Holtzmann and J. Réville, hold that he was a Hebrew Christian (see, further, notes on 4:27 and 18:15). With this goes, of course, the question of the linguistic style of the Gospel, from which the critics seek to determine the amount of "culture" (Acts 4:13) at the Evangelist's command. Some, as O. Holtzmann and Jülicher (after F. W. Newman in this country), speak of "monotony" characterising the discourses, whilst von Soden complains of "the poverty of vocabulary," which seems ill to accord with the same writer's saying that the Evangelist's mind was "rooted in the Greek culture in which he grew up" (p. 440). The device is, accordingly, adopted of supposing him to be a Hebrew Christian with a Gentile education. Dr. Briggs holds strongly that this Gospel was first written in Hebrew (p. 147). There is a great unwillingness to own Ewald's demonstration of its Hebraising style, or the justice of Lightfoot's very competent opinion that "a scholarly Greek could not have written as John" (see his *Biblical Essays*, pp. 16 *f.*, 128 *ff.*, 135 *ff.* for illustrations). Ewald supposed that the book was taken down by a friend from the Apostle's dictation; that the amanuensis had some control over the language used (*Johannine Writings*, p. 50 *f.*), thus rendering the Apostle service like the aid that another is believed to have given to Paul in the literary form of the Epistle to the Hebrews (*cf.* Salmon. p. 206). Dr. Barry finds no difficulty in assuming that "St. John gave the substance, which his Hellenistic secretary put into shape" (p. 169) [Professor Gregory (p. 312, *f.*) states that Prochorus (*cf.* Acts 6:5) is portrayed in several manuscripts as the amanuensis (*cf.* Zahn, *Exposition*, p. 28).]

NOTES ON THE INTRODUCTION

2 A decision as to the date of the publication of this Gospel, of course, depends mainly on the view that one takes of the authorship. The old Tübingen opinion, now happily dead, was that it arose in the latter half of the second century. This has been brought back by H. Holtzmann to the years from 100 to 140 (Schmiedel, between 132 and 140). But Dr. Plummer inquires: "If the Gospel was published between these years, why did not the hundreds of Christians who had known St. John during his later years denounce it as a forgery?" (p. xxxvii.). Other dates are J. Réville's, 100-125, Julicher's, 100-110, until we reach O. Holtzmann's convenient "not before 100" (because of alleged dependence on Luke's Gospel). There remain the views of the two specially representative scholars, all of whose writings, from different points of view, command English respect—*Harnack*, who does not conceal his dissatisfaction with nineteenth-century results, and puts the date at between 80 and 110; and *Zahn*, whose date is from 75 to 90. Eusebius says that the Gospel was written in the Evangelist's old age, with which Harnack's and Zahn's respective dates would sufficiently agree. And so W. Kelly: "God directed that the truth should be held back from his pen for fifty years at least" (*An Exposition of the Epistles of John the Apostle*, p. 6). "Repetition of phrases," as Barry says, "is characteristic of old age" (p. 161); see also note on 5:2.

The best short popular statement as to the authorship is that by Colonel Turton in his clearly written, sane, and, to opponents, markedly fair book (pp. 323-335).

3 See notes on 1:3-5, etc.

4 See note {19} on 1:14.

5 See note introductory to chapter 3.

6 It is clear that the latest of the Gospels supposes acquaintance with those which preceded it (see 2:12, 3:24, 11:2, 18:24, 28).

Renan started the absurd notion that this Evangelist bore testimony against whatever he omitted. Thus, the second chapter of the *Vie de Jésus* begins with "Jesus was born at Nazareth," with footnote referring to John 1:45 *f.* (see, further, in note 42 below).

O. Holtzmann enumerates certain omissions from this Gospel (as of any account of the Temptation), and says that such incidents were deemed derogatory to the Son of God. Nowhere, however, in the Synoptics is greater insistence placed on the Lord's humanity than in John's Gospel.

Dr. E. A. Abbott, in book iv. of his *From Letter to Spirit*, has a chapter on "The Silence of John," but Dr. Drummond shows, by an illustration taken from old ecclesiastical literature, how little the argument drawn from silence serves the purpose for which it is used (p. 157).

Nine-tenths of this Gospel is peculiar to itself, and five-sixths is composed of discourses.

On its relation in general to the Synoptic records, see Westcott, Introduction lxxviii.-lxxx., or Salmon, Lecture XVII., Milligan, xxix. *f.*, Reynolds, lxxxviii.-cxxviii. Ewald and Godet suppose that John designedly gave his narrative a supplementary character, whilst Weiss and Zahn consider that he did so without intending it, but Reuss rejects either view (see Introduction to the *Exposition of the Gospel of Mark*, p. 7, and note 12 there). Pfleiderer (as now Heitmüller) has differed from German critics in general with regard to the Johannine

Christ; these two writers hold that the fourth Gospel exhibits the "historical Jesus" (see, further, next note).

7 A very serious point is the claim of the fourth Gospel to be accounted *historical—i.e.*, as setting forth what our Lord actually said and did. This is discussed in Westcott's *Introduction*, p. liii. *Cf.* the Advent Lectures (1907) of the Dean of Westminster {Armitage Robinson}. Many critics depreciate it relatively to the Synoptic Gospels from the fancy that the "Jesus" of Paul (2 Corinthians 11:4) and John (1 John 4:3) is "another" than the "historical" Jesus of the Synoptists. The followers of Renan criticize by the light of this. All careful readers may discern, alongside of parallel statements in the Synoptists (Reuss, p. 226 *f.*), the difference between the Gospels according to Matthew, Mark, and Luke, on the one hand, and that going under the name of John on the other, in regard of (1) the duration of the Lord's ministry (see note on 2:13); (2) the scene of it (*ibid.*); (3) the style of our Lord's teaching (see note introductory to chapter 3), (4) the assertion of His Messianic claim (see notes on 1:33, 41). The personality of the writer does seem to enter more largely into the last than that of the writers of the earlier narratives into their respective texture. And yet if John was to portray the *inwardness* of our Lord's life and mind, how could he do so without projection of his own soul into the task of setting forth the way in which he had "learned Christ" (Ephesians 4:20)? Such even as Schmiedel talk of the application of their "own intellect" to analysis of the mind of Christ (*Jesus in Modern Criticism*, p. 36). Clement of Alexandria described the fourth Gospel as predominantly "spiritual" in contrast with the "bodily" Synoptic Gospels (Eusebius, vi. 14, 7), as to which see W. Kelly, *Elements of Prophecy*, p. 82, or Bruce, *Kingdom*

of God, p. 346. This may have referred to the inner spirit in contrast with the facts of the Lord's life (Milligan, Introduction, xix). *Cf.* T. H. Green, *The Gospel at its Highest Potency and in its Finest Essence* (iii. 171). It may be said to set before us "heavenly" rather than "earthly" things (3:12; *cf.* 7:46, 16:12). Nevertheless, as W. Kelly has written in his *Exposition of the Revelation*, the "general bent" of this Gospel is to trace what He was on earth rather than what He is in heaven (p. 100).

There may be a difference between theological *veracity* and scientific *exactness* (see F. W. Robertson, sermon on "The Kingdom of the Truth," vol. i. of *Sermons*) respectively expressed in Professor Kaftan's recent pamphlet (*Jesus and Paul*, p. 66) by *Wahrheit* (veracity) and *Wirklichkeit* (reality); but can one safely apply that distinction to the discourses in the fourth Gospel? With Robertson it is easy to go when he says (sermon on "The Sanctification of Christ," vol. ii., No. 17): "Feel a truth: that is the only way of comprehending it. St. John felt out truth. He understood his Lord by loving Him." So already Origen (Inge, *Christian Mysticism*, p. 45). However that may be, to use the words of Bishop Moule, "In the record as it stands I have a report revised by the ever-blessed Speaker" (p. 14). *Cf.* Bernard, *The Central Teaching of Jesus Christ*, p. 179.

That the material accuracy of its statements should be questioned is soul-corrupting in the light of the express assurance conveyed by 21:24. But it is the centre of the position of those who uphold New Testament revelation in general *(cf.* Lightfoot, *Biblical Essays*, p. 47), and so must be attacked. Dr. Salmon, moreover, has remarked that "critics nowadays trust far more to their own power of divination than to historical testimony" (p. 256). Intellectual honesty is incumbent on all of us. As says

NOTES ON THE INTRODUCTION

Bishop Gore: "We must all train ourselves in the very rare quality of submission to good evidence. This quality is as rare among sceptics as among believers" ("First Sermon on the Permanent Creed," etc., p. 17). It may be added, indeed, that the "free science" upon which some German professors flatter themselves belongs rather to the mythology of the nineteenth century. It is the duty of historians to hold the balance between the "objective" and "subjective"; but Kaftan, in his pamphlet already mentioned, remarks that those of the "Liberal" school "wish to know history not as it was, but as it ought to be—that is, according to their presuppositions, governed by the modern view of the world" (p. 56).

8 The various foregoing aspects of this Gospel will receive detailed consideration in the following notes on passages specially used by the "critical school" for the statement of their respective views, and, it is hoped, some aid win be given towards discrimination of that which is true from what is false in current theories. For example, the writer of *Supernatural Religion* has: "If the doctrines preached in the fourth Gospel represent Christianity, then the Synoptic Gospels do not teach it" (vol. ii., p. 463). There is an element of truth in these words. The three first Gospels supply us only with "the word of the beginning of Christ" (Hebrews 6:1). The late W. Kelly (*God's Inspiration of the Scriptures*, p. 524 {1st edition; p.422, Scripture Truth Publications, 2007 edition} note) would have associated himself entirely with the following extract from Sir R. Anderson's Reply to Harnack: "The *distinctive* doctrines of Christianity are not to be found in the teaching of the *Synoptics*, as they are called. The first two Gospels belong as much to the Old Testament as to the New. ... The Synoptical Gospels are divinely described as the records of what Christ

began to do and teach; of what *began* to be spoken by the Lord. And His voice, like that of Moses and the prophets then *spake on earth*. But to us He speaketh from heaven" (*Twentieth Century Papers*, p. 189). *Cf.* Professor Kaftan: "To proclaim the *Jesus religion* as the proper and true Christianity is contrary to history" (p. 50). *Cf.* Seeley "Ecce Homo," p. 78 *f.* (edition of 1908). The position taken up by Baur, later German professors, with Mr. W. R. Cassels, have but plagiarised. As the late Professor Schlottmann has said: "It is the right and duty of the Church to reject the popularising of crude hypotheses put forth with the semblance of scientific results" (*Compendium of Biblical Theology*, p. 137).

Without any reservation, the view, expressed towards the end of his life by W. Kelly, of the authorship of the Gospels and the Epistles going under the name of John, was that the Apostle so-called was the instrument of the Holy Spirit for furnishing the Church with these writings in succession, and that the Apocalypse was that which appeared last (*An Exposition of the Epistles of John the Apostle*, pp. 3-7).

This Gospel begins with a Preface ("Prologue"), which most writers regard as extending to 1:18 (so Tischendorf's Synopsis), and ends with an "Epilogue" (chapter 21). It is variously divided, as into seven parts (Milligan), or three parts (H. Holtzmann, Zahn). Some look upon the "Prologue" as the key to the whole, whilst Harnack thinks that it was intended only to engage the interest of Greek readers (p. 235).

NOTES ON THE FIRST CHAPTER

9 *Verse* 1.—"In the beginning ... WORD ... GOD." *Cf.*, of course, Genesis 1:1, where, "to begin with" (as to absence of the article, *cf.* W. Kelly's *In the Beginning*, p. 14), God is at once introduced, without the writer's pausing to prove His existence. That was supposed to flow from Creation, attributed to Him (*cf.* Romans 1:20), which is spoken of here also. Some evidential treatises have probably helped on unbelief as much as they have confirmed belief in GOD. Of recent books appealing to a wide circle of readers, mention may be made of Turton (chapters i. to iii.), Kinnear (chapter i.) both of which are really helpful, as also Lotze's work, of which there is an English edition.

As far back as research goes there has been RELIGION, however we may choose to define it, as with Bousset, "personal relation to God" (p. 23; *cf.* Liddon, *Elements*, p. 19). As to the discussion whether it lies in conduct (Kant), or knowledge (Fichte), or feeling (Schleiermacher), see Achelis, *Sketch*, pp. 98-100. Surely it extends to the whole man (Mark 12:30 and parallels).

For "Agnostics" (whose high priest was Herbert Spencer: see his *First Principles*, chapters iii., v.), not denying the existence of God, but saying that He is unknowable (*cf. Exposition*, p. 564 *f.*), DUTY takes the place of God; and so Ethical Societies have sprung up with their "Ethical Religion" (Mill's "Religion of Humanity"), a protagonist of which is Dr. Stanton Coit. [Has there ever been any *moral* revival without some *religious* impulse? asks Principal T. M. Lindsay (*The Reformation*).] As to the relation of morality to religion, see Wentscher, pp. 146 *f.*, and Achelis, *Ethics*, p. 42 *ff.*

For the Christian, as for the Jew, belief in God goes without saying (Hebrews 6:1, 11:6); it is experienced through His Word (Hebrews 4:12 *f.*). A man like F. W. Newman, who affected to believe in God apart from this, is by such pure rationalists as Mr. Benn deemed a "mystic." Even those who proclaim themselves without God feel the need of some equivalent, so ingrained in the human breast (as Comte knew) is the religious instinct, taking in the Far East the form of veneration of dead ancestors, as in the West of the memory of a wife (J. S. Mill), or of notable personages in the Positivist calendar. Scripture predicts general acquiescence in this last principle.

A momentous question still remains. Is JESUS, who is accounted to have revealed Him, Himself GOD? The fourth Evangelist affirms this, and some who are not conventional Trinitarians, such as Mr. Boyd Kinnear (chapter vii.), sustain his declaration. But it will be seen that this Gospel has much to say of the FATHER and also of the SPIRIT, the conjoint deity of whom is affirmed by the Nicene Creed so-called. The doctrines of the Godhead and of Redemption are closely knit together. See, further, note on 17:3.

NOTES ON THE FIRST CHAPTER

The WORD, *Logos*. Some moderns have identified the Evangelist's thought with that of his contemporary, Philo of Alexandria, a mystical Jewish philosopher. So Weizsäcker, Pfleiderer, O. Holtzmann, Wernle, Scott. It may be readily granted that such as Apollos (Acts 18:24) would carry the Alexandrian phraseology with them to Ephesus. But Harnack and Drummond have abandoned the theory that the writer of the Gospel was indebted to Philo for his doctrine, one holding that "the Logos of John has little more in common with the Logos of Philo than the name" (*History of Dogma*, i., p. 97), while the other says that "nothing can be more unlike than Philo and John" (*Inquiry*, p. 24). Our English writer has shown that, as far as his writings go, Philo never came to regard the Logos—an intermediate agent between God and man—as a *personal* agent. Meyer and others (including Bishop Gore, *Bampton Lectures*, p. 69) have traced the Logos to the *Memra* of the Targum, which is Philo's ῥῆμα (*cf.* Hebrews 11:3), used for God's mouth, voice, spirit, and face—all His relations with the world made and maintained by means of this. But, as Luthardt says, these Aramaic paraphrases of the Hebrew Scriptures (see note 20) in their present form belong to the third or fourth century of the Christian era. Some information about them could be derived from Edersheim, *Life of Jesus the Messiah*, i., p. 476, and ii. 659-664 (Appendix on "Philo of Alexandria and Rabbinic Theology"). The only satisfactory view is that of looking for the roots of the idea in the Wisdom books of the Old Testament: so Luthardt, Godet, Liddon (Lecture II.), Weiss (*Theology of the New Testament*, ii. 325, 347). The Evangelist's Preface no more witnesses to his having received a philosophical education than does use of such a word as "evolution" tell us anything about the intellectual antecedents of any person of the present day in whose mouth it is (Drummond, *Inquiry*, p. 23 *f.*). Nowhere does the Evangelist put "Logos" into the Lord's mouth, as any romancer or literary dreamer would certainly have done. Archdeacon Watkins, in a Bampton Lecture, has well remarked that the strain of the Prologue was as appropriate to an Ephesian as it would have been inappropriate to a Galilean circle of readers. Neither of these wanted nor would have cared for that which suited the other.

In the latter half of the second, or early part of the third, century certain people whom Epiphanius ({*Panarion*, or} *Adversus Hæreses*, LI., 3, 4) called Alogi (irrationalists), represented by one Caius of Rome, resisted the doctrine of the Logos, and "from the Evangelist's use of the term" they held that he must have been, not an Apostle, but Cerinthus or other Gnostic. Reference might be made to Stanton (pp. 198-212). Lightfoot remarks that their questioning the Johannine authorship of the Gospel is "just one of those exceptions which strengthen the rule" (p. 61). Large use was, of course, made of John's Preface in the Arian controversy; as to which see Dorner's standard work on *The History of the Person of Christ*, or Pullan's small but valuable book, *Early Christian Doctrine*. That Christianity itself was at stake Thomas Carlyle owned in his later life, stating to Froude that he had come to see that if the Arians had won it would have dwindled away to a legend (*Life in London*, ii., p. 462). Harnack adds his testimony: "The opponents were right: this doctrine leads back to heathenism."

See, further, Lightfoot's note on Colossians 1:15, Jowett, essay on "St. Paul and Philo" (p. 272 of reprint), and Inge, essay in *Contentio Veritatis*, p. 67 *f.*, which is a sequel to his Bampton Lectures, where the Logos is described as "the basis of Christian mysticism" (*cf.* note 278b.).

9a *Verse* 1 *f.*—"*With* God." The force of the preposition πρὸς is well brought out by Sanday: "face to face with" (*Outlines of the Life of Christ*, p. 41).

For the correspondence of the three great arguments for the existence of GOD to the three "Persons" of the Godhead, see Turton, p. 261.

For the Biblical cosmogony, see, of course, Genesis 1. The *geological* accuracy of the first chapter of the Bible has been impeached of late, in the columns of the *Guardian*, by the clerical Regius Professor of Hebrew at Oxford {Samuel Rolles Driver}, and his attitude upheld by another learned clergyman of the same University, who has written of "the utterly unscientific conception of the world presented in Genesis 1." *Contra*, a well-known German geologist, Professor Quenstedt, who does not pretend to any familiarity with Hebrew, but takes the Genesaic record according to its "plain meaning," in a lecture has been describing Moses as "a great geologist" (*einen grosser Geologen*), whose statements have "not yet been confuted" (*noch nicht widerlegt*). Will "conspicuous honesty" in Biblical interpretation, which Dr. Driver's henchman, Mr. F. H. Woods, claims that they represent, accept as an "ascertained fact" that *algæ* (see *Encyclopaedia Britannica*)—the marine plants used by Quenstedt as his illustration—were the primary organisms? That is, learn from Germans when these can really put English clergy right? Or are Germans to be followed only when they serve the cause of unbelieving criticism?

Again, *Darwinism*, some twenty years ago, might have served these English Hebraists as a refuge, but at a

German Natural History Congress of the present year (1907), the English scientist's characteristic doctrine (struggle for existence and sexual selection) was declared, without a single dissentient voice, to be *im Begriff abzusterben* (moribund).

May not the *Westminster Commentary* on Genesis within a few years' time be obsolete, so far as regards its physical science? An Oxford First Classman in Science, holder of the University Scholarship in Geology, and at the same time a Hall-Houghton Greek Testament Prize, who was a firm believer in the accuracy of Genesis, thirty years ago to the present writer described Huxley's *Elementary Lessons in Physiology* as "written in gold." The same friend's brother, himself a biologist, as the present century came in, spoke of that book as "entirely superseded." We have now a Senior Wrangler publicly declaring that he declines to take his science from Canon Driver. The "ordinary man," besides, as the *Athenæum* has just said, "believes the Mosaic incidents to be facts." Apart from reasons other than these, it is no wonder that churches are depleted of men. "*Knowledge comes*," indeed, but what if "*wisdom lingers*"?

As to alleged connection of evil with creation (*Exposition*, p. 57, {chapter 1,} note {c}), *cf.* Rashdall in *Contentio Veritatis*, pp. 43 *ff.* In Isaiah 45:7, it should be observed, "evil" means *adversity*.

9b *Verse* 3.—The preposition διά is commonly taken as instrumental, and yet in 1 Corinthians 1:9 it certainly is used of the original source (Kenrick).

On the concurrence of Aorist and Perfect (ἐγένετο, γέγονεν), see Lightfoot on Colossians 1:16.

NOTES ON THE FIRST CHAPTER

The punctuation by which γέγονεν is taken as part of this verse has had the approval of Meyer (as Alford), Luthardt, Godet and Zahn. Moulton went with Westcott and Hort.

10 *Verse 4.*—On the general question of the text of the Fourth Gospel, see Blass, *Philology of the Gospels*, chapter xii. This scholar, in his edition, has favoured more than most the "Western" text so-called, whilst Weiss differs from Westcott and Hort in always regarding the internal evidence.

11 Gnostics ascribed a distinct personality to both Life and Light. On such errors the standard English work is Mansel's *Gnostic Heresies*, but reference might be made also to Green, *Handbook of Church History*, pp. 171-176. Mr. E. F. Scott, adopting the theory that the Evangelist made incursions into philosophy (p. 256), imagines that the Life and Light are "related to the Platonic doctrine of Ideas" or archetypes (p. 253). That could only be by way of contrast. Why travel outside Biblical passages, such as Psalm 36:9?

God as Creator (Power or Force: *cf.* Mark 14:62) is the Hebrew (אֵל), Semitic idea, whilst the new revelation exhibits Him also as Light, establishing the Aryan notion (see note 90a on θεός). These are combined by the Evangelist in his Preface.

12 *Verse 6.*—"John." In this Gospel we have to distinguish (α) the Baptist, never so described by the Evangelist, to whom it does not occur that there could be any confusion of the son of Zacharias with himself; (β) the father of Andrew and Peter (verse 42).

12a *Verse* 7.—"All." For the universalism of this Gospel, *cf.* 3:16 and 12:32, also note {22} on verse 14 with regard to grace.

"Believe." In the fourth Gospel the verb only is used, not the noun "belief" or "faith." On the various constructions employed of the verb, see Abbott, *Johannine Grammar*, § 1480 *ff.*, in particular. On Faith as set forth by this Evangelist, see notes on 5:46 *f.*, 6:69, and 17:3. Reference may also be made to Sir R. Anderson's *The Gospel and its Ministry*, chap. iv., and to Illingworth's *Christian Character*, chapter iv.

13 *Verse* 9.—ὅ ... ἐρχόμενον. This connection of the words, followed in the Exposition, agrees with the opinion of Grotius, and seems to have the approval of Plummer. Luther adopted it for the first edition of his version. "Come into the world" was a Messianic phrase: *cf.* 11:27 and John the Baptist's "He that should come," from which Govett renders "was to come." The English Authorised Version has the support of Meyer, Ryle, and McRory, whilst "the true light was coming" represents the construction favoured by Weiss, H. Holtzmann, Godet, Westcott (see also Revised Version) and Zahn (p. 66 *f.*). That "the light lighteneth every man" remains certain. The words were quoted by the Gnostic Basilides exactly as they stand in this Gospel.

Mr. Carr refers to the ancient use of "enlightened" for the baptized; but only the Fathers, never Scripture, so spoke of them.

14 *Verse* 10.—"He was in the world." Origen, Chrysostom, Augustine, Cyril, and Theodoret agreed that these words speak of Christ pre-incarnate, or as Jehovah; so Milligan, Inge, etc. But *cf.* Zahn, pp. 57 *f.*, 66-68. As to the specially Johannine sense of the *world*,

NOTES ON THE FIRST CHAPTER

see *An Exposition of the Epistles of John the Apostle,* pp. 137-142, and note on 15:19 below. This verse bears on the philosophical doctrine of the *Transcendence* of God, exaggerated by Deists, and the scientific doctrine of His *Immanence,* exaggerated by Pantheists. As to the latter, see Wentscher, pp. 150-152, Mr. J. R. Illingworth's book, *Divine Immanence: An Essay on the Spiritual Significance of Matter,* and Bishop Gore's Third Lecture on "The New Theology." God is morally transcendent. And so Stevens: "The world is separate from God because of its sinfulness" (*Johannine Theology,* p. 97). *Cf.* T. H. Green, iii. p. 248. The immanence of God should rather be described as that of nature in Him (Acts 17:28; Colossians 1:17). The two notions find their reconciliation in the person of Christ, and in Him alone.

With this and the following verse, *cf.* 1 Corinthians 1:22 *f.*, and, of course, 16:8 of this Gospel. "He convicts them, not of mere unbelief in Messiah (as in Matthew), but of the common atheism of man" (Bellett, p. 10).

As to difference between Apprehension and Comprehension of the Infinite, see I. Taylor, *The World of Mind,* p. 822, and *cf.* Schofield, *The Knowledge of God,* p. 62.

15 *Verse* 11.—τὰ ἴδια, "His own door." Ségond's French version *(chez les siens* for this as for οἱ ἴδιοι) falls short of the conventional idiom of that language, *chez soi,* used in the *Version Nouvelle* by Mr. J. N. Darby.

16 *Verse* 12.—The vexed question as to universal "Fatherhood of God" comes in here (see F. W. Robertson, "First Sermon on Baptism," vol. ii., p. 59 *ff.*, and Bishop Gore, *Creed of the Christian,* p. 9 *ff.*). God is, of course, "Father of spirits" (Hebrews 12:9; *cf.* Acts 17:29). But Romans 8:16 is very clear, for all not hampered by reluctance to own the Evangelist's independence of Pauline doctrine (see general note on chapter 3) as a parallel to this passage, where "authority" (title) to become is so pronounced. "What is usually meant by the *Fatherhood* of God is really His *Godhood*" (Sir R. Anderson, *The Gospel and its Ministry*, p. 182).

Harnack writes ("The Essence of Christianity"): "God's Fatherhood is the main article in Jesus' message" (meaning the joint Synoptic record), as to which, however, see the English reply entitled *Christianized Rationalism*: "There was nothing new in the conception of the Divine Fatherhood so conceived" (p. 147). See, further, on {2:16,} 3:16 and on 16:26.

17 "Believe on (trust to) His name." Origen, on 3:18, regards "trusting to the name" as the initial form of faith (Abbott, *op. cit.*, § 1,486. *Cf.* note below on 2:23 *ff.*, and see 8:30-32). As to believing "His name" (without εἰς) in 1 John 3:23, see *An Exposition of the Epistles of John the Apostle*, p. 340 *f.* Salvation by His name alone, as set forth by the Evangelist's fellow-witness Peter in Acts 4:12, shatters the idea lately broached that all men are "potential Christs."

18 *Verse* 14.—"Became flesh." On the Incarnation, see such works as Bishop Gore's *Bampton Lectures*, Professor Orr's *Kerr Lectures*, No. VI., and Turton, p. 262 *ff*. It was either denied or undermined by Gnosticism, in its earliest form known as "Docetism," one of the representatives of which was *Cerinthus*, contemporary with the Apostle John. His errors Irenæus (iii., 11, 7) attributed to misuse of the Gospel of Mark. Cerinthus held that JESUS would rise again with the rest of mankind in the day of judgment {but "Christ" did not die}, for which Renan {*The Gospels*, p. 422} compares

NOTES ON THE FIRST CHAPTER

Qoran, iv. 156 {see also 157-158} (see Mansel, Lecture VIII.). The "Docetæ" derived their name from holding that our Lord had only an *apparent* body (see 1 John 1:1, 4:2 *f.*, 2 John 7). They made use of the Apostle's own writings, as of the Gospel (3:5 *f.*), in support of the evil of matter. The Apocryphal "Gospel of Peter" issued from this school (see *An Exposition of the Epistles of John the Apostle*, p. 251). *Basilides* (Mansel, Lecture X.) was an Alexandrian, active between 117-138 A.D.; *Valentinus* (Lectures XI., XII.) was doing his mischief from 140-155 A.D. He, too, quoted this Gospel. The error of *Nicolas* is referred to in Revelation 2:15 (see *Exposition of Revelation*, p. 51).

18a "Dwelt." See below under "glory" (note 20).

19 "We beheld." The writer was an eye-witness. There are many indications of this in the fourth Gospel. His use of the materials of others must not be mistaken for *dependence*, as by H. Holtzmann (*Manual Commentary*, p. 3). *Cf.* Von Soden: "What could have led him, the foremost of eye-witnesses, to depend upon an account second-hand such as the Gospel of Mark?" (p. 442). It were wiser to say that in all cases of such supposed reliance on existing written material the Apostle is confirming the narrative from his own knowledge (Hebrews 2:3).

20 "His glory" *(cf.* 12:41). The Targumic *Shekîna*, as at Exodus 25:8, where "dwell" (שׁכן) is represented by σκηνοῦν (John's, ἐσκήνωσεν) in the Palestinian Greek version by Aquila. See also references to LXX. in Zahn, p. 79. *Cf.* the Targum at Isaiah 53:3, etc., and note 9 above. An allusion seems to be made to the Transfiguration.

21 "Only begotten from beside a father." This striking form of expression is the Evangelist's way of alluding to the Virgin Birth. See Zahn, ii. 505, and p. 72 of his *Exposition*; also Blass, p. xii *f.* of Preface to critical edition, showing that Tertullian's text had "was born" (*cf.* old Lat. codex of Verona) without "who." Blass attaches importance to the first "and" of verse 14. *Cf.* papers of Mr. Carr in the *Expositor* and the *Expository Times*, 1907.

22 "Grace." It is only in the fourth of the Gospels that we meet with the revelation of grace. "It is not to be found in Mark or Matthew, although foreshadowed in Luke" (Sir R. Anderson, *Twentieth Century Papers*, p. 189). *Cf.* note 8 above, and, of course, Titus 2:11, one of the passages in Paul's writings by which some writers now imagine the Evangelist was influenced. See, further, general note {61} on chapter 3; also chapter ii. of Sir R. Anderson's *The Gospel and its Ministry*.

23 *Verse* 16.—On Gnosticism, see note 18 above, and for references in the Pauline epistles to the system in the hands of Jews, see Colossians 1:19, 2:9, 1 Timothy 6:20. The distinction made between "Jesus" and "Christ" has reappeared in the recent work entitled *Science and Health*, text book of "Christian Science" (110th edition, p. 229). The same work reasserts the evil of matter (p. 258, etc.).

24 "Grace upon grace." That is, grace taking the place of (ἀντί) old grace. The expositor here takes the same view as Bengel, Winer, Olshausen, Alford, Weiss and Zahn. The other view referred to in the text is that of Calvin, which is followed by Govett.

25 *Verse* 17.—"Jesus Christ" *(cf.* 1 John 1:3; Revelation 1:1). "Christ" had now become a personal name, in distinction from "*the* Christ" (see also on 17:3).

26 *Verse* 18.—There are four readings: (α) "The only begotten Son," to which Luthardt, as Kelly, adheres; (β) "The only begotten" (Latin copy, followed by Blass); (γ) "God only begotten" (Westcott and Hort, Weiss, Zahn); (δ) "the only begotten God." Westcott and Hort have in additional note: "The best attested reading has the advantage of combining the two great predicates of the word which have been previously indicated" (verses 1, 14). But the omission of the article before "God" tells against their reading. Carr (*Expositor,* April, 1907) avails himself of Dr. Hort's reading, but what he says on John 1:14 needs no such questionable support. Irenæus, Clement of Alexandria, and Origen all quote "God" (see Tischendorf, 8th edition, or Tregelles), so that the alteration must have been made early, and would secure some recognition when seen to lend itself to Arian views. But it was probably, as Paley says, "an error of transcription" (confusion of υσ and θσ). A recent commentator (Heitmüller) thinks υἱός the more probable reading.

26a Thus Mr. Ernest Scott writes: "Truth becomes another name for the Divine nature ... God the only true" (p. 254). But in John 17:3 the word for true is ἀληθινός, "genuine." Besides the remarks of Mr. Kelly on the present passage of John, reference should be made to his comment on 14:6, and to his *Exposition of the Epistles of John the Apostle,* p. 365 f.

26b *Verses* 16-18.—Origen, Athanasius, Augustine, Calvin, etc., suppose that these verses were spoken by the Baptist; but Cyril, Chrysostom, Grotius, Alford,

Wordsworth and Zahn take them to be the Evangelist's. Verse 19 clearly marks a resumption of the Baptist's testimony. Moreover, "who *is* in the bosom" would be said of the ascended Christ (Zahn, p. 96).

27 Much has been made by recent writers of the different way in which the unfolding of the claims of JESUS to be Messiah is treated in the fourth from its presentation in the other Gospels. Thus H. Holtzmann represents that, according to the Synoptists, it dawns on John the Baptist only when he is in prison that JESUS is the Christ! (*Manual Commentary*, p. 4). So also for the reserve of our Lord on this subject characteristic of the second Gospel, as to which see note on Mark 8:29 (No. 82). But already, according to that Evangelist's account in his first chapter (verse 44), the leper was told by the Lord to show himself to the priest "for a testimony to them." See now Garvie, *Studies in the Inner Life of Jesus*, chapter vi.: "Early self-disclosure."

28 *Verse* 19.—"The Jews." In verse 24 it is said that the Pharisees sent them. One of the fancies of current criticism is that when "Pharisees" are spoken of in this Gospel you have an earlier, when "Jews," as usually (2:6, 13, etc.) a later, recension. Apart from a special application of the name "Jews" to the Lord's opponents—those who were such only in name (Revelation 3:9)—distance of time and scene called for the designation even on the part of a writer himself a Jew by birth.

29 *Verse* 28.—"Bethany." Perhaps the Betonim of Joshua 13:26. The writer of *Supernatural Religion* impeached the Evangelist of ignorance of Palestinian topography, as though he confused the place here spoken of with the village by himself said to be near Jerusalem (11:18). There are other place-names, each of which is applied to more than one position in the country (*cf.* note in G. A. Smith's *Historical Geography of Palestine*, p. 496). For example, Emmaus in Luke 24:13 could not be the same as that spoken of in 1 Maccabees 3:40 (*cf.* note on Cana in 2:1 here). Moreover, places are liable to change of name. Drummond gives several instances of such variation in the British Isles. And so this Bethany may have become "Bethabara."

30 *Verse 23.*—One test of authorship of a New Testament book is the way in which the Old Testament is quoted by the writer. None of John's citations are from the LXX. against the Hebrew, whilst some are from the Hebrew against the LXX. Such are 12:14 *f.*, 40, 13:18 to 19:37. In this last, as Bishop Lightfoot notes, "the LXX. has not a single word in common with St. John's text." This bears on the question of whether a Gentile Christian could have been the writer of the Gospel (*cf.* notes 18, 92 on Mark).

31 *Verse 25.*—The Greek article, here as in verse 21, excludes the idea some have had that behind the Jew's inquiry was the superstitious notion (alluded to in Luke 9:19) that the old prophets would rise from the dead when Messiah came.

32 *Verse 26.*—"Standeth." Not that the Lord was just then in the crowd before the Baptist (*cf.* verse 29). It is, literally, "there hath stood." Bengel: "hath taken his stand."

33 *Verse 29.*—"Taketh away." So Meyer, Godet, Westcott, Weiss and Zahn. The word αἴρων was taken by Lücke and De Wette in the sense of "bearing" as the margin of A.V. With his exposition of the present passage *cf.* Mr. Kelly's treatment of 1 John 2:2 (p. 65 *f.*).

34 *Verse* 31.—"Knew Him not." Comparison with Matthew 3:14, which is cited as contradicting this, seems to show that οὐκ ᾔδειν here can scarcely mean absolutely unacquainted with our Lord, which in itself is very improbable, although allowance has to be made for the fact that they were brought up in different parts of the land. John did not previously know Him as Messiah. So Luthardt, Westcott, Milligan, Dods and Zahn; and see note 136 on Mark. *Cf.* also Carr's note. May we not also compare the last words of verse 26 in the Greek with the present passage? The Evangelist seems to speak of the same kind of knowledge here as there.

35 *Verse* 32 *ff.*—Several modern critics (e.g., Schmiedel, col. 2,538) treat this section of the first chapter as inconsistent with the Synoptists' representation of the Baptist's recognition of the Messiahship of JESUS. Such regard Matthew 11:2-6 (Luke 7:18-23) as indicating quite a different state of mind about this in John from what ordinary readers gather from those Gospels. The "critical" view is that the Baptist's belief in our Lord as the Christ was then not retrograde but hopeful. It is only by assuming that Matthew's account of the first official relations of the Baptist and JESUS was "doctored" that they can use the first Gospel in support of their theory (see last previous note).

Verse 32 contradicts the Gnostic theory that the Being who descended on JESUS was "the Christ," and declares that it was the "Spirit."

36 *Verse* 40.—"Simon Peter." The Evangelist assumes knowledge of this disciple from previous records (*cf.* his parenthetical note in 3:24).

NOTES ON THE FIRST CHAPTER

37 *Verse* 41.—"Messiah." Peculiar to this Gospel (see also 4:25). As to the bearing of this passage on Mark 8:29, see note 82 on that Gospel.

"First" is taken with "he" by Tischendorf (eighth edition), Meyer, Godet and Zahn (πρῶτος); with "brother" by Tregelles, Alford, W. and H. (πρῶτον; R.V.: "findeth first"). The Evangelist here intimates indirectly that he followed Andrew's example in bringing his own brother to JESUS (Zahn, p. 9).

38 *Verse* 42.—"Simon." Those bearing the name who come before us in the Gospels are (α) Simon Peter; (β) Simon the Cananæan, also described as Zealot; (γ) Simon Iscariot, father of Judas the Betrayer, as here; (δ) Simon one of the brethren of the Lord; (ε) Simon the leper; (ζ) Simon the Pharisee; (η) Simon of Cyrene.

39 "Kephas." This, his Aramaic surname, is peculiar to the fourth Gospel.

40 *Verse* 44.—"Bethsaida." There is a question as to whether there were two places of this name, as Trench thought (so now Staerk), one on the western shore of the lake, in Galilee, another on the eastern shore, in Gaulonitis. Thomson considered that there was but one (*The Land and the Book*, p. 373 *f.*). We have the name again in 12:21, where "Galilee" is added as if by way of distinction (*cf.* note 232).

41 *Verse* 45.—"Nathanael." Nathanael is mentioned again in 21:2, where he is said to have been of Cana, to which the Lord here proceeds. To imagine, as Mr. E. F. Scott does, that his name was used by the Evangelist symbolically, as a counterpart of Paul, is to carry the theory of the unhistorical character of the Gospel as far as the wildest of the Continental writers (see further in note 61). Others have, with no more reason, supposed that he was the disciple whom Jesus loved.

42 "Joseph." Under this name we have to distinguish (α) the husband of Mary, mother of the Lord; (β) one of the brethren of the Lord, introduced under the Greek form "Joses"; (γ) a brother of James the Little; (δ) the disciple from Arimathea. Trench notes "John's veracity in recording Philip's imperfect knowledge" (*Studies*, p. 68 *f.*). The Evangelist's admission to his record of such descriptions of our Lord (*cf.* 6:42) falls under what the late Dr. Salmon called John's "irony," as against the German suggestion that the Evangelist did not know of the Virgin Birth, or discredited it. This many-sidedness of John's narrative does but confirm the conviction of its never departing from, still less correcting, the common "historical" setting of the Synoptic Gospels. O. Holtzmann, whilst one of those lightly esteeming the historical value of the fourth Gospel (p. 108), hesitates not to appraise it highly, as occasion serves, like the present passage, for the belittling of the Synoptic narrative; here to support the idea of a human paternity of the Lord (see, further, on 6:42).

43 *Verse* 49.—"Son of God, King of Israel." With Psalm 2 *cf.* Isaiah 44:1-6; Zephaniah 3:13-20. For many Christians the Son of God's Kingship over Israel is a dead-letter. "To such Israel is a broken vessel never more to be used" (Govett, p. 50 *f.*). So they speak of His "reigning in the hearts of His spiritual people." But His death was to attest that He is "the King of the Jews," not "the King of the Church"; Scripture never so describes Him (*Exposition*, p. 531 *f.*)

NOTES ON THE FIRST CHAPTER

44 *Verse* 50.—"Verily, verily." This form of asseveration, characteristic of John's Gospel, regularly introduces a statement of special solemnity—we may say revelation (see 3:3, 11, 6:26, 32, 47, 53, 8:34, 51, 58, 10:1, 7, 13:16, 20, 21, 38, 14:12, 21:18).

45 *Verse* 51.—"Son of man." In this first chapter of John's Gospel we have had the Lord designated in about twenty different ways. For his title "Son of man," see note 30 on Mark 2:10, and in this Gospel, 3:13 *f.*, 6:27, 53, 62, 8:28 (9:35, doubtful reading), 12:23, 34. To the references in the note on Mark may here be added Bousset, *Religion of Judaism*, pp. 248-251, which introduces the reader to the Jewish literary sources belonging to the period between the Old and the New Testament, an early English authority on which was Prideaux, and by general readers chiefly but imperfectly known from the "Apocrypha." Staerk's little work is the most recent.

NOTES ON THE SECOND CHAPTER

46 *Verse* 1.—"The third day." *Cf.* with the remarks in exposition here the last paragraph but one of comment on chapter 20. The prevalence of the number *three* in this Gospel is noteworthy. Besides the three days here, we have the Lord going thrice into Galilee, thrice to Judæa; there are generally supposed to be three Passovers actually mentioned (but see on verse 13), and three other festivals; the discourse on the last day of the Feast of Tabernacles is divisible into three parts; Judas is thrice designated traitor; the Lord undergoes three judicial trials, and Pilate thrice tries to save Him from crucifixion; the Evangelist records three of the sayings from the cross; and the book may be divided into three parts (Holtzmann, *Introduction {to the New Testament}*, p. 438 *f.*). But "triads" are to be found also in the Gospel of Matthew. The number *seven*, in like manner (as in chapters 8-10), finds illustration in the fourth Gospel— "the seven signs", "these things have I spoken unto you" occurs seven times; there is sevenfold witness; "I am" has seven predicates if Resurrection and Life be taken as one, and likewise Way, Truth, Life (Abbott, *Encyclopædia Britannica*, § 52, col. 1,799). There is, however, nothing peculiar or unduly "artificial" in this,

NOTES ON THE SECOND CHAPTER

in the light of numerical arrangement running through other parts of the Bible. See an excellent pamphlet by R. Govett on *The Septenary Arrangement of Scripture*.

47 "Cana of Galilee." There was also a Cana in the tribe of Asher (Josephus, *Antiquities*, xv. 5, 1; *cf.* Joshua 19:28). Comparing 1:43, we may suppose that the Lord reached Cana from Peræan territory in one day's journey, its position on maps admitting of this.

48 "The mother of Jesus." Our Lord's humanity was not heavenly in the Gnostic sense; He did really take of His mother's substance. This Evangelist never mentions her name, although he gives that of His {legal} father {see page 198 *f.* and notes on 1:45 and 6:42}; all the others name her. It is one of the indications of John the Apostle's authorship. The name Mary was borne also by (α) the wife of Cleophas (Alphæus), (see note on 19:25); (β) the Magdalene; (γ) a sister of Lazarus.

49 Verse 4.—"What is there (in common) to Me and thee?" Blass remarks that this was "frequent in colloquial Greek of the time, quite in the meaning of our *Let me alone*" (*Philology of the Gospels*, p. 238).

50 Verse 6.—"Purifying of the Jews." *Cf.* Mark 7:4.

51 Verse 8 *f.*—Edersheim notes the absence of "friends of the bridegroom" in the custom of Galilee (*Life of Jesus the Messiah*, p. 155). Another indication of exact knowledge on the part of the writer.

52 Verse 11.—Trench has happily recalled the first miracle of Moses (Exodus 7:20), a turning of water into blood as a ministration of death, in contrast with this ministration of life (*Miracles*, p. 121 *f.*). It is significant that nearly all Christ's works of power reported in the canonical Gospels are those of benevolence. For the manifestation of Christ's glory, *cf.* Isaiah 40:5, and the version of the LXX. there with the Greek here; also note 99.

σημεῖα, "signs." This word is regularly used by the Evangelist in his comments;, whilst the Lord is recorded as always using ἔργα, "works." A strenuous endeavour has been made by writers of the negative tendency to set the fourth Gospel in an unfavourable light as compared with the Synoptists on the question of *miracles*. A difference has been set up, as by Harnack (see note 27 on Mark), between the way in which the Lord Himself regarded His works of power and the estimate of the writer of this Gospel. And so, as a recent British writer would have it, in the Synoptic records you have (1) belief, (2) miracles, with that order reversed in the fourth Gospel, the Evangelist's own point of view being distinguished from the Master's (Scott, p. 268). *Cf.* 14:11. How, then, are we to explain in the Synoptics the evidential value attached to His works, as in Matthew 11:4? Is not Luke 11:29 in exact agreement with the usual Johannine representation of miracles as performed to confirm the real, or raise the superficial, faith of those already disciples, as in the present passage? Again, how can "critics" explain the testimony of Christ's *word* being presented in John 8 and that of His *works* being postponed to chapter 9? According to the analysis in fashion, the arrangement of chapters in the fourth Gospel results from the Evangelist's arbitrary fancy. Although rearrangement of other parts of this Gospel has been proposed, the traditional order of those two chapters seems to remain unquestioned.

That in the Gospel "according to John" there are superficially apparent contradictions is recognised, but it is the critical interpretations of these which are at fault.

NOTES ON THE SECOND CHAPTER

Some, taken from H. Holtzmann's *Introduction*, will be examined in these notes.

On the general question of miracles, see J. N. Darby, *Collected Writings*, vol. xxxii., pp. 272 *ff.*; Green, iii., pp. 254 *f.*; Sir R. Anderson, *Silence of God*, chapter iii.; Nash, p. 141; Turton, chapter xviii.; Bishop Gore, Sixth Lecture on "The New Theology," etc.; and Von Gerdtell, "Burning Questions," etc., Nos. 2, 3 (published by Kielmann, Stuttgart). The last-named writer, like the lamented Count Andreas v. Bernstorff, having had both a juristic and a theological education, has preferred to remain a "layman," in order to "get the ear" of young men who, in Germany as in Britain, care not to listen to "pastors," either orthodox or heterodox, and, to use Count Bernstorff's words to the present writer, distrust the "professional mind." See, further, note 99.

53 Verse 13 *ff.*—It may be desirable here to consider the question of the length and the scene of our Lord's ministry as contemplated by the Synoptists and John respectively. Eusebius records an ancient observation that the Synoptists seem to tell us of only one Passover—*i.e.*, of but one year's ministry—whilst the fourth Gospel speaks of several Passovers, at least three (*cf.* 6:4, 12:1). Some, as W. Kelly (see note on 5:1), find four Passovers in this Gospel. Again, the earlier Gospels take us almost entirely to Galilee (and Peræa), but John's mainly to Judæa (*cf.* 5:1, 7:14, 10:22, 12:12). A great deal is made by "the critical school" of each of these admitted facts. It has been suggested by Blass (*Expository Times*, July, 1907) that, whilst the Church had its headquarters at Jerusalem, it was an account of the Galilean and of the Peræan ministry that Christians of Judæa in particular would require, the incidents of the Lord's work in Judæa being sufficiently familiar

there; but that, precisely when the Christian communities of Judæa were dispersed by political events, the need would arise of a record of the Judæan ministry, which John was able to supply. And, again, Briggs' recent book, *Fresh Light*, has earned the title adopted by the writer. He gives good ground for supposing that John's special fitness for his task came of his having companied with the Lord during the whole of an early Judæan ministry. Not only so, but that there was an early Galilean ministry of a less pronounced public character than that introduced by Matthew 4:12 and Mark 1:14. We shall recur to this in notes on the third Gospel, which seems to confirm Briggs' view. But Luthardt, Lightfoot, and others, had previously shown that Matthew 23:37 (as Luke 13:34) had already indicated by the ποσάκις ("how often") that the Lord's visits to Judæa were more frequent than might appear from the Synoptic records. Jülicher as to this caustically remarks: "To reconstruct several visits of Jesus to Jerusalem out of the Synoptists solely on account of the one prophetic utterance is childish" (p. 419). The "obvious intention" of the Synoptists supposed by him is very questionably obvious. A *tu quoque* might well be employed against such writers with regard to the use made of Luke 4:19 to establish a *single* year's ministry: nowhere do the Synoptists say that the ministry lasted only one year. Blass rightly observes: "It is John who first clears up the passage" (common to Matthew 23 and Luke 13) "and justifies it." There is no inconsistency, such as A. Réville sets up (ii. 20), between the Synoptists' account and John's representing that JESUS and the Baptist were at work for some time simultaneously. Moreover, as far as the Galilean ministry is concerned, John distinctly recognises it, whatever H. Holtzmann may say about such visits being "merely

NOTES ON THE SECOND CHAPTER

episodes" (John 2:1-12, 4:43-54, 6:1-7:10). Loisy (p. 64) asks: "How could Jesus have preached at Jerusalem *several years*, declaring Himself Messiah, without being arrested?" The words underlined do but savour of romance. At first no idea of a "permanent miracle," such as Loisy attributes to the Evangelist, is needed; the attitude of the "Jews" for some time was one of sceptical inquiry, of unwillingness to believe, rather than hostility. The incident in the Temple (chapter 2) will be discussed below. It is not until we reach chapter 8 that the "Jews'" threatening demeanour towards the Lord personally becomes acute. Even so, between the first (8:59) and second attempt to stone Him (10:31), we still find them asking Him, "How long dost Thou keep us in suspense?" (10:24). If He was to be arrested, it would be by the servants of the high-priest, but they served for protection, evidently sympathising with and giving effect to the feelings of many in the Judæan crowds, who had their spokesman in the Sanhedrin itself (7:40-52).

The second distinctly named Passover comes at 6:4, the third at 11:55, which speaks, in any case, of the last. According to this, the length of the whole ministry would be about two years (Irenæus, ii., 22, 3). So Delitzsch's article, "Passover," in Riehm's *Handbook*. Briggs, however, is of opinion that the scheme of the fourth Gospel in this respect coincides with that of the Synoptists, and that there were no other *distinct* Passovers than the one spoken of in the present passage and that mentioned in 11:55 (p. 54). *Cf.* Milligan's view.

54 Verse 13.—"The *Jews'* Passover." Critics use this as an indication that the writer was a Gentile. It seems, however, to mean no more than either that, as it in the first time the festival in mentioned by John, he so describes it for the information of his first readers—Gentiles—in

Asia Minor, or that it is used in distinction from the Christian Passover, which we know formed subject of controversy between East and West after his death. And yet, *pace* the neo-critics, Matthew (28:15), too, makes use of the word (*cf.* Luke 23:51).

Cf. Paul's way of speaking of Mount Sinai (not as "the mount of God") in Galatians 4:25.

55 *Verse* 14 *ff.*—See note 117 on Mark 11:15, parallel with Matthew 21:12 *f.* and Luke 19:45 *f.*, and W. Kelly's "Lectures on Matthew." Wendt says: "Such an act can only once be morally justified." Yet he recognises the differences in verses 16, 18-20 from the Synoptic accounts of the occasion with which the other Evangelists are concerned. Thus, comparing verse 18 with Matthew 21:23 *ff.*, anyone may see that while the leaders there also demand the authority of JESUS, He refers to the baptism of John, not, as here, to death and resurrection, as supplying it. Surprise has been expressed (*cf.* note 53) that there was no resistance offered, as to which, without resorting to the supposition that the Lord's supernatural manner overawed the traffickers, Carr says that it may be sufficiently explained by "the popular dislike to these *bazaars*, which were suppressed not long afterwards." So great was the odium which the family of Annas, in whose interest they were held, really earned. To this the Talmud witnesses. Horton (*Teaching of Jesus*, p. 215) well compares Mark 1:27 for "that air of authority observable from the outset" of the Lord's career.

56 *Verse* 16.—"My Father." This contradicts the Gnostics' idea that the God (Creator) of the Old Testament was not "the Father" spoken of by our Lord. Observe that in the cleansing of the Temple described by the Synoptists, instead of "My Father's house," we find "your house," because then the Jews had fully rejected Christ. For this designation of His opponents, here especially the leaders, *cf.* 7:15, 35, 8:22, 13:33, etc.

57 *Verse* 20.—The restoration of Zerubbabel's temple was completed only A.D. 64. Reckoning the forty-six years from Herod's commencement of the work B.C. 20 (Josephus, *Bellum Judaicum {The Jewish War}*, i. 21), we reach the year 26 of the new era—*i.e.*, the first of the Lord's ministry. For the force of the aorist οἰκοδομήθη here, Field aptly compares Ezra 5:16. The A.V., to which Mr. J. N. Darby's version adheres, is singularly close: the temple was not yet finished. Schmiedel, for once, supports Lightfoot on John's precision. For the use made of the Lord's words against Him judicially, see Mark 14:58.

58 *Verse* 21.—The minister of the Hampstead Congregational Church, Dr. Horton (following Reuss, Wendt, etc.), alleges against the Evangelist misinterpretation of the Master's mind (*Teaching of Jesus*, p. 164). As to such wanton treatment of this Gospel, the late Dr. Friedrich Blass, a happy representative of learned German "laymen," has sententiously remarked "that it becomes us moderns to query whether any can now know better than a contemporary." See also note {237} on 12:32 *f.*

58a *Verse* 22.—"The Scripture" seems to be Psalm 16:10.

59 *Verse* 23 *f.*—As to πιστεύειν εἰς τὸ ὄνομα, see note 17 above. It is a long cry from a miracle wrought to confirm those already believers (see verse 11) to another designed to impress sceptics. Ostensible discipleship, acceptance of instruction, is independent of living faith (6:60, 64; Matthew 28:19; Mark 16:16). The present passage shows that such faith may be superficial *(cf.* 7:31,

8:31 [proof of discipleship must be given], 10:38), which takes its character from the Lord's leaving them without excuse (11:45 *f.*). In the last, real fidelity to Him is in question. See also 6:68 *f.* and 17:21, 23, where, for disciples and the world alike, moral transcend physical impressions.

60 *Verse* 25.—This should be considered in connection with the Lord's choice of Judas and probable difficulties raised at the time this Gospel was written by unbelievers questioning His deity. *Cf.* Mark 2:8, where the same faultless insight is attributed already to the "historical Jesus."

{**60a**} Such as believe without confession of Christ appear again in 12:42 *f.* They had not yet learnt what discipleship was. Nicodemus, in the next chapter, was one of the better examples in that day.

NOTES ON THE THIRD CHAPTER

61 The beginning, with this chapter, of a series of discourses characteristic of the Gospel of John calls for some development of what has been said in note 7 upon the treatment these have received at the hands of critics. Westcott, in his conservative *Introduction to the Study of the Gospels*, has remarked that, as compared with the Synoptists, in the fourth Gospel there is a "transition from one world of thought to another ... a contrast in form and spirit between the earlier and later narratives" (p. 249). As the leading conservative scholar in Germany says, the Johannine teaching is "esoteric" (Zahn, ii. 528). It is, however, with the statement of the narrowly "scientific" writers that we have to deal.

One of the objections of F. W. Newman (following Strauss) was that the Evangelist makes our Lord and the Baptist speak in the same, his own manner (p. 153 *f.*). As to this, reference might be made to the Reply to the younger Newman made in *The Irrationalism of Infidelity* by J. N. Darby, whom Mr. Benn (in a footnote of his second volume) describes as "fanatical." The present writer, from twelve years' acquaintance with the "Irish clergyman" towards the close of his life, found him the very opposite of what one may suppose Tertullian as a Montanist or George Fox to have been, and singularly characterised by the Pauline σωφρονισμός (2 Timothy 1:7). For a balanced objective appreciation, see Cheetham, *History of the Christian Church since the Reformation* (1907), p. 306 f.

See, further, an interesting letter by the elder Newman in Plummer, p. 100, on the difference between the ancient and the modern mind with regard to the use of direct for indirect speech.

Renan, while accepting the historical character of the narrative portion of the Gospel, treated the speeches as romance. So Jülicher: a "philosophical fiction," "prose poem," and much to the same purpose you find in Weizsäcker, Pfleiderer, and the Holtzmanns. Wendt, on the other hand, attaches more credit to the discourses than to the incidents reported, and seeks to show the harmony between the Synoptic and Johannine teaching. But, asks Wernle, is it psychologically possible that Jesus preached alternately in the manner of the Sermon on the Mount and of John 14-16? (p. 421; *cf.* Gardner, p. 165). Goethe does not seem to have felt any such difficulty; *cf.* the great difference between the second part of his *Faust* from the first. Contrast the late Dr. Hort's *Dissertations*, etc., with his *Village Sermons*. We have to remember the very different audiences our Lord would have in Jerusalem from those in Galilee or Peræa. Of course, much depends for us on the way in which we regard the mystery of His Person.

Again, German writers raise a difficulty over the "eyewitness" of the Evangelist, impeaching this in respect of the conversations with Nicodemus, the Samaritan woman, and Pilate. Briggs' scheme of the ministry would get over this so far as regards Nicodemus, especially if we suppose (although the wind in the trees may suggest Olivet) that the Lord lodged in John's house at Jerusalem (*cf.* 19:27). The record in the fourth chapter is not prejudiced by the statement that "His disciples had gone away to the city," which are the Evangelist's own parenthetical words, besides being in accordance with his manner; and if he himself stayed behind, he would be reticent about it, whilst the propriety of language admits of exception from the *whole* number of the disciples. As for Pilate's judgment-hall, the fourth Evangelist records how "the beloved disciple" hovered about the scenes of this chapter of our Lord's sorrows, and the words exchanged between Him and Pilate may accordingly have well been within John's hearing.

The question of possible *interpolation* is discussed. Delff (*Fourth Gospel*, p. 11) has suggested that a considerable amount of matter has been added by a later hand, which H. Holtzmann and Jülicher will not allow, for they insist on the unity of the book; but Wellhausen, in his lately published monograph, supports the idea. Some of his supposed "interpolations" are taken seriatim in notes below. This idea of interpolation is a favourite resource of critics when stumbling on passages which contradict their theories.

The Evangelist's own comments are for the most part easily discerned. Such are 2:21 *f.*, 7:39, 8:6, 11:30, 51 *f.*, 12:6, 16, 33, 13:11, 18:2. Other alleged cases are uncertain, as 1:16-18, 3:13, 16-21, 31-36, where commentators differ as to who is the speaker.

Much is made of this Evangelist's supposed dependence on Paul's writings, the publication of all of which is generally supposed to have been intermediate between the appearance of the last of the Synoptic Gospels and that of the fourth. H. Holtzmann attributes the authorship of this to a John who was an Ephesian disciple of Paul, and quotes the Epistle to the Ephesians, as Jülicher that to the Romans, in support of this position. Holtzmann supposes that the "critical" John was afterwards confounded with the son of Zebedee, so that a later generation ascribed the writing of the Gospel to "the beloved disciple" (*Introduction*, p. 170). This notion is reflected in the American Professor Bacon's book (*Deutero-Pauline Christianity of Theologos*, etc.). Weiss (*New Testament Theology*, ii., p. 228), on the conservative side, sees the influence of the Epistle to the Hebrews on John's thought. There is a useful note in Salmon (p. 265) on the parallels gathered between the Pauline writings and the Johannine. See also Stevens, chapter xv., Bernard, p. 12 *f.* The recent English and American writers generally show scarcely more balance than the German and French (as Loisy). There is little to choose between Professor Wernle's saying that John is a mere plagiarist of Paul (*Beginnings {of Christianity}*, ii., pp. 262, 264, 274) and Mr. Scott's committal to the statement, "The Evangelist is everywhere indebted to Paul" (p. 46) "for almost all his larger doctrines" (p. 49). Of course, no one could deny that, as far as we can judge from *writings*, "it was Paul who first conceived of the glorified Christ as the real object of faith"; the manner of his conversion determined that. That the basis of the life of each of these two Apostles was "profoundly mystical" (Illingworth, chapter ix.) all would allow. But whilst Paul sets the believer in Christ before God, John sets God in Christ before the believer; in other words, the one instructs us in the Divine counsels, the other in the Divine nature. Scott speaks of John's advancing on Paul (p. 51), but this is gratuitous: the types of doctrine are throughout really distinct. The Church had already received the Pauline scheme; the Johannine, assuming the Synoptic accounts, was needed to complete the doctrine, not of the *Church*, but of the *Person of Christ*.

Even as regards the truths of redemption, Mr. Scott is at sea. A writer must be infatuated who can say that "sin has a subordinate place" in John's Gospel (p. 51 *f.*). The Evangelist's sense of the acuteness of it is evidenced by 16:8, 9. Paul's writings had sufficiently emphasised it in respect of man's *need*. On p. 52 we are told that Paul's doctrine of atonement has disappeared, in the sense of being transcended; and that John takes exclusive account of the Life as possessing the significance which Paul attached to the Cross. But this writer must have forgotten Romans 5:10: "Much more ... we shall be saved by His life." That John 8:33-39 flows from Romans 6:16-23 (*cf.* Galatians 4:30) there is no more ground for Mr. Scott's saying than any other writer's alleging the converse. Indeed, it is open to so-called "apologists" to suggest that, when in the company of this "pillar" during his stay in Judæa, Paul had opportunity of learning from him as to the Lord's ministry; for "imparted nothing to me" (Galatians 2:6) has reference to authority and capacity rather than to information.

62 Verse 1.—"Nicodemus." As to Abbott's identification of him with Nicodemon, son of Gorion, who was employer of the water-carriers in Jerusalem during the Passover, see Westcott, *contra*.

63 Verse 2.—"By night." See note 61 above. For Nicodemus' subsequent history, see 7:50 and 19:39. What we may learn from this state of mind in the present passage is that "it is not *learning*, but *life*, that man

needs" (Govett). For the function of signs, see note 52, and *cf.* 5:36, 10:25, 15:24.

64 *Verse 3 f.*—"Anew." So most commentators, as Godet, Westcott, Luthardt, Weiss and Zahn here and in verse 7, after the Peschito-Syriac, etc. Origen followed, amongst others, by Bengel, Meyer and Pfleiderer, prefers the meaning "from above"; "from heaven" is the interpretation put upon ἄνωθεν by most of the Greek writers. *Cf.* Abbott, *Johannine Vocabulary*, § 1,707e, referring to verse 31 and 19:11.

65 "The kingdom of God." This phrase is used only here in the fourth Gospel. For the connection between the Kingdom and Life *cf.* Mark 9:43, 45, 47, and Luke 18:18, 24; and in particular the *Exposition* at p. 484 *f*. As to other links between the second (critical first) and fourth Gospels, see notes 18, 94, 122, 130, 146 on Mark, and note {66a} on verse 5 below.

66 *Verse 5 ff.*—"Born of water and Spirit." Advanced critics oddly support the "Catholic" tradition that Christian Baptism is here spoken of (verse 22 *f.*); to this theory Scott adheres (p. 40). If Paul's doctrine is to control the interpretation of this Gospel, why do such writers ignore a passage like Ephesians 5:26? That the words bear some relation to the Baptism of John, which Nicodemus may have shirked, one may well believe (*cf.* Luke 7:30). As to ἐκ, "out of," and the one article in the Greek, see R. Govett's exposition of the passage. A reference to the Jewish baptism of proselytes owes its plausibility to that practice, which originated in part from the interpretation put on Ezekiel 36 cited in the Exposition. *Cf.* Seeley, *Ecce Homo*, p. 98.

66a "*Enter* into the kingdom." See note 99 on Mark. "Enter" seems to be always used of the time of recompense. *Cf.* Matthew 25:21, Luke 24:26, with, of course, Matthew 18:3, which links itself specially with this passage of John. The Messianic bearing of the first Gospel must always be kept in mind. Readers of Mr. Scott's book might derive from it an impression that the fourth Evangelist discards that point of view, which would be a mistake.

67 *Verse* 11.—The Lord takes up the "We know" of Nicodemus. "We" here seems used by Christ of Himself, as in Mark 4:30. So Theophylact of old, Ryle and McRory among moderns. If it mean John the Baptist as well as Himself (so Zahn), then there is a reference to the law's requirement of two witnesses (Govett). Luthardt, Godet and Westcott understand it of the disciples associated by the Lord with Himself.

68 *Verse* 13.—"That is in heaven." Words actually spoken by the Lord on earth; not supposing the Ascension accomplished, as Weiss thinks, apparently with 6:62 in mind (*cf.* Arnold, *God and the Bible*, chapter vi., § 5). It is probably the later passage that induces some to take verse 13 here as parenthetical, and as words of the Evangelist himself (note 61).

As to the note {e} on ὤν (p. 114, {chapter 3} of the *Exposition*), see Winer, p. 429. Bengel has been followed by Hofmann, Luthardt, Weiss, Barth and Zahn, some founding it on the passage in chapter 6, whilst the last-named writer refers to 9:25. Moulton is amongst those who reject these words.

69 *Verse* 15.—"Life eternal." Oosterzee, comparing this with 6:35, says that it expresses established personal communion with Christ (*Theology of the New Testament*, p. 170). *Cf.* notes 106, 110 on Mark. The rendering in R.V. results from acceptance of ἐν (see critical note), whilst Mr. Kelly has followed ℵ, etc.

70 *Verses* 16-18.—Tholuck, Luthardt, Godet, Westcott, Sadler, and Plummer, after Erasmus and others, take this and the following verses to 21 as words of the Evangelist himself (note 61). That, however, the third person is used does not tell against the Lord's speaking the words may be seen from 4:10, 5:19, 6:29. If they are His (Zahn), Christ speaks of Himself definitely as Son of God *(cf.* Sanday, "Son of God" in Hastings, *Dictionary of the Bible,* p. 572). He used the third person when speaking of Himself as Son of man also (Mark, as John).

On the significance of verse 16 for the *Biblical* doctrine of Atonement, see essay on that subject by Von Gerdtell, pp. 42, 77. He pulverises the theological travesty of it, to which unbelievers have rightly shown no mercy.

For the sentiment *cf.*, of course, Romans 8:32, 2 Corinthians 9:15. As to the scope of salvation here conflicting with the narrower outlook of the Synoptists (Matthew 10:5 *f.*, etc.), observe that it is precisely when the Lord is speaking in Judæa that He strikes the universalistic note, and when away from there that He speaks of His mission having been to the "lost sheep of the house of Israel." In verse 16 we have the compassion of the love of God as such *(cf.* note on 16:26).

Verse 17 is on the same lines as 12:47. As to 9:39, see note there.

71 *Verse* 19.—"Loved." Ryle, comparing 15:8 and also Romans 8:30, would take the aorist here as "proleptic"—that is, in a present sense. See however, Mr. Kelly's footnote on 13:31, where reference is made to the sixth verse of chapter 15.

NOTES ON THE THIRD CHAPTER

72 *Verse* 20 *f.*—*Cf.* 5:29, where the same distinction obtains between ποιεῖν, said of good, and πράσσειν, of evil.

73 *Verses* 22-30.—This passage Briggs regards as synchronising with Mark 2:18 *ff.*

74 *Verse* 22.—"He ... baptised." *Cf.* verse 26. Schmiedel (col. 2,538) sets against this 4:2. But what about Pilate's scourging JESUS, and his writing the superscription for the Cross?

75 *Verse* 24.—Wernle (*Sources*, p. 27 *f.*) treats this parenthetical note as "correcting" the Synoptists, as though they stated that the Lord's work in Galilee, with which His ministry opens in their Gospels, was the beginning of His public activity! Briggs, in his last book, raps the knuckles of a good many answerable for such "historical" criticism *(cf.* note {20} on Mark 1:13 *f.).*

76 *Verse* 26.—Schmiedel (col. 2,538), after H. Holtzmann, finds a contradiction here to verse 32. That is, the people say to the Baptist something, to be taken for what it is worth, to which he (or Matthew Arnold's "theological lecturer") takes exception. In any case, where is the self-contradiction on the part of the Evangelist? It is in connection with such cases, of course, that suggestions of dual authorship arise; but many are the cobwebs spun.

77 *Verses* 31-36.—The words are taken as the Baptist's by Luthardt, Godet, Plummer and Zahn. See, again, note 61, as for the last preceding note. Erasmus's view, that they are the Evangelist's, has been followed by Bengel, Tholuck, Westcott, Sadler, and Milligan. Nothing seems to be gained by the suggestion, nothing to need amendment in the older view, followed by the expositor. The words may have been suggested to the Baptist by those contained in Matthew 9:15.

Verse 32.—"No one receiveth His testimony." This has been set in conflict with verse 26, where, however, we meet with exaggeration of fervour: so Weiss and Westcott. The latter notes the singular darkness and hopelessness of the close of the Apostolic age *(cf.* 1 John 5:19).

78 *Verse* 32 *f.*—See J. H. Newman (*Apologia*, p. 199): "In religious inquiry we arrive at certitude by accumulated probabilities." *Cf.* the examination of that book by J. N. Darby. We have in verse 33 the touchstone of the quality of a man's "faith."

79 *Verse* 36.—Mr. Darby, in his version, has rendered ἀπειθῶν, "not subject," as supporting the view that the Baptist was the speaker *(cf.* Luke 3:7).

The words of this verse expose the delusion of a modern idea that, because God is love, He forgives as such, not because of the death of His Son.

NOTES ON THE FOURTH CHAPTER

80 Comparing Luke 9:51-56 with the contents of this chapter, Von Soden discredits the success among the Samaritans here recorded. That is, when one Evangelist speaks of the resistance shown to His ministry by Samaritans when the Lord is going in the direction of Jerusalem southwards, and another records a journey from Jerusalem northwards, which has a different result, the two accounts are held to clash. There is a good deal of the same superficial criticism in such literature. The writer named is silent upon the words of verse 9.

80a *Verse* 1.—Observe "the Lord" of the Evangelist, and "Jesus" of the Pharisees; and for "the Lord," *cf.* 6:23, 11:2, 20:20. "Knew," supernaturally (Milligan). *Cf.* 2:24.

81 *Verse* 2 *f.*—Wellhausen treats this as an editorial interpolation made to remove apparent discrepancy between the fourth Evangelist *(cf.* 3:22) and the Synoptists. If that, however, had been really felt, would not the course likely to be taken by any editor be to leave out the words "and baptizeth," which he found in the autograph? Here the Evangelist reverts to "Jesus," because he seems to be quoting a report. So Moffatt.

82 *Verse 5.*—"Sychar." Doubt was at one time felt as to the Evangelist's accuracy in this name. It was supposed to stand for Sichem, which is given by the Sinaitic Syriac, whilst the Harclensian recension has "Sychar." Eusebius, settled at Cæsarea, distinguished them. Thomson's identification of the place with the modern *Askar* was questioned by Grove, but it has been upheld by G. A. Smith in his *Historical Geography of Palestine*: "The author knew the place about which he was writing" (p. 368 *ff.*). That was not Shechem, the modern Nablûs.

83 *Verse 6.*—οὕτως, "thus." Field, apparently following Chrysostom—"as it chanced"—for which see also 5:30, 8:40. That is, *just as He was* (*cf.* Mark 4:36). The "wearied," as Zahn says (ii. 539), emphasizes His humanity.

84 "Sixth hour." As to John's way of reckoning hours, see note on 19:14.

85 *Verse 7 ff.*—Dr. Abbott, on the ground alleged that "no disciple was present," says that "it is practically certain that the dialogue did not occur in the exact words recorded" (*Encyclopædia Biblica*, col. 1,801). As to the absence of all disciples, see in note 61 above, to which may be added here the consideration that we are not to suppose all persons with whom Christ spoke kept the knowledge of such conversations to themselves. It is practically certain that they would reproduce at least the substance of Christ's words to them. For this *cf.* what the expositor has said in the volume on Mark (p. 10, foot) {see Appendix}.

86 *Verse 9.*—"A Jew." She knew Him to be such by His dress. See Schor, *Palestine and the Bible*. Here used in the broadest sense. So in verse 22, unlike 7:1, etc.

NOTES ON THE FOURTH CHAPTER

87 "For Jews have no intercourse with Samaritans." These words are treated as parenthetical in the R.V.—that is, as an explanatory comment of the Evangelist. Calvin considered them to be spoken by the woman.

88 "The gift of God." Luthardt, Govett and Zahn take this in the same way as the expositor. Godet, Westcott (referring to 3:16), and Carr follow Stier, who explains it of Christ. But Jeremy Taylor rightly described that as "too vague." "Christ, the smitten rock, was the source" (Govett).

88a *Verse* 14.—"Shall *not* thirst *for ever.*" So Govett, referring to Revelation 21:6.

89 *Verse* 20.—On προσκυνεῖν, see Abbott, *Johannine Vocabulary*, §§ 1,640-1,651.

90 *Verse* 22.—Olshausen, followed by Ryle, takes σωτηρία as equivalent to "the Saviour." *Cf.* Luke 19:9.

90a *Verses* 21-24.—"The hour." This present dispensation, which is only for a while: it will give place to the millennial. As to the character of worship on earth then, see Govett, pp. 145 *f.*

"God (θεός) is a Spirit (πνεῦμα)." The word θεός in latest philological research has been connected with "breath," "spirit." See article GOD in Hauck's *Encyclopædia*, vol. vi., p. 780.

91 *Verse* 25.—"That is called Christ." Here, again, brackets have been used in the R.V. to indicate a parenthesis, the Revisers understanding the words to be the Evangelist's addition, not used by the woman. "The woman expected a teacher, not a liberator" (Horton, p. 191).

92 *Verse* 26 *f.*—The first direct assertion by our Lord that He is "the Christ," and outside the Jewish territory. On the disclosure of this to a woman, Quesnel has remarked: "It is a great mistake to suppose that the knowledge of the mysteries of religion ought not to be imparted to women. ... The abuse of the Scriptures and the sin of heresies did not proceed from the simplicity of women, but from the conceited learning of men."

92a "Wondered," etc. The rabbinical rule, much quoted (from Dr. John Lightfoot), was that a man should not speak even to his wife in the street. See *Jewish Prayer-Book* (Eyre and Spottiswoode), p. 185. The knowledge of this prejudice shown by the Evangelist is one of the indications of his Jewish nationality. Others occur in 5:1 *ff.*, 7:22, 27, 49, 12:34, etc. (see note 1a, *ad fin.*).

93 *Verse* 28 *f.*—Origen calls her the "apostle of the Samaritans," whilst Cyril notes that after Christ had first bidden her call her husband, she finally of her own behest called all the men to Him, and receiving the talent of the glad tidings, she at once put it out to interest.

The R.V. has, "Can this be the Christ?" according to the form used in verse 33, but the older rendering practically comes to the same thing.

94 *Verse* 34.—Augustine here remarks that we should not be surprised by the woman's not understanding about the *water* of which Christ spoke to her when His disciples misunderstood what He said about *food*. This verse (*cf.* 9:4) explains the "must" of verse 4 above.

95 *Verse* 38.—Origen: "Did not Moses and Elias the sowers rejoice with the reapers, Peter, James, and John, when they saw the glory of the Son of God at the Transfiguration?"

NOTES ON THE FOURTH CHAPTER

96 *Verse* 43 *f.*—"His own country." It is difficult to determine whether this means Galilee or Judæa. Meyer, Hofmann, Luthardt, Govett and Zahn say Galilee, suggested by the like expression in the Synoptic Gospels (see note {22} on Mark 1:21), whilst Origen, Maldonatus, the approved Roman Catholic commentator (whom Kenrick follows), Westcott, Sadler, Milligan, Plummer, Norris, Reynolds, Wendt, Schmiedel and Carr (see his note) take it of Judæa. If the second view be right, we have here, of course, a recognition by the fourth Evangelist of the birth at Bethlehem, of which critics represent him as "knowing nothing."

Cyril, Calvin, H. Holtzmann, Field, and Briggs decide for Nazareth; Chrysostom and Euthymius, Capernaum. *Cf.* also Mark 6:4 for its bearing on the question.

97 *Verse* 48.—*Cf.* Mark 8:12 and note 27 on that Gospel; also Matthew 12:39. It is not a question so much of the Lord's own attitude or that of the disciples (which fluctuated) towards miracles as that of the mass of the people, which none of the Evangelists adopt, although critical works might lead one to suppose such was the case.

98 *Verse* 54.—This incident is not to be confused with that in Luke 7.

99 The working of "a sign" by way of display ("epideictic"), apart from some groundwork of antecedent faith *(cf.* 11:26 *f.* with verse 40 there), can no more be charged against the Johannine than the Synoptic miracles *(cf.* 2:11 and note 52).

NOTES ON THE FIFTH CHAPTER

100 *Verse* 1.—Most commentators (including the Reformers) follow Irenæus, Eusebius, and Theodoret, etc., in taking the feast here spoken of as a Passover. Jerome, followed by Norris, thought that it was *Pentecost*; Neander, Meyer, Weiss, McClellan and Milligan, *Purim*; Zahn (reading the article), *Tabernacles*. As to the number of Passovers during the ministry, see note 53.

101 *Verse* 2.—"There *is*." Blass (*Expository Times*, July, 1907) followed Bengel in accepting this as an indication of the date of the writing of the Gospel, as earlier than that of the Roman devastation.

102 *Verse* 8.—"Took up his couch." The simplicity of the process has been brought home to those visiting the recent Palestine Exhibitions. See Schor, *Palestine and the Bible*, p. 38. As to its taking place on the Sabbath day, (verse 10), *cf.* Jeremiah 17:21.

103 *Verse* 13.—For the apparently miraculous withdrawal here, *cf.* 10:39, as well as Luke 4:30. The word used in this place is a solecism. See Westcott or Govett, *in loc.*

NOTES ON THE FIFTH CHAPTER

104 *Verse* 14.—"Sin no more": a note of our Lord's omniscience.

105 *Verse* 18.—"Broke." Lit., "was loosing." *Cf.* Matthew 18:18, and see also 10:33 of this Gospel.

105a *Verse* 22.—As to alleged inconsistency with 15:2, see note there. The ascription of "judgment" to the Son (*cf.* verse 27) is by no means peculiar to the fourth Gospel. See Matthew 7:22 and other references in Turton, p. 448.

106 *Verse* 24 *f.*—De Wette, Olshausen, Meyer and Plummer explain this resurrection similarly to the expositor. The passage has been misused by such as those spoken of in 2 Timothy 2:18.

"Cometh." For this present tense, *cf.* 4:36, 6:46 *f.*, 54, and 12:25. In the last passage the future is used co-ordinately.

Observe that the Lord speaks of Himself a second time definitely as "Son of God" (see note 70 above, and *cf.* 9:35, 10:36, 11:4). It is a favourite notion of critics that such is language merely of the Evangelist.

107 *Verse* 26.—The all-important words are "in Himself" (*cf.* 6:57). Athanasius (*Orations against Arians*, iii.) says: "The word *gave* shows us that the Son is a distinct Person from the Father; but the use of the word "so" is a clear proof of His being the natural Son, equal to, co-essential with the Father. ... As the Father hath, so hath the Son from the Father, self-existence" (*cf.* note 9, *ad fin.*). Observe the aorist ἔδωκεν, "gave," not the perfect δέδωκεν, "hath given," for it transcends time.

108 *Verse* 28 *f.*—The difference of time in the two judgments is recognised by Meyer and Beyschlag. An objection made that the two resurrections take place in the same hour is rebutted by verse 25, where the spiritual resurrection which has gone on for nearly two millenniums is also called an "hour." A resurrection of the wicked does not emerge so clearly from the Synoptic accounts. That there is to be no general contemporaneous resurrection was foreshadowed by Psalm 1:5: "The wicked shall not *arise* in the judgment, nor sinners in the assembly of the righteous." See LXX. and Vulgate (*resurgent*). The German critics no more apprehend the sense of קוּם there than English translators, who alike adhere to "stand." But *cf.* Matthew 12:41, where all assign to ἀναστήσονται, in the same form of words, its natural meaning. The usual idea is that the Old Testament uniformly predicates resurrection of the righteous *alone*; but the point is that they who have done good and those that have done evil will *not* rise *together*. *Cf.* Simcox on Revelation 20:5. The Pharisees supposed that only the righteous would live again (Josephus, *Antiquities*, xviii. 14; 2 Maccabees 6:26; and other references in Bousset, *Religion of Judaism*, p. 259).

The present passage was so inconvenient to the Tübingen school that Scholten resorted to the usual makeshift—suggestion of interpolation—which feeble resource has had to do duty for several others since (see, *e.g.*, amongst recent writers, Briggs, p. 145).

109 *Verse* 30.—See note on 4:6.

109a *Verse* 31.—As to supposed conflict of this verse with 8:14, see note {160} there. Observe the use of the word "witness" throughout verses 31-39. It occurs, in one form or other, some fifty times in this Gospel; "believe" about one hundred times.

NOTES ON THE FIFTH CHAPTER

110 *Verse* 35.—*Cf.* Sirach {or Ecclesiasticus} 48:1. {"Then stood up Elias the prophet as fire, and his words burned like a lamp."}

110a *Verse* 36.—"Witness greater" representing μείζω, accepted by Blass, who understands "witness in greater measure." μείζων would mean "I the witness, a greater," etc. (see Zahn).

{**110b**} As to the evidence of "works" or "signs," see 3:2 and references there.

111 *Verse* 37.—The distinction of this witness from that of the Scriptures (verse 38) is maintained by Chrysostom. Bengel, and others, who refer it to the Lord's baptism, etc. Ryle (following Calvin, Tholuck, Alford, and Burgon) preferred to regard it as coalescing with the testimony borne by the Old Testament writings.

112 *Verse* 39.—The word ἐραυνᾶτε is taken as *indicative* by Cyril, Erasmus, Beza, Bengel, Meyer, Olshausen, Tholuck, De Wette, Burgon, Kenrick, Godet, Westcott (citing Hillel), Plummer, Govett, Kennedy, Manning, McRory, Carr and Zahn; as *imperative* by Chrysostom, Theophylact, Euthymius, Augustine, Luther, Calvin, Grotius, à Lapide, Stier, Luthardt, Alford, Wordsworth, Ryle, McClellan, and Field. The last-named very judicious scholar remarks that we should not stop short at "eternal life," as if the ὅτι had no influence beyond those words. The revisers, however, having decided to give up the A.V., their rendering will probably establish itself. J. N. Darby, in his versions, had adopted the indicative. Certainly the words "ye think" suggest it.

"Life eternal." This was a later development accepted by the Pharisees (Watson, *Inspiration*, p. 142).

113 *Verse* 43.—"Another." Bousset has rightly taken this of *Antichrist*, not of Bar Kochba (A.D. 132), as Pfleiderer, followed by Schmiedel (col. 2,551). The absurdity, again, of applying these words to the *Popedom* is clear from several New Testament passages, commencing with 2 Thessalonians 2. The Popes have never come in their own name, but in that of Peter; they own the Father and the Son (1 John 2:18-23), and Jesus Christ coming in the flesh (1 John 4:2). Bousset, in the *Encyclopædia Britannica* (vol. i., col. 177), following his work on Antichrist, takes 2 Thessalonians 2:1-12 as his starting-point; he sees that the Antichrist must be a Jew, and that any "præterist or historical interpretation is out of the question" (col. 181). Swete, in like manner, thinks that the "second beast" of Revelation 13 is in some sense Antichrist (*Commentary on Apocalypse, ad loc.*).

114 *Verse* 44.—The force of the aorist πιστεῦσαι is well brought out by Abbott: "to reach the threshold of belief" (§ 2,496 *f.*; *cf.* note on 12:39).

115 *Verse* 46 *f.*—In connection with the supremacy attached to Holy Scripture by our Lord, it may be helpful to consider what has been said by a few recent writers of repute on FAITH in general, and, in particular, its relation to SCRIPTURE. In the valuable Note 2 appended to Westcott's *Historic Faith* (pp. 73-77) he discriminates "a conviction of truth [knowledge], a quickening of love [feeling], a readiness for action [will]," which last is represented by "an advance into the unseen … wholly different from a belief in past facts which rests on testimony [intellectual assent]." The present Bishop of Birmingham, in his *Creed of the Christian* (p. 33), has said: "In order to act decisively, we must believe decisively," which is a repetition, in other words, of the prophet's teaching: "If ye do not hold fast, ye will not stand fast" (Isaiah 7:9). Dr. Gore, inquiring as to the essence of faith, answers that it is "the open hand or open mouth of the human soul" (p. 53). Next, where does Scripture come in? Dr. J. H. Newman shall reply. In a letter printed in Miss Mozley's *Letters and Correspondence* of this eminent man (vol. ii., p. 113), which he wrote to Hurrell Froude in 1835, we find: "The more I read of Athanasius, Theodoret, etc., the more I see that the ancients did make the Scriptures the *basis* of belief. ... The Fathers do certainly rest on Scripture, as upon two tables of stone." There is, happily, no reason for supposing that when he went over to Rome Newman had to abandon this conviction. And so we are prepared for what Professor Herrmann (a Ritzschlian) says in his *Faith and Morals* (p. 18): "The common idea [of Faith] is an acknowledgment of the whole Bible as God's Word and true, coupled with firm trust in its narratives and doctrines." He adds, critically: "That is no more than the Catholic idea of Faith," but then, as he says, Tradition is annexed to it by "Catholics." This it is which makes all the difference, for Superstition, which is purely carnal tends to swamp Faith. "For the writer of this Gospel," says Inge, "Faith is not an acceptance of a proposition upon evidence. It is the resolution to follow Christ wherever He may lead us" (*Christian Mysticism*, p. 50). See, further, note on 6:69; also Green, iii., pp. 253-276; and chapter iv. of Sir R. Anderson's *The Gospel and its Ministry*.

NOTES ON THE SIXTH CHAPTER

116 *Verses* 5-9.—As to the close connection of Philip and Andrew with John, see Lightfoot on Colossians, p. 45 *f.*

"A lad." On the baker's "boy," see Schor, *Palestine and the Bible*, pp. 32, 58.

117 *Verse* 11.—One miserable attempt to get rid of this miracle has been to suggest that JESUS and His disciples shared their provisions with some of the crowd, others following their example. From those who indulge in such explanations one may well ask for a reason why the people thought our Lord the Messiah, and wished to make Him King? That is significantly forgotten.

117a *Verse* 12 *f.*—"Fragments." Or "broken pieces," as R.V. The command is peculiar to this Gospel.

118 *Verse* 14.—"The prophet." See Deuteronomy 18:15, and *cf.* 11:27 (Matthew 11:3, Luke 7:19), 12:13. There the testimony is that of His works (*cf.* chapter 9), as in 7:40 of His teaching.

118a *Verse* 15.—As to kingship of JESUS, predicted in the Old Testament, see, further, Micah 5:2, Jeremiah 23:5, Psalm 89, etc., and *cf.* note {28} on Luke 1:32 *f.*

NOTES ON THE SIXTH CHAPTER

When our Lord did offer Himself as King, the Jews refused Him (Matthew 21:15). Godet would explain the "compelled" of Mark 6:45 (Matthew 14:22) by what we are told here.

119 *Verse* 15—H. Holtzmann criticizes "withdrew again to the mountain," because the Lord is not said previously to have left the mountain. And so Schmiedel and Heitmüller after him. One might well suppose that such writers are devoid entirely of imagination. A tract of hilly country is in question, into which Christ further penetrated. (So Weiss; *cf.* note 39 on Mark.) The "again" may suggest difficulty; but, as the critical note shows, that, to say no more, is a doubtful reading.

120 *Verse* 17 *ff.*—*Cf.* note 65 on Mark. For such power over sea and waves, *cf.* Psalm 107:23-31. Matthew's parallel (14:33) shows that the disciples worshipped Him as Son of God. Are we to be told of an *interpolation* there?

120a *Verse* 19.—"*On* the sea." The same Greek in 21:1 has been quoted for the meaning "at" (beside, on the bank of) the sea. But even there it may mean "on." In either case it expresses loose connection. As to attempts made, as by Paulus, to explain it away, see Turton, p. 412. Taking the miracle and the discourse which follows it in connection with the Lord's Supper (as do Catholics), certain critics have this notion so much on the brain that one of them—Schmiedel—will have it that the walking on the water was "intended to signify that exaltation of Jesus above the limitations of space necessary to render possible the presence of His glorified body at every celebration of the Eucharist!" (col. 2,521). Where "progress"—for it is imagination—beyond ecclesiastical tradition comes in it is indeed difficult to discover.

121 *Verses* 22-24.—Unbelievers of to-day are not seldom at issue with sceptics in the time of the Evangelist; those of old could not understand the Lord's walking *along the shore* within that short interval (verse 25). Some now, doubtless, would gladly discover differences in manuscripts here, so as to be able to suggest "accretions."

122 *Verse* 27 *ff.*—"Son of man." Not Christ, the Son of God, as Gnostics would have said: their Christ was not "Son of man" at all. Observe that, to meet their error, the Evangelist constantly speaks of our Lord as JESUS, and that here is the Son of *man* Whom the Father has sealed, attested, as *His* Son.

The Rabbins said that the seal of God was אמת, the three letters of which are respectively the first, the middle, and the last of the alphabet (Edersheim, ii. 29). Comparing verse 29 with Romans 1:5, may we not say that Paul's words are an echo of our Lord's here?

123 *Verse* 35.—The Lord here, for the first time, speaks of Himself as "the Bread," so that some, as Alford and Govett, would in verse 33 render by "that which" rather than by "He who," verse 34 indicating ambiguity. As to hunger and thirst, see on verses 51-56. For "ye believe not," *cf.* 16:9. Above all else, faith is due to God (*cf.* Mark 16:14 *ff.*). No quarter is given here to hyper-Calvinism.

124 *Verse* 42.—Forcible words of Von Hartmann should lead some to pause: "If one sees in Jesus only the son of the carpenter Joseph and his wife Mary, this Jesus and His death can as little redeem me from my sins as, say, Bismarck can do it" (*Dissolution of Christianity*, p. 92). Critics would have had the Lord here disclose His supernatural birth. But with what propriety to men in the state of mind that these were? It could but have excited their derision.

125 *Verse 47.*—For the "verily, verily," *cf.* 1 John 5:11-13.

126 *Verse 51.*—As to "living bread," see Carson, *On Interpretation*, p. 81. Much use has been made of the passage in the interests of a theory of the Incarnation, by which Christ, as the Word made flesh, is supposed to be "joined to universal humanity." Words of Irenæus (*Against Heresies*, v. 16, 2) about "Christ's raising humanity into God" by His incarnation, or of Athanasius, in his treatise *On the Incarnation*, where he speaks of our Lord's having "become man that we might be made God" (liv.), seem to have originated this notion. And so, on the one hand, Bishop Gore (*Sermon on Sin*, p. 21), as, on the other, Mr. Scott (p. 208, etc.). But the Lord does not speak here of His *taking*, but of His *giving* His flesh for us (so H. Holtzmann, but misapplying it); and such passages as Ephesians 5:30 and 2 Peter 1:4, which have been used in support of the theory, have nothing to do with the solidarity of the human race, but concern Christian believers only. The last words of verse 51—"for the life of the world"—are said, not of Christ's life, but His death; and "Unless ye shall have eaten the flesh of the Son of man, and drunk His blood, ye have no life in yourselves" (verse 53) means that we cannot be so associated with the "historical Christ" as the theory requires. Redemption is needed for it; whilst *bona fide* children of God alone are united to Him, and that in *resurrection*. Out of the Patristic theory has, beyond all doubt, arisen the whole remedial system of ordinances developed in the "historical" Church. The comradeship of sacerdotalists and critics in this matter tells its own tale: different poles of error unite for mutual aid. As to the use made of this text by Annihilationists, see Turton, p. 525; and on the Incarnation in general, Green, iii., pp. 207-220.

127 *Verses* 52-59.—The *Patristic* application (as by Chrysostom and Cyril, etc.) of this passage to the Eucharist for the doctrine adopted by Wordsworth, Burgon, Williams, Sadler and Gore, as already stated, has the unwonted and by no means edifying support of some critics, as H. Holtzmann, Pfleiderer and Harnack, followed by Burkitt (p. 224 *ff.*) etc., from the difficulty which they experience of understanding it in its present context. But, long ago, Augustine took a healthier view of it, as, in recent times, Meyer, Hofmann, Weiss (*Life of Christ*, iii. 71), Godet, and Westcott. Dr. John Lightfoot (*cf.* Bishop Boyd Carpenter, "Introduction to Scripture") showed that "eating" and "drinking" were used by Jesus metaphorically; a certain rabbi is recorded to have spoken of "devouring Messiah" (*Horæ Hebraicæ et Talmudicæ {Hebrew and Talmudical exercitations}*, iii. 307 *ff.*, Oxford edition). One will tell you that the Evangelist aimed at checking sacramental theory (so Scott); another that he himself held "high sacramental doctrine" (Burkitt); whilst a third would have it that the Lord observed the Eucharist from the beginning of His ministry (Wright)! Horton agrees with none of these (p. 298).

127a That the words were spoken to the Jews (verse 58) is, amongst others, recognised by Heitmüller, one of the latest writers on this Gospel. The lesson which they had to learn (that of Egypt and the wilderness: Bellett, p. 57) is the primary thing.

128 The reference is to Cardinal Wiseman, in his *Lectures on Doctrines and Practices*, No. XIV.; also in his *Lectures on the Real Presence*, p. 40 *f.*

NOTES ON THE SIXTH CHAPTER

Cardinal Manning's note on verse 54 says: "is here promised to the worthy receiver." There is not a word of qualification in the verse.

129 *Verse 56 f.*—"Abideth in Me, and I in him." One of the passages turned to account by those who make much of John's supposed dependence on Pauline doctrine ("in Christ," "Christ in us"). Again, let it be said, it is a *dead* Christ who gives to the believer life, as it is a *risen* Christ in whom he abides. See, further, on chapter 15:4 *ff.* Observe the use of the *present participle* here, as in verse 54, and compare the *present tense* (πιστεύετε) in verse 29: "live the life of faith" (Horton, p. 257).

"Shall live by reason of Me." See p. 208, and *cf.* Romans 5:10; also note 192. For both the Apostles it is the resurrection life, not that of the Lord on earth.

130 *Verse 62.*—*Cf.* note 68 above. This refutes Swedenborg, who held that the Lord was always casting off His manhood, so that at last only the Father remained; there was neither Son of God nor Son of man who could ascend! We are here told that Christ called Himself "Son of man," in view of *resurrection*. Swedenborg, in keeping with his theory of the Lord's earthly life, denied His *bodily* return from heaven—a negation which the Evangelist, in his Second Epistle, brands as a mark of Antichrist (verse 7; see R.V., and *cf.* 1 John 4:2). For further reference to the Ascension in this Gospel see 20:17. It is such passages as these that Wendt attributes to an "editor" (see note 1a on Introduction).

131 *Verse 67 ff.*—"The twelve." The first time that, in this Gospel, the apostolic band is so described.

131a Paley: "slanderer"—*i.e.*, to the rulers (verse 70).

132 *Verse* 68.—"To whom shall we go away?" Govett: "Before we leave what we hold, we should see what better can replace it" (p. 290). *Cf.* note 59, and see 17:8.

133 *Verse* 69.—*Cf.* note on 5:46 *f.* above. Note the force of the *perfect:* "We have been believing"—*i.e.*, they had acquired the habit in their hearts of thinking so of Him. For the disciples it was not a question of mere opinion, for which there is no assured permanence. *Cf.* Browning's *Bishop Blougram's Apology*: "With me faith means perpetual unbelief." A necessary element in it is knowledge of the truth, to which the Apostle Paul says some ever learning never attain (2 Timothy 3:7).

Martineau has well said: "Nothing so marks the degradation of our modern Christianity as the notion that faith is only opinion—that a man may have it or not without affecting his moral worth; that it is the result of intellectual accident or opportunity, for which God will never call him to account. ... Want of faith is the hypothesis of a coward, unaspiring heart. ... This presumption in favour of sanctity in human life is *faith*" (*Hours of Thought*, vol. ii., p. 90). See also Bishop Gore's *Creed of the Christian*, p. 53, and *Sermon on Sin*, p. 7. It should be remembered that in Lessing's *Nathan*, referred to by him, none of the three characters was a really typical representative of his own creed.

Weiss has written (*New Testament Theology*, ii. 364) that the doctrine of John on Faith in this connection, in distinction from the Pauline view, as that in the Epistle to the Hebrews, means the conviction of the truth of the fact that Jesus is the Christ, and not a trust in the love of God in Christ *(cf.* McGiffert, p. 498). This has, happily, been pronounced by Beyschlag (*New Testament Theology*, ii. 455 *ff.*) as "the greatest possible mistake";

for the Halle theologian, passages such as 14:1 set before us "a personal surrender to Christ leading to personal communion of life with Him" (*cf.* note on 5:46 above). Again, as he says: "The confident apprehension with the heart has to precede the deliberative apprehension with the mind." Scott's view (p. 52, etc.) is very much that of Weiss, for the British writer at one time treats faith and knowledge as identical (an intellectual assent: "acceptance of a given dogma," p. 267, as to which see note 374); but also because of passages in the First Epistle in particular (*e.g.*, 4:16) he treats knowledge as emphatically antecedent to faith, in which he seems to confound one element of faith which precedes knowledge with another which gives place to knowledge. Acquaintance with God and Christ certainly grows out of continued trust, for John as for Paul ("I know in whom I have believed"). The "act of belief" which, Scott says, "comes at the end of a religious experience" (p. 268), is the same with each Apostle. When this writer says, "The original demand for a simple childlike faith was no longer sufficient in a theology which had allied Christianity with a metaphysical doctrine" (p. 274), one wonders how he would attempt to make this tally with the classical passage in the First Epistle of this Evangelist (2:12-14), written subsequently to the Gospel, a knowledge of which is supposed throughout the Epistle. In singular, satisfactory contrariety to Scott's view is that of the late Dr. Martineau: "Religious faith is rather the first root of life than the last blossom of thought" (*op. cit.*). "As to what faith is psychologically," says Dr. McCosh, "no two metaphysicians explain alike" (*Gospel Sermons*, p. 73). This need cause no surprise.

133a "The Holy One of God." The writer referred to in the Exposition is Hengstenberg.

134 *Verse 70.*—"Chosen." Here, again, the Evangelist supposes knowledge of the earlier Gospels. The choice referred to is different from that spoken of in 13:18. In the present passage it is the appointment to apostleship (Mark 3:13 *f.*; Luke 6:13 *f.*). We have here an early disclosure of the character of Judas, but the rest of the Apostles seem not to have apprehended it at the time.

"Devil." See note 131*a*.

135 *Verse 71.*—"Judas, son of Simon *Iscariot.*" This seems to mean, *of Kerioth* (Joshua 15:25), in Judæa. He probably became a follower of the Lord during the early Judæan ministry. The question of his fate has been discussed lately in the *Interpreter* in his favour; but whatever may have been the belief of Judas as to the Lord's extrication of Himself, such a notion could only be fruit of unbelief in Christ's own words.

Besides the betrayer, we meet in the Gospels with (*a*) Judas, the Apostle otherwise called Lebbæus, or Thaddæus, and (*b*) Judas, brother of the Lord.

NOTES ON THE SEVENTH CHAPTER

136 *Verses* 1-5.—There is further recognition here of the Galilean ministry.

136a *Verse* 1.—"After these things." That is, about six months after the discourse of chapter 6.

"The Jews." *Cf.* 11:8, 54.

137 *Verse* 3.—As to the Lord's "brethren being uterine"—that is, His mother's children—see Psalm 69:8, and *cf.* Acts 1:14, 1 Corinthians 9:5. This belief is maintained, after Tertullian, by McClellan, Farrar (*Early Days of Christianity*, chapter 19), Mayor (Introduction to *Commentary on Epistle of James*), and by Professor Swete (Commentary on Mark). For the theory that Joseph was married previously, see Lightfoot ("Dissertation" in his edition of the Epistle to the Galatians) and Salmon. It must be borne in mind that Origen and Jerome, who supported the idea of Mary's continued virginity, were influenced by Apocryphal Gospels. Mr. Carr seems to have changed his opinion since he wrote the note in his Cambridge edition of Matthew's Gospel (see his note on present passage).

On what we are told in verse 5, Kinnear remarks: "His divinity was hidden in the absolute perfection of His humanity" (p. 71).

138 *Verse 8.*—The reading "not yet" seems to have arisen from a desire to meet Porphyry's imputation to JESUS of inconstancy. But the Lord's not going up then was but an illustration of what this Evangelist speaks of elsewhere—His dependence on the Father, by whose direction He was governed day by day, in respect both of speech (verse 16) and action (5:19). Any real difficulty is removed by the natural explanation of Westcott and Plummer—that the Lord meant, not to keep the feast.

139 *Verse 12.*—"Good": in the sense of "benevolent."

139a "The Jews." Here the special meaning that the title acquires in this Gospel is very clear.

140 *Verse 15.*—"Letters"—*i.e.*, rabbinical learning (Acts 26:24: πολλά γράμματα, "much learning"). In the Gospel records we are told of the Lord Jesus' *writing* (John 8:6), and of His *reading* (Luke 4:16). The one reading book of the synagogue school was the Bible. *Cf.* notes 23, 56 on Mark.

141 *Verse 21 f.*—"One." Heitmüller treats this as inconsistent with 7:31. But the Lord is not Himself the speaker there. The expositor takes "because of this" as part of verse 21, but Govett, as the revisers, with "Moses," as beginning of verse 22.

141a *Verse 23.*—The ὅλον goes with ἄνθρωπον rather than (as A.V. and R.V.) with ὑγιῆ—"a whole man" (so Wetstein).

142 *Verse 26.*—Observe that it is the *rulers* ("the Jews") who fail to recognise the Lord's Messiahship, and only those of the crowd influenced by them (verse 41).

NOTES ON THE SEVENTH CHAPTER

143 *Verse 27.*—See note at 9:29.

144 *Verse 28.*—"Cried." For the Lord's exceptional uplifting of His voice (Matthew 12:19), *cf.* verse 37 and 12:44.

"He allows that they have spoken *rightly* of His human origin" (Barth, *Chief Problems*, p. 162). We may suppose, however, that our Lord is but reminding them of their own words recorded in 6:42—*i.e.*, taking them on their own ground.

145 *Verse 31.*—See Micah 5:2.

145a *Verse 34.*— "I am." *Cf.* 3:13.

146 *Verse 37.*—"The great." According to Numbers 29:12, the feast was to last seven days; another day had been added by custom, but on this day no water was drunk from the pool of Siloam, to be poured on the altar. JESUS was the true Shiloh ("sent"). But *cf.* Jeremiah 2:13. This statement shows exact knowledge on the part of the writer.

147 "Stood ... thirst." His *attitude* now, as well as His manner, emphasized His words. Connect with this, "I will stand upon the rock in Horeb" (Exodus 17:6; *cf.* Numbers 20:11).

148 *Verse 38.*—"As the scripture said." Reference may be made to such passages as Isaiah 12:3, 35:6 (*cf.* Matthew 11:4-6), 44:3, 55:1, 58:11; Joel 3:13; Ezekiel 47:1.

149 *Verse 39.*—"Spirit was not yet." On this Schmiedel, who is followed by Burkitt (p. 248) and Scott (p. 336), has the following remark: "The Holy Spirit had no existence before the exaltation of Christ," and cites 2 Corinthians 3:17 (col. 2,530). One might fairly expect a writer of such pretension (he has edited Winer's *Grammar*) to be acquainted with a use of the negative which appears in other passages of this Gospel, such as 9:3 and 11:4, and also in 2 Corinthians 3:10. From there being no article before "Spirit," some (as Norris and Govett) would explain it of spiritual gift (1 Corinthians 12, 14), which now represents the gifts of the Spirit predicted of the days of Messiah. See, however, the *Exposition*, p. 598, {chapter 20,} note {i}. As to misunderstanding by the Evangelist of the Lord's utterances (alleged by Reuss and others), see note at 2:21.

150 *Verse* 40.—*Cf.* verse 46 for Christ's words being evidential. As to "the prophet," see note 118. For the connection of this verse with verse 52, see Carr, *Horæ Biblicæ*, p. 76 *ff.* He considers that "the" should be understood before "prophet" in the Pharisee's question (p. 83). This suggestion, which commends itself, is reproduced in the same writer's annotated edition of the R.V. of this Gospel. *Cf.* Abbott, *Johannine Grammar*, p. 358.

151 *Verse* 42.—"Bethlehem." Critics wonder why John (Wendt and others would say his "editor"), if he knew of the Bethlehem birth, did not here mention it. Perhaps we have in this an instance of what Dr. Salmon described as the Evangelist's "irony," as in 6:42. We have examples of something of the kind in the Pauline Epistles. The important point is that the Jews, as Govett remarks, "in this the chief of questions had not interest enough to push their inquiries."

152 *Verse* 43.— "Division." This illustrates Luke 12:51. So, again, in 9:16, 10:19 of this Gospel. The word in each passage is "schism."

153 *Verse* 45 *f.*—"The chief priests." These represent the Synoptic "Sadducees," who, together with the Pharisees, made up the Sanhedrin.

"Never man"—*i.e.*, a mere man (ἄνθρωπος).

NOTES ON THE EIGHTH CHAPTER

154 7:53 – 8:11.—Some of those rejecting this passage are influenced by the feeling that there is no clear connection with what comes before or follows it. As to this, see the Exposition. Difficulty over the connection has, however, not weighed so much as judgment formed on the diplomatic evidence. The expositor shows that the impeachment on that side of the case is not so formidable as is usually supposed. Eusebius says that he found the passage, not merely in the Gospel of the Hebrews, but in Papias, from whom Lightfoot supposes it was derived. It is markedly in harmony with 1:17, and was not likely to be inserted by a later hand. Whilst the early Reformers (Calvin, Beza, etc.) discredited it, Augustine before them, as Bengel afterwards, upheld it. The agreement of textual critics of such different schools as Tregelles and Scrivener, of course, is unfavourable to its being read in John; whilst some, acknowledging it as "Scripture," would place it at the end of Luke 21, as in the Ferrar group of manuscripts (but in these only); so Blass, the latest editor. Lightfoot's judgment was that "it is an interpolation where it stands" (*Biblical Essays*, p. 69). He regarded it as a marginal note to verse 15. We may, however, be morally certain that the Evangelist, if he did not actually put the incident in writing, told the story in his oral ministry. "Advanced" critics go with others in commendation of its spirit and teaching, Jülicher describing it as "the noblest of Agrapha" (p. 393). Its *Divine* wisdom is attested on all sides. See, further, notes 157, 159.

155 *Verse* 3.—Here only in this Gospel are the *scribes* spoken of. Instead of being against the genuineness, the word tells the other way; for, as some one has said, "it is in exact keeping with any attempt—the only one described in this Gospel—to entrap Him subtilely, in which the expertness of such men was needed."

156 *Verse* 5.—The Old Testament texts are Leviticus 20:10, Deuteronomy 22:22. Observe that "Moses in the law" is solely Johannine (1:45), not being found in the Synoptic Gospels. What about the absence in these Jews of concern as to the treatment to be dealt out to the *adulterer? Cf.* Seeley, *Ecce Homo*, pp. 117-120.

156a *Verse* 7.—See Deuteronomy 13:6-11.

157 *Verse* 11.—"Neither do I condemn," or, command execution of the law. Had early Christians discerned that these words have regard to the distinction between the Church and the world in its sentences, they could not have hesitated, as they did, to admit the passage into lectionaries. There is no "Go in peace," or "Thy sins are forgiven thee" here: the woman is governmentally respited (*cf.* the case of chapter 5). The Lord gave effect to the law which required two witnesses (Deuteronomy 17:2-7, 19:15). *Cf.* verse 17 of this chapter, which bears singularly on the authenticity of the passage, but seems to have been uniformly neglected by those who have questioned it.

158 Reference should here be made to *Lectures Introductory to the Study of the Gospels*, p. 462 *ff.*

159 *Verse* 12.—The "again" marks resumption of the interrupted discourse (verse 2). To whom could "them" refer but the angry Pharisees? If a passage like this (*cf.* 12:32) were editorial, might we not say that the interpolator was a prophet? Moreover, would not this verse be awkward if 7:53 to 8:11 were omitted?

159a *Verse 12 ff.*—"The light," referring probably to the sun, beaming out as He spoke (Bishop Andrewes and others), rather than to the golden lamp (Stier, etc.), or to the pillar of cloud and fire (Cyril, etc.).

160 "True." Here ἀληθής, but in 19:35 ἀληθινός: both words occur together there. Schmiedel, as others before him, pits verse 13 against 5:31, in which they have been anticipated by these very Jews here! The answer to the critical, as to the Pharisaic, objection turns on His Godhead, shown by what follows. Westcott puts it: "The *I* in the earlier passage marked the separate individuality; here it marks the fulness of the whole Person."

160a "Ye know not." This, again, has been set against 7:28: "Ye know." But there He says, "whence I *am*"; here, "whence I *come*." The objection is a mere quibble; the Lord was speaking previously of His earthly origin.

Burkitt (p. 227) characterises His attitude towards the Jews here as "mystifying, repellent," from not weighing the *moral* bearing of the words. See the Exposition.

161 *Verse* 17.—See Deuteronomy 17:6, 19:15. For "law of the Jews" ("your law"), *cf.* 10:34, 15:25 of the Gospel. It is a case of *argumentum ad hominem*. So Stevens (p. 35), whilst his countryman Bacon follows captious German criticism. *Cf.* note 157 above.

NOTES ON THE EIGHTH CHAPTER

161a *Verse* 18.—As to testimony to the two natures of the Lord, see *Exposition* (p. 248 *f.*), Mark 12:35-37, where, as Lord of David, we get His Deity, as in Son of David His humanity *(cf.* Romans 1:3).

162 *Verse* 19.—May not 7:28 have been slightly ironical, as Ryle suggests? See above {note 151} as to the irony, also ascribed to the Evangelist by Salmon.

163 *Verse* 20.—*Cf.* Luke 22:53. The Lord taught in the outer courts only, being, according to the flesh, of the tribe of Judah, not Levi (Hebrews 7:14).

164 *Verse* 24.—"I AM": Deuteronomy 32:39-41; Psalm 102:25-27; Isaiah 41:4, 48:12.

164a The American Revisers discredited the British marginal rendering, "How is it that I speak to you at all?" which was derived from Cyril and Chrysostom, and is approved by Zahn. *Cf.* Blass, *Grammar*, § 50. 5 (*Expository Times*, p. 176), who would render "(Do you reproach Me) that I speak to you at all?" Those taking it as "altogether" include Winer, Grimm, Stier, H. Holtzmann, Alford, Godet, Plummer, and Reynolds.

165 *Verse* 29.—This controverts Swedenborg's doctrine that there is only one "Person" in the Godhead, that the body taken was the Son; and that the Father, in His resistance to evil, put it off altogether! (*Cf.* note 130.)

165a *Verses* 30-32.—"Believed on Him ... believed Him." See note 17.

166 *Verse* 37.—"Maketh no way." So Westcott, who compares Wisdom 7:23-24 and Weiss, referring to 2 Maccabees 13:26; as Zahn also to 3:40, 15:37 there.

167 *Verse* 40.—"A man" ἄνθρωπος. Gnosticism denied (α) the Deity of Jesus, (β) the humanity of the Christ. It was the predicted parent of the apostasy spoken of in 1 Timothy 4:1-3.

167a *Verse* 41.—*Cf.* Malachi 2:10.

168 *Verse* 43.—*Cf.* Proverbs 8:9. What Alexander Carson, fifty years ago, remarked is true still: if men "are erroneous in their doctrines, they must be erroneous in their philology" (*On Interpretation*, p. 91).

169 *Verse* 44.—"Standeth" (ἔστηκεν), as the American revisers. The British committee adopted the imperfect of στήκω—*i.e.*, ἔστηκεν (אB^{pm}, DL, etc.); and so Blass. Horton criticizes the first part of the verse in the light of verse 30. But the Lord is speaking to the Jews referred to in verse 33. *Cf.* verses 40 and 45. Polycarp, in his *Letter to the Philippians*, echoed the words "of the devil."

170 *Verse* 46.—It is on the Lord's conscious sinlessness that Weiss would base His Messianic consciousness (*Life of Christ*, i. 290).

Professor Du Bose has revived the execrable doctrine of Edward Irving. Note the following terrible statements taken from the American writer: "There was that in His flesh which actively He had to put to death" (*Soteriology*, p. 320); "His lifelong death to sin created and constituted His sinlessness" (*The Gospel in the Gospels*, p. 159); "He had as much to hunger and thirst after righteousness which was not His own as we have" (*ibid.*, p. 164); "Jesus Himself, in His humanity, needed the salvation which all humanity needs" (*The Gospel according to St. Paul*, p. 127); "There was that in Him which He needed to deny, to mortify, to crucify" (*ibid.*, p. 173); "*As man*, our Lord was subject with us all to sin and death" (p. 228). To found such execrable language on anything from Paul or Peter (*e.g.*, Romans 8:3;

NOTES ON THE EIGHTH CHAPTER

2 Corinthians 5:21; 1 Peter 4:1) is, as one of them has written, to wrest the Scriptures to your own destruction. *Cf.* 5:23 of this Gospel. What a mercy that the Saviour (*pace* Schmiedel) has spoken of forgiveness extended to those blaspheming the "Son of man"! (Matthew 12:32).

With verse 47 *cf.* 1 John 4:6.

171 *Verse* 48 *f.*—Schmiedel (col. 2,541): "Had Jesus really possessed that exalted consciousness of His preexistence and Divine dignity which is attributed to Him in the fourth Gospel, the declaration that blasphemy against Him was incapable of forgiveness (Matthew 12:31 *f.*; Luke 12:10) could never have been attributed to Him." But it is to His character of Son of man that the Synoptic words as to forgiveness attach; and it is precisely in the earlier Gospels that the blasphemy against the Holy Ghost is said not to admit of forgiveness, attributing Christ's works to Beelzebub, as here His words to a demon. There is not a particle of such difference in the accounts: the Synoptists record nothing that detracts from the words "ye dishonour Me" given by John.

As to the Jews' insinuation, see Schofield, *Christian Sanity*, p. 14. *Cf.* 7:20 of this Gospel.

172 *Verse* 57.—"Fifty years old." What is one to think of Loisy, who follows Irenæus, saying that, "according to the Evangelist, the Christ was about fifty years old when He died" (p. 13)? as to which Schmiedel sensibly remarks that Irenæus was not trustworthy in respect of traditions of that kind. The "fifty" might be explained from Numbers 4:3, 39, 8:34, but probably means, what is generally supposed, that the blessed Saviour was prematurely old. *Cf.* Zahn, *ad loc.*

173 *Verse* 58.—"I am." See note 164, and *cf.* Psalm 90:2, 102:27. The Unitarian explanation is that "Jesus only meant that He existed as Messiah in God's counsels before Abraham." There would, however, be nothing peculiar in that, as true also of Adam and the Jews themselves, whom He was addressing. *They* understood His words very differently. The "wrangling, little in the style of Jesus," which is said to characterise this chapter (Horton, p. 164; *cf.* Burkitt) is, of course, primarily an utterance of German oracles.

NOTES ON THE NINTH CHAPTER

174 *Verse* 1—"Blind from birth." Symbolical of Israel as a people (Deuteronomy 29:4). D'Alma imagines that the Evangelist had Paul in his mind; but the Apostle of the Gentiles, instead of being "a proselyte of the gate," was "a Hebrew of the Hebrews."

175 *Verse* 2.—The Pharisees supposed that the souls of good men passed from one body to another (Josephus, *Antiquities*, xviii. 1, 3; *Bellum Judaicum {The Jewish War}*, ii. 8, 14). So Herod, of John the Baptist. By the "pious and learned author" referred to in the Exposition Tholuck would seem to be meant, for such is the view that he propounds.

176 *Verse* 6.—As to this Jewish remedy for eye disease, see Edersheim (*Life*, ii. 48). The next verse seems to show that it stands here for Jewish ordinances, which the people refused to give up for the word of Christ. Their "Sabbath" was their hindrance (*cf.* Isaiah 28:9-12).

177 *Verse* 7.—"Siloam." The Shiloah of Isaiah 8:6 (*cf.* Psalm 46:4). That the name meant "sent" has been questioned in *Supernatural Religion*, (p. 419), but not by Schmiedel, Mr. Cassels' German counterpart. Reference should here be made to 8:16-18, 26-29, besides verse 4 of this chapter. For the use of clay as eye-salve, *cf.* that made of the brazen serpent, and for the water here, *cf.* Acts 2:33, 38 *f.*, of the Holy Spirit sent down to dispel Jewish blindness.

178 *Verse* 16.—"How can," etc. See 3:2, the "we" of which finds further illustration here. There were some who agreed with Nicodemus. *Cf.* verse 33 of the present chapter.

179 *Verse* 22.—The opposition to our Lord's Messianic claim had now become acute, at an advanced stage of His ministry. As to exclusion from the fellowship of the synagogue, see Edersheim, ii. 184.

180 *Verse* 24.—"Give glory to God." This formula takes us back to the time of Joshua (7:19).

181 *Verse* 29.—"We know *not* whence He is." Schmiedel (following Holtzmann, etc.) says that the Evangelist "sometimes contradicts his own precise statements" (col. 2,537). The reference here is, of course, to 7:27. Westcott explains that here it is a question of His prophetic function of the commission, the authority by which JESUS comes. So the healed man's "the wonderful thing." Is it not simply a question of "the Jews," learned and acute as the man knew them to be, stultifying themselves? Govett's comment is: "Unbelievers will at last be condemned out of their own mouths and by their own principles." The "common sense" which governs men in ordinary concerns has a way of forsaking them in religious matters; the soundness of the head is here regulated so much by the state of the heart. Weiss notes the emphatic ἡμεῖς, "we." *Cf.* the man's ὑμεῖς, "ye"— "they, the people's spiritual leaders, who alone have to judge in such matters"! Have we not their analogues in our own day?

182 *Verse* 31 *f.*—The man's statement is supported by Psalm 66:18; Proverbs 15:29; Isaiah 1:15. *Cf.* the history of Elijah and Elisha. Observe that the knowledge of the constancy of Nature had already in the Apostolic Age filtered through to the people (Gerdtell, *Primitive Miracles*, etc., p. 30).

182a *Verse* 34.—This was the sole attempt the Jews made to disprove any of the Lord's miracles. *Cf.* 3:2, 11:47.

183 *Verse* 35.—"The Son of God." See 3:18, 5:25, 10:36, 11:4. For "Son of man," see 3:15, 6:27 (and Exposition), 34-36 (the same). It may be said, on the one hand, that any alteration would be more likely made from "man" to "God" than *vice versa*, because of the frequency of "Son of God" in this Gospel (so Zahn); but, on the other, that a copyist, from the fact that the "Son of man" was Christ's usual mode of designating Himself, would be very likely to alter "Son of God" into "Son of man." In support of "Son of *God*," see *Irrationalism of Infidelity*, p. 293. Godet, too, adheres to this reading, because of the worship rendered by the man. Indeed, 6:27, 29 seems to the present writer to settle the whole point. The "Son of man" is there said to be sealed (attested) as "Son of God" (*cf.* note 122). Before He could be Son of man He must have been *sent* as Son of God. By acknowledgment of the truth of this, the object of the miracle became the first "martyr" confessor of the new community (Carr). See also note 238.

184 *Verse* 39.—The Lord here fulfils Isaiah 29:9-13. The judgment is a sifting process. *Cf.* Luke 2:34: "for the falling and rising up of many in Israel," leaving men either better or worse, with "they that see not"; also 3:19 *ff.* Carr aptly compares the words of 7:49. "They that see" of course calls up Isaiah 42:19. Only those who fail to see the different bearing of 3:17 and the present passage "as to judgment" could, with H. Holtzmann, find a contradiction. *Cf.* McRory, *ad loc.*

185 Verse 41.—*Cf.* 15:22. "Remaineth," attacheth, is unforgiven. "Forgiveness" is not a term of this Gospel, which. however, expresses the idea in various ways, as in 8:32, "the truth shall make you free." For the attitude of unbelief towards the Christian doctrine of forgiveness, see Greg, *Creed of Christendom*, or *Essays* of Miss Edith Simcox in the same strain; and on the believing side Sir R. Anderson, *Christianized Rationalism*, p. 193.

Heitmüller: "Sin reposes essentially on ignorance; if a man have proper insight, he will act rightly" (p. 174). Such is Tolstoy's doctrine. See record of interview between him and the late Dr. F. W. Baedeker, in *Memoir* of the latter. The Russian Count had not reckoned with Luke 11:21 *f. Cf.* note 49 on Mark, as to Humanitarianism.

NOTES ON THE TENTH CHAPTER

186 *Verses* 1-18.—The Scriptures for reference are, in particular, Psalm 23, Isaiah 40, Zechariah 11. To be understood rightly, the close connection of this passage with chapters 8 and 9 must be seen, which the division of chapters tends to obscure.

187 *Verses* 1-3.—"The fold." "... leadeth them out." One of the "realistic scenes" given at the Palestine Exhibitions brings out those characteristics of an Eastern sheepfold stated in Carr's note, *ad loc.*—the high wall; entrance closed at night and guarded by "porter"; the mixture of flocks; and their separation each morning through the different voice of each shepherd. *Cf.* Isaiah 43:1 and Acts 2:39. By "the porter" it will be seen the expositor understands the Holy Spirit (so Stier, Alford, and McRory); Godet, the Baptist.

{187a} For the New Testament add, in particular, Luke 15:11-32. As to the relation of allegory to metaphor, see Carson on *Figurative Language of Scripture*, or *Encyclopædia Britannica*, vol. i., under "Allegory."

188 *Verses* 4-7.—"He goeth before them." The Lord severed His connection with the Temple before the disciples separated from it; their break with it was very gradual.

{188a} With *verse 6 cf.* 16:25 *ff.* and Mark 4:13; and with *verse 7*, Hebrews 10:20 (Norris).

189 *Verse 8.*—"Before me." These words seem to have been omitted in some leading manuscripts from the difficulty that attaches to the verse when they are read. The Manichees used them in support of their theories. If the words πρὸ ἐμοῦ are retained, one way of taking πρό is in the sense of "instead," "in place of," but then it will be necessary to take the statement prophetically, as none such presented themselves until *after* the Lord's first coming. Isaiah has used the past tense in this way (10:28-31). Other explanations are recorded in Alford's note, *ad loc.* Zahn combines the idea of both past and immediate future by supposing that the Asmonæan rulers and Herodian princes are meant.

190 *Verse 9.*—"Shall go in and shall go out." This is a Hebraism. See Numbers 27:17. *Cf.* Maclaren's remarks on Communion and Service in his *Exposition*, vol. ii., pp. 28 *ff.*

An Eastern shepherd acts as a door.

191 *Verse 10.*—"Abundantly." *Cf.* 2 Peter 1:11.

192 *Verse 11.*—The view of Pfleiderer (ii. 480), that Paul's doctrine of salvation resting on the death and resurrection of Christ was supplanted by John's emphasizing the whole redemptive activity of His earthly life, is reproduced by Scott. As to this theory, see the *Exposition* at p. 485 *f.*

"The *good* Shepherd": *cf.* (Hebrews 13:20) "the *great* Shepherd," and (in 1 Peter 5:4) "the *chief* Shepherd."

NOTES ON THE TENTH CHAPTER

Psalms 22, 23, 24 seem to answer respectively to these designations.

"Layeth down His life," or *soul* (*cf.* Isaiah 53:10). The word for "life" here is altogether different from that in verse 10 (life in contrast with death). The following "for," as Meyer says, indicates *substitution*, not only benefit, as in 1 John 3:16, with which *cf.* Romans 16:4 (decisive). It comes out strikingly in this Gospel (18:8), where see note.

Govett, on the present passage, well remarks: "He showed He had power to enforce that exchange." How can Scott get over the five-times repeated mention by Christ of His *death* in this short discourse? It carries as much emphasis as, *e.g.*, in Acts 20:28 or Hebrews 13:20, 1 Peter 1:19.

193 *Verse* 12.—See Ezekiel 34:11-23, etc. For the "wolf," *cf.* Matthew 10:16 and Acts 20:29. The "hireling" is exemplified in the conduct of the blind man's parents in chapter 9 here.

193a See the *Lycidas* of Milton.

194 *Verses* 14-16.—Here we have a link with the first Gospel: our Lord "in the days of His flesh" was "Minister of the circumcision" {Romans 15:8} (*cf.* 12:23-32 and note 8 above). Again, there is connection with the third Gospel. It would be nearer the truth to say that John was influenced by Isaiah (chapter 49) than by Paul.

With verse 14 *cf.* 17:20-22. The passage should correct the strangely serious notion that to doubt one's acceptance is the best proof of being a child of God!

As one has said, "To insist on the one *flock* (verse 16) and yet form a sacramental *fold* which is exclusive, instead of inclusive, is suicidal: always has been and ever will be."

195 *Verse* 17 *f.*—On the relation of these words of Christ to those of Paul in Galatians 3:13, see Gerdtell on "Substitution," p. 44 *f.* Criticism has been bestowed on J. N. Darby's writing that the Lord gave up His first human life, "to which sin attached," to take up in resurrection another life, in which the sin of mankind, reckoned to Him on the cross (2 Corinthians 5:21), has no voice. But it is of the ζωή that the writer of *Synopsis of the Books of the Bible* speaks—from no neglect of the Greek word used here—with reference to such passages as 1 Peter 4:1. Reference to Mr. Darby's treatment of Scriptures outside this Gospel, like those just referred to, should remove any misapprehension of his meaning. The words of these verses entirely meet the unholy view of the Atonement, according to which the Father is regarded as exposing Himself to the imputation of injustice. He and the Son combine.

195a Contrast the present passage with Psalm 89:48. "No *one* taketh it away from Me." This, of course, at the same time as human, excludes Satanic power; it is equivalent to "No one *can*," etc. And so for Hebrews 5:7 as bearing on the agony in Gethsemane (Luke 22:43 *f.*).

In 9:14 of that Epistle {Hebrews}, "an eternal spirit" speaks of Christ's own (Westcott). His own Deity was engaged in the work.

195b *Cf.* Horton, *Teaching of Jesus*, pp. 200 *f.*

196 *Verses* 19-21.—*Cf.* Psalm 146:7 *f.* From these verses of the Gospel we may learn that truth separates as a preliminary to uniting.

NOTES ON THE TENTH CHAPTER

Observe how the Lord's works were seen to reinforce His words, which stand or fall together. Jülicher admits that they are inseparable.

With verse 20, *cf.* Schofield, *Christian Sanity*, p. 15.

197 *Verse 22.*—The "Feast of Dedication," also called the "Feast of Lights," was instituted by the Maccabean Jews to commemorate the rededication of the Temple after the victories of Judas over Antiochus Epiphanes, who had desecrated it. See *Jewish Prayer Book*, p. 274. The *Chanuka* generally falls in the month of *Chisleu*, or December, and so the mention of "winter." Observe that the Evangelist does not speak of it as a "feast"—*i.e.*, as if it had Divine sanction.

198 *Verse 24 f.*—"Dost thou hold our soul in suspense?" These words serve to show that the progress of the Messianic claim is not really represented differently in the fourth from what it is in the earlier Gospels *(cf.* Horton pp. 190 *f.).*

John takes us more "behind the scenes," emphasizing more their responsibility; nevertheless, the Jews can still talk thus at this advanced stage of the ministry. Having regard to 9:22, their sincerity may well be questioned. It is much the same with the antecedent rejection of "the miraculous" in our day. "Openness of mind" alone will do in religious as in all other search after truth. *Cf.* Matthew 11:4 *f.*; Luke 11:33 *ff.*

198a *Verse 26 f.*—See verse 3 *f.*

199 *Verses 28-30.*—See note 110 on Mark, and *cf.* Deuteronomy 32:39, Isaiah 43:13. Hengstenberg: "Jesus assumes to Himself the possession of the power which belongs to Jehovah." See Hooker's notable sermon on the "Perpetuity of Faith in the Elect," which might suffice for "Anglicans."

"*We* are One," ἕν, neuter. It is not one in will or purpose only, for this in the case of Jesus might still be frustrated, but that will and *power* coalesce in the person of the Speaker. In these verses the distinction of Persons and unity of Nature alike come out. See, further, 12:45, 14:9 *f.*, 17:21; and *cf.* Hebrews 1:3. The Sabellian and Patripassian (Swedenborgian) theory breaks down when faced with the words: the Father and JESUS are not one "Person"; whilst the one *nature* contradicts Arians (Socinians). The contemporary Jews understood the Lord's statement, whilst their descendants and "Unitarians" miss its meaning.

200 *Verse* 31.—*Cf.* Leviticus 24:16, and see note on 19:7 below.

201 *Verse* 32.—*Cf.* Psalm 78:11 *f.*

201a *Verse* 33.—This may be regarded as the *locus classicus* on the way in which the Lord's claims were understood *at the time.*

202 *Verse* 35.—"The word of God came." *Cf.* Ezekiel 1:3; Luke 3:2.

203 *Verse* 36.—See note 30 on Mark {2:10}.

204 *Verse* 40 *ff.*—"Again." As to the Peræan ministry, see 1:28. As to John's performing no miracles, see Gerdtell, p. 70.

NOTES ON THE ELEVENTH CHAPTER

205 *The Resuscitation of Lazarus.*—This, the third and most notable case of Christ's raising the dead, has always excited sharp criticism by sceptics. Spinoza is said to have declared that if he could be satisfied that the miracle was actually performed he would become a Christian. But, of course, such an intellectual creed, several times spoken of in this Gospel, has never permanently profited anyone. At the present day the main objection taken to the incident is that John alone records it, which circumstance is considered to invest the story with suspicion, because it is alleged an incident represented to have brought about the death of the Lord (see note on verse 53) must have been known to one or other of the Synoptists if it really took place. So Cassels, Abbott, Burkitt, etc., after Strauss, Keim, and their Continental followers. It affords prominent illustration of a favourite "critical" canon—that if a biblical historian knows of an event he is bound to record it. The author of *Supernatural Religion* goes so far as to say that "each of the Synoptic Gospels professes to be complete in itself"—a principle that can only yield an absurd result. Not even does the preface of Luke lend itself to such an idea. That Evangelist's "all" is said of his resources, not of the things in which Theophilus had been instructed, for the accuracy of which Luke is prepared to vouch.

If there were any sound basis in the principle, it would, of course, apply all round. Matthew 27:52, for example, would fall under it; there alone are we told of the dead saints who left their graves and appeared in Jerusalem after the Lord's own resurrection. In respect of the present Gospel we should have to assume that, in the face of Synoptic declarations to the contrary, John himself knew nothing of the raising of Jairus's daughter, of the Transfiguration, of the agony in Gethsemane, or the forsaking on the Cross, all recorded by Mark, who was a witness of none of these! Two of such incidents are indirectly attested by John (see notes 20 above, and that on 12:27); and other such incidents as the Temptation (Matthew, Luke) some (as Reynolds) believe have parallels in his Gospel (chapters 1-4).

Keim treated the resuscitation of Lazarus as a fiction; O. Holtzmann (*Life of Jesus*, p. 275), followed by Burkitt, cannot fit it into the framework of Mark's, conceived to be the fundamentally historic, narrative. Schmiedel (col 2,521), as Abbott in the same work (col 1,805), after Bruno Bauer and Schenkel, regards it as a development of the parable of Lazarus in Luke 16:19-31; and so Wernle (*Sources*, pp. 42 *f*.). As to all this, see note 5 in the volume on Mark, and *cf.* Turton, p. 413. Remarks will be made below on individual features of the narrative, to show how worthless are such insinuations against its credibility. See, further, Weiss, *Life of Christ*, Bk. vi., § 6, or Westcott, *Study of the Gospels*, p. 164, who says: "It did not fall in with the common plan of the Synoptists, which excluded all working at Jerusalem until the final entry."

NOTES ON THE ELEVENTH CHAPTER

206 *Verse* 2.—The Evangelist assumes that an incident is already known from the earlier accounts which he will himself describe later (12:2). *Cf.* Luke's manner of writing in 4:23, 31 of his Gospel.

207 *Verse* 15.—"Let us go unto *him*." These words negative the idea of Swedenborgians and spiritualists that the disembodied is the final state of man, as if after death the body is no more resumed.

208 *Verse* 16.—"That we may die with *him*." As in the first edition, "him" has been printed with small initial letter, because of the uncertainty which attaches to its exact meaning. Zahn, as did Grotius, takes it of Lazarus; most commentators, however, understand JESUS. See verse 9 *f.*

209 *Verse* 18.—"Was." For the imperfect tense here, instead of the present as in 5:2, Lightfoot compares Luke 4:29 (*Biblical Essays*, p. 175). See also Blass in *Expository Times*, July, 1907.

210 *Verses* 24-26.—"The resurrection at the last day." Martha's belief was doubtless that propounded by the Pharisees from Isaiah 25:8, 26:19; Daniel 12:2; Hosea 13:14. For the novelty that the Evangelist was a "Christianized Sadducee," see Burkitt, p. 250.

With verse 26 *cf.* 6:40; Luke 20:35 *f.*; Philippians 3:11.

211 *Verse* 27.—"That should come into the world." See note on 1:9.

212 *Verse* 33.—"Where have ye laid Him?" If the Lord had not asked this question, would not unbelievers have said that He was only acting a part, or that there was collusion? As to the Lord being "moved in spirit," see Maclaren, ii. 99.

212a *Verse* 35.—"Jesus wept"—*i.e.*, shed tears simply, not "sobbed," as the word means which is used in verses 31, 33. The word employed in the present verse appears here only in the New Testament. For other occasions of the Lord's weeping, see Luke 19:41; Matthew 26:39. Chrysostom remarks that this Evangelist emphasizes His affections whilst making higher statements as to His nature than the other Evangelists.

Cassels has described our Lord's tears here as "the theatrical adjuncts of a dramatic scene" (*Supernatural Religion*, p. 461). Such writers have not profited by the lesson of Mark 10:13-16 and parallels. The propriety of those tears has been questioned because of the early removal of the cause of sorrow. But surely, as Christ thought of the vast area of misery brought in by Satan with sin, the sorrow shown here was natural and becoming. Indeed, had the Lord not wept, would not sceptics have suggested that it was not a representation of any true humanity?

213 *Verse* 38.—"A cave"—that is, a rock-hewn tomb (Schor, *Palestine and the Bible*, p. 34), as shown at the Palestine Exhibitions.

214 "Take away the stone." Had the Lord removed it miraculously, objectors would have insinuated that it evinced fraud; that Lazarus had done it from inside.

214a *Verse* 39.—"The sister of the deceased." Does not the Evangelist say this in order to remove the least shred of suspicion of imposture?

215 *Verse* 41 *f.*—Cassels: "Evidently artificial." But although no prayer by Christ is mentioned in previous cases of resurrection, the fourth Gospel aims at exhibiting Him as the SON submissive in all things to the

NOTES ON THE ELEVENTH CHAPTER

Father's will, not an independent Deity. Hence its propriety, which, of course, only a believer can appreciate.

215a Verse 43 *f.*—"Lazarus ... the dead." *The dead* is strictly applicable to the *body*, and so that attaches to man *risen*. Resurrection, therefore, is not, as some represent, emancipation of the soul from the body at death. But that notion, doubtless, is widely prevalent.

215b Verse 46.—Origen's view that the information was conveyed to the Pharisees with a friendly intention is, as Carr says, unlikely.

216 Verse 47 *f.*—Bengel: "Death more easily yields to Christ's power than unbelief" (*cf.* note 219). Observe that "many" miracles are spoken of.

217 Verses 49, 51.—"Being high priest of that year." Instead of election for life, the office was held at the whim of the Romans, according to Josephus, *Antiquities of the Jews*, xviii. 2. Eleazar and Simon (appointed in succession by Valerius Gratus, after the deposition of Annas) each held the office for only one year. The Evangelist, neither here nor in 18:13, uses the article before "high priest." It is, perhaps, another illustration of his "irony" (Salmon). "Twenty-eight held the position from the time of Herod's accession to the destruction of Jerusalem" (*cf.* Acts 23:5). Keim gave up the critical objection founded on the words. Holtzmann supposes a circle of readers accustomed to the naming of a year after the "Asiarch" (Acts 19:31) in office at the time being.

217a The decision as to the death of JESUS must rest with the high priest for the time being (Weiss).

217b "One of them." This may indicate that Caiaphas was not acting as president of the Sanhedrin (Godet).

The brusqueness here of this Sadducean illustrates what Josephus tells of his party (*Bellum Judaicum {The Jewish War}*, ii. 8, 14). Here it was a case of "Sadducee *versus* Pharisee."

218 *Verse* 50.—"For the nation." This is clearly substitutionary, not "in behalf of"; ὑπὲρ, "instead of." Our Lord died as Saviour or Redeemer of Israel (Isaiah 45, 49), as well as of the Church. "For the transgression of My people was He stricken." Not that He was made a curse for Israel alone, as Kaftan supposes (*Dogmatics*, pp. 461 *f.*). See Galatians 3:13, and *cf.* Orr, p. 73.

219 *Verse* 53. *Cf.* note 216. Use has been made of this verse for the supposition that it is to the raising of Lazarus we must attribute the Crucifixion, so as to heighten any difficulty about the silence of the other Evangelists. The Lord's death, however, had been determined on long before (see 7:1, 25 *f.*, 44; again in 8:40, and 10:31, 11:8, 16). This incident did not bring matters to a crisis and lead the rulers to give definite shape to their plans, because the characteristic tenet of the high-priestly family had been shaken to its foundations, so as to discredit them to the utmost.

220 *Verse* 54.—This place is identified with the modern *El-Taiyibeh*, about twenty miles from Jerusalem, on the road from Jericho north-westwards. It was from here, probably, that the Lord went to Jericho, and thence to Bethany (12:1; *cf.* Mark 10:46; Luke 18:31, 35).

NOTES ON THE TWELFTH CHAPTER

220a *Verse* 1.—Matthew 20:17-24; Mark 10:32-52; Luke 18:31 - 19:20 will immediately precede this section of the Gospel (see Carr's note).

The Lord's arrival at Bethany would be on the evening of the Friday—*i.e.*, technically, on Saturday, the 9th Nisan. "*Six* days before the Passover" is terminology characteristic of the *Roman* calendar.

221 *Verse* 2.—"They." Indefinite. *Cf.* Matthew 5:15, 10:19, 13:48, and 15:6 of this Gospel.

222 *Verse* 3.—*Cf.* Psalm 23:5. Origen and Chrysostom considered that there were three anointings: (α) in house of Simon the Pharisee (Luke 7); (β) in house of Simon the leper (Mark 14); (γ) in Martha's house (John 12). Some find but two, regarding Martha as wife of Simon the leper. There seem to be seven Simons mentioned in the Gospels (see Note 38).

223 *Verses 4-6.*—For the words of Judas here, *cf.* Psalm 55:21. The Lord was not bound to keep temptation out of the way of the traitor, who must have forgotten the petition which he had been taught: "Bring us not into temptation." Judas, it may be observed, betrayed his

Master for one-tenth the value of that which Mary lavished upon Him.

224 The word γλωσσόκομον does not mean "bag," but a chest (R.V., margin "box"); and ἐβάσταζεν may be rendered "used to take away" (steal). The papyri inscriptions recently discovered throw light on the Evangelist's statement.

225 *Verse 7.*—The word τηρήσῃ seems to mean that Mary had reserved it from the ointment used for Lazarus's funeral. See Field, who does not follow Alford. Had we not Martha here, this alone would tell against the identification of Mary with the Magdalene.

226 *Verse 9.*—Abbott (*Johannine Grammar*, §1,739) contrasts the ὁ ὄχλος πολὺς used here and in verse 12 with the better Greek of Mark (12:37), ὁ πολὺς ὄχλος. This militates against the idea (see first note on Introduction) that the Greek of this Gospel was not such as a Galilean fisherman would have had at his command.

227 *Verse 12 f.*—"On the morrow." This brings us to the first day of the last week—the 10th Nisan (*cf.* Exodus 12:3; Zechariah 11:12; Mark 11:15). With respect to the "palms," is it not striking, as regards the question of the authorship of the Gospel and of the Apocalypse, that these two books alone in the New Testament speak of them? (see Revelation 7:9-17). Leaves of the palm-tree are associated with the Feast of Tabernacles, type of the Kingdom. *Cf.* Zechariah 14.

228 *Verse 14.*—Besides verse 9 of Zechariah 9, *cf.* also Zephaniah 3:13-20. The disciples were *not* taught by the Holy Spirit that Zion stands for the Church (according to the Patristic interpretation, which was Pusey's).

NOTES ON THE TWELFTH CHAPTER

229 *Verse* 17.—The reading ὅτι, adopted by the Revisers, as by Mr. Kelly may have sprung from the difficulty felt over the multitude ("crowd") present when the Lord performed the miracle. *Cf.*, of course, 11:42: a crowd was gathered by Him on His journey from Ephraim to Bethany.

230 *Verse* 19.—The same doubt attends θεωρεῖτε here as ἐραυνᾶτε in 5:39. Ryle takes the word here as imperative.

231 *Verse* 20.—"Of." This is surely preferable to the "among" of the R.V., which would imply inclusion of Jews. It means, of the Greeks that came up. For such devout Gentiles, *cf.* Acts 17:4.

232 *Verse* 21.—"Bethsaida *of Galilee*." G. A. Smith: "This need not mean that it lay west of the Jordan, for the province of Galilee was right round the lake" (*Historical Geography of the Holy Land*, p. 458). The existence of two Bethsaidas is however, a question likely to remain uncertain. The present writer inclines to Trench's view. *Cf.* note 65 on Mark. Professor Smith's "*need* not" is significant. Why should "of Galilee" be added by the Evangelist, unless there were two or more places of the same name?

232a *Verse* 24.—We have here the antitype of the sheaf of firstfruits (Delitzsch). The way in which the Lord expressed Himself seems to have been adapted to the system of thought familiar to Greeks of that day. See J. G. Frazer, *The Golden Bough*, iii. 130 *ff.*, for "dying God" and "corn spirit." *Cf.* Achelis, *Sketch*, p. 32. Researches such as Prof. Frazer's do but by illustration confirm rather than, as he supposes, impair revealed truth. The fourth Gospel was the divinely suited vehicle for the record of such words of Christ. As to protest from Germany against such interpretation as Frazer's of the play of heathen conception in primitive Christianity, see Knowling, p. 86.

233 *Verse* 23.—"Son of man." See note on verse 34. In 11:4 it was glorification of the Son of God.

234 *Verse* 25.—*Cf.* Matthew 10:39, 16:25; Mark 8:35; Luke 9:24, 14:26, 17:33. "In this world." For κόσμος the Synoptists use αἰών, which connects itself with the Kingdom, a term that the fourth Evangelist uses only in 3:3-5, because, as here, he regards eternal life in its future aspect as beginning with that. He is concerned characteristically with its present significance.

235 *Verse* 27.—Milligan, for the ἐκ, "out of," compares Hebrews 5:7. See also Reynolds, *ad loc.* Many critics make use of what they conceive to be the fourth Evangelist's omission of the Synoptic agony in Gethsemane, of which John should have had some special knowledge, for their argument against his authorship of the book. We seem, however, in these words to have an allusion to it. The vicious principle that governs such writers has been already considered. See the *Exposition* at p. 517 *f.*

236 *Verse* 31.—"This world." See 1:5-10. "Shall be cast out." Bishop Gore speaks of Satan's "hiding his face in hell" (*The Christian Creed*, p. 68). But see Revelation 2:13 ("earth"), 12:10 ("heaven").

237 *Verse* 32 *f.*—The expositor, it will be seen, explains by "crucified" (see verse 33). "Out of." After some Fathers, Meyer, Milligan, and Dods (*cf.* Zahn, *in loc.*) regard it as covering the Ascension. *Cf.* Genesis 40:13, 19.

NOTES ON THE TWELFTH CHAPTER

Wendt (p. 69) refers to verse 23. See also Carr's note. Reuss and others, as Horton in England, make use of verse 33 for the wretched theory of the Evangelist's imperfect understanding of our Lord's meaning (see note on 2:21). John is evidently emphasizing the world's side of this greatest of tragedies.

238 *Verse* 34.—See Luke 24:26 and note 30 on Mark {2:10} as to Son of man. From this passage we learn that the title was not familiar to the Jews, and that it was not used for "Messiah." The present passage seems to support the reading "God" in 9:35.

"Abideth for ever." See 1 Chronicles 17:12, Psalm 89:24, {28,} 29, 110:4; Isaiah 9:7, 53:8; Ezekiel 37:25; Daniel 7:14; Micah 4:7.

239 *Verse* 36.—"The light." JESUS meant Himself (1 John 1:5)—that is, that He is GOD. See Deuteronomy 32:20, Psalm 78:11 *f.*, for "hid Himself from them."

240 *Verse* 37 *ff.*—"So many signs"—four in Galilee, three in Judæa—with tacit reference to the earlier Gospels.

"Could not believe." The present infinitive ($\pi\iota\sigma\tau\varepsilon\acute{\upsilon}\varepsilon\iota\nu$), "to form a habit of belief" (Abbott, §2,496). *Cf.* note 114 (5:44), and see Milligan's remarks on the judicial blinding of these Jews. Observe that "Isaiah" is named as source, and no critical "Second Isaiah."

241 *Verse* 40.—Isaiah 6:9 *f.* is quoted in all four Gospels. It is given here (*cf.* 9:39) in the same form as in Mark and Luke. See volume on Mark, note 45.

242 *Verse* 42 *f.*—Amongst such, probably, was Joseph of Arimathæa, as well as Nicodemus. *Cf.* note 59 above. The Evangelist's words in verse 43 carry us back to those of the Lord in 5:44.

243 *Verse* 44.—For "cried" (ἔκραζεν), *cf.* Matthew 27:50 (Mark 15:39), and 7:28, 37 of this Gospel.

244 *Verse* 46.—See verse 9 of the Preface (chapter 1), and *cf.* Ephesians 5:14.

245 *Verse* 48.—"Slighteth" is in the Greek (ἀθετῶν) peculiar to this passage of John. It is used also in Luke 10:16.

"The last day." This term is peculiar to the fourth Gospel (6:39 f., 44, 54 and 11:24). It is one of the "interpolations" alleged by Wendt, etc.

246 *Verse* 50.—*Cf.* 1 John 3:22 f.

NOTES ON THE THIRTEENTH CHAPTER

247 *Verse* 1.—"Before the Feast of the Passover." The question, by many always considered so difficult, here presents itself of the agreement or otherwise of the fourth Gospel with the preceding records in regard to the character of the last meal of which our Lord partook with His disciples. The subject has already been discussed in note 142 on Mark (14:12 *f.*). Here may be added reference to Dalman, *Aramaic Grammar*, p. 248 *f.*, פסח being used in post-Biblical Jewish literature for the whole feast; also to Andrews, pp. 542-581. The general question can be dealt with most conveniently in the present volume, in connection with the expositor's own note on 19:14 below.

248 *Verse* 2.—Field and Govett adhere to the reading of A.V.: γενομένου. Alford renders "supper being prepared" (or, going on), and compares Matthew 26:6. Mr. Kelly, as the Dean and the Revisers: γινομένου. It affords a good instance of the different ways in which copyists, writing from dictation, heard a word uttered by the reader.

249 *Verses* 4, 5.—This is manifestly the narrative of an eye-witness. There are seven steps, all engraven on the Evangelist's memory. Note the graphic ἐγείρεται ... βάλλει. As to the "girding," *cf.* Luke 12:37.

Those who deny that it was a strictly *paschal* supper make use of the fact of the "rising": "standing" had been prescribed for that, but it would seem for the first occasion alone.

250 For "washing from iniquity," *cf.* Psalm 51:2, and 1 Corinthians 6:11.

251 See on verse 12 below.

252 *Verse* 10. Calvin's idea of continued reconciliation was doubtless in the minds of King James's New Testament company concerned with the rendering "to make reconciliation" in Hebrews 2:17. It has reappeared in teaching of recent years, based on an interpretation of 2 Corinthians 5:20, which the expositor combated.

253 *Verse* 12.—The "know" means *understand* (γινώσκετε). *Cf.* verse 7, where οἶδας and γνώσῃ occur together.

254 *Verse* 13.—See Luke 5:8.

255 *Verse* 17.—Schmiedel remarks: "If read in the Synoptic Gospels, would cause no difficulty." What, then, about Matthew 7:21, which is to the same effect?

255a *Verse* 18.—The quotation is from the Hebrew, from which the Septuagint varies.

256 *Verse* 19.—*Cf.* Isaiah 43:11-13 and 8:24, 28, 58 of this Gospel.

NOTES ON THE THIRTEENTH CHAPTER

257 *Verse* 21.—It is supposed that this is the point at which the Lord's Supper would come in. For "troubled in His spirit," *cf.* 11:33, 12:27.

258 *Verse* 22.—"Doubting," perplexed (ἀπορούμενοι).

259 *Verse* 23.—"At table." The posture was that of reclining. Leonardo da Vinci's picture, which represents the guests as sitting, represents quite a wrong idea.

260 Here is the first mention by the Evangelist of the disciple understood to mean himself. Westcott, Drummond, Loisy and others concur, at any rate, in this opinion. Scholten started the notion, which Bacon advocates, that an ideal disciple is meant. Imagination may employ itself *ad infinitum*, but fruitlessly.

261 *Verses* 24-27.—A critical canon, as to the shorter readings being preferable, here favours the T.R.

262 As to the morsel, or "sop," given and received in token of a covenant of peace, see pamphlet of Mr. Khodadad (London Jews' Society), pp. 32 *f.*

263 *Verse* 29.—"For the feast." It is used here for the whole feast, as in 2:13, 23, 6:4, 11:55, 12:1, and the first verse of this chapter. See, further at 18:28 {note 336}.

263a *Verse* 30.—"Having received the morsel." *Cf.* Luke 22:21. "It was night." *Cf.* Exodus 12:42.

264 *Verses* 31-34.—See note 154 on Mark 14:62. For love as element of Christian character, see Illingworth, chapter v.

265 *Verse* 31 *f.*—"Is [was] glorified." For the aorist, *cf.* 15:6, 8, and 17:4; also at 3:19, in purpose, if not in reality.

266 *Verse* 33.—"Little children": a solecism in the Gospel. Judas is by this time excluded. "The Jews": the only time in which the Lord uses the term to *His disciples*.

267 *Verse* 35.—The Christian is not to be known by his wearing a cross, as the South Sea Islander a tattoo, or the Brahmin a blue thread.

268 As to discrepancies alleged by Strauss and others in respect of Peter's denials, see McClellan, pp. 494-503.

NOTES ON THE FOURTEENTH CHAPTER

269 *Verse* 1.—"Let not your heart be troubled." Hengstenberg finds *seven* encouragements in this chapter: verses 2 *f.*, 4-11, 12-14, 15-17, 18-24, 25 *f.*, 27.

270 "Ye believe," as in A.V.; supported by Erasmus, Grotius, Olshausen, etc. The Syriac of Sinai treats the verb as in the imperative the first time also; so Cyril, Augustine, Stier, Alford, Revisers' Margin, Norris, Bernard and Zahn (comparing 1:46, 7:52, 11:34).

271 *Verse* 3.—"I am coming." This is understood by Meyer, Ewald, Luthardt, Hofmann, Westcott, H. Holtzmann, Weiss and Zahn, of the παρουσία (personal "Second Advent," note 134 on Mark): one happy instance of representative agreement. So Cyril in the past, and Bishop Hall. Neither by the Paraclete nor other "spiritual" coming (De Wette, Stier, Wendt), nor, as supposed by many ordinary readers, inspired by Tholuck, etc., of a coming at death. *Cf.* 21:22.

The Tübingen idea was that the fourth Evangelist was "so spiritual that he did not believe in a visible Second Coming of Christ." The reader would find this reflected *ad nauseam* in Mr. E. F. Scott's recent book (chapter x.). Some remarks will be made on his version of German views when commenting on chapters 17 and 20 of this Gospel. How melancholy the words of Bishop Westcott: "A few enthusiasts from time to time bring the thought of Christ's return into prominence, but for the most part it has little influence upon our hearts and minds" (*The Historic Faith*, p. 38).

On the παρουσία (the word itself does not occur in the Johannine writings), see also Mr. Kelly's *An Exposition of the Epistles of John the Apostle*, p. 163, and his books specially devoted to the "Second Coming" in its various aspects. There is a very instructive treatise on the "Rapture" in particular by the late R. Govett, where the sense of the word παρουσία, by that writer always translated "Presence" (as R.V., margin), and of cognate terms, is skilfully determined from Scripture. See also *The Lord's Coming*, etc., by the late T. B. Baines of Leeds (6th edition, 1890).

The terms ἡ πρώτη παρουσία and ἡ δευτέρα παρουσία seem to have been first used by Justin Martyr in his *Dialogue with Trypho*. In his *Apology* also he often speaks of the "First Coming." *Cf.* note 88 on Mark (9:1).

272 *Verse* 4.—Field defends the T.R. (and so A.V.), supposing that an οἴδατε ("ye know") was omitted through *homœoteleuton*.

273 *Verse* 8 *ff.*—As to Philip and his "son of Joseph," see 1:45. Christ must have been GOD to speak as He does here.

274 *Verse* 11.—"If not ... for the very works' sake." Here, it must be borne in mind, our Lord is addressing

NOTES ON THE FOURTEENTH CHAPTER

His disciples. It is His works, not as Messiah (Matthew 12:23), but as Son of God.

275 *Verse* 12 *f.*—"Greater things than these." See, for example, Acts 2:41. Because of verses 17 *f.* of Mark 16 there is the greater readiness on the part of those with loose views of Scripture to get rid of the last twelve verses of that Gospel. See last note {168} under Mark. The second Evangelist goes even beyond the fourth in this particular, only that, according to John, as we see here, it was promised to believers in general. To say, as do some critics, that the portion questioned does but proceed from Church experience, aggravates the unbelief concerned. As to the effect of prayer, see Kinnear, pp. 176 *f.*

276 *Verse* 15.—For the Lordship of Christ, which has been described as "the first principle of the Christian faith," *cf.* 1 John 2:4 and Romans 10:9.

277 *Verse* 16.—English scholars (Alford, Christopher Wordsworth, Westcott and Lightfoot, etc.) have generally accepted, as did the expositor, the distinction made between these synonyms by Trench. It has been questioned, not only by the American scholar Ezra Abbot in his *Critical Essays*, but also by Field, *ad loc.*, referring to Luke 14:32, Acts 3:2 *f.*, 1 John 3:16 *f.*, for their equivalence. The two words occur together in the Gospel at 16:26 *f.* Abbott is of opinion that ἐρωτᾶν implies inquiry whether accomplishment of the wish is possible. A good example would be found in 12:21 of this Gospel. The word is one of the examples used by Deissmann (article "Hellenistic Greek" in Hauck's *Encyclopedia*, vol. vii., p. 638) of the widespread colloquial language of the period.

277a The three Persons of the Holy Trinity are clearly distinguished in this verse. Scott is one of those who, questioning the personality of the Holy Spirit, acknowledge only an influence (p. 343). But the terms in which the Evangelist speaks of the "Comforter" scarcely need, for the support they give to the language of the Creeds, the aid of Paul's doctrine—*e.g.*, his words as to not *grieving* the Spirit (*cf.* Ephesians 4:30).

The idea of the personality of the Holy Spirit was already making itself felt among the Jews when the Psalms of Solomon appeared (see 17:42 there {"And (relying) upon his God, throughout his days he will not stumble; For God will make him mighty by means of (His) holy spirit, And wise by means of the spirit of understanding, with strength and righteousness." (Translated from Greek and Syriac manuscripts by G. Buchanan Gray in R. H. Charles, ed., *The Apocrypha and Pseudepigrapha of the Old Testament in English* (Oxford: Clarendon Press, 1913) 2: 631-652)}). Pfleiderer conceives that "Paraclete" came from Philo (p. 488). This fancy also is worked out in E. F. Scott's book.

On the Spirit as "the truth" (1 John 5:6 {verse 7 in R.V.}), see Godet, ii. 177, Bernard, 164 *f.*

278 *Verse* 18.—This "coming" is also taken of the Holy Spirit by Tholuck, Meyer, Luthardt, Godet, Plummer and Charles. Zahn, after Augustine, understands it as that spoken of in verse 3; whilst Ewald and Weiss take it here of the appearance of the Lord to His disciples after His resurrection.

278a *Verse* 20.—*Cf. An Exposition of the Epistles of John the Apostle*, p. 87 *f.*

NOTES ON THE FOURTEENTH CHAPTER

278b *Verse* 23.—As to Mysticism (variously represented by Bernard, Tauler, Teresa, Law, etc.), of which this Gospel has been described as "the charter," see the article "Mystical Theology" in Hauck's *Encyclopedia*; the two books of Inge and chapter in Illingworth, *Christian Character*; also James, *Varieties of Religious Experience*, Lect. xvi. *f.*; Cheetham, *History of the Christian Church, etc.*, pp. 132-134, 249. Mrs. Bevan's *Three Friends of God* and *The Quiet in the Land*; and Schofield, *Christian Sanity*, ch. vii. Professor Inge prefers the shortest definition of all, "the love of God"; Mr. Illingworth has described it as the belief that the human spirit is capable of an immediate apprehension of God and His truth; whilst, from the "rationalist" side, Benn speaks of it as "inward illumination caught straight from the central heart of things." Ritschl rightly held that there is no *immediate* "communion" with God without the mediation of His word (*Theology and Metaphysics*, p. 476). Many need ever to be reminded of this.

The system of thought designated after the last-named writer regards Christianity, in the words of Inge, as a primitive Puritanism spoiled by the Greeks, who brought into it their intellectualism and their sacramental mysteries. "True Christianity," on the other hand, "is faith in the *historical* Christ" (*Christian Mysticism*, p. 346). But for Kaftan, one of this school, "the centre of gravity is the glorified Christ, the Christian's life being *a life hid with Christ in God*" (Orr, *Essays*, p. 66). The Berlin professor here, accordingly, forsakes the general trend of Ritschl's followers.

On Divine immanence, see note 14, and *cf.* F. B. Meyer, pp. 76-82.

279 *Verse* 26.—*Cf.* 16:13. Mahomet, his English followers tell us, claimed to be the predicted Paraclete (Qoran, chapter lxi. {6}, "Ahmed"). See the writings of Mr. Quilliam of Liverpool.

In the last words of this verse we have the *rationale* of the fourth Gospel.

280 *Verse* 28.—"The Father is greater than I." *Cf.*, of course, the words of the Athanasian Creed so-called: "inferior to the Father as touching His manhood." Men of intellectual pretension—Unitarians and their followers—sometimes read Scripture very superficially. These words in the fourth Gospel are constantly used by such in support of their theory that our Lord was inferior in essence (nature) to the Father. But He is here speaking of *station*. "I go unto the Father." The reference is plainly to His exaltation on Ascension, after that He had first humbled Himself in becoming Son of man. He is then given a name above every name (Philippians 2:9). It has nothing whatever to do with His nature. *Cf.* Bernard, p. 171. The alleged repudiation of Ascension in the Johannine record (*cf.* note on 20:17) is part of current rubbish of "critical exposition" popularised in such books as the last of Wernle.

281 *Verse* 30.—"Hath nothing *in* Me." These words meet the blasphemous doctrine of Irvingites, Christadelphians, etc., which represents that the Lord had evil propensities, but that these were never allowed to break out. We have to remember that "the *thought* of evil is sin." Not only were the Jews unable to convict JESUS of overt evil, but Satan, He affirms, could find no vulnerable point within Him.

282 *Verse* 31.—"Let us go hence." The Saviour here associates His disciples with Him in His conflict: Satan is their foe as well as His. *Cf.* Mark 14:42.

NOTES ON THE FIFTEENTH CHAPTER

283 *Verse* 1 *f.*—"I am the true [genuine] Vine." Cf. Psalm 80:8-16; Jeremiah 2:21. As to the difference between ἀληθής and ἀληθινός used here (as in 17:3 of God), see Trench, *Studies*, p. 274, or his work on *Synonyms of the New Testament*. So of Christ as the genuine Bread in 6:32. It speaks of what is original, archetypal, the Vine of heaven. Alford's idea that we here have the "Visible Church" is, as Ryle, in his excellent *Expository Thoughts*, has said, altogether unsatisfactory. For "Husbandman" *cf.* Luke 13:7, only that there the word used is ἀμπελουργός, as to which, and the use made by Arians of it, see Trench, *op. cit.*, p. 276, note. The "vine of the earth" John sets before us in the Apocalypse: a terrible ending it will have. Many do not clearly distinguish between the harvest and the vintage there (14:18).

284 *Cf.* Paul's doctrine of "in Christ," upon which Alford touches at the end of his note.

Use of this verse has been prominent in the "Arminian" controversy.

If H. Holtzmann could but apprehend the distinct bearing of 5:22, he would not venture to pit that passage against this, as if they were inconsistent.

285 *Verse* 3.—Observe the emphatic "ye," the ὑμεῖς being expressed for the disciples' comfort. *Cf.* 13:10. The expositor's remarks here call for special attention.

"I have spoken." *Cf.* 5:24, 8:31 *f.* Man is not to judge ("criticize") God's word, but to let it search his conscience (12:48). What was then the spoken is now for us the *written* word. When justified, the Christian needs *practical*, following on *positional*, sanctification, which detaches from much that would otherwise hinder "advance in grace" (2 Peter 3:18). Few things can be more blighting than what passes as "Higher Criticism," putting Scripture into man's mortar and applying his pestle to it. Is there not pride, self-satisfaction, which is "of the world" (1 John 2:16) behind it all? God forbid that, in writing so, one should even seem to assume a "superior tone." All by nature alike are tarred with the same brush.

286 *Verse* 4 *ff.*—"Abide in Me … much fruit." *Cf.* Colossians 1:27; 2 Peter 1:5-11. It is manifestly a question of "laying up in store" against "the time to come," the "day of Christ," the time of recompense (1 Timothy 6:19—τὸ μέλλον—and 2 Timothy 4:8). McGiffert would have it that the Evangelist here represents the Lord as saying that He dwelt in His followers even during His earthly life (p. 493).

287 *Verse* 6.—ἐβλήθη. *Cf.* ἐδοξάσθη in verse 8. Winer: "immediate result." Abbott would regard this use of the Greek tense as a "Hebraic instantaneous aorist" (*Johannine Grammar*, § 2,445: he compares Isaiah

NOTES ON THE FIFTEENTH CHAPTER

40:6-8). "*They* gather ... cast." *Cf.* Matthew 5:15; Mark 1:30; Luke 16:9.

Alford follows Meyer, who refers it to the "day of judgment."

288 *Cf. An Exposition of the Epistles of John the Apostle*, p. 229 *ff.*

289 *Verse* 7 *f.*—For the bearer of our Lord's words here on the "Higher Criticism," see *ibid.*, pp. 144-147; and as to "Development," p. 154. See, in particular, 2 John 9, and observe that in the present passage Christ's words are inseparable from Himself (verse 4).

290 *Verse* 11.—Ryle (p. 122) quotes a happy remark of Cyril, *ad loc.*: "Christians find their joy in that over which Christ rejoices."

290a *Verse* 12.—This is developed in 1 John 3:14. Illingworth: "The essence of the life is love" (chapter v.).

290b *Verse* 13.—This would be the highest reach of what is now called "Altruism." But *cf.* Matthew 5:44. The present writer has heard Dr. Coit admit that "ethical religion" has in this a hard task in rivalry with Christianity.

291 *Verse* 15.—*Cf.* Luke 12:4 for a previous occasion when the Lord called the disciples His "friends." A striking illustration of the difference between "friend" and "servant," as regards communications made, presents itself in the incident recorded of Jonathan in contrast with his attendant (1 Samuel 20).

291a {*Verse* 18.}—From here to 16:20, *cf.* Matthew 10:17-22.

291b *Verse* 19.—"The world." This, in the words of Westcott, stands for "the organization of society alien from, and opposed to, God" *(cf.* 1 John 2:15). "Chosen you out": here is the idea of the Church (ἐκκλησία).

292 Verses 22-24.—In verse 22 note the *words*; in verse 24, the works.

Verse 22.—*Cf.* 16:9. Scott writes: "To the mind of John sin in itself involves no moral culpability; sin is in itself a mere privation" (p. 220). The "City Temple" homilies have offered the same withering sentiment for the delectation of "the man in the street." In his First Epistle the Evangelist lays down, "Sin is lawlessness," which should be read in connection with the words immediately preceding (3:3 *f.*). Such ministers are at direct issue with both Paul and John. One of these Apostles uses language in that same letter (4:6) which might warn them to reconsider their position in view of the βῆμα of Christ. The Epistle supposes throughout acquaintance with the Gospel.

292a {*Verse* 25.}—The Lord avoided needless irritation of the Jews. How could the words of the Psalm quoted be made to agree with Burkitt's remarks on the discussion in Chapter 8?

293 Verse 26.—For this *"procession"* the Gnostics substituted their "emanation." Norris has a good note on the Catholic doctrine.

The witness that the Holy Spirit bears is another evidence of personality. Observe that the Lord has sent, not merely, as an influence, imparted the Spirit. For later Scriptural designations of the third "Person" of the Trinity, *cf.* Acts 16:7; Galatians 4:6; Philippians 1:19.

NOTES ON THE SIXTEENTH CHAPTER

294 *Verse 2.*—Those acquainted with the history of the "Inquisition" will remember that the slaughter of "heretics," so-called, was described as an "act of faith" (*auto da fé*).

294a As to persecution, see note on the last verse of this chapter.

295 *Verse 5.*—H. Holtzmann, with others, finds in this a contradiction of 13:36. To this there is no need of any English, for his countryman B. Weiss has an adequate reply: "No one any longer asks, because it had become only too clear to them that the '*I go back to the Father,*' of which He was constantly speaking, concerned His definite departure from the earth." There is no reproach in the Lord's words. Nevertheless, as the expositor puts it, desire for some further communication would have been the expression of simpler faith.

296 *Verse 7.*—*Cf.* note 134 on Mark.

297 *Verse 8 ff.*—"Afford proof." ἐλέγχειν (verse 8) may here be rendered by "indict," "charge." For the crowning sinfulness of unbelief, see 15:22 and note 292.

Blindness of soul comes out also in Matthew 6:23 (Luke 11:34 f.).

298 *Verse* 10.—"Righteousness." Stevens (p. 214 f.), after Chrysostom, with most (Luthardt, Zahn, and H. Holtzmann alike), takes this of the Saviour's righteousness; H. Holtzmann, referring to 9:24, 18:30. And certainly, as one spiritual writer has said: "Righteousness comes in graciously between sin and judgment" (Govett). Mr. Kelly, it will be seen, understands by it the Pauline "righteousness of God," as Mr. J. N. Darby before him. As to this, *cf.* Liddon, *Analysis of the Epistle to the Romans*, p. 71, and also Reynolds, *ad loc.*; for Augustine it was "The Righteousness of Faith." The present passage alone should be enough to meet Du Bose's assertion that "God raised Him from the dead by His *grace*" (*The Gospel in the Gospels*, p. 184).

299 *Verse* 12 *f.*—"From Himself." Here again comes out the distinct *personality* of the Holy Spirit. *Cf.* the same form of expression by Christ of Himself in 5:19. For spoken words of the Spirit, *cf.* 1 Timothy 4:1 (λέγειν); 1 Peter 4:11 (λαλεῖν), "His instruments." The Scriptures have to suffice us now (2 Timothy 3:16). *Cf.* Note 13 on Mark. "All bodies of Christians have tended to imagine that they are in the same stage of religious development as the first believers" (Jowett, *Essays*, p. 484). Whether this be true or not, we may well echo the words of F. B. Meyer: "The cry should be, '*Up* to Christ' rather than 'Back to Him'" (p. 125). The exposition should correct Westcott's interpretation of τὰ ἐρχόμενα, "the constitution of the Christian Church," for see Revelation 1:19.

300 *Verse* 16.—"Behold" (θεωρεῖν) and "see" (ὁρᾶν), the one relating to "things external" (as Matthew 27:55), the other to "things spiritual." The word for vision (ὄψις) is connected with the latter (Carr).

300a The difficulty which seems to have produced the omission of the last clause (retained by Govett) is easily appreciated. How could the Lord's departure be the cause of their seeing Him? For *spiritual* sight, see Ephesians 1:18. That Epistle is charged with mention of the Holy Spirit.

300b That which the expositor describes as "the enigma" of "the little while" is resolved in the same way by Luther, Hengstenberg, Ewald, Luthardt, and Weiss. It does not set before us the παρουσία, as Augustine, followed by Hofmann, supposed. See also the helpful remarks of Maclaren, p. 120 *ff.*

301 *Verse* 20.—"Grieved." *Cf.* Luke 23:27, and for their joy 24:41, 52 of the same Gospel, as also 20:20 here.

302 *Verse* 23.—The word ἐρωτᾶν is here taken as "to question" by Meyer, Trench, Alford, Godet, Westcott, H. Holtzmann, Plummer, and Carr, but "to make request" by Weizsäcker, Weiss, O. Holtzmann, and Abbott. *Cf.* note on 14:16.

As to prayer in Christ's name, see Martensen, *Christian Dogmatics*, p. 415 *f.*

302a See note {n} on p. 422, {chapter 14}, and notes 275, 277 of Appendix.

303 *Verse* 25.—The use of "hour" in this verse bears on the interpretation of 5:28 *f.* See note there.

304 *Verse* 26.—*Cf.* 8:42, and observe how these Scriptures discredit the modern theory of "the Fatherhood of God" and the cognate "Union in Incarnation." The difference between 3:14-17 and the present passage is that between love of *compassion* and of *complacency* (delight). That which was true of "the Jews" then, according to 7:7-19, 15:24 *f.*, has been true of "the world" in general since the Ascension (Luke 19:14).

305 *Verse* 27.—"Came forth from (beside) God." Already the disciples not only believed, but had come to know this (*cf.* 6:69, 17:8).

306 *Verse* 29 *f.*—These verses should be read with reference to "the little while" which had perplexed the disciples, but which they now supposed they understood. It is clear, however, that, as the expositor says, they felt that He read their hearts, and Divinely.

307 *Verse* 31.—Those (as Alford) who take "believe" affirmatively regard it as indicating the Lord's own glad appreciation of progress in their thoughts (*cf.* 17:8). The Revisers, however, seem to have acted wisely in retaining the interrogation in A.V., as do the critically revised texts.

308 *Verse* 32.—"His own." For the sense, see margin of R.V., comparing 19:27.

"Should leave Me alone." See Chapter 18. Critics question how the words following tally with the Synoptic, "My God, My God, why hast Thou forsaken Me?" (Matthew 27:46; Mark 15:34). Such people talk of "psychological" difficulties, if not impossibilities: so arbitrary are they; but their psychology sits easily upon them. English readers of our national history need only be reminded of King Henry IV.'s state of mind when informed of his son's delinquency before one of the royal judges. He was a prince as well as a father. Here, in the fourth Gospel, it is of God as His Father that our Lord speaks.

308a See notes 205, 235.

309 *Verse* 33.—Compare 1 Corinthians 15:57. There must be tribulation for the people of God until the time comes predicted in Isaiah 25. There can be no real truce in the meantime between the "World" and the "Church," as pictured to us in Scripture. One of Luther's fine sayings was: "The World's enmity is the court-dress of Christians."

NOTES ON THE SEVENTEENTH CHAPTER

310 Modern critics are very ready to speak of that which they deem *impossible* where Scripture is concerned, yet some of these display rank perversion of their own "psychology" by conceiving it *possible* that some unknown writer of Greek education, whether aided by Pauline teaching at Ephesus or not, composed that which, among *bona fide* Christians, goes by the name of the Lord's "High-priestly Prayer." The credulity of such people is amazing. Moreover, if to any unsophisticated reader it seem, at any rate, improbable that even a highly educated Hellenist or Hellenistic Jew could have put together such a prayer, how much more unlikely that the critics' Galilean provincial, John, son of Zebedee, could have indulged in a reverie of his own to manufacture such a composition or idealize the Lord's utterances!

310a The prayer divides itself into three parts: (1) Of the Lord for Himself; (2) for those in whose hearing it was spoken; (3) for those who should believe on Him through their word.

NOTES ON THE SEVENTEENTH CHAPTER

Milligan well says: "It would be as difficult to account for it from the pen of the Evangelist as from the lips of Jesus."

Bishop Chase, in his book on the Lord's Prayer (so called) in the early Church, has very suggestively compared the petitions of that formula with the prayer of this chapter as follows:

"Our Father who art in Heaven" with "Father" in verses 1, 5, 21, 24; with "Holy Father" in verse 11; and with "Righteous Father" in verse 25.

"Hallowed be Thy Name" with verses 6, 11, 12, 26. [We might add, "that Thy Son may glorify Thee" in verse 1.]

"Thy kingdom come" with verses 1 *f.*

"Thy will be done" with verses 4 *f.*, 11, 21.

"Bring us not into temptation" with verses 12, 15.

Cf., passim, Bishop Moule's volume on this chapter, recently published, which is in his best style.

311 *Verse* 1.—"Glorify Thy Son." How could this have been said, or put into the mouth of one no more than man?

"That Thy Son," etc. Govett: "That He may expend what is given in the glorifying of the Father Himself."

312 *Verse* 3.—"This is the eternal life." Weiss and Westcott suppose that we have here a definition; but Beyschlag rightly says that it would be incongruous in such utterances (*New Testament Theology*, i. 263 *f.*). Theosophy seeks to turn to account our Lord's words here in the service of its theory. Thus Mrs. Besant: "The heavenly root [of all religions] is the Wisdom, the knowledge of God, which is Eternal Life. ... From any one of its branches a man may pluck a leaf for the healing of the nations" (*Theosophist*, July, 1907). And yet, even "many *Christians* do not know God" (Schofield, *The Knowledge of God*, p. 32): see 1 Corinthians 15:34; Titus 1:16.

312a The knowledge which, as Westcott points out from the present tense used, is eternally progressive, is the knowledge of intimate communion, or fellowship, as said Luther. It is realised in the present, according to 5:24 *f.* and 6:47, 54, but only by foretaste (*cf.* Mark 10:30; Luke 18:30). See Note 110 on Mark. It is not that faith (*cf.* 20:31) and knowledge are coextensive (Scott); for faith is temporal, knowledge eternal. As Professor Inge puts it: "Eternal life is not γνῶσις, knowledge and possession, but the state of acquiring knowledge." The knowledge is dependent on the life, rather than the life on the knowledge. *Cf.* Walpole's *Vital Religion*, ninth edition, 1907, chapter i. As to difference between apprehension and comprehension of the Infinite, see Isaac Taylor, *The World of Mind*, p. 822, and *cf.* Job 36:26.

312b "True" (ἀληθινός), in contrast with what is imperfect, rather than the false, which would require ἀληθής, as in Romans 3:4.

312c "Jesus Christ." This is the only place in the Gospels where our Lord speaks thus of Himself, so that it has been a quarry for critics. H. Holtzmann says, "The historic Christ cannot have spoken so," and refers it to the same influence on the text as that alleged for Matthew 28:19 *f.* So Horton.

Godet, happily, adheres to the unimpeachable credibility of the Evangelist's "These words spoke Jesus"; as does also Bernard (p. 345 *ff.*). Not so Westcott and

NOTES ON THE SEVENTEENTH CHAPTER

Plummer, who bow to German ruling. Those who love the Scriptures may hold fast the assurance that our Lord's *own* self-designation here was the source of that so often afterwards used by the Holy Spirit in the New Testament. And so, to begin with, Matthew 1:1; Mark 1:1. For the Lord's naming Himself, *cf.* the Synoptic self-designation as "Son of man." On the verge of the close of His life He called Himself by the name JESUS, given to Him by the angel at its outset; and that He did call Himself "the CHRIST" is vouched for by Matthew 23:10. It is not, therefore, correct to say, as Carr, on the present passage of John, "Here only does our Lord apply the term 'CHRIST' to Himself," for in Matthew's Gospel the Lord does more than "accept" the title, as in 16:17 there; also Mark 14:61 *f.*

Finally, by what philosophy or romance could knowledge of a creature, as Unitarians and their critical allies regard Christ, be needful for life eternal? A like question is, of course, applicable to the words "glorify Thy Son" in verse 1, as to verses 10 *f.*, etc.

313 See note 232*a*.

313a The Exposition here meets a point raised by Pfleiderer and, in English guise, Scott (note 192).

313b *Verse 5.*—"The glory which I had," etc. If this, as Unitarians suggest, had meant merely the glory that Christ had in the counsels of the Father before living in this world, how could such a being have known of glory destined for him? *Cf.*, of course, 1:3.

314 *Verse 6.*—"I manifested Thy Name." *Cf.* Psalm 22:22.

314a *Verse 8.*—"Knew"—*i.e.*, learned. Not conscious knowledge, as εἰδῆτε in 1 John 5:13, etc. However closely "believe" may approach "know" in this way, they are not interchangeable words.

315 *Verse* 9.—"I request for them." The preposition is περί, not ὑπέρ, "in behalf of" (*cf.* the Greek, both verb and preposition, at 18:19), which occurs in verse 19. It is not intercession, but the Lord putting forth a claim.

316 *Verse* 11.—"We." Christ puts Himself on a perfect level with the Father.

"One." "Not manifested ecclesiastical oneness, but in the spirit of their minds" (Bellett, p. 124). *Cf.* note on verse 21.

317 *Verse* 12.—Alford, Wordsworth and Burgon use this verse for the idea that Judas had at one time been a true believer (verse 6). This is not only to hazard their reputation as commentators, but to bring "divinity" into contempt. See 18:9.

317a *Verse* 15.—Milligan and Bernard would render "out of the Evil One" (*cf.* 1 John 5:18 *f.*). This rendering Mr. Kelly preferred for Matthew 6:13.

318 *Verse* 17.—As to "disunion of the Church" being an incentive to unbelief, see T. Pearson on *Infidelity*, Part II., chapter vi.; also Isaac Taylor, *Spiritual Christianity*, p. 149. *Cf.* notes 316, 319*a*.

318a *Verse* 18.—"I also sent." This may be proleptic.

319 *Verse* 19.—Our Lord does not speak of "consecration of humanity" as such, but of His setting Himself apart for the sake of disciples. *Cf.* 10:36, of which this is correlative.

319a *Verse* 21.—"One." *Cf.* note on verse 11. Bishop Moule (p. 177) happily compares Romans 14:19. The still continuing tendency is unfavourable to this; indeed, ecclesiastical dissension might seem to retard the Second Coming of the Church's Head. As to "believe," see note on verse 23.

320 *Verse* 22.—"The glory," as future (*cf.* Romans 8:18).

321 *Verse* 23.—"Perfected into one." *Cf.* Ephesians 4:13.

"Know." Here is an advance on verse 21, "believe." *Cf.* note 314*a*. Heitmüller treats the words as "almost identical." Such a notion breaks down when applied to their context. Indeed. the critical reading of 10:38, as of 1 John 5:13, shakes it severely.

322 *Verse* 24.—Scott: "He is not thinking primarily of a future meeting with His disciples in heaven" (p. 305 *f.*). How does that comport with the preceding verse, which does not yield to the German view (see last preceding note) that the Johannine "know" and "believe" are practically equivalent. To hark back to verse 15 is a long cry. Again: "He has taken them to dwell in heavenly places with Himself" (p. 306). But this only introduces Paul's doctrine (Ephesians 2:6), of which John's is independent, although the writer labours to prove the contrary. With reference to the notion that Paul's belief had undergone material change since he wrote his First Letter to the Thessalonians (Charles, *Eschatology*, p. 385 *ff.*), we have but to compare 2 Thessalonians 2:8 with 2 Timothy 4:8. The word ἐπιφάνεια is common to both of these letters, and in the earlier letter the Apostle has combined παρουσία with it. John has in no sense "corrected" Paul.

NOTES ON THE EIGHTEENTH CHAPTER

323 *Verse* 2.—We have here manifestly the comment of an eye-witness. All attempts to forge a weapon against such testimony must come to nought.

324 *Verse* 6.—"Went away backward" *(cf.* Psalm 40:14). These words, as others elsewhere, may well have been directed against the Gnostic theory (Irenæus., bk. iii.) that "the Christ" forsook "Jesus" in the hour of need.

325 *Verse* 7 *f.*—Deuteronomy 22:6 here finds its spiritual counterpart. The Lord seems to say: "Take either Me or them; you cannot have both" (Govett). How Frederick Robertson's unhappy words, "He drew too near to a whirling wheel," etc., witness against a preacher whose utterances have been much in vogue! Conspicuous is the truth of *substitution*, assailed like so much else in the words of Christ Himself.

326 *Verse* 10.—The fourth Evangelist alone supplies the names. *Cf.* note above on verse 2.

327 *Verse* 11.—"The cup," etc. Whilst these words are peculiar to John's narrative, they afresh illustrate his way of subdued reference to Synoptic accounts. *Cf.* Matthew 26:39.

328 *Verse* 12 *f.*—"To Annas first." How, in the light of the Synoptic account could any but an eye-witness, the Evangelist himself, have recorded this without contradiction?

329 *Verse* 13.—"Who was high priest of that year." See note {217} on 11:49.

330 *Verse* 15.—"Known to the high priest." Bleek and Ewald (*History of Israel*, vi., p. 118; *Johannine Writings*, i., p. 400) supposed that the Evangelist was related to the high-priestly family. This idea has been used by Delff for his theory that the writer had himself been a priest, as by Burkitt (p. 250) for the notion that he had been a Sadducee. Such fancies have been generated by a statement (in Eusebius) of Polycrates, Bishop of Ephesus A.D. 190, that John of Ephesus wore a πέταλον—i.e., plate, coronet, or mitre (*cf.* Exodus 39:30). This may, however, have referred to one of the same name who, we know, was "of the kindred of the high priest" (Acts 4:6). Whilst Chrysostom and Cyril regard the disciple "known to the high priest" as the Evangelist, Augustine and others have questioned the identity. Bengel supposed Nicodemus to be meant; Zahn thinks, James. "The" before "other" is doubtful: it is not in אABD, the Syriac, and Memphitic. Anyhow, γνωστὸς must be distinguished from συγγενής (verse 26). If it be the Evangelist, any trade-connection he may have had with the high priest would sufficiently explain the word here used.

331 *Verse* 19.—"The high priest." Augustine, Chrysostom, Alford, Ellicott and Luthardt understand

Annas (*cf.* verses 13, 24); but Zahn, as most, takes it of Caiaphas. See note on verse 24.

332 *Verse* 20.—"In secret I spoke nothing." See Isaiah 45:17-19, 48:12-18. It will be observed that the Lord is silent as to His disciples.

333 *Verse* 22.—The record of this is peculiar to John.

334 *Verse* 24.—Most commentators are of opinion that this should come in between verses 13 and 14, as in some Greek and Syriac manuscripts, and as it was read by Cyril of Alexandria; and that the questioning and smiting took place before Caiaphas and the Sanhedrin. Some writers, however, suppose that John describes only the informal hearing before Annas, and accordingly passes over the trial by Caiaphas. *Cf.* Zahn, *ad loc.*

The verse comes twice in Cod. A. of the Syriac of Jerusalem lectionary, the first time after verse 13, and again after verse 23: this, of course, represents the work of harmonists. Luther's Bible contains a marginal note by himself at the earlier verse that it "has been misplaced in turning the page, as often happens," and at verse 24: "This verse ought to follow immediately after verse 14." Verses 19-24 are absent from the Syr^{sin}. See Mrs. Lewis's remarks in *Expositor*, vol. xii., p. 519 ("Verses 13, 24, and 14 are really one"). *Cf.* Blass, *Philology of the Gospels*, p. 59, on "blundering scribes." In his text this last of recent editors has placed verse 24 between verses 13 and 14.

335 *Verse* 28 *ff.*—The seven stages in the trial before Pilate, according as it was conducted outside or inside the "prætorium," are verses 28-32 of this chapter, outside; verses 33-37 inside; verses 38-40 outside;

NOTES ON THE EIGHTEENTH CHAPTER

19:1-3 inside; verses 4-7 outside; verses 8-11 inside; verses 12-16 outside (Westcott).

336 *Verse* 28.—"That they might eat the Passover." The difficulty about the last Passover, already discussed in a note on Mark 14:12 {Mark note 142}, and touched on here in connection with the opening words of chapter 13, is dealt with by the expositor in a long note on 19:14, where the view is taken that it *was* allowable to partake of the paschal meal within the twenty-four hours of the same technical day. And so Milligan, who supposes that the Jews' celebration was interrupted. *Cf.* Bernard, pp. 49-54. It may have been to secure strict compliance with primitive usage that the rubric in the Talmudic treatise *Zebbach* (verse 2) was afterwards framed. Delitzsch (in Riehm) questions the explanation given by Dr. John Lightfoot, the learned Rabbinic scholar of the seventeenth century, who says that the Evangelist here adopts the popular language—*i.e.*, speaks of the *Chagigah*, or peace-offering (*Works*, ii. 670). Zahn, however, is of opinion that Lightfoot was probably right, and that the day here intended was the fifteenth of Nisan (*Introduction*, ii., p. 514; *Exposition*, p. 622 *f.*). The learned Erlangen professor remarks that φαγεῖν is used for celebration, and that the standing expression for the fourteenth day of Nisan was ποιεῖν. *Cf.* "This *do* in remembrance of Me"; Exodus 12:48; Numbers 9:2; Deuteronomy 16:1; Matthew 26:18; Hebrews 11:28. Note that Numbers 28:16-18 (as Leviticus; see note {142} on Mark) distinguishes between the paschal meal and "the Feast." See, further, Khodadad, p. 20 *f.*, and note 346 below *(ad fin.)*.

337 *Verse* 31 *f.*—"It is not lawful for us," etc. According to the Talmud, it was in the year immediately preceding this that the Romans had deprived the Jews of execution of capital punishment—*i.e.*, exactly "forty years" before the Fall of Jerusalem.

338 *Verse 37.*—"King." See Luke 23:2, and *cf.* 1 Timothy 6:13, the "good confession."

"Of *the truth*": *cf.* 1 John 3:19 and 4:6, 5:19. "Of *God*," in the last references does not justify its being said that the terms are practically equivalent, as by Heitmüller (so Scott). See *Exposition*, p. 38.

339 *Verse 38 ff.*—"I find no fault in Him at all." *Cf.* Exodus 12:5; Deuteronomy 17:1; 1 Peter 1:19.

339a One of the latest crazes is to drag in here the Feast of Purim, so that Barabbas should represent Mordecai, and the rôle of Haman be taken by our Lord (Frazer, *Golden Bough*, iii. 188-198). Even Benn hesitates to accept such a suggestion. Conjuring with the name of the Jewish anarchist cannot be a self-satisfying, to say nothing of a creditable, service to society, for either an authority on folk-lore or a writer of romance.

NOTES ON THE NINETEENTH CHAPTER

340 *Verse 2.*—For the "robe" Herod's men put on our Lord, in which He was sent back to Pilate, see Luke 23:11. Evidently Pilate's soldiers, in the first instance, combined with Herod's in this indignity, and readjusted the same garment on returning to their own guardroom. It was not merely Herod's men who engaged in that horseplay, as Frazer represents (*op. cit.*, iii., p. 190).

341 *Verse 5.*—*Cf.* 11:50. He was so portrayed by Correggio in the picture exhibited at the National Gallery, and in the later famous picture in the Doré Gallery.

342 *Verse 6.*—The Jews disguised from Pilate that the punishment prescribed in Leviticus 24:16 was "stoning," which they had already several times attempted.

343 *Verse 7.*—As to the alleged blasphemy, *cf.* 5:18, 8:59, 10:33. Here is their final deliberate judgment of His claims (*cf.* Matthew 26:65; Mark 14:64; Luke 22:71).

344 *Verse 11.*—By "he" Caiaphas is meant (11:49 *ff.*).

345 *Verse* 13.—Pilate now took his seat, it would seem for the first time. Some would treat ἐκάθισεν as "seated"—*i.e.*, "Jesus"—but the verb is nowhere else used transitively (Westcott, Zahn).

"*Gabbatha*." Bishop Lightfoot (p. 143) follows Ewald in taking this, not of a "raised" place, but as connected with a root yielding the idea of *mosaic*.

346 *Verse* 14.—"The preparation ... the *sixth* hour." The expositor, in his note attached to this verse, leaves really very little to add beyond recording that Alford, as Bengel, has followed Eusebius's idea that the text was altered. The present writer, accordingly, whilst referring the reader to note 142 in the volume on Mark's Gospel, and that on 18:28 of this Gospel, may confine his remarks here pretty much to the question of the hours, Sir William Ramsay's treatment of which seems not to have come under Mr. Kelly's notice.

To begin with, it should be noticed in Luke 22:7-13 that John was one of the two concerned in making the actual Passover "preparation." Schmiedel writes: "John corrected by insertion what Mark and Luke corrected by omission" (col. 1,773). To this the present remarks shall be directed. The leading passage referred to by Mr. Kelly may be transcribed in an English rendering.

Pliny (ii. 79): "The days have been computed by different peoples in different ways. The Babylonians reckoned from one sunrise to the next; the Athenians from one sunset to the next; the Umbrians from noon to noon; the multitude universally from dawn to darkness; while the Roman priests and those who presided over the Civil Day (as also did the Egyptians and Hipparchus) from midnight to midnight." Aulus Gellius (*Noctes*

Atticæ) refers to a work of Varro, whose statement is to the same effect.

Sir W. Ramsay (*Expositor*, 1893, fourth series, vol. vii., pp. 216-223, and 1896, fifth series, vol. iii., pp. 457 *ff.*; *cf.* article in Hastings, *Dictionary of the Bible*, extra vol., p. 475 *ff.*) holds that *sixth hour* indicated *mid-day* at all seasons of the year, so that "about the sixth hour" would be "somewhere between 11 a.m. and 1 p.m.", and that the Roman civil day "was not divided into hours." Further, that "there is no justification for the theory that the ancients reckoned the hours in two ways— (1) beginning from sunrise; (2) beginning from midnight." Accordingly, he gives up the usual reconciliation. He believes that "the numbering of hours began invariably from daybreak or sunrise." Zahn is like-minded.

If the Roman reckoning differed in Italy and the Roman province of Asia Minor, the third hour of Mark living in Italy would be identical with "about the sixth hour" of John living at Ephesus in his old age. *Cf.* Plummer (*ad loc.*).

Besides Nonnus, spoken of in the original note, Theophylact conjectured the true reading to be "third," and so Bengel, Usher, Alford and McRory; but the textual evidence is strongly against it. *Cf.* Zahn, p. 718.

Wordsworth and Burgon's belief, as that of Tholuck, Ewald, Westcott and Milligan, that John followed the Roman computation of time (in some form or other), so that "sixth hour" would be our 6 a.m., whilst Mark's was the Jewish (for this purpose reckoned from sunrise), and the same as modern 9 a.m., might seem to be sustained by the fourth Gospel itself. As Ryle says, there would remain three hours to account for. These would be taken up with the preliminaries of crucifixion. That excellent writer himself inclines to the view of Calvin, Hammond, Hengstenberg, Ellicott, etc., that, from the Jews' division of their day into twelve hours of four parts (Maimonides), Mark's "third hour" would work out at about 9 a.m., and John's "sixth" at between 9 and 12.

According to old Jewish modes of thought, the day spoken of in 20:19 would have to be a "Monday," but everyone knows that John is speaking of the *first* day of a week. On the whole, the present writer cannot but think that resort to a recondite explanation, of which none of the ancients seems ever to have dreamed, is best avoided.

To what has been said on the general question of alleged discrepancy in note {142} on Mark 14:12 may be added that Chwolson, a Hebrew Christian, in his *Last Passover of Christ* (1892), maintains that the Pharisees ate their Passover on the 13th, the Sadducees on the 14th Nisan.

Zahn holds that John says substantially the same as the Synoptists (*Introduction*, ii., pp. 523-526; *Exposition*, pp. 637-640). As to the "Paschal Controversy" (A.D. 165-170), see Eusebius, v. 24; Stanton, 173-197; Zahn, ii. 522 *f.*, with his notes 16-18.

The date of the Lord's death seems to have been April 7 in the year 30 of our era.

347 *Verse* 15.—Here probably Matthew 27:24 comes in. Some, however, put the incident there between 18:40 and 19:1 of this Gospel.

348 *Verse* 17.—"Went out." See Leviticus 6:12-21, 16:27; Hebrews 13:12.

349 *Verse* 19.—Of the four forms of inscription, John's is the fullest, and is most like Matthew's, so that proba-

NOTES ON THE NINETEENTH CHAPTER

bly these were both in Hebrew. Pilate would perhaps employ different scribes to write the several inscriptions. Observe that no part of any of them is excluded by or inconsistent with any part of the other three. Its being put in different languages is in keeping with the glory of the "Son of man" (Bellett, p. 148).

350 *Verse* 23.—A coat of one piece only is still worn by Northern peasants (Schor, p. 48).

351 *Verse* 25.—Most commentators take Mary, wife of Cleopas, as sister of the Lord's mother; but Bengel, Meyer, Alford, Norris, Weiss, Mayor and Zahn regard Salome as sister of the Lord's mother (*cf.* Matthew 27:56 and Mark 15:40), so making four women. According to their view, the Evangelist and his brother James would be cousins of our Lord.

351a *Verse* 26.—Bishop Lightfoot, in his second Dissertation appended to edition of the Epistle to the Galatians, regards the Lord's committal of His mother to the care of John as "fatal" to the "Helvidian" theory that His kinsmen were His *uterine* brethren. But surely His marking their unbelief in this way may be accepted in explanation.

The statement of Origen, cited by this learned writer, is certainly wrong—that Scripture nowhere speaks of them as Mary's children: see Psalm 69:8, the Messianic character of which, presumably, neither of these truly great scholars would have denied (*cf.* note 137).

352 *Verse* 31.—The day was "great" because on it were offered the firstfruits (Leviticus 23:10-14; *cf.* Deuteronomy 21:23).

Paraskeue, the Christian name of Friday, "could to Greek Christians suggest nothing else" (Milligan).

353 *Verse 35 f.*—"He knoweth." This has been taken by Weizsäcker of a confirmatory witness, and Schmiedel, a complacent follower, questions how the witness already spoken of could be sufficiently authoritative. Although Luthardt has cited 9:37 as closely parallel, Abbott, Zahn, etc., follow Erasmus's paraphrase in taking ἐκεῖνος of our Lord. On the other side, reference may be made to Buttmann (against Hilgenfeld). As usually taken, the pronoun illustrates the characteristically redundant style of this Evangelist.

See "Not a bone of Him shall be crushed." *Cf.* Psalm 139:16 (Bellett).

354 *Verse 37.*—The Evangelist here follows neither the present Hebrew text of Zechariah 12:10 (which has "on Me") nor the Septuagint. If we regard the matter from the merely literary point of view, he may have been acquainted with some Aramaic paraphrase.

354a {*Verse 38.*}—John alone says that this Joseph was "a disciple of Jesus, but secretly for fear of the Jews." *Cf.* note {166} on Mark 15:43; Luke 23:50; Matthew 27:57. It will be found that each of the Evangelists furnishes some statement peculiar to himself.

354b {*Verse 41.*}—*Cf.* Luke 23:53.

355 *Verse 42.*—"They put Jesus." This, again, controverts such views of human destiny as Swedenborg's, which represent the body as for ever abandoned at death. The Lord's body is spoken of as *Himself.*

NOTES ON THE TWENTIETH CHAPTER

356 The RESURRECTION.—For the order of appearances (see Table in Turton, p. 357) of the risen Lord, see West on the Resurrection {Gilbert West, *Observations on the History and Evidence of the Resurrection of Jesus Christ*, 1747}, Birks's *Horæ Apologeticæ*, Ryle's valuable note, and a pamphlet by R. Govett, *The Saviour's Resurrection: Events of the First Day*, as also a powerful book by the same, published by Maclehose, Glasgow. Colonel Turton's chapter (xvii.) on the whole subject is excellent; see in particular p. 362 as to St. Paul's reference to the various occasions in groups. Reference should also be made to Swete, *The Appearances of the Lord after the Passion*, p. 51 *ff.*

357 *Verse 1 f.*—See note 167 on Mark 16:1-8. Here is John's first mention of the stone.

"Dearly loved," ἐφίλει, for which ἠγάπα is used elsewhere, as in 13:23.

358 "We know not." This assumes knowledge of the earlier Gospels. The fourth Evangelist, like each of the rest, knew more than he has recorded. *Cf.* note on verse 30.

359 *Verse* 3.—*Cf.* Luke 24:12, where sceptical writers, as is their wont in such cases, find a contradiction. There (α) Peter is *alone*, (β) does not enter the tomb (see verse 6 here). But the earlier Evangelist is speaking of a second visit of Peter, on returning from which he met the Lord Himself (verse 34 there).

360 *Verse* 5.—"Stooping down"—*i.e.*, sideways (παρακύψας). Had he not done so, he would have stood in his own light. As to such a tomb, see Schor, p. 34.

361 *Verse* 7.—The word ἐντετυλιγμένον speaks volumes. It means "folded *inwards*"—*i.e.*, turban-shaped (Govett), or twirled (Latham). What was it that entranced him? The remarkable appearance that the vesture presented in the position of the various parts towards each other. The Lord had detached Himself from the napkin and the shroud without dishevelling them, to say nothing of handling them. A miracle alone could explain the phenomenon. The common notion (as of Dr. Torrey, *Talks with Men*) that He had just calmly folded up the napkin afresh in a different place, so as to indicate that there had been no haste, no removal of the body by friend or foe, is feeble in comparison with the full reality. "A place apart" refers to the different position consistent with the unity, which had not been disturbed. *Cf.* Carr: "The napkin perhaps rested on a stone which had served as a pillow." So apparently, Bishop Gore understands it (*New Theology*, iii., p. 123), as does Prof. Swete. Further reference may be made to Govett or Latham (*The Risen Master*, p. 43 *ff.*, ed. of 1901).

362 *Verse* 8.—A question has been raised as to the Lord's vesture as risen. A change must take place if Leviticus 16:23 was to be fulfilled.

NOTES ON THE TWENTIETH CHAPTER

362a "Saw" (εἶδεν). This time with intelligence.

362b As suggested by Lake (*Historical Evidence for the Resurrection of Jesus Christ*, p. 133).

363 Verse 9.—"From"—i.e., from *among* (ἐκ).

363a See note on 6:69, and as to Divine faith founded on Scripture giving infallible certainty, Bishop Pearson on the words of the Creed, "I believe."

363b *Cf.* 17:8, 1 John 5:13.

364 *Verses* 11-16.—These and the two following verses are peculiar to John. *Cf.*, again, note 167 on Mark. Some have carped at the absence of any record of fright on Mary's part. But, writes Bellett, "What was such splendour to her?" (p. 155).

365 *Verse* 13.—"I know not." In verse 2 it was "We know {not}." She had spoken with the other women in the meantime. John's account supposes knowledge of Matthew 28:1, 5 *f.*; Mark 16:1-5; Luke 24:1-10 (Zahn, ii. 509). One may see that the fourth Evangelist attaches himself especially to the account given by the second.

366 *Verse* 14.—Athanasius, Chrysostom and Bishop Andrewes suppose that Mary thought, from the altered manner of the angels, that there was another on the scene, and that, accordingly, she turned to see the newcomer.

367 *Verse* 17.—"The Christ" had not yet ascended. The Gnostics alleged that He did so when "Jesus" was arrested (note 324). Scott supposes that he reproduces the Evangelist's own interpretation when he represents the Lord's ascension as "accomplished from the time of His meeting with Mary", that for John "there was no room for what is described by the writer of the Acts";

and that "the παρουσία was taken out of its Apocalyptic setting." Such writers evidently should leave 21:22 alone, for *their* system "has no room" for it. Observe that the words "till I come" (or, "while I am coming") are independent of any theory as to the three closing verses of the Gospel. See notes 394 *ff.*

"Do not go on touching Me." For denial of historical support to the bodily resurrection of the Lord, see Lake, *op. cit.* For St. Paul's position, *cf.* Colossians 2:9, Philippians 3:21.

"My God." The Lord is "Son of man" still. *Cf.* notes {68 and 130} on 3:13, 6:62.

368 *Verse* 19.—"When it was evening." See note {346} on 19:14 *(ad fin.)*.

"The doors were shut," etc. The question as to the properties of the Lord's body in resurrection leads to the suggestion of a "four-dimensional world," of which Mr. R. J. Campbell has availed himself for a system of ideas very different from the views of the propounder of it (Dr. A. T. Schofield).

369 *Verse* 20.—"The disciples." Luke shows that others were present besides the Apostles. As to his saying that they were "terrified" whilst John speaks of their being "glad," see sensible remarks of Turton, p. 359.

370 *Verse* 23.—See note {149} on 7:39. It would be found that each form of the commission in the Gospels illustrates the design of the respective record (Bellett, p. 162 *f.*).

371 This act of administrative forgiveness, Augustine said, holds of all believers everywhere. So even Pusey on *Absolution*, p. 32. *The Second Book of Homilies*, {"Of Repentance"}: "The priests are as much bound to confess to the lay people as the lay people to the priests." After such *dicta*, who could call the late Dean Stanley revolutionary when he wrote: "The clergyman needs the advice and pardon of the gifted layman quite as much as the layman needs the advice and pardon of the gifted clergyman"? (*Christian Institutions*, p. 179).

Observe that Thomas was absent on this occasion. This lends support to the view of Augustine and others, to which reference has been made; otherwise that Apostle's commission must have been defective.

Instances of such retention of sin are Ananias and Sapphira, the incestuous person at Corinth, Hymenæus and Alexander.

For power conferred on the ἐκκλησία as such, see Matthew 18.

372 "Didymus." This is not a surname: Thomas in Syriac means "twin."

373 *Verse 29.*—*Cf.* 1 Peter 1:8.

374 *Verse 30 f.*—"Signs." The great question of controversy between the Church and the Jewish rulers had been as to the Messianic claims of JESUS, and in the first period miracles played the chief part in establishing them. It was to the interest of Jewish opponents to upset the reality of these. Why, it may be asked, if truth was on their side, did they not put the Apostles to open shame? (Gerdtell, *On the Miracles*, etc., p. 53). Martineau thought that these verses indicate that the writer did not intend his work to be taken as strictly "historical" (*Seat of Authority in Religion*, p. 435). In them, however, we have inspired expression to the difference between merely human and Scripture biography. Contrast Boswell's *Johnson*, Lockhart's *Scott*, Morley's *Gladstone*,

with the very limited scope of the fourth Gospel. Such a statement as that contained in these verses, of course, discredits theories like those of Wellhausen, who, accordingly, in his recent monograph, treats them as from a later hand (p. 27).

The last words afford us a pre-eminent instance of what is meant by "dogma." "A truth which every one who would be a Christian is bound to believe" (Gore, *The Creed of the Christian*, p. 16). But Creeds are, after all, "only human expositions" (Kinnear, p. 163). As to Dogma, see Green, iii. 165-185, Lotze, § 94 *ff.*

There were two departments of error with which the Apostles had to deal: (α) *Jewish*, to which the Gospel of Matthew is directed; (β) that of *Gentile* speculation, rife around John at Ephesus, which treated matter as evil, and questioned the omniscience and goodness of the Creator. The fourth Evangelist has shown that sin is a matter of man's heart, and that the Lord Jesus was the Creator's accredited agent and witness. Again, reason as man may about the character of the Lord's body in resurrection, that this was not merely phenomenal is patent to all but bigots.

The Lord has been shown to be Son of God and Son of man in one (see verses 14-18). *Cf.*, again, 3:13 and 16 with 11:27 and 17:3. In 1:32 the Dove was not "the Christ," but the Spirit.

As for Eternal Life, Christ's word was saturated with mention of it (6:68, 10:27 *f.*). He is Himself that Life (5:26, 11:25 *f.*).

With verse 31 here *cf.*, of course, 1 John 5:9, 13, which in like manner informs us of the object the Apostle had in writing that letter.

NOTES ON THE TWENTIETH CHAPTER

375 Grotius thought that the last chapter was written by John the Presbyter, as do Harnack and others now. The opinion that the Gospel originally ended with chapter 20 seems to go back to Tertullian (*Adversus Praxean*, 25). It is that of Germans in general, including Zahn (§ 66 *ad init.*).

375a Ewald's opinion was that it was John's own composition, dating some ten years after the rest of the Gospel, but added before its publication, the uncompleted part in the meanwhile having a sort of private circulation. It is rather a summary, like that at the close of chapter 12 (Reynolds).

NOTES ON THE TWENTY-FIRST CHAPTER

376 As far as we know, writes Zahn, the Gospel has never circulated without this chapter (ii., p. 484). Tatian's *Diatessaron* used the essential parts of it down to verse 25. Some think that the closing verses proceeded from those around the Apostle, with his sanction (Zahn, p. 493).

Scarcely any German writer now follows Hengstenberg's defence. Even Luthardt regards it as an Epilogue, although probably from John's own hand. So Meyer and Godet. Weiss is one of those who think that it was by another hand (see note 394*a*). Happily, most reject the view of Baur, Strauss and Keim, that it represents a vindication of John as a rival of Peter.

Mr. Kelly, it will be seen, defends every verse of the chapter as an integral portion of the Gospel written by John himself, reprobating the idea that it is a supplement.

377 *Verse* 1.—"Manifested Himself." *Cf.* 2:11, 7:4.

"At the sea of Tiberias." It was so called already in the time of Josephus. Observe John's combination of the

NOTES ON THE TWENTY-FIRST CHAPTER

Lucan and Matthæan different scenes of the appearances.

378 *Verse 2.*—"The sons of Zebedee." The only distinct mention in the Gospel of James and John, and, of course, not by name. Zahn regards it as indication of editorship (ii., p. 485).

379 Godet suggests that these may have been Papias's John the Elder and Aristion, whom the ancient writer speaks of as "disciples of the Lord." Observe that there are *seven* disciples in the scene (see note 46). Germans are embarrassed in accounting for the number.

379a *Verse 3.*—Bacon: "Unconscious of the Resurrection" (*Hibbert Journal*, October, 1907, p. 141). How, then, explain the readiness of the words of the disciple to Peter in verse 7?

380 *Verse 4 ff.*—There seems to be a designed comparison with Luke 5:1-9, whilst verse 7 reminds of Matthew 14:28-31, and verses 9-12 recall 6:9-11 of this Gospel.

{380a} John's account is different from that of the incident described in Luke 5, from the very fact that they were distinct occasions. Thus, in the earlier Gospel Peter says, "Depart from me," etc., whilst here he girds his fisher's smock about him and strikes out for the shore to go to the Lord. On the previous occasion his confession of sinfulness was superficial; experience acquired of what he is has now the rather moved him to be silent about it. On that first occasion the net was being rent and the fish not secured; here all is tranquilly brought to land. See, further, in Harnack, *Luke the Physician*, English translation, p. 227, where dissent is expressed from the view taken by Wellhausen in commentary on Luke.

381 *Verse* 7.—This verse makes it certain that the Evangelist John was intended by "the disciple whom Jesus loved."

382 "One hundred and fifty-three." No better explanation has ever been found for this number than Hengstenberg's, that it was the number of nations of the world known at the time.

383 *Verse* 13 *f.*—The Gnostic condemnation of animal food is here disposed of.

384 "The third time." That is, to the Apostles as a company.

385 *Verses* 15-17.—Who but John could have written these verses? *Cf.* 13:37.

386 *Verse* 15 *f.*—Adolphe Monod: "Give me thine observances, says the God of Pharisaism; give me thy personality, says the God of Hegel; give me thy reason, says the God of Kant. It remains for the God of Jesus Christ to say, Give Me thy heart ... the unmistakable feature of a genuine conversion" (from sermon on *Dieu demandant le Coeur de l'Homme*, cited by Bishop Moule in his devotional book on *Jesus and the Resurrection*).

The difference between ἀγαπᾷν and φιλεῖν is that "φ. is so far lower than ἀ. that it indicates less of insight and more of emotion" (Moule, p. 181, aptly comparing 1 Peter 1:8). Reference may be to Trench, Westcott, Abbott. Augustine calls attention to "My" (not "thy").

"Feed ... tend." The difference between βόσκειν and ποιμαίνειν being one of sustenance, as compared with guidance.

387 *Verse* 18 *f.*—*Cf.* 2 Peter 1:14. The words here are from the same hand as 12:33 (Lightfoot, p. 194).

NOTES ON THE TWENTY-FIRST CHAPTER

388 *Verse* 18.—"When thou wast young." There is a *prolepsis* in these words. The Lord is speaking of "Peter's life then present" (Moule, pp. 190 *f.*). *Cf.* 1 Corinthians 13:12.

389 *Verse* 19.—*Cf.* 13:36.

390 *Verses* 20-23.—John was still alive when these verses were written (Zahn, ii. p. 488).

Drummond, from these words, vindicates the Evangelist against the Tübingen charge (note 376) of depreciation of Peter (p. 395 *f.*).

391 *Verse* 21.—*Cf.* Mark 10:39.

392 *Verse* 22.—Bengel: "Peter, the foundation; John, the crown."

393 "Come." At death, say Augustine, Grotius, Ewald, Olshausen, etc.; at destruction of Jerusalem, Luthardt, Alford, Godet, Westcott, etc.; but De Wette, Meyer, Weiss, H. Holtzmann, Gloag and Zahn, at the "Second Coming."

Instead of negativing Paul's distinction of two classes, those who shall have fallen asleep and those who remain, these verses rather confirm it.

A question has been raised whether John the Apostle died a natural death as generally supposed, or was, like his brother, martyred by Jews (*cf.* Matthew 20:23; Mark 10:38 *f.*), as alleged in a Fragment of Philip of Sidé of the fifth century. See English edition of Schürer (p. 59), and a Chronicle of George the Sinner of the ninth or tenth century. *Cf.* Stanton, p. 167; Burkitt, p. 252. The statement of George the Sinner, which had already been given in Harnack's *Apostolic Fathers* (p. 87 *ff.*), that distinguished scholar himself discredits (*Chronology,*

p. 665 *f.*), because of the silence of Eusebius and Irenæus. Heitmüller, one of the latest writers, joins Schmiedel and others in crediting this mythology. Drummond (p. 223) had remarked, with reference to the Syrian martyrology in Burkitt (p. 254), that it does not imply that the brothers came by their deaths at the same time and place.

394 *Verses* 23-25.—Harnack supposes that the Evangelist was already dead when verse 23 was added (p. 676), and (as Ewald) that the writer is expressly distinguished from the disciple that "beareth witness and wrote." From verse 23 a curious notion has been derived by Pfleiderer (Scott follows suit), that the Evangelist gave up the chiliastic expectation (Revelation 20:4).

394a THE EPILOGUE (verse 24 *f.*).—Weiss and many other students of Scripture regard verses 24 and 25 as alone written after the Apostle's death. But how could a third person, or even a company of John's friends or followers, attest the truth of his record, whether personally acquainted with him or not? As Dr. R. G. Moulton sensibly remarks, "endorsement is of no value without names" (*The Modern Reader's Bible*, p. 1706). Bacon's quotation of Romans 8:16 is not in the least to the point. *Cf.* 19:35 and note {353}. The difficulty, moreover, that some raise over "we know" (verse 24) is not felt by those who compare the same form of expression in chapter 1 of the First Epistle (see also 2 Corinthians 1:13). Observe that there is no emphatic pronoun (ἡμεῖς) used, which would have given colour to the "critical" argument. Again, the transition from the third person we meet with in 3 John 1 of the "elder"—it becomes the first plural in verses 9, 12; whilst the final use of the first singular is paralleled by 1 Thessalonians 2:18; Hebrews 13:18 *f.* So that there is no need whatever to take "we know" of Ephesian elders or friends (as Westcott, from comparison of 19:35), or "I suppose" of an amanuensis. Even if such were necessary, the direct association by the Apostle of others with himself would be paralleled by joint-writers of Pauline epistles. One need do no more than just record the ingenious proposal of Chrysostom and Theophylact to read, instead of οἴδαμεν, οἶδα μέν, so as to preserve the first person singular.

Weizsäcker (vol. iii., p. 209 *ff.*) and some others regard the whole of the Gospel as written after the Apostle's death. This, it is hoped, has been sufficiently dealt with in note 1a on the Introduction.

395 "Contain." See Matthew 19:11 in the Greek. As to the Oriental hyperbolism of Scripture, reference might be made to Ryle, vol. iii., p. 529. Amongst other passages, that writer refers to our Lord's own language as to Capernaum, and reproduces a helpful remark of Calvin.

{**396**} Tregelles upheld the verse as written by the first hand in the Sinaitic manuscript.

AN EXPOSITION OF THE GOSPEL OF JOHN

Indexes to the Notes

Index of Scripture Quotations in the Notes 819

Index of Greek and Hebrew Words in the Notes 824

Index of Subjects in the Notes 826

References in these indexes are to note numbers in the preceding Notes.

AN EXPOSITION OF THE GOSPEL OF JOHN

Index of Scripture Quotations in the Notes

Genesis
1 9a; 1. 9
40:13, 19. 237

Exodus
7:20. 52
12:3. 227; 5. 339; 42. 263a; 48. 336
17:6. 147
25:8. 20
39:30. 330

Leviticus
6:12-21. 348
16:23. 362; 27. 348
20:10. 156
23:10-14. 352
24:16. 200, 342

Numbers
4:3, 39. 172
8:34. 172
9:2. 336
20:11. 147
27:17. 190
28:16-18. 336
29:12. 146

Deuteronomy
13:6-11. 156a
16:1. 336
17:1. 339; 2-7. 157; 6. 161
18:15. 118
19:15. 157, 161
21:23. 352
22:6. 325; 22. 156
29:4. 174
32:20. 239; 39. 199; 39 ff. 164

Joshua
7:19. 180
13:26. 29
15:25. 135
19:28. 47

1 Samuel
20 291

1 Chronicles
17:12. 238

Ezra
5:16. 57

Job
36:26. 312a

Psalms
1:5. 108
2 43
16:10. 58a
22 192; 22. 314
23 186, 192; 5. 222
24 192
36:9. 11
40:14. 324
46:4. 177
51:2. 250
55:21. 223
66:18. 182
69:8. 137, 351a
78:11 f. 201, 239
80:8-16. 283
89 118a; 24, 28, 29. 238; 48. 195a
90:2. 173
102:25 ff. 164; 27. 173
107:23-31. 120
110:4. 238
139:16. 353
146:7 f. 196

Proverbs
8:9. 168
15:29. 182

Isaiah
1:15. 182
6:9 f. 241
7:9. 115
8:6. 177
9:7. 238
10:28-31. 189
12:3. 148
25 309; 8. 210
26:19. 210
28:9-12. 176
29:9-13. 184

35:6. 148
40 186; 5. 52; 6-8. 287
41:4. 164
42:19. 184
43:1. 187; 11-13. 256; 13. 199
44:1-6. 43; 3. 148
45 218; 7. 9a; 17-19. 332
48:12. 164; 12-18. 332
49 194, 218
53:3. 20; 8. 238; 10. 192
55:1. 148
58:11. 148

Jeremiah
2:13. 146; 21. 283
17:21. 102
23:5. 118a

Ezekiel
1:3. 202
34:11-23. 193
36 66
37:25. 238
47:1. 148

Daniel
7:14. 238
12:2. 210

Hosea
13:14. 210

Joel
3:13. 148

Micah
4:7. 238
5:2. 118a, 145

Zephaniah
3:13-20. 43, 228

Zechariah
9:9. 228
11 186; 12. 227
12:10. 354

INDEX OF SCRIPTURE QUOTATIONS IN THE NOTES

14 227

Malachi
2:10. 167a

Ecclesiasticus (Sirach)
48:1. 110

Wisdom
7:23. 166

1 Maccabees
3:40 29

2 Maccabees
3:40. 166
6:26. 108
13:26. 166
15:37. 166

Psalms of Solomon
17:42. 277

Matthew
1:1. 312c
3:14. 34
4:12. 53; 21 f. 1
5:15. 221, 287; 44. 290b
6:13. 317a; 23. 297
7:21. 255; 22. 105a
9:15. 77
10:5 f. 70; 16. 193; 17-22. 291a; 19. 221; 39. 234
11:2 ff. 35; 3. 118; 4 ff. 52, 148, 198
12:19. 144; 23. 274; 31 f. 170 f.; 39. 97; 41. 108
13:48. 221
14:22. 118a; 28-31. 380; 33. 120
16:17. 312c; 25. 234
18:3. 66a; 18. 105, 371
19:11. 395
20:17-24. 220a; 23. 393
21:12 f. 55; 15. 118a; 23 ff. 55
23 53; 10. 312c; 37. 53
25:21. 66a

26:6. 248; 18. 336; 39. 212a, 327; 65. 343
27:24. 347; 46. 308; 50. 243; 52. 205; 55. 300; 56. 1, 351; 57. 354a
28:1. 365; 5 f. 365; 15. 54; 19 f. 59, 312c

Mark
1:1. 312c; 13 f. 75; 14. 53; 20. 1; 21. 96; 27. 55; 30. 287
2:8. 60; 10. 45; 18 ff. 73
3:13 f. 134; 17. 1
4:13. 188a; 30. 67; 36. 83
6:4. 96; 45. 118a
7:4. 50
8:12. 97; 29. 27, 37; 35. 234
9:1. 271; 43, 45, 47. 65
10:13-16. 212a; 30. 312a; 32-52. 220a; 38 f. 393; 39. 391; 46. 220
11:15. 55, 227
12:30. 9; 35-37. 161a; 37. 226
14:3 ff. 222; 12. 336, 346; 12 f. 247; 42. 282; 58. 57; 61 f. 312c; 62. 11, 264; 64. 343
15:34. 308; 39. 243; 40. 1, 351; 43. 354a
16:1 ff. 357, 365; 14 ff. 123; 16. 59; 17 f. 275

Luke
1:32 f. 118a
2:34. 184
3:2. 202; 7. 79
4:16. 140; 19. 53; 23, 31. 206; 29. 209; 30. 103
5:1-9. 380; 1-11. 1; 8. 254; 10. 1
6:13 f. 134
7:1-10. 98; 18-23. 35; 19. 118; 30. 66; 36 ff. 222
8:51. 1

821

9:19. 31; 24. 234; 28. 1;
  51-56. 80
10:16. 245
11:21 f. 185; 29. 52; 33 ff. 198;
  34 f. 297
12:4. 291; 10. 171; 37. 249;
  51. 152
13 53; 7. 283; 34. 53
14:26. 234; 32. 277
15:11-32. 187a
16:9. 287; 19-31. 205
17:33. 234
18:18, 24. 65; 30. 312a;
  31, 35. 220; 31 ff. 220a
19:9. 90; 14. 304; 41. 212a;
  45 f. 55
20:35 f. 210
21 154
22:7-13. 346; 21. 263a;
  43 f. 195a; 53. 163; 71. 343
23:2. 338; 11. 340; 27. 301;
  50. 354a; 51. 54; 53. 354b
24:1-10. 365; 12. 359; 13. 29;
  26. 66a, 238; 34. 359;
  41. 301; 52. 301

Acts
1:14. 137
2:33, 38 f. 177; 39. 187; 41. 275
3:2 f. 277
4:6. 330; 12. 17; 13. 1a
6:5. 1a
15 1
16:7. 293
17:4. 231; 28. 14; 29. 16
18:24. 9
19:31. 217
20:28. 192; 29. 193
21 1
23:5. 217
26:24. 140

Romans
1:3. 161a; 5. 122; 20. 9
3:4. 312b
5:10. 61, 129
6:16-23. 61
8:3. 170; 16. 16, 394a; 18. 320;
  30. 71; 32. 70
10:9. 276
14:19. 319a
15:8. 194
16:4. 192

1 Corinthians
1:9. 9b; 22 f. 14
6:11. 250
9:5. 137
12 149
13:12. 388
14 149
15:34. 312; 57. 309

2 Corinthians
1:13. 394a
3:10. 149; 17. 149
5:20. 252; 21. 170, 195
9:15. 70
11:4. 7

Galatians
2:6. 61; 9. 1
3:13. 195, 218
4:6. 293; 25. 54; 30. 61

Ephesians
1:18. 300a
2:6. 322
4:13. 321; 20. 7; 30. 277a
5:26. 66; 14. 244; 30. 126

Philippians
1:19. 293
2:9. 280
3:11. 210; 21. 367

INDEX OF SCRIPTURE QUOTATIONS IN THE NOTES

Colossians
1:15. 9; 16. 9b; 17. 14; 19. 23; 27. 286
2:9. 23, 367
4:13. 1a

1 Thessalonians
2:18. 394a

2 Thessalonians
2:1-12. 113; 8. 322

1 Timothy
4:1. 299; 1-3. 167
6:13. 338; 19. 286; 20. 23

2 Timothy
1:7. 61
2:18. 106
3:7. 133; 16. 299
4:8. 286, 322

Titus
1:16. 312
2:11. 22

Hebrews
1:3. 199
2:3. 19; 17. 252
4:12 f. 9
5:7. 195a, 235
6:1. 8, 9
7:14. 163
9:14. 195a
10:20. 188a
11:3. 9; 6. 9; 28. 336
12:9. 16
13:12. 348; 18 f. 394a; 20. 192

1 Peter
1:8. 373, 386; 19. 192, 339
4:1. 170, 195; 11. 299
5:1. 1a; 4. 192

2 Peter
1:4. 126; 5-11. 286; 11. 191; 14. 387

3:18. 285

1 John
1 394a; 1. 18; 3. 25; 5. 239
2:2. 33; 4. 276; 12-14. 133; 15. 291b; 16. 285; 18-23. 113
3:3 f. 292; 14. 290a; 16. 192; 16 f. 277; 19. 338; 22 f. 246; 23. 17
4:2. 113, 130; 2 f. 18; 3. 7; 6. 170, 338, 292; 16. 133
5:6, 7. 277a; 9. 374; 11-13. 125; 13. 314a, 321, 363b, 374; 18 f. 317a; 19. 77, 338

2 John
1. 1a; 7. 18, 130; 9. 289

3 John
1. 1a, 394a

Revelation
1:1. 25; 19. 299
2:13. 236; 15. 18
3:9. 28
7:9 ff. 227
12:10. 236
13:11. 113
14:18. 283
20:4. 394; 5. 108
21:6. 88a

Index of Greek And Hebrew Words in the Notes

ἀγαπᾶν, φιλεῖν, 357, 386
ἀθετεῖν, 245
αἰτέω, 277
ἀληθής, ἀληθινός, 160, 283, 312b
אמת, rabbinic use of, 122
ἀναστήσονται, 108
ἀντί, 24
ἄνωθεν, 64
ἀπειθῶν, 79
ἀπορούμενοι, 258

βαστάζειν, 224
βόσκειν, ποιμαίνειν, 386

διὰ, use of, 9b

ἐβλήθη, 287
ἐδοξάσθη, 287
εἶδεν, 362a
ἐκ, 66, 235, 237, 363
ἐκάθισεν, 345
ἐλέγχειν, 297
ἕν, 199
ἐντετυλιγμένον, 361
ἐπιφάνεια, 322
ἐραυνᾶτε, 112

ἐρχόμενα, 299
ἐρχόμενος, 13
ἔργα, 52
ἐρωτᾶν, 277, 302
γέγονεν, ἐγένετο, 9b
γινώσκειν, 253
γλωσσόκομον, 224
γνωστὸς, 330
γράμματα, 140

κόσμος, αἰών, 234

λαλεῖν, λέγειν, 299
λόγος, 9

οἶδα, use of, 253
οἴδαμεν, 394a
οἰκοδομήθη, 57
ὁρᾶν, 300

παρακύπτειν, 360
παρουσία, 271, 322, 367
περί, ὑπὲρ, 315
φαγεῖν, 336
πιστεύειν εἰς τὸ ὄνομα, 17, 59
πιστεύειν, 240
πιστεῦσαι, 114

INDEX OF GREEK AND HEBREW WORDS IN THE NOTES

ποιεῖν, 72, 336
πράσσειν, 72
πρός, force of, 9a

קום, 108

ῥῆμα, Philo's use of, 9

σημεῖα, 52
שכן, 20
σκηνοῦν, 20
σωτηρία, 90

τηρεῖν, 225
θεός, etymology of, 90a
θεωρεῖν, ὁρᾶν, 300
θεωρεῖτε, 230

ὑπὲρ, 218

Index of Subjects in the Notes

Abbot (Dr. Ezra), 1, 1a, 277
Abbott (Dr. E. A.), 1, 1a, 6, 12a, 17, 46, 62, 64, 85, 89, 114, 150, 205, 226, 240, 287, 302, 353, 386
Achelis (Dr T.), 9, 232a
Agnosticism, 9
Alford (Dean), 9b, 24, 26b, 37, 111, 112, 123, 164a, 187, 189, 225, 248, 270, 277, 283 f., 287, 302, 307, 317, 331, 346, 351, 393
"Alogi", 1a, 9
American revision, 164a, 169
Altruism, 290b
Anderson (Sir R.), 1a, 8, 12a, 16, 22, 52, 115, 185
Andrewes (Bp.), 159a, 366
Andrews (S. J.), 247
Annas, trial before, 328
Aorist, force of, 107
Aquila, version of, 20
Arianism, 26, 199
Aristion, 379
Arnold (M.), 1a, 68, 76
Athanasian Creed, 280
Athanasius, 26b, 107, 115, 126, 366
Augustine, 14, 26b, 94, 112, 127, 154, 270, 278, 298, 300b, 330, 331, 371, 386, 393

Bacon (Prof.), 1a, 61, 161, 260, 379a, 394a
Baedeker (Dr. F. W.), 185

INDEX OF SUBJECTS IN THE NOTES

Baines (T. B.), 271
Bar Kochba, 113
Barry (Dr. W.), 1, 1a, 2
Barth (Prof.), 1a, 68, 144
Basilides, 1a, 13, 18
Bauer (B.), 205
Baur (F. C.), 1a, 8, 376
"Believe", 17, 59, 109a, 115, 133, 314a, 321 *f.*
Bellett (J. G.), 14, 127a, 316, 349, 353, 364, 370
Bengel (J. A.), 24, 32, 64, 68, 77, 101, 111, 112, 154, 216, 330, 346, 351, 392
Benn (A. W.), 9, 61, 278b, 339a
Bernard (T. D.), 7, 61, 270, 277a, 280, 312c, 317a, 336
Bernard of Clairvaux, 278b
Bernstorff (A. von), 52
Bethany, 29
Bethlehem, 151
Bethsaida, 40, 232
Bevan (Mrs.), 278b
Beyschlag (W.), 1a, 108, 133, 312
Beza, 112, 154
Birks, 356
Blass (F.), 1a, 10, 21, 26, 49, 53, 58, 101, 110a, 154, 164a, 169, 209, 334
Bleek (F.), 1a, 330
Boanerges, 1
Born of water, etc., 66
Bousset (Prof.), 1, 1a, 9, 45, 108, 113
Brethren of the Lord, 137
Bretschneider (C. G.), 1a
Browning (R.), 133
Briggs (Prof.), 1a, 53, 61, 73, 75, 96, 108
Bruce (Dr. A B.), 7
Bunsen (Chevalier), 1a
Burgon (Dean), 111, 112, 127, 317, 346
Burkitt (Prof), 127, 149, 160a, 173, 205, 210, 292a, 330, 393
Buttmann (P. C.), 353

Caiaphas, "high priest of that year", 217;
   trial before, 334, 344

Caius of Rome, 9
Calvin, 24, 26b, 87, 96, 111, 112, 154, 252, 346, 395
Campbell (R. J.), 368
Cana, 47
Carlyle (T.), 9
Carpenter (Bp. Boyd), 127
Carr (A.), 13, 21, 26, 34, 55, 88, 96, 112, 137, 150, 183, 184, 187, 215b, 220a, 237, 300, 302, 312c, 361
Carson (A.), 126, 168, 187a
Cassels (W. R.), 1a, 8, 29, 177, 205, 212a, 215
Cerinthus, 1, 1a, 9, 18
Chagigah, 336
Charles (Prof.), 278, 322
Chase (Bp.), 310a
Cheetham (Archd.), 61, 278b
"Chief priests", 153
Chiliasm, of the Evangelist, 394
Christ, as personal name, 312c;
    not detached from "Jesus" before death, 23;
    Lordship of, 276
Christadelphianism, 281
"Christian Science", 23
Chrysostom, 14, 26b, 83, 96, 111, 112, 127, 164a, 212a, 222, 298, 330, 331, 366, 394a
Church, idea of, 291b
Chwolson, 346
Clemen, 1a
Clement of Alexandria, 1a, 7, 26
"Coming into the world", 13
Coit (Dr. S.), 9, 290b
Comte (A.), 9
Corn of wheat, in recent researches, 232a
Correggio, 341
Cosmogony, Biblical, 9a
Creation, by the WORD, 9
Credner (C. A.), 1a
Creeds, 9, 277a, 280, 363a, 374
Cyril of Alexandria, 14, 26b, 93, 96, 112, 127, 159a, 164a, 270, 271, 290, 330, 334

INDEX OF SUBJECTS IN THE NOTES

D'Alma, 174
Dalman, 247
Darby (J. N.), 15, 52, 57, 61, 78, 79, 112, 183, 195, 298, 330
Darwinism, 9a
Davidson (Dr. S.), 1a
Da Vinci, Leonardo, 259
Dedication, the Feast of, 197
Deissmann (Prof.), 277
Delff (H.), 61, 330
Delitzsch (F.), 53, 232a, 336
De Wette (W. M. L.), 1a, 33, 106, 112, 271, 393
"Disciple whom Jesus loved," 1, 260, 381
Discourses, the Johannine compared with Synoptic, 61
Docetæ, 18
Dods (Dr. M.), 34, 237
Dogmas, 374
Dorner (A.), 9
Driver (Canon), 9a
Drummond (Dr. J.), 1a, 6, 9, 29, 260, 390, 393
Du Bose (Prof.), 170, 298
Duty, as substitute for God, 9

Ebion, 1
Edersheim (Dr. A.), 9, 51, 122, 176, 179
Ellicott (Bp.), 331, 346
Emanation, 293
Emeth, Jewish use of, 122
"Encyclopædia Britannica", 9a, 187a
Ephraim, city of, 220
Epiphanius, 1, 9
Erasmus, 70, 77, 112, 270, 353
Eternal life, 69, 112, 312, 312a, 374;
   connection with Kingdom, 65
Ethical Religion, 9
Eucharist, not in Chapter 6, 127
Eusebius, 1, 1a, 2, 7, 53, 82, 100, 154, 330, 346, 393
Euthymius Zigabenus, 96, 112
Evanson (E.), 1a
Ewald (H.), 1a, 6, 271, 278, 300b, 330, 345, 346, 375a, 393, 394

Faith, in relation to scripture, 115;
  relation to knowledge, 133, 314a, 321 *f.*;
  creeds, merely human, 374
Farrar (Dean), 137
Fatherhood of God, 16, 304
Ferrar MSS., 154
Field (Dr. F.), 57, 83, 96, 112, 225, 248, 272, 277
Forgiveness of sin as presented in the fourth Gospel, 185
Frazer (Prof.), 232a, 339a, 340
Froude (H.), 9, 115

Gabbatha, 345
Gardner (Prof. P.), 61
Garvie (Princ.), 27
Gellius, Aulus, 346
George the Sinner, Chronicle of, 393
Gerdtell (L. von), 52, 70, 182, 195, 204, 374
Gethsemane, allusion to agony in, 195a, 235
Gloag (Dr.), 1a, 393
Glory of Son of man dying, 126, 233
Gnosticism, 11, 18, 35, 56, 122, 167, 293, 324, 367, 383;
  in "Christian Science", 23
God, His existence everywhere assumed in Scripture, 9;
  the Truth not coextensive with, 338
Godet (F.), 1a, 6, 9, 9b, 13, 33, 37, 64, 67, 70, 77, 88, 112, 118a,
  127, 164a, 183, 187, 217b, 277a, 278, 302, 312c, 376, 379, 393
Goebel (Prof.), 1a
Goethe, 61
Gore (Bp.), 7, 9, 14, 16, 18, 52, 115, 126, 127, 133, 236, 361, 374
GOSPEL OF JOHN, authorship, 1a;
  date, 2;
  compared with Synoptists, 27, 35, 52, 53, 61, 70, 358;
  whether supplementary to them, 6;
  historical character, 7;
  comments of Evangelist, 61, 159, 374;
  alleged interpolations, 374;
  alleged Paulinism, 61, 129;
  alleged inconsistencies, 76 *f.*;
  errors met by, 374;
  the Greek of, 226;

INDEX OF SUBJECTS IN THE NOTES

real close of, 376, 385, 394
Doctrine (see main index entries):
CHRIST; Eucharist; Eternal life; Faith; GOD, GODHEAD; HOLY SPIRIT, the; Incarnation; JESUS; Knowledge; Messiah; Miracles; Religion; Resurrection; Son of man; Truth; Word; World
Gospel of Peter, the Apocryphal, 18
Govett (R.), 13, 24, 43, 46, 63, 66, 67, 88, 88a, 90a, 96, 103, 112, 123, 132, 141, 149, 151, 181, 192, 248, 271, 298, 300a, 311, 325, 356, 361
Green (S. G.), 11
Green (T. H.), 7, 14, 52, 115, 126, 374
Greg (W. R.), 185
Gregory (Prof.), 1a
Grimm (C. L. W.), 164a
Grotius, 13, 26b, 112, 208, 270, 375, 393
Grove (G.), 82

Hall (Bp.), 271
Hammond, 346
Harnack (Prof,), 1, 1a, 2, 8, 9, 16, 52, 127, 375, 380, 393, 394
Hartmann (E. von), 124
Haussleiter (Prof.), 1a
Heitmüller (W.), 6, 26, 119, 127a, 141, 185, 321, 338, 393
Hengstenberg (E. W.), 1a, 133a, 199, 269, 300b, 346, 376, 382
Heracleon, 1a
Herrmann (Prof. W.), 115
Hilgenfeld (A.), 1a, 353
Hillel, 112
Hofmann, 68, 96, 127, 271, 300b
Holtzmann (Prof. H.), 1, 1a, 2, 7, 8, 13, 19, 27, 46, 52, 53, 61, 76, 96, 119, 126, 127, 164a, 181, 184, 217, 271, 284, 295, 298, 302, 312c, 393
Holtzmann (Prof. O.), 1a, 2, 6, 9, 42, 61, 205, 302
Holy Spirit, personality of, 299
Homilies, the, second book of, 371
Homœoteleuton, 272
Hooker (R.), 199
Hort (Dr.), 26, 61
Horton (Dr. R. F.), 55, 58, 91, 127, 129, 169, 173, 195b, 198, 237, 312c

Hours, in the Fourth Gospel, 346
HyperCalvinism, 123

Ideas, Platonic doctrine of, 11
Illingworth (J. R.), 12a, 14, 61, 264, 278b, 290a
Immanence of God, 14, 278b
Incarnation, union in, 126
Inge (Prof.), 7, 9, 14, 115, 278b, 312a
Inquisition, 294
Irenæus, 1, 1a, 18, 26, 100, 126, 172, 324, 393
Irvingism, 170, 281

James (Prof.), 278b
Jerome, 100, 137
JESUS, omniscience of, 104;
    King, 43, 118a;
    "the Lord", 80a;
    full humanity emphasized, 6, 83
"Jesus Christ", 25, 312c
Jews, those specially so called in fourth Gospel, 28, 54, 56, 86, 139a, 142, 266
John the Apostle, an eye-witness, 249, 312c, 328, 333, 346;
    career of, 1;
    called "Theologos", 1a;
    alleged Paulinism of, 61;
    alleged martyrdom of, 393
John the Elder, 1a, 61, 379
John, father of Andrew and Peter, 12
Joseph, the name, 42
Joseph, a brother of the Lord, 42;
    a brother of James the Little, 42
Josephus 47, 57, 108, 175, 217, 217b, 377
Jowett (B.), 9, 299
Judas, the name, 135
Judas Iscariot, treason of, 135, 223
Judæa, whether "His own country", 96
Jülicher (Prof.), 1a, 2, 53, 61, 154, 196
Justin Martyr, 1a, 271

Kaftan (Prof.), 7, 8, 218, 278b
Keim (C. T.), 1, 1a, 205, 217, 376

INDEX OF SUBJECTS IN THE NOTES

Kennedy (Dr. B. H.), 112
Kenrick (Archbp.), 9b, 96, 112
Kephas, the name, 39
Khodadad (K. E.), 262, 336
"King of Israel", 43
Kingdom of God, 65;
    connection with Life, 65;
    "entering into", 66a
Kinnear (J. B.), 9, 137, 275, 374
Knowledge, Christ's supernatural, 80a;
    relation to Faith, 133, 314a, 321 f.
Knowling (Prof.), 232a

Lake (Prof.). 362b, 367
Lapide, Cornelius à, 112
"Last Day", the, 245
Latham (H.), 361
Law, 278b
Lazarus, raising, 205
Leonardo da Vinci, 259
Lessing (G. E.), 133
Lewis (Mrs. A. S.), 334
Liddon (Dr. H. P.), 9, 298
Life, of Christ regarded as redemptive, 192
Lightfoot (Dr. John), 92a, 127, 154, 336
Lightfoot (Bp. J. B.), 1a, 7, 9, 9b, 30, 53, 57, 116, 137, 154, 209, 277, 345, 351a, 387
Lindsay (Prof.), 9
Loisy (A.), 1a, 53, 61, 172, 260
Lotze (H.) 9, 374
Lücke (G. C. F.), 1a, 33
Luthardt (Prof.), 1a, 9, 9b, 26, 34, 53, 64, 67, 68, 70, 77, 88, 96, 112, 271, 278, 298, 300b, 331, 353, 376, 393
Luther, 13, 112, 300b, 309, 312a, 334

Maclaren (Dr. A.), 190, 212, 300b
Mahomet, claimed to be the Paraclete, 279
Maldonatus, 96
Mansel, 11, 18
McClellan, 100, 112, 137, 268
McCosh (Dr J.), 133

McGiffert (Prof.), 133, 286
McRory (Prof.), 13, 67, 112, 184, 187, 346
Manichees, 189
Manning (Card.), 112, 128
Martensen (H. L.), 302
Martineau (Dr. J.), 1a, 133, 374
Mary, 48;
    others bearing the name, 48;
    of Cleopas, 351
Mayor (Dr. Joseph B.), 137, 351
Memra, 9
Messiah, title peculiar to fourth Gospel, 37;
    Baptist's recognition of, 34 *f*.;
    disclosure of person of, 92, 198
Meyer (H. A. W.), 1a, 9, 9b, 13, 33, 37, 64, 96, 100, 106, 108, 112, 127, 192, 237, 271, 278, 287, 302, 351, 376, 393
Meyer (F. B.), 278b, 299
Mill (J. S.), 9
Milligan (W.), 6, 7, 8, 14, 34, 53, 77, 80a, 96, 100, 235, 237, 240, 310a, 317a, 336, 346, 352
Milton (J.), 193a
Ministry, length of the, 53;
    Judæan, 53;
    Peræan, 53
Miracles, in general, 52, 99, 274;
    feeding the Five Thousand, 117;
    resurrection of Lazarus, 205, 219;
    as testimony to disciples, 52, 99
Moffatt (Dr. Jas.), 81
Monod (Adolphe), 386
"Mother of Jesus", the, 48
Moule (Bp.), 7, 310a, 319a, 386, 388
Moulton (Dr. R. G.), 394a
Moulton (Dr. W. F.), 9b, 68
Mozley (Miss), 115
Muratorian fragment, 1a
Mysticism, 9, 278b

Nash (Prof.), 52
Nathanael, 41

INDEX OF SUBJECTS IN THE NOTES

Neander (A.), 1a, 100
Newman (Card.), 61, 78, 115
Newman (F. W.), 1a, 9, 61
Nicene Creed, 9
Nicodemus, 62
Nicolaitans, 18
Nonnus, 346
Norris (Archd.), 96, 100, 149, 188a, 270, 293, 351
Nouvelle (A.), 1a

Olshausen (H.), 24, 90, 106, 112, 270, 393
Omissions in fourth Gospel, 206, 235
"One hundred and fifty-three", 382
"Only-begotten", 21, 26
Oosterzee (J. van), 69
Origen, 1a, 7, 14, 17, 26, 26b, 64, 93, 95, 96, 137, 215b, 222, 351a
Orr (Prof.), 18, 218, 278b

Paley (F. A.), 26, 131a
Papias 1a, 154, 379
Passover, the last, 336
Passovers, 53
Paul, the doctrine of, 61, 129
Pearson (Bp.), 363a
Pearson (T.), 318
Pentecost, Feast of, 100
Peræa, ministry in, 53
Pfleiderer (Prof.), 1a, 6, 9, 61, 64, 113, 127, 192, 277a, 313a, 394
Pharisees, as equivalent to "Jews", 28;
 and life eternal, 108, 112
Philip the Apostle, 42
Philip of Sidé, 393
Philonism, 9, 277a
Pilate, trial before, 335
Pliny, 346
Plummer (Dr. A.), 1a, 2, 13, 61, 70, 77, 96, 106, 112, 138, 164a, 278, 302, 312c, 346
Polycrates, 330
Polycarp, 169
Porphyry, 138

Positivism, 9
Prayer Book, Jewish, 92a, 197
Present tense, use of, 106
Prideaux, 45
Prolepsis, 388
Pullan, (L.), 9
Purim, Feast of, 100, 339a
Psychology as applied to fourth Gospel, 61, 308, 310
Pusey (Dr.), 228, 371

Qoran, 18, 279
Quenstedt (Prof.), 9a
Quesnel, 92
Quilliam, 279
Quotation, manner of, 30

Ramsay (Sir W.), 346
Rashdall (Dr.), 9a
Religion, essentials of, 9
Renan (E.), 1a, 6, 7, 18, 61
Resurrection, of body, not emancipation of spirit, 215a; how treated by Evangelists, 356
Reuss (E.) 1, 6, 7, 58, 149, 237
Réville (Prof. A.), 53
Réville (Prof. J.), 1a, 2
Reynolds (Dr. H. R.), 6, 96, 164a, 205, 235, 298, 375a
Ritschl (A.), 1a, 278b
Robertson (F. W.), 7, 16, 325
Robinson (Dean), 7
Routh (Dr. M.), 1a
Ryle (Bp.), 13, 67, 71, 90, 111, 112, 162, 230, 283, 290, 346, 356, 395

Sabatier, (A.), 1a
Sabellianism, 199
Sadler (M. F.), 1a, 70, 77, 96, 127
Salmon (Dr. G.), 1a, 6, 7, 42, 61, 137, 151, 162, 217
Sanday (Prof.), 1a, 9a, 70
Schanz, 1a
Schenkel, 205
Schleiermacher, 1a

INDEX OF SUBJECTS IN THE NOTES

Schlottmann (A.), 8
Schmiedel (Prof.), 1, 1a, 2, 7, 34, 57, 74, 76, 96, 113, 119, 120a, 149, 160, 170, 171, 172, 177, 181, 205, 255, 346, 353, 393
Schofield (Dr. A. T.), 14, 171, 196, 278b, 312, 368
Scholten, 1, 1a, 108, 260
Schor (S.), 86, 102, 116, 213, 350, 360
Schürer (Prof.), 1a, 393
Scott (E. F.) 9, 11, 26a, 41, 52, 61, 66, 66a, 126, 127, 133, 149, 192, 271, 277a, 292, 312a, 313a, 322, 338, 367, 394
Scribes, 155
Scrivener (F. H.), 154
Second Coming of Christ, 271
Seeley (Sir J. R.), 8, 66, 156
Ségond (Dr. L.), 15
Seven, the number, 46
Shekina, 20
Siloam, 146, 177
Simcox, (Miss E.), 185
Simcox (W. H.), 108
Simon, the name, 38
Smith (Prof. G. A.), 29, 82, 232
Soden (Prof. the Baron von) 1a, 19, 80
Son of man, 45, 122, 367
Spencer (H.), 9
Spinoza, 205
Staerk (Dr. W.), 40, 45
Stanley (Dean), 371
Stanton (Prof.), 1a, 9, 346, 393
Stier, 88, 112, 159a, 164a, 187, 270, 271
Stevens (Prof.), 14, 61, 161, 298
Strauss (D. F.) 1a, 61, 205, 268, 376
Substitution, 325
Swedenborg, 130, 165, 199, 207, 355
Swete (Prof.), 113, 137, 356, 361
Sychar, 82

Tabernacles, Feast of, 46, 100, 227
Talmud on execution of capital punishment, 337
Targums, 9, 20
Tatian, 1a, 376

Tauler, 278b
Taylor (I.), 14, 312a, 318
Taylor (J.), 88
Temple, building of the, 57
Tense, the historical: see under "Aorist"
Teresa, 278b
Tertullian, 1, 21, 137, 375
Text, the Greek, 10, 248
Theodoret, 14, 100, 115
"Theologos", 1a
Theophilus of Antioch, 1a
Theophylact, 67, 112, 346, 394a
Theosophy, 312
Tholuck (A), 70, 77, 111, 112, 175, 271, 278, 346
Thomson (W. M.), 40, 82
Tiberias, Sea of, 377
Tischendorf, 8, 26, 37
Tolstoy (L.), 185
Torrey (Dr.), 361
Transcendence of God, 14
Transfiguration, 20
Tregelles (S. P.), 26, 37, 154, 396
Trench (Archbp.), 40, 42, 52, 232, 277, 283, 302, 386
Trinity, the Holy, 277a
Triplets, 46
Truth, God not said to be the, 26a;
Turton (Col.), 2, 9, 9a, 18, 52, 105a, 120a, 126, 205, 356, 369

Union in Incarnation, 304
Unitarianism, 173, 199, 280, 312c, 313b
Universalism of the fourth Gospel, 12a
Usher, 346

Varro, 346
Valentinus, 18
"Verily, verily", significance of, 44
Vintage, harvest and, 283
Virgin Birth, 21, 42

Walpole (Canon), 312a
Watson, 112

INDEX OF SUBJECTS IN THE NOTES

Watkins (Archd.), 9
Wellhausen (Prof.), 61, 81, 374, 380
Weiss (Prof. B.). 1, 1a, 6, 9, 10, 13 24, 26, 33, 61, 64, 68, 77, 100, 119, 127, 133, 166, 170, 181, 205, 217a, 271, 278, 295, 300b, 302, 312, 351, 376, 393, 394a
Weisse (C. H.), 1a
Weizsäcker (C.), 1a, 9, 61, 302, 353, 394a
Wendt (Prof.), 1a, 55, 58, 61, 96,130, 151, 237, 245, 271
Wentscher (Prof.), 9, 14
Wernle (Prof.), 1a, 9, 61, 75, 205, 280
West (G.), 356
Westcott (Bp.), 1a, 6, 7, 9b, 10, 13, 26, 33, 34, 37, 61, 62, 64, 67, 70, 77, 88, 96, 103, 112, 115, 127, 138, 160, 166, 181, 195a, 205, 260, 271, 277, 291b, 299, 302, 312, 312a, 312c, 335, 345, 346, 386, 393, 394a
Wetstein, 141a
Wiclif, 161, 162, 270, 478
Williams (I.), 127
Winer (G. B.), 24, 68, 149, 164a, 287
Wiseman (Card.), 128
Witness, frequent use of, 109a
Woods (F. H.), 9a
WORD, the, 9
Wordsworth (Bp. Chr.), 26b, 112, 127, 277, 317, 346
World, the, its hatred for those confessing Christ, 309; alienation from God, 291b
Wright (Dr. A.), 127

Zahn (Prof.), 1, 1a, 2, 6, 8, 9b, 13, 14, 20, 21, 24, 26, 26b, 33, 34, 37, 61, 64, 67, 68, 70, 77, 83, 88, 96, 100, 110a, 112, 164a, 166, 172, 183, 189, 208, 237, 270, 271, 278, 298, 330, 331, 334, 336, 345, 351, 365, 346, 353, 375, 376, 378, 390, 393
Zebbach, Talmudic treatise, 336
Zebedee, sons of, 378

Referenced Notes on the Gospels of Mark and Luke

The following appendices include those Notes from E. E. Whitfield's editions of William Kelly's *Exposition of the Gospel of Mark* and *Exposition of the Gospel of Luke* to which reference is made in the *Exposition of the Gospel of John*.

AN EXPOSITION OF THE GOSPEL OF JOHN

Notes on the Gospel of Mark

Notes from *An Exposition of the Gospel of Mark* by William Kelly, edited, with additions, by E. E. Whitfield referenced in *An Exposition of the Gospel of John*.

NOTES ON THE INTRODUCTION

§1.

2 The treatment of incidents in which Peter is prominent strikes all readers: that which would be honourable to the Apostle is passed over, whilst anything discreditable to him is emphasized. If this be not seen, some support might attach to the Tübingen "tendency theory." Peter's connection with this Gospel acquired, however, a legendary character, more and more as the actual circumstances receded. Papias (A.D. 125) and Irenæus (A.D. 180) having represented the Gospel as finished after the death of Peter, Clement of Alexandria (A.D. 200) spoke of it as written in his lifetime; Eusebius as with the Apostle's sanction; whilst Jerome (A.D. 420) makes out that Peter dictated it (Pfleiderer, i. 398 *f.*).

As to the extent of the circulation of Mark's Gospel in the early Church, see Burkitt, p. 260 *f.* The earliest Greek commentary upon it which is extant was that of Victor and others of Antioch (about A.D. 400); the earliest Latin that of our venerable Bede. See, further, note **168**.

§2.

3 Since the middle of the second century of our era (with the exception of a statement by Clement of Alexandria, that the two Gospels with genealogies were the first written), the Gospel of Mark has taken the *second* place, intermediate between those of Matthew and Luke, of the Gospels called "Synoptic" by Griesbach (1790). So in typical authorities such as Muratori's fragment in the West, Athanasius's list of books in the East, neither Mark nor Luke is placed first in a single document. The traditional idea, followed by Origen (third century), has been that Matthew's was the Gospel first of all written, then Mark's; and this belief was accepted by post-Reformation writers of repute, such as Grotius and Bengel. In the nineteenth century Greswell (i., p. 16) adhered to the old view, and it underlies Bernard's esteemed Bampton Lectures on "Progress of Doctrine," where (p. 143 *f.*) Matthew's close link with the Old Testament and his treatment of the Gospel preached first to "the circumcision" (Romans 15:8), have been emphasized. Archbishop Thomson, in his introduction to the first volume of the "Speaker's Commentary" (p. xxxvii. *f.*), did not depart from it. Roman Catholic opinion, represented by Hug (1808) and Schanz, maintains the precedence of Mark over Luke. That W. Kelly's conviction was the same as that of these various writers appears in his "Lectures on Matthew" (p. 376. *f.*).

From the time of Herder (1780), however, the notion arose that Mark's, the shortest and simplest of the three, was the earliest of the Gospels written. Lachmann (1835) gave formal expression to this belief (see Burkitt, p. 37). For a time, in the hands of the dominant

Tübingen school (Baur, Hilgenfeld, etc.), Matthew's priority held its ground, and as late as the year 1885 H. J. Holtzmann could describe this as a "burning question." It is still an open one, although the suffrages of most experts, including Westcott in England (p. 190), are for Mark (see below under "Synoptic Problem" {note 6}). Some of these, nevertheless, allow that passages such as Matthew 5:17, 10:6, 15:24, tell against their opinion. Certain modern writers have held that Mark was last of the three, whilst some Germans in the middle of the last century have assigned to Luke priority over both Matthew and Mark. Such was already Beza's opinion at the time of the Reformation: he could not believe that Matthew and Mark wrote before Luke, because of the third Evangelist's apparent criticism, in his Preface, of all predecessors. But it has not been generally supposed that Luke included Matthew and Mark in what he there says. Matthew, at any rate, was an "eye-witness," an "attendant on the Word" (Greswell, p. 75), whilst Mark's Gospel is in close relation to the Apostle Peter's ministry (note 2).

Dean Robinson adopts Professor Harnack's earliest date for Mark, which is A.D. 65; Professor B. Weiss's date is A.D. 67. The corresponding date for Matthew is A.D. 70 (the Epistle of Barnabas, quoting Matthew's Gospel, refers to the destruction of Jerusalem as quite recent); and for Luke, A.D. 80. Zahn's dates are, for Mark, A.D. 67; for Luke, A.D. 75; for Matthew, A.D. 85.

The chief result of assigning the earliest date of all to Mark has been that the critics' view of the development of Christian doctrine has been shaped by their interpretation of this Gospel in particular, which is regarded as exhibiting the teaching of the "historical" in distinction from the "Pauline" Christ. Mr. F. W. Newman, in his last book, "Hebrew Jesus," remarked (p. 57): "No one can reasonably doubt that the whole essence of the faith and religion of Jesus of Nazareth finds its expression in the *Lord's Prayer.*" Strange to say, the prayer is not contained in the Gospel of Mark! For reply to the same writer's remarks in "Phases of Faith," p. 173, on the Synoptists in relation to the Deity of Christ, see J. N. Darby, "Irrationalism of Infidelity," p. 287.

5 The "fragmentary" view was advocated by the celebrated Schleiermacher (1817), whose Essay on Luke was translated into English by Bishop Thirlwall (1832). But Mark's Gospel (6:14) will show us that the Evangelists, selecting their materials (*cf.* John 20:30), did not go to work with mere fragments which came to their hand haphazard. Their omissions were due to an entirely different cause from that alleged by writers who measure their knowledge of words and deeds by the limits of their respective records.

A crucial instance is that of the raising of Lazarus. Professor Burkitt writes as to this: "Where are we to put the scene into the historical framework preserved by St. Mark? Can any answer be given except *there is no room?*" (p. 222). Already had Professor Sanday, in his "Fourth Gospel" (p. 166), written: "The vague, shifting outlines of the Synoptists allow ample room for all the insertions made in them with so much precision by St. John" (*cf.* John 4:2, 3). Professor Tischendorf, in his "Synopsis Evangelica," placed the incident between the end of the ninth and beginning of the tenth chapters of Mark, and that without awakening sense of dislocation on the part of most students, including Greenleaf, the standard American writer on Evidence, who assigns the same position to it in his "Harmony." But Burkitt goes on to say that the event could not have been unknown "to a well-informed personage like *Mark,* nor could he have had any reason for suppressing a narrative at once so public and so edifying. ... Is it possible," he asks, "that anyone who reads the story of Mark can interpolate into it the tale of Lazarus and the notable sensation? ... Must not the answer be that Mark is silent about the raising of Lazarus because *he did not know of it?*" (p. 222 *f.*). Hear now W. Kelly: "Why should the resurrection of Lazarus be omitted in the first three Gospels? Man, if these accounts had been his work, would not have omitted it; he would deem the insertion of it in each Gospel necessary for a full and truthful account. ... The omission of so stupendous a miracle in Matthew, Mark, and Luke, points out clearly that it is the Spirit of God who wrought sovereignly, and writes by each with a special purpose. ... This miracle of raising Lazarus does not show us Jesus as the Messiah, or the SERVANT, or the Son of man, but as the Son of God, who gives life and raises the dead, a grand point of doctrine in John 5, and there found alone in the Gospels" ("Lectures on Matthew," p. 437 *f.*). The difference between the "sayings" of Jesus and "public events" in His life (Burkitt) is of no significance whatever from this point of view. So it is with the whole texture of the Gospels, from Matthew 1 to John 21. Various incidents are recorded by those who did not actually witness them, whilst one or other who did is silent about them. *Cf.* another quotation in note 7 from an earlier part of Professor Burkitt's book.

6 We here reach one of the two determining elements of the so-called "Synoptic Problem," which has engaged men's minds since the time of Le Clerc (1716), more particularly since the thirties of the last century. It is the conjunction of agreements and differences which makes the problem, from the merely literary point of view, so "complex and difficult," as Professor Sanday has described it in his Bampton Lectures (p. 281). Professor H. J. Holtzmann remarks that, while the idea of inspiration (see note **13**) governed scholars' minds, it was the differences which exercised them; that now they canvass the *agreements*, which the older writers ascribed to the *autor primarius*. W. Kelly, however, would explain the differences in the same way.

Archbishop Thomson refers agreements to a common source. That there was any such written one is purely hypothetical. Luke's ἄνωθεν (1:3) does not tell us, as Newman's "Phases of Faith" (p. 127) might lead unwary readers to suppose, that the third Evangelist used such (*cf.* "Irrationalism of Infidelity," reissue, p. 162 *f.*). If there be any truth at all in a story, we look for substantial agreement in the witnesses.

7 For a historical student, as for a lawyer, it is *differences* which demand the more consideration. When we have to estimate the value of any statements, as Chrysostom long ago said, the very differences may remove all suspicion of collusion on the part of the witnesses. Now, if "each of the three Gospels represents a different view of our Lord's life and teaching" (Burkitt, p. 131), the solution of differences should usually not be far to seek, even if it seem not at first entirely adequate; and this because we do as yet but "know in part."

A solution of some difficulty of this kind often proposed is that the diversity arises from difference in *translation* from the Aramaic speech of Christ or of those reporting Him (so Eichhorn: see Schmiedel, col. 1850). There is, says Salmon, the tendency of different translators of a common document to vary in both words and constructions (p. 105 *f.*). The reference there is to Mark 12:38, compared with Luke 20:46. At verse 40 of Mark (as verse 47 of Luke) we have "prayers," but in Matthew 23:5 "phylacteries": the word *"tephillin"* means both.

The following simple cases may be taken in further illustration:

1. Reporting the Parable of the Sower, Mark 4:15 has "Satan," Matthew 13:19 the "wicked one," Luke 8:12 "the devil."

2. In the account of the Transfiguration, Mark 9:5 has "Rabbi," Matthew 17:4 "Lord," Luke 9:33 "Master" (as to which last, see Burkitt, p. 113 *f.*). It is easy to see that for these a mere difference of translation may arise.

3. The superscription on the cross, written in three languages. Mark's narrative (Mark 15:26), probably read in particular by Roman Christians, would follow the Latin form, the most concise.

4. The parallels to Mark 12:15 in Matthew 22:18 and Luke 20:23 used by Westcott are very interesting, because they exhibit a difference of both verbs and nouns throughout.

But the difference may be one of enlargement or contraction, as in the report of Peter's great confession. Mark 8:29 has simply "the Christ," but Luke 9:20, "the Christ of God," whilst Matthew 16:16 gives "the Christ, the Son of the living God." Here is a case in which Mr. Kelly's difference of "Divine design," of which the respective writers were instruments, alone will help us. Reference may be made to his "Lectures on the Gospels," and to those specially on Matthew, in a separate volume.

12 On the "supplemental" view, see Westcott, p. 183 *f*. The history of the whole problem, of which this is the last phase discriminated by W. Kelly in the text, would be found lucidly given in H. J. Holtzmann's "Introduction." The Fathers and traditional theology held that Matthew's Gospel was intended to prove the Lord's Messianic claims; that Mark made use of Matthew, according to Augustine, whom Erasmus followed, as an epitomizer; but Koppe, in 1782, rightly denied that such was the case. The Roman Catholic scholar Hug held that Mark gave a chronological arrangement to the materials that he found in Matthew's record; and that Luke, besides using his predecessors' work, as assumed by Augustine in his "De consensu Evangelistarum," i. 2, 4, where "co-operation" is spoken of (said by Schanz, p. 25 *ff.*, to have continued to be the prevalent idea), availed himself of further sources. From the extracts used by Greswell (p. 55 *f.*) it would seem that Luke was actually acquainted with Matthew's Gospel as well as Mark's. In the third Evangelist's account of the institution of the Lord's Supper some find combination of Matthew and Mark's records with Paul's (1 Corinthians 11:23-25).

Biblical writers do seem to have made use of each other's work: (1) in the Old Testament, for example, Jeremiah of Deuteronomy, Micah of Isaiah, or *vice versa*; (2) in the New Testament, where the First Epistle of Peter is cognate with the Roman and Ephesian Epistles of Paul, Second Peter with Jude. Paul is supposed by W. Kelly, in his exposition of 1 Timothy (5:18), to have used Luke's Gospel (10:7). Zahn connects Mark 10:9 with 1 Corinthians 7:10. As to this use by one writer of another, see "Irrationalism of Infidelity," p. 165.

13 The INSPIRATION of the Bible is a topic which, unhappily, at the present day awakens dissension amongst Christians. The older view is represented by such writers as Bishop Wordsworth of Lincoln. Archdeacon Lee of Dublin, and Dean Burgon; that now prevalent, by the British and American Higher Critics and their adherents of the "modern" pulpit.

The slur which imputation of "Bibliolatry" carries with it no more attaches to those cherishing the same conviction as that of W. Kelly than to all Christians worthy of the name who venerate the Bible as an altogether unique sacred Book. The superstitious respect in which a *volume* of the Bible is held by the Russians is something quite different from the allegiance of such as the lecturer, for whom there is no exchange of the thraldom of "historical Christianity," as it is called, for bondage to the *letter* of Scripture, so often alleged against the English Reformers. Those who emphasize the guidance of the Spirit are not prone to make that mistake.

Gardner is right in saying, "All compromises are unavailing; we must have either verbal inspiration or scientific criticism, with its results, whatever they may be" ("Exploratio Evangelica," p. 469). It will be seen that the present book unreservedly accepts this issue.

A bogey has been made of plenary (verbal) inspiration by reason of ill-advised statements of extremists (see Ladd, vol. ii., pp. 182, 206 *f.*, 218). To contend for the inerrancy of Hebrew vowel-points and accents (ii. 177), which tyros in that language at the present day know were invented only after the Canon of Scripture was closed, and to set up other like indefensible positions, have brought discredit on the phrase, from which there is difficulty in emancipating it. The "mechanical" view, so called, that God "took possession of every faculty, suspending and superseding it" (Thomson, "Introduction," p. lv.), is negatived by 1 Corinthians 7:40, 2 Corinthians 11:17. As the Archbishop rightly says, "the sacred writers were not machines. ... If his mind was logical, he reasoned as Paul did; if emotional, he wrote as John wrote." That theory carried with it the idea of *dictation*, which was a mistake: it is, to begin with, inconsistent with reminiscence (John 14:26). As to style: "If God has expressly formed the instrument, He can use *it* for the purpose for which He has formed it. That is *style*" ("Irrationalism of Infidelity," p. 147). Of course, the Holy Spirit has no special language of His own: He did but use the particular writer's language, which none the less bears the impress of the Spirit. One may take 1 Corinthians 15:2 in R.V.: "in what *words* I preached it unto you." A spiritualist will tell you that a "medium" gives him the spirit's *words*. Why not, then, God His own in the Bible? To say, as do advocates of the "illumination" theory (as to which see Farrar, "The Bible," etc., p. 111), that inspiration extends only to doctrine, not at all to the language of Scripture, traverses 1 Corinthians 2:13. The word $\lambda\alpha\lambda\varepsilon\tilde{\iota}\nu$ used there is not applied by Biblical writers exclusively to oral speech (see Romans 7:1, Hebrews 4:8, 2 Peter 3:16, comparing Acts 28:25). Reference may here be made to the note {140} below on Mark 14:9, in respect of which Wellhausen has tripped. Few will question the supernatural value of the Lord's own words on earth, and the claim they make upon His disciples. As a Synoptic passage we may take Mark 8:38, and compare 1 Timothy 4:6, 6:3, where probably the Apostle speaks of his own utterances or communications as "words of our Lord Jesus Christ." That there is a difference between "the word" and "words" appears from John 8:43 (*cf.* Davidson, article

"Prophecy" in "Hastings' Dictionary" and note **69**). That inspiration attaches to the ῥῆμα as used in Acts 28:25, where "one" such extends to verse 28, is beyond dispute. Dr. Clifford (p. 88) objects to the American sceptic Ingersoll's remark: "It will not do to say that it (the Bible) is not verbally inspired. If the words are not inspired, what is?" The infidel was perfectly right. It is not those who defend "plenary" inspiration that need any commiseration, but certainly those that deny it. Instead of such concessions conciliating infidelity, they do but encourage it, as the present writer found when concerned with intelligent workmen at Chatham, whose hostility to conventional religion has not been removed, but rather strengthened, by certain summer courses of cathedral sermons in the neighbourhood.

Ancient opinion as to inspiration may be seen in Westcott ("Introduction" Appendix B). Justin Martyr, Tertullian, and Origen certainly went further than moderns; Basil, Chrysostom and Jerome allow for individuality.

After Luther had already expressed his opinion against the idea (Dorner, "History of Protestant Theology," i., 254), a decree of the Council of Trent declared for dictation, somewhat to the embarrassment of the recent Papal Commission. As to the present Catholic position, see Schanz, "A Christian Apology," ch. xiii. Calvin was of much the same mind as the German reformer (Dorner, i., p. 390). Calov and Quenstedt, of the Wittenberg school, in the following century held the most extreme view of "mechanical" inspiration (ii. 128, 131, 136). With them agreed the divines who drew up the Helvetic Confession (1675).

As far as writers like W. Kelly are to be classified, it will be with those whose sympathies go with the "dynamic" view, of "the immediate and indefeasible guidance of the Holy Spirit"; but the miserable idea of mistakes on the part of the Biblical writers is for such entirely excluded. Schaff's moderate statement is to be commended: "We cannot say that the thoughts only are Divine, while the words are altogether human. Both thoughts and words, contents and form, are Divine and human as well." It is the same, he says, as with the Person of Christ.

Leading British theologians, for the most part, now are influenced by the views of Coleridge, which underlie the "general" view (see Farrar, p. 112) represented by Dean Alford, and fostered in the academic teaching of the Old English Universities, as well as Nonconformist theological colleges. It recognises "the action of the Holy Spirit on the heart of the writers, *not distinct* from the analogous influence on all Christian men." But this is to confound *positive* inspiration with a strain of high fervour. Nobody could wisely deny a Divine "afflatus" to Christian hymns which impress the spiritual nature of people of different nations in somewhat the same way as Scripture does: such is the hymn by Bernard of Clairvaux, put into English verse by Josiah Conder, which begins, "Thou art the everlasting Word." Hymns and spiritual songs of that high quality go into every hymn-book. Some writers, from the names used by the Apostle appearing in the titles of the LXX, have supposed that the "hymns and spiritual songs" Paul mentions in his Ephesian and Colossian letters were the Old Testament Psalter alone. But with this view W. Kelly could not agree (see his "Reply to Rees").

The school of opinion on inspiration last discriminated in Farrar's book attaches "no attribute of infallibility to

Bible phrases and references." As this position is very much the one taken by Martineau and Emerson, it is manifest that with it "Higher Criticism" acquires wide scope, and few safeguards remain. "Calling it inspiration," wrote W. Kelly, "only adds to the delusion" ("An Exposition of the Gospel of John," p. 570). Doubtless the Spirit is, as A. B. Bruce said, "the only true guardian of orthodoxy" ("Kingdom of God," p. 336); but, at the same time, you have leading Higher Critics claiming that the movement engineered by themselves is a "breathing of the Spirit." It rather behoves the "spiritual" to acknowledge than to criticize Scripture (1 Corinthians 14:3; cf. John 7:17, and Psalm 112:4).

Professor Sanday ("Oracles of God," p. 36) says: "There is a grave question whether its history is altogether infallible," although Dr. Clifford writes: "Historians were seers, and went down below the surface of things." Réville (i. 257) alleges misreporting and misrepresentation of the Lord's sayings by the Evangelists; and so Dr. Horton in "Revelation and the Bible" (p. 233 f.): "Historical criticism may challenge the accuracy of the Evangelists." He himself has assailed that of John ("The Teaching of Jesus"). How any responsible writers can, in the face of Luke 1:4, state that the Biblical writers do not claim accuracy is an enigma. Thus Wright ventures to say that "the Scriptures themselves protest against the traditional view of the Gospels that they are absolutely true," and his Scripture reference is none other than 1 Corinthians 13:9f., which does but speak of what is true as far as it goes—i.e., covers nothing in any way false; it concerns what as yet remains unrevealed. Moreover, such use of Paul's words is surely perilous in the light of Mark 13:32. In the same strain as Dr. A. Wright, Dean Robinson speaks of "an inspiration which does not carry with it the entire accuracy of every detail of historical narrative" ("Thoughts on Inspiration," p. 10).

The unity of the Scripture is manifestly impaired by the very prevalent error that the historical element is purely human. What is one to think of the use made by some of James 3:2 as evidence of a disclaimer by Biblical writers of infallibility? How, in the name of such British common sense as exists outside of a modern minister's study, can one conceive that the readers of that epistle (in accordance with a favourite canon of interpretation) understood the Apostle's words in that fashion? For them, as for Luther, his letter would only have been one of "straw."

Associated, strangely enough, with misrepresentation by the Evangelists of the Lord's teaching is the alluring cry of "back to Christ" (the *new*, Ritschlian, theology). Wellhausen tells you that such a thing is impossible; that the "historical *Christ*" (*cf.* note 3 at end) is so much overlaid by "historical *Christianity*" as to be "played out." Amidst all this wreck, let writer and reader hold fast 1 John 4:6. What *can* we know of Christ save as instructed by His commissioned first followers?

Much depends on the use which we make of the Bible for the particular view we take of inspiration. If the word be our daily food, that view will be high; if it is only "studied," a very low view will satisfy. As far as there is any fault, it must be in ourselves. Principal Fairbairn has well said, "Unless God be heard in the soul, He will not be found in the word" ("Christ in Modern Thought," p. 499).

A profound student of Holy Scripture has written: "We are only sure of the truth when we retain the very language of God which contains it" (Darby, "Synopsis of the Books of the Bible," on 2 Timothy 1:13). It was from sharing this conviction that men like Tregelles and Burgon, widely divided in their views of textual criticism, went to work in the same spirit, the former wearing himself out with lifelong devotion to an attempt to arrive at an approximately pure text of the New Testament. Such pains taken by anyone with lower views of inspiration than his it is difficult to appreciate.

As to "the word of God" being "contained in Scripture," see note {**69**} on 7:13. Reference may further be made to Sir R. Anderson's trenchant remarks on the whole subject of the present note in his "Bible and Modern Criticism," pp. 83, 177-184.

NOTES ON THE FIRST CHAPTER

17 Mark 1:1. — "Gospel of Jesus Christ, the Son of God." Some, as Meyer and Wellhausen, treat this as a title, corresponding to that in the beginning of Matthew, which view H. J. Holtzmann discredits because of the "according as." "Gospel" here is not used in the literary sense of "book," a meaning which it did not bear until well into the second century, when Justin Martyr, writing about the year 150, speaks of the Gospels as "Memoirs" (ἀπομνημονεύματα). Some writers—the Germans, misled by Luther's version (kept up in the joint critical translation of 1899)—take Mark's words to mean "Gospel *concerning* Jesus Christ." Zahn, however, sees that the real force is "beginning of the Gospel" as ministered, good news brought, by Him. *Cf.* Acts 1:1, Hebrews 2:3, Revelation 19:10 ("testimony of Jesus Christ"). It is a portraiture of His service, a model for His workmen (*cf.* 1 Peter 2:20 *ff.* with 8:35, 10:29 here). Zahn well says that for doctrine about Him the Biblical manner of expression would show περί, as in Acts 28:31,

Romans 1:3. See also Hosea 1:2, referring likewise to W. Kelly's "Exposition of the Epistles to Timothy," p. 4.

18 Mark 1:2. — With regard to the quotation, Klostermann points out that "prepare the way" in Malachi is, in fact, characteristic of the latter part of Isaiah, and that the absence of "and" is significant—that Mark meant a single prediction (p. 176). Large use of "and" (parataxis) is certainly peculiar to this Gospel, for which, besides the opening chapter (*passim*), see in particular 3:13-16 and 10:32.

Lee (p. 339), after Hengstenberg ("Christology of the Old Testament," iii., p. 608), supposes that Malachi used Isaiah—that is, not to have given an independent prediction (*cf.* note **12** above).

"Thy [for My] way." J. Weiss (p. 197 *f.*) remarks that "the Christology of Mark is related to that of John more closely than is generally supposed." As to this, reference may be made to verses 41 and 44 of Mark's opening chapter, 2:10 (see note {**30**} there), 3:15, 6:7, and to note **3** above. The "priority" of Mark lends no assistance to the theories of writers like Martineau about growth of "mythological attributes of the person of Jesus" ("The Seat of Authority in Religion," ii. 360).

18a In ἐβάπτισα we have a good instance of the flexibility of the later aorist, scarcely differing here from the present. It is not a mere Hebraism.

20 Mark 1:13, 14. — Between these two verses a position may very well be found for the early Judean ministry of the Lord recorded by the fourth Evangelist. Greswell supposes that it lasted six months at least (p. 19). *Cf.* John 3:24, John 4:1{-}3, and Acts 10:37, with Mark 3:7, 8. In Luke 4:44 there is a striking variant reading—"the synagogues of *Judea*"—which finds place in the text of the "Workers' New Testament" and in the margin of the R.V.

22 Mark 1:21. — Capernaum (*cf.* Matthew 9:1, "His own city"). Trench quotes Chrysostom ("Homily on Matthew"): "Bethlehem bare Him, Nazareth nurtured Him, Capernaum had Him continuously as inhabitant."

23 Mark 1:22. — For the scribes, see the article "Scribes" in the American "Jewish Encyclopædia," vol. xi. A stupendous fact of the Lord's life on earth is that He had no education commonly so called, although Josephus ("Contra Apion," ii. 25) tells us that "Moses gave commandment to instruct children in the elements of knowledge (γράμματα)." Graetz ("History of the Jews," ii. 148) quotes from the Talmud that "a fatherless child was not brought to be taught" in any synagogue school. Indeed, "there is no evidence," writes Fairbairn, "that in the time of Jesus any schools existed in Nazareth. The wonder both at Nazareth (Mark 6:2) and Jerusalem (John 7:15) how He knew His letters proves that He had not been educated in any school" ("Studies in the Life of Christ," p 52; *cf.* his "City of God," p. 226). The Lord spoke the Aramaic dialect of a Galilean peasant, but Fairbairn goes probably too far in saying that He did not know Greek ("Manchester Lectures on the Miracles of Christ," p. 17). If so, how did He communicate with the Greek woman of {Mark} 7:26? Sepphoris, a Greek city, was within five miles of Nazareth, and Greek was spoken throughout that region. Even so, His would be only colloquial Greek, like that which we meet with in the Gospel of Mark. See, further, note **56**.

H. J. Holtzmann ("New Testament Theology," p. 129 *f.*) speaks of the importance of students of the Gospels being acquainted with the vernacular of JESUS. *Cf.* Burkitt, p. 5 *f.*, where reference is made to Wellhausen's application of such knowledge to the interpretation of the Gospel records, the Cambridge Professor stating that things imperfectly understood by students knowing only Hellenistic Greek are "immediately clear" to those so further equipped. As far as the German Professor's "Commentary on Mark" is concerned, we are not struck with the result as profitable. His treatment of "Son of man" is based on a view of the Aramaic background which Dalman, the leading expert in this branch, rejects (see note {**30**} on 2:10). Is it helpful to anyone to be told by Wellhausen (on 1:4) that the Aramaic equivalent of a Greek passive is an active intransitive (reflexive), illustrated in baptism by "the one baptized" of the classical language being equivalent to "the one dipping (himself)" in the vernacular of Christ? Leaving eccentricities or tricks of language alone, we may recall a solemn question of the Lord at Jerusalem, and His own answer (John 8:43): "Why do ye not know My speech ($\lambda\alpha\lambda\iota\alpha\nu$)? Because ye cannot hear My word ($\lambda\acute{o}\gamma o\nu$)."

As to the scribes (Sir A. F. Hort, "Divinity Professors"), reference may be made to Edersheim, "Life of Jesus the Messiah," if not to Schürer, "History of the Jewish People in the Time of Jesus Christ," § 25. As to Christian "theology," see note **35**.

27 Mark 1:43, 44. — Harnack ("What is Christianity?") uses this passage in support of his idea that the Lord "did not assign that critical importance to His miraculous deeds which even the Evangelist Mark attributed to them." On the miraculous, see note **58**.

"Say nothing to anyone": lest the priests, hearing of it by anticipation, should discredit the hand of JESUS in it (J. Wesley).

NOTES ON THE SECOND CHAPTER

29 Mark 2:7. — *Blasphemy* is one of the New Testament Greek words which acquired an extension of meaning among the Jews beyond that which they had in the classics. There it meant simply "speaking against" a person, a "blasphemy" thus being the opposite of a "euphemism" (Trench, "Miracles," p. 219). *Cf.* its use in 14:64 of this Gospel, and for the thought *cf.* Philippians 2:6. Bengel has a good note in his "Gnomon" at Matthew 9:3. Another such word is αἰώνιος, used in 3:29 here, where the "Workers' New Testament" renders "age-abiding." Such words illustrate Psalm 12:6: "The words of Jehovah are pure words, silver tried in the furnace of earth, purified seven times."

30 Mark 2:10. — Here we meet, for the first time in Mark, with the title *Son of man,* used characteristically by the Lord of Himself. The lecturer sets forth at the end of this chapter (verse 27 f., *cf.* the note {35} there) what is undoubtedly its true significance. But the phrase exercises "divines" still, as of old the "scribes" (John 12:34). H. J. Holtzmann says that the meaning intended is "one of the most intricate questions in New Testament theology" ("Introduction," i., p. 246); and the article "Son of Man" in Hastings (vol. iv.) certainly shows the perplexity prominent contemporary writers feel in dealing with it (p. 586). How could anyone really be satisfied with such enlightenment as this article affords? It is, however, like *exposés* of "modern thought," which Mrs. Humphry Ward deems instruments of a "liberal education." A summary of the points at issue may be useful:

1. Whether "Son of man" does or does not bear a Messianic meaning. Bousset (chapter x.) avers that the majority of scholars regard it as a true Messianic title. Harnack, on the affirmative side, agrees not only with H. J. Holtzmann, but with B. Weiss, whom Stalker (Lect. ii.) and Stevens follow. They are influenced by such passages as Mark 14:61 *f.*, John 3:13, and 1 Corinthians 15:45, 47—some, accordingly, seeing a reference in it to Christ's heavenly origin (so also Dalman). The negative side is taken by Westcott ("Commentary on John's Gospel") and Wendt ("The Teaching of Jesus"). Neander limited himself to saying, "It is certain that this name was not amongst the more usual or best-known names of Messiah" (p. 98).

2. As to the meaning which "Son of man" bears in the Old Testament. The passages discussed are Job 25:6, Psalms 8:5 and 80:17, Ezekiel 2:1, etc., Daniel 7:13. Job 25:6 and Psalm 8, as well as the passages of Ezekiel, are supposed to describe inferiority. A. B. Bruce on Matthew 9:6 would connect the parallel passage here with those of the Ezekiel type ("humiliation"). Daniel 7:13, it is generally agreed, stands for superiority. However this may be, H. J. Holtzmann, Dalman, Schmiedel, etc., trace the New Testament use of the title to Daniel; not so Westcott, etc.

3. The relation of the Evangelists' "Son of man" to that in the apocryphal book of Enoch ("Similitudes," chapters xxxvii.-lxxi.) is discussed. This book was for long known only in Ethiopic, but for the last twenty years the first thirty chapters of it have been available in Greek. Deane, in his "Epigrapha," has dealt with so much as concerns the present topic (pp. 49-95; see in particular pp. 62, 89 *f.*). Amongst others, Réville (i. 192 note) is of opinion that the picture of the "Son of man" in this book

"differs entirely from that common to the four Gospels." Stanton and Drummond agree in considering the book post-Christian.

4. With regard to the meaning being *(a)* "mankind," or *(b)* simply a "human being." Grotius took it in the first sense; later writers, as Neander (p. 99), Westcott, Stanton ("Jewish and Christian Messiah," part ii., chapter ii.), and Farrar, understand by it the "Ideal of Humanity," and practically a new title, although Psalm 8:4 and Psalm 80:17 might seem, from the parallelism in each, to countenance that sense already in the Old Testament. H. J. Holtzmann ("Introduction," p. 39 *f.*; "New Testament Theology," i., p. 255), Pfleiderer (i. 341, referring to Matthew 9:8), Wright, Wellhausen ("Jewish and Hebrew History," p. 346), hold that the use of *Bar Enosh* in Aramaic determines "human being" as the sense, on the ground that B-E is the only equivalent in that language for "man." This view naturally suits such as Martineau ("Seat of Authority in Religion," p. 335 *f.*). Holtzmann's view, however, Dalman, the leading expert, describes as "a grievous error," "a mare's nest," because in Biblical Aramaic *Enosh* alone, not B-E, stands for "man," and with him Schmiedel and some others agree.

Theology—call it "systematic" or "scientific"—is certainly not at its best in such uninspiring treatment of this title, after which it is refreshing to find Fairbairn writing that "Son of man" is "no man's son"; that He "has no fellow"; that Christ is "*the* Son of man"; and, further, "As Son of God, Christ interprets God to man; as Son of man, He interprets man to God" ("Christ in Modern Theology," p. 364).

Following up the lecturer's remarks, which introduce the reader to a very different atmosphere from that of conventional scholarship, we may develop these by reference to the "Synopsis of the Books of the Bible," by Mr. J. N. Darby. The second psalm, he explains, in the light of Acts 4:25 *ff.*, as exhibiting to us the Son of God, rejected in His character of Messiah; the eighth as setting Him forth "the Son of man," with a higher glory (*cf.* John 1:49 *ff.*, 12:23, 34). In Mark 9 (see also notes {**93**} on that chapter) Peter, having confessed Jesus as *Messiah,* the Lord thereupon *drops* that title for the time being, to introduce His sufferings as *Son of man.* In Ezekiel the title "suited the testimony of a God who spoke outside of His people." "It is Christ's own title, looked at as rejected and outside of Israel. He would not, thus rejected, allow His disciples to announce Him as the Christ, for the Son of man was to suffer" (ii., p. 370 *f.*). "He could not be rejected as Christ without His having a more glorious place destined to Him" (*ibid.,* p. 78). On Daniel 7 the same writer remarks: "It is not now the Messiah, owned as King in Zion, but ONE in the form of the Son of man, a title of far greater and more wide significance. It is the change from Psalm 2 to Psalm 8 brought about by the rejection of the Messiah" (p. 437).

In his "Lectures on Matthew" W. Kelly has remarked, with reference to the use of this title in Acts 7:52-56, that when the Lord "was refused as Messiah, Stephen, finding that the testimony was rejected, is led of God to testify of Jesus as the exalted Son of man at God's right hand" (p. 352).

Attempts are made to divorce the Synoptic from the Johannine treatment of the Lord's ministry in general; but a comparison of Mark 14:64 with John 10:36 would show what a link this title forms between the three first and the fourth Gospels. *Cf.* Schanz, "A Christian

Apology," ii., p. 521. Thus in John 6:27 we are told that in His baptism (Mark 1:10 *f.* and parr.) the Lord was "sealed" as Son of man. Moreover, not only in John's, but in all the other narratives the distinction between the titles "Christ" and "Son of man" is maintained. This is especially noticeable in Luke 9:26 (*cf.* Matthew 10:23), but we meet with it also in Mark 9:31 *f.* See also 13:34, and compare Westcott's note on p. 34 of his "Commentary on John."

In all four Gospels the sufferings of the Son of man as well as His exaltation, are spoken of; His being future Judge (John 5:22) is but one form of the latter.

Outside the Gospels, besides Acts 7:52 *ff.*, already mentioned, reference may be made to 1 Corinthians 15, Ephesians 1, and Hebrews 2, and, of course, to Revelation 1:13 and 14:14. On Matthew 9:6, Bengel connects "on earth" with "Son of man" (as here). *Cf.* John 3:13. Neander also accepts the idea of the connection with heaven in the title itself. The Lord, he says, indicated thereby "His elevation above all other men, the Son of God in the Son of man" (p. 100).

See, further, notes {**35** and **155**} on verses 27, 28, and 14:64; also note {**81**} on 8:27 *ff.* as to the claim of JESUS to be Christ, which, as so much else at the present day, has been wantonly questioned.

35 Mark 2:27, 28. — The questions raised in respect of the designation "Son of man" have been already discussed in note **30** (on verse 10), in anticipation of the lecturer's remarks at this place. Grotius would apply the rules of formal logic to the "man" of the first of these two verses, followed by the "Son of man" of the other (*cf.* note **29** above); and so H. J. Holtzmann *(ad loc.)*. Bousset likewise finds it "obvious" that Son of man here means "man in general" (p. 185). But much that is "obvious" to any not going beyond the surface of a passage is illusion. The application of logic, which we have to correct in life by our experience, has been baneful in "theology": see as to this Professor Julius Kaftan's standard book on "The Truth of the Christian Religion" (1894), or his recent pamphlet "Jesus and Paulus," especially at pp. 33, 36. All know how forcibly this consideration applies to Calvin's system of doctrine. It is curious that learned men should be anxious to foist conventional logic into the interpretation of such a homely narrative as Mark's is throughout. The reader may look for like treatment by "advanced" writers at 10:18, 12:37, where see notes {**107** and **124**}.

It may be desirable here to note the characteristics of theology, or reasoned development of Biblical doctrine, which it has been since the time of Origen. One whose writings are not sufficiently known shall speak. "When a man's mind apprehends the truth, and he seeks to give it a form, he does it according to the capacity of man, which is not its source; the truth as he expresses it, even were it pure, is separated in him from its source and its totality; but, besides this, the shape that a man gives it always bears the stamp of the man's weakness. He has only apprehended it partially, and he only produces a part of it. Accordingly, it is no longer *the* truth. Moreover, when he separates it from the whole circle of truth in which God has placed it, he must necessarily clothe it in a new form, in a garment which proceeds from man: at once error mixes with it. Thus it is no longer a vital part of the whole: it is partial, and thereby not *the* truth; and it is, in fact, mixed with error. That is *theology*" (J. N. Darby, Synopsis," vol. v., on 2 Timothy).

NOTES ON THE THIRD CHAPTER

39 Mark 3:13. — "*The* mountain." Wernle ("Sources of the Life of Jesus," p. 58) here indulges in miserable criticism of the use of the definite article; as if Mark, from vague acquaintance with the land, thought that there was only one mountain in the district. The definite article in the colloquial style is used to mark mountainous country, highlands. It is the same in more or less classical Hebrew, as at Genesis 12:8, 14:10, Deuteronomy 1:24 ("ins Gebirge" in German, Kautzsch's "Textbibel," 1899, for which French has a like fitting expression, "à la montagne"). So at {Mark} 6:46, Matthew 5:1, etc.

It is at this point that "the Sermon on the Mount" fits in with Mark's narrative. See, further, last verse of the chapter and note **43**.

43 Mark 3:35. — Adeney (p. 46) notes the obvious implication that the Lord did not, "could not, regard other people in the same light" as the responsive hearers spoken of in this passage. For the "will of God," see the Sermon on the Mount (Matthew 5-7).

NOTES ON THE FOURTH CHAPTER

45 Mark 4:10-12. — Compare Matthew 13:10-17, where the Divine motive behind the Lord's words is made quite clear. The "remnant" is discriminated from the nation at large, whose wilful repudiation of Him as the Messiah, as represented by its leaders, brings upon the mass ("the many" of Daniel 9:27, Mark's "those without," Luke's "the others") that judicial sentence of blindness which Isaiah (chapter 6) proclaimed, but modern critics, such as Schmiedel (col. 1866) and Bousset (p. 42), are slow to apprehend. A diatribe of one of these is against the "preposterous dogmatic pedantry of a later age." Jülicher pronounces the words reported by Mark as "impossible in the mouth of Jesus." Compare with such infatuated views Neander's remarks: "There is here expressed a moral necessity that those destitute of the right will (on which all depends, and without which the Divine *drawing* is in vain) could understand nothing of the things of the Lord which they saw and heard. So long as they remained as they were, *the whole life of Christ*, according to the same general law, remained to them an inexplicable parable" (p. 107 *f.*). *Cf.* the judicious remarks of Burkitt (p. 88) on the subject. Menzies refers to Romans 11:8, comparing Mark 3:5. Salmond cites Matthew Henry: "A shell that keeps good fruit *for* the diligent, but keeps it *from* the slothful." — J. Wesley: *(a) would* not, *(b) could* not.

In verse 12 Mark for "that" has ἵνα, for which Matthew has ὅτι. Bengel, nevertheless, would take ἵνα also as consecutive ("so that"), referring to Genesis 22:14 in the LXX. {The quotation here is from the LXX of Isaiah 6:9-10} (*cf.* Luckock, *ad loc.*, the "more merciful rendering"), according to which the people must be supposed to make their own heart fat. See also Sadler's note on Matthew's parallel. Gould thinks that "it is only ironically that God commands the prophet to harden the people by his pungent preaching." Plumptre had already written: "The acceptance of a foreseen result was in Hebrew forms of thought expressed as the working out of an intention" (*cf.* John 3:19). At the passage in Matthew he refers to John 12:40 and Acts 28:26. With this view agrees what Schanz says on the subject.

NOTES ON THE FIFTH CHAPTER

49 Deliverance from the world, writes Professor Kaftan, is the keynote of Paul's doctrine of Redemption ("Jesus and Paulus," pp. 50-54), a thought that seems being echoed in these days within the State Church of Prussia.

Amelioration of the world, whether of its moral state or of the material interests of mankind, which goes under the name of "Humanitarianism," and is, according to Cotter Morison and his school, to provide "the religion of the future," is a poor copy of what Christianity left to itself would effect. It is not, of course, to be denied that φιλανθρωπία was known to the pre-Christian moralists; it belongs to the vocabulary of Xenophon and Plato (*cf.* Acts 28:2). But, to his credit, Professor Percy Gardner in his book (p. 187) has questioned whether humanitarians from mere "love for man" accomplish what Christ did for man from love of God. See Titus 3:4, and *cf.* Acts 10:38, besides, for the Old Testament, Micah 6:8.

54 Mark 5:36. — *Cf.* Luke 8:50. "Only believe" carries faith in Himself, whose power (Mark 9:23) is ever involved in any question concerning it, and yet is but one element of it (*cf.* 8:4 {and notes **58, 82, 92a** on 6:5-6, 8:29 and 9:24}). But His Person as such is not so much in the forefront in Mark's as it is in Luke's Gospel. In Mark 9:42 the words εἰς ἐμέ are rejected by the editors, although well attested—by ABC^{corr} and later uncials, with 1, 69, Jerome's Vulgate, Syrr., as against ℵC^{pm}, D and Δ. See, further, note {**58**} on verses 5 and 6 of the next chapter, and *cf.* Sir R. Anderson's reply to Harnack's "What is Christianity?" in "Christianized Rationalism" (*Twentieth-Century Papers,* 1903).

NOTES ON THE SIXTH CHAPTER

56 Mark 6:2. — Some remarks have already been made in note **23** upon the "education" (speaking κατὰ ἄνθρωπον) of our blessed Lord. It is quite needless to consider whether He in youth ever entered the portals of such an academy as in the Talmud is called a *yesheybah* (ישיבה), for the accuracy of the Jews in the taunt recorded in the passage of John cited in the earlier note may remain unquestioned. His "new doctrine" (Mark 1:27) was His *prophetic* word, as to which *cf.* Amos 7:14 *f.* It was creative, not created (Schlottmann, § 144; *cf.* John 7:46). Wernle, in "Beginnings of Christianity," vol. i., p. 36, describing the Lord as "Layman," says that He "redeemed His listeners from the theologians" (p. 99). May we not add that such redemption is to be had in our day from the critics likewise? As Sir R. Anderson has said in a recent book, we do not propose to exchange thraldom to the one set of men for bondage to the other. Wernle's book has been translated by one cleric and edited by another. "All laymen," we are told by him, "accept the most obvious contradictions, and *do not strive after any inner harmony*" (p. 379). Surely those who live in the proverbial glass house might withhold their stones. "Laymen" are not so idiotic (see Greek of 1 Corinthians 14:23). Wernle's countryman Weizsäcker ("Textbibel") has rendered ἰδιῶται by *Uneingeweihte*, "uninitiated" (shall we say in "mysteries"?). *Cf.* 2:14 there. The writer of that Epistle co-ordinates them with ἄπιστοι, *Ungläubige*, "unbelievers." Lawyers, describing critics as "laymen," will tell these that they are miserable judges of *evidence* in statements that seem to conflict.

57 Mark 6:3. — "The carpenter." As to the humiliation of this pursuit, see {Sirach, or} Ecclesiasticus 38:24-34, and *cf.* Delitzsch, "Jewish Artisan Life in the Time of Christ" (1902).

In Matthew 13:55 we have the "carpenter's Son." That is one of the variations from Mark's record found in the

NOTES ON THE GOSPEL OF MARK: CHAPTER 6

first and third Evangelists which some critics idly imagine represent a later tendency to tone down Mark's language, so as to divest the record of the Master of what was considered derogatory to it; whilst others represent Mark as "secondary," because he does not speak of Christ as son of Joseph (Schmiedel, col. 1846). True, such is what "literary analysis" can accomplish. How very appropriate to the second Gospel is the disclosure that the servant Son of God thus wrought with His own hands, sanctifying all human *service,* and doubtless maintaining a widowed mother!

It is on record that when the Emperor Julian ("the Apostate") was engaged in his last campaign, a Christian soldier was asked by a scornful officer, What was the Carpenter doing just then? The answer received was, "Making a coffin." The Emperor fell in that very battle (Sozomen, "Ecclesiastical History," v. 8).

"The son of Mary" (*cf.* Luke 4:22, "the son of Joseph"). It is common for critics to allege against the virgin-birth of the Lord being historical the fact that Mark is silent about it. In this strain writes Menzies. Mary herself "knows nothing of His having been born in any extraordinary way." If, however, our second Gospel were the earliest, what could be more reasonable than to conclude that during the lifetime of the Lord's mother the circumstances of His birth Divine wisdom and propriety of human feeling combined to withhold? The perfection of the Bible does, of course, lie in its matchless fusion of Divine and human, a truism constantly urged by critics, but feebly apprehended in any helpful, fruitful way by themselves. The Tübingen scholar Baur, who adhered to Matthew's priority, used this verse in support of *his* idea that Mark did know of the virgin-birth! See, further, note in Farrar, "Life of Christ," p. 63.

As to there being no genealogy in Mark, W. Kelly has written: "Who would ask the pedigree of a *servant*?" ("An Exposition of the Gospel of John," p. 21).

58 Mark 6:5, 6. — Faith in the Person of Christ attaches in the second Gospel to His function as Prophet; in Luke's to that of Priest; in Matthew to His being the King. With Mark's narrative *cf.* Peter's words in Acts 3:22.

A comparison of this place with Matthew 13:58 affords some critics another illustration of their fad that Matthew, or the "editor" of his Gospel, revised Mark's too naïve statements!

A distinction may be made between the "supernatural" and the "miraculous" in respect of the efficacy of ordinary prayer (Drummond, p. 13 *f.*). Some answers to prayer, however, may fall under the miraculous.

On the general subject of miracles, see notes **27, 54** above.

Schmiedel's discrimination of certain passages of Mark which for him constitute the "foundation pillars for a truly scientific life of Jesus" (cols. 1881-1883 of his article in "Biblical Encyclopædia"), Fairbairn well characterises as an illusion that mistakes critical ingenuity for historical science ("Philosophy of the Christian Religion," p. 304).

With reference to the passage under consideration, Bousset (p. 56; E.T., p. 49) makes the Lord's being unable all a matter cognizable by human psychology. For the believer it suffices to know the method of the "psychology" which is Divine. Men may have pressure put on them to come within the range of spiritual blessing (Matthew 20:17-19), but faith is a gracious gift, in no way the result of compulsion. In the first Gospel (11:12) force is exerted by men themselves, who seek God with all their heart (Deuteronomy 4:29). According to Matthew 22:11, 12, a man already in the presence of the Host is found not to have accepted that vesture which, according to the custom of ancient princes, was offered by them to their guests *(cf.* Philippians 3:12).

One may be sure that Richard Hooker did not foresee the use which would be made in our day of his position in the "Ecclesiastical Polity" that God is Himself governed by His own laws.

59 Mark 6:8. — "No money in their belt." Dr. R. F. Horton, according to his "Revelation and the Bible" (p. 367), has allowed himself to be strangely misinformed as to the practice of Christians whom he describes as "the most emphatic in maintaining the Divine infallibility of the Bible." He alleges that they "reject the inference of St. Paul in favour of paid ministry." He would be right if by "paid" he merely meant *stipulated* remuneration, which is unknown in the community amongst whom W. Kelly laboured. It contains most of the few who really act upon the precepts of Scripture bearing on *hired* ministry (1 Corinthians 9:9, etc.). Material *support* of ministry exercised in faith is a Divine obligation which they ever recognise.

65 Mark 6:45. — Wellhausen here avails himself of an old difficulty created by comparison of John 6:17 with Mark's statement. In Mark we find πρός, "Bethsaida"; in John εἰς, "Capernaum." Indeed, εἰς τὸ πέραν, which is sufficiently accredited by the textual evidence (its omission in the Sinaitic Syrian version is insignificant), exhibits the difference of prepositions involved. They occur together again in 11:1, where εἰς stands for the *direction* taken; πρός for the point arrived at or actually reached (*cf.* the quotation in Luke 4:26). There is no inconsistency, nor "conversion of B. into C.," as Wellhausen puts it. Trench ("Miracles," p. 296) says: "This Bethsaida (*cf.* John 1:44) lay on the west side of the lake, *in the same direction* as Capernaum, and near to it." Wellhausen himself has "not far from Capernaum."

NOTES ON THE SEVENTH CHAPTER

69 Mark 7:13. — "The word of God." From the time of the Reformation much has been written as to the connection of this phrase with Scripture, some holding that the two terms are now co-extensive, whilst others maintain the ancient distinction between "the word" as *oral* and as *written*. Happily, in this country "the judicious Hooker" wrote, now three hundred years ago, that "we have no word of God but the Scripture." He opposed the Puritans' idea that mere reading of Scripture cannot be effectual ("Ecclesiastical Polity," v. 21, 1, 2).

This standard Anglican writer has expressed himself as follows on the subject of *interpretation*: "I hold it for a most infallible rule in exposition of sacred Scripture that when a literal construction will stand, the farthest from the letter is commonly the worst" (*cf.* notes **88, 134**). There is, of course, a logical connection between inspiration (note **13**) and interpretation.

It is no doubt correct that, as A. B. Davidson has said for the Old Testament (Hastings, vol. iv., p. 127), "the word" stands for the *spiritual meaning* of the "words" (see John 8:43, and *cf.* John 17:8, 14). It is, however, an exaggeration on the part of Farrar ("The Bible," etc., p. 134 *f.*; *cf.* Beet, "Manual of Theology," p. 65) to represent that "nowhere in the New Testament is the Old Testament called *the word of God*"—that this phrase is used of

Christ alone. That "the word of God" is used in the New Testament *chiefly* of the contemporary oral word, as in Mark 2:2 (*Cf.* 2 Timothy 4:2) and Hebrews 13:7, is unquestionable. But even if such a passage as Hebrews 4:12 could be shown not to refer to Scripture, it seems certain that Mark 7:13 distinguishes "the word of God" from aught oral. *Cf.* "it is written in your law": this last word, we know, applies in the New Testament, not only to the Pentateuch, but to the Psalms (John 10:34). As for the New Testament, when Timothy was enjoined to "preach the word" (2 Timothy 4:2), this precept was given in close connection with what the Apostle says of the *Scriptures* (end of chapter 3—*i.e.*, in the same context), so that the material of the written word can scarcely be excluded from the preaching. Professor Theodor Zahn, in a sermon on James 1:16 *ff.*, has said: "When we talk of the word of God, we first think of the Bible, the word of God reduced to writing for His community (Church). But James is not speaking of the Bible. ... It is possible to honour the Bible, and not to hear thus the voice of God."

Moreover, God does of course speak to His creatures otherwise than by Scripture. We have, however, to be guided by intimations on the subject (as in the case of the raising up of Cyrus), not by the influence of great names, as Luther (Dorner, "History of Protestant Theology," p. 244). Note here the extravagance of Zwingli: "He who is born of the Spirit requires a book no longer" (Dorner, i. 290 *f.*; *cf.* Barclay's "Apology for the Quakers"). It is through the word that any are so born, so that it is the vital principle (which needs sustaining), if we listen to Apostles (1 Peter 1:23); and those not of God are characterised by ears closed to the inspired writers (1 John 4:6).

A further momentous question is the interrelation of the Bible and the Church. And, first, does the Church's "sanction" impart to the Scriptures their authority? The Church has not formed the Bible, but it was through Christ's word which we have in the Bible that the Church was "gathered." "If the Bible," writes Fairbairn, "is made to depend on the Church, is it not evident that it is not the Bible conceived as a revelation? What the canonizing process produced was not a revelation, but a book." And again: "Hebrews was precisely as much inspired, and possessed exactly as much authority, before as after its incorporation in the Canon," whilst "the continuance of the Spirit is the source of the authority of the word of the living God" ("Christ in Modern Thought," p. 505 *ff.*). Dorner had already written that the Bible is itself a revelation, "not merely the record of a revelation previously given" ("History of Protestant Theology," ii. 128).

Bishop Gore has written that, for his school, "it becomes more and more difficult to believe in the Bible without believing in the Church" ("Lux Mundi," p. 248; *cf.* his sermon in 1900 at Westminster Abbey for the British and Foreign Bible Society), which means, doubtless, as Fairbairn puts it, that "as the supremacy of the Bible is weakened, the position of the Church is strengthened." If men thus tell us that our faith must be rooted in the Church's testimony, we need only reply by inquiring, How are we to know that "the Church" is to be trusted? Any rejoinder that the Church rests on the authority of the Bible would he manifest reasoning in a circle.

For the views of such as Dr. James Martineau on Scripture as authority, reference might be made to his "Seat of Authority," book ii., chapter ii. The Deism which passed from this country to Germany, to beget there the Rationalism of the eighteenth century (see Cheyne, "Founders of Criticism"), returned hither in the nineteenth in the form of "Higher Criticism," now running its course; with such a movement Unitarians naturally are in sympathy. They claim as virtual adherents the German leaders of this unholy cause, who, as their comrades in Great Britain, remain in outward conformity to *officially* orthodox Churches.

The "critics" at present in vogue find no proper place in their vocabulary for Paul's "in part" (1 Corinthians 13:9). With such limitations as they themselves seek to impose, there can be no true progress, no fully scientific because no sufficient accuracy (*cf.* Sir William Ramsay in the *Expositor,* December, 1906). Many of them, like souls of old, will not "enter in," nor allow others to do so who lean upon them.

For Roman Catholic treatment of Tradition, see Schanz, "A Christian Apology," ii., ch. xi.

NOTES ON THE EIGHTH CHAPTER

76 Mark 8:1-9. — *Cf.* parallel in Matthew. Having had in chapter 6 the record of the feeding of five thousand men, we here meet with the description of another like work of power in behalf of four thousand persons. This time it is not JESUS in the character of Messiah among Israelites as such. The significance of numbers in Scripture is allowed more or less by even German writers (as Ewald); it is illustrated here by the difference between seven baskets as compared with twelve in the previous case, appropriate in a Jewish connection. Chapter 6 sets before us that which was dispensational; in chapter 8 we find the Lord acting as "Creator and Preserver of all mankind." This was seen of old by Hilary amongst others (see Trench).

Modern critics, who never rest on their oars in the quest of novelties, find a "doublet" here. Menzies, amongst British writers, treats the two accounts as only different versions of the same incident. As in most other questions of criticism, our scholars, for the most part, are content to echo the Germans. Wernle ("Sources," p. 66) offers the hypothesis that Mark "was told something of the kind twice over," and will have it that "the similarity of the two accounts is disguised by the interposition of other stories." B. Weiss, adhering to the distinction between them—which it requires only "eyes to see" (see below, note 79)—supposes that there were divergencies in the "Petrine tradition." What a balanced English writer of the first rank says on the subject may be seen by consulting Sanday ("Outlines," p. 123).

79 Mark 8:19 *f.* — The baskets in the earlier miracle were κόφινοι (hand-baskets); in the second, σπυρίδες (hampers). This closely accurate distinction has been often remarked, as by H. J. Holtzmann ("Manual Commentary," p. 191). Some have supposed that it militates against the theory of essentially oral tradition (Burkitt, p. 35).

81 Mark 8:27-30. — *Cf.*, of course, parallels in Matthew 16 and Luke 9. This passage has been somewhat anticipated in note **30**.

82 Mark 8:29. — The literature now most in vogue ignores the impressions which must have been left on those disciples who had come to Christ in the first instance through John, by his testimony to Messiah (John 1:34-51). Difference of judgment as to the historical value of the fourth Gospel becomes vital. How is one to understand their alacrity in Mark 1:16-20, which implies belief in some human testimony, but for John's narrative? That belief has now ripened into conviction, issuing in confession, which is Divine (Schlottmann, p. 111).

Martineau (most original of the English school) held that the Lord never Himself claimed to be Messiah; that it was "a position made for Him and palmed upon Him by His followers" ("Seat of Authority," p. 331 *f.*). Réville calls this "proving too much" (ii. 185). Harnack has sense enough to abstain from this negation ("What is Christianity?" p. 133); for the Berlin professor the entry into Jerusalem is decisive.

86 Mark 8:38. — Farrar shows from this that "Son of man" was not a synonym of "Messiah" ("Life of Christ," p. 333). But he seems not to have apprehended its full significance.

NOTES ON THE NINTH CHAPTER

88 Mark 9:1. — "*Come* in power." The Greek form (ἐληλυθῦιαν) expresses "come in its completeness" as the end of a gradual process (Plumptre).

Trench ("Studies in the Gospels," pp. 185 *ff.*) rightly rejects the idea that Pentecost was the fulfilment of these words. But he falls short of the truth when he sees the fulfilment in the destruction of Jerusalem (*cf.* J. Scott Russell's views). Even so, partial fulfilment, as he puts it, is "a rehearsal of the final." Pentecost in Acts 2 was that. As to the same writer's connection of Matthew 24:34 with the complete fulfilment, see notes {**135**} below on Mark 13:30. Here, as there, we have illustration of an Apostolic principle as to ἰδία ἐπίλυσις (2 Peter 1:20).

That the first Christians looked for the return of the Lord in their lifetime, as Bishop Robertson says in his Bampton Lectures, one may suppose to have been the case previously to the fall of Jerusalem. That event, being unattended by His παρουσία, must have widened their understanding of His words.

Dr. Horton, on the same page of his "Revelation and the Bible" where already an error of his has been pointed out (note **59**), goes wrong with Alford over Paul's words in 1 Thessalonians 4:15. Neither the elastic use of the Greek present participles there nor the English idiom of the common translation requires our understanding the Apostle to say that he would be one of those alive at the time of the παρουσία. The form of words, it is certain, may be equivalent to "those of us who," etc. So Theodoret, Chrysostom, Bengel, Dean Vaughan, and others (*cf.* Greek at Hebrews 10:39). Moreover, the Apostle employs the Old Testament formula: he was speaking ἐν κυρίῳ—*i.e.*, oracularly. It was of God, for the benefit of believers throughout the dispensation, that he expressed thus vaguely the "blessed hope" of that event. See, further, note **134**.

92 Mark 9:13. — According to Matthew's parallel, the Lord here made use of Malachi 4:5, as well as of 3:1 of the same prophet in chapter 11:10 there (*cf.* Mark 1:2); whilst the Baptist, according to John 1:23, quoted Isaiah 40:3, to which alone he appeals. Isaiah set forth the witness of the forerunner.

92a Mark 9:24. — For other than personal faith inducing grace, *cf.* Luke 5:20.

93 Mark 9:31. — The ἄνθρωποι into whose hands the Lord was to be betrayed were Gentiles. It is impossible to get a satisfactory explanation of the title "Son of man" in a passage like this from the collocation of Son of man and men as treated from the point of view now popular. The Lord was rejected (1) as Christ by the Jews; (2) as

Son of man by the Gentiles as well. Under such circumstances, the modern conception of Him as ideal is feeble in the extreme (see notes **30, 35**).

94 Mark 9:37. — The language here resembles that of John's Gospel (Sir A. F. Hort).

99 Mark 9:43 *ff.* — "Enter into." See Dalman, p. 95, on this terminology.

NOTES ON THE TENTH CHAPTER

106 Mark 10:17. — *"Inherit* life eternal." *Inherit* stands for "take possession of," as in Matthew 25:34 (Dalman). So in Luke 18:18. In the Synoptic Gospels it is regarded as in reserve; so in Paul's Epistles. Luke 18:22 tells us that the young man was to have *treasure in heaven. Cf.* Colossians 3:3.

Some have supposed that there is a difference between "life" and "life eternal," but this is a mistake. See Matthew 19:16, 17, and Dalman, who shows that in the early and in part contemporary Jewish literature "life" without qualification stands for "life eternal." Outside the Bible (Psalm 133:3 and Daniel 12:2) we meet with the expression in the apocryphal Psalm of Solomon (3:16 {"But they that fear the Lord shall rise to life eternal, And their life (shall be) in the light of the Lord, and shall come to an end no more."}), 2 Maccabees (7:9 {"And when he was at the last gasp, he said thus: You indeed, O most wicked man, destroy us out of this present life: but the King of the world will raise us up, who die for his laws, in the resurrection of eternal life."}), and the Book of Enoch (37:4 {"Till the present day such wisdom has never been given by the Lord of Spirits as I have received according to my insight, according to the good pleasure of the Lord of Spirits by whom the lot of eternal life has been given to me."}), as also in the Aramaic paraphrases ("Targums") used in the synagogues, as at Leviticus 18:5, Deuteronomy 33:6. See, further, note **110**.

107 Mark 10:18. — Much use has been made of this verse by those interested in obtaining evidence for the notion that, in respect of the Deity of the Saviour, as of much else, there are *layers* of narrative, in the earliest of which there is no recognition of aught beyond simple humanity. Christ here seems to be taking the position predicted of Him in Psalm 16:2. The emphasis is not on "Me," but on "good" (Swete). Nothing further need be added to the words of the lecturer here, although reference may be made to his "Lectures on Matthew" (p. 415 *f.*) for remarks on "goodness" in the parallel passage there; also to "Introductory Lectures," p. 358 *f.* One may readily see in either passage an intended appeal to the man's sanctified reason. It was a question to be answered by *himself.* For the use made by Bishop Chase, after Germans (*cf.* Wernle, p. 42; Bousset, p. 202, E.T.), of the Matthew passage, as if it betrayed the moulding influence of the editor's hand, see Burkitt, p. 17 *f.*, and *cf.* notes **57**, **59** above.

110 Mark 10:30. — "In the *coming age* life eternal." For the Jew all blessing is connected with this earth, and expressly in connection with Messiah's reign. The Synoptic Gospels do not go beyond the Old Testament use of the phrase "life eternal" (note **106**). In general, says Dalman, "the life of the world to come took the place of eternal life" (*cf.* Nicene Creed). It is nowhere, however, regarded as lapsing when the eternal state sets in, as some in recent years have supposed. The fourth Gospel regards the title to it as indefeasible ({John} 10:28 *f.*).

NOTES ON THE ELEVENTH CHAPTER

117 Mark 11:15-18. — *Cf.* John 2:14 *ff.* Farrar says rightly that it is "*impossible to* believe that the narratives refer to the same event." Miss Bramston (perhaps echoing Wright or others) says that "it is *improbable* that He did it twice," but *why* is not stated ("Sunrise of Revelation").

NOTES ON THE TWELFTH CHAPTER

122 Mark 12:8. — It is common, with regard to the question of *probation,* either (1) to uphold the idea that Christians are under the law, or (2) to deny man's complete moral ruin before God, in either alternative impairing Pauline doctrine (Galatians 5:18, Romans 6:14, 7:18, 8:8). The alleged antithesis between the Synoptic teaching of the Lord on this subject and that of the Apostle is one of the novelties of "modern thought" with which the present generation is harassed. Anyone may understand that the full truth as to human depravity must have become clearer after the Crucifixion; yet the germs of Paul's doctrine, like that of John (chapter 3), are to be found in Mark 10:15, the truth of which Matthew's στράφητε (18:3) does but emphasize.

124 Mark 12:35-37. — We are here told that David *himself,* and that by inspiration (for the Greek, *cf.* Revelation 1:10), said that which modern critics deny to him as his words. The old Jewish idea of the authorship of Psalm 110 was that, in David's old age, when he could no longer go out to battle, a Court poet composed it in order to console him. But the Evangelist here tells us that the Lord cited the Psalm definitely as David's own. Not content with the denial of such authorship, some writers go on to represent that Christ here disavowed His being Himself "Son of David" (Réville i., p. 47 note,

303 f., 381; Bousset, p. 182). Compare what Professor Sanday says on this subject (article "Son of God," p. 573 in Hastings); Neander (p. 402) "to oppose a one-sided adherence to the one at the expense of the other"; and, for the relation of sonship of God to the Lord's Messianic claims, the article in Hastings just referred to, p. 576.

NOTES ON THE THIRTEENTH CHAPTER

129 Mark 13:10. — "The Gospel." As to supposed reflex influence of the theological language of the early Church on the Synoptic vocabulary, see Sanday, "Son of God," in Hastings, p. 573.

130 Mark 13:11. — In this early Synoptic Gospel we meet already with the promise of the Spirit in the Johannine sense (*cf.* note **94**).

134 Mark 13:26. — *Cf.* 8:38, and note {**86**} *ad loc.* Here we have what Paul in one of his very earliest letters (2 Thessalonians 2:8), speaks of as the ἐπιφάνεια of the Lord, "the *appearing* of His coming (παρουσία)." The "coming" in its initial stage he has described in his first letter to the same Christians (4:15). It may be useful at this point to state the ideas of some critics on the subject. We shall take H. J. Holtzmann as a now long-accredited spokesman. In his somewhat famous "Synoptic Gospels," published just before these lectures appeared in the *Bible Treasury*, this scholar discriminated three aspects of the Second Advent—of His return as dealt with by the Lord when on earth; *(a)* for judgment (Luke 17:24), *(b)* a historical coming (Mark 9:1), *(c)* a spiritual coming (Matthew 18:20, to which we may add John 14:18, 16:7). All this, it is believed, is very much in accordance with the facts which the Gospel records supply. To the view thus gained we have to add

Paul's revelation (1 Thessalonians 4), which speaks of that not to be confounded with any of Holtzmann's comings. The Apostle's first statement many Christians, misled by the majority of commentaries—e.g., Alford on 2 Thessalonians 2:1—wrongly merge in his supplementary declaration, made to correct the Thessalonians' understanding of his first (see 2 Thessalonians 2:2, R.V.). *Cf.* note **88** above.

135 Mark 13:30. — "This generation ... all these things. ..." From taking "generation" in the temporal sense of the word, Strauss and De Wette represented the Lord as fallible. Others, as Meyer, A. Wright, Swete, preserve their "orthodoxy," while still explaining the word of a period of some thirty to thirty-three years. The difficulty of determining when such a generation should *begin*—the Lord's contemporaries belonged to different generations relative to their age—is altogether ignored. These writers, to begin with, have to assume that such a generation as they think of commenced with His ministry, without anything in the Gospels to appeal to for support. Origen and Chrysostom of old, followed by Wordsworth and Alford (as equivalent to γένος) of recent English commentators, with Dorner and Stier amongst Germans, take "generation," as it must be taken, in its moral meaning. Not only is it so used in the Old Testament (as in Deuteronomy 32:5, Psalms 24:6 and 73:15, Jeremiah 8:3 {LXX}), but in the Gospels themselves (Mark 9:19, Matthew 17:17, Luke 16:8), as elsewhere (Acts 2:40, etc.; *cf.* Galatians 1:4). Is not "that day" in verse 32 suggestive of "something at a distance"? (Beet, "Manual of Theology," p. 446 *f.*).

Verse 10 must be borne in mind in connection with the words "all these things." The convenient makeshift of critics has been mentioned in note **129**.

136 Mark 13:32. — "Nor the Son." *Cf.* Matthew 24:36 in the critical text, followed in the "Workers' New Testament." These words have been supposed by writers of Unitarian tendency to impair the Lord's omniscience, in which they are followed by several in high ecclesiastical position in the English Establishment. The κένωσις (emptying) of the Lord spoken of in Philippians 2:7 has a bearing on the words.

"It is of course difficult," writes Dean Strong, "to understand how two kinds of consciousness can have been present at one time in one Person" ("Manual of Theology," p. 119). Again, Bishop Gore: "He willed to observe the limits of the science of His age, and He puts Himself in the same relation to its historical knowledge" ("Lux Mundi," p. 205). This idea had already been countenanced by a living prelate. "When He quoted passages from the Old Testament, He might have no more knowledge of their age and actual authors than that which was current in His own time" (Bishop Moorhouse, "Teaching of Christ," p. 47). See, however, more healthy remarks than these in Schaff, "Christ and Christianity," pp. 107-119.

The American writer Gould speaks of the passages having given rise to much "theological tinkering." He does not himself, certainly, afford any help on the subject.

Augustine (quoted by Wordsworth *in loc.*) refers to the elastic force of the word "know," undeniable as regards both Hebrew and Greek. Here the word is οἶδεν (not γινώσκει). Its use may be seen in "I know you not," "the Lord knoweth them that are His," "I knew Him not" (said by John Baptist of Christ, evidently not denying any ordinary previous acquaintance with JESUS (John

1:31, 33, Matthew 3:14, and Luke 1:36)). *Cf.* Peter's "I know not this Man" (14:71 here).

Some have repudiated explanations offered on the ground that these virtually supported a Docetic view—that is, that our Lord "feigned a condition which did not actually exist for the benefit of His disciples." The Docetists, such as Cerinthus, held that the flesh of Christ was not real (see Strong, p. 99, and *cf.* Fairbairn, "Christ in Modern Thought," p. 353). Réville (ii. 313), condemning words of a sermon by Bossuet, questions the authenticity of the words, which he supposes were due to Arian influence on the manuscripts of the Gospels. Worst of all, Schmiedel (article on "Gospels" in "Encyclopædia Biblica," col. 1881) boldly says, "In the person of Jesus we have to do with a completely human being," and that "the Divine is to be sought in Him only in the form in which it is capable of being found in a man." He seems to seek to blunt the edge of these soul-corrupting words by adding what is true—that the *historical* value of the Gospels goes with the presence of such passages in them.

The devout Bengel's explanation, which most commends itself of all put forth on the "orthodox" side, is that the Lord had no command from the Father to declare that day. For the "authority" of His words, see Mark 1:22, John 12:48-50, 14:24, and *cf.* Acts 1:7 (Greek), Revelation 1:1 *ff.*, and see remarks of Professor Sanday (article "Son of God" in Hastings), also Dorner, "Person of Christ," i. 54. As to correlative use of the "Father and the Son," reference may be made to {Mark} 9:37, 14:36, comparing Matthew 11:27, 28:19, Luke 10:22, all of which bear on Harnack's proposition that "the Gospel as Jesus proclaimed it has to do with the

Father only, and not with the Son" ("What is Christianity?" p. 147).

With this question is connected that of silence (see Mark 15:5).

A few words of the late J. N. Darby may be welcome as a conclusion to this note. "In the historical presentation of Christianity the Son is always presented as down here in servant and manhood estate all through John, though in heaven and one with the Father. ... In Matthew 3 the whole Trinity is revealed, and, we may say, for the first time fully. ... Hence, *No! not the Son,* has no difficulty" ("Notes and Comments," vol. ii., from p. 416).

NOTES ON THE FOURTEENTH CHAPTER

140 Mark 14:8 *f.* — Allowing the Aramaism, it is only necessary to remark that τὸν καιρόν is understood as object of the verb προέλαβε, "seized in good time her opportunity of embalming with myrrh," etc. Whatever Wellhausen may think, it is accurate, idiomatic Greek.

As to "Gospel," see note **17**. Here it is, of course, the Gospel of "service," as elsewhere in Mark, not doctrine about Christ (Carpenter, p. 204, and Wellhausen, *ad loc.*), save as His service and that of the woman to Him are reproduced in the devotion of His followers.

Chrysostom already (about 400 A.D.) in Homily on Matthew 8, spoke of "those who inhabit the British Isles publishing abroad an act done in Judea privately in a house by a woman" (I. Williams, ii. 19).

J. Weiss (p. 5) uses this verse to show how far distant for Mark was the παρουσία (see note **88**).

142 Mark 14:12 *f.* — *Cf.* verse 1 *f.* "The first day of unleavened bread, when they used to sacrifice the

Passover" (*cf.* Matthew 26:17, "on the first day of the feast of unleavened bread"; Luke 22:7, "the day of unleavened bread"; John 13:1, "*before* the *feast* of the Passover"). This introduces a long-debated question—whether the Passover partaken of by our Lord on the verge of His crucifixion was, as the Synoptists represent, the *ordinary* Paschal meal, or one in anticipation of it, as John's Gospel some have thought requires us to believe. It will be desirable first to seek to determine the meaning of the expressions used by the Synoptists before considering any specially found in the fourth Gospel.

1. "The first day of unleavened bread." The patristic Greeks took Matthew and Mark's πρώτῃ as equivalent to προτέρᾳ (we might say προτεραίᾳ), "the day before" (the ἄζυμα, "unleavened bread")—a view that was unwittingly confirmed by the Jewish medieval commentator Rashi on Exodus 12:15, who says that "first day" there means "the day before" (Schanz), the 15th of Nisan being technically the first of these days. As for Luke's "the day," we may compare Genesis 2:4, noting the words of the third Evangelist, "called the Passover," which are exactly those used by Josephus in his "Antiquities." If "days of unleavened bread" were called "Passover," we have to do with a whole *season*.

2. The "*feast* of the Passover" (John). Leviticus 23:5 *f.* requires our distinguishing in the original institution the initial "Passover" from the "feast" annexed to it—the "feast of unleavened bread." Each term has to be understood not only in its own proper narrower meaning, but also according to its conventional elastic meaning. The learned Dr. John Lightfoot (seventeenth century) has shown in his "Horæ Hebraicæ et Talmudicæ" (Gandell's edition, vol. ii., p. 467 *f.*) on the present passage of Mark that, according to Jewish

phraseology, considered with reference to Deuteronomy 16:2 (*cf.* Numbers 28:17), oxen ("herds"), or the sacrifices offered *after* the lamb eaten, were called the "Passover," as well as the lamb itself; and in his notes on John 18:28 (vol. iii., p. 420 *f.*) he shows, from expressions used by the Rabbins, that it is the *chagigah*, or festive offering, brought on the fifteenth day (not fourteenth) of Nisan to which John's word "Passover" refers. "Feast" speaks of the whole season, but specifically of that prescribed in Leviticus 23:6 (*cf.* Edersheim, "Life and Times of Jesus the Messiah," chapter ix., p. 489).

The American "Jewish Encyclopædia" (article "Passover," by Emil Hirsch) shows that what was strictly the "Passover" and the "Feast of Unleavened Bread" came naturally to be looked upon as one season, and therefore to have the same designation.

3. All four Evangelists fix the *day of the Crucifixion* as a Friday, with which agrees the tradition recorded in the Talmud. Wellhausen at Mark 15:42 renders παρασκευή as "Friday," in accordance with old Syriac, and also modern Greek. This leads us to inquire what the "preparation" was for. Westcott and others have replied, for the Passover in the narrow sense of the word, but Purves ("Hastings' Dictionary," under "Preparation") holds that it was for the Sabbath, and so "preparation of the Passover" would stand for "the preparation in Passover week." Whilst the technical word "preparation" seems to have been in standing use for a weekly function (with Mark 15:42 *cf.* Josephus, "Antiquities," xvi. 6, 2, referred to in Grimm's "Lexicon," *s.v.*), some preparation would be needed for various festivals, and the preliminaries for the Passover in that year would blend with those for the Paschal Sabbath, called "high day" in John 19:31.

The "Jewish Encyclopædia" discredits Chwolson's idea that the present calendar for Passover, which excludes Friday as a day for its observance, was in existence then, stating that it is not generally accepted.

To sum up: The Lord and His disciples may be confidently regarded as having taken the initial meal substantially at the same time as the rest of the Jews, within the limits of what Wellhausen (on "Luke") calls the same "official day," referring to {Luke} 22:34 there (*cf.* Mark 14:30, yet more explicit). The language of John 18:28 is, in the light of Jewish usages, in no way incompatible with that of Mark 14:12; and John 19:14 does but fix the day and hour of what is spoken of in the latter passage, whilst 19:31 speaks of preparation simply with manifest reference to the Sabbath alone. The "mistake" that critics have attributed to the Synoptists is a "mare's nest." Most are singularly wanting in what Huxley called "scientific imagination."

Grotius, Hengstenberg, Alford, Wordsworth, Westcott, Ellicott, Farrar, Edersheim, W. Kelly ("An Exposition of the Gospel of John," p. 554 *f.*, {chapter 19,} note {f}), Drummond and Sanday have in turn discussed the question. Grotius supposes that no lamb was used by the Lord (so Luckock, Carr, etc.). Even if it were so, the case would be in line with that of the Jews outside the land. Hengstenberg (on John) follows Lightfoot; Alford settles nothing; Wordsworth is content to follow Chrysostom, who supposes that the Jews broke the law by deferring their observance of the supper until after midnight of the 14th of Nisan. Sir R. Anderson's treatment of the subject in his "Bible and Modern Criticism" (chapter viii.) is excellent.

Wright ("Synopsis," p. xxxi.) hesitates not to speak of John as "correcting Mark"; Gardner, of its being "impossible to reconcile the two in accordance with the canons of history" (p. 152 *f.*). But the language and ways of the period have to be thoroughly investigated before a "reconciliation" can be deemed needful. If it be "quite uncertain," as Professor Gardner says, "which date for the Crucifixion is the true one," does not such "uncertainty" affect only the minds of those who imagine reconciliation is required? Again, there is no excuse for an arch-offender, Schmiedel, saying that the Synoptists (he speaks of Luke) confound the preparation and the Passover itself. It is only those in confusion over the παρασκευή who could say so; the two could certainly be coincident, and did in that year fall unquestionably on the same day.

See further {note 145} at verse 18 here, and as to Mark's "third hour," considered in relation to John's "sixth," refer to note {162} on {Mark} 15:25 below.

The two disciples, Luke tells us (22:8), were Peter and John.

145 Mark 14:18 — The Jews had adopted the Roman custom of *reclining* at meals.

146 Mark 14:19 *f.* — The allusion to the betrayer becomes intelligible on reference to John 13.

154 Mark 14:61 *f.* — As to the Lord's reticence when first interrogated, see Stalker, p. 151, and Sir R. Anderson's book on "The Silence of God." Observe the association here of the three titles, Christ, Son of God, Son of man. Martineau (p. 133), as Wendt, allows the Messianic sense of Son of God in this place alone (*cf.* Luke 22:67-70).

155 Mark 14: 64. — The felt blasphemy is very noticeable in connection with the title "Son of man" (*cf.* note 30). On the aorist ἠκούσατε, see note 18a.

NOTES ON THE FIFTEENTH CHAPTER

162 Mark 15:25. — *Cf.* John 19:14, and {Mark} note **142**. Mark's "third hour" is by "critics" set against John's "sixth hour." Such do not see that, while the second Evangelist is speaking of the Crucifixion, the fourth refers to the outcry before Pilate (Kelly, "An Exposition of the Gospel of John," p. 555 *ff.*, {chapter 19,} note {g}). It is usual for "reconcilers" to suppose that the Synoptists' statements are based on the strictly Jewish day, those of John on the Roman way of reckoning the civil day. The Jews took the hours from sunrise (our six a.m.), the Romans from midnight, with whom the sixth hour, accordingly, was the same as ours. Then three hours would elapse before the crucifixion (nine a.m.), and these would be taken up by the events recorded in the three first Gospels: the sentence of death, the journey to Golgotha, and the preparations there for the crucifixion. See, however, papers of Sir W. M. Ramsay in the *Expositor,* referred to by Professor Sanday in "Outlines of the Life of Christ," p. 147. As to Wieseler's idea, see Farrar, "Life of Christ," p. 112 note, where reference is given to Justinian's "Digest" (xli., Tit{le} iii, 6, 7).—The present writer believes that it means the third hour after the last watch of the night ({Mark} 13:35).

166 Mark 15:43. — "Took courage," etc., τολμήσας. Such is Dr. Field's rendering, based on that of the "New Translation," by J. N. Darby, to which the learned editor of the "Hexapla" refers in his "Notes on the Translation of the New Testament" at this passage.

NOTES ON THE SIXTEENTH CHAPTER

167 Mark 16:1-8. — The accounts of the Resurrection given by the four Evangelists have always been closely scrutinised in the service of unbelief, so that the most has been made of apparent discrepancies. The late Professor Rawson Birks, in his "Horæ Evangelicæ," vol. iii., chapter iii., p. 449 *f.*, entered into an "examination of charges of inconsistency of Mark's account with that of one or other of the rest of the Evangelists," to which any reader may be referred, as also to the later work of Christlieb, "Modern Doubts," p. 468 *f.*

It is desirable closely to compare the four accounts, and to make sure of the right meaning of the exact expression used by each Evangelist. Something like the following scheme may aid any reader of a book like O. Holtzmann's "Life of Jesus," in which the different accounts are represented as inconsistent with one another.

Mary Magdalene (accompanied by "the other Mary") visited the sepulchre whilst it was yet dark (Matthew 28:1, John 20:1). The word ἐπιφώσκειν used by Matthew refers, not to morning, but to evening twilight—"as it began to grow dusk"—*i.e.*, on the Sabbath evening which preceded the morning of the resurrection. See its like use in Luke 23:54, where Wellhausen remarks that in the Syriac liturgies the expression bears the same sense.

Mary Magdalene goes to tell Peter and John, who come and go again (John 20:3-10, Luke 24:12—omit "then" of A.V.), but Mary Magdalene on her return remains, and sees JESUS (Mark 16:9, John 20:11 *f.*). The other Mary, it seems, in whose company she revisited the sepulchre, carried information to Salome (Mark 16:1).

Then other women (Luke 24:10) come, who see the angels and flee, saying, whilst on their flight, nothing to anyone until they meet JESUS, whose words rally them, so that they deliver their message to the eleven as to Galilee (Mark 16:5-8, Matthew 28:5-10, Luke 24:9). *Cf.* Bp. Chase, Camb. Essays, p. 393.

Mary Magdalene delivers the message confided to her by JESUS to the disciples in general as to the Father (John 20:17, 18, Mark 16:9-11).

Luke 24:13-35 (*cf.* Mark 16:12, 13) tells us of the interview between JESUS and the two journeying to Emmaus, and verses 36-49 (Mark 16:14 *f.*) of His appearance to the eleven, which was on two consecutive Sundays (John 20:19-29). Within the next five weeks the disciples must have gone to Galilee, and returned to Judea for the Ascension scene recorded by Luke.

And so, if Mark's "Salome" is set against Luke's "Johanna," the common-sense explanation is that Luke must have included Salome among "the others" he speaks of in the same verse (24:10).

Again, in verse 5 here, "a young man." Against this "critical" writers use Luke's "two men" (24:4). The women were trembling. Only one of the angels, presumably, was spokesman; to him their attention was attracted.

168 Mark 16:9-20. — The textual criticism of the closing verses of Mark has been fully discussed by Tregelles, Scrivener, Burgon, Westcott and Hort, Sadler, Salmon, and others. A recent statement will be found in Swete's Introduction to his edition of Mark.

They appear in AC and fifteen other uncials, all cursives, and versions except Syr[sin]. D has as far as verse 15, whilst Syr[cm] shows verses 17-20. Hippolytus quotes verse 19, Irenæus verse 20. Their place in the Gospel has been recognised by Wetstein and Bengel among the older scholars; by Scheiermacher, De Wette, Bleek, Strauss, Hilgenfeld, Olshausen, Ebrard, Ellicott, Salmon, Wace, etc., among the more recent—in particular by Scrivener and Burgon. Scrivener deals with the *external* evidence in his "Introduction," pp. 337-344, fourth edition; Burgon with the *internal* in his, chapter ix. Salmon writes: "We have no evidence that any writer anterior to Eusebius remarked that there was anything abrupt in the conclusion of St. Mark's Gospel, or that it gave no testimony to our Lord's resurrection" (p. 146). He, too, discusses the internal evidence, holding that it favours reception of the verses; Morison, the same emphatically, calling the question as to these verses a "romance of criticism, which must, as time goes on, yield to sober truth" (lxxiii).

The following scholars, amongst others, have been more or less adverse to the belief that Mark was the writer: Tischendorf, Tregelles, Westcott and Hort, B. Weiss and Zahn.

Tregelles, while questioning that Mark was the writer, treats the verses as authentic and a part of canonical Scripture. He compares them with the last chapter of Deuteronomy ("Printed Text of the New Testament," p. 246 *f.*).

By those English scholars who do not defend Mark's authorship they are supposed to have been written by Aristion, spoken of by Papias as "a disciple of the Lord."

Dr. Hort's views will be found in "Introduction to Greek New Testament," Appendix, pp. 28-51.

Wright suggests that Mark's Gospel was not copied in his lifetime, and would therefore be little used, thus "narrowly escaping extinction" (Synopsis XIV., *cf.* Burkitt, p. 260 *f.*).

Professor Sanday writes: "The most probable view, I think," regarding these verses, "is that they were written to make good a loss through the frayed end of a roll" (Bampton Lectures, p. 380).

Zahn's opinion, that the book remained uncompleted, he rests on the critical canon that, where two mutually exclusive texts, the origin of each of which may be a shorter, well-attested text, compete with this, the shorter must be regarded as the original recension ("Introduction to the New Testament," vol. ii., p. 227).

Pfleiderer (i. 395) compares these verses with verses 58-60 of the "Gospel of Peter," which has a like abrupt ending. See also Dean Robinson's lecture on that apocryphal work (p. 29).

So much for the views of those not defending the verses. Since the appearance of the Revised Version, it has been discovered that they are included in Tatian's "Diatessaron," of the early part of the second century. This later phase of the question may have led to some modification of the case against them.

W. Kelly to the end of his life shared Burgon's conviction as to the inordinate respect in which the most ancient copies have in general been held, whilst feeling, perhaps yet more strongly than the late Dean of Chichester, that the text was really tampered with here, as was always the lecturer's belief with regard to another dozen verses in the fourth Gospel (7:53-8:11).

Reference in Note 6 of John

An Exposition of the Gospel of Mark,
Introduction, § 2. Divine Design, p. 7

"On the same principle we may account for a vast deal of intermediate matter given in the central parts of the first and third Gospels, which does not appear in the Gospel of Mark. We are thus delivered from the theories which have occupied many learned men, to the hurt of themselves and of those who trust them. For they have sought on human grounds to explain the different phenomena of the Synoptic Gospels, some advocating a common document, others only a general apostolic tradition. Again, a supplemental intention has been attributed to those that followed successively the first, for his own contribution to the sum as it gradually appeared and grew. Had they believed in the special design imprinted by the Holy Spirit on each and every one of them, erroneous speculation had been spared, to the honour of God's word and to the spiritual profit of His children. The differences which undoubtedly occur would then have been known to be in no case discrepancy, but springing from God's wisdom, not man's weakness, and adding incalculably to the witness of Christ, and consequently to the spiritual intelligence of him that accepts all from God in faith of His truth and love."

Reference in Note 85 of John

An Exposition of the Gospel of Mark,
Introduction, § 2. Divine Design, p. 10, foot

"The Spirit of God in recording does not limit Himself to the bare words that Jesus spoke. This I hold to be a matter of no little importance in forming a sound judgment of the Scriptures. The notion to which orthodox men sometimes shut themselves up, in zeal for plenary inspiration, is to my mind altogether mechanical; they think that inspiration necessarily and only gives the exact words that Christ uttered. There seems to me not the slightest necessity for this. Assuredly the Holy Spirit gives the truth, the whole truth, and nothing but the truth. The differences are owing to no infirmity, but to His design, and what He has given us is incomparably better than a bare report by so many hands, all meaning to give the same words and facts."

EDITIONS OF AUTHORS USED

N.B.—Foreign works existing in English translations are recorded under the titles of such; all are cited in the notes by English titles. An asterisk (*) is attached to the name of any Roman Catholic writer, a dagger (†) to that of any professed Unitarian and a double dagger (‡) to that of any Jewish writer.

BRITISH.

ABBOTT, DR. E. A.:
  Article "Gospels" in Encyclopædia Britannica, 9th ed., vol. x. (1879).
  Article "Gospels" in Encyclopædia Biblica, "Descriptive and Analytic" (1901).

ADENEY, PRINCIPAL:
  Theology of the New Testament (1894).

ANDERSON, SIR R.:
  The Bible and Modern Criticism (1902).
  Pseudo-Criticism (1904).

BEET, DR. A.:
  The Last Things (1905).
  A Manual of Theology (1906).

BENNETT, PROFESSOR:
  The Mishna as illustrating the Gospel (1884).
  A Primer of the Bible (1897).

BERNARD, T. D.:
:   Progress of Doctrine in the New Testament (Bampton Lectures, 1864; 5th ed., 1899).
BIRKS, T. R.:
:   Horæ Evangelicæ (1852, 1892).
BRUCE, DR. A. B.:
:   The Synoptic Gospels (1897).
:   The Kingdom of God (1899).
BURGON, DEAN:
:   The Last Twelve Verses of the Gospel of St. Mark (1871).
BURKITT, PROFESSOR:
:   The Gospel History and its Transmission (1906).
†CARPENTER, PROFESSOR:
:   The First Three Gospels (1904).
CLIFFORD, DR. J.:
:   The Inspiration and Authority of the Bible (1892).
DARBY, J. N.:
:   Irrationalism of Infidelity (1853; reissue, abridged, 1890).
:   Synopsis of Books of the Bible (included in Collected Writings, 1867-1883, but also published separately).
:   The Bible: is it a Revelation of God, and is it inspired of God? (1882).
:   Inspiration and Interpretation (in vol. ix. of Collected Writings).
DAVIDSON, A. B.:
:   Article "Prophecy" in Hastings' Dictionary of the Bible, vol. iv. (1903).
DRIVER, PROFESSOR S. R.:
:   Article "Son of Man" in Hastings' Dictionary of the Bible, vol. iv. (1903).
EDERSHEIM, DR. A.:
:   Life of Jesus the Messiah, 4th ed. (1887).
:   The Temple: its Ministry and Services in the Time of Christ (1900).
ELLICOTT, BISHOP:
:   Historical Lectures on the Life of our Lord (1876).

FAIRBAIRN, PRINCIPAL:
: The City of God (1883).
: The Place of Christ in Modern Theology (1893).
: Studies in the Life of Christ (9th ed., 1896).
: The Philosophy of the Christian Religion (1902).

FARRAR, DEAN:
: History of Interpretation (1886).
: The Bible: its Meaning and Supremacy (1897).
: The Life of Lives (1900).
: The Life of Christ, memorial ed. (1903).

FIELD, DR. F.:
: Notes on the Translation of the New Testament (Otium Norvicense, Pars 3^a, 1899).

GARDNER, PROFESSOR P.:
: Exploratio Evangelica (1899).

GLOAG, DR. P.:
: Introduction to the Synoptic Gospels (1895).

GORE, BISHOP:
: Lux Mundi, Essay VIII., 12th ed. (1891).

GRESWELL, E:
: Dissertations, vol. i. (1837).

HORT, DR. F. J. A., with WESTCOTT:
: New Testament in Greek, Introduction (1891).
: The Christian Ecclesia (1897).

HORT, SIR A. F.:
: The Gospel according to St. Mark (1902).

HORTON, DR. R. F.:
: Revelation and the Bible (1892).

KELLY, W.:
: Lectures Introductory to the Study of the Gospels (1874).
: Lectures on the Gospel of Matthew (1896).
: Exposition of the Gospel of John (1898 {3rd edition, 2013}).

LUCKOCK, DEAN:
: Footprints of the Son of Man according to St. Mark (1886).

†Martineau, Dr. J.:
   The Seat of Authority in Religion (1890).
Mason, Dr. A. J.:
   The Faith of the Gospel, 3rd ed. (1889).
Menzies, Professor A.:
   The Earliest Gospel (1901).
Moorhouse, Bishop:
   The Teaching of Christ (1891).
Morison, Professor:
   Practical Commentary on the Gospel of St. Mark, 3rd ed. (1882).
Newman, F. W.:
   Phases of Faith (1850).
   The Hebrew Jesus (1895).
Plumptre, Dean:
   Commentary on St. Mark's Gospel (Bishop Ellicott's Commentary on New Testament, 1884).
Robertson, Bishop:
   Regnum Dei—Bampton Lectures on the Kingdom of God (1901).
Robinson, Dean:
   Lectures on the Gospel of Peter (1892).
   The Study of the Gospels (1902).
   Some Thoughts on Inspiration (1905).
Rushbrooke, W. G.:
   Synopticon (1880).
Sadler, M. F.:
   The Gospel according to St. Mark (1884).
Salmon, Dr. G.:
   Introduction to the New Testament, 7th ed. (1894).
Salmond, Principal:
   Articles "Mark" and "Eschatology" in Hastings' Dictionary (1900).
   The Century Bible: Mark (1903).
Sanday, Professor:
   The Oracles of God (1891).
   Bampton Lectures on Inspiration (1893).

Article "Gospels" in Smith and Fuller's Bible Dictionary (1893).
Article "Son of God" in Hastings' Dictionary (1902).
Outlines of the Life of Christ (1905).

SCRIVENER, DR. F. H.:
A Plain Introduction to the Criticism of the New Testament, 4th ed. (1894).

STALKER, PROFESSOR:
The Christology of Jesus—Synoptic Gospels (1899).

STANTON, PROFESSOR:
Article "Gospels" in Hastings' Dictionary, vol. ii. (1899).

STRONG, DEAN:
A Manual of Theology (1903).

SWETE, PROFESSOR:
The Gospel according to St. Mark, 2nd ed. (1902).

THOMSON, ARCHBISHOP:
Article "Gospels" in Smith's Bible Dictionary (1863).
Introduction to Gospels in Speaker's Commentary on New Testament, vol. i. (1878).

THOMSON, W. M.:
The Land and the Book, 3 vols. (1881-1886).

TREGELLES, DR. S. P.:
Account of the Printed Text of the New Testament (1854).

TRENCH, ARCHBISHOP:
Studies in the Gospels (1867).
Notes on the Parables, 15th ed. (1881).
Notes on the Miracles, 13th ed. (1886).

WESTCOTT, BISHOP:
Introduction to the Study of the Gospels, 4th ed. (1872); see also under HORT, F. J. A.

WRIGHT, DR. A.:
New Testament Problems (1898).
Synopsis of the Gospels in Greek, 3rd. ed. (1906).

AMERICAN.

GOULD, PROFESSOR:
Commentary on Mark (1896).

GREENLEAF, PROFESSOR:
  The Testimony of the Evangelists examined by the Rules of Evidence (1874).
‡JEWISH ENCYCLOPÆDIA:
  (Funk and Wagnalls, 1901-1906).
LADD, PROFESSOR:
  The Doctrine of Sacred Scripture (1883).
STEVENS, PROFESSOR:
  The Teaching of Jesus (1901).

GERMAN.

*ABERLE, PROFESSOR M. VON:
  Einleitung in das Neue Testament (1877).
BENGEL, J. A.:
  Gnomon of the New Testament (T. & T. Clark's ed.).
BLASS, F.:
  Philology of the Gospels (1898).
  Grammar of New Testament Greek (1905).
BOUSSET, PROFESSOR W.:
  Jesus (1906).
CHRISTLIEB, T.:
  Modern Doubts (1875).
DALMAN, PROFESSOR G.:
  The Words of Jesus (1902).
DELITZSCH, F.:
  A Day in Capernaum (1889).
  Jewish Artisan Life in the Time of our Lord (1902).
DORNER, J. A.:
  History of Protestant Theology (1871).
EWALD, HEINRICH:
  Revelation: its Nature and Record (1884).
  Old and New Testament Theology (1888).
‡HAMBURGER, RABBI:
  Real-Encyclopädie für Bibel und Talmud (1886).
HARNACK, PROFESSOR A.:
  What is Christianity? (1904).
HOLTZMANN, PROFESSOR H. J.:
  Die Synoptischen Evangelien (1863).

Einleitung in das Neue Testament (1885).
Handcommentar zum Neuen Testament (1891).
Lehrbuch der N. Ttlichen Theologie (1897).
Die Entstehung des Neuen Testamentes (1904).

HOLTZMANN, PROFESSOR O.:
The Life of Jesus (1904).

JÜLICHER, PROFESSOR:
Article "Marcus im Neuen Testament" in Hauck's Encyclopädie u. s. w.
Introduction to the New Testament (1904).

KAFTAN, PROFESSOR J.:
The Truth of the Christian Religion (1894).
Jesus und Paulus (1906).

KLOSTERMANN, PROFESSOR:
Das Marcusevangelium u. s. w. (1867).

MEYER, WEISS: Commentary on Mark (T. & T. Clark's ed., 1901).

NEANDER, A.:
The Life of Jesus Christ (4th German ed., 1871).

PFLEIDERER, PROFESSOR O.:
Das Urchristentum u. s. w. (1903).

*SCHANZ, PROFESSOR P.:
Commentar über das Evangelium des h. Marci (1881).

SCHLOTTMANN, A.: Kompendium der Biblischen Theologie (1889).

SCHMIEDEL, PROFESSOR:
Article "Gospels," Historical and Synthetical, in Encyclopædia Biblica (1901).

SCHÜRER, PROFESSOR E.:
History of the Jewish People in the Time of Jesus Christ (1885).

STIER, R.:
The Words of the Lord Jesus (1864).

TISCHENDORF, C.:
Synopsis Evangelica (7th ed., 1898).

WEISS, PROFESSOR B.:
Das Marcusevangelium (1872).
Introduction to the New Testament (1885).

WEISS, PROFESSOR J.:
   Das älteste Evangelium (1903).
WELLHAUSEN, PROFESSOR J.:
   Das Evangelium Marci (1903).
   Einleitung in die drei ersten Evangelien (1905).
WERNLE, PROFESSOR P.:
   The Beginnings of Christianity (1903).
   Die Quellen des Lebens Jesu (1905).
ZAHN, PROFESSOR T.:
   Einleitung in das Neue Testament (1897).

FRENCH.

RÉVILLE, PROFESSOR A.:
   Jésus de Nazareth (1897).

Note on the Gospel of Luke

Note from *An Exposition of the Gospel of Luke* by William Kelly, edited, with annotations, by E. E. Whitfield, referenced in *An Exposition of the Gospel of John*.

NOTE ON THE FIRST CHAPTER

28 Luke 1:32. — "The Highest." The Old Testament *Elyon*. It was the usual designation of GOD among the Hellenistic Jews of the Dispersion. Again in verses 35, 76.

"His father David." Mary was probably of the tribe of Judah (B. Weiss).

EDITIONS OF AUTHOR USED.

GERMAN.

WEISS, PROFESSOR B.:
 Life of Christ (E. T., 1883, 1884).
 Introduction to the New Testament (E. T., 1885).
 The Gospels, Greek Text with Short Exposition (cited as "Manual Commentary") (1902): American adaptation (1906).
 Sources of Luke's Gospel (1907).
 Sources of Synoptic Tradition (in series of "Texts and Investigations," edited by Harnack and Schmidt (1908).

www.ingramcontent.com/pod-product-compliance
Lightning Source LLC
Chambersburg PA
CBHW070752300426
44111CB00014B/2379